Humor in Eighteenth- and Nineteenth-Century British Literature

A Reference Guide

DON L. F. NILSEN

GREENWOOD PRESS
Westport, Connecticut • London

Library of Congress Cataloging-in-Publication Data

Nilsen, Don Lee Fred.
  Humor in eighteenth- and nineteenth-century British literature : a
reference guide / Don. L. F. Nilsen.
      p.   cm.
  Includes bibliographical references and index.
  ISBN 0–313–29705–3 (alk. paper)
  1. English wit and humor—History and criticism—Bibliography.
2. English literature—18th century—History and criticism—
Bibliography.   3. English literature—19th century—History and
criticism—Bibliography.   4. Humorous stories, English—History and
criticism—Bibliography.   5. Humorous poetry, English—History and
criticism—Bibliography.   6. Comic, The, in literature—
Bibliography.   I. Title.
Z2014.W57N56   1998
[PR935]
016.827009—dc21   98–14819

10 0145 5546

British Library Cataloguing in Publication Data is available.

Library of Congress Catalog Card Number: 98–14819
ISBN: 0–313–29705–3

First published in 1998

Greenwood Press, 88 Post Road West, Westport, CT 06881
An imprint of Greenwood Publishing Group, Inc.

Printed in the United States of America

The paper used in this book complies with the
Permanent Paper Standard issued by the National
Information Standards Organization (Z39.48–1984).

10 9 8 7 6 5 4 3 2 1

Dedicated to the Nilsen and Wickman Families
    Alleen Pace Nilsen, Wife and Critic
    Kelvin and Sean Nilsen, and Nicolette Wickman, Children
    Lorrain and Kath Nilsen, and Jeff Wickman, Spouses
    Taryn, Britton and Kami, Iowa Grandchildren
    David and Lauren Nilsen, Kentucky Grandchildren
    Jim and Luke Wickman, Utah Grandchildren

Contents

Preface

    This book is arranged chronologically according to the birth year of the author being discussed. Note that for ease of reference the birth and death dates of the various authors are given both in the text and in the index. The main body of the book is divided into four chapters. The first chapter deals with the eighteenth century, a century filled with satire, burlesque, and parody both in art and in literature. The second chapter deals with the first third of the nineteenth century. This is the period of the witty and gently satiric comic novels of Jane Austen and William Makepeace Thackeray. It is the period of the witty poetry of Charles Lamb, George Gordon, Lord Byron, Percy Bysshe Shelley, Thomas Hood, and Alfred Lord Tennyson. This is also the period when Thomas Love Peacock and Jane Austen began to develop the comic Gothic novel. The third chapter deals with the middle third of the nineteenth century. During this period, Robert Browning and Matthew Arnold refined the tradition of witty and ironic poetry started by Lamb, Byron, and Shelley. This is also the period when Charles Dickens established the tradition of the "humors character" in his vernacular comic novels, and also expanded the tradition of the comic gothic. The Brontë sisters also expanded the comic gothic tradition, as did George Eliot. This was also the period of Edward Lear who began the development of the genre of "Benign Humor." This is a genre in which the author plays with the ironies, parodies, and general slipperiness of words. The middle of the nineteenth century is also the period when Anthony Trollope started to combine comedy with pathos, and when George Meredith, the Brontë sisters, and others further developed the notion of feminine comedy that had been so well established earlier by Jane Austen. The last third of the nineteenth century is dealt with in the final chapter of this book. This is the period of Charles Dickens, Sir William Schwenck Gilbert, and George and Weedon Grossmith, four splendid "Benign Humorists" who all made important contributions to the refinement of various techniques of word play. This is the period of Samuel Butler's tongue-in-cheek <u>Erewhon</u> satires, and also the period when Thomas Hardy further developed the pathos of comedy. But the dominant figure of this period was probably Oscar Wilde, who took the genre of "Comedy of Manners" to a completely new level.

Acknowledgments

I would like to express my appreciation to members of the Arizona State University Humanities Computing Facility--Peter Lafford, Ahmad Rafiq, Glenn Trombly, and Gary Walker--for managing the facility in such a way as to make it convenient to provide high quality camera-ready copy to the publisher. I would also like to express my appreciation to Nancy Gutierrez, Willis Buckingham, Karen Adams, Dawn Bates, Lee Croft, Kenneth L. Donelson, Barbara Lafford, Roy Major, Elly van Gelderen, and Wendy Wilkins, for their encouragement and support of scholarly research.

Special thanks goes to O. M. (Skip) Brack and Taylor Corse for their help with Restoration and 18th-century British humor, and to Daniel Bivona, L. Randel Helms, Mary Green, Mildred Green, Alan P. Johnson, Kathryn Kent, Thais Morgan, Sandra Nagy, and Gene Valentine for their constant input on Romantic and Victorian British humor, and for reading extensive portions of the manuscript and offering suggestions for expansion and revision. Special thanks goes to Nicolette (Nilsen) Wickman for reading the manuscript and offering many important suggestions for revision. Extra special thanks goes to my wife, Alleen, who has seen or heard the manuscript in many forms and has offered as much constructive criticism as I was able to handle.

Without the above support, and without a sabbatical leave from Arizona State University, there is little hope that this project would ever have been completed.

Introduction

In relating eighteenth-century English satire to satire in general, J. D. Browning states that the aim of satire was to reform the world through perceptive ridicule. "The satirist saw what was wrong with the world; the reader reciprocated by agreement and amendment" (Browning 1). Both in literature and in the fine arts, satire had a double audience--the person attacked, and the spectators to the assault. Almost by definition, satire is about "other people." "The person attacked is an assumed, rather than an actual reader." Furthermore, the moral value of satire may come after the time of enjoyment and appreciation (Browning 2). Browning feels that the reading of satire is a form of "ethical education."

> In the celebrated "contract" scene of Hogarth's Marriage à la Mode, for example, all the participants are vacuously self-absorbed, at once tense and inactive. The groom takes snuff, the bride fiddles with a kerchief and a ring, the father gestures to himself and his family tree; all are stiff, ill-at-ease and awkward. But Hogarth's patterns draw the eye not to a contrasting image of genuine family love or mutual human respect. Rather he directs us, in the bottom left-hand corner, to two dogs, side by side, relaxed, healthy, and alert. Their attractive vitality throws into contrast not the folly of the humans but their discomfort. Like all great satirists, Hogarth is not lashing vice or pointing out defects; he is reminding us of the tension of human life and the pity of it. (Browning 4)

Browning also notes that the satire of eighteenth-century cartoonists is richly parodic in nature. "Gillray's statesmen loll gracelessly in attitudes only minutely differing from those of Rubens's self-assured burghers. Cruikshank's Prince Regent, savagely etched in such a series as The Queen's Matrimonial Ladder, has, as it were in pentimento, the images of Van Dyck's Stuart court" (Browning 6).

There is a great range in the satire that has come out of the British literary tradition. C. S. Lewis said the following: "A satiric portrait by Pope or Swift is like a thunderclap; the Addisonian method is more like the slow operations of ordinary nature, loosening stones, blunting outlines, modifying a whole landscape with 'silent overgrowings' so that the change can never quite be reversed again" (Berry 3).

Satire is a powerful weapon, and Isaac D'Israeli has noted that "Satirists, if they escape the scourge of the law, have reason to dread the cane of the satirized." "Dryden was beaten up by the hired thugs of the Earl of Rochester...Swift seems to have been denied a bishopric because Queen Anne was too literal-minded a reader to follow the religious parable in A Tale of a Tub. Defoe's heavily ironic pamphlet, The Shortest Way with the

Dissenters, misfired with still more adverse consequences to the author, who was pilloried for seditious libel. Thereupon, cheered by the people who witnessed his official disgrace, he wrote an unregenerate "Hymn to the Pillory," along with a Brief Explanation of his intentions: "If any man take the pains seriously to reflect upon the contents, the nature of the thing, and the manner of the style, it seems impossible to imagine that it should pass for anything but an irony." Yet, taken at face value, it had been denounced by fellow Dissenters, while being hailed by the Tory extremists whose bigotry it mocked" (Levin Playboys 201-202).

Michael DePorte compares satirists to James Bond in that they both have "a kind of license to kill." He says that Partridge never recovered from Bickerstaff's predictions even though he did continue for a while to write almanacs. Dryden ruined Shadwell's reputation as a dramatist by caricaturing him as the gross, dull-witted successor to Flecknoe. In the role of the injured and long-suffering moralist of the "Epistle to Dr. Arbuthnot," Pope was able to say many nasty things about Addison and Hervey.

Perhaps no satirist has ever taken more advantage of the aggressive possibilities of satire than Swift. Swift subjects some victims to imagined deaths. In The Battle of the Books he fells Descartes with a spear through the eye, has Davenant trampled underfoot, Perrault's and Fontennelle's brains dashed out, and Wotten and Bentley skewered on a single lance. In pieces written much later Swift depicts the unfortunate William Wood boiled in oil, scaled to death by molten copper, and three times sent to the gallows. (DePorte 53)

Bret Harte wrote parodies of a number of British works in his Sensation Novels Condensed. Most of the novelists pilloried in this work are nothing more than a vague allusion to Harte's reading public (Kitchin 280). Harte parodied Thackeray, and he also parodied Charlotte Brontë, and to a lesser extent Charles Dickens. On the quality of Harte's parody, Kitchin states, "We would place his Miss Mix (Jane Eyre) beside Evoe's parody of Miss Sheila Kay Smith. They both provoke boisterous laughter. The caricature of Rochester--the eternal "He-Man"--is "almost too funny" (Kitchin 281). Kitchin concludes that Bret Harte's parodies of British authors contain a great deal of clowning and farce, but the parodies are at the same time adequately shrewd (Kitchin 282).

Leigh Hunt suggests that there are basically six rhetorical methods for achieving wit, and British authors have used them all. The author may use the direct simile or metaphor, as Jonathan Swift did when he said that epithets are like stepping stones, or like a heel-piece used to support a cripple because one of his legs is too short, or like a bridge that joins a marsh to a moorland (12-13). Or the author may leap to a conclusion, leaving out the intermediate logical steps. This results in the juxtaposition of two incongruous ends of thought. During Joseph Addison's day, it was the fashion for ladies to wear a patch on their faces, to show the fairness of their skin by contrast. Through time, the location of the patches started to indicate the lady's political leanings--as Tories, or as Whigs. Addison could then say that "Rosalinda, a famous Whig partisan, has most unfortunately a very beautiful mole on the Tory part of her forehead" (Hunt 15).

About the beginning of the eighteenth century, a group of writers of Scottish vernacular verse emerged in Edinburgh. Prior to this time, belles lettres had been lying dormant in Scotland. James Watson's Choice Collection of Comic and Serious Scots Poems was typical of the revival of vernacular poetry. The first part appeared in 1706; this was followed by a second part in 1709 and a third part in 1711 (Walker 252). Gavin Douglas's allegory King Hart is an arresting poem of meditation and mild playfulness. Its humor is very similar to that of much modern poetry, though it still contains some of the didacticness of its day. Another Scottish poet is David Lyndsay. Louis Cazamian considers Lyndsay's John the Common Weal of The Satire of the Three Estaitis to be the

Scottish counterpart to William Langland's <u>Piers Plowman</u> (Cazamian 94).

Introduction Bibliography

Berry, Reginald. "Modifying a Whole Landscape: False Humour, Good Nature, and Satire in the <u>Spectator</u>." <u>Thalia: Studies in Literary Humor</u> 3.1 (1980): 3-10.

Browning, J. D., ed. <u>Satire in the 18th Century</u>. New York, NY: Garland, 1983.

Cazamian, Louis. <u>The Development of English Humor</u>. Durham, NC: Duke University Press, 1952.

DePorte, Michael. "Swift and the License of Satire." <u>Satire in the 18th Century</u>. Ed. J. D. Browning. New York, NY: Garland, 1983.

Hunt, Leigh. <u>Wit and Humour Selected from the English Poets</u>. London, England: Smith, Elder and Co. 1882.

Kitchin, George. <u>Survey of Burlesque and Parody in English</u>. New Haven, CT: Yale University Press, 1959.

Levin, Harry. <u>Playboys and Killjoys: An Essay on the Theory and Practice of Comedy</u>. New York, NY: Oxford Univ Press, 1987.

Walker, Hugh. <u>English Satire and Satirists</u>. London, England: J. M. Dent, 1925.

1

Humor in Eighteenth-Century British Literature

Eighteenth-Century English Humor

Charles Dickens said of the eighteenth century, "It was the best of times; it was the worst of times" (Bigaldi and Achtert 48). About the beginning of the eighteenth century, a group of writers of Scottish vernacular verse emerged in Edinburgh. Prior to this time, belles lettres had been lying dormant in Scotland. James Watson's Choice Collection of Comic and Serious Scots Poems was typical of the revival of vernacular poetry. The first part appeared in 1706; this was followed by a second part in 1709 and a third part in 1711 (Walker 252). Gavin Douglas's allegory King Hart is an arresting poem of meditation and mild playfulness. Its humor is very similar to that of much modern poetry, though it still contains some of the didacticness of its day. Another Scottish poet is David Lyndsay. Louis Cazamian considers Lyndsay's John the Common Weal of The Satire of the Three Estaitis to be the Scottish counterpart to William Langland's Piers Plowman (Cazamian 94).

In England, the novel developed mainly during the eighteenth century. According to Bernard Kreissman,

> The English novel traces its roots beyond the medieval romance, but it first began to assume recognizable form early in the eighteenth century with such books as Defoe's Robinson Crusoe, Roxanna, and Moll Flanders; Mrs. Behn's Oroonoko and Swift's Gulliver's Travels. It was not until mid-century, however, that it took on its full lineaments in the works of Richardson, Fielding, Smollett, Sterne, and their followers. The first of these "true" novels, published on November 6, 1740, was Richardson's Pamela: or, Virtue Rewarded. Pamela caught on, enjoyed a great popular vogue, started several schools of fiction, and was directly responsible for a

vast array of imitation, adaptation, burlesque, parody, translation, commendation, and vilification--in short, a veritable literary warfare. (Kreissman 1)
There was much satire and burlesque written during the eighteenth century, and V. C. Clinton-Baddeley comments on the difference between these two genres: "Satire is the schoolmaster attacking dishonesty with a whip. Burlesque is the rude boy attacking pomposity with a peashooter. Satire must laugh not to weep; burlesque must laugh not to burst" (Clinton-Baddeley 2).

For hack writers, the literary center of London during the eighteenth century may well have been Grub Street (which was renamed in 1830 to Milton Street, and which was later swallowed up by the Barbican Building). Grub Street was noisy, squalid, crowded, and teeming with moral decay. Many hack writers of the day, Swift and Pope included, lived in Cripplegate Ward Without, in and around Grub Street. "The milieu of Duncehood was, first and foremost, the parish of St. Giles', Cripplegate, in the liberties of the City of London" (Rogers 1).

Much of the eighteenth century can be classified as "neo-classical." This is a movement which contended that "whatever is, is right," and proponents of this philosophy include Pope, Swift, Fielding, Johnson, Goldsmith, and Austen (Demarest 51).

All of the authors mentioned above play a game similar to Pope's: they will advance a given moral view so fervently that we cannot doubt authorial conviction, and then, suddenly we are told, "Look again; things are not as simple or as clear as you thought"--and we feel that the author is correcting himself as he is correcting us.... The rationalism of the Age of Reason is not dogmatic, and it does not dictate simple attitudes. Its principle is the energy of re-examination and qualification. Even--or especially--our most dearly loved convictions are not as certain and as simple as we would like to think.... Eighteenth-century satire is founded upon a tolerance, an acceptance, indeed an affirmation of man as he is; again--in a more profound sense than meets the eye--"Whatever is, is right." (Demarest 52)

Early in the eighteenth century the titles of periodicals suggest and even require a multiplicity of view points and perspectives. There is The Spectator, and The Observator, and The Intelligencer, and The Plain Dealer, and The Inspector, and The Mirror. But such titles can be found only at the beginning of the eighteenth century. The writings of Laurence Sterne illustrate the growing difficulty in the eighteenth century of being able to separate the author from the characters. "At certain times, indeed, Sterne is synonymous with Shandy or with poor Yorick. The mask and the masker become interfused" (Clark 41). By the end of the eighteenth century, "poets cannot be dramatic," and they "seldom write effectually in the tragic, comic, or satiric modes" (Clark 42).

David Nokes feels the literature of the entire century from 1660 until 1760 to be dominated by satire, starting with Dryden and Rochester, and concluding with Charles Churchill, Samuel Johnson, and Laurence Sterne (Nokes xi). Many different types of satire were written during the eighteenth century. There were prose satires as well as verse satires. There were also operas, novels, poems, pamphlets, and tragi-comi-pastoral farces (Nokes x). Eighteenth-century satire was filled with teasing paradoxes and allusive parodies. Since many of the allusions were either to classical literature, or to contemporary politics, modern readers have difficulty with the genre (Nokes ix).

Bernard Kreissman points out that even much of the polite literature of the eighteenth-century shocks modern readers. It follows then that the burlesques and parodies of that period would be even more shocking. This is confirmed by Swift's Directions to Servants and by Defoe's Law to Enact the Castration of Popish Ecclesiasticks. According to Kreissman, such satires and burlesques are "meat too strong for the modern stomach"

(Kreissman 2).

The travels of Baron Münchausen were first published in 1786, and their popularity and esteem were documented by the large number of editions, and of translations into foreign languages which these travels underwent. The author of these travels is probably Raspi, a German who fled from Germany to England to escape persecution (L'Estrange 136-137). One incident, for example, happened while Baron Münchausen was travelling over deep snow in Poland. He fastened his horse to a post, but this post later turned out to be the top of a church steeple. By morning he was able to see his mistake, since the snow had melted, and his horse was hanging on the top of the church by its bridle (L'Estrange 138).

In some of the best satires written in the late seventeenth century, the dunce was a common theme. The dunce can be seen in Scriblerus, and in A Tale of a Tub, and in Dunciad. Such works are part of the "perennial war between wits and 'dunces,' between humanist and pedant, a war which became particularly vehement in the late seventeenth and early eighteenth centuries in England, because of the general shift in the structure of society resulting from the rise of the middle classes" (Stedman 53).

Book IV of Pope's Dunciad paints a picture of Chaos ruled by the "uncreating" Word, the babble of the Dunce. Laurence Sterne's Tristram Shandy, in its way, is an extension of Pope's vision. It gives an account of human life not as a tale told by an idiot but as the story of a Cock and a Bull.... Swift attacked the Grub Street hack by parodying his style; Pope sallied against the pedantic dunce by burlesquing his method; and Sterne, in his turn, donned cap and bells in order to show up foolishness by playing the fool. (Stedman 64-65)

In Tristram Shandy, Walter, Toby, and Tristram are all manifestations of the dunce. "Sterne, like Swift and Pope, was keenly interested in preserving the rule of 'wit' by pricking the pretentious windbags of pedantry whose hold over the great public was obviously growing" (Stedman 53). The "Slawkenbergian Story" is about a man with a nose so long that it fascinated the people of Strasburg to the extent that they could think of nothing else. Stedman suggests that this story "serves not only to titillate Sterne's readers, but also provides an excellent example of the futility of pedantry, and, even more, of its danger" (58). According to Alfred Gu L'Estrange, "Sterne exceeded Smollett in indelicacy as much as in humorous talent. He calls him Smelfungus, because he had written a fastidious book of travels.... But Sterne is more immediately associated in our minds with Swift, for both were clergymen, and both Irishmen by birth, though neither by parentage" (99).

At the turn of the century, during the reigns of William (1689-1702) and Anne (1702-1714), there developed a clear sense of duty and of citizenship in England, and this can be seen in the Spectator, where the goods and evils of life were "embedded in the very conscience of the people" (Cazamian 387). "Genuine humor, which has more to do with seriousness than with mirth, lost less than it gained through such changes, one aspect of which was the pronounced decline of 'merry England' " (Cazamian 388). The most famous comedian in England between 1710 and 1738 was Joe (Josias) Miller. Although he was unable to read or write, he had a considerable native talent, and many popular jest books were written anonymously, and attributed to him. Realizing that any book with Joe Miller's name on it would be well read, compilers were quick to place his name on their humorous collections. The name of Joe Miller has become a symbol for any jokes that are broad and pointless (L'Estrange 95).

Early in the eighteenth century, there was a rising debate about the legal status of women and about this time there was also a reform made in the divorce laws. This made discordant marital humor an important topic in the plays written during this period.

Restoration comedy tended to be rather hostile to marriage, since both males and females were against the institution--males were exerting their libertinism, and females their independence. But although the plays themselves tended to be discordant, the endings of the plays often begrudgingly supported the institution of marriage. In Congreve's The Way of the World (1700), for example, Millamant wonders if she must "dwindle to a wife" (Hume 176-177).

In 1709 Richard Steele became the founding editor of the Tattler, which after two hundred and seventy-one issues became the Spectator, mainly to promote the fact that Joseph Addison had become a more important contributor. The Spectator in turn changed to the Guardian after another six hundred and thirty-five issues. The only difference worth noting between the Spectator and the Guardian was the prominent appearance of Pope as an essayist (L'Estrange 86). In the Guardian, Pope said that poetry was beginning to become composed "upon mechanical principles, in the same way that house-wives make plum-puddings." Pope then goes on to give a recipe for making an epic poem, and this is followed by a recipe for making the "fable," and the "comedy of manners" (L'Estrange 87).

According to William Myers, Ben Jonson is replaced by William Hogarth as representative satirist, as the seventeenth century becomes the eighteenth century. At the same time, Thomas Hobbes is replaced by John Locke as the representative philosopher, and power and appetite are replaced by reason and law as the "fuel of politics" (Myers 76). "Typically, the eighteenth-century satirist's viewpoint is that of the private observer moving at random through a complicated, densely populated society, looking for striking, but, once properly seen, not puzzling social and psychological forms. Jonsonian comedy, concerned with a sequence of events in a single place and time, is irrelevant to such a search" (Myers 77).

Jonathan Swift punned greatly as he compared himself to a king in a letter written to Orrery in 1735, during the reign of George II: "As to writing in verse or prose, I am a real king, for I never had so many good subjects in my life; and the more a king, because like the rest of my rank (except King George) I am so bad a governor of them, that I do not regard what becomes of them, nor hath any single one among them thrived under me these three years past" (Ulman 13).

In discussing the role of religion in British literature, Robert Polhemus says that since the beginning of the eighteenth century, the comic artist who openly broke from the religious tradition of sexual repression has always risked "quick and firm censorship." He further suggests that one of the important reasons why such comic masters of the eighteenth century as Fielding, Sterne, and Smollett turned to writing novels instead of plays is that in the novel they could "get the comedy of physical life into print" in a way that would not be possible in a stage play (12-13). According to Polhemus,

> Fielding's Parson Adams, Goldsmith's Vicar of Wakefield, Smollett's satire of Humphry Clinker's preaching, and Sterne's mockery of Dr. Slop's Catholicism all show that by the start of the nineteenth century, comic fiction has a history of touching upon religious matters and characters. Everywhere in eighteenth-century fiction we find both humor and the comic dream of earthly abundance and rising social status being used to bolster the Christian vision of regeneration. (Polhemus 17-18)

John Ashton discusses the relationship of chapbooks not only to the development of humor specifically, but to the development of literacy more generally in eighteenth-century London.

> These little books more than any other evidence we have open a window on the world of the eighteenth century poor. In chapbooks we find the tales which enthralled them, the ballads which had been passed on from one generation to another, and a good deal of the lore of the weather and of

primitive medicine which was part of the background which they took for granted. It is hard to envisage a more important source for the history of popular culture. (Ashton 6)

The ballads, romances, and lore of these chapbooks were unsophisticated, and their straight-forward natures created little controversy. Furthermore, they stood in sharp contrast to the street ballads of nineteenth-century London, which did exhibit various political and religious points of view in linguistically sophisticated and complex ways. But there would have been very small audiences for these sophisticated nineteenth-century street ballads if the chapbooks had not aided the people in their language skills.

Without the eighteenth century chapbook, opportunities for reading would have been very much more restricted, and thus might this skill have withered amongst those whose poverty precluded the purchase of any literature other than these little books available so cheaply, and designed so specifically to appeal to them. As it was, the skill developed; and as the nineteenth century dawned the mere fact that they were able to read political pamphlets meant that politics at working class level were not simply a matter of a demagogue haranguing a mob. (Ashton 9-10)

Many eighteenth-century scholars were very careful about the rules of English usage. In a book entitled An Essay Towards Fixing the True Standards of Wit, Humor, Raillery, Satire and Ridicule (1744), Corbyn Morris distinguished between raillery and ridicule by the seriousness of the subject matter, and by the intended response: "Raillery is used on slight subjects and its purpose is to give pleasure by causing only 'a little embarrassment of a person,' whereas ridicule aims at more serious faults and its aim is 'to degrade the person attacked and to render him contemptible' " (Bullitt 95). Morris's definition of "raillery" concentrates on "good humor," and seems close to the definition of the Oxford English Dictionary as "good humored ridicule." During the eighteenth century, raillery was considered to be a "genteel, poignant attack of a person upon any slight foibles, oddities, or embarrassments of his, in which he is tender, or may be supposed to be tender, and unwilling to come to a free explanation" (Bullitt 95).

According to John Stedman, "early eighteenth-century satire, such as that of Swift and Pope, launched attacks on the misuse of reason and on those who allowed themselves to be dominated by their passions. As the century advanced, such satire softened into sentimental comedy" (Stedman 48). For example, Stedman considers the tone of Sterne's Tristram Shandy to be very different from that of Swift's A Tale of a Tub, in that it is much less biting and much more good-humored (Stedman 48). In a book entitled The Amiable Humorist, Stuart Tave discusses the benevolent virtues of "good nature" and "good humour" and the resultant cheerfulness, innocent mirth, and restrained raillery, satire and ridicule that occurred during the eighteenth century. During Restoration times, the tradition of the English was to copy the foolish and knavish originals of the age, and to expose, ridicule, and satirize them. Authors in the seventeenth century viewed humor and satire as ways of attacking society's aberrations; however, eighteenth century authors had developed more of a national pride, and more of an enjoyment of English "humors." They had also developed a genuine delight in good-natured humor for its own sake, and an enjoyment of the variety and incongruity of the "picturesque, unique, and even infinite qualities of humor." As a result, there developed a close interrelationship between jest and earnestness, of tragedy and tears, of melancholy and sympathy with pathos (Tave viii-ix). "Between the seventeenth and the nineteenth centuries, certain conventions of comic theory and criticism were so altered as to produce a new group of conventions which, for need of a name, I have called amiable humor" (Tave viii).

Eighteenth-century Sentimental Comedies were ruled by a benevolent providence, and most of the plays in this genre ended by paying tribute to this providence. Compare in this regard the ending of Richard Steele's The Conscious Lovers with the ending of Cumberland's The West Indian. Steele's Sir John Bevil says, "Now ladies and gentlemen, you have set the world a fair example. Your happiness is owing to your constancy and merit, and the several difficulties you have struggled with evidently show. Whate'er the generous mind itself denies, the secret care of Providence supplies" (Rayner 98). Providence is also an important part of the ending in The West Indian, as Cumberland's Belcour says, "I beseech you, amiable Louisa, for the time to come, whenever you perceive me deviating into error or offence, bring only to my mind the providence of this night, and I will return to reason, and obey" (Rayner 98).

Eighteenth-century German author Jean Paul gives evidence in support of Stuart Tave's contention that eighteenth-century humor tends to be amiable. He disagrees with those philosophers who believe that humor is the result of a feeling of triumph, and he offers as evidence the fact that the more people there are who laugh at our joke, the better we are pleased, "and this does not seem as though the enjoyment came from a feeling of triumph. But what is really laughed at is the humour, and not the humorist" (L'Estrange 311).

As eighteenth-century humor became gentler, it also became less ironic. In an article entitled, "The Decline of Irony in the Eighteenth Century," John R. Clark points out that during the eighteenth century the English developed a "slowly maturing sense of self." As the Eighteenth-century English became more interested in themselves, they became increasingly "unable to identify with others, to assume a variety of roles, or to manage or even comprehend complex irony" (Clark 39). Clark says that poets of the later eighteenth century write more and more about themselves and their immediate experiences. They may still have "masks," but "the autobiographical strain has come of age" (Clark 40). Clark traces the development of "self" just described. Shakespeare's plays were dramatically diverse, and were filled with irony. As examples of complex characters, Clark mentions Hotspur, Lear, Richard III, Polonius, Bottom, and Touchstone. Somewhat later, Ben Jonson, Edmund Spenser, and John Donne were able to write in three or four, even six or seven modes, and they were able to change their identifications from one mode to another with ease. Elizabethan drama was filled with multiplicity, fluidity, and flux. This multiplicity, fluidity, and flux were largely missing, however, from eighteenth-century writing. John Keats lived in an "age devoid of aesthetic distance, of irony, and of multiple points of view." He must have yearned for more dramatic variety, as he said, "A Poet is the most unpoetical of any thing in existence, because he has no Identity--he is continually...filling some other body." Clark feels that Keats is defining his age, an age which "prevented a man from transcending the barriers of the self" (Clark 40-41). According to Clark, the period between the time of Shakespeare and that of Keats "may be delineated as the falling-off of ironic consciousness" (Clark 41). Jonathan Swift, who inhabited a middle ground between Shakespeare and Keats, had irony, but it was what Clark termed a "neurotic irony," whereby a person not being himself was "as nervous as a filly and as strained as constipation at stool" (Clark 41). Clark admits that Swift was skilled in being a chameleon whereby he was constantly playing at being somebody else--"a Partridge, a Mistress Frances Harris, a lunatic Grub-Street Scribbler, a Modern City Poet, a Nominal Christian, a gallows bird, a Drapier, a Modest Proposer--even the elegiac epitaph-maker of himself" (Clark 41). Swift was able to take on these different persona, but only with great effort. "The very fact that Swift must labor mightily--and self-consciously--to attain to irony suggests an effort of will unknown to the Elizabethans" (Clark 41). Furthermore, there was a clash between Swift and his audience in terms of his irony, for it was imperceptible to many of his readers, and his meanings were frequently misunderstood. If irony is defined as "the capacity deliberately to conceive and to sustain a variety of (even potentially conflicting) points of view," then the eighteenth century can be distinguished in "its increasing incapacity to be witty, cosmopolitan, and ironic" (Clark 41).

Oliver Goldsmith's Honeywood, and Richard Sheridan's Lydia Languish and Joseph Surface are instances of characters designed to satirize the sentimental comedy of the eighteenth century. Other eighteenth-century authors who satirized sentimental comedy were George Colman in his Polly Honeycombe, Samuel Foote in his The Devil upon Two Sticks, and William Whitehead in his A Trip to Scotland. These were all considerably successful, and were all explicitly satires on the tradition of romantic sentimentalism (Hume 350). But it is basically Goldsmith and Sheridan who are known as the developers of laughing comedy and the attackers of sentimental comedy, even though Murphy, Foote, Macklin, Colman, Garrick, and others must be added to this list, for "laughing comedy" so-called was a thriving movement in the days of Goldsmith and Sheridan. "To say that the two of them...reacted against excessive emphasis on sensibility is perfectly accurate. But the old 'revolutionary' hypothesis is bunk" (Hume 354-355). Allan Rodway would agree with Hume. In an article ironically entitled "Goldsmith and Sheridan: Satirists of Sentiment," Rodway states that "their anti-sentimental plays must seem, to anyone familiar with the Restoration mode they purported to revive, to be themselves affected by the usurping Genteel or Sentimental mode they purported to attack." Rodway later states that this ambiguity of attitude is present in all of their comedies (Rodway 65). Rodway contrasts the humor in Goldsmith's plays with that in Sheridan's plays:

> The Rivals and School for Scandal are both comedies, not farces. Goldsmith's characters--in She Stoops to Conquer anyway--know they are only there for fun and often play up to, rather than play, their allotted parts.... Sheridan's personages, in fact, are not humour-characters so much as wit-characters.... Goldsmith shows absurd character in action--in a situation springing from, and dependent on the 'humour'--Sheridan shows it in speech. (70-71)

Alice Rayner suggests that the ruling genre of the eighteenth century was sentimental comedy. "The appeal of the sentimental comedy is that of moral content in character. The comedy reaches out toward the subjectivity of the bourgeois or sentimental audience. As in melodrama, good and evil are easily distinguished, and no ambiguity arises. Sentimental comedy eliminates the friction between moral order and characters in action" (Rayner 101).

These eighteenth-century sentimental comedies were founded on the myth that the purpose of a play is to create good examples for the audiences. The sentimental playwrights refused to make the social world intelligible or the fictional world "dangerously delightful." Oliver Goldsmith points out that in sentimental comedy the virtues of private life are exhibited, and the vices of private life are left unexposed. Goldsmith suggests that sentimental comedy "has taken over the pathetic aspects of tragedy and has lost the capacities of comedy to criticize and delight. For plays in which distress is the focus of delight and rescue is the example for instruction, the playwright asks the audience to invest a subjective pathos" (Rayner 101). Comedy is optimistic "in spite of its capacity for bitterness and satire because it refuses to let the world rest in self-satisfaction" (Rayner 102). "Sentimental comedy consumes some of tragedy's timeless territory by making indistinguishable the personal, the social, and the metaphysical levels of moral action" (Rayner 102-103). Sentimental comedy caters to the sphere of "bourgeois certainty" in the realm of "romance myth."

> Sentimentality is the utilitarian method for mythologizing the mundane. As a consequence it loses the comic capacity for the criticism that makes society and human nature intelligible. In appealing to the brimming eyes and the bursting heart, it is no longer a comic response to the contradictions

in human beings and society but a demand to feel, not think, to identify, not
disengage. (Rayner 103)
   In "An Essay on the Theatre: or, A Comparison between Laughing and Sentimental
Comedy" (1772), and later in The Critic, Goldsmith complained about a new sort of
Dramatic Composition which had the following three characteristics: 1. The plots or lines
of action in these plays were designed to evoke tears of distress or joy; they were therefore
called "sentimental comedies." 2. The faults and foibles of the comic characters were
always forgiven in these plays, because of the characters' "good hearts." 3. These
"sentimental comedies" did not contain any bawdiness, or indelicacy, nor any of the
improbabilities of farce, nor any vulgar characters. There was an emphasis on the refined,
sensitive, dignified, and morally uplifting (Auburn 24-25). The end of the eighteenth
century, and the beginning of the nineteenth century not only promoted these "sentimental
comedies," but it also disallowed many non-sentimental comedies:
      Consider some enduring comedies which were not popular in the Georgian
      repertory: Volpone, The Man of Mode, The Country Wife, and The Plain
      Dealer. Each of these plays lacks a comic plot productive of the sort of
      anxiety typical of, say, the Claudio-Hero line of Much Ado about Nothing
      or the Shylock-Antonio line of The Merchant of Venice. Each presents
      humours characters who are satirically attacked. And each deals with
      matters of sexuality with frankness and even license. The Georgian period
      did recognize the great comic potential of each of these plays; either
      adaptations or near analogues such as Cibber's innocuous fop plays held the
      board throughout the era. (Auburn 10)

Eighteenth-Century English Humor Bibliography

Appleton, William W. "The Double Gallant in Eighteenth-Century Comedy." English
   Writers of the Eighteenth Century. Ed. John H. Middendorf. New York, NY:
   Columbia Univ Press, 1971, 145-157.
Ashton, John. Chap-Books of the Eighteenth Century. New York, NY: Augustus M. Kelley,
   1970.
Auburn, Mark, S. Sheridan's Comedies: Their Contexts and Achievements. Lincoln, NE:
   University of Nebraska Press, 1977.
Auty, Susan G. The Comic Spirit of Eighteenth-Century Novels. Port Washington, NY:
   Kennikat, 1975.
Baker, Sheridan. "Humphrey Clinker as Comic Romance." Papers of the Michigan
   Academy of Science, Arts, and Letters 46 (1961): 645-654.
Bateson, F. W. English Comic Drama, 1700-1750. New York, NY: Russell, 1963.
Berman, Ronald. "The Comedy of Reason." Texas Studies on Literature and Language 7
   (1965): 161-168.
Bernbaum, Ernest. The Drama of Sensibility: A Sketch of the History of English
   Sentimental Comedy and Domestic Tragedy 1696-1780. Gloucester, MA: Smith,
   1958.
Bevis, Richard. The Laughing Tradition: Stage Comedy in Garrick's Day. Athens, GA:
   University of Georgia Press, 1980.
Bigaldi, Joseph, and Walter S. Achtert, eds. MLA Handbook for Writers of Research
   Papers. 2nd edition. New York, NY: MLA, 1984.
Bond, Richmond P. English Burlesque Poetry, 1700-1750. Cambridge, MA: Harvard
   University Press, 1932.
Brownell, Morris. "Poetical Villas: English Verse Satire of the Country House, 1700-1750."
   Satire in the 18th Century. Ed. J. D. Browning. New York, NY: Garland, 1983, 1-8.

Browning, J. D. ed. Satire in the 18th Century. New York, NY: Garland, 1983.
Bullitt, John M. "Swift's 'Rules of Raillery.'" Veins of Humor. Ed. Harry Levin.
    Cambridge, MA: Harvard University Press, 1972.
Buss, Robert William. English Graphic Satire and Its Relation to Different Styles of
    Painting, Sculpture, and Engraving: A Contribution to the History of the English
    School of Art. London, England: Virtue and Company, 1874.
Cazamian, Louis. The Development of English Humor. Durham, NC: Duke University
    Press, 1952.
Clark, John R. "The Decline of Irony in the Eighteenth Century." Thalia: Studies in
    Literary Humor 2.1-2 (1979): 39-44.
Clinton-Baddeley, V. C. The Burlesque Tradition in the English Theatre after 1660.
    London, England: Methuen, 1952.
Demarest, David P., Jr. "Reductio Ad Absurdum: Jane Austen's Art of Satiric
    Qualification." Six Satirists. Pittsburgh, PA: Carnegie Mellon University, 1965, 51-
    68.
Draper, John W. "The Theory of the Comic in Eighteenth-Century England." Journal of
    English and Germanic Philology (1938): 207-223.
Fujimura, Thomas H. The Restoration Comedy of Wit. Princeton, NJ: Princeton Univ
    Press, 1952.
Green, Mary Elizabeth. "Cabbage-heads, Maggots, and Gnawing Rats: Gentlemen and
    Scholars in the Eighteenth Century." WHIMSY 1 (1983): 160-163.
Grego, Joseph. Rowlandson the Caricaturist: A Selection from His Works, with Anecdotal
    Descriptions of His Famous Caricatures and a Sketch of His Life, Times, and
    Contemporaries. London, England: Chatto and Windus, 1880.
Hume, Robert D. The Rakish Stage: Studies in English Drama, 1660-1800. Carbondale, IL:
    Southern Illinois Univ Press, 1983.
Jack, Ian. Augustan Satire: Intention and Idiom in English Poetry 1660-1750. Cambridge,
    England: Cambridge University Press, 1952.
Kenny, Shirley Strum. "'Elopements, Divorce, and the Devil Knows What': Love and
    Marriage in English Comedy, 1690-1720." South Atlantic Quarterly 78 (1979): 84-
    106.
Kenny, Shirley Strum. "Humane Comedy." Modern Philology 75 (1977): 29-43.
Kitchin, George. "Burlesque of Eighteenth Century Lyric Kinds, and The Rolliad." Survey
    of Burlesque and Parody in English. London, England: Oliver and Boyd, 1931, 123-
    151.
Kitchin, George. "Eighteenth Century Verse Parody." Survey of Burlesque and Parody in
    English. London, England: Oliver and Boyd, 1931, 99-122.
Kitchin, George. "Early [Eighteenth Century] Prose Parody and Burlesque." Survey of
    Burlesque and Parody in English. London, England: Oliver and Boyd, 1931, 152-
    175.
Kreissman, Bernard. Pamela-Shamela: A Study of the Criticisms, Burlesques, Parodies, and
    Adaptations of Richardson's "Pamela." Omaha, NE: University of Nebraska Press,
    1960.
Krutch, Joseph Wood. Comedy and Conscience after the Restoration. New York, NY:
    Russell, 1967.
Kunzle, David. The Early Comic Strip: Narrative Strips and Picture Stories in the European
    Broadstreet from C. 1450 to 1825. Berkeley, CA: University of California Press,
    1973.
L'Estrange, Alfred Gu. History of English Humour. New York, NY: Burt Franklin, 1878.
Levin, Harry, ed. Veins of Humor. Cambridge, MA: Harvard Univ Press, 1972.
MacMillan, Dougald. "The Rise of Social Comedy in the Eighteenth Century." Philological

Quarterly 41 (1962): 330-338.

Muir, Kenneth. The Comedy of Manners. New York, NY: Humanities, 1970.

Myers, William. "Plot and Meaning in Congreve's Comedies." William Congreve. Ed. Brian Morris. London, England: Ernest Benn, 1972, 73-92.

Neill, Michael. "Heroic Heads and Humble Tails: Sex, Politics, and the Restoration Comic Rake." The Eighteenth Century: Theory and Interpretation 24 (1983): 115-139.

Nokes, David. Raillery and Rage: A Study of Eighteenth Century Satire. Sussex, England: Harvester Press, 1987.

Palmer, John. The Comedy of Manners. New York, NY: Russell, 1962.

Polhemus, Robert M. Comic Faith: The Great Tradition from Austen to Joyce. Chicago, IL: University of Chicago Press, 1980.

Priestley, J. B. "Eighteenth-Century Giants." English Humour. New York, NY: Stein and Day, 1976, 39-48.

Rayner, Alice. Comic Persuasion: Moral Structure in British Comedy from Shakespeare to Stoppard. Berkeley, CA: University of California Press, 1987.

Rodway, Allan. "Goldsmith and Sheridan: Satirists of Sentiment." Renaissance and Modern Essays. Ed. G. R. Hibbard. New York, NY: Barnes and Noble, 1966.

Rogers, Pat. Hacks and Dunces: Pope, Swift, and Grub Street. New York, NY: Methuen, 1972.

Ruttkay, Kálmán G. "The Crisis of English Comedy in the Early Eighteenth Century." Studies in Eighteenth-Century Literature. Eds. Miklos J. Szenczi and László Ferenczi. Budapest: Akadémiai Kiadó, 1974, 83-115.

Sampson, H. Grant. "Terence, Comic Patterns, and the Augustan Stage." All the World: Drama Past and Present. Ed. Karelisa V. Hartigan. Washington, DC: Univ Press of America, 1982, 85-92.

Scouten, A. H. "Notes toward a History of Restoration Comedy." Philological Quarterly 45 (1966): 62-70.

Seidel, Michael. "Satire and Metaphoric Collapse: The Bottom of the Sublime." Satire in the 18th Century. Ed. J. D. Browning. New York, NY: Garland, 1983, 116-123.

Semple, Hilary. "Molière and Restoration Comedy." English Studies in Africa. 18 (1975): 63-84.

Shafer, Yvonne Bonsell. "The Proviso Scene in Restoration Comedy." Restoration and 18th Century Theatre Research 9.1 (1970): 1-10.

Sharma, R. C. Themes and Conventions in the Comedy of Manners. New York, NY: Asia Publishing, 1965.

Shaw, Sharon Kaehele. "The Burying of the Living in Restoration and Eighteenth Century Comedy." Ball State University Forum 11.4 (1971): 74-79.

Simon, Irène. "Restoration Comedy and the Critics." Revue des Langues Vivantes 29 (1963): 397-430.

Sitter, John. Arguments of Augustan Wit. New York, NY: Cambridge University Press, 1991.

Smith, John Harrington. "Tony Lumpkin and the Country Booby Type in Antecedent English Comedy." Publication of the Modern Language Association 58 (1943): 1038-1049.

Stathis, James J. "Striking an Early Blow for Personal Freedom: A View of Restoration Comedy." To Hold a Mirror to Nature: Dramatic Images and Reflections. Ed. Karelisa V. Hartigan. Washington, DC: Univ Press of America, 1982, 115-126.

Staves, Susan. "A Few Kind Words for the Fop." Studies in English Literature, 1500-1999. 22 (1982): 413-428.

Stedman, John M. The Comic Art of Laurence Sterne Toronto, Canada: University of Toronto Press, 1967.

Stubbs, John Heath. "The Eighteenth Century." The Verse Satire. London, England: Oxford University Press, 1969, 51-96.

Tave, Stuart M. The Amiable Humorist: A Study in the Comic Theory and Criticism of the Eighteenth and Early Nineteenth Centuries. Chicago, IL: University of Chicago Press, 1960.

Thackeray, William Makepeace. The English Humourists of the Eighteenth Century. New York, NY: Henry Holt, 1900.

Thorndike, Ashley H. "Pantomime, Opera and Farce, 1730-1760." English Comedy. New York, NY: Macmillan, 1929, 377-409.

Thorndike, Ashley H. "The Return of Sentiment, 1700-1730." English Comedy. New York, NY: Macmillan, 1929, 342-376.

Thorndike, Ashley H. "The Revival of Comedy, 1760-1800." English Comedy. New York, NY: Macmillan, 1929, 410-438.

Thorndike, Ashley H. "Sentimentality Triumphant, 1760-1800." English Comedy. New York, NY: Macmillan, 1929, 439-471.

Ulman, Craig. Satire and the Correspondence of Swift. Cambridge, MA: Harvard University Press, 1973.

Urwin, G. G., ed. Humorists of the Eighteenth Century. London, England: John Murray, 1962.

Walker, Hugh. English Satire and English Satirists. New York, NY: J. M. Dent, 1925.

Wardroper, John. "The Hell-Begotten Jacobins." Kings, Lords, and Wicked Libellers: Satire and Protest, 1760-1837. London, England: John Murray, 1973, 141-166.

Wardroper, John. Lovers, Rakes, and Rogues. London, England: Shelfmark, 1995.

Thomas D'Urfey (1653-1723)

Alfred Gu L'Estrange points out that Thomas D'Urfey wrote more Odes than Horace wrote, and four times as many Comedies as Terence wrote. Nevertheless, D'Urfey was "reduced to great difficulties by a set of men who had furnished him with the accommodations of life, and [he] would not, as we say, 'be paid with a song' " (L'Estrange 326). D'Urfey wrote through the reigns of King Charles II, King James II, King William and Queene Anne, and into the reign of King George I. His plays were thought attractive at the time, but they contained much that would now be considered gross. They were furthermore deficient in both humor and power (L'Estrange 327). D'Urfey's short songs and poems, however, were another matter. They were his most successful genres. His "Pills to Purge Melancholy" sometimes "approached humour," and D'Urfey often introduced fresh and pleasant glimpses into English country life. In fact, his writing often degenerated into a type of maudlin and indelicate love-making between pseudo-Roman Corydons and Phyllises (L'Estrange 329).

Thomas D'Urfey Bibliography

Graham, C. B. "The Jonsonian Tradition in the Comedies of Thomas D'Urfey." Modern Language Quarterly 8 (1947): 47-52.

L'Estrange, Alfred Gu. "Poetry--Sir Richard Blackmore--D'Urfey--Female Humorists--Carey, etc." History of English Humour. New York, NY: Burt Franklin, 1878, 312-339.

John Oldham (1653-1683)

Hugh Walker feels that Oldham's best writing is his satires. He is best known for his Satires upon the Jesuits, written in 1679 and published in 1682. Because of their violence and intensity, Walker considers these satires to be Juvenalian. Oldham's temperament tended to be violent, and in fact Walker feels he confused violence with strength. This can be seen in his A Satire upon a Woman, which states

Vilest of that vile sex that damn'd us all!

Ordain'd to cause, and plague us for our fall! (Walker 148).

Oldham is equally violent in his Satires upon the Jesuits, the Prologue to which refers to Jesuits as "the vile brood of Loyola and Hell" (Walker 148). Oldham was conscious of his indebtedness to Juvenal, and in fact wrote The Satire in Imitation of the Third Satire of Juvenal, in which he exposed local town life. This satire, and his A Satire Addressed to a Friend that is about to Leave the University are well written because they are both based on personal experiences (Walker 149).

John Oldham Bibliography

Walker, Hugh. English Satire and English Satirists. New York, NY: J. M. Dent, 1925.

Daniel Defoe (c1660-1731)

One of the things that Daniel Defoe is famous for has to do with his being sentenced to stand in the pillory and suffer a fine and imprisonment. But such suffering did not put Defoe in low spirits as might be expected. Rather, he employed part of his time composing a piece entitled, "Hymn to the Pillory" (L'Estrange 24).

Daniel Defoe, like Samuel Pepys, enjoyed life to the hilt. For this reason, his irony was infrequent, and it was mild, but it was nevertheless present, for Defoe lived in an age when irony was to be expected. "Embracing irony as a necessary and established form, he added to it an admirable sense of humour, enlivened by an almost roguish persistence." Turner continues by saying that Defoe's irony, "...lacks the unemotional detachment, often so effective in irony. Here, as in everything else to do with Defoe, cheerfulness was always breaking in, and if not cheerfulness, some other disturbance equally disruptive of irony, a new idea, or the sudden accession of enthusiasm for what things ought to be like" (Turner 46-47). Defoe liked people too much to bear any feeling of contempt or malice toward them, and the fact that his irony bears no bitterness was to his credit (Turner 50-51).

Hugh Walker feels that Daniel Defoe was the first journalist in England who deserves serious consideration as a satirist. The earliest satires that have been identified as Defoe's were two pieces of poetry, A New Discovery of an Old Intrigue (1691), and The True-Born Englishman (1699) (Walker 182). The True-Born Englishman was a verse satire written in honor of King William and the Dutch, and it targeted the nobility of Holland, who didn't appreciate the foreign court. It is a rough piece, filled with rude sarcasm (L'Estrange 22).

In fact, Hugh Walker suggests that satire can be found in most of Defoe's writings, though it is often difficult to determine the precise spirit in which Defoe was writing. Defoe's best satire is The Shortest Way with the Dissenters (1702) (Walker 183). This was originally a pamphlet and the irony is formal and continuous throughout. Here as elsewhere, Defoe's irony is only intended to ridicule, and it is therefore of an unprovocative nature (Turner 48). Although the irony is obvious in The Shortest Way, many of Defoe's contemporaries read the piece as a literal statement of the opinions of a high churchman (Walker 183).

In 1706 Defoe published Jure Divino, a satire which is more substantial in size but not in literary merit.
> Jure Divino is surpassed both by The Mock Mourners, with its severe comments on those who "never value merit till 'tis dead"; and, still more, by The Diet of Poland, which under a transparent disguise, deals with English politics and politicians in the reign of Anne. Perhaps the liveliest passage is that which ridicules the book of travels by William Bromley, afterwards Speaker and Secretary of State. (Walker 183)

Defoe's The Political History of the Devil is probably the richest in mild irony and satire of all that Defoe wrote. A short pamphlet entitled, What if the Pretender should Come? is also quite amusing because of the irony it contains; this pamphlet, however, cost Defoe a number of days in prison before the true meaning of the pamphlet became clear, at which time Defoe was released from prison (Turner 51). Defoe also wrote Comical Pilgrim which contains quite a bit of coarse humor (L'Estrange 25). There is also some satire in Defoe's The Complete English Tradesman, and in his pamphlet entitled Everybody's Business Is Nobody's Business he "made everybody's business his own" (Turner 51).

One of Defoe's most important pieces is The Fortunes and Misfortunes of the Famous Moll Flanders (1721). It is filled with ironies such as the following: "To give the history of a wicked life repented of, necessarily requires that the wicked part should be made as wicked as the real history of it will bear, to illustrate and give a beauty to the penitent part, which is certainly the best and brightest, if related with equal spirit and life" (Defoe viii).

Defoe was the target of a great deal of criticism during his day. In fact, James Sutherland suggests that Defoe was one of the most frequently abused authors of his generation (Rogers 312), and Pat Rogers further suggests that he was "a born dunce who happened to have literary genius" (Rogers 313). In The Dunciad, Pope said "earless on high, stood un-bash'd Defoe" (Rogers 311). Swift made a barbed allusion to Defoe when he referred to him as "one of these authors (the fellow that pilloried; I have forgot his name)." Alexander Pope commented to Joseph Spence that the first part of Robinson Crusoe was "good." He qualified the evaluation by saying, "DeFoe wrote a vast many things, and none bad, though none excellent" (Rogers 311). Pope said that Defoe "figures among the ostriches." He means by this that Defoe is one of those writers "whose heaviness rarely permits them to raise themselves from the ground." "Their motion is between flying and walking; but then they run very fast" (Rogers 311).

Defoe began his days as the son of a tallow chandler on Grub Street, and ended his days on Grub Street as well. But in the meantime he became England's first great novelist, and the first great urban writer, with such books as Colonel Jack, Moll Flanders, and Journal of the Plague Year (Rogers 315). At first the novel was not much respected in England. Not only was it a new genre, but also it tended in the direction of romance, and stooped to borrowing from a variety of sources, such as journalism, biography, picaresque tales, and popular theology. This miscellany gave the novel much of its appeal, but it also detracted from its prestige (Rogers 324).

James Sutherland, Defoe's biographer, probably gives the best summary of Defoe's contribution:
> The contempt with which writers like Pope allude to Defoe is instructive; they sneer because they are secretly uneasy. Here was this fellow, throwing off book after book, and he had no business to be writing at all. He was outside the "ring"; he had not graduated from the recognized school of authorship. His Latin was contemptible, he paid far too little attention to polite diction--he actually wrote more or less as he spoke--and he was full

of vulgar sentiments that appealed to the lower orders. And yet Pope felt that he was a remarkable writer. (Rogers 326-327)

Daniel Defoe Bibliography

Defoe, Daniel. The Fortunes and Misfortunes of the Famous Moll Flanders. London, England: Constable and Company, 1923.
L'Estrange, Alfred Gu. "Defoe." History of English Humour. New York, NY: Burt Franklin, 1878, 22-43.
Rogers, Pat. "Defoe as a Dunce." Grub Street: Studies in a Subculture. London, England: Methuen, 1972, 311-326.
Turner, F. McD. C. The Element of Irony in English Literature. Cambridge, England: Cambridge University Press, 1926.
Walker, Hugh. English Satire and Satirists. London, England: J. M. Dent, 1925.

Anne Finch (1661-1720)

Martha Rainbolt says that about one half of Anne Finch's work is either satiric or humorous. Her humorous work can be divided into three categories: the playful and whimsical poems about loving, writing, and being a woman; the satiric fables; and the humorous satires, often about women and fashion (Rainbolt 366). Myra Reynolds describes Finch's fables as "vignettes of social satire." They are beast fables in which the main characters are owls, eagles, sows, or cats. These animals talk as if they were human, and they behave in funny and disastrous ways. The fables often conclude with a two-line aphorism (Rainbolt 367). In an article about Anne Finch as a feminist, Katharine M. Rogers emphasizes her distinctively female kind of satire (Rainbolt 369), and says, "In her satire on women, the satirist is not a censor scolding or instructing an inferior class, but a right-minded person criticizing other human beings for degrading themselves below the standards which all should meet" (Rogers 46). Myra Reynolds says that Anne Finch's antipathies are lively, and that her insight is acute, "yet her satire is seldom personal, and seldom really acrimonious. Much of it is in the fables and even those with the most caustic morals are often marked in the narrative portions by a gaiety, a humorous lightness of touch, and a tolerance far enough removed from a genuinely pessimistic view of human nature" (Reynolds 120-121).

"The Circuit of Apollo" is typical of Finch's writing, in that her tone is light, playful, and comic. "The Circuit of Apollo" is a satire which asks who the greatest woman poet is. This piece mocks the inflated seriousness of some poets, as Apollo, unlike Paris, avoids his responsibility as a judge and awards the prize to all four. Here Finch is gently chiding the poets for their jealousy of each other (Rainbolt 366-367). In "La Passion Vaincue," the poet is contemplating suicide because her beloved has betrayed her, but she decides against it. The comic tone of this poem is established by the pastoral setting, the French title, and the serious subject as contrasted with the last line of the poem which reads, "Since the Swains are so Many, and I've but One Life" (Rainbolt 367). In "Sir Plausible," Finch discusses the linguistic wimp, saying that "Sir Plausible" doesn't have any opinions of his own, but rather adopts the opinions of other people in his environment "Fast as chameleons change their dye" (Rainbolt 368).

Anne Finch Bibliography

Rainbolt, Martha. "Anne Finch." Encyclopedia of British Humorists, Volume I. Ed. Steven

H. Gale. New York, NY: Garland, 1996, 365-369.
Reynolds, Myra, ed. The Poems of Anne, Countess of Winchilsea. Chicago, IL: University
of Chicago Press, 1903.
Rogers, Katharine M. "Anne Finch, Countess of Winchilsea: An Augustan Woman Poet."
Shakespeare's Sisters: Feminist Essays on Women Poets. Ed. Sandra Gilbert and
Susan Gubar. Bloomington, IN: Indiana University Press, 1979, 32-46.

Sir Samuel Garth (1661-1719)

In 1699 Sir Samuel Garth published The Dispensary, written in the mock-heroic
form of satire. It was well received by Garth's contemporaries; however, Hugh Walker
suggests that while the work did not deserve the panegyrics of Garth's contemporaries,
more recent literary critics have perhaps gone too much the other way. Although we now
care little about the quarrel between the physicians and the apothecaries which was the
main theme of Garth's satire, Garth's work foreshadowed that of John Philips, and even
that of Alexander Pope in his development of the mock-heroic genre.

Sir Samuel Garth Bibliography

Walker, Hugh. English Satire and Satirist. New York, NY: Dutton, 1925.

Richard Bentley (1662-1742)

Richard Bentley became the Master of Trinity College, Cambridge University in
1700, and he remained in that position for thirty-nine years. During that time he was in
a constant feud with the Fellows of Trinity College, both in and out of print, in and out of
court, and in and out of faculty meetings, where he used such epithets as "caustic drudge,"
"cabbage-head," "insect," "worm," "maggot," "vermin," "gnawing rat," "snarling dog," and
"ignorant thief" on his learned opponents. During a meeting of college heads, for example,
one of the heads observed that the matter under discussion was "not yet clear to him."
After a short pause, Bentley retorted, "Are we to wait here until your mud has subsided?"
Mary Green suggests that such language is rather strong, especially when it occurs during
the "Age of Reason" (Green 160).

Richard Bentley Bibliography

Green, Mary Elizabeth. "Cabbage-Heads, Maggots, and Gnawing Rats: Gentlemen and
Scholars in the Eighteenth Century." WHIMSY 2 (1983): 160-161.

Thomas Brown (1663-1704) SCOTLAND

Tom Brown, who was born in 1663, acquired the reputation of a humorist. At
Christ Church, Oxford, Brown became known for his quickness and proficiency, and for
the irregularity of his conduct. During Brown's time, men of letters often obtained patrons,
but Brown's temper and the coarseness of his writing, excessive even in that day, made him
ineligible for this sort of promotion (L'Estrange 315). On one occasion, he was found
guilty of a particularly objectionable frolic, and he was about to be expelled, when he wrote
a letter of penitence to the Dean, who was already familiar with the quality of his talent.

The Dean forgave him if he would do an extemporaneous translation of an epigram by
Martial which read as follows:
Non amo te, Zabidi, nee possum dicere quare;
Hoc tantum possum dicere non amo te.
Brown's translation came out as follows:
I do not love you, Dr. Fell,
But why I cannot tell,
But this I know full well,
I do not love you, Dr. Fell.
Brown was allowed to continue his studies at Oxford (L'Estrange 313).
    In "Lectures on the Philosophy of the Human Mind," Brown observes that the
ludicrous is often a combination of a feeling of gladness and a feeling of astonishment
(L'Estrange 279). In his lectures on "The Human Understanding," Brown observes that the
ludicrous is designed more for admiration than for condemnation. For Brown, the ludicrous
is a result of the contemplation of incongruities, and Brown is puzzled by the fact that
incongruities in science--in chemistry for example--don't make people laugh or smile
(L'Estrange 310-311).

Thomas Brown Bibliography

L'Estrange, A. G. History of English Humour. New York, NY: Burt Franklin, 1878.

Matthew Prior (1664-1721)

    Frances Rippy says that Matthew Prior wrote in an "impressive array of genres:
prose dialogues of the dead, serious philosophical poems, laureate verse, burlesques,
fabliaux, epigrams, satires, [and] comic eroticism" (Rippy 885). The most remarkable
aspect of Matthew Prior's humorous writings might be their astonishing range. Rippy says
that Prior is unexcelled in two types of comic verse, the "Hudibrastic," and the "vers de
société." The "Hudibrastic" was boisterous, exaggerated, pretentious, and doggerel, but the
"vers de société" in contrast was "polished, sophisticated, graceful, refined, playful, and
easy" (Rippy 884). Even beyond these two genres, Prior also produced a number of other
humorous types, such as prose dialogues of the dead, epigrams, comic eroticism, satires,
burlesques, and fabliau-like tales.
    Matthew Prior has many champions. R. P. Blackmur praises Prior for his metrical
variety (octosyllabics and anapests), and for his being of the category of "homo ludens."
Richmond Bond praises Prior's ability to write burlesque and hudibrastic tone (Rippy 886).
T. K. Meier likes the "gentle irony" and the "amused worldliness" of Prior's "Christian,
mythological, classical and heroic traditions" in Henry and Emma. Edward Richards also
praises Prior's Hudibras in the Burlesque tradition (Rippy 887). Frances Rippy says of
Prior's writing, "His classicism repeatedly jests at the striking of heroic poses in an
unheroic and domesticated middle-class world" (Rippy 888).
    Sir Walter Scott felt that "in the powers of approaching and touching the finer
feelings of the heart, he [Prior] has never been excelled, if indeed he has ever been
equalled" (L'Estrange 11). In a section entitled, "Booth's Passion, Locke's Will, Prior's
Predestination," John Sitter suggests that there are basically three ways that Matthew Prior's
Predestination relates to the development of comic characters in England. First, Prior's
Jack and Joan are unrelieved by prayer, or by any other form of introspection, and they end
up in despair or at least in uncomprehending oblivion. They tend to be sketched from a
perspective which Prior extrapolates from Augustine and Calvin, as "reasonable machines,"

and as "puppets danc'd upon this earthly scene." In the second place, the characters' roles
are assumed and superficial. "The characters' compulsions, rationalizations, and rote
responses amuse only by being more schematic than the imputed observer's train of
uneasiness and successive, hurried attempts at ease." Third, Prior's brooding, like Pope's
hypothesizing, and Locke's quandary, all help the audience to realize, in comic form, some
of the deepest fears of the eighteenth century--fears about how determinism and mechanical
operations of fate have profound effects on the unwitting characters (Sitter 39). William
Makepeace Thackeray feels that Prior's lyrical poems were some of the easiest, the richest,
and the most charmingly humorous in all of England (Thackeray 137).

Prior's Dialogues of the Dead were not published until 1907. In all four of these
dialogues, Prior selects two conflicting characters whose values and lifestyles are strikingly
different, and he pits one against the other. Even though Prior may have a favorite in each
pairing, neither character is a clear victor in the debate, because each is successful only in
terms which he himself values, and which his opponent despises. Thus Charles V, the King
of Spain values military victories, but he is pitted against Nicolas Kleynaerts, who values
peace and scholarship. John Locke, a systematic, methodical person who believes that man
should know himself is pitted against Michel de Montaigne, an unsystematic, unmethodical,
person who is convinced that man can never know himself. The third debate is between
Sir Thomas More, who was beheaded because he held fast to his faith and his conscience,
and the Vicar of Bray who achieved success by changing his faith three times so that it
would be more consistent with those who had power over his life. The fourth debate was
between Oliver Cromwell and his porter who went mad on the day that Cromwell executed
Charles I. In these four dialogues, Prior "achieves much of his comic effect by permitting
disparate value systems to collide in a world which is itself chaotic, mad, and disorderly."
The language of these debates is colloquial, plain, and persuasive (Rippy 880).

Prior was also an excellent epigramist. His epigrams are "terse, polished versions
of the same comic value conflicts seen in the prose dialogues," and they "strike out at folly,
hypocrisy, ingratitude, or vanity, in belles, professions, patrons, spouses, knaves, and fools"
(Rippy 880). Some of Prior's funniest stories "depend for their final witty turn upon our
knowledge of human (particularly female) anatomy" (Rippy 881). Prior also wrote comic
treatments of various individuals which Frances Rippy calls "personal satires." These
include "A Satyr on the Modern Translators," and "Satyr on the Poets. In Imitation of the
Seventh Satyr of Juvenal." The Hind and the Panther Transvers'd ridicules Dryden's The
Hind and the Panther, which had been published just two months earlier. It diminishes
Dryden's beasts to two Horatian mice. Bayes comes across as vain, tedious, and fatuous
as he quotes lines from his own poems, with the key terms often altered, always for the
worse. This burlesque ridicules by exploiting an imaginative distance between subject and
style. Subject is lofty, while style is debased. Thus The Hind and the Panther Transvers'd
burlesques Dryden's serious The Hind and the Panther (Rippy 881). Prior's "Satyr on the
Poets," is an attack on Dryden, and his "A Satyr on the Modern Translators" is in part an
attack on Dryden and in part an attack on the Duke of Buckinghamshire, but it is also a
"rueful statement that England is no country for poets--it permits them to starve, whether
they write well or ill" (Rippy 881).

Prior's Alma: or, the Progress of the Mind (1718) is also Hudibrastic, but it also
operates as a burlesque, as it makes fun of philosophical system-building by being written
in a kind of verse language that is generally used only for comic topics (Rippy 881).
Alma: or, the Progress of the Mind gets its title from Samuel Butler's three-part poem
Hudibras (1662-1678) which was itself a mock-romance that ridiculed the Puritans, both
the Presbyterians and the Independents, and which was purposefully erudite, digressive, and
couched in octosyllabic doggerel, containing many clumsy rhymes. Rippy says that, "Prior
captured the Hudibrastic so effectively in Alma: or, The Progress of the Mind that the

eighteenth century came to think of the Hudibrastic in terms of Prior rather than Butler." Rippy continues that, "Its comic octosyllabic couplets, with far-fetched and perilous rhymes and absurdly colloquial tone, suited his own liking for an art which mocked art." In Prior's time, the Oxonian and the Cantabrigian natural philosophers disagreed as to where the mind was located. Following Aristotle, the Oxonians argued that the mind or the soul was everywhere throughout the body. But following Descartes, the Cantabrigians, believed that the mind was entirely in the brain. In Alma, Prior sets up a dialogue with Richard Shelton in which he proposes a compromise theory: "that the mind moves upward through the body throughout life, from its dwelling in the feet of the child to its final residence in the head of the old man." This proposition is presented "in the rollicking semi-doggerel of the Hudibrastic." Thus Alma burlesques as it ridicules. It mixes epigrams with seemingly uncontrolled ramblings. The outrageous rhyming of the couplets frequently doubled, or even tripled (Rippy 883).

One of Prior's funniest burlesques is "An English Ballad, On the Taking of Namur by the King of Great Britain, 1695," in which he mocks Nicolas Boileau-Despreaux's "Ode Sur la Prise de Namur, Par les Armes du Roy, L'Anee 1692." Boileau-Despreaux's piece was written to celebrate the French victory at Namur, but three years later, when Prior's parody appeared, it was the English who had won at Namur. Prior printed Boileau-Despreaux's poem on the left of the page, and his own poem facing it on the right of the page, thus parodying and mocking Boileau-Despreaux's pretentious claims and pretentious diction stanza by stanza (Rippy 881). Another of Prior's funny burlesques is his "Idle Tales," five of which show Prior doing what he does best, "domesticating classical myths." These five are named "Cupid and Ganymede," "The Dove," "Mercury and Cupid," "Protogenes and Apelles," and "Daphne and Apollo." "Closely related to burlesque, these five mythical domesticatings simultaneously mock both the classical materials and the modern society which has no use for them" (Rippy 882). The tales which were most famous in Prior's own day were his "Merry Tales," and included "Hans Carvel," "The Ladle," and "Paulo Purganti and His Wife: An Honest, but a Simple Pair" (Rippy 882). These tales are colloquial, bawdy, and lively, as the narrator tells about unhappy and incompatible marriages and the sexual disasters that result. Frances Rippy says that "The Turtle and the Sparrow" is especially Chaucerian in its tone and flavor (Rippy 883).

Matthew Prior Bibliography

Blackmur, R. P. "Homo Ludens." Kenyon Review 21 (1959): 662-668.
Bond, Richmond P. English Burlesque Poetry, 1700-1750. Harvard Studies in English, No. 6. Cambridge, MA: Harvard University Press, 1932.
L'Estrange, Alfred Gu. "Burlesque--Parody--The'Splendid Shilling'--Prior--Pope--Ambrose Philips--Parodies of Gray's Elegy--Gay." History of English Humour. New York, NY: Burt Franklin, 1878, 1-21.
Meier, T. K. "Prior's Adaptation of 'The Nutbrown Maid.'" Moderna Sprak (Stockholm) 68 (1974): 331-336.
Richards, Edward Ames. Hudibras in the Burlesque Tradition. New York, NY: Octagon Books, 1972.
Rippy, Frances Mayhew. "Matthew Prior as the Last Renaissance Man." Studies in Medieval, Renaissance, American Literature: A Festschrift. Fort Worth, TX: Texas Christian University Press, 1971, 120-131..
Rippy, Frances Mayhew. "Matthew Prior." Encyclopedia of British Humorists, Volume II. Ed. Steven H. Gale. New York, NY: Garland, 1996, 875-889.
Sitter, John. Arguments of Augustan Wit. New York, NY: Cambridge University Press, 1991.

Thackeray, W. M. "Prior, Gay, and Pope." The English Humorists: Charity and Humour: The Four Georges. New York, NY: Dutton, 1912, 133-181.
Thackeray, William Makepeace. "The English Humorists of the Eighteenth Century: A Series of Lectures. Lecture the Fourth: Prior, Gay, and Pope." The Complete Works. Standard Library Edition. New York, NY: Harper and Brothers, 1854.

Sir John Vanbrugh (1664-1726)

Sir John Vanbrugh is an English author of Dutch extraction. He was dubbed "Easy" Vanbrugh, not in reference to his virtue, but rather because of the grace of his writing, "for his dialogue seemed so natural that the actors could learn their lines with scarcely any trouble at all" (Faller 17). Vanbrugh is the author of nine dramatic comedies, of which two--The Relapse (1696), and The Provok'd Wife (1697)--and a fragment of a third--A Journey to London (1728)--are original. The rest are translations and free adaptations of eighteenth-century French comedies. Even though he wrote very little, Vanbrugh is frequently classed with Etherege, Wycherley, Congreve, and Farquhar as among the most talented writers of the Restoration comedy of manners, but of these authors, Vanbrugh's writing has received the least critical attention. In the accounting of history, Vanbrugh will probably be better remembered as an architect than as an author, since there have been more extended studies of his buildings than of his plays (Berkowitz 346).

Vanbrugh was one of the few English authors who was able to acquire a fortune, but this was more for his skills as an architect than for his skills as an author. He constructed a grand theatre on the site of the present Haymarket Opera House. He also built Blenheim, Castle Howard, and a half dozen stately halls in England. In addition he built several houses for himself, one of which was near Whitehall, and was called by Swift, "a thing like a goose pie." Vanbrugh himself describes another house which he built for himself, this one near Greenwich, as "the mince pie" (L'Estrange 340-341).

Relapse was the first play that made Vanbrugh well known, and it is also one of his most humorous comedies. In it there is an effective caricature of the fops of the day, as "Lord Foppington in his fashionable twang gives us his views, and sketches his mode of life" (L'Estrange 341). Lord Foppington is not a totally unsympathetic character. He is genuinely witty, he has a sophisticated sense of humor, and he is always able to retain his "cool." As others are criticizing Lord Foppington in the novel, Amanda responds, "Now it moves my pity more than my mirth to see a man whom nature has made no fool be so very industrious to pass for an ass" (Faller 18). Lincoln Faller suggests that Vanbrugh has given Lord Foppington a dignity that is more than comic, a dignity which lifts him above contempt. When Lord Foppington tells Amanda that he is desperately in love with her and asks her to strike him speechless, she responds by boxing his ear. Amanda's husband responds by drawing his sword. Everything here "bespeaks a low and primitive state of society" (L'Estrange 341). There is some swordplay which follows between Amanda's husband and Lord Foppington, and Lord Foppington falls to the floor. A quack doctor at the scene suggests that the wound may be fatal, and as Lord Foppington is carried off he generously forgives his assailant. This is a comic scene because Lord Foppington is not dying at all; he has only been slightly tweaked in the side. It is also comic because the play suggests that Amanda's reproof would have been more than adequate for the offence (Faller 18).

Vanbrugh (like Farquhar) is a transitional writer who wrote mainly during the turn of the century (1695 to 1705). He is transitional between the high comedy of manners of William Wycherly and the fullblown sentimentality of Richard Steele, but he was actually not a very good adherent of either of these schools (L'Estrange 346). "He accepts the conventions of the comedy of manners, but works subtle variations on their context or application so that they are turned against themselves. He thereby exposes their limitations, demonstrating that they are barely able to do what they set out to do" (L'Estrange 347). Vanbrugh's treatment of the wit-duel motif is a good example of his approach. In The Provok'd Wife, Constant (the hero), and Lady Brute (the heroine) match their wits as they verbally spar with each other:

> LADY BRUTE: Sure you think me scandalously free, Mr. Constant. I'm afraid I shall lose your good Opinion of me.
> CONSTANCE: My good Opinion, Madam, is like your Cruelty, never to be remov'd.
> LADY BRUTE: But if I shou'd remove my Cruelty, then there's an end of your good Opinion.
> CONSTANCE: There is not so strict an Alliance between 'em neither. 'Tis certain I shou'd love you then better (if that be possible) than I do now; and where I love, I always esteem. (L'Estrange 348)

A. G. L'Estrange notes that in this exchange, each speech is at the same time a defensive parry and an offensive thrust, "a response to the preceding speech that twists its image or argument (often by repeating a key word) in order to score a point for the opposite side" (L'Estrange 348).

Lincoln Faller suggests that Lord Foppington anticipates the amiable fools of Oliver Goldsmith and Frances Sheridan, but it is difficult to compare Sir John Brute either with the comedy of manners that came before, or the sentimental comedy which came afterwards. Sir John Brute's wife has "grown so dainty of late [that] she finds fault even with a dirty shirt," and she becomes vexed when her husband returns home "all dirt and bloody." When he demands a kiss, she refuses him. "Delighted by her obvious aversion to him--"I see. Goes damnably against your stomach"--he demands another, and then he grabs and "tumbles" her, besmearing her with his own filth. "So," he says, paying no attention to the presence of her confidante, 'now you being as dirty and as nasty as myself, we may go pig together'" (Faller 18-19). Sir John Brute is an obscenity even in those scenes where he appears without his wife. He prowls the night streets with Lord Rake and Colonel Bully, "abusing the citizenry, breaking their windows, and beating the watch" (Faller 19).

Lincoln Faller suggests that we can see the essence of Vanbrugh's comedy in the characters of Foppington and Brute. His comedy is a blending of "jest and earnest." "Thus, his delight in Foppington's ripe folly is mellowed with a certain sympathy, and his pleasure in Brute is tainted with disgust. In the case of Sir John especially, Vanbrugh displays a sensibility exceptional among the comic writers of his age" (Faller 19).

Vanbrugh's plays contained much more realism than did the plays of Etherege or Wycherley, and this often worked against him. Since the world that Etherege and Wycherley developed in their plays was an artificial one, their characters and plots could be manipulated with little regard for realism or probability, but by adhering to the higher standard of realism, Vanbrugh could not manipulate his plots or his characters, and his plays therefore characteristically end with no resolution at all (L'Estrange 360). But although this lack of resolution made Vanbrugh's audiences uncomfortable, history gives him a higher evaluation.

> By modifying and breaking with the conventions of the comedy of manners, Vanbrugh frees his plays and his characters from the "compelling internal mechanism" that limited the depth and scope of Restoration comedy. His plays, and those of his one major artistic heir, Farquhar, are marked by an unmistakable vitality and expansiveness, as well as a new ability to deal with serious issues. (L'Estrange 361)

Much of Vanbrugh's humor is very rough and indelicate, more like the humor of Aristophanes than that of English writers. One of his gentleman characters calls another gentleman character an "Old Satan," and Vanbrugh's elegant ladies often indulge in rather strong oaths (L'Estrange 341).

Sir John Vanbrugh Bibliography

Berkowitz, Gerald M. "Sir John Vanbrugh and the Conventions of Restoration Comedy." Genre 6 (1973): 346-361.
Faller, Lincoln B. "Between Jest and Earnest: The Comedy of Sir John Vanbrugh." Modern Philology 72 (1974): 17-29.
Finke, Laurie A. "Virtue in Fashion: The Fate of Women in the Comedies of Cibber and Vanbrugh." From Renaissance to Restoration: Metamorphosis of the Drama. Eds. Robert Markley and Laurie Finke. Cleveland, OH: Bellflower, 1984, 154-179.
L'Estrange, Alfred Gu. "Vanbrugh--Colley Cibber--Farquhar." History of English Humour. New York, NY: Burt Franklin, 1878, 340-354.
Perry, Henry Ten Eyck. The Comic Spirit in Restoration Drama: Studies in the Comedy of Etherege, Wycherley, Congreve, Vanbrugh, and Farquhar. New Haven, CT: Yale Univ Press, 1925.

John Arbuthnot (1667-1735) SCOTLAND

John Arbuthnot and Jonathan Swift engaged in many pleasantries and childish fancies together, but whereas Swift, being more impetuous preferred practical jokes, Arbuthnot preferred conundrums and riddles (Turner 54). Speaking about the most eminent writers during the reign of Queen Anne, Samuel Johnson said, "I think Dr. Arbuthnot the first man among them." Johnson considered Arbuthnot to be a universal genius, being an excellent physician to Queen Anne, a man of deep learning, and a "man of much humour" (Turner 45). Even though Arbuthnot did not identify himself with any public movements, his satire nevertheless dealt with current topics. Arbuthnot's Law is a Bottomless Pit was later changed to The History of John Bull. It is from this piece that the term John Bull, the generic title of all Englishmen, was derived (Turner 53). The History of John Bull is a satire about the war of the Spanish Succession and about European politics. It is "especially convincing as a satire upon England and English behavior during the war." "By far the most telling parts of John Bull are not so much ironical as rather bitterly satirical" (Turner 54-55). Arbuthnot combined a certain amount of irony to his wit to give it a keener edge. Only in The Memoirs of Scriblerus is there any really bitter irony. Possibly the most successful of Arbuthnot's ironic works is his essay on The Art of Political Lying (Turner 55). Arbuthnot, together with Addison and Steele combined with their irony and wit a sense of kindliness and tolerance that was not common in their day. "They had a profoundly humanizing influence, not on literature alone, but on their age in general" (Turner 57).

John Arbuthnot Bibliography

Turner, F. McD. C. The Element of Irony in English Literature. Cambridge, England: Cambridge University, 1927.

Susanna Centlivre (1667-1723)

In the preface to Love's Contrivance (1703), Susanna Centlivre explains that she does not write plays the way a man would write them.

> The Criticks cavil most about Decorums, and cry up Aristotle's Rules as the most essential part of the Play. I own they are in the right of it; yet I dare venture a wager they'll never persuade the Town to be of their Opinion, which relishes nothing so well as Humour lightly tost up with Wit, and drest with Modesty and Air.... I do not say this by way of condemning the Unity of Time, Place, and Action; quite contrary, for I think them the greatest Beauties of a Dramatick Poem; but since the other way of writing pleases full as well, and gives the Poet a larger Scope of Fancy..., why should a Man torture, and wrack his Brain for what will be no Advantage to him? (qtd in Kinney 86-87).

Susanna Centlivre and Aphra Behn were both very popular eighteenth-century women playwrights. Centlivre's Busie Body (1709) was performed in London 475 times between 1709 and 1800 (Frushell 16). Behn's The Rover (1677) was also a very popular play, having 158 performances between 1700 and 1760 (Link xiii). Suz-Anne Kinney says that both Centlivre and Behn were accused of plagiarism for having used other playwrights' ideas in their own plays, and they both suffered virulent criticism as a result. Because of this they both tried unsuccessfully to publish plays anonymously. More important than this, however, is the fact that both of these women authors were forced to support themselves through the money that they earned from their writing of plays (Kinney 82).

Susanna Centlivre Bibliography

Centlivre, Susanna. The Busie Body. (1709). Los Angeles, CA: University of California Press, 1949.

Frushell, Richard C. "Marriage and Marrying in Susanna Centlivre's Plays." Papers on Language and Literature 22 (1986): 16-38.

Kinney, Suz-Anne. "Confinement Sharpens the Invention: Aphra Behn's The Rover and Susanna Centlivre's The Busie Body. Look Who's Laughing: Gender and Comedy. Ed. Gail Finney. Amsterdam, Netherlands: Gordon and Breach, 1994.

Link, Frederick M. ed. "Introduction." The Rover by Aphra Behn. Lincoln, NE: University of Nebraska Press, 1967. ix-xvi.

Jonathan Swift (1667-1745) IRELAND

Peter Schakel says that Swift took on a lofty sense of superiority, and used his digressive story-telling style, his reductive argument, his classical references, and his sarcastic asides to produce his excellent satire (Schakel 324). Swift's Advice to Grub-Street Verse Writers is a poem which gives mock advice, and as such represented a very popular form in early eighteenth century writing. A Meditation upon a Broomstick, And Somewhat Beside (1710) is a parody on the popular forms of religious meditation during Swift's day. A Modest Proposal is Swift's most famous satire, and in some ways anticipates the absurd irony of Franz Kafka and Samuel Beckett. His The Battle of the Books, his Gulliver's Travels, and A Tale of the Tub are masterpieces of allegory, but Swift was also fond of puns, riddles, and whimsical verse, or what he liked to call "bagatelles" (Washington 1086).

Gene Washington suggests that the "persona" is Swift's main satirical device, and is the source of most of his humor. It is such personas as Gulliver, and the Modest Proposer who tend to be dogmatic, proud, and argumentative. The persona in A Tale of a Tub is a Grub-Street bookseller who is mainly interested in promoting modern literature.

In A Modest Proposal, the persona is a "projector" whose "main 'intention' is to 'provide' for the poor children of Ireland and their parents and to bring some pleasure to English landlords." In Directions to Servants, the persona is the Footman, and in The Bickerstaff Papers it is the astrologer. The motives of such persona are expressed with demonic intensity, and they rise from basic and prosaic emotions such as the need to pontificate or to force an opinion (Washington 1089). Gulliver's persona is more complicated. His nature changes from voyage to voyage. When he is in Lilliput, he is gentle and obliging to his hosts, and very much naive. In Brobdingnag, on the other hand, he is nervous, impatient, and sometimes shrill. In Laputa he has very little interaction with the natives, so he is much like a modern tourist, looking around and wandering from place to place as he tries to figure out the local customs. In his fourth and final voyage to Houyhnhnmland, he becomes very misanthropic, a persona that could not have been predicted from the personas he had established in the earlier voyages (Washington 1090).

Swift was a master at "mundus inversus" or turning the world upside down. In Lilliput, Gulliver is confronted be people who are twelve times smaller than he is. This same inversion is repeated in Brobdingnag, but her it is Gulliver who is twelve times smaller than the natives. In Houyhnhnmland it is the horses who are the rulers, thus inverting the man-as-master, horse-as-servant relationship. Before visiting Houyhnhnmland, Gulliver had considered white to be the best color, but in this land, the equine color of black is the best color. "Among the Houyhnhnms, the white, the sorrel, and the iron-grey were not so exactly shaped as the bay, the dapple-grey and the black" (Washington 1090).

Swift had three main concerns about England: the first concern was with reason vs. the lack of reason. The second concern was with politics. The third concern was with language and style. The first concern (with reason vs. the lack of reason) can be illustrated in the Yahoos vs. Gulliver vs. the Houyhnhnms of Gulliver's last voyage. The Yahoos were irrational, while the Houyhnhnms were rational; and Gulliver was neither fully rational like the Houyhnhnms, nor fully irrational like the Yahoos (Washington 1086). Swift was very much concerned that the established church was being threatened, and he concluded that among the Catholics there was too much Whiggish tolerance, and that this was being reinforced by such dissenting groups as the Presbyterians and the Quakers. It was against such groups that Swift wrote A Tale of a Tub, and Mechanical Operation of the Spirit, satires not only against religious fanatics, but also against the reducing of religion to dogmatism and enthusiasm (Washington 1087). Swift's second concern (with politics and politicians) is seen throughout Gulliver's Travels in that Gulliver is everywhere alienated from power. Gulliver's proper name, Lemuel Gulliver, is not used anywhere in the entire novel. Instead, he is addressed by such temporary titles as "Man Mountain," or "Relplum Scalcath" or merely with such pronouns as "you," "he," or "it." Swift's concern with politics can also be seen in the relationship between Swift's life and that of Gulliver. Swift wrote Gulliver's Travels after he had returned to England from Ireland, and in his personal correspondence dated August 10, 1716, he said, "I am in an obscure scene, where you know neither thing nor person...the scene and the times have depressed me wonderfully." In a later letter, dated December 1, 1731, Swift said, "I am in so obscure a corner, quite thrown out of the present world, and within a few steps of the next" (Washington 1087). Swift's third concern (with language and style) can be seen in several of his minor humorous pieces such as his Hints Towards an Essay on Conversation (1710), his A Modest Defense of Punning (1716), and his Polite Conversation (1738). These three pieces attack language corruption, and establish the need to preserve linguistic integrity between the speaker and the listener or the writer and the reader. Note also that in Gulliver's Travels, Gulliver describes the writing of the Lilliputians as being "very peculiar; being neither from the left to the right, like the Europeans; nor from the right to the left, like the Arabians, but aslant from one corner of the paper to the other, like ladies in

England" (Washington 1089). One aspect of language that especially intrigued Swift was the "reification" of an idea, in which for satirical purposes, a thing is used to represent an idea (Washington 1090). The best example of this process is in the Academy of Lagado, where all words have been substituted by actual things (Washington 1091).

A Tale of a Tub, Written for the Universal Improvement of Mankind (1704) contains some of Swift's most original and brilliant satire (Schakel 324). A Tale of a Tub has two satiric targets. In the "Apology" to the fifth edition, Swift describes his first target as "the numerous and gross corruptions in religion and learning." Thus Swift was attacking behavior which he considered to be deviant from the pure ancient Christianity. He was attacking the additions to the original Christian doctrine which he felt lacked biblical basis, such as the papacy, purgatory, and transubstantiation. He was also attacking the deviations of the Presbyterians and the other "dissenters" who had broken off from the Church of England, especially their rejection of liturgy and music, and their reliance on individual interpretations of the scriptures. Peter, Martin, and Jack are the three brothers in A Tale of a Tub. When the father of the three brothers dies, each of them is given a new coat (symbolic of the doctrine and the faith of Christianity), and a Will (symbolic of the New Testament), and instructions that they are not to alter their coats in any way. Peter (who represents the Catholic Church) convinces the brothers that they should add some shoulder knots and some lace to their coats, and then he tries to convince them that he is the sole heir to their father's fortune, and imposes various restrictions on his brothers. Martin (Martin Luther), and Jack (John Calvin) eventually rebel against Peter (the Rock). Jack, the more radical of the two Protestants rips every ornament off from his coat, leaving it torn and tattered and becoming mad in the process. Martin (who stands not only for Martin Luther, but who also stands for the Anglican Church) removes the worst of Peter's ornaments, but with caution and moderation. The Tale of the Tub is thus meant to be a strong rejection of Catholicism and radical Protestantism, and a defense and an endorsement of the Church of England, and its extension the Church of Ireland (Schakel 327).

In his An Account of a Battel Between The Antient and Modern Books in St. James's Library (1704), Swift uses the process of reification to turn abstractions into physical things as a way of ridiculing the ideas. This book is in three parts, each in a different literary form. The first part is a pseudo-academic discourse that outlines the background of the battle. The quarrel began on Parnassus Hill; the Modern books were inhabiting a lower place on the hill than the Ancient books, and they asked to exchange places, or else to cut the hill down to their level. The second part of the book is an allegorical fable about a spider and a bee (Schakel 324). The spider was modern in its thinking in looking inside himself for answers, while the bee, like ancient thinkers looked outward toward nature for answers. The third part of the Battle of the Books is the battle itself, as described in mock-epic terms that are rich with allusions to the Iliad and the Aeneid (Schakel 325). The bee is developed as a gentlemanly English figure of Enlightenment, while the spider is portrayed as an "outsider," who is vulgar, explosive, and rebellious (Schakel 326).

The Bickerstaff Papers (1708-1709) are witty and amusing. Predictions for the Year 1708 is written in a style which parodies the style of Almanacs. In this paper, Isaac Bickerstaff predicts the death of John Partridge, an almanac maker whose views were different from those of Swift. "I have consulted the Star of his Nativity by my own Rules; and find he will infallibly die upon the 29th of March next, about eleven at Night, of a raging Fever." The 29th of March came and went, and at the end of March a new edition appeared entitled The Accomplishment of the First of Mr. Bickerstaff's Predictions, in which Bickerstaff announced that Partridge had indeed died at the time and in the manner he had foretold. At this point, Partridge was forced to issue an announcement that the reports were false, and that he was still perfectly alive (Schakel 330).

In August of 1710, Swift became the editor of The Examiner, and in this position, he adapted the Addison and Steele devices of writing letters to the journal. Some of these letters were stand-alones; others were answered, often ironically, using fables and other narrative devices within the answers, and invoking the world of the coffeehouse as the location of the writing and the source of the information (Schakel 335). Swift used similes, homespun analogies, lists, rhetorical questions, exaggeration, and sarcasm in The Examiner (Schakel 336).

Between September of 1710 and June of 1713 Swift wrote his "journal" to Stella (Schakel 339). These letters were intimate in flavor and employed a tone which Swift referred to as his "little language." it was filled with baby talk in which the l's and the r's were interchanged, as in "Go play cards & be melly...& rove pdfr who roves Md bettle zan his Rife. Farewell deelest Md." Swift used "MD" to mean "My Dear," or "My Dears." Stella is referred to as "Ppt," which stood either for "Poppet," or for "Poor Pretty Thing." Swift referred to himself as "Pdfr," which was to be pronounced as "Podifar," and which stood for "Poor Dear Foolish Rogue," or "Poor Dear Fellow." Much of the charm of the writing came from the colloquial and conversational style (Schakel 340). Even the handwriting exhibited a certain carelessness that again contributed to the intimacy of the effect. Here as in other Swift writings, Swift was able to develop a playful "voice" that was not entirely his own (Schakel 341).

Peter Schakel considers Swift's "An Argument Against Abolishing Christianity" to be his finest satirical essay. It was published in Miscellanies in Prose and Verse (1711), and says that freethinkers had proposed a bill in Parliament for the abolishment of Christianity and that they had written pamphlets telling the advantages to be gained from doing so. Swift's essay is written as a reply to these non-existent pamphlets, questioning the so-called advantages to be gained from abolishing Christianity, and explaining what disadvantages would come about if such a proposal were to be enacted, but he does so as an unreliable narrator, and he does not properly present the opposing case. The first hint that the "I" is not to be relied on comes at the end of the opening paragraph, "in the present Posture of our Affairs at home or abroad, I do not yet see the absolute Necessity of extirpating the Christian Religion from among us." Thus, he does not yet see the absolute necessity of eliminating Christianity (Schakel 332). He then goes on to say that there is no real need of exterminating "Christianity" as a label; what needs to be extinguished instead is the faith and commitment that influence a person's values and actions. Once these are eliminated, the term "Christianity" should be allowed to remain. The essayist "dismisses 'real Christianity' as outdated and impractical: 'I hope, no Reader imagines me so weak to stand up in the Defense of real Christianity; such as used in primitive Times.'" Schakel says that much of the wit and humor of this piece comes from the reasons that the essayist gives in rebuttal to the advantages which his opponents claim for abolishing Christianity. "Nominal Christianity should be retained because it gives the Wits a trivial target to attack and diverts them from attacking important things like the government and political policies." Phillip Harth suggests that Swift is here satirizing both freethinkers and nominal Christians, both of which in Swift's eyes threaten Christianity, the first from the outside, the second from within (Schakel 333).

In 1722, England awarded William Wood a patent that authorized him to coin and distribute a hundred thousand pounds worth of Irish copper farthings and halfpence. But Ireland was not allowed to have its own mint to make its own money, and it incensed the Irish that the authority to coin money for Ireland could be given without even consulting the Irish. So in 1724, Jonathan Swift wrote the first of his "Drapier's Letters," entitled A Letter To The Shop-Keepers, Tradesmen, Farmers, and Common People of Ireland. In this letter Swift took on the voice of a dealer in cloth and dry goods, or a drapier, to persuade people not to accept the new coins. Swift exaggerated and pushed to the extremes as he dramatized with vivid examples what would happen if people used the coins. He said that Mr. Woods had made his half-pence of base metal, and of a size that was so much smaller than the English ones that "the Brazier would not give you above a Penny of good money for a Shilling of his." The Drapier prophesied that soon a country squire would have to use five or six horses laden with sacks of the money when he came to town to shop (Schakel 345). And he further prophesied that in order to pay his annual rent, a landowner would require twelve hundred horses to carry the money. He alluded to the biblical statement that people should not touch anything that was "unclean," and said that these half-pence were "like the accursed thing," and that they would "run about like the Plague and destroy every one who lays his hands upon them." The Drapier predicted that soon the butchers, the brewers, and the bricklayers, and even the beggars would offer declarations that they would refuse to accept the new coins. The Drapier letters caused a great stir, and England offered the huge reward of three hundred pounds for information leading to the Drapier's identity. But even though it was common knowledge throughout Ireland that Swift had written the letters, the reward was never claimed, because Swift was regarded as a national hero. Flyers were circulated in Dublin quoting from 1 Samuel 14: "And the people said unto Saul, Shall Jonathan die, who hath wrought this great salvation in Israel? God forbid: as the Lord liveth, there shall not one hair of his head fall to the ground." Thus did the Irish unit, and finally they gained victory. The English government was forced to withdraw Wood's patent; this happened in August of 1725 (Schakel 346).

Samuel Holt Monk has noted that Travels Into Several Remote Nations of the World, In Four Parts, by Lemuel Gulliver, First a Surgeon, and then a Captain of Several Ships (1726) (hereafter referred to as Gulliver's Travels is a satire about the four aspects of man--the physical, the political, the intellectual, and the moral (Monk 70). Monk says that in the adventures to Laputa, Swift was ridiculing the pursuit of science over moral sense. The seventeenth century was the "Age of Enlightenment," an age when Galileo Galilei challenged the church teachings over the Heliocentric universe, and Sir Isaac Newton developed many new theories in the field of physics, one of which was gravity. They both favored experimentation and observation over faith and tradition. During the Enlightenment, scientists were obsessed with new discoveries at the expense of the old. "Laputa" is probably a term coming from Spanish "La Puta" which means "the whore." The heads of the scientists in Laputa "were all reclined either to the right or to the left; one of their eyes turned inward, and the other directly to the zenith" (qtd. in Greenburg 174). They were introspective. They lacked grounding. The scientists had flappers who would hit them on the mouth or the ear with bags to bring them back to reality. After Gulliver gives an account of the history of seventeenth-century England, the King responds by describing Gulliver's account as "only a heap of conspiracies, rebellions, murders, massacres, revolutions, banishments; the very worst effects that avarice, faction, hypocrisy, perfidiousness, cruelty, rage, madness, hatred, envy, lust, malice and ambition could produce" (Quinnell 148).

The voyage to Laputa, Book Three of Gulliver's Travels is regarded by many critics to be less interesting than the other books for four reasons. First, in this book the objects of Swift's satire are more particular to his age. Second, in this book the satiric attack is delivered on too many different fronts to have a strong effect. And third, it is only in this book that Gulliver is an observer and not an actor (Monk 72). K. M. Williams, however, notes that in this book Swift is showing his readers how the eighteenth-century rationalists were misusing their powers of reason. In this book, speculative thought is aimless, ridiculous, and without any practical ramifications. Those engaged in it have their eyes turned inward and upward and have to have their mouths and ears flapped by bladders in order to be roused from their deep thoughts. The Laputans "have cut themselves off completely from all that is humanly creative and constructive.... In fact, their flying island represents their desertion of the common earth of reality" (Williams 66). Chitra Duttagupta notes that in Chapter Two and Chapter Three of this book, the Laputans are devoted to useless work such as cataloguing stars and comets, cutting their food according to mathematical shapes, using compasses and rulers for measuring clothes and describing the beauty of a woman in terms of rhombs, circles, parallelograms, ellipses, and so forth. Duttagupta notes that the projects in Chapter Five and Chapter Six are equally impractical. One project is investigating ways of extracting sun beams out of cucumbers; another project is designed to change human excrement back into its original food and another project connects the mind to the intestinal tract so that knowledge becomes the end-product of the digestive process. There are projects designed to make fire malleable and to soften marble for pin cushions, and to breed naked sheep, and to begin the building of houses at the roof and work down to the foundation. There is still another project designed to cut polysyllabic words down to a single syllable; a later stage in this project is to abolish words altogether and to carry things around instead to represent these words. There is even a plan for curing the ills of party government by slicing in half the brains of two opposing party members and interchanging them, and still another project whereby the political complexion of a man could be determined by examining the complexion of his stool.

Chitra Duttagupta notes that the satire gets darker and darker with each book of Gulliver's Travels. W. E. Yeomans suggests that in the last book of Gulliver's Travels the "horse-over-man superiority of Houyhnhnmland [is] far greater than the man-over-horse superiority of Europe" (Yeomans 263). In Gulliver's Travels Swift's purpose was "to vex the world rather than divert it." In a letter to Alexander Pope dated September 29, 1725, Swift confessed that "principally I hate and detest that animal called man.... Upon this great foundation of misanthropy the whole building of my Travels is erected" (Case 101).

A Modest Proposal (1729), one of Swift's best known pamphlets, was written in the form of an economic essay (Schakel 346). As an economic essay, it first establishes the problem, and then offers a solution, outlining the advantages of the proposal, and refuting any possible objections. Swift thus mimics the style and the language of a serious proposer. In typical Swift fashion, the proposal contains an abundant amount of concrete detail. The imagery compares the Irish to cattle, as the child is "dropt from its Dam." Butcher imagery is later employed as they "flay the Carcase" and use the skin for the making of fine gloves and books. Cooking imagery is also employed as when the child would make "a most delicious nourishing, and wholesome Food; whether Stewed, Roasted, Baked, or Boiled" (Schakel 347). In keeping with the economic essay, there is also much statistical imagery: "I have already computed." What all of this imagery has in common is that it is all dehumanizing. "It treats human beings as things to be used for someone else's benefit." And it therefore appropriately reflects England's attitude toward the Irish. "She dehumanizes them, uses them to her advantage without regard for their welfare." Swift merely takes metaphors of the day and changes them from metaphorical to literal in their effect. Two such metaphors are "devoured" and "eat up." Thus Swift extends this metaphor: "I grant this Food will be somewhat dear, and therefore very proper for Landlords; who, as they have already devoured most of the Parents, seem to have the best Title to the Children" (Schakel 348).

See also Nilsen, Don L. F. Humor in Irish Literature: A Reference Guide. Westport, CT: Greenwood, 1996.

Jonathan Swift Bibliography

Bullitt, John M. Jonathan Swift and the Anatomy of Satire: A Study of Satiric Technique. Cambridge, MA: Harvard University Press, 1953.
Carnochan, W. B. "Swift's Tale: On Satire, Negation, and the Uses of Irony." Eighteenth-

Century Studies 5 (1971): 122-144.

Case, A. E. Four Essays on Gulliver's Travels. Princeton, NJ: Princeton University Press, 1945.

Davis, Herbert. Jonathan Swift: Essays On His Satire and Other Studies. New York, NY: Oxford University Press, 1964.

Davis, Herbert. The Satire of Jonathan Swift New York, NY: Macmillan, 1947.

Davis, Herbert. "Swift's Use of Irony." The World of Jonathan Swift. Ed. Brian Vickers. Oxford, England: Blackwell, 1968, 154-170.

Duttagupta, Chitra. "Swift's Satire in Gulliver's Travels. Unpublished Paper. Tempe, AZ: Arizona State University, 1996.

Eddy, William Alfred, ed. Swift: Satires and Personal Writings. New York, NY: Oxford University Press, 1932.

Elliott, R. C. "The Satirist Satirized." Twentieth-Century Interpretations of "Gulliver's Travels." Ed. F. Brady. Englewood Cliffs, NJ: Prentice-Hall, 1968, 41-53.

Greenburg, Robert A., et al. eds. The Writings of Jonathan Swift. New York, NY: W. W. Norton, 1973.

Leavis, F. R. "The Irony of Swift." Swift: A Collection of Critical Essays. Ed. E. Tuveson. Englewood Cliffs, NJ: Prentice-Hall, 15-29.

Mack, Maynard. "The Muse of Satire." Yale Review 41 (1951): 80-92.

Monk, S. H. "The Pride of Lemuel Gulliver." Twentieth-Century Interpretations of "Gulliver's Travels." Ed. F. Brady. Englewood Cliffs, NJ: Prentice-Hall, 1968, 70-79.

Palmeri, Frank A. "'To Write upon Nothing': Narrative Satire and Swift's A Tale of a Tub." Genre 18 (1985): 151-172.

Peterson, Leland D. "Swift's Project: A Religious and Political Satire." PMLA 82 (1967): 54-63.

Quinnell, P., ed. Jonathan Swift's Gulliver's Travels. Calcutta, India: Rupa, 1726.

Quintana, Ricardo. "Situational Satire: A Commentary on the Method of Swift." University of Toronto Quarterly 17 (1948): 130-136.

Rawson, Claude. "The Character of Swift's Satire: Reflections on Swift, Johnson, and Human Restlessness." The Character of Swift's Satire. Ed. Claude Rawson. Newark, DE: University of Delaware Press, 1983, 21-82.

Rosenheim, Edward W. Jr. Swift and the Satirist's Art. Chicago, IL: University of Chicago Press, 1963.

Schakel, Peter J. "Jonathan Swift." British Prose Writers, 1660-1800. Ed. Donald T. Siebert. Detroit, MI: Gale Research, 1991, 319-351.

Siebert, Donald T., Jr. "Masks and Masquerades: The Animus of Swift's Satire." South Atlantic Quarterly 74 (1975): 435-445.

Starkman, Miriam K. Swift's Satire on Learning in "A Tale of a Tub." Princeton, NJ: Princeton University Press, 1950.

Steele, Peter. Jonathan Swift: Preacher and Jester. Oxford, England: Clarendon Press, 1978.

Stout, Gardner D., Jr. "Satire and Self-Expression in Swift's Tale of a Tub." Studies in the Eighteenth Century, ii: Papers Presented at the Second David Nichol Smith Memorial Seminar, Canberra, 1970. Ed. R. F. Brisenden. Canberra, Australia: Australian National University Press, 1973, 323-339.

Stout, Gardner D., Jr. "Speaker and Satiric Vision in Swift's Tale of a Tub." Eighteenth-Century Studies 3 (1969): 175-199.

Washington, Gene. "Jonathan Swift." Encyclopedia of British Humorists, Volume II. Ed. Steven H. Gale. New York, NY: Garland, 1996, 1085-1093.

Williams, K. M. "Conclusion to Jonathan Swift and the Age of Compromise. Swift: A Collection of Critical Essays. Ed. E. Tuveson. Englewood Cliffs, NJ: Prentice-Hall,

1964, 115-122.
Yeomans, W. E. "The Houyhnhnm as Menippean Horse." Swift: Modern Judgements. Ed.
A. N. Jeffares. London, England: Macmillan, 1966, 258-266.

William Congreve (1670-1729) IRELAND

Satire was an important aspect of William Congreve's humor; nevertheless, his most
important quality was wit. His language and his actions were filled with a kind of paradox
that provokes both laughter and thought (Rosenblum 266).
    The Old Batchelor (1693) is filled with impostors. Heartwell pretends to slight
women, but in fact he is secretly in love with Sylvia. Sir Joseph Wittol and Captain Bluffe
are the play's greatest fools. Their names reveal their characters. Sir Joseph has such a
high opinion of himself that he believes that Araminta, a fine lady, has fallen in love with
him. Captain Bluffe pretends to be brave. Fondlewife, the Puritan banker, becomes a
cuckold when he marries someone who is very much his junior (Rosenblum 266).
Bellmour has slept with Silvia, but he nevertheless maintains that Silvia has remained true
to Vainlove because she thought she was sleeping with Vainlove and not Bellmour.
Bellmour argues further that Silvia is even more true to Vainlove because in his absence
she showed her fondness for him by choosing a lover as much like him as possible.
Bellmour argues that If anyone is abused in this case, it is the lover, not the husband, "for
'tis an argument of her great zeal toward him, that she will enjoy him in effigy"
(Rosenblum 267). Later, when Fondlewife and Laetitia are reconciled, Laetitia puts her
arms around Fondlewife's neck, and this allows Bellmour to kiss her hand behind
Fondlewife's back. This scene, plus the scene involving Heartwell's inability to move out
of Silvia's doorway, and the scene of Silvia's pretense of innocence, and Bluffe's pretense
at bravery are all considered by Joseph Rosenblum to be "entertaining spectacles"
(Rosenblum 268). In The Old Batchelor, the targets are the dissenters, the "citizens," the
country bumpkins, and the old men. At the end of the fifth act the witty couple is
rewarded with marriage (Rosenblum 267).
    In a letter written to William Walsh, John Dryden said that Congreve's The Double
Dealer (1693) hit too close to the mark to be appreciated. "The women think he has
exposed their bitchery too much; and the gentlemen are offended with him for the
discovery of their follies, and the way of their intrigues, under the notion of friendship to
their ladies' husbands" (Rosenblum 266). The tone of The Double Dealer is rather dark,
and the targets of satire are not marginal characters, but rather London society itself. It is
London's lords and knights who appear as foolish as the Wittols and the Fondlewifes
(Rosenblum 269). The title of The Double Dealer comes from the behavior of Maskwell,
who is Lady Touchwood's servant and lover. Maskwell appears to be helping Mellefont
with the Touchwoods, but in truth, he is double dealing (Rosenblum 268). According to
Rosenblum, The Double Dealer contains a great deal of witty dialogue and a number of
enjoyable scenes. In the second act, when Lady Froth asks her husband to show Cynthia
how he bowed when he was given a picture of his future wife, he seems so fond of the
image that his wife becomes jealous of her own image. Lady Plyant may have sex with
most men in the play, but she refuses to have sex with her husband. Instead, "she has him
swathed down, and so put to bed; and there he lies with a great beard, like a Russian bear
upon a drift of snow" (Rosenblum 269).
    The sharpest satire in Love for Love (1695) appears in the fourth act, when
Valentine pretends to think himself to be "Truth." He asks a lawyer, "Does thou know
me?" and when the lawyer responds that he does, Valentine says, "Thou liest, for I am
Truth." Later, when Foresight asks what is going to happen at court, Valentine responds,

"I am Truth. I never come there." Foresight in Love for Love is an astrologer, and his name is ironic, for he cannot tell who is "in conjunction" with his wife. Foresight is a foolish figure who believes in fortune-telling, and who has married a young and sanguine wife. In Love for Love, Tattle initiates Prue into the art of love. This is funny because Prue is such an adept pupil. Tattle asks if she will kiss him and she responds "No indeed; I'm angry at you." But at the same time she runs over and kisses him. By the end of the scene, Prue announces that she is going to hide from Tattle behind her bed curtains, and that he would have to push her down to get into her room (Rosenblum 270).

In The Way of the World (1700), Millament has to forfeit half of her fortune if she marries Mirabell without the consent of her aunt, Lady Wishfort. Lady Wishfort had formerly been in love with Mirabell herself, and so she opposes the match, especially when she learns that he was courting her to gain access to her niece (Rosenblum 270). Congreve notes that some members of the audience have had difficulty distinguishing between the truewits and the pretenders in The Way of the World. Even Alexander Pope questioned whether Congreve's fools were fools indeed. Fainall, for example, is witty and intelligent, but he is also malicious. "As the discussion turns to Marwood, Mirabell emerges as both the better man and keener wit." In The Way of the World, Sir Wilfull Fitwoud is a country squire that is so innocent and ignorant of urban ways that he is unable to fit into sophisticated society. For example, he mistakes Millamant's allusion to the poet Suckling as a reference to a young edible pig. In The Way of the World, Lady Wishfort says to Foible, "I look like an old peeled wall," thus indicating that she is all façade. Lady Wishfort stands between Mirabell and Millamant. She is too old for the young Mirabell, so she tries to cover up her wrinkles by caking on her makeup so thickly that it "cracks and peels like old paint." Witwoud and Petulant are two of the false wits in The Way of the World. They are both preoccupied with their appearances. Witwoud memorizes clever sayings so that he will be considered intelligent. Petulant pays people to call on him so that he will be considered to be popular (Rosenblum 271). Petulant even leaves a group of people, puts on a disguise, and returns to "call for himself, wait for himself; nay, and what's more, not finding himself sometimes [leave] a letter for himself." At the end of The Way of the World, the true wits are united, and the false wits are exposed. The villains are driven from the stage. Nevertheless, at the end of the play, Mrs. Fainall remains married to a man who has tried to run her through with a sword. The ending of the play is ambiguous in its moral in that each of the Fainalls has deceived the other (Rosenblum 272).

See Nilsen, Don L. F. **Humor in Irish Literature: A Reference Guide**. Westport, CT: Greenwood, 1996.

William Congreve Bibliography

Fujimure, Thomas H. The Restoration Comedy of Wit. Princeton, NJ: Princeton University Press, 1952.

Kronenberger, Louis. "Congreve." The Thread of Laughter: Chapters on English Stage Comedy from Jonson to Maugham. New York, NY: Hill and Wang, 1952, 117-145.

Loftis, John. Comedy and Society from Congreve to Fielding. Stanford, CA: Stanford University Press, 1958.

Markley, Robert. Two-Edg'd Weapons: Style and Ideology in the Comedies of Etherege, Wycherley, and Congreve. Oxford, England: Clarendon, 1988.

Muir, Kenneth. "The Comedies of William Congreve." Restoration Theatre. Ed. John Russell Brown, and Bernard Harris. London, England: Edward Arnold, 1965, 220-237.

Novak, Maximillian E. "Love, Scandal, and the Moral Milieu of Congreve's Comedies."

Congreve Considered. Los Angeles, CA: William Andrews Clark Library, 1971, 23-50.
Rosenblum, Joseph. "William Congreve." Encyclopedia of British Humorists, Volume I. Ed. Steven H. Gale. New York, NY: Garland, 1996, 264-274.
Wertheim, Albert. "Romance and Finance: The Comedies of William Congreve." Comedy from Shakespeare to Sheridan: Change and Continuity in the English and European Dramatic Tradition. Ed. A. R. Braunmuller. Newark, DE: University of Delaware Press, 1986, 255-273.

Colley Cibber (1671-1757)

Colley Cibber was poet laureate of England. He wrote four original comedies. His Love's Last Shift (1696), and his The Careless Husband (1704) have gained Cibber some reputation because they address questions which are urgent to contemporary audiences, marital discord, the balance between personal liberty and social adjustment, and the balance between material security and individual feeling in choosing a marriage partner. Cibber had a hostility against women which became progressively worse from Love's Last Shift in 1696 to The Provoked Husband (1728). Both in Love's Last Shift and in The Provoked Husband the women are scolded by being told about "unnatural" women stepping out of their proper places who were appropriately humiliated for their actions. But in The Lady's Last Stake, which is a reply to female critics of Lady Easy's wifely "patience," "the various mortifications attendant on Lady Wronglove's resentment and mannishness are set out in strong and crude colours." Twenty years later, Cibber's resentment seems to be increasing even more in The Provoked Husband, where the dialogue on the harm that comes in spoiling wives is described by Vanbrugh as "shrill and bitter" (Drougge 61-62). Nevertheless, Cibber's comedies are filled with hope and sentimentality.

Cibber's sentimentality, his brash early version of "eighteenth-century optimism," retains a measure of interest by virtue of its (still earlier) images of emergent social attitudes: in Love's Last Shift, the reformation of the anarchistic, libidinal Loveless into a provident and prosperous husband, and in The Careless Husband the collapse from these economic realities into "careless" and "easy" domesticity, presided over by the genteel wifeliness of Lady Easy. (Drougge 79)

Richard Brown has written an article entitled "The Fops in Cibber's Comedies." He describes Sir Novelty Fashion in Love's Last Shift (1696) as a "fool carefully and conscientiously self-made. He has brains, and his fopperies and affectations are merely a deliberate experiment in self-advertisement" (Brown 31).

In the three comedies which Cibber published in 1707, the fops became protagonists, and their personalities determined the shape of the action as their love interests provided the comic resolutions (Brown 31). Some of Cibber's fops are charming. Lord Foppington in The Careless Husband (1704) presents a sang froid that almost makes him heroic, and he gestures magnificently in his absurdity. Lord George Brilliant in The Lady's Last Stake (1707) and Celadon in The Comical Lovers (1707) are characters who persuade their associates to appreciate them as special--strange but wonderful. Philautus in Love in a Riddle (1729) is the only one of Cibber's fops whose exhibitionism comes more from insecurity than from self-delight (Brown 31).

Colley Cibber's greatest fame comes from his being the "hero" of Pope's Dunciad. Pope's treatment of Cibber was biting and relentless. In his epistolary response to Pope, Cibber said that he was under a disadvantage of having only the blunt and weak weapon of literal prose whereas Pope had used the stronger weapon of satiric and ironic poetry.

Cibber also acknowledged that his writing skill was unequal to that of Pope. In this war of words, Cibber compares himself to a famous boxer at the Bear-Garden by the name of "Rugged and Tough," who would stand and be drubbed for hours until his opponent was worn out from hitting him, noting that by keeping his wind and his composure Rugged and Tough sometimes came off victorious. History has shown, however, that Cibber was not so fortunate as was Rugged and Tough (Cibber 8).

Colley Cibber Bibliography

Brown, Richard E. "The Fops in Cibber's Comedies." Essays in Literature 9 (1982): 31-41. Cibber and the Dunciad: 1740-1744. New York, NY: Garland, 1975.
Drougge, Helga. "Colley Cibber's 'Genteel Comedy': Love's Last Shift and The Careless Husband." Studia Neophilologica 54 (1982): 61-79.
Finke, Laurie A. "Virtue in Fashion: The Fate of Women in the Comedies of Cibber and Vanbrugh." From Renaissance to Restoration: Metamorphosis of the Drama. Eds. Robert Markler and Laurie Finke. Cleveland, OH: Bellflower, 1984, 154-179.
Fone, B. R. S. "Love's Last Shift and Sentimental Comedy." Restoration and 18th Century Theatre Research 9.1 (1970): 11-23.
L'Estrange, Alfred Gu. "Vanbrugh--Colley Cibber--Farquhar." History of English Humour. New York, NY: Burt Franklin, 1878, 340-354.

Joseph Addison (1672-1719)

Joseph Addison made a number of important contributions to the development of British humor. Along with Steele he developed such high standards for periodical essays, that his style and his topics were frequently emulated. Second, he created an impressive cast of humorous characters who mildly satirized the social situations of the day. And third, his philosophy of "wit and propriety defined early eighteenth-century culture and literature" (Athey 11). It was probably Addison who shifted the focus of the Tatler from news and politics to society and humor. The characters which he created had charm and diversity. In the Tatler, Addison attacked pedants who ignore the textual sense of a book in order to focus on textual details by creating Tom Folio, the pretentious "book connoisseur." Addison also created the character of Ned Softly, a poet who is "truly English," in that he is does not admire the masterful strokes of the art of poetry, but is instead pleased with the little Gothic ornaments of epigrams, conceits, turns, points, and quibbles which are so frequently admired in the English poets. Then there is Sir Timothy Tuttle who is devoted to former critics and to ancient authors. When his lady friend laughs heartily at the last new comedy, Sir Timothy Tuttle finds much fault with this same comedy, and says, "But Madam...you ought not to have laughed; and I defy any one to show me a single rule that you could laugh by" (Athey 12).

Addison was fascinated by laughter. In a description of religious wax-work display in Tatler 257, he stated,

> Just opposite to this Row of Religions, there was a Statue dressed in a Fool's Coat, with a Cap of Bells upon his Head, laughing and pointing at the Figures that stood before him. This Idiot is supposed to say in his Heart, what David's Fool did some Thousands of Years ago, and was therefore designed as a proper Representation of those among us who are called Atheists and Infidels by others, and Free-thinkers by themselves. (Ingram 36)

For Addison, laughter was appropriate whenever the targets of the laughter were those who would deny the common hope of mankind. For Addison, laughter was most inappropriate when it was the "sound the free-thinker would make if such gloomy creatures could be conceived of as laughing" (Ingram 36).

It was Addison who said, "when a man of wit makes us laugh, it is by betraying some oddness or infirmity in his own character" (L'Estrange 271). Addison argued that the test of true wit is translation; for Addison, genuine humor should not be bounded by frontiers. Harry Levin suggests, however, that there is much to be learned from the untranslatable or from a foreign perspective. "Mr. Punch may embody the typically English figure of fun, yet he was born in Naples, and acquired his beak and hump in France.... The particularity of English humor seems, at all events, to have been universally acknowledged. Locally it was a matter of self-recognition--and of self-congratulation, too" (Levin 5).

After two hundred and seventy-one issues of the Tatler had been printed, Richard Steele decided that it should be modified to make the publication more important. First, it was to become a daily paper. Second, it would contain only one essay on a single subject in each issue. Third, a more impressive title was needed, so the Tatler became the Spectator. But the most important difference was that Joseph Addison became a much more important contributor (L'Estrange 77). Addison wrote a number of essays for the Spectator on the subject of wit, in which he condemned much of that which normally passes under that name. Addison also criticized that which was of poor quality in verbal humor, and such absurd devices connected with verbal humor as the rebus. For Addison, the rebus was merely a bad attempt at humor, a sort of pictorial pun (L'Estrange 79).

The humor in the Spectator frequently came from the character sketches and the social satire. Addison is especially well known for his characters, which served as prototypes for the early English novels of Henry Fielding, Oliver Goldsmith, and Tobias Smollett. The first of his characters is Mr. Spectator, the narrater, who said in the first issue of the Spectator, "I have acted in all the parts of my life as a looker-on, which is the character I intend to preserve in this paper." Captain Sentry, the military advocate is another of Addison's characters, as is the Clergyman who is a vociferous speaker but neglects his office, and the Templar, who does not care for legal studies, and Will Honeycomb, who is a throwback to the gallants of the Restoration. Sir Roger de Coverley, the Tory landowner often repeated the phrase, "much might be said on both sides," which was Addison's way of saying that the old Tories were too obsolete to be trusted to run the country (Athey 11). In one issue of the Spectator, Addison provides a fictional history of the "cat-call," a small instrument that was used for whistling inside the theater. Addison says that the instrument is very well suited to British theater because "it very much improves the sound of nonsense." He says describes two kinds of cat-calls, the base and the treble. The base should be used for tragedy, and the treble for comedy. Only in tragi-comedies should both cat-calls be used together (Athey 12).

In the Spectator, Addison's humor satirized London life and London people. Joel Athey says that his social commentary was not polemical, but was rather reflective. His characters were "humours characters," modeled in the tradition of Ben Jonson. In number 10 of the Spectator, Addison's stated his intention as to "enliven morality with wit, and to temper wit with morality." Some issues of the Spectator were devoted almost entirely to humor. Issues 35, 47, and 249 were devoted to humor, while Issues 58-63 were devoted to wit. In Spectator 35, Addison said, "as true humour generally looks serious whilst everybody laughs that is about him, false humour is always laughing whilst everybody about him looks serious." For Addison, False Humor is outside of the realm of reason. It ridicules the individual rather than the vice, and it is indifferent to the target it attacks (Athey 13).

In a series of Spectator essays (especially numbers 58 to 63), Addison developed a distinction between "True Wit" and "False Wit." Reginald Berry suggests that the purpose of the Spectator was not so much to build consistently logical theories as it was to illuminate, to entertain, and to reform. Berry notes that in the Spectator, Addison was responsible for most of those issues related to satire, and that in these issues Addison discussed the types, the range, the effects, the dangers, and the origins of the satiric mode (Berry 3). Although both Joseph Addison and Richard Steele were responsible for the writing in the Spectator, it should be noted that "except for Steele's essay on 'Raillery' (Spectator 422), the authorship of all the papers which concern aspects of satire is Addison's, and it is quite evident that, as far as the statements on satire are concerned, Addison's is the face behind the mask of Mr. Spectator" (Berry 9).

In the Spectator, Addison is building on John Locke's earlier opposition of "Wit" and "Judgment" (Sitter 50). This is based on Locke's distinction between "Wit" and "Judgment," in which Locke shows that these qualities are not always the talents of the same person (Sitter 62). Locke had considered wit to be an "assemblage of ideas"; however Addison considered true wit to be a resemblance and congruity of ideas." For Addison, true wit generally but not always offers delight and surprise to the reader. According to John Sitter, "Addison's emphasis on the surprise of wit suggests pleasure from the discovery of real resemblances (and appositions) in place of Locke's 'beauty at first sight' (Sitter 63). Addison later proposed that the basis of all wit is truth. Addison felt that true wit consisted not only of resemblances, but of oppositions as well; about this Sitter notes the following irony: "If it is true that wit discerns differences as well as similarities, then the dichotomy between wit and judgment collapses. Having enlisted it in an argument for the truth of wit, Addison leaves Locke's distinction, so to speak, without judgment" (Sitter 64). Addison did not feel that verses, acrostics, quibbles or puns constituted true wit, and this is clear in his statement that "True wit consists in the resemblance of ideas, and false wit in the resemblance of words" (Sitter 63).

In both the Tatler and the Spectator, the targets of the satire ranged from duelling to gaming to ladies fashions to stage immorality to John Milton. Sometimes the entire issue would consist of letters from readers, and according to Joel Athey, this was the beginning of participatory journalism (Athey 11). During his time, Addison was more popular than either Alexander Pope or Jonathan Swift, and in 1975, Louis Milic wrote an article entitled "The Reputation of Richard Steele: What Happened?" which explains in part why this perception has changed (Athey 14).

Joseph Addison Bibliography

Athey, Joel. "Joseph Addison." Encyclopedia of British Humorists, Volume 1. Ed. Steven H. Gale. New York, NY: Garland, 1996, 10-14.

Berry, Reginald. "Modifying a Whole Landscape: False Humour, Good Nature, and Satire in the Spectator." Thalia: Studies in Literary Humor 3.1 (1980): 3-10.

Cazamian, Louis. "Congreve, Shaftesbury, Steele, and Addison." The Development of English Humor. Durham, NC: Duke University Press, 1952, 400-407.

Ingram, Allan. Intricate Laughter in the Satire of Swift and Pope. New York, NY: Macmillan, 1986.

L'Estrange, Alfred Gu. History of English Humour. New York, NY: Burt Franklin, 1878.

Levin, Harry, ed. Veins of Humor. Cambridge, MA: Harvard University Press, 1972.

Milic, Louis. "The Reputation of Richard Steele: What Happened?" Eighteenth-Century Life 1 (1975): 81-87.

Sitter, John. Arguments of Augustan Wit. New York: Cambridge University Press, 1991.

Thackeray, William Makepeace. "Congreve and Addison." The English Humorists: Charity and Humour: The Four Georges. New York, NY: Dutton, 1912, 47-87.

Thackeray, William Makepeace. The English Humorists of the Eighteenth Century: A

Series of Lectures. New York, NY: Harper and Brothers, 1853.

Richard Steele (1672-1729) IRELAND

Joseph Addison and Richard Steele deliberately avoided the harsh and bitter satiric style of Jonathan Swift as they attempted to increase the size of their reading audience. Swift nevertheless influenced their writing in positive ways. Steele's Isaac Bickerstaff, is the same name that Swift had used in his Bickerstaff Papers. Addison and Steele tended to satirize groups rather than individuals, and they attempted to be temperate or even gentle in their satire. Sir Roger de Coverley is their most famous creation, and is typical of their characters. Sir Roger owns land, and is a Tory, a political position that is opposite the positions of Addison and Steele. Sir Roger falls asleep during church services after he has earlier admonished all members of the congregation to stay awake. Sir Roger also makes speeches about legal matters that he does not totally understand (McCrea 1053).

Thomas Macaulay says that Steele's writings "have been well compared to those light wines which though deficient in body and flavor, are yet a pleasant drink if not kept too long, or carried too far" (Macaulay 106). Austin Dobson says that Steele's humor is "so cheerful and good-natured, so frank and manly that one is often tempted to echo the declaration of Leigh Hunt--'I prefer open-hearted Steele with all his faults to Addison with all his essays'" (Dobson 217, 225). Steele reacted against the cynicism and the ribaldry of Restoration Comedy. He made it his goal to write comedy that contained pure diction without the salaciousness of double entendre (McCrea 1054). Steele developed a kind of "sentimental comedy" that works outside of the Aristotelian principle of the separation of styles (McCrea 1054). Steele pioneered a new genre for humor called the "Periodical Essay." He also changed the course of English stage comedy and changed it in a "very basic and profound way." During Steele's time the literary world shifted from being dominated by the great patrons of literature, to being dominated by entrepreneurial booksellers. This was a shift from the elitist, stylized and cynical humor of the Restoration to the tolerant and more conversational humor of sentimental comedy. "Perhaps Steele's greatest achievement is his use of humor to mediate social change and thus to avoid social conflict" (McCrea 1055). Brian McCrea says that the Tatler and the Spectator provided readers with "a model for accommodation between the landed men and the moneyed men, between tradition and innovation, between the aristocracy and the bourgeoisie--accommodation of the sort that British society as a whole would move toward in the years after Steele's death" (McCrea 1056).

Early in The Tender Husband (1705), Biddy Tipkin is "laughable in her affections." But in the end she is rewarded for her virtues (McCrea 1054). Steele is serious when he deals with characters of humble social origins. He reserves comic treatments for such servants as Tom in The Conscious Lovers (1723) who tries to be like his social superiors because such characters assume that their "superiors" are their "betters" (McCrea 1055). In the "Preface" to The Conscious Lovers, Steele explains that he wants to overturn the traditions of Restoration comedy with its emphasis on base motives and duplicitous means of realizing them. Steele felt that in Restoration comedy the laughter is Hobbesian in that it comes from "sudden glory," and is an expression of "superiority." For Steele, laughter should not be the goal. Rather, the goal should be "virtuous tears, tears that bespeak compassion and sympathy rather than superiority."

See also Nilsen, Don L. F. Humor in Irish Literature: A Reference Guide. Westport, CT: Greenwood, 1996.

Richard Steele Bibliography

Dobson, Austin. Richard Steele. London, England: Longmans Green, 1888.
Kenny, Shirley Strum. "Richard Steele and the Pattern of Genteel Comedy." Modern
    Philology 70 (1971): 22-37.
Loftis, John. Comedy and Society from Congreve to Fielding. Stanford, CA: Stanford
    University Press, 1959.
Macaulay, Thomas Babington. Essays on Milton and Addison. Ed. Thomas Marc Parrott.
    New York, NY: Globe School Book Company, 1901.
McCrea, Brian. "Richard Steele." Encyclopedia of British Humorists, Volume II. Ed.
    Steven H. Gale. New York, NY: Garland, 1996, 1050-1057.
Thackeray, William Makepeace. "Richard Steele." The English Humorists of the Eighteenth
    Century: A Series of Lectures. New York, NY: Harper and Brothers, 1853, 171-
    129.

Ambrose Philips (Namby-Pamby)(c1675-1749)

Alexander Pope said that Ambrose Philips was "a man who could write very nobly,"
but later Pope and Philips became rivals, and the relationship got so bad that Pope called
Philips "a rascal." In response, Philips hung a rod up on the wall, with which he said he
planned to chastise Pope. Alfred Gu L'Estrange suggests that Philips resorted to a physical
response because "he felt that he was worsted by his adversary in wordy warfare, having
little talent in satire" (L'Estrange 14). Samuel Johnson feels that Ambrose Philips was
responsible for the introduction of the parody form in England; however Alfred Gu
L'Estrange feels that eighteenth-century parody is a revival of the parody which he sees in
the fifteenth century (L'Estrange 361). In 1714 John Gay wrote a good travesty of
Ambrose Philips's pastoral poetry, in which he stated,
        I quaintly stole a kiss; at first, 'tis true,
        She frowned, yet after granted one or two.
        Lobbin, I swear, believe who will my vow,
        Her breath by far excelled the breathing cow. (L'Estrange 17)
Ambrose Philips was a lively writer of successful burlesque, but he was less
successful as a serious poet, though he "devoted himself to it with a scholarly dullness
which he would probably have seen the folly of in anyone else." Philips's burlesques were
in the style of John Milton's Paradise Lost (Hunt 255).

Ambrose Philips (Mamby-Pamby) Bibliography

Hunt, Leigh. Wit and Humour. New York, NY: Folcroft Library Editions, 1972.
L'Estrange, Alfred Gu. "Burlesque--Parody--The 'Splendid Shilling'--Prior--Pope--Ambrose
    Philips--Parodies of Gray's Elegy--Gay." History of English Humour. New York,
    NY: Burt Franklin, 1878, 1-21.

John Philips (1676-1709)

John Philips was the transitional author between Samuel Garth (1661-1719), and
Alexander Pope (1688-1744) in the development of the mock-heroic genre. Philips was
an imitator of Milton both in his serious and in his burlesque verse, and did much to
develop the blank verse style of poetry (Walker 167). Philips's most important contribution

to the field of humor studies was his invention of the "mock-Miltonic mode," a particular type of the mock-heroic that was later used by John Gay, Alexander Pope, and other "Augustan scribblers." Kevin Cope says that the "mock-Miltonic mode" was a satiric verse description of city life and that this mode was perfected by Ambrose Philips [no relation to John] and ironized by Jonathan Swift. The "mock-Miltonic mode" employed "comic juxtaposition of heroic, iambic pentameter, pseudo-Homeric verse against undignified subject matter had already been attempted by John Dryden in MacFlecknoe and Samuel Garth in The Dispensary, but the humorous application of Miltonic blank verse to trivial, fanciful topics originated with Philips." When Philips says that a person "sinks found'ring in the vast Abyss," he is invoking Milton's "hieratic" style. He is also invoking one of Milton's favorite topics, the great abyss between heaven and earth, but the mocking tone is obvious when we discover that this "Abyss" is actually a tear in his trousers (Cope 845).

Hugh Walker considers Philips's The Splendid Shilling (1701) to be a very good burlesque of the poet Milton, and in fact, this is more than a burlesque. It is a travesty of epic proportions. According to Walker, "The debtor, the dun, and the catchpole are material suitable for comic treatment, and the similes in which the catchpole is compared to the cat and the spider are an excellent burlesque of the epic simile" (Walker 168). The expression The Splendid Shilling, is actually only a subtitle of John Philip's poem. The proper, and commonly recognized true title was An Imitation of Milton (Cope 845). Philips's Blenheim (1706) is just as much a burlesque of Milton as is The Splendid Shilling even though on the surface the tone seems to be perfectly solemn (Cope 845).

The light and comic tone of Cerealia (1706) seems natural for Philips. It deals with the making of malt liquor from English grains, and contains a "hard-edged, unexpectedly aggressive wit, defaming inferior continental wines while lauding homegrown brews." Much agricultural and geological imagery is developed as Philips experiments with a sarcastic tone in this "crabby comedy of dialect" (Cope 845). The conclusion to Cerealia is described by Kevin Cope as "climactically vulgar," as "Philips stoops to body-humor of the Animal House variety (Cope 846).

Cyder (1708) is filled with gentle wit that is reminiscent of bucolic times when the term "clown" referred to a peaceful countryman as well as a colorful circus performer. This poem is about the growing and the harvesting of apples, and the pressing of the apples for juice, and the fermentation of hard cider, and the merry revelry that is associated with the consumption of this hard apple cider. According to Cope, a lot of the comedy of Cyder is either "neurotic," or it is "external to the poem," or it is both. During much of the poem, Philips is marveling at how humor, ribaldry, and burlesque can be interpreted as encyclopedic learning, or even as epic verse (Cope 846).

In conclusion, John Philips wrote six of what Kevin Cope calls "celebratory pieces," in which he "perfected the art of simultaneously revivifying and burlesquing the greatest of English epic writers, John Milton. Philips's verse "laughs respectfully" at the verse that it is poking fun of. It "laughs respectfully" at the "triviality of modern life and its incongruity with the heroic tradition. John Philips's writing is both urbane and witty (Cope 846).

John Philips Bibliography

Bond, Richmond P. English Burlesque Poetry, 1700-1750. Cambridge, MA: Harvard University Press, 1932.
Cope, Kevin L. "John Philips." Encyclopedia of British Humorists, Volume II. Ed. Steven H. Gale. New York, NY: Garland, 1996, 844-847.
Walker, Hugh. English Satire and Satirists. New York, NY: E. P. Dutton, 1925.

George Farquhar (1678-1707) IRELAND

George Farquhar helped to institute a new stage morality which was to become
"Sentimental Comedy" (Athey 352). He began by writing in the tradition of Comedy of
Manners, but he ended up by developing the Comedy of Sentiment. Thus he "transported
comedy out of the drawing room of high society and into country inns" (Athey 355).
    Love and a Bottle (1699), was an exaggeration of earlier plays in the respect that
it had a total of three mock marriages. In the play, Leanthe, the Heroine, is disguised as
a boy. Roebuck, the Hero, is an Irish rake who has recently arrived in London. Roebuck
is coarse, and he is a rake both in practice and in principle. Love and a Bottle could be
considered to be a burlesque of Restoration comedy (Athey 352). In The Constant Couple,
or the Trip to the Jubilee (1700), Lady Lurewell is a callous jilt, and Sir Harry Wildair is
an urbane and graceful rake. The satire of The Constant Couple targeted pedants, marriage,
and scandalous behavior, and was the success of the London season (Athey 352).
    The Recruiting Officer (1706) is a sprightly military satire on the exaggerations and
bribery that are used to recruit new soldiers. The minor plots in The Recruiting Officer
revolve around the romantic intrigues of rakes who by the end of the piece are shown not
to be as rakish as they first appeared. The satire is directed at the recruitment process in
particular, but is more generally directed at military life, and in fact at the shams and
hypocrisy of society at large (Athey 352). Captain Plume, the central figure, is a lusty and
saucy recruiter whose strategy is to "kiss the prettiest country wenches, and you are sure
of listing the lustiest fellows." He says, "I tell'e what, I'll make love like a platoon," and
continues that his recruiting officers had, "lampooned all the pretty women in town,"
adding, "I thought 'twas a maxim among them to leave as many recruits in the country as
they carried out." In The Recruiting Officer, Farquhar develops the metaphor that SEX IS
WAR. in that both of these activities require adjustments in order to preserve the stability
of society. Farquhar is masterful in working out the parallels (Athey 353).
    The Beaux' Stratagem (1707) is a play which employs both the wit of manners, and
the wit of sentiment. The play operates on a number of levels, ranging from farce to wit
(Athey 353). There is much ribaldry in the play, as in the "Love's catechism" scene
between Archer, who is pretending to be a footman, and Cherry, the country lass. The
scene satirizes Cherry's love of reading novels, and their repartee ends with, "And now, my
dear, we'll go in, and make my master's bed." The play also uses such allegorical names
as Freeman, Sullen, Bellair, Lady Bountiful, and Aimwell. Aimwell is a fortune hunter
who "is decent and aims for the good." Some of the wit involves visual and tactile
imagery. Mrs. Sullen describes her marriage in the following way: "He came home this
morning at his usual hour of four, waken'd me out of a sweet dream of something else.
He comes flounce into bed, dead as a salmon into a fishmonger's basket; his feet cold as
ice, his breath hot as a furnace, and his hands and his face as greasy as his flannel night-
cap.--Oh matrimony!" But the play also has examples of intellectual wit, and literary
allusions, and biting ripostes. This is contrasted with the "low dialogue." "The humor thus
produced realism that audiences identified with and also gave some degree of complexity
to the characters" (Athey 354). The Beaux' Stratagem takes place in a country inn, where
two impoverished rakes pose as a peer and his servant. One of them falls in love with a
wealthy daughter, and the other one with Mrs. Sullen, who is unhappily married. They
save their lovers from robbery and then reveal their true status. Mrs. Sullen relates the two
plots by crying out "thieves" to save her house from the intrusion of Hounslow and
Bagshot, and in so doing she aligns the intrusion of Archer and Aimwell with virtue. In
the end the fortunes of the Protagonists are restored, and all is harmonized, as the boorish
Mr. Sullen departs (Athey 353).
    See also Nilsen, Don L. F. Humor in Irish Literature: A Reference Guide.

Westport, CT: Greenwood, 1996.

George Farquhar Bibliography

Athey, Joel. "George Farquhar." Encyclopedia of British Humorists, Volume I. Ed. Steven
H. Gale. New York, NY: Garland, 1996, 351-355.
Nelson, James E. The Development of George Farquhar as a Comic Dramatist. The Hague,
Netherlands: Mouton, 1972.

John Winstanley (1678-1750) IRELAND

See Nilsen, Don L. F. **Humor in Irish Literature: A Reference Guide.** Westport,
CT: Greenwood, 1996.

John Gay (1685-1732)

William Lilly notes that what distinguishes a humorist from other artists is a sense
of playfulness. He furthermore notes that this sense of playfulness can have many forms,
and he contrasts the "grim playfulness of the tigre" as in Jonathan Swift with "the sportive
playfulness of the kitten" as in John Gay (Lilly 6). William Makepeace Thackeray
describes John Gay's humor as follows: "He laughs at you over his shoulder with an
honest boyish glee--an artless sweet humour. He was so kind, so gentle, so jocular, so
delightfully brisk at times, so dismally woebegone at others, such a natural good creature,
that the Giants loved him" (Thackeray 142). John Gay wrote twelve plays that were mostly
humorous, and included four farces, two comedies, and three ballad operas (Evans 436).
John Gay liked to mingle high style with low subject matter in order to show the satiric
truth about rural and urban life respectively. His most original achievement was the
invention of a new kind of drama which is the parodic and satirical ballad opera (Evans
439).
John Gay's Wine (1708) is a burlesque in blank verse written to parody John
Milton. Gay signals that it is a parody by using a sublime style while talking about a
trivial subject (Evans 435). The Mohocks, a Tragi-Comical Farce (1712) presents a "comic
confrontation between street bullies called Mohocks, swaggering in blank verse, and a
Shakespearean group of watchmen, easily intimidated by them" (Evans 436). Rural Sports
(1713) is a mock pastoral. The Wife of Bath (1713) is a five-act prose comedy about
sexual intrigue. A number of characters from Chaucer's The Canterbury Tales appear in
the play, including the Wife of Bath, who is the play's protagonist (Evans 436).
The Fan (1714) is a mock epic ridiculing the beau monde. In this poem, the
goddess Venus presents a fan to Strephon. The idea is that he can use the fan to win the
heart of the vain Corinna. The Shepherd's Week (1714) is a mock pastoral of six poems
designed to parody the "realism" of Ambrose Philip's Pastorals (1709). The Shepherd's
Week was also supposed to bring to mind Virgil's Eclogues. The shepherds and
shepherdesses are given such homely names as Lobbin Clout, Cuddy Marian, Sparabella,
Hobnelia, Bumkinet, Grubbinol, and Bowzybeus. The poems contain country superstitions
and proverbs, and there is also a comic incongruity of language and action, especially in
"Wednesday."
The What D'Ye Call It: A Tragi-Comi-Pastoral Farce (1715) is a parody of
seventeenth- and early eighteenth-century tragedy (Evans 437). John Gay collaborated with
Alexander Pope and John Arbuthnot in the writing of another farce, this one entitled, Three

Hours after Marriage (1717). Three Hours after Marriage is a three-act prose comedy about an aging antiquarian who marries a young wife. Two rakes attempt to seduce the young wife, and even go so far as to disguise themselves as an alligator and a mummy in order to gain entrance into the house. The main characters include the virtuoso, the town lady, the rakes, the female author, and the critic, and all of these characters are ridiculed in the play (Evans 437).

     Trivia: or, The Art of Walking the Streets of London (1716) is a mock-georgic poem. James Evans says that it is a "palimpsest" of Hogarthian detail, and that it is reminiscent of Virgil's "depiction of rural life in the Georgics to survey the disorder of eighteenth-century urban existence." Trivia consists of three books. The first is subtitled, Of the Implements for Walking the Streets, and Signs of the Weather. The second is subtitled, Of Walking the Streets by Day, and the third is subtitled, Of Walking the Streets by Night. "The 'art' of the poem is humorously presented through vignettes of place or character within London. For example, the walker is warned to avoid chimney-sweeper, dust-man, chandler, and butcher by day and pick-pocket, ballad-singer, whore, watchman, and rake by night. He is taught to know the day of the week by detecting the smells of the tradesmen" (Evans 436).

     Poems on Several Occasions (1720) is a group of humorous eclogues with such titles as "The Toilette," "The Tea-Table," and "The Funeral." These poems were written to ridicule the affectations of upper-class London women (Evans 436). Fables (1727) were John Gay's most popular poems during his lifetime. This was a collection of fifty poems in tetrameter couplets which were written for and dedicated to Prince William who was then four years old. John Gay was good at writing fables, because they were a good genre for him to present his ridicule of human folly. The animal characters, and the inanimate characters allowed Gay enough comic distance that he could effectively ridicule such human traits as ambition, hypocrisy, and greed. This comic distance also allowed him to satirize the Court which had ignored him for so many years. And all of this was done under the guise of gentle instructions for the young prince (Evans 436).

     William Empson discusses the irony of The Beggar's Opera (1728), and the deflection of the heroic tradition, and the pastoral tradition as well (Evans 440). David Nokes notes that many critics consider Gay's Beggar's Opera to be a lightweight work in terms of social criticism. Nokes precedes his treatment of Beggar's Opera with a treatment of The Shepherd's Week, a mock pastoral which would again seem to place Gay in the lightweight division. Both works are linked by their ironic reversals of pastoral themes and conventions. Nokes, however, concentrates on Gay's language, and finds a level of verbal sophistication not often associated with Gay's writing (Nokes xi-xii). The idea for The Beggar's Opera had been suggested by Jonathan Swift, and it is said by some critics that this piece gave birth to the English Opera. "This opera, or musical play, brought out by Mr. Rich, was so remunerative that it was a common saying that it made 'Rich gay, and Gay rich' " (L'Estrange 19). In The Beggar's Opera the humor is based on Polly's falling in love with a highwayman. Harry Paddington is a member of the highwayman's gang. He is "a poor, petty-larceny rascal, without the least genius; that fellow, though he were to live these six months would never come to the gallows with any credit." Tom Tipple, another member of the gang was "a guzzling, soaking sot, who is always too drunk to stand, or make others stand." Peachum, Polly's father, and his wife lament over their daughter's choice of Captain Macheath (the highwayman), and there are numerous songs with lyrics like, "Our Polly is a sad slut! nor heeds what we have taught her. I wonder any man alive will ever rear a daughter" (L'Estrange 19).

     The Beggar's Opera is a parody of Italian opera, of English tragedy, and of English sentimental comedy. It satirizes the moral disorder that results from self interest and politicians who take advantage of that particular vice. Such characters as the highwaymen and the prostitutes, the fences, and the prison keepers are low-class characters. These characters are hypocrites, and their songs of love and of honor have a mock-heroic effect. Through the heroic posturing of the protagonist, the highwayman Macheath, The Beggar's Opera ridicules tragedy. There are ironic allusions to such tragic plays as John Dryden's All for Love. Gay is satirizing the Sentimental Comedy of Richard Steele, by undermining the play's optimistic assumptions about human nature and about middle-class virtue (Evans 437). Gay is also satirizing the politics of the Court, especially Robert Walpole, the corrupt Prime Minister. Walpole is satirized both by the scheming Peachum, who is interested only in his own profit, and by the self-aggrandizing Macheath. One of the points of this comic opera is that the people of the road are neither better nor worse than are the gentlemen of the Court. It is difficult to know for sure whether Polly Peachum, the heroine of The Beggar's Opera is a romantic fool, or a character of some integrity, but she so interested Gay that he made her the title character of Polly (1729), which is the sequel of The Beggar's Opera. In this sequel, Polly pursues Macheath to the West Indies, where he has been transported (Evans 438).

Achilles (1733) is a burlesque in the form of a ballad opera about a Greek hero who must be disguised as a woman because Thetis, his goddess mother, wants to keep him out of the Trojan war (Evans 438). The Distress'd Wife (1734) is a five-act prose comedy. It is a Comedy of Manners written in the style of the preceding age. In The Distress'd Wife, Sir Thomas Willit is a country gentleman who finds himself and his wife in financial trouble because of her extravagant life of fashion. As a solution to his dilemma, he compels his wife to return to the country (Evans 438). Finally, The Rehearsal at Goatham (1754) is a brief farce.

"Alexander Pope wrote the couplet that serves as the epitaph on John Gay's tomb in Westminster Abbey. It reads as follows: "With native Humour tem'pring virtuous Rage, / Form'd to delight at once and lash the age" (Evans 434). Twelve years before his death, John Gay had written his own epitaph. It read, "Life is a jest; and all things show it, / I thought so once; but now I know it." About these two epitaphs, James Evans says, "Pope's antithesis--humor / rage, delight / lash--are complemented by Gay's single word "jest," which nicely identifies his achievement as the author of burlesque, mock pastoral, mock georgic, fable, farce, comedy, and ballad opera" (Evans 435).

John Gay Bibliography

Bronson, Bertrand. "The Beggar's Opera." Studies in the Comic. Berkeley, CA: University of California Publications in English, Volume 8, Number 2, 1941, 197-231.
Donaldson, Ian. "'A Double Capacity': The Beggar's Opera." The World Upside-Down: Comedy from Jonson to Fielding. Oxford, England: Clarendon, 1970, 159-182.
Empson, William. "The Beggar's Opera: Mock-Pastoral as the Cult of Independence." Some Versions of Pastoral. London, England: Chatto and Windus, 1935, 195-250.
Evans, James E. "John Gay." Encyclopedia of British Humorists, Volume I. Ed. Steven H. Gale. New York, NY: Garland, 1996, 434-440.
Irving, William Henry. John Gay: A Favorite of the Wits. Durham, NH: Duke University Press, 1940.
L'Estrange, Alfred Gu. "Burlesque--Parody--The 'Splendid Shilling'--Prior--Pope--Ambrose Philips--Parodies of Gray's Elegy--Gay." History of English Humour. New York, NY: Burt Franklin, 1878, 1-21.
Lilly, William Samuel. Four English Humourists of the Nineteenth Century. London, England: John Murray, 1895.
Nokes, David. Raillery and Rage: A Study of Eighteenth Century Satire. Sussex, England: Harvester Press, 1987.

Sitter, John. Arguments of Augustan Wit. New York, NY: Cambridge University Press, 1991.
Thackeray, W. M. "Prior, Gay, and Pope." The English Humorists: Charity and Humour: The Four Georges. New York, NY: Dutton, 1912, 133-181.

Allan Ramsay (1686-1758) SCOTLAND

Allan Ramsay was a master of a poetic metre called the "standart Habby," in which there are six lines containing two rhymes. This metric tradition originally came from the Troubadours, and it was well known in medieval England, but it had been forgotten until it was reintroduced in Scotland (Walker 253). Ramsay's Elegy on John Cowper is directed against the "kirk session's jurisdiction of morals," and Walker feels that this could be regarded as a "tentative and cautious prelude to [Bobbie] Burns's great satires" (253).

Allan Ramsay Bibliography

Walker, Hugh. English Satire and Satirists. New York, NY: E. P. Dutton, 1925.

Henry Carey (c1687-1743)

Henry Carey's importance to the field of humor studies lies in his burlesque farces, the two best known of which are The Dragon of Wantley, and Chrononhotonthologos (Rainbolt 206). Martha Rainbolt maintains that both The Dragon of Wantley, and Chrononhotonthologos are funny even today, as they burlesque the heroic drama of Carey's time, and join John Gay's The Beggar's Opera in spoofing Italian opera (Rainbolt 207). Joseph Addison very much liked Carey's poetry, especially his "Sally in Our Alley," because it was a "plain, simple copy of nature" (Wood 24). Rainbolt says that Carey was ingenious in his word play, and that his rollicking mockery of sentimental comedy, and the bombastic mock heroism in Carey's writing "confirm Carey's place in this tradition of nonsense literature" (Rainbolt 208).

Carey is the author of A Learned Dissertation on Dumpling (1726), and of Pudding and Dumpling Burnt to Pot, or, a Compleat Key to the Dissertation on Dumpling (1727). These contain satiric pieces that attack both such political figures as Robert Walpole, and such writers as Jonathan Swift. In one of the pieces, "Of Stage Tyrants," he complains that when he writes a bad play, the critics say that his work is not acceptable, but if he writes a good play, they deny that he wrote it, "Because 'twas good, 'twas thought to good for mine" (Carey 16).

The Dragon of Wantley (1737) is a parody of heroic drama. The dragon must be killed, and the fair maiden must be rescued. Moore of Moore-Hall is the Valiant Knight who kills the dragon by kicking it on the backside (Rainbolt 207). Henry Carey wrote a number of burlesques, including Hanging and Marriage (1722), Betty or The Country-Bumpkins (1732), and The Honest Yorkshire-Man (1735). Carey's The Dragoness (1738) is a Burlesque Opera.

Chrononhotonthologos (1743) is filled with extravagant word play, such as the title of the play, "Chrononhotonthologos," who is the King of "Queerummania," and "Bombardinian," his General, and "Aldiborontiphoscophornio," and "Rigdum-Funnidos," two Courtiers, and "Fadladinida," the Queen of Queerummania, and "Tatlanthe," her favorite. Frederick Bateson describes such word play as "happy nonsensicality," adding that it "pokes fun at bombastic language and melodramatic episodes" (Rainbolt 207).

Henry Carey Bibliography

Bateson, Frederick W. "Henry Carey." English Comic Drama, 1700-1750. Oxford, England: Clarendon, 1929, 104-114.
Carey, Henry. A Learned Dissertation on Dumpling and Pudding and Dumpling Burnt to Pot. Los Angeles, CA: UCLA Augustan Reprint Society, 1970.
Clinton-Baddeley, V. C. "Henry Carey." The Burlesque Tradition in the English Theatre after 1660. London, England: Methuen, 1952, 65-71.
Rainbolt, Martha. "Henry Carey." Encyclopedia of British Humorists, Volume I. Ed. Steven H. Gale. New York, NY: Garland, 1996, 206-209.
Wood, Frederick T. The Poems of Henry Carey. London, England: The Scholartis Press, 1930.

Alexander Pope (1688-1744)

Sir Samuel Garth (1661-1719), and John Philips (1676-1709) both helped to develop the mock heroic style, and were in that way predecessors of Alexander Pope; however, it was Pope who perfected the genre (Walker 168). From the beginning of his writing career, the mock-heroic style came to him easily, partly because he was so well read in heroic verse, and enjoyed playing with the form, and partly because he "correctly recognized that mock-heroic is an apt vehicle for emphasizing key discrepancies in people and situations and attitudes" (Anderson 198).

According to Alfred Gu L'Estrange, Pope did not engage in travesty, because his object was not to ridicule the piece he was criticizing, but rather "to assist himself by borrowing its style. His productions are the best examples of parodies in this latter and better sense." Pope's borrowings give a classic air to his satires, and this classic air is further reinforced by Pope's basing the arrangement of his satires on Horace's arrangement of his satires (L'Estrange 11).

Pope's addition of sylphs and gnomes to The Rape of the Lock, An Heroic-Comical Poem in Five Cantos (1712) is a mock epic in which Pope uses satire to ridicule many of the qualities of the epic. Pope uses both a diminished style and a diminished content. The gods become tiny and powerless sylphs. A shield becomes a petticoat; the theft of Helen becomes the theft of a lock of hair; and the epic battle becomes a card game (Adler 866). There is also the epic question, "Say, what strange motive, Goddess, could compel / A well-bred Lord t'assault a gentle Belle?" (Adler 866), and there is the epic sacrifice, "three garters, one glove, and three sighs" (Adler 867).

The Rape of the Lock raises the genre of the mock heroic to a new plane, by providing an inexhaustible resource for scintillating wit. The piece "sparkles in every line," is filled with "gay good humor," and there is great irony that the powers of air, as well as of earth, are centered in a mere lock of hair (Walker 168). Pope is skilled in mingling the great with the trivial, and he juxtaposes the puffs, powders, patches, bibles, billets-deux, and other objects that clutter the toilet table with the seriousness of heaven and earth. The shriek announcing that the lock has been severed is so strong as to rend the skies and is compared to the time "when husbands, or when lapdogs breathe their last" (Walker 169). Pope was aware of the extreme symbolic power that "hair" has had throughout history, and was aware also that "beauty draws us with a single hair" (Walker 169).

Leigh Hunt considers Pope to be an "admirable wit and satirist" (Hunt 260). There are many ways of interpreting Alexander Pope's most important satire, written in the mock-heroic style, The Rape of the Lock (1712). In Alexander Pope (1985), Laura Brown presents it as a celebration of consumer fetishism in an emerging imperialistic culture. In

The Poetics of Sexual Myth (1985), Ellen Pollak gives a feminist reading to the poem, as does Brean Hammond in his Pope (1986). "Pollack argues that while Belinda appears to be the subject of the poem, she is in fact marginalized in the text as a figure of phallocentric myth. Hammond, less harshly, sees the poem as a satire on the exaggerations of sexually stereotypical forms of behavior" (Nokes x-xi).

In the view of William Anderson, Pope used a rapier wit in The Rape of the Lock to target many of the major defects of the elegant London society during Pope's day. Pope's satire had the effect of eliciting the delight and admiration of its audience (Anderson 198).

> Pope mocks Belinda's vain ideas of conquest, her elaborate arming for victory, her battle at cards, and her later battle with the bodkin. Behind the amusing façade, however, spectacularly masked by the witty verse form, lies a more serious application of the epic material: no heroic, not even a valid ethical motive, impels Belinda. She cares more for her trivial honor than for real virtue, for broken china than for broken chastity, for a lock of hair more than a worthwhile existence. (Anderson 210)

Anderson goes on to compare Pope's Belinda with the epic heroine Dido, who was the star-crossed lover of Aeneas (Anderson 210).

The Rape of the Lock is about Belinda, who in her morning dream sees visions containing elves, and sylphs and especially the powerful Ariel, the guardian sylph. Belinda's dream world is presided over by airy sylphs, and this dream world is juxtaposed to the real world to which it is feared that Belinda might awake. To keep her from awakening, Ariel enters Belinda's dream to tell her not to bind her narrow view just to things below. Belinda is further told to "Think what an Equipage thou hast in Air, / And view with scorn Two Pages and a Chair" (Guilhamet 101). The sylphs reinforce Belinda's "violent addiction to chastity," and aid in Belinda's undergoing a metamorphosis whereby "her toilet transforms her into an amazon of sorts, prepared to resist sexual advances" (Guilhamet 101-102). This transformation by making Belinda more formidable, also increases her sex appeal, and in fact, she becomes so attractive that the Baron is made into a desperate thwarted lover. Because he has no chance for success as a lover, he must have his way by guile and force (Guilhamet 102).

The ironic or satiric tone of The Rape of the Lock is achieved mainly through the fact that rape is an unnatural and violent act, while in Pope's piece the object of passion is only a lock of hair. "Thus the seriousness of satire and the triviality of comedy are linked from the outset" (Guilhamet 100). Belinda does not respond to the Baron the way an adult would respond, so the Baron treats her like a child. Ariel also treats her like a child, and speaks of her "infant thought." In evoking his fantasy world, Ariel says, "Some secret Truths from Learned Pride conceal'd, / To Maids alone and Children are reveal'd." It is clear from this statement that one of the duties of sylphs is to "preserve maidens from their natural progress toward maturity, a maturity marked by sexual surrender and the assumption of the name of woman" (Guilhamet 104). Gnomes serve a similar function. The gnome Umbriel journeys into the Cave of Spleen in order to ensure that Belinda's heart remains hardened against the Baron. Umbriel is a former prude, who may (like Ariel) be male in his present form, but who was a female in his mortal state. "The confusion of gender is another result of metamorphosis that terminates in unnatural sexlessness" (Guilhamet 105).

The Rape of the Lock is not merely mock heroic; it is mock-lyric as well: "We laugh at the hyperbole of the heroes, but we laugh as well at the hyperbole of the hair. In other words, in this disruption of contexts, neither world, of heroes or lovers, can be taken seriously. Each generic context acts as a distorting mirror to the other" (Guilhamet 104). According to Guilhamet, the juxtaposing of the mock-heroic and the mock-lyric creates comic ridicule which is directed mainly against Belinda as representing all members of the fair sex who reject their adult sexuality. Since the Baron is also implicated in the satire, however, the satire is balanced. Yet satire does emerge because of the stress laid on Belinda's rejection of "her natural role" (Guilhamet 108). The deus ex machina at the conclusion of The Rape of the Lock may be brilliant, but it resolves nothing, for both Belinda and the Baron remain committed to their own perversities. "As in many satires, nothing really occurs. The Baron's rape has left Belinda a virgin. That is precisely the point" (Guilhamet 108).

The true successor to John Dryden in the genre of satiric verse was not Thomas Shadwell, nor Elkanah Settle, nor Samuel Pordage, nor Matthew Prior, nor any of the other writers who most imitated and satirized Dryden's writings during Dryden's times, but it was instead Alexander Pope.   Hugh Walker suggests that Dryden's influence in The Dunciad (1728) is so conspicuous that "Pope seems to have been a little uneasy as to his debt to MacFlecnoe.... The Dunciad is just MacFlecnoe broadened out in scope from the individual to the class" (Walker 166). David Nokes considers Pope's The Dunciad to be a "comic palimpsest of ancient heroes and modern hacks." He also discusses Pope's sober style of satire in the Moral Essays and the Imitations of Horace, where he combines the idealism of a moral philosopher with the censoriousness of a one-man tribunal" (Nokes xi). Pope was a mature poet when he wrote The Dunciad, and here again he resorted to the mock-heroic style.

Pope exhibits a marvelous sense of play in The Dunciad, both in the scenes he contrives and the vast quantity of pseudo-learning which interlaces the satire (Anderson 198). The following sentence epitomizes the ironic method of Pope's attack: "As Virgil is said to have had Ennius, out of his dunghill to draw gold, so may our author read Shakespeare, Milton, and Dryden for the contrary end, to bury their gold in his own dunghill" (Anderson 211). The Dunciad is about Colley Cibber, poet-laureate of England, and about other anti-intellectuals of the time who controlled the publishing, the speaking, and the thinking in literary channels. The games in The Dunciad are designed to "honor King Cibber," and dung is the end of each contest. Dung is the prize for which the contestants compete, and into which in one instance they "plunge, dive, or sink" (Anderson 212). The funeral games are intended to be not only mock-heroic, but mock-pastoral as well:

> Full in the middle way there stood a lake.
> Which Curl's Corinna chanc'd that morn to make. (Guilhamet 112)

A mud-covered form is seen rising up from this lake to tell about his subterranean love:

> First he relates, how sinking to the chin,
> Smit with his mien, the Mud-nymphs suck'd him in. (Guilhamet 113)

Pope begins Book 2 of The Dunciad with a witty travesty of the first five lines of Milton's Paradise Lost, as in these lines he says that Cibber is "high on a gorgeous seat," comparing him to Satan, Prince of Darkness, who in Paradise Lost is "high on a throne of royal state."

> The games in Book 2 which celebrate the choice of King Cibber to be poet-laureate derive from the games in Aeneid 5 commemorating the death of Anchises, Aeneas's father, and from those in Iliad 23 in honor of Patroclus....   Both epic contexts honor dead heroes, dwellers in the Underworld. Accordingly, one important implication of the allusion is that Cibber is "dead," an uncreative spirit, or, as the opening of the book indicates, a prince of Darkness. The dunghill imagery only reinforces that implication. (Anderson 212-213)

The avowed function of The Dunciad is to remove the imperial seat of dullness from the city to the polite world (Guilhamet 109). Pope's depiction of Cibber is similar to Dryden's earlier depiction of MacFlecknoe. Like MacFlecknoe, Cibber is constantly trying to produce a literary work. The outcome, however, is never acceptable. In Pope's poem, Cibber blasphemed.

> Then gnaw'd his pen, then dash'd it on the ground,
> Sinking from thought to thought, a vast profound!
> Plung'd for his sense, but found no bottom there,
> Yet wrote and flounder'd on, in mere despair.
> Round him much Embryo, much Abortion lay,
> Much future Ode, and abdicated Play.

And Cibber's hard work does not pay dividends.

> How Prologues into Prefaces decay,
> And these to Notes are fritter'd quite away. (Guilhamet 110)

Pope's poem, like Dryden's before him, turned the writer's own life and language against him. Pope's "Take up the Bible, once my better guide" is based on the fact that Cibber's father had intended for him to become a clergyman. Pope's references to "Fiddle," and to "christian progeny" point to eccentricities in Cibber's expression, and Pope's mentioning of "smutty sisters" might be an allusion to Mrs. Charlotte Charke, Cibber's scandalous daughter (Guilhamet 110). Pope is also making a comment about Cibber's narrow horizons when he states,

> Small thanks to France, and none to Rome or Greece.
> A past, vamp'd, future, old, reviv'd, new piece,

and Cibber is classed not with major authors, but rather with the minor authors in

> Twixt Plautus, Fletcher, Shakespeare, and Corneille,
> Can make a Cibber, Tibbald, or Ozell.

The Dunciad is a satiric attack on dullness and boredom. It is a mock epic reminiscent of Homer's Iliad; it is what Jacob Adler calls "an Iliad of dunces." The opening line is "Books and the man I sing," and this is based on the opening line of Virgil's Aeneid, "Arms and the man I sing." The entire poem deals primarily with books and authors, but only bad books, and bad authors (Adler 868). There is a place where bad works are written by bad authors and published by bad publishers, and this place is ruled over by the goddess of Dullness. The Dullness includes "ineffective and inappropriate similes and metaphors, inappropriate mixtures of comedy and tragedy, and inappropriate mixtures also of epic and farce." As additional examples of bad writing, Pope mentions puns, and the Gothic, which were hated in Pope's day, and he says that Tibbald sacrifices bad books to the goddess of Dullness (Adler 869).

Pope's maxim--"Whatever is, is right"--defines the neo-classical movement in eighteenth-century satire. In his An Essay on Man, Being the First Book of Ethic Epistles. To Henry St. John, L. Bolingbroke (1747), Pope notes that if we affirm the grotesqueness of our own identities, it is only logical that we must affirm the grotesqueness of other people's identities as well. If we are right, then they are also right:

> What e're the Passion, knowledge, fame or pelf,
> Not one will change his neighbor with himself.
> The learned is happy nature to explore,
> The fool is happy that he knows no more;
> The rich is happy in the plenty given,
> The poor contents him with the care of Heaven.
> See the blind beggar dance, the cripple sing,
> The sot a hero, the lunatic a king;
> The starving chemist in his golden views
> Supremely blest, the poet in his Muse. (Demarest 53)

David Demarest notes that in the view articulated by Pope here, the satirists of the eighteenth century tend to be very tolerant. In fact, Demarest notes that during this period, the only unequivocal sin is intolerance of philosophical differences (53).

Samuel Johnson writes about the personal habits and physical infirmities of "the great little Pope":

His body was crooked; he was so short that it was necessary to raise his chair in order to place him on a level with other people at table. He was sewed up in a buckram suit every morning, and required a nurse like a child. His contemporaries reviled these misfortunes with a strange acrimony, and made his poor deformed person the butt of many a bolt of heavy wit. The facetious Mr. Dennis, in speaking of him, says, 'If you take the first letter of Mr. Alexander Pope's Christian name, and the first and last letters of his surname, you have A. P. E.' " (Thackeray 176)

Although this may be considered to be a scathing criticism, Pope did not cower before such charges, and in fact William Makepeace Thackeray suggests that "Pope was more savage to Grub Street than Grub Street was to Pope" (Thackeray 178). "The thong with which he lashed them was dreadful; he fired upon that howling crew such shafts of flame and poison, he slew and wounded so fiercely, that in reading the Dunciad and the prose lampoons of Pope, one feels disposed to side against the ruthless little tyrant, at least to pity those wretched folk on whom he was so unmerciful" (Thackeray 178).

Thackeray continues: "There were great prizes in the profession which had made Addison a Minister, and Prior an Ambassador, and Steele a Commissioner, and Swift all but a Bishop. The profession of letters was ruined by that libel of the Dunciad" (Thackeray 178). The conclusion to the Dunciad supports Thackeray's contention:

As, one by one, at dread Medea's strain
The sick'ning stars fade off the ethereal plain;
As Argus's eyes, by Hermes's wand oppress'd,
Closed, one by one, to everlasting rest;-- (Thackeray 178).

Frederick Keener suggests that in the course of his writing career, Alexander Pope's sense of himself "became more and more himself, more and more self-conscious; that, in short, his ironic aloofness diminished until we discern, in the later poems, a poet active, involved, immersed in the dramatic scenes he portrays" (Clark 40).

John Clark, believes that Keener was wrong in this assessment. He believes that Pope "had managed, throughout his career, to sustain a degree of witty aloofness that we still identify--however Romantically--as exemplary of 'the Gloom of the Tory Satirists' " (Clark 40). Pope's wit, like that of Dryden was "the propriety of words and thoughts adapted to the subject," for Pope said,

True wit is nature to advantage dressed,
What oft was thought, but ne'er so well expressed,
Something whose truth convinced at sight we find.
That gives us back the image to our mind. (L'Estrange 309)

William Anderson sums up Alexander Pope's writing career in the following way:

Pope explored basic themes of the Aeneid and Paradise Lost, elaborately working out his controlling metaphor of darkness in his travesty of Rome's fated founding as the seat of civilization, of the Miltonic overthrow of Satan. The mock-heroic describes the destruction of civilization and the triumph of Satan, but we experience the triumph of Alexander Pope, and we sense that his special "heroism" will survive. (Anderson 213)

There are those who would stigmatize Pope as waspish, venomous, and malignant, and with some justification. But there is another side to his character. Even though he was a bitter enemy, he was also a warm friend. "What is peculiar in the case of Pope is the sharpness of the contrast." According to Walker, "for energy Dryden, and for polish Pope, are the culminating points of classical satire in English verse" (Walker 179).

Alexander Pope Bibliography

Adler, Jacob. "Alexander Pope." Encyclopedia of British Humorists, Volume II. Ed. Steven H. Gale. New York, NY: Garland, 1996, 865-871.

Anderson, William S. "The Mock-Heroic Mode in Roman Satire and Alexander Pope." Satire in the 18th Century. Ed. J. D. Browning. New York, NY: Garland, 1983, 198-213.

Clark, John R. "The Decline of Irony in the Eighteenth Century." Thalia: Studies in Literary Humor 2.1-2 (1979): 39-43.

Demarest, David P., Jr. "Reductio Ad Absurdum: Jane Austen's Art of Satiric Qualification." Six Satirists. Pittsburgh, PA: Carnegie Mellon University Press, 1965, 51-68.

Guilhamet, Leon. "Pope." Satire and the Transformation of Genre. Philadelphia, PA: University of Pennsylvania Press, 1987, 100-124.

Hunt, Leigh. Wit and Humour. New York, NY: Folcroft Library Editions, 1972.

Ingram, Allan. Intricate Laughter in the Satire of Swift and Pope. Hampshire, England: Macmillan, 1986.

L'Estrange, Alfred Gu. History of English Humour. New York, NY: Burt Franklin, 1878.

Nokes, David. Raillery and Rage: A Study of Eighteenth Century Satire. Sussex, England: Harvester Press, 1987.

Powell, Dilys. "Alexander Pope." English Wits. Ed. Leonard Russell. London, England: Hutchinson, 1940, 1-26.

Quintana, Ricardo. "The Rape of the Lock as a Comedy of Continuity." Review of English Literature 7.2 (1966): 9-19.

Rogers, Pat. Hacks and Dunces: Pope, Swift, and Grub Street. New York, NY: Methuen, 1980.

Rogers, Robert W. The Major Satires of Alexander Pope. Folcroft, PA: Folcroft, 1955.

Rosenblum, Michael. "Pope's Illusive Temple of Infamy." The Satirist's Art. Eds. H. James Jensen, and Malvin R. Zirker, Jr. Bloomington, IN: Indiana University Press, 1972, 28-54.

Schmidt, Johann N. Satire: Swift and Pope. Berlin, Germany: Verlag W. Kohlhammer, 1977.

Sitter, John F. "Abstraction from the Body in Pope and Prior." Arguments of Augustan Wit. New York, NY: Cambridge University Press, 1991, 138-142.

Sitter, John F. "Big Bodies and Little Bodies (Swift, Gay, Pope). Arguments of Augustan Wit. New York, NY: Cambridge University Press, 1991, 101-113.

Sitter, John F. The Poetry of Pope's Dunciad. Minneapolis, MN: University of Minnesota Press, 1971.

Thackeray, W. M. "Prior, Gay, and Pope." The English Humorists: Charity and Humour: The Four Georges. New York, NY: Dutton, 1912, 133-181.

Walker, Hugh. "Pope." English Satire and Satirists. New York, NY: J. M. Dent, 1925, 166-179.

Williams, Aubrey L. Pope's Dunciad. Hamden, CT: Shoe String, 1968.

Wolfe, Humbert. "Pope and His Successors." Notes on English Verse Satire. London, England: Leonard and Virginia Woolf, 1929, 96-114.

Samuel Richardson (1689-1761)

Richardson's Pamela: or, Virtue Rewarded was written in the form of a series of long and detailed letters from Pamela Andrews, a poor country girl who is in service to a rich family. When her mistress dies, Pamela is in the position of being forced to resist the continued advances of the young master of the house. When he fails to seduce her, he attempts rape on a number of occasions, but he is always thwarted at the last moment. Finally, in a desperate state, he proposes marriage, and Pamela happily accepts his offer, thus receiving the reward for her virtue. The book was published on November 6, 1740, and by September of 1741, five editions had been published, not to mention a pirated edition in Ireland (Kreissman 3-4). In the winter of 1740-1741, Horace Walpole remarked, that Pamela was like the snow in that it covered everything with whiteness (Kreissman 4).

Although Pamela was extremely popular as a novel, its significance went far beyond its simple popularity, for it was responsible for starting several schools of fiction, and it was also directly responsible for a large number of imitations of various kinds (Kreissman 1). It is Richardson's ethical outlook, and his artistic ability that is the base of all of the burlesque, parody, criticism, objection and condemnation that Pamela has evoked. The two most successful attacks of Richardson's Pamela are Henry Fielding's Joseph Andrews, and his Shamela (Kreissman 1).

Richardson spent his next eight years working on Clarissa. Clarissa's death is foreshadowed in the novel from the first pages when Anna Howe assures her, "...I am fitter for this world than you: You for the next [more] than me" (Lansbury 10). This is followed by what Coral Lansbury describes as "unquestionably the longest death scene in English literature." Lansbury adds that it is "also the most exhilarating, fired by the conflicting perturbations of grief, anger, and rapturous excitement" (Lansbury 11). Clarissa is destined not so much to die as to become a divine bride.

> The six who kneel and witness her transfiguration hear her joyful acceptance of her bridegroom. Every earthly comfort has been denied her, even the pardon of her parents, because "...God Almighty would not let me depend for comfort upon any but himself." She has learned true submission, not to man, like Pamela, but to Jesus, who cannot be imagined to possess any of the failings of a Mr. B. (Lansbury 11)

For Richardson, it is not a tragedy but a comedy when Clarissa's corpse is carried home, for it is "a savage exultation over those who defy God and take up arms against virtue" (Lansbury 12). The reading of the will is also comic for Richardson, since the will is "a set comic piece and sure test of familial feeling in any age. All of Clarissa's enemies are in turn chastised and broken like clay" (Lansbury 13). This part of the novel can be described as jubilant in that it "speaks to barely repressed impulses in all of us--the desire for retribution, the urge to inflict punishment" (Lansbury 13). According to Lansbury, "we enjoy the downfall of Clarissa's enemies; we delight in the orchestrated grief of her family" (Lansbury 13). We are especially delighted at Lovelace's punishment. "From the night that he raped Clarissa, his body is stretched on a rack of pain, his mind flickering like a fire" (Lansbury 13). Only Lovelace, with his magnificent arrogance could demand, with his last breath, that his death should atone for his sins. For someone with Richardson's faith, a person did not get off so easy as that. "Lovelace died seeing Clarissa and calling to her for mercy: 'Sweet Excellence! Divine Creature! Fair Sufferer!' And once he said, 'Look Down, Blessed Spirit, look down!'--And there stopped; his lips however, [still] moving" (Lansbury 15).

The final passages of the novel pronounce all of the living characters to be dead, and all of the dead characters alive. This ending "was a spiritual transubstantiation that has proved singularly resistant to modern psychological and sociological interpretation" (Lansbury 10). Richardson was always puzzled and irritated when people insisted on reading Clarissa as a tragedy. The novel had a happy ending, and he himself considered it to be a "divine comedy."

Samuel Richardson Bibliography

Kreissman, Bernard. Pamela-Shamela: A Study of Criticisms, Burlesques, Parodies, and
    Adaptations of Richardson's Pamela. Lincoln, NE: Univ of Nebraska Press, 1960.
Lansbury, Coral. "The Triumph of Clarissa: Richardson's Divine Comedy." Thalia: Studies
    in Literary Humor 1.1 (1987): 9-18.

Lord Philip Dormer Stanhope Chesterfield (1694-1773)

In the history of humor studies, Lord Chesterfield's chief claim to fame is that he
condemned vocal laughter for its "democratic vulgarity" (Levin 12). Nevertheless,
Chesterfield admired wit, and said of it, "Wit is so shining a quality that everybody admires
it; most people aim at it; all people fear it; and few love it, unless in themselves" (Nicholls
xi).

Lord Chesterfield was a close personal friend of Jonathan Swift, and when Swift lie
dying in Dublin, Chesterfield came to his bedside. Swift lay ruined, deprived of most of
his career, his health, and his intellect, but Chesterfield observed that "life is like that." He
went on to say that the prize goes to the diplomat, not the genius, and then added that if
Swift had wanted to end his life in any other way, he would have learned to shrink himself
to the size of the company he was in, and to take their tone as his own (Eddy xxxii).

Lord Philip Dormer Stanhope Chesterfield Bibliography

Eddy, William Alfred, ed. Satires and Personal Writings by Jonathan Swift. London,
    England: Oxford University Press, 1949.
Levin, Harry, ed. Veins of Humor. Cambridge, MA: Harvard Univ Press, 1972.
Nicholls, Mark. The Importance of Being Oscar: The Life and Wit of Oscar Wilde. New
    York, NY: St. Martin's Press, 1980.

Matthew Green (1696-1737)

Matthew Green's "Remedies for the Spleen" was admired by Alexander Pope, and
quoted by Samuel Johnson. Green was subject to depression, and he often got himself into
a better mood by relying on his wit and good sense. The "spleen" that Green refers to was
a common preoccupation of eighteenth-century writers, though it often had other names like
"biliousness," "melancholy," "hypochondria," "vapours," "hyp," "the nerves," or just "low
spirits" (Hunt 313). Leigh Hunt feels that Green's wit was sometimes "more laboured than
finished," but he also feels that Green should be praised for his brevity and for the
originality of his similes. Green wrote in the school of Butler, and Hunt remarks that "no
man since Butler has put so much wit and reflection into the same compass of lines" (Hunt
308).

Matthew Green Bibliography

Hunt, Leigh. Wit and Humour. New York, NY: Folcroft Library Editions, 1972.

Robert Dodsley (1703-1764)

Robert Dodsley was the son of a schoolmaster who went into domestic service as a footman. He wrote about his experiences in "A Muse in Livery." Dodsley also wrote "The Devil's Dance," which was directed against the Pope, written on the occasion of the Pope's absolving a rich person for his sins, but not absolving a poor person with nearly the same sins. The poem offers a kind of literary poetic justice that was not obtainable in real life:

> Home goes the man in deep despair,
> And died soon after he came there,
> And went 'tis said to hell: but sure
> He was not there for being poor!
> But long he had not been below
> Before he saw his friend come too.
> At this he was in great surprise
> And scarcely could believe his eyes. (L'Estrange 115)

Dodsley was an epigramist, and the church was one of his favorite targets:

> Cries Sylvia to a reverend dean
>   "What reason can be given,
> Since marriage is a holy thing,
>   That there are none in heaven?"
>
> "There are no women," he replied,
>   She quick returns the jest,
> "Women there are, but I'm afraid
>   They cannot find a priest." (L'Estrange 115)

Robert Dodsley Bibliography

L'Estrange, Alfred Gu. "Dodsley, Fielding, and Smollett." History of English Humour. New York, NY: Burt Franklin, 1878, 113-126.

Arthur Dawson (c1700-1775) IRELAND

See Nilsen, Don L. F. Humor in Irish Literature: A Reference Guide. Westport, CT: Greenwood, 1996.

Henry Fielding (1707-1754)

Between 1728 and 1737, Henry Fielding wrote twenty-six plays, all of them comedies (Trainor 359). They ranged from farce to ballad opera to burlesque to comedy of manners to satire to parody. George Meredith had a great deal of respect for Henry Fielding as a writer. In fact, Fielding is the only English writer which Meredith includes as writers who are able to invoke the Comic Spirit: "O for a breath of Aristophanes, Rabelais, Voltaire, Cervantes, Fielding, Molière when you do call." This inclusion of Fielding among the masters of intellectual comedy strikingly departs from the Victorian perspective. Fielding's work for Meredith's contemporaries represented coarseness, the "jolly old England of cakes and ale," and the farce of muddy roads and fights in inns" (Stewart 234).

The Victorian English responded to Fielding's "noisy enormity," and they overlooked the "mental richness" which Meredith admired. Meredith says in Essay on Comedy that Fielding is "a master of the comic both in narrative and in dialogue." Meredith approves of Fielding's parody of the sentimental Richardson, and he "focuses on Fielding's presentation of character as a central example of the comic distinguished from the satiric, the ironic, or the humorous treatments" (Stewart 234).

George Levine feels that dramatic irony was very prominent in Fielding's early satiric plays such as The Author's Farce; and the Pleasures of the Town (1730), The Temple Beau (1730), Tom Thumb (1730), The Grub-Street Opera (1731), The Modern Husband (1732), Pasquin (1736) and The Historical Register (1737). In addition to being satires, all of the plays written during this period are burlesques, except for Rape Upon Rape (a satirical comedy), and The Letter-Writers (a farce) (Levine 145). The Mock Doctor, for example, attacked a Dr. John Misaubin, and it was a burlesque of Molière's Le Médecin malgré Lui. Here, Fielding praises Misaubin for qualities which most 18th-century readers immediately recognized to be false (Levine 146). These comedies were noted for their severe satire, and some of them became so political as to be instrumental in leading Chamberlain's supervision of the stage (L'Estrange 118). Fielding's plays were not very successful. Although they abounded in witty sallies and repartee, and although the characters were rough, farcical, and jolly, the plots themselves were not humorous (L'Estrange 118).

The tension which is often developed between the author or narrator on the one hand and the characters and audience on the other hand is a characteristic feature of Fielding's works. But there can be different kinds of tension. Trapwit, a character in Pasquin is not aware of many of the implications of his own play, and this is intended to be ironic, as Trapwit is the butt of much of Fielding's ridicule. On the other hand, Medley, a character in The Historical Register, is fully aware of the implications of his own work, and this results in a very different kind of satire.

Fielding said that "of all kinds of writing, there is none on which variety of opinions is so common as in those of humour, as perhaps there is no word in our language of which men have in general so vague and indeterminate an idea" (Tave vii). Fielding wrote a number of humorous songs, one of which is entitled, "Pleasures of the Towne," in which he wrote,

> Betwixt the quack and highwayman,
> What difference can there be?
> Tho' this with pistol, that with pen,
> Both kill you for a fee. (L'Estrange 118)

Fielding's "Journey from this World to the Next" also contained a considerable amount of humor. Here, he introduced the character of Julian whose reincarnation brings him back as a king, a fool, a tailor, a beggar, etc. As a tailor, he talks about the dignity of his profession, saying that "the prince gives the title, but the tailor makes the man." As a tailor, Julian divides courtiers into two classes, those who never intend to pay for their clothes, and those who do intend to pay for them, but are never able to do so (L'Estrange 120). As a beggar, Julian observes how similar he is to the politicians of the day:

> No profession requires a deeper insight into human nature than a beggar's. Their knowledge of the passions of men is so extensive, that I have often thought it would be of no little service to a politician to have his education among them..., it being equally their business to delude and impose on mankind. It must be admitted that they differ widely in the degree of advantage, which they make of their deceit, [however], for whereas the beggar is contented with a little, the politician leaves but a little behind. (L'Estrange 120)

Fielding viewed affectation as "the only Source of the true Ridiculous." However, when he explicitly addressed the subject of humor in The Covent-Garden Journal, he emphasized the vagueness of the word, and the variety of opinions that people have about the concept (Levin 3). In the Preface of Joseph Andrews, Fielding talks about the limits of the ridiculous: "What could exceed the absurdity of an author who should write 'The Comedy of Nero,' with the merry incident of ripping up his mother's belly, or what would give a greater shock to humanity." This is an example of what Erich Segal would call Schadenfreude (Levine 73). David Nokes looked at two features which helped to make Fielding's satire unique--the language and imagery of violence, and the language and imagery of food (Nokes xii). F. McD. C. Turner considers Fielding second only to Swift as an ironist and satirist. "Early as he stands among our novelists, his work, nevertheless, possesses a vivacity that makes it very readable still, and there is something about his characters singularly true to human nature in spite of their many absurdities and overdrawn propensities" (Turner 59). H. Barton Baker considers Henry Fielding to be the "father of modern burlesque," as he explains that his The Tragedy of Tragedies was an effective burlesque of the heavy tragedies of the day (Baker 213).

The Tragedy of Tragedies; or The Life and Death of Tom Thumb the Great (1731) is a masterpiece of dramatic burlesque targeting the popular playwrights of Fielding's day. It is such an amusing travesty that it made Jonathan Swift "laugh for only the second time in his life" (Trainor 360). Alan Downer says that the elaborate annotations of sources in Tom Thumb is part of Fielding's mockery of aesthetic theories (226). Frank Whiting says about this play that "reading the script is probably more enjoyable than seeing it performed on the stage, for the copious footnotes are half of the fun" (84). Whiting points out that after Tom has cried, "Oh happy, happy, happy, happy, Thumb!" a footnote "solemnity informs us that Tom is exactly one-fourth happier than Masinissa, a well-known character in the tragedy "Sophonisba," who was only "happy, happy, happy!" (Whiting 84).

The Author's Farce (1730) is a good-humored satire in which Fielding gives the playgoer an amusing view of the relationship between booksellers and hack-writers who were working for the booksellers. The tone of this satire is more benign than that of Jonathan Swift or Alexander Pope (Trainor 362). The Covent-Garden Tragedy (1732) is a blank-verse parody of neoclassical drama (Trainor 360). The Mock Doctor (1732) is a farce adapted from Molière, and so is The Miser (1733).

H. Barton Baker suggests that Fielding's Pasquin, and The Historical Register may have been responsible for having provoked Minister Walpole to introduce the famous "Licensing Act" of 1737. In effect, this act gave the official government stamp of approval to certain plays considered respectful to the government. Ironically, the public responded by rejecting the approved plays, simply because they had be so approved (Baker 66-67).

Between 1739 and 1741, Fielding edited The Champion, which was published three times a week. Fielding assumed the persona of Captain Hercules Vinegar (Trainor 360). While Fielding was editor of The Champion, in 1740, Samuel Richardson wrote Pamela: or Virtue Rewarded, an epistolary novel about a maidservant who defended her virtue, and was later able to marry the gentleman whose advances she had successfully rejected. Richardson's Pamela became a cult phenomenon of his day. The readers hung breathlessly on every turn of events, and Aaron Hill's family and friends were said to have been so moved by Hill's reading of the novel that they frequently had to leave the room and weep in privacy. The villagers in Slough are said to have rung the church bells when their reader came to Pamela's marriage. Fielding's first novel, Shamela (1741), was an indictment of Pamela's totally ethical view. "It seems contradictory to refer to such a bawdy book as serving the cause of morality, but Fielding's sexual comedy is free and open and hearty, unlike the pornographic melodrama of Richardson's bedroom scenes where a sensual leer hides behind a mask of gentility. Of all the remedies against a hyperactive libido, there is none better than laughter" (Battestin xvi). Battestin goes on to suggest that there is something essentially healthier in Shamela's lusty good humor than in the prurient sobriety of Pamela.

Charles Trainor says that Shamela was the first and by far the best satire of Richardson's Pamela. It is a ribald and very clever parody which undercuts what Fielding considered Richardson's "spurious morality." It also reveals the "sham" of Richardson's heroine, who is "exposed as a calculating hussy, utterly without morals although always ready to talk for 'a full hour and a half about my fartue" (Trainor 361).

George Levine excluded Shamela from his study of English irony because "it is a work of almost pure sustained parody, containing very little irony" (7). Much of the satire of Shamela targets religion, and centers on the Methodist Parson Williams, who preaches "convenient doctrine" about the "sufficiency of faith." (Rothstein 389). The parson says to Shamela, "I propose to give you a Sermon next Sunday, and shall spend the evening with you, in pleasures, which, tho' not strictly innocent, are however to be purged away by frequent and sincere repentance" (Rothstein 389).

Fielding's Shamela was a direct attack on Richardson's Pamela, but his The History of the Adventures of Joseph Andrews, and of His Friend Mr. Abraham Adams, Written in Imitation of the Manner of Cervantes (1742) was also an attack, although rather than being frontal, it was an attack to the flank. Whereas Shamela attacked the novel itself, Joseph Andrews attacked the sentimental readers of the novel.

> A certain type of reader of Joseph Andrews--the sentimentalist--allows himself to become so emotionally entangled with the narrative that he fails to see that he is as much the butt of Fielding's ridicule as the fictional characters themselves. Thus when Fielding stops the action in III, x in order to "divert" the reader with an apparently irrelevant dialogue between the poet and the player, he is doing more than merely imitating Marivaux's elaborate delaying tactics; his verbal irony is, in effect, a means of engaging in a cat and mouse game with the sentimental reader who would take seriously the battle of the chamberpot and the dirty mop and the peculiar array of combatants: a trouserless parson, a resolute male virgin, a pandering captain, and a trembling but chaste milkmaid. (Guthrie 149)

In the preface to his book on Joseph Andrews, Martin Battestin says that "What is most memorable about Fielding is not his morality or his religion, but his comedy--the warm breath of laughter that animates his fiction" (Guthrie 91). Joseph Andrews probably began as a parody of Samuel Richardson; however, it developed into a "sympathetic and sensitive bildungsroman" in its own right (Browning 7). James Evans compares Joseph Andrews to Don Quixote. Both Andrews and Quixote seem foolish because they act on the basis of texts they have read, remembered, and oftentimes quoted. But while it is Amadis of Gaul and other chivalric romances which have made Quixote mad, Andrews owes most of his folly to the reading of the Bible and other theological texts (Evans 50). Robert Polhemus also compares Fielding with Cervantes in that they both target chivalric romance. Cervantes writes about mad knight-errantry in a mundane world, as he contrasts Don Quixote's blind idealism against Sancho Panza's peasant materialism. This contrast allows the reader "to infer a potentially subversive message about living by blind faith in the supposed word of God" (Polhemus 14). Cervantes manages to give readers "an option of respecting and loving a truly ridiculous and eccentric character--that is, an option of embracing the humorous." Fielding was very much a disciple of Cervantes, and his Joseph Andrews sets out to parody the "romantic nonsense and hypocritical morality of Richardson's Pamela." But something happens as the story unfolds:

> The center of his novel becomes the quixotic knight-cleric of Christianity, Parson Adams. In the figure of Adams he uses comedy to humanize

Christian faith, and Adam's benevolence and charity make the humor "amiable." Fielding works to fuse Christian and comic vision by making Adams at once ridiculous and an admirable defender of a sacred and humane faith. (Polhemus 15)

When Joseph Andrews boxes Beau Didapper soundly on the ear for offending Fanny, Beau draws his sword, and the Parson Adams snatches up the lid of a pot in his left hand and uses it to cover himself as with a shield, though he doesn't have any weapon of offence in his other hand. "The hilarity of the scene, the antiheroic description of the combatants (especially the mundane nature of Adams's equipage), all contribute to a comic effect which obscures the real courage and devotion to his friend which marks Adam's action. The reader is required to make the vital distinction between the amusing and the ridiculous" (Berland 98).

In the "Preface" of Joseph Andrews, Fielding argued for a comic catharsis the same way that Aristotle had argued for a tragic catharsis. For Fielding, Mirth and laughter "are probably more wholesome Physic for the Mind [than is tragic catharsis], and conduce better to purge away Spleen, Melancholy and ill Affections, than is generally imagined." Joseph Andrews is what Trainor calls a "sweeping social comedy, in which Fielding "unmasks uncharitable clergymen, grasping innkeepers, and affected fops." It is nevertheless filled with benevolent humor that centers on the gullible Parson Adams. It is a romance, but it is also a burlesque, a drama, an epic, and it is picaresque fiction as well. The result is an amalgam which Fielding himself describes as "a comic epic-poem in prose" (Trainor 361).

The two most important ironic or satiric devices of The Life of Mr. Jonathan Wild The Great (1743) are blaming by praise, and praising by blame. In this novel, he praises by blaming only when he is describing nonfictional characters which are so obviously praiseworthy that there is no possibility of mistaking his intention (Guthrie 155). To this Guthrie adds a third ironic device, "complimentary connotation." And in Jonathan Wild, all of these devices, but especially the first one, are substantially reinforced through constant repetition. Thus, whenever Fielding says "great" or talks of "greatness," he really means "mean" and "meanness." and whenever he says "hero," he really means "villain" (Guthrie 151).

Fielding's characterizations are filled with "complimentary connotations," used ironically. In Jonathan Wild, Fireblood is described in terms of what he is not. "We shall therefore (which is the properest way of dealing with this kind of GREATNESS) describe him negatively, and content ourselves with telling our Reader what Qualities he had not: In which Number were Humanity, Modesty, and Fear, not one Grain of any of which was mingled in his whole Composition" (Guthrie 153). Tom Smirk in the same novel is described by how he dressed:

> He wore, then, a Pair of white Stockings on his Legs, and Pumps on his Feet; his Buckles were a large Piece of Pinchbeck Plate, which almost covered his whole Foot. His Breeches were of red Plush, which hardly reached his Knees; his Wastecoat was a white Dimity richly embroidered with yellow Silk, over which he wore a blue plush Coat with Metal Buttons, a smart Sleeve, and a Cape reaching half way down his Back. His Wig was of a brown Colour, covering almost half his Pate, on which was hung on one side a little laced Hat, but cocked with great Smartness. (Guthrie 152)

Jonathan Wild is a devastating political satire targeting Walpole. It is written in the form of a mock-heroic biography of a notorious criminal of the day, Jonathan Wild. It uses inflated rhetoric, Homeric similes, and mock battles to develop the mock-heroic tone. Wild's execution was written up in a style which burlesques the high style of heroic drama and romance (Trainor 361).

Between 1747 and 1748, Fielding was the editor of Jacobite's Journal, which presented current affairs from an ironic or slightly sarcastic point of view. In The History of Tom Jones, a Foundling (1749) Fielding expresses his allegiance to Aristophanes, Cervantes, Rabelais, and Shakespeare in having the ability not only to laugh at the follies of others, but also to humbly grieve at their own follies as well (Evans 47). A number of critics have suggested, in fact, that Tom Jones is presented as a moral lesson on how not to be; however, William Guthrie sees Tom Jones as a "comic celebrant of life." In the first chapter of the novel, Fielding introduces the motif of festive comedy with his description of a feast. According to Guthrie, "The feast metaphor suggests that the reader must as readily consider the actions of men an entertaining banquet to be enjoyed as good food is enjoyed." As Tom Jones himself exclaims, "What can be more innocent than the indulgence of a natural appetite? or what more laudable than the propagation of our species?" (Guthrie 93).

Indeed, Tom Jones has animal spirits, and William Guthrie suggests that Tom is a "walking symbol of the life-spirit whose physical charms no woman can resist" (Guthrie 98). Sophia says of Tom, "I know none with such perfections. So brave and yet so gentle; so witty, yet so inoffensive; so humane, so civil, so genteel, so handsome!" (Guthrie 98). Sophia's maid, Mrs. Honour, also admires Tom, and also gives enthusiastic testimony to his many admirable characteristics, and Molly Seagrim is still another lover and adulator of Tom, as is Mrs. Waters. Guthrie discusses the relationships that Tom has with these various women. "Like Sophia, Honour, and Molly, Mrs. Waters also recognizes Tom's masculine assets, and she, too, resolves to partake of the sensual pleasure offered by him. Just as he endears himself to Sophia through his gallant rescue of her from her runaway horse, so he performs another chivalrous act in his rescue of Mrs. Waters from Northerton" (Guthrie 98). But after the encounter, Mrs. Waters's clothes are torn from the upper part of her body, and her breasts,

> ...which were well formed and extremely white, attracted the eyes of her deliverer, and for a few moments they stood silent, and gazing at each other.... Thus our hero and the redeemed lady walked in the same manner as Orpheus and Eurydice marched heretofore; but though I cannot believe that Jones was designedly tempted by his fair one to look behind him, yet as she frequently wanted his assistance to help her over stiles, and had besides many trips and other accidents, he was often obliged to turn about. However, he had better fortune than what attended poor Orpheus, for he brought his companion, or rather follower, safe into the famous town of Upton. (Guthrie 99)

Tom's life-force can also be seen in the various women whom he encounters. Guthrie suggests that if we accept Tom Jones's sensual nature as healthy, we are at first inclined to accept Lady Bellaston's pursuit of Tom also as an expression of the same comic life-force. But Lady Bellaston is not like Tom's other lady friends. "What Fielding develops in Lady Bellaston is a symbol of passion and social power that is a serious threat to the comic life-spirit" (101). In the novel, Tom is continually in Lady Bellaston's power, first because she can lead him to Sophia, and second because he needs her money (Guthrie 101). Furthermore,

> unlike Mrs. Waters, Lady Bellaston is totally unwilling to share Tom. Her own ill-natured and selfish passion causes her to try to destroy the happiness and even the life of others. Thus she is the antithesis of Tom, whose sexuality is always coupled with his good-natured concern for his partner whether she be Molly Seagrim, Mrs. Waters, or even Lady Bellaston herself. (Guthrie 102)

In contrast to the actions of Tom Jones, there are the actions and attitudes of Reverend Allworthy, who condemns the natural passion by saying that such passions are undesirable because they are animalistic. "Like Allworthy, Fielding relates the indulgence of sexual appetites to animals. But here the similarity ends, for what Allworthy described to Jenny Jones as vile and low, Fielding regards as natural, noble, festive, and free" (96). Guthrie feels that there is a moral lesson being presented in the novel, but it is not the moral lesson of Reverend Allworthy. "Fielding's portrayal of Allworthy suggests that the moral lesson of the novel may be directed not mainly at imprudent youths like Tom Jones, but more seriously at the Allworthys who make prudence a necessity" (97). In the novel, Allworthy reads Tom a lecture on morality, and then he banishes him. "But Fielding's comment on the lecture suggests that he sees Allworthy's morality as comically rigid, not as admirable" (Guthrie 97).

Dowling Campbell feels that <u>Tom Jones</u> has its share of flatulence. Lady Western is in the company of Squire Western, and the Squire's sophisticated, dignified, prim, and proper sister. The Squire has just redressed Lady Western, who responds as follows:

"Thou art one of those wise men," cries she, "whose nonsensical principles have undone the nation; by weakening the hands of our government at home, and by discouraging our friends and encouraging our enemies abroad."--"Ho! are you come back to your politics?" cried the squire: "as for those I despise them as much as I do a F__t." Which last words he accompanied and graced with the very action, which, of all other, was the most proper to it. (Campbell 147-148)

William Guthrie feels that the primary function of festive comedy is to affirm the joy of living, and the ending of <u>Tom Jones</u> is an affirmation of the festive comic tradition. Tom triumphs, and he and Sophia are reconciled. William Thackeray, in fact, does not like the ending of <u>Tom Jones</u> precisely because the novel <u>is</u> celebrant of life, and <u>does</u> fall into the category of Dionysian festive comedy: Thackeray says that Tom does not repent and is "not half punished enough before the great prize of fortune and love falls to his share." Thackeray therefore declares, "I am angry with Mr. Jones" (Guthrie 103). Guthrie continues, "Thackeray's artistic sense made him realize that if Fielding wanted to stress a moral lesson he should not reward Tom so quickly and generously at the end" (Guthrie 103).

<u>Tom Jones</u> is Fielding's masterpiece. It is a mock-epic burlesque, but it is also an all-out farce filled with buffoonery that is made all the more effective by its concentration with the sophisticated writing style. Fielding's satiric devices were influenced by Jonathan Swift land William Hogarth, but <u>Tom Jones</u> is written as a warm-hearted comedy, and is about good-natured characters like Tom Jones, who may go wrong from time to time, but they are filled with the desire to go right. "And throughout it all there is the irony that is the mainstay of the novel." Tom Jones has many witty allusions, apt quotations, and rhetorical flourishes, but it is never pretentious or pedantic. Instead, Fielding's style is urbane and playful as he develops in Tom Jones a character that is an infectious blend of gusto, good humor, and comic energy. The novel offers a "vivid panorama of society high and low, urban and rural, in eighteenth-century England" (Trainor 362).

The end of <u>Tom Jones</u> is especially indicative of the fact that it is festive comedy. In the end "All were happy, but those the most who had been unhappy before" (Guthrie 104). The novel ends with a series of marriages which William Guthrie sees as the triumph of the life-force. It is true that Fielding concludes the novel with praise not of Tom, but of Allworthy; Allworthy says of Tom that "he hath also, by reflection on his past follies, acquired a discretion and prudence very uncommon in one of his lively parts" (Guthrie 104), implying that Tom has finally become a perfect gentleman by learning Allworthy's lesson. But Guthrie feels that this is not the whole story. "Fielding's reference to Tom's 'lively parts' playfully reminds the reader of Tom's vigor just when Tom is supposed to be the reformed man of prudence.... Tom's 'very uncommon' transformation is simply

Fielding's way of saying that Tom Jones, the prudent gentleman, is not as believable or interesting as Tom Jones, the 'good natured' celebrant of life" (Guthrie 104). The tone of Amelia (1751) is rather dark, and the satire is bitter, as Fielding attacks both social and political abuses (Trainor 362). In Journal of a Voyage to Lisbon (1755), published post-humously), Fielding approaches the end of his life with intellectual vigor that is undiminished by the pains of his crippled body (Trainor 362). Throughout his life, Fielding had chosen "to laugh humankind out of its favorite follies" (Trainor 363).

Henry Fielding Bibliography

Baker, H. Barton. History of the London Stage. New York, NY: Benjamin Bloom, 1969.
Baker, Sheridan. "Henry Fielding's Comic Romances." Papers of the Michigan Academy of Science, Arts, and Letters 45 (1960): 411-419.
Battestin, Martin. Joseph Andrews. Boston, MA: Houghton, 1961.
Berland, K. J. H. "Satire and the Via Media: Anglican Dialogue in Joseph Andrews." Ed. J. D. Browning. New York, NY: Garland, 1983, 83-99.
Campbell, Dowling G. "Flatulence from Chaucer to Salinger." WHIMSY 1 (1983): 147-150.
Castillo, Rosa. " 'Wit and Humour' in Henry Fielding." Literary and Linguistic Aspects of Humour. Barcelona, Spain: Univ of Barcelona Dept of Languages, 1984, 41-45.
Coley, William B. "The Background of Fielding's Laughter." ELH 26 (June, 1959): 229-252.
Donaldson, Ian. The World Upside-Down: Comedy from Jonson to Fielding. Oxford, England: Clarendon, 1970.
Downer, Alan S. The British Drama. New York, NY: Appleton-Century-Crofts, 1973.
Evans, James E. "Bilfil as Tartuffe: The Dialogic Comedy of Tom Jones." Comparative Literature Studies 27.2 (1990): 101-112.
Evans, James E. "Comedy and the 'Tragic Complexion' of Tom Jones." South Atlantic Quarterly 83 (1984): 384-395.
Evans, James E. "The World According to Paul: Comedy and Theology in Joseph Andrews." Ariel: A Review of International English Literature 15 (1984): 45-56.
Fielding, Henry. Joseph Andrews and Shamela. Boston, MA: Riverside Press, 1961.
Goggin, L. P. "Development of Techniques in Fielding's Comedies." Publication of the Modern Language Association 67 (1952): 769-781.
Guthrie, William B. "The Comic Celebrant of Life in Tom Jones." Tennessee Studies in Literature 19 (1974): 91-105.
Hume, Robert D. "Marital Discord in English Comedy from Dryden to Fielding." The Rakish Stage: Studies in English Drama 1660-1800. Carbondale, IL: Southern Illinois Univ. Press, 1983, 176-213.
Irving, W. R. "Satire and Comedy in the Works of Henry Fielding." Journal of English Literary History 13 (1946): 168-188.
Knight, Charles A. "Fielding and Aristophanes." Studies in English Literature, 1500-1900 21 (1981): 481-498.
L'Estrange, Alfred Gu. "Dodsley, Fielding, and Smollett." History of English Humour. New York, NY: Burt Franklin, 1878, 113-126.
Levine, George R. Henry Fielding and the Dry Mock: A Study of the Techniques of Irony in His Early Works. The Hague, Netherlands: Mouton, 1967.
Loftis, John. Comedy and Society from Congreve to Fielding. Stanford, CA: Stanford Univ Press, 1958.
Polhemus, Robert M. Comic Faith: The Great Tradition from Austen to Joyce. Chicago, IL: University of Chicago Press, 1980.

Reid, B. L. "Utmost Merriment, Strictest Decency: Joseph Andrews." Sewanee Review 75 (1967): 557-584.

Rothstein, Eric. "The Framework of Shamela." ELH 1968: 381-402.

Schneider, Daniel J. "Sources of Comic Pleasure in Tom Jones." Connecticut Review 1 (1967): 51-65.

Sitter, John. "Prose Character Progresses and the Novel: Swift and Fielding." Arguments of Augustan Wit. New York, NY: Cambridge University Press, 1991, 39-44.

Spilka, Mark. "Comic Resolution in Fielding's Joseph Andrews." College English 15 (1953): 11-19.

Stewart, Maaja A. "Techniques of Intellectual Comedy in Meredith and Fielding." Genre 8 (1975): 233-247.

Thackeray, W. M. "Hogarth, Smollett, and Fielding." The English Humorists: Charity and Humour: The Four Georges. New York, NY: Dutton, 1912, 182-221.

Thornberry, Ethel Margaret. "Fielding's Theory of Comedy." Henry Fielding's Theory of the Comic Prose Epic. Madison, WI: Univ of Wisconsin, 1931, 151-163.

Trainor, Charles "Henry Fielding." Encyclopedia of British Humorists, Volume I. Ed. Steven H. Gale. New York, NY: Garland, 1996, 358-364.

Whiting, Frank. An Introduction to the Theater. New York, NY: Harper and Row, 1978.

John Armstrong (c1709-1779)

An Essay for the Abridging of the Study of Physick (1735) demonstrated John Armstrong's "sharp, bumpkinish, scatological humor." According to Kevin Cope, we can "hear the cadences of great future novelistic buffoons like Smollett's Lieutenant Bowling or Frances 'Fanny' Burney's Captain Mirvan" in this poem. Armstrong's The Oeconomy of Love (1736) was written to discourage masturbation, and it is said that it is "the most 'nauseous' poem ever written." Employing Miltonic style, Armstrong strikes with ringing blank-verse iambs in his attempt to warn against excessive self-induced pleasures. By the middle of the eighteenth century, however, the Miltonic style had been linked with mock-heroic poetry, so Armstrong's poem, which had not been written as a humorous poem, was suddenly causing a great deal of "nervous laughter" (Cope 42). By using such extraordinary periphrases as calling the penis a "tumid Wonder," Armstrong also picked up the reputation of being a pornographer and a panderer (Cope 43).

Sketches or Essays on Various Subjects (1758) describes a program used to produce humorous personal histories (Cope 43). In these Sketches, Armstrong presents light parodies of a wide range of literature, from almanacs to medical handbooks. In typical English understatement, Armstrong suggests that we should "abstain from hemlock, henbane, deadly mandrake, arsenic, sublimate, etc., for most physicians agree, that all these plants are more or less unwholesome" (Cope 44).

The narrator of The Muncher's and Guzzler's Diary (1748) is Noureddin Ali. This is a parody of farmer's almanacs, and one of the rhetorical devices used to establish the parody is what Cope terms the "scaffold of tautologies." "If the wind does not blow from the south this month, we shall have it from the east or the north, except it comes from the west." The complete title of this piece is what Cope calls "an amusing orgy of onomastic emissions." It reads: The Muncher's and Guzzler's Diary: The Wits', the Critics', the Conundrumist's, the Farmer's, the Petit-Maitre's Pocket Companion: The Jacobite's, the Whig's, the Freethinker's, the Methodist's Breviary: The London, the Rome, the Constantinople, the Pekin, the Cairo, the Mexican, the Brentford Calendar: The Gentleman's, the Lady's, the Old Woman's, the Child's Manual: The Male, the Female, the Hermaphrodite Prognosticator: The Mole's, the Salamander's, the Butterfly's, the Whale's, the Alligator's, the Phoenix's, in a Word, The Universal Almanac (Cope 44).

John Armstrong Bibliography

Cope, Kevin. "John Armstrong." Encyclopedia of British Humorists, Volume I. Ed. Steven
H. Gale. New York, NY: Garland, 1996, 41-45.

Samuel Johnson (1709-1784)

Hester Thrale, in her Anecdotes of the Late Samuel Johnson, LL.D., says that
Samuel Johnson was an admirer of Joshua Reynolds (1723-1792) who in 1764 suggested
founding a Literary Club having such members as Johnson, Garrick, Goldsmith, Burke,
Boswell, and Sheridan. Johnson first met Reynonds at the house of Frances and Charlotte
Cotterell, where the two women were lamenting the death of a person who had helped them
greatly. Reynolds remarked, "You have, however, the comfort of being relieved from the
burthen of gratitude." The women were shocked, but Johnson was impressed by
Reynolds's sharp insight into the truth of human nature. Hester Thrale's account of this
event goes as follows: "When I one day lamented the loss of a first cousin killed in
America,--'Prithee, my dear, (said he,) have done with canting; how would the world be
the worse for it, I may ask, if all your relations were at once spitted like larks, and roasted
for Presto's supper?'--Presto was the dog that lay under the table while we talked"
(Rosenblum 586). Johnson felt that life was something that mainly had to be endured,
rather than enjoyed, so he resented those who intentionally added to the burden of sorrow,
as Mrs. Thrale had done in summoning up the memory of a distant relative just as a subject
of conversation, and out of no deep-felt sympathy. Johnson's humor was grounded in the
"bedrock of common sense. He delighted in puncturing pretensions (Rosenblum 587).
Johnson is aware of life's uncertainties and blames them on "frolic beings" who
"take a man in the midst of his business or pleasure and knock him down with an
apoplexy." It is the nature of these "frolic beings" to "see a man tumble with an epilepsy,
and revive and tumble again, and all this he knows not why" (Topsfield 13). Early in his
writing career, Dr. Johnson wrote two ironic works on comical subjects. These two works
were called Marmor Norfolciense and A Complete Vindication of the Licensors of the
Stage. It is true that Dr. Johnson was witty and had a sense of the ridiculous. It is true
that he had the sentimentalist's warmth of heart. It is also true that sophisticated wit, a
sense of the ridiculous, and empathy for the subject are all important ingredients in
humorous irony. But these two early works of Johnson failed nevertheless, because
Johnson did not have the gift of sustained irony (Turner 60-61). Johnson's irony was based
on the creed of sincerity and understanding. He had a firm belief that people should not
meddle with things they do not understand, and it was in support of this belief that most
of Johnson's irony was composed (Turner 64).
Later, Johnson wrote poetry, and his London: A Poem, In Imitation of the Third
Satire of Juvenal (1738) represents Johnson's ability at both satire and at parody
(Rosenblum 592). Juvenal had mocked those who pursue vain wishes, but Johnson had
sympathy for these people. Juvenal painted a ludicrous portrait of an old man who would
not die; whereas Johnson's old man arouses pity (Rosenblum 587). Johnson's The Vanity
of Human Wishes (1749) says, "There mark what ills the scholar's life assail / Toil, envy,
want, the garret and the jail" (Rosenblum 588). Samuel Johnson considered linguistic
change as "degeneration"; however, he acknowledged that such change was inevitable and
confessed that the lexicographer was unable "to change sublunary nature, and clear the
world at once from folly, vanity, and affection" (Rosenblum 589).

Johnson did not sympathize with the American Revolution, and in his <u>Taxation No Tyranny</u> (1775) asked, "How is it that we hear the loudest yelps of liberty from the drivers of Negroes?" (Rosenblum 590). William Adams considered Samuel Johnson to be "a gay and frolicksome fellow." James Boswell remembers his first meeting with Johnson in the following way: "He has great humour and is a worthy man." On one occasion Boswell was trying to impress Johnson with the "amenities of Scotland" by showing him the water closet in a very old castle. Johnson responded, "You take very good care of one of a man, but not of the other." Sir John Hawkins considered Johnson to be "the most humorous man I ever knew," and David Garrick said, "Rabelais and all other wits are nothing compared with him. You may be diverted by them; but Johnson gives you a forcible hug, and shakes laughter out of you, whether you will or no." Samuel Johnson had an unhappy first marriage; nevertheless, he married a second time. He described such experience as "the triumph of hope over experience" (Rosenblum 591).

In the middle part of the eighteenth century, the French, the Spanish and the Italians all had national dictionaries, so the English desired one too. In 1746, a group of booksellers asked Johnson to prepare this work, and after some hesitation he took on the project. It is interesting that the forty members of the Academie Français had taken more than forty years to produce their dictionary. When he was asked about this French experience, Johnson is said to have replied, "Let me see; forty times forty is sixteen hundred. As three to sixteen hundred, so is the proportion of an Englishman to a Frenchman." And Johnson, with some help from six aides, accomplished the task in nine years. Some of Johnson's definitions do not make matters simpler, however. He defines "cough" as "a convulsion of the lungs, vellicated by some sharp serosity." And his "network" is "any thing reticulated or decussated, at equal distances, with interstices between the intersections." Johnson at one point said, that a lexicographer should not be feared--that he was merely a "harmless drudge." He also said that patriotism is all too often, "the last refuge of the scoundrel" (Rosenblum 588).

It is interesting to note that the first of nine definitions of "humor" listed in Samuel Johnson's <u>A Dictionary of the English Language</u> (1755) is quite literally "moisture," hearkening back to pre-Ben-Jonson days. This definition referred more specifically, to the ancient and medieval uses of the term as it related to physiology, and thereby denoted the four fluids of the human body--choler (or bile), melancholy, phlegm, and blood, which had in turn been derived from the four elements (Levin 7). According to Harry Levin, Samuel Johnson had "bouts of jocularity" and was an advocate of the vocal laughter which Lord Chesterfield had condemned for its "democratic vulgarity." Sir John Hawkins said that Johnson was the most humourous man he had ever seen (Levin 12-13).

Much of Johnson's humor was short and pithy. Johnson was schooled in the classics, and his rhetorical style was Augustan in nature. Johnson was very much offended by the simplified style of writing that was emerging at his time, and he parodied this simplistic style in one of his impromptus:

I put my hat upon my head
And walk'd into the Strand,
And there I met another man
Whose hat was in his hand. (MacDonald 560-561)

Johnson's parodies reduced literature to the ludicrous. Authors like Thomas Wharton wrote "pseudo-medieval ballads," and such ballads especially appealed to Johnson's sense of the ridiculous, and inspired such verses as the following:

Hermit hoar, in solemn cell,
Wearing out life's evening gray,
Smite thy bosom, sage, and tell,
Where is bliss? and which the way?

Thus I spoke; and speaking sigh'd;
--Scarce repress'd the starting tear;--
When the smiling sage reply'd,--
--Come, my lad, and drink some beer. (Rosenblum 588)

Dr. Johnson was the master of the retort. When he was young, Johnson spent about two years selling books in a bookstore. Some of the wealthy customers were annoyed at being neglected by Johnson, because Johnson refused (in his own words) to "supersede the pleasures of reading by the attentions of traffic" (Pearson 53).

On one occasion after he had eaten a dinner he had been invited to, Johnson said, "This was a good dinner enough, to be sure, but it was not a dinner to ask a man to" (Knox 45). On another occasion, after reading a manuscript which one of his contemporaries gave to him to criticize, he said, "Your manuscript is both good and original, but the part that is good is not original, and the part that is original is not good" (Helitzer 128; McPhee 17). When a particular individual defended Dominicetti's vapor baths, Johnson said, "Well, Sir, go to Dominicetti, and get thyself fumigated, but be sure that the stream be directed to thy head, for that is the peccant part" (Knox 30). When Boswell and Johnson were talking about forcing a certain spendthrift to leave London, Johnson told Boswell to go and visit him: "If that does not drive a man out of his house, nothing will" (Knox 31). But most of Johnson's jabs are not so much at individuals as at their ethnicities. "Johnson hardly ever scored a real success with a purely personal repartee. He never made Boswell look a fool qua Boswell, only qua Scot. His genius was for generalization, not for satirizing the individual" (Knox 31).

But Dr. Johnson did get many good jabs at the Scots, because he felt that they betrayed their king during the Civil War, and because such Scots as Hume, Beattie, Robertson, Macpherson, Reid, and Adam Smith were spreading all over and pretty much having their own way about it. When Johnson lost his oak staff on the isle of Mull, he said, "It is not to be expected that any man in Mull who had got it will part with it. Consider, Sir, the value of such a piece of timber here" (Knox 42). Johnson considered the learning of the Scottish people like the bread in a besieged city: "Every man gets a little, but no man gets a full meal" (Knox 42).

Johnson especially liked to tease Boswell, but this was a delicate thing to do, because if the humour was too broad, the Scottish laugh came too easily; if it was too subtle, there was the distinct danger that Boswell would not see the joke at all. There is no question that Boswell was, at times, a nuisance. And Johnson showed remarkable self-restraint in many of his gentle reprimands. When Boswell offered to "explain" Allan Ramsay's "Gentle Shepherd" to Johnson, Johnson mildly retorted, "No, Sir, I won't learn it. You shall retain your superiority by my not knowing it." He also said on one occasion, "Boswell, lend me sixpence, not to be repaid." Boswell was constantly requesting confirmation of Johnson of his good will, so often in fact that Johnson finally said, "My regard for you is greater almost than I have words to express, but I do not choose to be always repeating it; write it down in the first leaf of your pocket-book, and never doubt of it again" (Knox 44).

Another of Johnson's targets was religion. He was a preacher himself, and he therefore didn't like to see the preaching profession abused. "Johnson's semi-skeptical, semi-superstitious nature was horrified by a clergyman's mental licentiousness, revolted by his worldliness, and scared by his profanity. "This merriment of parsons is mighty offensive," he once said when a group of the clergy were enjoying one another's jokes" (Pearson 52).

One of the reasons that Johnson was so critical of Swift was that they both were preachers. "Boswell tells us that Johnson had "an unaccountable prejudice against Swift" and never missed an opportunity of attacking him. But the prejudice is not unaccountable.

Johnson, a puritan, hated coarseness of language and loose conversation with women, and Swift could be very coarse both with men and women" (Pearson 52).

Dr. Johnson did not like puns. "People that make puns," he said, "are like wanton boys that put coppers on the railroad tracks. They amuse themselves and other children, but their little trick may upset a freight train of conversation for the sake of a battered witticism" (Morris 128). When James Boswell suggested that Johnson disliked puns because he couldn't make them, Johnson replied, "If I were punished for every pun I shed, there would not be left a puny shed of my punnish head" (Morris 128).

At the beginning of an age of sentimentalism, many of Johnson's jabs were against cant. Johnson was also in revolt against the "noble savage," and against, in fact, the emerging field of modern anthropology. Probably his greatest ability as a conversationalist was that of being able to provide effective illustrations on the spur of the moment. He said, "If a physician were to take to eating horseflesh, nobody would employ him, though one may eat horseflesh, and be a very skilful physician" (Knox 39). When a shy boy was sent to a public school, Johnson commented, "Placing him at a public school is forcing an owl upon day" (40). And of course the comment which Johnson is most famous for concerns the preaching of a particular Quaker lady. Johnson said that this was "like a dog's walking on his hinder legs. It is not done well, but you are surprised to find it done at all" (Knox 40). Occasionally there was a wit who was able to get back at Johnson, and one of these was David Garrick. Garrick had lived with Samuel and Tetty Johnson during the autumn of 1735 in Edial, and for years afterwards, Garrick was the life of many of the parties he attended by imitating Johnson's elephantine love-making and odd mannerisms (Pearson 55).

Johnson considered it his duty in any argument to take the unpopular side. Johnson was also not against contradiction if it suited his purposes. "I have all my life long been lying till noon, yet I tell all young men, and tell them with great sincerity, that nobody who does not rise early will do any good." According to Ronald Knox, "Johnson did not merely say that; he thought it" (34).

Samuel Johnson Bibliography

Beaurline, L. A. Johnson and Elizabethan Comedy: Essays in Dramatic Rhetoric. San Marino, CA: Huntington Library, 1978.

Butterick, George F. "The Comedy of Johnson's Rasselas." Studies in Humanities 2.1 (1970-71): 25-31.

Cazamian, Louis. "The Doctrine of 'Humors' about 1600; Johnson's Two 'Humors' Comedies." The Development of English Humor. Durham, NC: Duke University Press, 1952, 309-316.

Helitzer, Melvin. Comedy Writing Secrets. Cincinnati, OH: Writer's Digest Books, 1987.

Knox, Ronald A. "Dr. Johnson." English Wits. Ed. Leonard Russell. London, England: Hutchinson, 1940, 27-46.

Kronenberger, Louis. The Thread of Laughter: Chapters on English Stage Comedy from Johnson to Maugham. New York, NY: Hill, 1970.

L'Estrange, Alfred Gu. "Sterne, and Dr. Johnson." History of English Humour. New York, NY: Burt Franklin, 1878, 99-112.

Levin, Harry. Veins of Humor. Cambridge, MA: Harvard University Press, 1972.

MacDonald, Dwight, ed. Parodies: An Anthology from Chaucer to Beerbohm--and After. New York, NY: Random House, 1960.

McPhee, N. The Book of Insults, Ancient and Modern. New York, NY: Penguin, 1978.

Morris, Scot. "In Search of the Perfect Pun." Omni 8.2 (November, 1985): 128-129.

Pearson, Hesketh. "Samuel Johnson." Lives of the Wits. New York, NY: Harper and Row,

1962, 52-69.
Rosenblum, Joseph. "Samuel Johnson." Encyclopedia of British Humorists, Volume I. Ed.
    Steven H. Gale. New York, NY: Garland, 1996, 585-594.
Topsfield, Valerie. The Humour of Samuel Beckett. New York, NY: St. Martin's Press,
    1988.
Turner, F. McD. C. The Element of Irony in English Literature. Cambridge, England:
    Cambridge University Press, 1926.

Laurence Sterne (1713-1768) IRELAND

Gene Washington says that Laurence Sterne's Tristram Shandy and his Sentimental
Journey are now recognized as masterpieces of comedy and irony (Washington 1059).
These two books are satires on styles of writing that were common during Sterne's day.
They especially target eighteenth-century methods of telling a story (Washington 1060).
Sterne was sensitive to "polysemy," which is the ability that language has to represent more
than one thing or one idea with a single term. When Sterne uses the word "place," for
example, he is exploiting the word's polysemy. He does the same with the word "purse,"
which is a container for money and is also a term used to refer to the female genitals. And
"bridge" is something in the mouth, and a military fortification, and "auxiliary" is a part
of speech and a military unit. "Without polysemy his work would lose much of its humor--
especially that effected by punning and innuendo." Sterne also exploits what C. S. Peirce
calls the "thirdness" of language. This "thirdness" is the tendency of the human mind to
use language in structuring the memory, the experience, and this "third" thing, "the thing
between two other things." To illustrate this "thirdness," Sterne says in Tristram Shandy
that conscience is "neither Protestant nor Catholic" (Washington 1064). Gene Washington
says that Sterne's achievement as a humorist, his sense of play, the self-referential nature
of his fiction, and his mixing of the sacred and the secular all add to the effectiveness of
his writing (Washington 1065).
      In The Life and Opinions of Tristram Shandy (1760), Tristram Shandy says, "I
declare I have been at it [the story of his life] these six weeks, making all the speed I
possibly could--and am not yet born" (Washington 1060). Knowing that the reader is
always wondering what is going to happen next, Tristram at one point tells the reader that
he "will never be able to guess." At another point, he tells the reader that Walter's
"propagation of children is 'not worth talking about,'" and in yet another place he tells the
reader that he may "skip" this part of the book if he wishes to do so (Washington 1061).
Sterne subverts the plot of Tristram Shandy by skipping from one generation to another and
from one family member to another. "Modern readers see in this structure a clever, and
successful, strategy for the comic writer. It gives Tristram, for one thing, great time-depth
and with that an opportunity for Sterne to move between generations and among the
members of one generation, and to poke fun at such common matters as the family arms
and familial pride, marital disagreements, and the naming of children." Tristram Shandy
is a comedy of synchronic events. It deals with simultaneous events that occur in different
places. To show this, Sterne often uses parallel sentence structure in the narrative
(Washington 1063). Since these simultaneous events often feature "domestic
arrangements," Tristram describes things that are happening simultaneously in different
parts of the Shandy house. Sterne was very aware of what he was doing, and in fact wrote
to Robert Dodsley, his publisher, that "all locality is taken out of the book, the satire
[made] general" (Washington 1063).
      In Tristram Shandy, Sterne is satirizing not only the plot of the novel (and its way
of telling a story), but also the qualities that are traditionally given to an eighteenth-century

hero. When Tristram is telling the story about the mid-wife, he is interrupted by Yorick's story. He is also interrupted by Uncle Toby, who says, "I think, says he." Thus he is interrupted, and not allowed to finish until about thirty pages later in the novel. The grammar is also satirical. The subjects and the predicates are frequently separated from each other by long parenthetical comments marked by dashes, parentheses, or asterisks. "In fact, punctuation serves not to establish order and succession as in traditional written narrative but rather fragmentation and disruption" (Washington 1060). In Tristram Shandy, Sterne exposes the writer's paradox. The writer "can't write fast enough to catch up." He "loses writing time in the necessity of fleeing from death." He knows that while writing is linear, one sentence after another, his life and opinions are everywhere, recursive and non-linear, 'running parallel,' both in the parlor and the kitchen" (Washington 1064).

The target of the satire in A Sentimental Journey (the Sermons, Political Romance, and Journal to Eliza) (1768) is travel writing. Sterne is here following the satiric pattern established by Swift in parts of his Gulliver's Travels, and specific targets of Sentimental Journey are the styles of eighteenth-century novelists in general, and travel writers in particular, and more specifically Tobias Smollett, who goes by the name of "Smelfungus" in the narrative (Washington 1060).

See also Nilsen, Don L. F. **Humor in Irish Literature: A Reference Guide.** Westport, CT: Greenwood, 1996.

Laurence Sterne Bibliography

Cash, Arthur H. Sterne's Comedy of Moral Sentiments: The Ethical Dimensions of the Journey. Pittsburgh, PA: Duquesne University Press, 1966.
New, Melvyn. Laurence Sterne as Satirist: A Reading of "Tristram Shandy." Gainesville, FL: University of Florida Press, 1969.
Washington, Gene. "Laurence Sterne." Encyclopedia of British Humorists, Volume II. Ed. Steven H. Gale. New York, NY: Garland, 1996, 1057-1067.

William Shenstone (1714-1763)

Shenstone's Poems Upon Various Occasions were written while he was in college. These poems are short, clever lyrics imitating the styles of Samuel Butler, Jonathan Swift, and Alexander Pope. Randall Calhoun says that it is impossible to read the humorous poetry of William Shenstone without "hearing echoes of the English poets who immediately preceded him." "A Simile" is written in octosyllabic couplets and is a doggerel verse form known as "Hudibrastic." "A Simile" satirizes inflated epitaphs by being a mock "Inscription" about a squire who died from embarrassment because he had passed wind in public." "Colemira, A Culinary Eclogue" is a burlesque in which the humor is directed at the ignorance of a stable hand and a kitchen wench who try to imitate their betters. The Beau in "The Beau to the Virtuoso" is the narrator and is also the target of the ridicule, but he is not so ridiculous as the virtuoso in the poem whose life is dedicated to the propagation of flies and moths:

And speak with some respect of beaux,
Nor more as triflers treat 'em;
'Tis better learn to save one's cloathes,
Than cherish moths that eat 'em.

In "The Rape of the Trap," Shenstone mocks education and politics. It is a mock-heroic poem about a rat who comically drags away the elaborate trap that had been set for it. The sixteen stanzas of this poem show that we have just as much need for good mousetraps as we have for good scholars, and effective politicians (Calhoun 968).

William Shenstone Bibliography

Calhoun, Randall. "William Shenstone." Encyclopedia of British Humorists, Volume II. Ed. Steven H. Gale. New York, NY: Garland, 1996, 967-969.
Pagliaro, Harold. "The Aphorisms of William Shenstone." Unpublished Ph.D. Dissertation. New York, NY: Columbia University, 1961.

Thomas Gray (1716-1771)

In keeping with the eighteenth-century tradition of light-verse-with-moral-attached, Thomas Gray's most famous comic poem is entitled "Ode on the Death of a Favorite Cat." This poem humorously philosophizes on one of Horace Walpole's cats which had drowned while attempting to catch some goldfish for supper. The cat is first seen preening vainly at its own reflection in the water, but suddenly it catches sight of two gold objects swimming by, and the poem suddenly becomes an allegory satirizing the "weaker sex's love of glitter and money":

> The hapless nymph with wonder saw:
> A whisker first and then a claw,
> With many an ardent wish,
> She stretched in vain to reach the prize.
> What female heart can gold despise?
> What cat's averse to fish?

Gray didn't like his humorous poems to be published. At first he allowed "A Long Story" to be published, but he later repressed the republication of the poem. William Gentrup feels that the reason Gray didn't write more humorous poems is that they contained "too much of himself." Almost all of his humorous poems were dependent on a particular incident that affected his personal life, and none of his humorous poems were meant to be read outside of his own inner circle.

Thomas Gray Bibliography

Gentrup, William. "Thomas Gray's Humorous and Satiric Verse." WHIMSY 1 (1983): 162-163.

David Garrick (1717-1779)

Even though David Garrick was one of the first important comic actors, the only humorous pieces which he wrote and published were a few "indifferent farces" (L'Estrange 112).

David Garrick Bibliography

L'Estrange, Alfred Gu. History of English Humour. New York, NY: Burt Franklin, 1878.

Horace (Horatio) Walpole (1717-1797)

It was Horace Walpole who said, "The world is a comedy to those that think, a tragedy to those that feel." (Levin 9). In a similar vein, Ralph Waldo Emerson later said that all lies and all vices, if seen from sufficient distance, where our moral sympathies do not interfere, become ludicrous. Emerson expanded on this observation by saying, "The presence of the ideal of right and truth in all action makes the yawning delinquencies of practice remorseful to the conscience, tragic to the interest, but droll to the intellect" (Bullitt 5). But Emerson needed the Walpole insight in order to provide his refinements of the insight.

Horace Walpole was capable of very dark humor. John R. Clark notes that a traditional theme of satire that has been constant from the eighteenth century to the present day is cannibalism. Clark then goes on to describe what he calls "one demented tale that has weathered the test of time." This is Horace Walpole's "The Peach in Brandy," and the title describes a still-born foetus of a royal heir to the throne which was retained in a pickle jar. The Archbishop mistook the foetus for a peach, and ate it. A horrified witness to the snack exclaimed, "He gulped it all down at once without saying grace. God forgive him!" whereupon the princess wailed, "Mamma, mamma, the gentleman has eaten my little brother" (15).

Horace Walpole Bibliography

Bullitt, John M. Jonathan Swift and the Anatomy of Satire: A Study of Satiric Technique. Cambridge, MA: Harvard University Press, 1953.

Clark, John R. "Chafing Dish: Satire's Adulteration of Language and Style." Thalia: Studies in Literary Humor 5.1 (1983): 14-26.

Levin, Harry. Playboys and Killjoys: An Essay on the Theory and Practice of Comedy. New York, NY: Oxford Univ Press, 1987.

Charlotte Lennox (1720-1804)

Charlotte Lennox wrote a comedy, and a number of humorous poems and novels. Her most remarkable humorous production, however, The Female Quixote: or, The Adventures of Arabella, is a novel about female quixotism. In this novel a young lady develops strange attitudes about male-female relationships by reading romances. The work is a close imitation of Don Quixote; however, Lennox's protagonist is not so natural as is the original Don Quixote developed by Cervantes (L'Estrange 112). It is interesting to note that Tabitha Gilman Tenney's Female Quixotism, Exhibiting in the Romantic Opinions and Extravagant Adventures of Dorcasina Sheldon is based on Lennox's earlier novel (Nilsen 26).

In the Introduction to Lennox's The Female Quixote, Margaret Doody writes, "Lennox laughs at the romances for the repetitive improbability of the events...their inflated diction and their jargon of superlatives" (xvi-xvii). Regina Barreca expands Doody's statement by saying that Lennox does more than write gentle mocking and didactic satire. "Lennox's use of comedy throughout the work makes it a template for dealing with feminine inscriptions of humor." Barreca compares Lennox's writing to that of Jane Austen. Like Austen, Lennox's habitual irony distances her from her own society, but at the same time it unites her with her readers by forming what Barreca calls a "conspiracy of intellect." Robert Polhemus adds, "Whoever does not perceive it becomes its target" (Polhemus 41).

Patricia Meyer Spacks contrasts The Female Quixote with Cervantes's original by saying that the female Quixote, unlike the male Quixote, cannot "travel through the world"

(Spacks 130). Leland Warren would agree with Spacks, and explains the underlying pathos of The Female Quixote in the following way, "Driven to an ideal world by being denied actuality, its heroine must deny the self she has created in order to be allowed once more a place in actuality" (Warren 378).

Charlotte Lennox Bibliography

Barreca, Regina. "Dearly Loving a Good Laugh: Humor in Charlotte Lennox and Jane Austen." Untamed and Unabashed: Essays on Women and Humor in British Literature. Detroit, MI: Wayne State University Press, 1994, 34-60.
Doody, Margaret Anne. "Introduction." The Female Quixote or The Adventures of Arabella. by Charlotte Lennox. New York, NY: Oxford University Press, 1989, xi-xxxii.
L'Estrange, Alfred Gu. History of English Humour. New York, NY: Burt Franklin, 1878.
Nilsen, Don L. F. Humor in American Literature: A Selected Annotated Bibliography. New York, NY: Garland, 1992.
Polhemus, Robert M. Comic Faith: The Great Tradition from Austen to Joyce. Chicago, IL: University of Chicago Press, 1980.
Spacks, Patricia Meyer. Adolescent Idea: Myths of the Young and the Adult Imagination. New York, NY: Basic Books, 1981.
Warren, Leland F. "Of the Conversation of Women: The Female Quixote and the Dream of Perfection." Studies in Eighteenth-Century Culture 11 (1982): 367-380.

William Collins (1721-1759)

In an ode entitled "The Manners," William Collins includes a patriotic tribute to the subject of humor:
O Humour, Thou whose Name is known
To Britain's favor'd Isle alone. (Levin 3)
This poem contributed to the Merry-Olde-England stereotype.

William Collins Bibliography

Levin, Harry, ed. Veins of Humor. Cambridge, MA: Harvard University Press, 1972.

Samuel Foote (1721-1777)

Samuel Foote played comedy roles at Drury Lane, and was successful as a mimic of prominent persons. Simon Trefman, Samuel Foote's biographer, describes Foote as "the most notorious wit and prodigal of his day" (Trefman 1). Trefman says that Foote is a buffoon, but adds that he "has wit too, and is not deficient in ideas, or in fertility and variety of imagery.... Then he has a great range for his wit; he never lets truth stand between him and a jest, and he is sometimes mighty coarse" (Trefman 69). In Bons-Mots of Samuel Foote and Theodora Hook, Walter Jerrold collected a number of Samuel Foote's epigrams, which tend to be both witty and acerbic. Samuel Foote's humor is not so much comedy as it is farce (Rainbolt 379). Samuel Johnson said that Foote had "a great deal of humour," but he denied Boswell's contention that Foote had a "talent for exhibiting character. About Foote's humor, Johnson said, "It is not a talent; it is a vice; it is what others abstain from. It is not comedy, which exhibits the character of a species, as that of a miser gathered from many misers: it is farce, which exhibits individuals" (Rainbolt 380). Samuel Foote was interested in comedy, and in fact wrote The Roman and English Comedy Consider'd and Compared (1747). Foote's The Knights (1749) ridicules Italian opera. His The Englishman in Paris (1753) mocks the Englishman, who when he goes abroad refuses to modify his behavior in any way in order to accommodate what may be a more refined set of customs and manners (Rainbolt 380). In The Minor, Foote attacks religious hypocrisy in general, and the Methodist preacher Whitefield in particular. On Stage, Foote played the role of Mrs. Cole, who amply demonstrated the trait of religious hypocrisy. She professed to be a deeply religious woman, but she was also very bawdy, and advertised for servants under the age of seventeen in rural newspapers so that she could entice these young women into prostitution (Rainbolt 380).

Mrs. Aircastle in The Orators (1762) satirizes the English trend that promoted manners without morals, and grace without substance (Rainbolt 381). The focus of The Mayor of Garratt (1763) is on corrupt politics, the fickleness of the mob, and the trials of married life (Chatten 79). Jerry Sneak is a caricature of a henpecked husband "whose wife is affectionate to other men but cold, haughty, and shrewish to her spouse" (Rainbolt 380). In The Mayor of Garratt, Foote is satirizing married life, political corruption, and the stupidity of the mob (Rainbolt 381).

Foote lost one of his legs in a hunting accident, and made fun of having only one leg in The Devil upon Two Sticks (1768) and The Lame Lover (1770). In The Devil upon Two Sticks, Foote satirizes the "blue stockings" and other aspects of eighteenth-century English life. The play ridicules the medical profession, especially in its debate about which universities would be allowed to train the doctors, and who should be admitted to the Royal College of Physicians. At the end of each performance, Foote would perform a monologue on recent happenings around England. In The Nabob (1772) Foote satirized East India Company servants. In The Trip to Calais (1776), Foote did such a successful caricature of the Duchess of Kingston (who was Kitty Crocodile in the novel) that he was charged and indicted for libel (Neilson 538). In The Cozeners (1774), Foote attacks Lord Chesterfield's idea of grace (Rainbolt 381).

Samuel Foote Bibliography

Chatten, Elizabeth N. Samuel Foote. Boston, MA: G. K. Hall, 1980).

Hill, G. B., and L. F. Powell, eds. Boswell's Life of Johnson: III. Oxford, England: Clarendon, 1934-1964.

Jerrold, Walter, ed. Bons-Mots of Samuel Foote and Theodora Hook. London, England: Dent, 1894.

Neilson, William Allan. Webster's Biographical Dictionary. Springfield, MA: G. and C. Merriam, 1971.

Rainbolt, Martha. "Samuel Foote." Encyclopedia of British Humorists, Volume I. Ed. Steven H. Gale. New York, NY: Garland, 1996, 378-382.

Trefman, Simon. Sam Foote, Comedian, 1720-1777. New York, NY: New York University Press, 1971.

Tobias Smollett (1721-1771) SCOTLAND

Like Henry Fielding, Tobias Smollett felt that humor resulted from unexpected behavior (Rosenblum 1031). Paul-Gabriel Boucé feels that Tobias Smollett "introduces his readers to a world swarming with rogues, crooks, thieves, prostitutes and highwaymen." He feels that Smollett's novels are surrealistic, and that evil is exaggerated for satiric ends

(Boucé 300). Smollett's writing is a blend of sentimentalism and satire. Most of his characters are malicious, but there are enough benevolent characters to thwart them. In Peregrine Pickle, Strap and Hauser Trunnion are models of virtue. The same can be said of Renaldo in Ferdinand Count Fathom, and Launcelot Greaves in Sir Launcelot Greaves, and Matt Bramble and Humphry Clinker in Humphry Clinker. Furthermore, many of Smollett's villains come across more ludicrous than evil (Rosenblum 1030).

Advice: A Satire (1746), and Reproof: A Satire (1747) are Tobias Smollett's first important publications. They are both satires written in verse form. In Advice, Smollett wrote that the intent of these poems was to "fix the brand of infamy on vice." Just as Pope had done before him, Smollett lampoons a series of individuals, including the Duke of Newcastle, the Duke of Grafton, the Earl of Granville, and the Earl of Bath. Smollett also attacks certain "vices" such as homosexuality and sycophancy. In Reproof, Smollett targeted Theatre Manager Rich, and particular financiers and writers, but he especially targets Henry Hawley, and Thomas Thompson whom he considered to be a quack (Rosenblum 1028).

In the "Preface" to The Adventures of Roderick Random (1748) Smollett links the novel to satire and says that he wants to "animate the reader against the sordid and vicious disposition of the world." One of the reasons that the characters are more comic than dark is that they are ruled by a benign providence. Whenever Random most needs help, it appears, sometimes in the appearance of Tom Bowling, the devoted friend, or Random's rich and resurrected father, or his beloved Narcissa, we observe at the end of the book that Random's sudden good fortune, "seemed to have been brought about by the immediate direction of providence" (Rosenblum 1030). But Roderick doesn't seem to be respected. A cabman intentionally splashes him with mud, and a servant considers himself to be a great wit for directing Random to the River Thames instead of the address he is looking for (Rosenblum 1028). Random is wounded and captured by a press gang, and when he asks a fellow prisoner to take a handkerchief out of his own (Random's) pocket so he can make a bandage, the fellow instead steals the handkerchief to sell for a dram of gin (Rosenblum 1029). In Roderick Random, Roderick describes Launcelot Crab as "about five foot high, and ten round the belly; his face was capacious as a full moon, and much of the complexion of a mulberry; his nose resembling a powderhorn, was swelled to an enormous size, and studded all over with carbuncles; and his little grey eyes reflected the rays in such an oblique manner, that while he looked a person full in the face, one would have imagined he was admiring the buckle of his shoe" (Rosenblum 1030).

In Roderick Random, Random and Strap, who are on their way to London, spend a night in an inn with four other people, Captain and Mrs. Weazel, Jenny, and Isaac Rapine. Strap mistakes Captain Weazel's room for his own, and gets into bed with Captain Weazel's wife. Captain Weazel had gone to use the chamberpot, and when he returns he feels a man's head in his bed. He assumes that he has mistaken Jenny's bed for his own, and that she is entertaining someone. Angered by this, he throws the contents of the chamberpot on the couple. Strap and Mrs. Weazel jump up, and the captain begins to strangle Strap. At the same time, Mrs. Weazel hits her husband's head with a shoe to punish him for dousing her. It is at this time that Jenny, who has been sleeping with Isaac, yells, "Rape! Murder! Rape!" (Rosenblum 1031).

An important comic device for Smollett is the use of jargon, and in Roderick Random, he uses legalese to create double entendres. When a lieutenant and a prude go off together, the lawyer says, "I suppose the lady knows him to be an able conveyancer, and wants to make him a settlement intail." Smollett also uses the jargon of sailors for comic effect. When Tom Bowling confronts Random's cousin, he warns him, "Look 'ee, you lubberly son of a w--e, if you come athwart me, 'ware your gingerbreadwork. I'll be foul of your quarter, d--n me." And Morgan flaunts a Welsh accent, with its love of

repetition, "I will impeach, and accuse, and indict him for a roppery" (Rosenblum 1032).
Robin Bates describes The Adventures of Peregrine Pickle (1751) as an "unorganized mass of humorous, obscene or violent incidents and vividly drawn caricatures, all of which overwhelm the romance plot which concludes it. Gameliel Pickle could be described as "John-Bullish," and filled with "Roast-Beef-of-Old-England complacency." Bates suggests a similarity between Gameliel Pickle and Fielding's Squire Allworthy. Both men are introduced in syntactically similar sentences at the beginning of their respective books. "The comparison is further prompted by the fact that each man has an old maid for a sister and a Jonsonian humour for a neighbor. Such plot similarities, however, are less important than certain thematic parallels" (Bates 27). Bates concludes that Gam is not a parody of Allworthy, but rather a substitution.
This unimaginative, sluggish, and non-committal squire, Gameliel Pickle, is the type of person against which Peregrine must rebel, since Peregrine Pickle is a member of the progressive bourgeoisie class, and Peregrine embodies much energy, drive, and desire for freedom and independence. Smollett uses satire to condemn Peregrine's drives, and Peregrine himself is schizophrenically torn between conservative and liberal views (Bates 26). "Throughout the book, Peregrine's pranks frequently overflow the satiric context, and at one point Smollett calls him a reformer, amends the label to 'castigator,' and concludes by saying that Peregrine exercises his talents among those 'who chanced to incur his displeasure' " (Bates 27). Bates notes that Peregrine's pranks are constantly going bad. "What begins as a simple joy at disrupting the order of things threatens to have disastrous consequences: Grizzle almost dies of poisoning; an exciseman is whipped; a farmer is beaten to 'within an inch of his life' and laid up for two months" (Bates 28).
One of Smollett's rhetorical devices is caricature, and another is providing insights into characters by their peculiar uses of language. Trunnion's language, for example, is described as follows: "This composition of notes at first resembled the crying of quails, and croaking of bull-frogs, but as it approached nearer, he could distinguish articulate sounds pronounced with great violence, in such a cadence as one would expect from a human creature scolding thro' the organs of an ass. It was neither speaking nor braying, but a surprising mixture of both" (Bates 30). Walter Allen considers Hauser Trunnion to be one of the greatest English comic characters. "He has his genesis in a simple joke executed with infinite ingenuity." Commodore Trunnion is a retired naval officer who insists on living as if he were on the bridge of one of His Majesty's ships at sea even though he is now on dry land. He is the epitome of the inability and refusal to adjust. "He continues in his retirement to feel, think, talk, behave entirely in terms of his profession of naval officer." The incongruities resulting from this failure to adjust constitute the structure of the joke he is living. On his wedding morning, Trunnion sets out to navigate his way to church on horseback and on the way he is caught in a fox-hunt.

> Trunnion says nothing that is not in character, but the character--the sailor on dry land, both nouns existing as it were in the abstract--is the narrowest conceivable. Trunnion is the simplest kind of Jonsonian humour; and what he says--the translation, for instance, of his horse into a frigate--is implicit in the basic situation. To maintain the nautical metaphor, Trunnion is firmly anchored to his creator's intellectual conception of him. (Allen 14-15)

Joseph Rosenblum says that the sailors in Peregrine Pickle are very much out of their element when they are on land. Hauser Trunnion, for example, "rides a horse as if he were navigating a ship, tacking in a stiff wind" (Rosenblum 1032).
Smollett's approach to experience is totally empirical, and his emphasis is on the facts of each situation rather than on the conclusions which can be drawn (Bates 25). Bates considers this totally empirical approach to be both the major strength and the major weakness of Smollett's work.

Smollett does not pace his book to maintain suspense. To pace the book would require judgmentally giving weight to some things and not to others. Suspense, meanwhile, is a highly artificial strategy often achieved by withholding certain information from the reader, or at least subordinating the present to the future. Trying to articulate a new reality, Smollett minutely examined the present and achieved in intensity what he lost in suspense. (31)

Sir Cadwallader Crabtree is another character in Peregrine Pickle. Alan Dugald McKillop describes this character as "the malcontent and misanthrope of post-1600 English comedy, and the sequence in which he sets up as a necromancer and derides and gulls those who expose themselves by consulting him is thoroughly Jonsonian" (McKillip 161).

Smollett was very aware of Fielding's work, and he confronted head-on issues which Fielding only skirted. Because of this, the contradictions in Peregrine Pickle clash violently and, in fact, almost alienate the reader permanently from the hero, as Peregrine attacks parental authority, the institution of marriage, and offers to substitute in its place "unfettered love, which is delicate, refined and, to give it substance, backed by 12,000 pounds in bank notes" (Bates 28). Fielding had another influence on Smollett as well. Since Smollett was put off by Fielding's constant and extended intrusions, he parodies Fielding by writing an intrusion of his own. Ironically, this intrusion is directed against intrusions, and especially against the introductory chapters of Tom Jones. Smollett's intrusion ends as follows, "I have too much matter of importance upon my hands, to give the reader the least reason to believe that I am driven to such paultry shifts, in order to eke out the volume" (Bates 25).

In The Adventures of Ferdinand Count Fathom (1753), Smollett is trying to "subject folly to ridicule, and...vice to indignation." He also wants to "brand iniquity with reproach and shame." It was Smollett's aim to show that "without money there was no respect, honour, or convenience to be acquired in life; that wealth amply supplied the want of wit, merit and pedigree...and that the world never failed to worship the flood of affluence" (Rosenblum 1028). In The Adventures of Sir Launcelot Greaves (1762) and also in Humphry Clinker (1771), Smollett praises Alexander Pope and Jonathan Swift, both of whom he used as literary models for his own writings (Rosenblum 1028). There are a number of comic incidents in Sir Launcelot Greaves, as when Vanderpelft concludes his speech with the words, "This...is the solid basis and foundation upon which I stand." At this point, the barrel on which he had been standing collapses, and Vanderpelft disappears. The supporters of Valentine Quickset shout, "Stole away! stole away!" (Rosenblum 1031).

In 1766 Smollett described the French common people as diminutive, meager, withered, dirty and half naked. He described the artisans as lazy, needy, awkward and void of all ingenuity. He had compared the noblesse as to Jonathan Swift's Yahoos, had said that French churches were sanctuaries for all kinds of criminals, and had described French art and culture as almost a total blank. Frank Felsenstein indicates that in England, Smollett's work was "lauded for its sturdy defence of British values over the foppish and effeminate habits that were likely to be imbibed by the traveller in France and Italy," and adds, "early reviews emphasize in chauvinistic terms the extent to which the Travels (1766) could be considered as scoring a hit against our 'natural enemy,' the French" (Felsenstein xiii).

The Expedition of Humphry Clinker (1771) portrays a world filled with selfishness and ignorance (Rosenblum 1029). Smollett was very adept at characterization, and visual imagery. Lismahago, in Humphry Clinker, for example, is described as "about six feet in height, had he stood upright; but he stooped very much; was very narrow in the shoulders, and very thick in the calves of his legs, which were cased in black spatterdashes. As for his thighs, they were long and slender, like those of a grasshopper" (6-7). Smollett enjoyed practical jokes, fighting, and violent language. In Humphry Clinker, he describes the ladies at a party in Bath, "Some cried, some swore, and the tropes and figures of Billingsgate were used without reserve in all their native rest and flavour" (L'Estrange 126). Humphry Clinker concludes with not one, but three marriages, and the death of Baynard's wasteful wife allows him to recoup his fortune. In the final letter of the book, Winifred Jenkins Loyd writes, "Providence hath bin pleased to make great halteration in the pasture of our affairs" (Rosenblum 1030).

The malapropisms in Humphry Clinker were used to show the deep truth that lay beneath the comic illiteracy. The letters of Tabitha Bramble and Winifred Jenkins are filled with hilarious solecisms, many of them with sexual or scatological implications, as when Tabitha is so angry at Dr. Lewis that she swears that she will never write to him again even if he "beshits me on his bended knees." Talking to Mary Jones, Tabitha expresses her wish that Clinker may "have the power given to penetrate and instill his goodness, even into your most inward parts." Tabitha wants Roger to "search into, and make a general clearance of the slit holes which the maids have in secret" (Rosenblum 1031).

Sir Walter Scott said, "Smollett's humour arises from the situation of the persons, or the peculiarity of their external appearance, as Roderick Random's carroty locks, which hung down over his shoulders like a pound of candles; or Strap's ignorance of London, and the blunders that follow it. There is a tone of vulgarity about all his productions" (L'Estrange 124).

Tobias Smollett Bibliography

Allen, Walter. Dickens 1970. New York, NY: Stein and Day, 1970.

Baker, Sheridan. "Humphry Clinker as Comic Romance." Papers of the Michigan Academy of Science, Arts, and Letters 46 (1961): 645-654.

Bates, Robin. "Smollett's Struggle for a New Mode of Expression." Thalia: Studies in Literary Humor 1.3 (1989): 25-32.

Boucé, Paul-Gabriel. "Structures of the Comic." The Novels of Tobias Smollett. London, England: Longman, 1976, 302-342.

Felsenstein, Frank, ed. Tobias Smollett: Travels through France and Italy. New York, NY: Oxford Univ. Press, 1981.

Folkenflik, Robert. "Self and Society: Comic Union in Humphry Clinker." Philological Quarterly 53 (1974): 195-204.

L'Estrange, Alfred Gu. "Dodsley, Fielding, and Smollett." History of English Humour. New York, NY: Burt Franklin, 1878, 113-126.

McKillop, Alan Dugald. "Tobias Smollett." The Early Masters of English Fiction. Lawrence, KS: University of Kansas Press, 1956.

Rosenblum, Joseph. "Tobias George Smollett." Encyclopedia of British Humorists, Volume II. Ed. Steven H. Gale. New York, NY: Garland, 1996, 1026-1034.

Thackeray, W. M. "Hogarth, Smollett, and Fielding." The English Humorists: Charity and Humour: The Four Georges. New York, NY: Dutton, 1912, 182-221.

Frances Sheridan (1724-1766) IRELAND

See Nilsen, Don L. F. **Humor in Irish Literature: A Reference Guide**. Westport, CT: Greenwood, 1996.

Arthur Murphy (1727-1805) IRELAND

See Nilsen, Don L. F. Humor in Irish Literature: A Reference Guide. Westport, CT: Greenwood, 1996.

John Wilkes (1727-1797)

Olga Venn notes that at Ludgate Circus there is a small and dingy obelisk dedicated to "the Right Honourable John Wilkes, Esq., Lord Mayor." Venn considers this to be an "appropriate symbol," because today this obelisk marks a comfort station for gentlemen (199). Venn considers Wilkes to be a prototypical example of the person who tries to be too clever, or too witty. He represents what can happen to a person who tries to be too funny, a person who jokes about serious things (200).

John Wilkes was an unnaturally ugly gentleman. His forehead was described as low and short; his nose was too short, and too low. His upper lip was long and projecting, and his eyes were sunken and squinted horribly. Wilkes, however, accepted his ugliness saying that his wit made up for it. He claimed that it took him only half an hour to talk away his face (Venn 201).

John Wilkes Bibliography

Venn, Olga. "John Wilkes." English Wits. Ed. Leonard Russell. London, England: Hutchinson, 1940, 197-234.

Edmund Burke (1729-1797)

F. McD. C. Turner indicates that Edmund Burke's Reflections on the Revolution in France is filled with excellent irony, in spite of Burke's passionate cry of alarm that invades the book. "Yet on the whole it may be said of him, and not of Swift or even of Milton, that his wrath, although it lost him personal respect and not infrequently hurried him into gross metaphor, nevertheless gave such fire to his expression that the gain was greater than the loss" (Turner 64-65).

Edmund Burke Bibliography

Turner, F. McD. C. The Element of Irony in English Literature. Cambridge, England: Cambridge University Press, 1926.

Oliver Goldsmith (c1730-1774) IRELAND

Oliver Goldsmith argued that comedy "should excite our laughter by ridiculously exhibiting the Follies of the Lower Part of Mankind" (Balderston 210). In 1759, Goldsmith contributed eight essays to The Bee, Being Essays on the Most Interesting Subjects which was a weekly magazine. In its second issue is an Oliver-Goldsmith essay with the title, "On Dress" which is a humorous experience of two older characters displaying their fine clothes in the Mall. By ridiculing this event, "On Dress" gently ridicules affectations in general. Goldsmith's "A Reverie," which appeared in the fifth issue of The Bee mocked the pretensions of some contemporary authors who were trying to get a coach to take them to the "temple of fame" (Evans 453).

The Citizen of the World; or Letters from a Chinese Philosopher, Residing in

London, to His Friends in the East (1762) is a series of letters written by a character named Lien Chi, a philosopher from China. The letters represent English life from a Chinese point of view, and therefore create an ironic distance that is then used to highlight English and European folly. It is this ironic distance that is responsible for much of the humor in The Citizen of the World. When Lien Chi visits the law courts in Westminster Hall, or the races at Newmarket, and Westminster Abbey, he always finds things that are ridiculous. He considers the rivalry of two London theaters, and the fashion in funeral elegies, and the people attending various dinners, or belonging to certain clubs quite hilarious. Goldsmith adds to the texture of The Citizen of the World by adding some letters from Hingpo, Lien Chi's son, and by introducing two recurrent characters, Beau Tibbs, and the Man in Black (Evans 453). Beau Tibbs is a shabby character whose affectation of gentility can be considered to be comical (Evans 454). Katherine Balderston considers The Man in Black to be "an humourist in a nation of humourists" (Balderston 109).

The Reverend Charles Primrose in The Vicar of Wakefield: A Tale, Supposed to be Written by Himself (1766) is both an ironic observer, and a fool. He is wise enough to mock the affectation of his wife and his daughters, who try to imitate the gentry. But although he is able to see the affectations of his family, he is unable to see his own affectations. The family portrait in Chapter 16, for example, is much too large for the Primrose house (Evans 454).

In the "Preface" to The Good Natur'd Man: A Comedy (1768), Goldsmith's first play, Goldsmith expresses his regret that "refinement" was threatening to elevate English comedy so much that it would lose its humor. Goldsmith also defended the "necessary lowness" of humor by having his readers remember the period before such "genteel comedy" when "little more was desired by an audience than nature and humour" (Balderston 13).

In She Stoops to Conquer: or, The Mistakes of a Night, A Comedy (1773), Tony Lumpkin is an amiable humorist, a good-natured jokester who enjoys deception, and by doing so allows Goldsmith to ridicule the affectation of Marlow and Hastings, two gentlemen from London whom Tony Lumpkin tricks into thinking that his stepfather's country house is actually an inn. Thus, Lumpkin makes it possible for Kate Hardcastle, his stepsister, to play the part of the inn's maid, and thereby to test the suitor Kate's father has chosen for her to marry. Hastings and Miss Neville are the play's other pair of lovers; they are involved in a conventional comic subplot in their attempt to outwit the foolish Mrs. Hardcastle, who wants Miss Neville to mary her son, Tony. Mr. Hardcastle, her husband, is a humorous eccentric, but he is a sympathetic character because he allows his daughter Kate to marry the man of her choice (Evans 456). Samuel Johnson made the following statement about She Stoops to Conquer: "I know of no comedy for many years that has so exhilarated an audience, that has answered so much the great end of comedy--making an audience merry" (Boswell 525).

Oliver Goldsmith wrote many humorous poems. In Retaliation (1774) Goldsmith responds to the friendly mockery of his club at St. James's Coffee House. When he is provoked to answer a comic epitaph, he retaliates with humorous sketches of nine friends (Evans 455). James Evans considers The Haunch of Venison (1776) to be a "Horatian epistle to his patron Lord Clare." Goldsmith is here influenced by Jonathan Swift, and also by the Nicolas Boileau-Despreaux, the French satirist. Before the dinner, the poet of The Haunch of Venison romanticizes what a fine dinner it will be with all of his literary friends, but then the poet describes in comic detail the disappointing meal, and his ill-bred acquaintances (Evans 455).

See also Nilsen, Don L. F. Humor in Irish Literature: A Reference Guide. Westport, CT: Greenwood, 1996.

Oliver Goldsmith Bibliography

Balderston, Katherine C., ed. The Collected Letters of Oliver Goldsmith. Cambridge, England: Cambridge University Press, 1928.

Bevis, Richard. The Laughing Tradition: Stage Comedy in Garrick's Day. Athens, GA: University of Georgia Press, 1980.

Boswell, James. Life of Johnson, Revised Edition. London, England: Oxford University Press, 1953.

Evans, James E. "Oliver Goldsmith." Encyclopedia of British Humorists, Volume I. Ed. Steven H. Gale. New York, NY: Garland, 1996, 452-458.

Hume, Robert D. "Goldsmith and Sheridan and the Supposed Revolution of 'Laughing' against 'Sentimental' Comedy." The Rakish Stage: Studies in English Drama, 1660-1800. Carbondale, IL: Southern Illinois Univ Press, 1983, 312-355.

Charles Churchill (1731-1764)

James Hannay considers Charles Churchill to be a fine satirist. He says that Churchill's writing contained "warm feeling, penetrating sense, bright wit, and fancy." Unlike most authors who wrote in the heroic metre during the eighteenth century, Churchill did not imitate Pope. It was Dryden who most influenced his writing (Hannay 194). Churchill's Prophecy of Famine is a satire written in the pastoral form. The target is Scotland:

> Far as the eye could reach no tree was seen,--
> Earth, clad in russet, scorned the lively green;
> The plague of locusts they secure defy,
> For in three hours a grasshopper must die;
> No living thing, whate'er its food, feasts there,
> But the chameleon, that can feast on air. (Hannay 195)

Charles Churchill Bibliography

Hannay, James. Satire and Satirists. Folcroft, PA: Folcroft Press, 1969; originally published in 1854.

William Cowper (1731-1800)

Alfred Gu L'Estrange believes that the writings of William Cowper would not have made it into the twentieth century were it not for his humor (127). Playfulness was a natural trait of Cowper, and in his first volume of poems there are some quite-humorous pieces, such as "The Report of an Adjudged Case not to be found in the books." Another humorous Cowper poem is entitled, "Hypocrisy Detected," and in this poem a number of Muslims try to decide which part of the pig the prophet commanded them not to eat, but each Muslim abstains from eating a different part.

> Much controversy straight arose
> These choose the back, the belly those;
> By some 'tis confidently said
> He meant not to forbid the head;
> While others at that doctrine rail,
> And piously prefer the tail.

Thus conscience freed from every clog,
Mohometans eat up the hog.
The moral is that each of us makes an exception in favor of his or her own particular transgressions (L'Estrange 129).
Another of Cowper's poems is entitled "On the Death of Mrs. Throckmorton's Bulfinch." This poem satirizes female sentimentality, and in the poem there is a discrepancy between the pretentiousness of the language and the triviality of the subject. Robin Headlam Wells suggests that the formal language suggests that the subject is not as trivial as it first appears. "Imbued as he was with a Calvinist belief in special providence, it was natural enough that Cowper should regard such trivia as symbolic of an underlying religious truth" (Wells 3). After all, God knows when even the smallest of the sparrows falls. Vincent Newey suggests that the poem has even more import, since it is possibly an expression of unresolved childhood fears in which the aptly named "Bully" represents a schoolboy tyrant who had persecuted Cowper. It follows from this that the persecutor with whom the poem's subject is identified in Cowper's mind might be the Calvinist deity himself (Wells 3).
"On the Death of Mrs. Throckmorton's Bulfinch" is a darkly comic poem; it is a witty adaptation of the classical rules of composition to a trivial subject. More specifically, in the tradition of Greek and Roman literature, Cowper's poem is an epitaph for a dead animal. Consider, for example, Catullus's lament for the sparrow whose death has made his mistress's eyes red with weeping, and Ovid's witty elegies on Corinna's parrot. In quite some detail, the poem follows Quintilian's advice on how to compose a funeral piece in praise of some noble personage: The eligiast should first deal with the subject's lineage. He should then deal with the subject's special gifts of mind and body. Finally, the elegiast must relate the special circumstances of how the deceased departed this world. Cowper follows this traditional elegy formula very closely. As to Bully's ancestry, Cowper says the following:
Where Rhenus strays his wines among,
The egg was laid from which he sprung. (qtd. in Wells 5)
As to his special qualities, Cowper writes,
And though by nature mute,
Or only with a whistle blest,
Well-taught, he all the sounds express'd
Of flagelet or flute. (qtd. in Wells 5)
Again following the formula are the details about Bully's assassination. Because Bully's death was not a natural death, the poet is required to evoke the pity and the indignation of the audience; this Cowper does. Cowper's narrative of the assassination is "descriptio," which can be defined as "an evident declaration of a thing, as though we saw it even now done" (underlining Wells's). The assassination took place in darkness--strong symbolism here. The assassin is described as follows:
Long-back'd, long-tail'd, with whisker'd snout,
And badger-colour'd hide. (qtd. in Wells 5)
But the reader discovers even more pathos in learning that the bird was caged, and thus unable to protect itself. Asleep in its cage, the bird starts to dream of terror. It awakes from its dream to discover that it is a helpless assanination victim. It is being eaten by a rat.
Ah, Muse! forbear to speak
Minute the horrors that ensued;
His teeth were strong, the cage was wood--
He left poor Bully's beak. (qtd. in Wells 6)
Looking at Bully's remains, Cowper is reminded of another singer--Orpheus. "The

absurdity of using the Orpheus myth to lionize a bullfinch has little to do with the poet's personality." The death of the bullfinch, like the death of Orpheus is symbolic of the death of the poetic imagination. "What more appropriate figure to link bird and poet than the legendary singer Orpheus, himself the victim of such cruel ironies?" (Wells 6). After Bully's death, only the beak remains; compare this to Orpheus: "In one of the cruellest stories of the Metamorphoses, Ovid tells how, his mind having been turned against women by the bitter experience of losing Eurydice, the singer is finally torn limb from limb by the Thracian Maenads until only his head is left, still singing" (Wells 7).

Wells concludes by contrasting Cowper's mock-elegy with the tradition of the Christian elegy: "Where the purpose of the Christian elegy is to offer consolation and to justify the ways of God to man, 'Mrs. Throckmorton's Bulfinch' suggests the opposite. Belying the surface comedy of this mock heroic elegy for a dead bird is a sense of fate's malignancy" (Wells 8). While Cowper's "Mrs. Throckmorton's Bulfinch" does not fit into the genre of the Christian elegy, it does fit well into the tradition of the mock elegy, as can be seen in the "moralitas" which is amended to Cowper's "The Raven."

> Fate steals along with silent tread,
> Found oft'nest in what least we dread,
> Frowns in the storm with angry brow,
> But in the sunshine strikes the blow. (qtd. in Wells 8)

William Cowper Bibliography

L'Estrange, Alfred Gu. "Cowper, and Goldsmith." History of English Humour. New York, NY: Burt Franklin, 1878, 127-140.
Newey, Vincent. Cowper's Poetry: A Critical Study and Reassessment. Liverpool, England: Liverpool University Press, 1982.
Wells, Robin Headlam. "William Cowper as Mock Epideictic Elegist." Thalia: Studies in Literary Humor 9.1 (1986): 3-9.

Cumberland (1732-1811)

Cumberland's first name is not known. He was a dramatist who wrote farces, tragedies, essays, and novels, but who is most remembered for his writing of sentimental comedies. Cumberland is ridiculed in Sheridan's The Critic as Sir Fretful Plagiary. Cumberland's The West Indian is a perfect example of sentimental comedy. Alice Rayner notes one of the most salient features of this genre: "because there is virtually no friction between the individual and the social order, we find a utopia. Character, feeling, action, and ethical principles are so closely connected that there is no dialectical level with which to open this world to criticism" (86). Rayner also notes that in sentimental comedies, the characters tend to be very simple, but the plots tend to be notoriously complex, and The West Indian is again a good example of sentimental comedy because the characters are very simple and the plot is very complex (87). In The West Indian, as in other sentimental comedy, "we the audience are privy to secrets that will affirm clear moral divisions--who is deserving, who is not; what partners belong together; who is just and righteous. Knowing those secrets puts the audience in the position of omniscient sympathy, and morality is felt rather than thought" (Rayner 90).

Cumberland Bibliography

Rayner, Alice. "Cumberland and Steele's Aphorism: Use in Utopia." Comic Persuasion:

Moral Structure in British Comedy from Shakespeare to Stoppard. Berkeley, CA:
University of California Press, 1987, 81-103.

John Wolcot (Peter Pindar)(1738-1819)

Robert Vales considers Peter Pindar to be the most important satirist between
Jonathan Swift and Lord Byron (iii). Peter Pindar's real name was John Wolcot. Leigh
Hunt feels that Pindar wrote a lot of trash, even in his humorous writing, and this was
because his stories, like the razors in one of his compositions, were composed "to sell."
Hunt considers Wolcot's versification in "Conversation on Johnson, by Mrs. Piozzi (Thrale)
and Mr. Boswell" to be masterful and straightforward, and the mock-heroic inversions in
this piece are also very effective. Hunt continues, "I am thrown into fits of laughter when
I hear these rhyming Johnsoniana. I can hardly, now this moment, while writing about
them, and glancing at the copy which lies before me, help laughing to myself in private"
(Hunt 327).

Some of Peter Pindar's titles are compelling: "Ode to Ugliness," "The Young Fly
and the Old Spider," "Sir Joseph Banks and the Boiled Fleas," "Ode to my Ass," "To my
Candle," "Perapathetic Razor-Seller," "Bozzy and Piozzi," "Apple Dumplings and a King,"
"Solomon and the Mousetrap" and "Frogs and Jupiter" (L'Estrange 150, Zall v). Peter
Pindar was the chief verse satirist during the reign of George III, an age that "appreciated
verse much as ours appreciates television" (Zall vii). George III was the chief target of
Pindar's satire and wit. Pindar's popularity and his career therefore rose and fell inversely
with the popularity of George III. He wrote comic descriptions of the King's eccentricities
and mannerisms, and his peculiar speech, and at one point Pindar confessed "The King has
been a good subject to me, but I have been a bad subject to his Majesty" (Zall vii).

Another of Pindar's targets was William Pitt, who was the Prime Minister during
Pindar's day who went against strong public opinion in raising taxes to pay for a war at
a time when bad harvests and inflation had spread misery across the land. In his satires,
Pindar often referred to the minister as "Bottomless Pitt" (Zall 3). Pindar was able to keep
a clear distinction between satire of the monarch and subversion of the monarchy, and he
tried not to cross the line. On frequent occasion he escaped arrest for libel and treason by
using the simple defence that the material he used was common knowledge. During his
lifetime there were constant rumors circulated that Pindar hired spies in the King's
household, and according to Peter Zall, Pindar encouraged such notoriety, but Zall further
notes that most of his material was "readily available in the columns of the daily
newspapers" (2).

Pindar enjoyed targeting celebrities in his satires, such as Boswell and Dr. Johnson,
and the Royal Academicians, and politicians, and not only King George III, but also his
German Court with its mannerisms which Pindar found comical (Zall vii-viii). Pindar
sometimes calls the Academicians "Sons of Canvas"; at other times he calls them "Tagrags
and bobtails of the sacred brush." In his Epistle to Boswell (1786), and in his Bozzy and
Piozzi (1786), for example, Pindar mocked James Boswell and also Boswell's literary style.
Pindar wrote epigrams, parodies, political songs, imitations, inscriptions, fables, epistles,
mock-heroic epics, verse essays and songs in the style of Greek Anthology. Pindar's style
was varied and flexible. He could imitate Milton in one stanza and Butler in the next (Zall
4). Pindar attacked the Royal Academy in four poems written between 1782 and 1786, and
in 1786 also wrote The Lousiad, a satire directed at George III. He ridiculed James
Boswell in Journal of a Tour to the Hebrides with Samuel Johnson (1785). And he also
wrote at least one pamphlet each attacking the works not only of James Boswell, but of
Thomas Warton, Henry James Pye, James Bruce and Hannah More. "In these satires, John

Wolcot utilizes, primarily, the manner of Horace in attacking human foibles and the content of the works under observation. He does not rant, rave, or sadistically slash his victims; instead, he is urbane, stands somewhat at a distance, and speaks with a mocking smile upon his face. He questions the meaning and value of each work" (Vales 38). Wolcot's satiric technique employs mainly the "mock encomium" or "mock eulogy" for its effect. He frequently compares people to animals and uses disabling adjectives, and exaggerated examples (Vales 39).

Pindar's satire was topical, and during his day he was extremely popular. There were "...seven or ten editions in a year of his burlesques and lampoons, the booksellers falling over each other to print his works. When Haydn appeared in London, Peter was called on to write the libretto of his oratorio 'The Storm.' And when the Polish patriot Kosciusko was in prison in St. Petersburg, his jailer lent him a volume of Peter's works. There was fame!" (Zall vii). He wrote a huge number of verses, and most of them were bawdy jests and scurrilous gossip "as timely as the morning papers, and produced with no care for polish or accuracy." Pindar wrote with "rapidity, fluidity, and buffoonish disregard for any standard, moral or aesthetic. His public loved him for it" (Zall 1). Peter Pindar, né John Wolcot lived to the ripe old age of ninety-one, and although he was blind in his later years, he was mirthful to the end (Hunt 326).

John Wolcot (Peter Pindar) Bibliography

Hunt, Leigh. Wit and Humour. New York, NY: Folcroft Library Editions, 1972.
L'Estrange, Alfred Gu. History of English Humour. New York, NY: Burt Franklin, 1878.
Vales, Robert L. Peter Pindar (John Wolcot). New York, NY: Twayne, 1973.
Zall, P. M., ed. Peter Pindar's Poems. Somerset, England: Adams and Dart, 1972.

Sir Boyle Roche (c1740-1807) IRELAND

See Nilsen, Don L. F. Humor in Irish Literature: A Reference Guide. Westport, CT: Greenwood, 1996.

Hannah Cowley (1743-1809)

Hannah Cowley's The Belle's Stratagem (1780) is a comedy in which Letitia Hardy uses a strategy of varied female personas to successfully win the affections of her fiancé, Doricourt. Letitia is able to orchestrate her own romance by assuming various female identities, thereby tricking Doricourt into his role of the faithful hero. The personas change from vulgar to witty to proper. Letitia's various identities are perpetrated not only through clothes and facial disguise, but more significantly by language. Through her choice of vulgar, witty, or proper language, Letitia controls the comedy by herself (Isikoff 100). People living during the eighteenth century wanted their women to choose modesty (which was respectable and unsexual) over masquerade (which was degrading, sexual, and dangerous). Nevertheless, The Belle's Stratagem demonstrates that modest demeanor and a masquerade costume are merely types of trappings that can be put on and taken off as the occasion demands. The Belle's Stratagem leaves open the question as to which of these two strategies is better (Isikoff 100).

Hannah Cowley Bibliography

Hannah Cowley (1743-1809)   1

Isikoff, Erin. "Masquerade, Modesty, and Comedy in Hannah Cowley's The Belle's Stratagem. Look Who's Laughing: Gender and Comedy. Ed. Gail Finney. Amsterdam, Netherlands: Gordon and Breach, 1994. 99-118.

John O'Keefe (1747-1833) IRELAND

See Nilsen, Don L. F. **Humor in Irish Literature: A Reference Guide.** Westport, CT: Greenwood, 1996.

Henry William Bunbury (1750-1811)

Bunbury's style tended to teeter delicately between true horror, and humorous excess. Bunbury was trying to "reduce the Gothic ballad to absurdity by pushing it to its grotesque limits." The fifth stanza of Bunbury's ballads was "a veritable compendium of Gothic cliches" and is an indication that Bunbury was "playing with the conventions of the form for comic purposes" (O'Connor 166). Henry Bunbury enjoyed lampooning fashionable bad taste, and beginning in 1796, he began publishing a series of Gothic ballad parodies, designed to ridicule earlier ballads of Matthew Gregory "Monk" Lewis, Robert Southey, Walter Scott, Samuel Taylor Coleridge, and others (O'Connor 166).

Henry Bunbury did such satiric engravings as "La Cuisine de la Poste" (1771), and "View on the Pont Neuf at Paris." In both of these engravings, Bunbury's figures are costumed in such a way as to overwhelm individual identity, and to suggest social station. Bunbury's angular and shrunken faces serve merely as pedestals for wigs and for oversized hats. The thin shanks of the figures serve to display their ostentatious hose, their gargantuan boots, and their other preposterous footwear. Bunbury's engravings are in the same tradition as are those of William Dickinson. Dickinson's "Richmond Hill" (1782) also pokes fun at British dandyism, but does so not only in the exaggerated clothing of the people, but in the equipage of the horses as well. Bunbury's "A Long Minuet as Danced at Bath" (1787), and his "The Propagation of a Lie" (1787) are only a few inches high, but "A Long Minuet" is seven feet long, and "The Propagation of a Lie" is six feet long. Both of these pictures display couples of comically diverse physique and physiognomy who are elegantly dressed. The couples are attempting to strike the graceful poses demanded by the dance, and some are more successful than others in this regard. The figures in "The Propagation of a Lie" are fashionably costumed and appropriately bewigged, but the humor of their facial expressions, and their awkward poses are enhanced by Bunbury's captions, which are very much like the captions of modern comic strip dialogue (O'Connor 165).

Bunbury's An Academy for Grown Horsemen (1787), and his Annals of Horsemanship (1791) both contribute to the humor of sport (O'Connor 168). Tales of Terror (1801) is a collection of poetry, and the last poem in this collection is entitled "The Mud-king, or Smedley's Ghost." In this poem, "one of those hapless bards whose fates and fortunes are celebrated in the Dunciad" is able to lure a moon-struck balladeer to leap into the slime of Fleet Ditch. This poem is attacking the bad taste of such poets as Alexander Pope (O'Connor 167). Tales of the Devil (1801) is a collection of poetry that goes beyond Gothic parody and on to grotesque humor. Such poems as "Earl Widgeon," "The Phantom of Funkinberg," "Simon Sniggle," and "The Hospodar" are humorous because they juxtapose everyday experience, especially the everyday experience of the aristocrat or the sportsman, against something which is quite diabolical. Robert O'Connor feels that these poems present a kind of "grotesque comedy that can be enjoyed for its own sake as well as for its momentary satiric purpose" (O'Connor 167).

Henry William Bunbury Bibliography

Buss, Robert William. English Graphic Satire and Its Relation to Different Styles of Painting, Sculpture, and Engraving: A Contribution to the History of the English School of Art. London, England: Virtue and Company, 1874.
Grego, Joseph. Rowlandson the Caricaturist: A Selection from His Works, with Anecdotal Descriptions of His Famous Caricatures and a Sketch of His Life, Times, and Contemporaries. London, England: Chatto and Windus, 1880.
Kunzle, David. The Early Comic Strip: Narrative Strips and Picture Stories in the European Broadstreet from C. 1450 to 1825. Berkeley, CA: University of California Press, 1973.
O'Connor, Robert H. "Henry William Bunbury." Encyclopedia of British Humorists, Volume I. Ed. Steven H. Gale. New York, NY: Garland, 1996, 164-168.

Robert Fergusson (1750-1774) SCOTLAND

Robert Fergusson joined such authors as Allan Ramsay, and Robert Burns in generating the eighteenth-century Scots vernacular revival. These Scottish poets used the force of satire to counter the puritanism of the Calvinist church and the "Anglicization of the Scots language and Scottish culture." Gerard Carruthers says that Fergusson wrote some of the most effective satire in the Scots dialect in any period. His satire is directed against the cultural encroachments of the Whigs, and to a lesser extent against puritanical religion. (Carruthers 356). Fergusson's poetry is farcically funny, but it is culturally biting as well. Fergusson uses "a range of Scots registers, including urban working-class Scots and peasant dialects, and works in the most energetic Scottish stanzaic traditions to produce slanted, sardonic, sneering comment on the socio-cultural condition of Scotland" (Carruthers 358).

The King's Birth-Day in Edinburgh (1772) is a parody, written in the sprightly "Standard Habbie" metre. Here Fergusson is satirizing the Edinburgh magistrates, and the highland militia, both of which are grotesquely caricatured. "This poem highlights the farcical surface of much of Fergusson's poetry, but underneath there lies a serious point arising from the poet's eighteenth-century Tory sensibilities: the bad behavior of the lower orders is made possible by the unsociableness of officialdom" (Carruthers 357). The Rising of the Session (1773) and The Sitting of the Session (1773) also target Edinburgh's legal system. In these farces, the satire is oblique, but there is a range of explicitly stated satiric targets (Carruthers 357). The "standart Habby" was a favorite stanza of Robert Fergusson, who was more gifted in the form than was Allan Ramsay, from whom he acquired this particular style of poetry. Both Ramsay and Fergusson are considered by Hugh Walker to be more humorists than satirists. Walker considers Fergusson's writing to be more from the perspective of a keen-eyed, dispassionate, amused spectator than from the perspective of a critic or a satirist. Even though the themes of The Rising of the Sessions, and The Sitting of the Session are themes which "invite to satire," Fergusson is just not a satirical poet. He is even less satirical in The Farmer's Ingle and Leith Races, though in all of these poems there are satirical touches. Fergusson's Home Content proclaims itself as satire, but it is mild satire (Walker 253). In his Braid Claith, the thesis is that fine clothing paves the way to fame and love. In Hugh Walker's words, "the lady will not look at the lover unless he wears fine garments" (Walker 254).

The Election (1773) was Fergusson's first political satire to be written in the "Christis Kirk" stanza. Here Fergusson "sneers at the corruption of 'rotten borough' practices" (Carruthers 357). To the Principal and Professors of the University of St.

Andrews, on their Superb Treat to Dr. Samuel Johnson (1773) is written in reaction to Samuel Johnson's disparagement of Scottish cuisine and culture. Here Fergusson imagines changes in the menu at the banquet St. Andrews held in Johnson's honor. In Fergusson's fantasy, the Englishmen are fed haggis, sheep's head, and other "Scottish delicacies" (Carruthers 357). Fergusson's Mutual Complaint of Plainstones and Causey (1773) is a humorous debate between the sidewalk and the road. His To the Tron-kirk Bell (1772) features a personified church-bell. In both of these poems, therefore, there is the personification of inanimate objects (Fergusson 357). Braid Claith (1772), On Seeing a Butterfly in the Street (1773), and To My Auld Breeks (1773) are "three of Fergusson's most general social satires." In each of these Fergusson is attacking the extent to which we are impressed by materialism, especially at the extent to which clothing affects our mental perceptions (Carruthers 357).

Robert Fergusson Bibliography

Carruthers, Gerard C. "Robert Fergusson." Encyclopedia of British Humorists, Volume I.
    Ed. Steven H. Gale. New York, NY: Garland, 1996, 355-358.
Walker, Hugh. English Satire and Satirists. New York, NY: E. P. Dutton, 1925.

John Philpot Curran (1750-1817) IRELAND

See Nilsen, Don L. F. **Humor in Irish Literature: A Reference Guide.** Westport, CT: Greenwood, 1996.

Richard Brinsley Sheridan (1751-1816) IRELAND

Mark Auburn considers Sheridan's The Rivals and School for Scandal to be "the two most memorable plays of the late eighteenth century and two of the best examples of what has been called "comedy of manners" (Auburn 972). The Rivals: A Comedy (1775) opened on January 17, and closed on January 18, 1775. It was considered to be smutty, and poorly cast. Eleven days later it reopened, and the rest is history. The Rivals is an amusing story of Captain Jack Absolute's wooing of Lydia Languish. Its comic characters include the irascible father, and the amorous widow, but it is Mrs. Malaprop who steels the scenes by creating such "malapropisms" as a "nice derangement of epitaphs." It is Mrs. Malaprop who describes Jack as "the very pine-apple of politeness." In addition to Mrs Malaprop, there is Squire Bob Acres, a foppish and therefore humorous outsider from the country. There is also Sir Lucius O'Trigger who is a typical Irish fortune hunter, but who is also good-humored and pugnacious (Auburn 970).
    The Duenna (1775) is Sheridan's second major hit. It is a Comic Opera in Three Acts, in which Margaret, the Duenna, uses trickery to be able to marry Isaac. There is a great deal of dramatic irony in which the audience is always in on the jokes (Auburn 971). St. Patrick's Day; or, The Scheming Lieutenant (1775) is a Comic Opera in which the title character must don a series of disguises. It is a farce, and it is also a virtuoso piece in which the title-role character can display his control over a wide variety of comic impersonations (Auburn 971).
    Mark Auburn describes The School for Scandal, A Comedy (1777) as "the finest comedy of manners in the English language." It is the story of Sir Peter Teazle, and his wife, Lady Teazle in a December-May marriage relationship. The play is filled with witty dialogue, but there are also other types of humor. Joseph's name is ironic, because he is

not nearly so pure as is the Joseph in the Bible after whom he is named. Joseph speaks "sentiments, which are scraps of morality that convince Sir Peter that he is a good person. But about four-fifths of the way through the play, there is a scene in which Lady Teazle visits Joseph in his apartment, and when Sir Peter and Charles also come to Joseph's apartment, he hides Lady Teazle behind a screen (Auburn 972). But Lady Teazle is discovered, and Sir Peter now realizes that his wife has been having an affair with the "chaste" Joseph. Sir Peter further discovers that "his low estimation of Charles has been as wrong as his respect for Joseph." In the fifth and final act, Sir Peter and Lady Teazle are reconciled. Lady Sneerwell and the scandalmongers are banished, and sentimental Charles is rewarded with the hand of the long-suffering Maria, Sir Peter's ward (Auburn 972). That The Critic (1779) is a comedy of manners can be seen in the first scene, in which Mr. and Mrs. Dangle receive theatrical visitors. The scene then moves to a rehearsal of Mr. Puff's play, "The Spanish Armada." In The Critic there is a burlesque of "almost every commonplace of bad theater" (Auburn 972).

   See also Nilsen, Don L. F. Humor in Irish Literature: A Reference Guide. Westport, CT: Greenwood, 1996.

Richard Brinsley Sheridan Bibliography

Auburn, Mark, S. Sheridan's Comedies: Their Contexts and Achievements. Lincoln, NE: University of Nebraska Press, 1977.

Auburn, Mark S. "Richard Brinsley Sheridan." Encyclopedia of British Humorists, Volume II. Ed. Steven H. Gale. New York, NY: Garland, 1996, 969-973.

Davidson, Peter, ed. Sheridan: Comedies. London, England: Macmillan, 1986.

Dulck, Jean. Les Comedies de R. B. Sheridan: Etude Litteraire, Paris, France: Didier, 1962.

Francis (Fanny) Burney (1752-1840)

   Francis Burney's satire and her humor are her greatest strengths as a writer (Rainbolt 173). Burney's first three novels are social comedies about young women without mothers who must find their way in the world on their own. These three novels mimic and show the absurdities of the middle-class characters. They also contain a number of farcical episodes (Rainbolt 173). Martha Rainbolt considers Francis Burney to be a comic writer who "like Henry Fielding before her, mocks the superficiality, hypocrisy, and affectation of her society" (Rainbolt 176).

   Evelina, or, A Young Lady's Entrance into the World (1778) is Burney's first and most popular novel. Lady Louisa is a shallow and silly woman who comments on her own weakness, and Mr. Coverley responds, "for egad I'd as soon see a woman chop wood, as hear her chop logic." Many of the characters in Evelina consider Mrs. Selwyn to be a negative character, but readers love this character, and they cheer as she "chops logic" with the men. There are many humorous episodes in Evelina, such as when a monkey is introduced as a relative, and as when two old ladies have a race. There is also "the extravagant satire on middle-class values and speech" (Rainbolt 174).

   The Witlings (1779) is Burney's second novel. Margaret Doody says that Burney satirizes the "blue-stockings" by creating such characters as Lady Smatter. Doody considers these characters to be in a tradition which includes the "knowledgeable ladies" in Molière's Les Femmes Savantes, and Lady Froth in William Congreve's The Double Dealer, and Phoebe Klinket and John Gay and Alexander Pope's Three Hours After Marriage. It is Lady Smatter who says, "I declare, if my pursuits were not made public, I should not have any at all, for where can be the pleasure of reading books...if one is not to have the credit of talking of them?" (Doody 80).

Cecilia: or, Memoirs of an Heiress (1782) is a four-volume novel which continues the satire on eighteenth-century anti-feminism. Here Burney ridicules the shallow values and life of party goers (Rainbolt 175). Cecelia's uncle, the Dean, left her a lot of money, but gave the control of this money to three guardians, Mr. Harrel, the dissipated man of fashion, Mr. Briggs, the vulgar miser, and the Honorable Mr. Delvile, the haughty aristocrat. Bothered by the extent to which men had control over women's lives, Burney in this novel was able to turn hopelessness and frustration into humor as she deconstructed the authority of these men and the society which supported them (Rogers 88). Cecilia was depicted as a mature, sensible heroine, who was under the guardianship of three males, not one of whom was qualified to control anyone. Some of the humor of Cecilia comes from long "truisms" like,

> the best way to thrive in the world is to get money; but how is it to be got? Why, by business: for business is to money, what fine words are to a lady, sure road to success. Now I don't mean by this to be censorious upon the ladies, being they have nothing else to go by. When they are taken in by rogues and sharpers, the fault is all in the law, for making a proviso against their having money in their own hands. (Cecilia, Volume 4, 255)

Burney's deflation of the pompous Delvile, the prime representative of the patriarchal aristocracy, is very funny. Delvile is convinced that he is a superior and busy person, but only because he is accustomed to being deferred to. He believes that he is surrounded by people who are unable to act without his orders, though in fact, everyone wishes he would stay out of their way. When Cecelia calls on Delvile to get him to intercede with Briggs so that he will give her some of her own money to pay a bill owed to Cecelia's bookseller, Delvile tells her that a young lady has no need for books, because her future husband will have collected a library for her to read (Rogers 89). Much of the humor of Briggs, the comic miser, comes from his being played off against Delvile. It takes Briggs's crudity to tell off Delvile when he needs to be told off. Mr. Albany, the moralist, and Mr. Hobson, the well-fed businessman, are two other male authority figures that are made to look ridiculous in Cecelia (Rogers 91).

One delightful scene in the novel consists of bringing four of these various male authority figures together. The traditional aristocrat, the preacher, and the two representatives of the rising power of money are played off from each other in a satiric way. This scene happens when Cecelia has come of age and is eager to conclude her business and take control of her own money. It has already been established that Briggs takes pride in saving every penny possible, while Hobson takes equal pride in living comfortably. "As Briggs and Hobson quarrel over whether a successful businessman should or should not indulge in oysters, Albany bursts in: 'Once more I come to prove thy sincerity; now wilt thou go with me where sorrow calls thee?' "(Rogers 93). Albany's high-flown and archaic language makes him appear ridiculous, especially because this is played against the prosiness of Hobson's speech, and the crudity of Briggs's speech.

After a while the busy Mr. Delvile arrives on the scene. He doesn't greet anyone or apologize for his lateness. He comes forward in his usual stately manner, and ponderously explains his motives for coming. Burney comments that his speech "was directly addressed to no one, though meant to be attended to by every one." When everyone in the room responds with dead silence, Delvile interprets this silence as "the effect of his awe-inspiring presence." As Delvile becomes more affable, Briggs begins to bait him. Kay Rogers notes that these wildly different representatives of male power over women nevertheless "agree on their priorities--as they pursue their preoccupations, oblivious to a woman's eagerness to complete business essential to her. This book dramatizes the subjection of women in a patriarchal society--and every man in it is undisciplined, irresponsible, wrong-headed, or stupid" (Rogers 95).

Most recent critics considered Camilla, or, A Picture of Youth (1796) to be a "festive" work, filled with irony and satire targeting the idea that "women are mainly objects of moral and physical scrutiny" (Doody 227). Margaret Doody argues that this novel contains a pervasive "game-and-play motif" (Rainbolt 175). Love and Fashion (1799) is a comic play, A Busy Day (1801), and The Woman Hater (1801) are comic plays. Love and Fashion is a satire which targets materialistic society with its emphasis on fashions, manners, and show. A Busy Day is the most comic of these three dramas. "It has the funniest and most light-hearted scenes of any of the three." In A Busy Day, Eliza Watts is an heiress who has just returned from Italy. In this play, "Burney uses the contrast between the behavior and language of the well-bred young lady and that of the vulgar relations to provide much of the comedy. Eliza's modesty is completely misunderstood by her boorish relative, Miss Watts" (Rainbolt 175). The Woman Hater employs such traditional comic stratagems as confused identities and problems with inheritance. In fact, "Mistaken identities, confusion of fathers and daughters, provide the comic plot line." It is Sir Roderick who is the "woman-hater" of the title. He says, "'Why, what does a woman spend her life in? D'ye know? Doing nothing but mischief; talking nothing but nonsense, and listening to nothing but flattery! Sitting, with her two hands before her, all day long, to be waited on; and sighing and moping, because her noodle pate can't hit upon things to give trouble fast enough!'" (Rainbolt 175).

Francis (Fanny) Burney Bibliography

Burney, Francis. Cecilia: or, Memoirs of an Heiress. London, England: Cadell, Davies, and
    Payne. 1809, 4 vols.
Doody, Margaret. Frances Burney: The Life in the Works. New Brunswick, NJ: Rutgers
    University Press, 1988.
Rainbolt, Martha. "Francis 'Fanny' Burney." Encyclopedia of British Humorists, Volume
    I. Ed. Steven H. Gale. New York, NY: Garland, 1996, 172-176.
Rogers, Kay. "Deflation of Male Pretensions in Fanny Burney's Cecelia." Last Laughs:
    Perspectives on Women and Comedy. Ed. Regina Barreca. New York, NY: Gordon
    and Breach, 1988. 87-96.

Thomas Maurice (1754-1824)

Thomas Maurice's reputation as a humorist derives from two parodies of John Philips's "The Splendid Shilling. These poems are "The Schoolboy, A Poem in Imitation of Mr. Philips's 'Splendid Shilling.'" (1775), and "The Oxonian: A Poem. In Imitation of the 'Splendid Shilling.'" (1778). In "The Schoolboy," Maurice "self-consciously imitates Philips's imitation of Milton's emulations of antiquity." By so doing, Maurice "strikes a poignantly paradoxical pose," a pose that is a combination of "nostalgia, envy, sense of inferiority, respect, emulation, zeal, and aplomb." Both "The Schoolboy" and "The Oxonian" are satires targeting English Education, and in fact, The Oxford Sausage, a compilation of popular college poems very well may be the source of "The Oxonian." "The Schoolboy" is about the terrors of a student who is about to be switched by the master. In contrast, "The Oxonian" tells about the disobedience and the confinement of rambunctious college students (Cope 745). Many of the terms in these poems are marked, and therefore bring attention to themselves. "Conn" is used instead of the more common term, "know." "Chronologic Page" is used instead of "history book." This is one of the devices which Maurice uses to imitate himself imitating Philips imitating Milton imitating the ancients. Another device Maurice uses is direct transcriptions from Milton. "The comic effect of these passages comes straight from England's greatest epic bard and is thus all the more ridiculous when imported into the little red schoolhouse" (Cope 746).

Thomas Maurice Bibliography

Cope, Kevin L. "Thomas Maurice." Encyclopedia of British Humorists, Volume II. Ed. Steven H. Gale. New York, NY: Garland, 1996, 744-747.

William Godwin (1756-1836)

Burton Pollin considers "Modern Philosophy and the Godwynian System" to be one of the keenest and wittiest examples of anti-Jacobin poetry. This piece appeared in the March 1803 issue of the Christian Observer, and is considered by Pollin to be "a trenchant criticism of the views of William Godwin, as expressed in his Enquiry Concerning Political Justice and Its Influence on General Virtue and Happiness (1793)" (31). It is interesting that some of the lines parallel certain passages of Prometheus Unbound, written by Percy Bysshe Shelley who was Godwin's son-in-law. The anti-Godwin poem is first published in Pollin's article, and the tone can be seen by referring to the following excerpt:

> [Godwin] Fashions a new Utopia's blest domain
> Uncurst with laws, exempt from Custom's rein,
> Where Reason reckless spurns at love and hate,
> and Justice holds with Apathy her state.
> Connubial ties, parental cares and fears,
> And every charity that life endears,
> Love, friendship, gratitude, the pleasing glow
> Of pity melting at a brother's woe,
> The Philosophic Hierophant proclaims
> Phantoms of weakness, visionary names. (Pollin 37)

The same tone of strong criticism for Godwin's liberal stance can also be seen in another poem published at about the same time, ironically entitled, "The Modern Philosopher." It was reprinted in the December 1802 Anti-Jacobin Review in a review of Rhyme and Reason. This is an anonymous collection of "short and original poems" by an Oxford clergyman [Philip Smith]. The twenty-line satire on Godwin is written from the first-person perspective, as if to represent Godwin's own views.

> Religion I hate--for I hate all restraint,
> And whatever I have been, I'm no longer a faint:
> Each volume of Ethics may rest on the shelf
> For the mainspring of action is center'd in self. (Pollin 34)

William Godwin Bibliography

Pollin, Burton R. "Verse Satires on William Godwin in the Anti-Jacobin Period." Satire Newsletter 2.1 (Fall, 1964): 31-40.

William Blake (1757-1827)

There is much irony in William Blake's art and writing. His "An Island in the Moon" contains a passage where priests collect money from some children. This results in the children being in poverty, so one of the priests gives them charity from the church

(Eaves 70). Blake's "The Marriage of Heaven and Hell" is one of his longer works, and it is both vigorous, and deliberately outrageous. In places, it is a comical onslaught against conventional and self righteous people, especially people associated with the Church. In this poem, Blake's satire is deceptively simple (Abrams 53).

William Blake Bibliography

Abrams, M. H., et al. eds. "William Blake's 'The Marriage of Heaven and Hell.'" The Norton Anthology of English Literature, 6th Edition. New York, NY: Norton, 1993, 18-79.
Eaves, Morris. William Blake's Theory of Art. Princeton, NJ: Princeton University Press, 1982.

Robert Burns (1759-1796) SCOTLAND

The poetry of Robert Burns was influenced by the poetry of such Scottish Chaucerian poets as William Dunbar and Robert Henryson. But the humor of Burns's poetry goes back more specifically to the eighteenth-century Scottish poetry of Allan Ramsay, and Robert Fergusson. "With these masters as guides, he evolved into one of the greatest humorists of the English language" (Roy 179). G. Ross Roy says that "Burns's humor runs the gamut from erotic (both specific and suggestive), through political satire, religious satire (but never vicious satire), the bacchanalian, and on to songs which gently chide his fellow beings." Ralph Waldo Emerson said about Burns that "he grew up in a rural district, speaking a patois unintelligible to all but natives, and he has made that Lowland Scotch a Doric dialect of fame. It is the only example in history of a language made classic by the genius of a single man" (Roy 183).

Robert Burns wrote satirical verses, ballads, squibs and epigrams, and he wrote them from the heart. He did everything from the heart: loving, hating, praying and drinking (Hannay 232). Of all British writers, it was Robert Burns who first gained firm control of verse satire.

He handled the two measures (one stave of six lines and another of nine) in which the majority of his satires are written with such skill and power as to make him one of the very foremost of British satirists, and he wove in with the satire such pure poetic beauty as no satirist had ever mingled with it before, and as only Byron combined with it afterwards. It is this mingling of poetic beauty with satiric keenness which is the special feature of the new satire. (Walker 254)

Robert Burns had a great influence on Scotland, and on Scots and friends of Scots. Raymond Grant tells a story about Robert Burns. The story has many forms and is retold daily around the world. It speaks to the fame of Robert Burns. It is a story which Scots understand deeply, and which non-Scots don't understand at all.

One beautiful April evening, the minister of a remote Highland parish called on one of the farmers in his congregation and found that worthy leaning on a gate and lost in contemplation of the lovely vista before him of heather-clad slopes and craggy peaks. Sharing the pleasant experience with the old man for several minutes, the minister was finally constrained to whisper softly, "I to the hills will lift mine eyes" "Aye," replied the old farmer, misty-eyed, "Aye, Rabbie Burns was the boy!"

Scots find the joke hilariously funny, but non-Scots don't quite understand what is going on. In Scotland the joke is funny because there the people develop a keen familiarity with the metrical version of Psalm 121 preached by the Church of Scotland. The hearers of the joke therefore understand the minister's allusion as a reference to scripture, and they are therefore amused that the old farmer has mistaken it for a quote from "Rabbie Burns." Raymond Grant gives the following variant of this joke, this time not in the form of a story, but rather in the form of a mocking response in a dialogue: "Ye've never heard o' Rabbie Burns? Awa', man, an' read yer Bible!" (5).

Robert Burns is so quintessentially Scottish that he has become Scotland's national poet. But at the same time his appeal is so universal that he also has received world-wide acclaim. "No other poet from any other country has this twin impact on his native heath and on the world as a whole, and the puzzle begs solution just as much as the joke craves explication" (Grant 6). Raymond Grant's The Laughter of Love: A Study of Robert Burns is an attempt to explain the joke, and an attempt to use the poetry of Robert Burns to explain his immense popularity (6).

In 1786, Robert Burns published such satiric poetry as "To a Mouse," "To a Mountain Daisy," and "To a Louse, On Seeing One on a Lady's Bonnet at church." This last poem begins:

Ha! whare ye gaun, ye crowlan ferlie? [crawling wonder]
Your impudence protects you sairly [indeed].

And after the poet follows the progress of the louse all the way up the body of Jenny, it finally reaches her bonnet. Jenny is still unaware that the louse is there, and Burns comments on this fact with the famous lines,

O wad some Pow'r the giftie gie us
To see oursels as others see us! (Roy 179).

This illustrates Robert Burns's satiric gift of being able to paint the particular in such a way that it allows the reader to see the general. This same satiric gift can be seen in "Holy Willie's Prayer," in which Gavin Hamilton is brought before the Presbytery of Ayr because of his "unnecessary absences from church" and because of his "setting out on a journey on the Sabbath," and because of his "habitual neglect of family worship." Burns's poem is about the consternation of William Fisher, one of the most fundamentalist of the Elders of the Kirk when Hamilton is absolved of these "crimes." In the poem, William Fisher is praying after the Hamilton case has been decided, and his words are as follows:

Thou might hae plunged me deep in hell,
To gnash my gooms, and weep, and wail,
In burning lakes,
Yet I am here, a chosen sample,
To shew thy grace is great and ample.

"Holly Willie's Prayer" has been called the "greatest short satire in the English language" (Roy 179). But many of Burns's other satiric poems have a similar power. Burns targets the follies of his church in "Auld Lichts" (old lights), which condemned William McGill of Ayr for writing The Death of Jesus Christ (1786). "The Kirk's Alarm" is also a splendid satire in which Burns names many of the principals in the "undignified debate which ensued." The disagreement between two ministers over their parish boundaries became immortalized in Burns's "The Twa Herds: or the Holy Tulzie [quarrel]" (Roy 180). "The Holy Fair" ends as follows:

There's some are fou o' love divine;
There's some are fou o' brandy;
An' monie jobs that day begin,
May end in Houghmagandie [fornication]. (Roy 181)

Burns was also a writer of funny songs, such as "What can a Young Lassie do wi' an auld man?" describes the dilemma facing a young girl after she has been forced to marry an old man. "Hey for a Lass wi' a Tocher [dowry]" is filled with irony, and "Death and Doctor

Hornbook" is a satire which targets the medical profession (Roy 181).
"Love and Liberty--A Cantata" (1785) is normally referred to as "The Jolly
Beggars," and G. Ross Roy says that "nothing else that Burns wrote can compare for sheer
Rabelaisian abandon." The scene of this "bacchanalian revelry" is Poosie Nansie's tavern
in Mauchline. Here, a group of vagabonds have come together for a night of boisterous
abandon. Each member of the party comes forward to sing his or her song, after which
there is a recitativo (Roy 181). The soldier says,
> I am a Son of Mars who have been in many wars,
> And show my cuts and scars wherever I come;
> This here was for a wench, and that other in a trench,
> And welcoming the French at the sound of the drum.

The soldier's stanza is followed by that of his paramour, who says,
> I once was a Maid, tho' I cannot tell when,
> And still my delight is in proper young men:
> Some one of a troop of Dragoons was my dadie,
> No wonder I'm fond of a Sodger Laddie.

The round ends with the chorus singing about how little they care for the niceties of life:
> A fig for those by law protected!
> Liberty's a glorious feast!
> Courts for Cowards were erected,
> Churches built to please the Priest.

Matthew Arnold wrote that "The Jolly Beggars" had "breadth, truth, and power," and even
goes so far as to say that these verses are "only matched by Shakespeare and Aristophanes"
(Roy 182).

"Tam o' Shanter" tells the story of Tam's getting drunk after a particular market day
in Ayr. Tam arrives at the ruins of the Alloway Kirk, and there he sees a dance of
supernatural beings:
> Warlocks and witches in a dance;
> There sat auld Nick, in shape o' beast [the Devil];
> A towzie tyke, black, grim, and large [shaggy dog],
> To gie them music was his charge:
> He screw'd the pipes and gart them skirl [made them scream].

The graves open and the ghosts come out as Tam stares at the sight. "The Mirth and fun
grew fast and furious." Then Tam shouts out, "Weel done, Cutty-sark! [short skirt]," and
at this point, the entire "hellish legion" starts chasing him. But Maggie, the mare that Tam
is riding is able to cross the keystone bridge, and the supernatural pursuers are not able to
cross this bridge. But before Maggie can get all of the way across, Cutty-Sark snatches her
tail, and the mare is left with a stump of a tail for the rest of her life. Burns ends the poem
with this warning to his readers:
> Whene'er to drink you are inclin'd,
> Or cutty-sarks run in your mind,
> Think, ye may buy the joys o'er dear,
> Remember Tam o'Shanter's mare.

G. Ross Roy reminds us that this warning is ironic. "A mare's tail would be a small price
to pay for such an evening of fun and adventure" (Roy 182).

Robert Burns wrote many bawdy poems and songs, such as The Merry Muses of
Caledonia; A Collection of Favourite Scots Songs, Ancient and Modern (1799). G. Ross
Roy says that "the best of the bawdry written by or collected by Burns is humorous, some
of it outrageously so." An example is "When Princes and Prelates" (1792), which ends,
> Here's George our gude king and Charlotte his queen,
> And lang may they tak a gude mowe! [fornication] (Roy 183).

On January 25th of every year all around the world there is a celebration in honor of Robert Burns; this is called the "Address to the Haggis." At this supper, always dedicated to Robert Burns,

> ...the food must include the traditional fare of haggis, neeps and tatties, and must be attended by suitable ceremonies--the saying of one of the Burns graces, the piping in of the haggis, the addressing and ritual cutting of the haggis, the toast to the Queen, the toast to the lassies, the lassies' reply, the toast to the Twa Lands of Scotland and Canada (or its equivalent in other countries boasting Scottish heritage), and the extended proposal of the toast to the Immortal Memory of the poet. (Grant 9)

The feast of the haggis always gets attention, but it does not always get respect, for as Alistair Maclean states in his Introducing Scotland, "for the majority of people at the majority of such gatherings Burns is synonymous not with poetry but with haggis and an endless river of Scotch; it is compulsory, nay, it is a sacred duty, to drink to the poet's memory and hopeful health in the hereafter: no such ludicrous degree of obligation attaches to the actual reading of his poetry" (Grant 10).

Robert Burns Bibliography

Cazamian, Louis. "Scottish Writers; Skelton." The Development of English Humor. Durham, NC: Duke University Press, 1952, 89-96.

Grant, Raymond J. The Laughter of Love: A Study of Robert Burns. Calgary, Alberta, Canada: Detselig, 1986.

Hannay, James. Satire and Satirists. Folcroft, PA: Folcroft Press, 1969; originally published in 1854.

Roy, G. Ross. "Robert Burns." Encyclopedia of British Humorists, Volume I. Ed. Steven H. Gale. New York, NY: Garland, 1996, 177-185.

Walker, Hugh. "The English and Scottish Chaucerians; and Skelton." English Satire and Satirists. New York, NY: J. M. Dent, 1925, 24-38.

Walker, Hugh. "The New Satire: Burns and Byron." English Satire and Satirists. New York, NY: J. M. Dent, 1925, 252-277.

Thomas Lovell Beddoes (1760-1808)

Robert McCartney considers Beddoes's last play, Death's Jest-Book to be his best. The play contains many incongruities, and much humor, and self-parody. Beddoes is using the term "jest book" to mean a book filled with jests, and in this play, death is the person who owns this particular jest book. It should be noted that when someone dies, the body does not remain intact, but disintegrates, and is often converted into other forms of life, resulting in a sort of resurrection. The story is told from the perspective of the body itself:

> Thread the nerves through the right holes,
> Get out of my bones, you wormy souls.
> Shut up my stomach, the ribs are full:
> Muscles be steady and ready to pull
> Heart and artery merrily shake
> And eyelid go up, for we're going to wake--
> His eye must be righter--one more rub!
> And pull up the nostrils: his nose was snub. (68)

Here, death is being mocked. Death is seen as a parody of life, first striking at the spiritual, and then at the physical aspects, as in the dance-of-death scene, where the stage directions read as follows: "The Deaths, and the figures paired with them come out of the walls, and dance fantastically to the rattling music, singing: some seat themselves at the table and drink and with mocking gestures, mask the feast" (McCartney 68).

Death is seen to effect everyone from the most significant in the kingdom to the least significant:

> The emperor and empress, the king and the queen,
> The knight and the abbot, friar fat, friar thin...,
> We'll dance and laugh at the red-nosed gravedigger,
> Who dreams not that Death is so merry a fellow. (McCartney 69)

The humor here is ironic, since there is a reversal of the expected mood from appropriate solemn dread into inappropriate light gaiety. This same kind of irony can be seen in the description of the gravedigger, who doesn't realize that he and Death share the "merry" pastime of drinking, since the gravedigger is imbibing the wine that is turning his nose red, while Death is drinking up the fluids of life (McCartney 69).

Thomas Lovell Beddoes Bibliography

McCartney, Robert. "The Parody of Universal Analogy in Death's Just-Book by Beddoes." WHIMSY 2 (1984): 67-69.

Edward Lysaght (1763-1810) IRELAND

See Nilsen, Don L. F. Humor in Irish Literature: A Reference Guide. Westport, CT: Greenwood, 1996.

Isaac D'Israeli (1766-1847)

In 1796, at the age of thirty, Isaac D'Israeli wrote a verse defense of the Poet Laureate entitled, "On the Abuse of Satire" which created something of a scandal. D'Israeli had a very modern view of John Skelton that partly explained his taste for the witty and the satirical (Hayes 316). D'Israeli had a kind of creativity that gave color and vitality to his treatments of contemporary subjects. Both his non-fiction and his fiction contain various elements of humor. "His non-fiction is enlivened by a witty, capricious, and ironic style, but in the fiction these pleasant features are supplemented by an altogether grosser humor, sarcasm, and outright personal attacks" (Hayes 317).

D'Israeli's compendium of quirky information in such works as Curiosities of Literature (three volumes, 1791) is the cornerstone of his popularity. Curiosities contains such titles as "Anecdotes of Errata" and "Of Literary Filchers" (Hayes 316). In Curiosities, the reader learns about Rabbi Benjamin of Tudela who "describes a journey, which if he ever took, it must have been with his night cap on, being a perfect dream" (Hayes 317). D'Israeli later wrote a sequel to Curiosities of Literature, and it was entitled A Second Series of Curiosities of Literature (three volumes, 1823) (Hayes 318).

D'Israeli's Vaurien, or Sketches of the Times (1797), and his Flim-Flams! Or the Life and Errors of My Uncle, and the Amours of My Aunt! (three volumes, 1805) are novels which made D'Israeli famous because they were both obviously depictions of prominent people living during D'Israeli's time, and they therefore created minor scandals (Hayes 316). Vaurien is a satirical novel which attacked the English who were still in sympathy with the French Revolution. The characters are modeled on the major politicians of the day. William Godwin became Mr. Subtile in the novel. Thomas Holcroft became

Mr. Reverberator (Hayes 317). Vaurien is about Charles, an innocent country person, who comes to town, and is shocked to find a prostitute who is a virtuous and affectionate parent. He is also shocked about an old thief who has the office of a Justice, and about a pickpocket who is an esteemed gentleman (Hayes 318).

Flim-Flams! is a light satire which deals with important contemporary people and events (Hayes 317). It is a satire, but parts of it are parody, and other parts are farce, and throughout there is a sly wit and humor that can also be found in D'Israeli's non-fiction works. Flim-Flams! is a parody of the excesses of scholarship. "My Uncle" is an avid scholar who, "whatever the world knew least and wished to know less, this great man knew most, and wished to know more." Flim-Flams! has four prefaces, each addressed to a different readership (Hayes 318). Miss Eleanor knows a great deal more about the body of man "than was thought decent." Dr. Della Lena is a crafty Italian who "humiliated his ear close to the key-hole." The landscape gardener is Mr. Contour. "My Uncle" of the subtitle has such adventures as bleaching his Negro servant. My Uncle marries Miss Eleanor, who then becomes "My Aunt," and it is My Aunt, then, who gives birth to an ape. My Aunt is a particularly offensive character, and is based on the life of an astronomer by the name of Caroline Herschel. Edmund Cartwright, the inventor of the power loom, could also see himself in the novel, but "he took the joke at his expense in good humor." (Hayes 318). There are more general targets of satire as well. For example, Kent, the landscape gardener in Flim-Flams! wants to have a nice looking garden, so in order to get the effect he is after, he plants some "dead trees" (Hayes 318).

Calamities of Authors (2 volumes, 1812), and Quarrels of Authors (3 volumes, 1814) are D'Israeli's best known and most popular books (Hayes 316). These five volumes contain such titles as "Pope and his Miscellaneous Quarrels," and "Influence of a Bad Temper in Criticism" which was about John Dennis (Hayes 317). Important characteristics of D'Israeli's writing style include his detached irony, his humor, and his modesty. These three qualities brought D'Israeli many important readers during his day. His satires were similar to those of Voltaire, and are deeply linked to the issues of his day (Hayes 318).

Isaac D'Israeli Bibliography

Hayes, Michael. "Isaac D'Israeli." Encyclopedia of British Humorists, Volume I. Ed. Steven H. Gale. New York, NY: Garland, 1996, 315-319.

Henry Luttrell (c1766-1851) IRELAND

See Nilsen, Don L. F. Humor in Irish Literature: A Reference Guide. Westport, CT: Greenwood, 1996.

2

Humor in Early Nineteenth-Century British Literature

NINETEENTH-CENTURY MONARCHS OF GREAT BRITAIN:

George III (William Frederick)	Hanover	1760-1820
George IV (Augustus Frederick)	Hanover	1820-1830
William IV (Silly Billy)	Hanover	1830-1837
Victoria (Alexandrina)	Hanover	1837-1901

Nineteenth-Century English Humor

Robert Martin notes that the conception of humor for the Romantics and the early Victorians had to do with "sublime shared ruggedness, grandeur, and, finally, the transcendental lineaments of the divine" (Martin 28). Charles Lamb discusses the nature of the transition in English comedy from the eighteenth century to the nineteenth century in England. Near the end of his Elia essay "On Some of the Old Actors," Lamb establishes the distinction between the "absolute, strict, downright concretion of the nineteenth-century theatre," and the "dreamy, playful, specious combinations of artificial comedy." This dichotomy was to become the subject for a later article entitled, "On the Artificial Comedy of the Last Century," in which Lamb labels his one era as "the age of seriousness" and associates it with "literal-mindedness, over-active morality, a propensity to judge everything by rigid laws" (Heller 149-150). Lamb contrasts this with the eighteenth century which possessed what he called "pleasurable faculties." According to Lamb, the writing of the eighteenth century possessed a dreamlike quality. Lamb talks about "the paradoxical realm of artificial comedy where everything is relative" (Heller 150).

> The dichotomy established in the essay between "Caledonian" absolutism and Elian relativism implies that the sensibilities of the literalist nineteenth-century audience are flawed. The laws and morality of daily life are imposed upon artificial comedy with disastrous results. Instead of being entertained, the spectator sits in judgment over the antics of fictitious characters, afraid to abandon himself to another level of reality. (Heller 151)

Lamb is very critical of nineteenth-century "realistic drama" because he feels that it results in a conscience that is "dulled and blunted from overuse," from "eternal tormenting unappeasable vigilance." In contrast, eighteenth-century comedy of manners is comparable to dreams, or shadows, or phantoms, or fairyland for Lamb. "The shape of such drama has only an oblique relationship to real life, and thus allows one to escape from its burdens and restrictions" (Heller 152).

In an article entitled "Peacock, Thackeray, and Jerrold: The Comedy of 'Radical' Disaffection," Roger Henkle says that these three authors were all acutely aware of the social disjunctions of the transition into the Victorian period, but their humor was nevertheless different. "Peacock engages in an essentially satiric exposure of the 'philosophies' and attitudes of the times; Thackeray first parodies and then elaborates on the fictions of the period; and Jerrold savagely attacks the Establishment mentality of early Victorianism." All three authors were acerbic commentators who had the tendency, in the last analysis, to retreat into "their own varieties of conservatism" (Henkle Comedy 68).

In a book entitled Four English Humourists of the Nineteenth Century, William Lilly points to humor trends that can be attributed to the nineteenth century. The first trend, "the humorist as Democrat" is represented by Charles Dickens. The second trend, "the humorist as philosopher" is represented by William Makepeace Thackeray. The third trend, "the humorist as poet" is represented by George Eliot. And the fourth trend, "the humorist as prophet" is represented by Thomas Carlyle (ix-xxiii). Dickens, Thackeray, Eliot, and Carlyle are considered to be "typical English humourists of the nineteenth century." The nineteenth-century is also the time when Punch was founded (1841), and flourished with its group writers, illustrators, and journalists, all of them effective wits. This group included Douglas William Jerrold, Mark Lemon, Charles Dickens, William Makepeace Thackeray, and John Leech (Worth 581).

Hugh Walker claims that the period between the death of George Gordon, Lord Byron--1824--until the present day marks the poorest period in literary history for satire. Walker suggests that this period is not congenial to satire. "Perhaps the age had grown more tolerant: it is certain that many themes which a century earlier would have been treated satirically are dealt with humorously or in the vein of sentiment. When satire is used it is generally of the lighter sort" (278).

George Kitchin considers the 1840s to have been "the great age of burlesque." It was during this period that Dickens published his Pickwick Papers, a burlesque of the sporting club in general, and of numerous things in particular. "The burlesque character of the work is most noticeable at the start, the founding of the club, but throughout we are treated to a joyous medley of burlesque, every public institution providing an occasion for fun." Kitchin considers Pickwick to be something of a "Don Quixote" figure, running eagerly from place to place attempting to redress evils and in the process covering himself with ridicule (Kitchin 279). W. L. Burn describes the "Age of Equipoise" (1852-1867) as basically paradoxical. Jerome Buckley describes this period by listing the opposing truths about the period: The Victorians were "complacent" yet torn by doubt; materialistic but idealistic; conformists and iconoclasts; sentimental yet hard-boiled (Henkle Comedy 181-182).

In the late nineteenth and early twentieth centuries, there developed a small-but-important group of writers referred to by Richard Carlson as the "benign humorists." This group included Lewis Carroll, Edward Lear, Kenneth Graham, P. G. Wodehouse, Walter de la Mare, Beatrix Potter, and A. A. Milne. Many people read the works of these authors; however their work has gone relatively unaddressed by most literary critics, who have tended to turn their critical energies toward literary satire and wit (ix). Many pleasant hours may be spent reading Lewis Carroll's Alice in Wonderland, Edward Lear's verses and limericks, Kenneth Grahame's The Wind in the Willows, P. G. Wodehouse's Bertie Wooster-Jeeves cycle of stories, Walter de la Mare's fantastic verses and songs, Beatrix Potter's animal adventures, and/or A. A. Milne's Winnie the Pooh stories, but that seems to be the end of it. Richard Carlson suggests that "the language and resulting literature of the benign humorists says a great deal about the nineteenth- and twentieth-century English society by saying nothing at all" (xi).

During the nineteenth century, gender roles were also being explored, and an excellent article on this subject is Karen Gindele's "When Women Laugh Wildly and (Gentle)Men Roar: Victorian Embodiments of Laughter." In this article, Gindele examines Victorian laughter as it correlates with gender roles in William Makepeace Thackeray's Vanity Fair (1848), Margaret Oliphant's Miss Marjoribanks (1866), and George Meredith's Diana of the Crossways (1885), noting how the gender-related laughter in these novels relates to desire. Gindele argues that,

> the representation of laughter as expressive defines a gender- and class-coded body as much as a mind. Both laughing bodies and minds can threaten, even though laughter is also held to be cohesive and communal. But laughter simultaneously establishes and disrupts boundaries beyond the sense in which it organizes a group of people around an object at a given moment. (Gindele 140)

In his Comic Faith: The Great Tradition from Austen to Joyce, Robert Polhemus traces the relationship between religion and humor through British literature, and suggests that the strong puritanical strains of Christianity in post-Renaissance Britain, as can be seen in the various seventeenth-century nonconformist Protestants, the Irish Catholics, the eighteenth-century Methodists, and the nineteenth-century evangelicals, provided a strong religious basis on which the religious comedy in Victorian and modern British fiction could flourish.

> Puritanical religion's repressiveness, its rigidities, its hostility to various kinds of artistic expression, its distrust of levity, its very success in coercing people to accept certain codes of moral behavior, and its sometimes unintentional assault on the Established Church's role in guarding truth and faith all helped to arouse longings for the vision, release, and ridicule of comedy. (Polhemus 18)

Polhemus suggests that puritanical religion provoked a desire for comic literature, and that although it tried, it could not stop the provoked comic writers from reaching the public (Polhemus 18).

Robert Martin says that the people in the Victorian Age, like those in any age of considerable sentimentality, believed that the highest form of sympathy and of love often resulted in shared tears. For them, the humor was grounded in sympathy and pathos. The chief defining characteristics of Victorian humor, therefore, were amiability, sympathy, naturalness, and pathos, and the significance of these characteristics for the Victorian age can be verified in nine-tenths of Victorian critical commentary. But attitudes toward humor were changing, and in 1870 Percy Fitzgerald wrote that the follies and the eccentricities that had once been the substance of serious comedy had become so exaggerated that there was no longer any comic effect. Only the French comedies had any "sparkling" or "epigrammatic" comedies, and during this time London playwrights were busy bringing these plays from across the channel and adapting them to the London stage. According to Fitzgerald, "All that the native writers could produce was increasingly mechanical spectacle that went by the name of comedy" (qtd. in Martin 38-39). Robert Martin has written a book entitled The Triumph of Wit: A Study of Victorian Comic Theory in order to "document the change of comic theory in the Victorian period, from a belief in amiable, sentimental humour to an acceptance of intellect as the basis of comedy" (Martin vii).

Polhemus discusses a trend in British literature to combine the religious with the comic. This trend lasted from the end of the nineteenth century into the beginning of the twentieth century, and can be especially well seen in the writings of Jane Austen (1775-1817), Thomas Peacock (1785-1866), William Makepeace Thackeray (1811-1863), Charles

Dickens (1812-1870), Anthony Trollope (1815-1882), George Meredith (1828-1909), Lewis Carroll (1832-1898), and James Joyce (1882-1941). "These specific comic visions...appear in a period spanning a little more than a century, running roughly from the end of the Napoleonic wars to the aftermath of World War I" (4).

From each work there emerges, upon close reading, a clear organizing pattern of human nature and procedure that illuminates its comic vision. It can often be summed up in one word. For Dickens, for example, it is "expression"; for Thackeray, "perspective"; for Carroll, "regression"; for Meredith, "egoism".... Later writers learn directly or indirectly from earlier ones; it is hard, for example, to conceive of Trollope's comedy without Austen's, Meredith's without Peacock's, Joyce's without Dickens's and Carroll's. (Polhemus 21)

In a chapter entitled, "Hood, Gilbert, Carroll, Jerrold, and the Grossmiths: Comedy from Inside," Roger Henkle notes that Thomas Hood, W. S. Gilbert, and Lewis Carroll all began with social grievances, but expressed these grievances in very personal terms.

They launched directly into artistic caprice, into plays on words, curious fantasies, exotic variations. There is something rather elemental about the art of these three that accounts for its expression as adult play, as dream, as remote fantasy, as pure concoction. Similarly, there is something elemental about their feelings that explains the penchant for incidents of brutality, perversity, madness, and pure anguish. (Henkle Comedy 218)

Although there has always been a tension and conflict between Christian orthodoxy and comic imagination, this tension was overlooked, or perhaps exploited during this century of divine comedy (3). Polhemus indicates that the best nineteenth-century comic novels discussed religion not so much from a standpoint of faith as from a standpoint of criticism, as they expressed "a deepening social need to supplement, broaden, mock, attack, revise, and transmute orthodox faith and the moral order established by traditional theological institutions" (4). What made this marriage between humor and religion possible was the realization that a sense of humor plays an important social role both for the individual and for society as a whole. Polhemus indicated that a new attitude had developed where it became shameful not to have a sense of humor. Another reason for the marriage between humor and religion was that they attempt to do the same thing. The main uses of religion are

...to honor creation; to provide hope; to reconcile people to their harsh fates; to smooth over social enmity and to defend culture by authoritative moral sanction against selfish and destructive behavior; to organize and discipline the energies and emotions of people; to make people feel that they are important and part of a "chosen" group; to institutionalize ways of getting rid of guilt; to allow people to identify with righteousness and let loose wrathful indignation and hostility in good conscience; to assure them of the possibility of future well-being; to lift them out of themselves and free the spirit. (Polhemus 5)

According to Polhemus, the functions of wit, humor, and satire are frequently exactly the same as those of religion mentioned above (Polhemus 5).

In an article entitled "Wilde and Beerbohm: The Wit of the Avant-Garde, The Charm of Failure," Roger Henkle discusses the fin de siécle humor of Oscar Wilde and Max Beerbohm. "Even as they flourish their artistic elaborations, they display a high degree of social consciousness. They speak in terms of alternative life styles of art's influence on life, of the play of human social behavior (Henkle Comedy 297). Robert Martin notes that during the last quarter of the nineteenth century authors began once again to recognize the importance of wit, comedy, and intellect as valid types of humor (Martin

29). Roger Henkle says that one of the most important aims of comedy during this period was to "furnish a release from having to make judgements about weighty issues of politics and morality." This humor served to insulate the audiences from the threat of disruptive powers which it refused to take seriously (Henkle "Pooter" 176).

The Romantic Period dates from 1785 to 1830. The Romantic period partly coincides with the Age of Reason, however, the Romantic writers focused on the physical beauty of nature, realization in tranquility, and a connection with God and nature that was often referred to as "complex harmony." Poets such as George Gordon, Lord Byron; Percy Bysshe Shelley, and William Blake possessed humor and made effective use of irony, satire, and contrast to lighten their ideas and make them more palatable during the Romantic Period (Taber 1).

Nineteenth-Century English Humor Bibliography

Auburn, Mark S. Sheridan's Comedies: Their Contexts and Achievements. Lincoln, NE: University of Nebraska Press, 1977.

Barreca, Regina. Untamed and Unabashed: Essays on Women and Humor in British Literature. Detroit, MI: Wayne State University Press, 1994.

Carlson, Richard S. The Benign Humorists. New York, NY: Archon, 1975, 16-30.

Gindele, Karen C. "When Women Laugh Wildly and (Gentle)Men Roar: Victorian Embodiments of Laughter." Look Who's Laughing: Gender and Comedy. Ed. Gail Finney. New York, NY: Gordon and Breach, 1994. 139-160.

Gray, Donald. "The Uses of Victorian Laughter." Victorian Studies 10 (December, 1966.

Gray, Donald. "Victorian Comic Verse; or, Snakes in Greenland." Victorian Poetry 26.3 (1988): 211-230.

Heller, Janet Ruth. "The Breeze of Sunshine: A Study of Lamb's Essay 'On the Artificial Comedy of the Last Century.' " Charles Lamb Bulletin 16 (1976): 149-156.

Henkle, Roger B. Comedy and Culture: England 1820-1900. Princeton, NJ: Princeton Univ Press, 1980.

Henkle, Roger B. "From Pooter to Pinter: Domestic Comedy and Vulnerability." The Critical Quarterly 16.2 (1974): 174-189.

Jerrold, Walker, and R. M. Leonard. A Century of Parody and Imitation. London, England: Oxford University Press, 1913.

Kitchin, George. Survey of Burlesque and Parody in English. London, England: Oliver and Boyd, 1931.

Krieger, Murray. "Postscript: The Naive Classic and the Merely Comic." The Classic Vision: The Retreat from Extremity in Modern Literature. Baltimore, MD: Johns Hopkins Press, 1971, 221-252.

Lilly, William Samuel. Four English Humorists of the Nineteenth Century. London, England: Norwood, 1978.

MacDonald, Dwight, ed. Parodies: An Anthology from Chaucer to Beerbohm--and After. New York, NY: Random House, 1960.

Martin, Robert Bernard. The Triumph of Wit: A Study of Victorian Comic Theory. Oxford, England: Clarendon, 1974.

Mayhew, Athol. A Jorum of Punch. London, England: Downey, 1895.

Miles, Alfred H., ed. The Poets and the Poetry of the Nineteenth Century: Volume 10: Humour. London, England: George Routledge and Sons, 1967.

Polhemus, Robert M. Comic Faith: The Great Tradition from Austen to Joyce. Chicago, IL: University of Chicago Press, 1980.

Previté-Orton, C. W. "The Elevated Satire of the Nineteenth Century." Political Satire in English Poetry. New York, NY: Russell and Russell, 1968, 193-232.

Price, R. G. G. A History of PUNCH. London, England: Collins, 1957.
Priestley, J. B. English Humor. New York: Stein and Day, 1976.
Savory, Jerold J. "Punch." British Literary Magazines: The Victorian and Edwardian Age,
    1837-1913. Ed. Alvin Sullivan. Westport, CT: Greenwood, 1984, 325-329.
Sewell, Elizabeth. The Field of Nonsense. London, England: Chatto and Windus, 1952.
Spielmann, M. H. The History of "Punch." New York, NY: Cassell, 1895.
Stubbs, John Heath. "The Victorians." The Verse Satire. London, England: Oxford
    University Press, 1969, 97-105.
Taber, Julia. "Irony among the Romantics." Unpublished Paper. Tempe, AZ: Arizona State
    University, 1997.
Tave, Stuart M. The Amiable Humorist: A Study in the Comic Theory and Criticism of the
    Eighteenth and Early Nineteenth Centuries. Chicago, IL: University of Chicago
    Press, 1960.
Thorndike, Ashley H. "The Illegitimate, Melodrama, Romance, and Claptrap, 1800-1840."
    English Comedy. New York, NY: Macmillan, 1929, 472-505.
Thorndike, Ashley H. "The New Birth of Comedy, 1890-1900." English Comedy. New
    York, NY: Macmillan, 1929, 560-584.
Thorndike, Ashley H. "The Victorian Era." English Comedy. New York, NY: Macmillan,
    1929, 506-539.
Walker, Hugh. "The Nineteenth Century." English Satire and Satirists. New York: J. M.
    Dent, 1925, 278-316.
Wardroper, John. Lovers, Rakes, and Rogues. London, England: Shelfmark, 1995.
Wolfe, Humbert. "The Dawn of the Nineteenth Century." Notes on English Verse Satire.
    London, England: Leonard and Virginia Woolf, 1929, 115-133.
Wolfe, Humbert. "The Victorians and Ourselves." Notes on English Verse Satire. London,
    England: Leonard and Virginia Woolf, 1929, 134ff.

George Canning (1770-1827) IRELAND

See Nilsen, Don L. F. Humor in Irish Literature: A Reference Guide. Westport,
CT: Greenwood, 1996.

James Hogg (1770-1835) SCOTLAND

In The Mountain Bard (1807), James Hogg says that when he read his play entitled,
The Scotch Gentleman (1796), to an Ettrick audience he realized that "it never fails to
produce the most extraordinary convulsions of laughter" (Mack 530). Although Hogg's
The Justified Sinner is a chilling story that tells about a murder, possession by the devil,
and damnation, it nevertheless contains "some richly funny scenes" (Mack 530). Hogg's
reputation as "one of the great parodists of the English language" comes largely from his
The Poetic Mirror (1816). Here he parodies not only William Wordsworth, but also
Samuel Taylor Coleridge, George Gordon Lord Byron, and Sir Walter Scott. "The
wickedly accurate, and very funny, parodies of The Poetic Mirror demonstrate a remarkable
talent for mimicry" (Mack 530).
David Tait's prayer in The Brownie of Bodsbeck (1818) is a striking and well-
known example of a comical scene. There are also a number of memorable comic passages
in Hogg's The Three Perils of Man (1822) (Mack 530). The Three Perils of Woman
(1823) tells about some farcical adventures that happened to a farmer named Richard
Rickleton during the 1820s. He becomes engaged to a number of different young women

at the same time, and he fights a series of absurd duels (Mack 530). "Willie Wastle and his Dog Trap" (1832) is one of Hogg's shorter works which is predominantly comic in tone. It is a prose tale about a dog that dances and talks, and Douglas Mack considers it to be "pleasant," and "genuinely funny" (Mack 531). Mack feels, however, that Hogg's chief achievement as a humorist is a result of his "remarkable comic poems," which "combine a mad, high-spirited energy with a vein of wild, fantastic absurdity." A Queer Book (1832), for example, contains "The Witch of Fife" which is a well-known example of comic exuberance. A Queer Book also contains "The Good Man of Alloa" a poem which is about an earthy old man who is taken by a mermaid to the floor of the ocean to hunt for pleasure. The supernatural setting adds to the comic entertainment (Mack 531).

James Hogg Bibliography

Mack, Douglas S. "James Hogg." Encyclopedia of British Humorists: Geoffrey Chaucer to John Cleese Ed. Steven H. Gale. New York, NY: Garland, 1996, 529-531.

William Wordsworth (1770-1850)

Ironically, the most important mark which Wordsworth left on the world of humor came from his being so solemn and unhumorous. William Wordsworth had a serious and distinctive writing style which was very easy to parody. Jackie Hayes notes that ten of Lewis Carroll's little songs in Alice Through the Looking Glass are "wicked and cunning parodies or burlesques of well-known contemporary poems, and she notes that one of the finest of these parodies is entitled "Knight's Song." This is "a sort of crazy-house mirror image of Wordsworth's "Resolution and Independence" ode. Hayes considers Carroll's "Night's Song" to be funny and fanciful enough to amuse any reader, but it is, of course, much funnier to the reader who is familiar with Wordsworth's original. "Resolution and Independence" is more commonly known as "The Leech Gatherer" because of its central image, and Carroll plays with the fact that Wordsworth's poem has both an official and an unofficial name, by having the Knight explain to Alice that the name of his song is "Haddock's Eyes," although it is called "The Aged Aged Man" (76).

Wordsworth has a romantic reverence for nature, childhood, and the common man, but Carroll's parody changes the tone from romantic to scientific--from reverence to skepticism, as he has a classical suspicion for the romantic view of life. Alexander Taylor explains the scientific tone of the following:

> And now, if e'er by chance I put
> My fingers into glue,
> Or madly squeeze a right-hand foot
> Into a left-hand shoe,
> Or if I drop upon my toe
> A very heavy weight,
> I weep, for it reminds me so
> Of that old man I used to know....

Taylor explains that the idea of dropping an object on the toe is an illustration of Newton's law of gravity, and the right-hand foot into the left-hand shoe is an illustration of Kant's idea of "incongruent counterparts," and he goes on to connect this with Pasteur's discoveries, and the scientific idea that the universe is disymmetric (Hayes 77).

Wordsworth had a way of taking things very seriously, and this left him wide open to parody. The images in the "Knight's Song" name real things, but in delightfully surprising contexts to create a world of surreal juxtapositions. There is also an ungrounded and incongruous hostility in Carroll's parody, as the old man is not treated with proper respect. "I shook him well from side to side / Until his face was blue," and later, "I cried come tell me how you live! / And thumped him on the head." Wordsworth had a kind of reverence toward his leech gather. He respected the leech gatherer's independence, and considered him something of a hero. But Carroll's turning the hero into a roguish tramp is both perverse and funny. He is demoted in status, as glamorizing images are changed into freakish ones. Wordsworth writes about "the sable orbs of his yet-vivid eyes," but for Carroll, this becomes "eyes, like cinders, all aglow." Wordsworth's leech gatherer uses "Choice word and measured speech, above the reach / Of ordinary men; a stately speech," but under Carroll's pen, the protagonist's speech is "muttered mumblingly and low, / As if his mouth were full of dough," and he "snorted like a buffalo" (Hayes 75). Wordsworth had to ask the old man twice who he was and what he did. Carroll parodies this by talking about an old man, "Who seemed distracted with his woe, / Who rocked his body to and fro, / and muttered mumblingly and low.... That summer evening long ago, / A-sitting on a gate" (Hayes 77).

Wordsworth wrote,
     The old man still stood talking by my side;
     But now his voice to me was like a stream
     Scarce heard; nor word from word could I divide
and Carroll parodied, "His answer trickled through my head like water through a sieve." Both Wordsworth's original, and Carroll's parody are lyrical narratives told from the first person point of view of a bourgeois gentleman who meets a poor old man and asks him how he lives, and in both poems the speakers are too preoccupied with their own thoughts to hear the answers to their own questions. But there is a difference between the poems in that Wordsworth's old man survives through work, while Carroll's old man survives through play (76). Jackie Hayes says that Wordsworth's speaker is "afflicted with a near terminal case of poet's melancholy, whereas the Knight's and Alice's is a mock melancholy." Carroll saw something in Wordsworth's writing of which Wordsworth himself seemed to be totally unaware, "wrapped up as he was in his solemn romantic haze" (Hayes 77).

William Wordsworth Bibliography

Hayes, Jackie. "Wordsworth's 'Resolution and Independence' Ode Seen 'Through the Looking Glass' of Lewis Carroll." WHIMSY 2 (1984): 76-78.
Turner, John. Wordsworth: Play and Politics: A Study of Wordsworth's Poetry, 1787-1800. New York, NY: St. Martin's Press, 1986.

Sir Walter Scott (1771-1832) SCOTLAND

George Kitchin notes that some of Scott's earliest contributions to the field of historical fiction were burlesques continuing the tradition of Joseph Strutt's Queenho Hall (1808). Scott's early burlesques are also like the early burlesques of Thomas Peacock in being a precarious blend of travesty and sincere enthusiasm. In his Quentin Durward, Scott turned a humorous eye on his "mere hero puppets...usually smothering them in elephantine humour" (Kitchin 253).

Scott was also engaging in ironic inversion when he describes Athelstane as pretender to the throne of Anglo-Saxon England, and the only logical candidate for the hand of the fair Rowena, for Athelstane was "...in the flower of his age--yet inanimate in expression, dull-eyed, heavy-browed, inactive and sluggish in all his motions, and so slow in resolution that the soubriquet of one of his ancestors was conferred on him, and he was generally called Athelstane the Unready" (Lamberts 71). There is also irony in Scott's description of the two-day tournament at Ashby-de-la-Zouche. Ivanhoe, who is disguised as the Disinherited Knight, wins the first-day's competition. The second day is more of a free-for-all, however, and although Ivanhoe's knights win the day, Ivanhoe is severely wounded, and many of his knights as well are wounded or killed. "Although only four knights, including one who was smothered by the heat of his armor, had died upon the field, yet upward of thirty were desperately wounded, four or five of whom never recovered. Several more were disabled for life; and those who escaped best carried the marks of the conflict to the grave with them" (Lamberts 71). Scott ironically sums up the event as follows: "Hence it is always mentioned in the old records, as the Gentle and Joyous Passage of Arms at Ashby."

Sir Walter Scott served for many years as the sheriff and legal arbiter in Liddesdale, and in this capacity, Scott was a collector of legends in the oral traditions of Scotland. Reverend Fraser of Rymour Club in Edinburgh interviewed a number of people who knew Sir Walter Scott. One of them said, "An old man also told me that, when a boy, he served in a house where Sir Walter used to visit--Mr. Cadel's of Cockenzie, and where the old man lived all his life. Waiting at the table he remembered Sir Walter well. 'He was la rale cheery man, an' many a lauch we got wi' him, but he did'na mind what he said.'" (Tucker 2). Another gave this account. "'Yes, I kenned the Shirra fine. I wrocht five years for him at Abbotsford. He likit fine to come oot an' sit doon on a stane an' set us crackin'. I think he whiles likit better to hear oor crack than to see us workin'. He was a queer man. He wad far rather hear us say shule than shovel, an' an auld-farrant oot o' the way word was often as guid as a day's wage'" (Tucker 2).

As sheriff, Scott came into contact with many independent-minded and brusque people who relieved the monotony of their lives by telling stories. These people lived in isolation from their neighbors, because the roads at the time were so incredibly bad that even the stagecoach drivers shunned them. Scott nevertheless made forays into the country, and W. E. Wilson says that these forays make for racy narrative. "The impression one derives is one of high animal spirits, mirth, jest, and jollity. Much liquor seems to have been consumed, but it was an age of heavy drinking that did not always mean drunkenness, and Shortreed is careful to point out that his companion was not often 'fou' " (Wilson 270). Scott called these forays "raids," and during them Scott collected much fascinating folklore. "He had a most peculiar, and, it may even be said, mysterious mode of committing these [instances] to memory. He used neither pencil nor pen, but seizing upon any twig or piece of wood which he could find, marked by means of a clasp-knife, with various notches, which his companion [Mr. Shortreed] believed to represent particular ideas in his own mind" ("Obituary" 367). Shortreed later recounted the experience:

> "Aye! We had great doings and then Sir Walter had sich an endless fund o' humour and drollery as never was the like. We never travelled ten yards t'gither, that we warna either talkin' or roarin' and singin'. And he could suit himsel sae brawlie to the way o' livin' o' everyone he was in the company o', just aye did as they did, and never made himsel the great man or shewed himsel off or apparently took the lead in the Company. I have seen him in all moods, in these jaunts--grave and gay, daft and serious, drunk and sober. He never was but good-humoured and agreeable." (qtd. in Wilson 272)

Many of the names of characters in Ivanhoe are humorous, and sometimes this humor is ironic as well. The name "Front-de-Boeuf," for example means "Oxface," and it is appropriate for a character whom Scott fleshed out with total depravity. Then there is the name of "Philip deMalvoisin" which means "bad neighbor." This is an appropriate name for this character as well. Two unadventurous and fat swineherds in Ivanhoe are appropriately named "Wamba" and "Gurth." Jack Lamberts notes that the word "wamba" meant "stomach" or "belly" in Anglo-Saxon times (the times portrayed in Ivanhoe), and this word has come into modern English as "womb." Wamba "is a mental defective who calls himself Wamba the son of Witless, the son of Weatherbrain, the son of an alderman" (Lamberts 70). Of course Gurth's name is an oblique reference to the circumference of his waistline (70).

Some names in Ivanhoe are used ironically by Sir Walter Scott. "Isaac knows no joyful moments; he is constantly torn between tears and terror." As a Scotch Presbyterian, Sir Walter Scot knew the story of Isaac in the Bible, who was given his name because Sarah was given a preposterous prophesy. In Hebrew, the expression "itzak" means "he laughs" (Lamberts 70). There is also irony, plus a touch of dark humor, in the name of "Higg, the son of Snell." The character Higg, like Scott himself, was a cripple. Since the name of "Higg" is derived from Anglo Saxon higian, which means "to hasten," and snell is the germanic word for "swift" Scott was engaging in ironic inversion in the naming of Higg.

Sir Walter Scott Bibliography

Kitchin, George. Survey of Burlesque and Parody in English. London, England: Oliver and
        Boyd, 1931.
Lamberts, J. J. "The Humor of Ivanhoe." WHIMSY 2 (1984): 70-72.
"Obituary--Sir Walter Scott." Gentleman's Magazine. October, 1832: 367.
Tucker, Regina. "Using Humor to Collect Humor: Sir Walter Scott and the Oral Tradition."
        Unpublished Paper. Tempe, AZ: Arizona State University, 1995.
Wilson, W. E. "The Making of the 'Minstrelsy.' Scott and Shortreed in Liddesdale." The
        Cornhill Magazine. September, 1932: 265-283.

Sydney Smith (1771-1845)

Sydney Smith had a melancholic disposition, but he was determined to make the best of everything, so he used his wit and his humor to expose the ridiculousness of human behavior and to become what Sheldon Halpern calls "the foremost wit and humorist of his day, in and out of print" (Halpern 1018). Smith was almost always to be found in an atmosphere of laughter, good humor, and high spirits (Pearson 127). He was known for his mental agility and his verbal facility; and in all of his controversies he is fortunate "never to [have] come up against an enemy as nimble and artful as himself" (Newman 103). One of his most important encounters was with the Bishop of Peterborough who had convinced the clerical world to prepare eighty-seven test questions for candidates for holy orders in his diocese. Smith immediately saw the possibility for fun in comparing the significance of the questions on the questionnaire with the amount of space allowed for providing the answer. "The Bishop not only puts the questions but he actually assigns the limits within which they are to be answered. Spaces are left in the paper of interrogations, to which limits the answer is to be confined--two inches to original sin; an inch and a half to justification; three-quarters to predestination; and to free will only a quarter of an inch" (Newman 120).

Mark Nicholls suggests that Oscar Wilde was very much influenced in his acerbic talents by "the inimitable Sydney Smith" whom Nicholls considers "Wilde's only rival in the area of real humor in the late eighteenth and early nineteenth centuries." Smith said things like, "Macaulay has occasional flashes of silence that make his conversation perfectly delightful." It was also Smith who provided literature not only with his celebrated Letters of Peter Plymley, but also with "what is perhaps a matchless analysis of wit and humor of clarity and sense" (Nicholls 161). In his dissertation on humor Smith gave an example of a humorous incident: "If a tradesman of a corpulent and respectable appearance, with habiliments somewhat ostentatious, were to slide down gently into the mud, and decorate a pea-green coat, I am afraid we should all have the barbarity to laugh. If his hat and wig, like treacherous servants, were to desert their falling master, it certainly would not diminish our propensity to laugh" (Nicholls 162). Smith explains that every aspect of this incident heightens the humor of the scene--"the gaiety of his tunic, the general respectability of his appearance, the rills of muddy water which trickle down his cheeks, and the harmless violence of his rage." But Smith adds that "if, instead of this, we were to observe a dustman falling into the mud, it would hardly attract attention because the opposition of ideas is so trifling, and the incongruity so slight" (Nicholls 162). Hesketh Pearson suggests that only Sydney Smith could outdo Oscar Wilde as a wit (Pearson 171). Pearson continues that some of Sydney Smith's imaginative outbursts were so intense that they actually prostrated people, making them ill with laughter (Pearson 175).

Smith was a clergyman whose humor was pleasant and without animosity or instruction. There were never hidden motives, and mirth seemed to be his sole objective. His mild tone can be seen from an exchange he had with Lord Dudley. Dudley said "You have been laughing at me constantly, Sydney, for the last seven years, and yet in all that time, you never said a thing to me that I wished unsaid" (L'Estrange 200). Smith's humor was what Alfred Gu L'Estrange called, "continuous," where the subject continues, but "the shape and the color change to many forms and hues" (L'Estrange 201). This can be seen in Smith's reaction to the plans of a small Scotchman to marry a lady of rather large dimensions. Smith exclaimed,

> Going to marry her?--You mean a part of her; he could not marry her all. It would be not bigamy but trigamy. There is enough of her to furnish wives for a whole parish. You might people a colony with her, or give an assembly with her, or perhaps take your morning's walk round her, always providing there were frequent resting-places and you were in rude health. I was once rash enough to try walking round her before breakfast, but only got half way, and gave up exhausted. (L'Estrange 200-201)

Smith founded The Edinburgh Review, and wrote articles for the journal which were irreverent, frivolous, and/or satirical. Smith felt that "it requires a surgical operation to get a joke well into a Scotch understanding" (Pearson 126). Smith used ridicule to attack all of the oppressive laws and the obsolete conventions of the time. "All the evils exposed by the Review were eventually rectified by the reform party when it came to power a generation later" (Pearson 127). In The Edinburgh Review, Smith liked to use humor in describing the fauna of exotic places. "The sloth in its wild state," he said, "spends its life in trees. He lives not upon the branches but under them. He moves suspended, rests suspended, sleeps suspended, and passes his life in suspense--like a young clergyman distantly related to a bishop" (Halpern 1023).

By the late eighteenth century, there were many laws in England which forbade non-Anglicans from holding public office, or high military rank. Between 1806 and 1829, when the Parliament finally passed Catholic emancipation, Smith used his humor and wit in The Edinburgh Review to attack these laws. Smith made an ironic proposal that was very reminiscent of Jonathan Swift, when he suggested that the Church of England could enhance its self-esteem by persecuting some minority that was smaller and weaker than the Catholics. Smith reasoned, "Why torture a bull-dog when you can get a frog or a rabbit?" and then he continued, "I am sure my proposal will meet with the most universal approbation. Do not be apprehensive of any opposition from [Cabinet] ministers. If it is a case of hatred, we are sure that one man will defend it by the Gospel; if it abridges human freedom, we know that another will find precedents for it in the Revolution" (Halpern 1021). This is ironic, because Smith didn't like the Catholic Church, and often ridiculed "the thumbs and offals of departed saints" and "the enormous wax candles, and superstitious mummeries, and painted jackets of the Catholic priests." On one occasion he Daniel O'Connell introduced Smith to a group of Catholics by calling Smith "the ancient and amusing defender of our faith." Smith quickly interrupted, "Of your cause, if you please; not of your faith" (Halpern 1022). Smith didn't like the Protestants any more than he liked the Catholics. He ridiculed their religious enthusiasm, their sense of personal salvation, their extreme moralism, and their exaggerated rhetoric, qualities which were common to all of the Evangelic sects (Halpern 1022). Smith's personal brand of political liberalism was based not so much in dogma as it was based in good humor (Halpern 1025).

The Church of England proposed many reforms, one of which was a plan to strip the cathedrals of much of their wealth and patronage in order to raise the income of the clergy. These clergy were appointed by bishops who were equally corrupt. In fact, Smith had a lifelong maxim: "A Bishop must always by in the wrong." In such ways, Smith poked fun at religion; sometimes the poking was gentle, but sometimes it was more bruising, especially when it was aimed at the Commissioners "as they went about redistributing Cathedral property but preserving their own Episcopal income and patronage" (Halpern 1023).

In 1850 Smith's "On Wit and Humour" was published posthumously in Elementary Sketches of Moral Philosophy. Much of the popularity of these sketches was due to Smith's reputation as a wit. The cautious approach to comedy in his lectures "On Wit and Humour" resulted from his awareness that his reputation as a wit did not help his path to ecclesiastical preferment (Martin 67). Tongue in cheek, Smith tells the reader that wit can be deliberately cultivated: "I am convinced a man might sit down as systematically, and as successfully, to the study of wit, as he might to the study of mathematics: and I would answer for it, that, by giving up only six hours a day to being witty, he should come on prodigiously before midsummer, so that his friends should hardly know him again" (Smith 129; qtd. in Martin 68).

Smith says that wit and poetry share a number of qualities; however, surprise is necessary for wit, but not for poetry. Surprise is such an important ingredient of wit that wit cannot bear repetition. As Smith states it, "the original electrical feeling produced by any piece of wit can never be renewed" (Smith 122; qtd. in Martin 68). For Martin, another way that wit and poetry differ is that wit must not be mingled with ideas of the beautiful, sublime, angry, or pathetic, but must instead be concerned with the bringing together of disparate ideas. Wit is dependent on what Robert Martin calls a "display of talent" (Martin 68). "Whenever there is a superior act of intelligence in discovering a relation between ideas, which relation excites surprise and no other high emotion, the mind will have the feeling of wit" (Smith 128; qtd. in Martin 69).

Smith then talks about puns, or what he calls the "wit of words," saying that "the wit of language is so miserably inferior to the wit of ideas, that it is very deservedly driven out of good company" (Smith 130; qtd. in Martin 69). In spite of making such pronouncements, Smith himself was notoriously addicted to punning. Smith goes on to define "irony" as "the surprise excited by the discovery of that relation which exists between the apparent praise and the real blame" (Smith 131; qtd. in Martin 69), and he says that "sarcasm consists in the obliquity of the invective" (Smith 133; qtd in Martin 69). Smith notes that surprise "is as essential to humour as it is to wit" (Smith 137; qtd. in Martin 69); he adds, however, that humour and wit are very different in regard to manner, subject, and result. The basic difference between wit and humor is that wit is involved with comparison, while humor is involved with contrast: "Wit and humour, though the first consists in discovering connection, the latter in discovering incongruity, are closely and nearly related to each other. The respective feelings, both depend upon surprise, are both incompatible with serious and important ideas, and both communicate the same sort of pleasure to the understanding" (Smith 146; Martin 70). Wit for Smith is concerned with the relationships of ideas, while humor is concerned with character, incident, facts, objects, and other externals (Martin 70). Laughter, the result of both wit and humor is also discussed by Smith: "Laughter is not so long and so loud in wit as it is humour." Finally, "wit excites more admiration than humour" (Martin 71).

Sydney Smith's reputation of being the leading with of his day was based more on his conversation and his letters than on his published writings. Smith is quoted twenty-six times in Bartlett's Familiar Quotations, and all but one of these twenty-six quotes come from his conversations and his letters. The only quotation taken from his published works comes from Elementary Sketches of Moral Philosophy, where he described the mismatch between people's personalities and their roles in life by saying that they were "square pegs in round holes." As an example of a quote taken from a conversation consider Smith's casual statement that Thomas Babington Macaulay's dialogue was much improved by his "brilliant flashes of silence" (Halpern 1025).

Smith was aware that his wittiness often prevented him from being taken seriously. Bishop Blomfield of London once called Smith, "my facetious friend," and Smith replied with a letter to The Times which contained the following statement, "You must not think me necessarily foolish because I am facetious, nor will I consider you necessarily wise because you are grave" (Halpern 1023).

Sydney Smith Bibliography

Halpern, Sheldon. "Sydney Smith." Encyclopedia of British Humorists, Volume II. Ed. Steven H. Gale. New York, NY: Garland, 1996, 1018-1026.

L'Estrange, Alfred Gu. "Theodore Hook, Sydney Smith, Thomas Hood, et al." History of English Humour. New York, NY: Burt Franklin, 1878, 196-206.

Martin, Robert Bernard. "Chapter V: Sydney Smith, Leigh Hunt, and Thackeray." The Triumph of Wit: A Study of Victorian Comic Theory. Oxford, England: Clarendon Press, 1974, 67-81.

Newman, Ernest. "Sydney Smith." English Wits. Ed. Leonard Russell. London, England: Hutchinson, 1940, 99-122.

Nicholls, Mark. The Importance of Being Oscar: The Wit and Wisdom of Oscar Wilde Set Against his Life and Times. New York, NY: St. Martin's Press, 1980.

Pearson, Hesketh. Lives of the Wits. New York, NY: Harper and Row, 1962.

Samuel Taylor Coleridge (1772-1834)

In a lecture on Shakespeare's punning, Coleridge noted tongue-in-cheek that punning "may be the lowest, but at all events is the most harmless kind of wit, because it never excites envy" (Morris 128). Coleridge also said, "All men who possess at once active fancy, imagination, and a philosophical spirit, are prone to punning (Coleridge, 610). Coleridge was a very witty person. He felt that wit is impersonal in the sense that it can be remarked by any observer, whereas humor, according to Coleridge, "always more or less partakes of the character of the speaker" (Levin 10). Coleridge said further about humor that "in humor, the little is made great and the great little, in order to destroy both, because all is equal in contrast with the infinite" (Holland 101). Throughout his writing career,

Coleridge wrote a significant body of light verse and epigrams, and his letters and conversations also are a testament to his comic wit (Prescott 258). Much of Coleridge's poetry is very humorous. His "Monody on a Tea-Kettle" (1790) was written "to mark the passing of his kitchen's 'sooty swain' tossed in the garbage to 'rust obscure midst heaps of vulgar tin.'" His "On Imitation" (1971) is an epigrammatic poem that ends, "Tho' few like Fox can speak--like Pitt can think-- / Yet all like Fox can game--like Pitt can drink." In 1791 Coleridge also wrote three odes about how uncomfortable it was to travel by carriage. In "Music" (1791), he wrote about the "scrape and blow and squeak and squall" of the Tiverton Church Choir. In such poems, Coleridge uses hyperbole, wordplay, and "the pleasing shock of irreverence" to achieve his effects. The most abusive of Coleridge's poetry is entitled "Written After a Walk Before Supper" (1792). This poem is about the Reverend Fulwood Smerdon, who replaced Coleridge's father as the vicar at Ottery St. Mary in 1781. In the poem, Reverend Smerdon is referred to as "Jack Sprat" and his wife, "Mrs. Sprat." Both are enshrined in blubber and vulgarity. Jack is described as "a meager bit of littleness." He is so thin, and the wife is so fat that "In case of foe, he well might hide / Snug in the collops of her side" (Prescott 258).

In "Sonnets Attempted in the Manner of Contemporary Writers" (1797) which appeared in Monthly Magazine, Coleridge parodies himself. He exposes the "affectation of unaffectedness," and the "jumping" and the "misplaced accent in common-place epigrams," and the "flat lines" that are "forced into poetry by italics." He also ridicules the "puny pathos," and so on. Robert Preston feels that here Coleridge is giving the advice to young poets that they should not take themselves too seriously (Prescott 259).

Coleridge's "Recantation" (1798) first appeared in the Morning Post. The poem is an indirect political satire of the French Revolution which is humorously described as an Ox. This allegory is then fully developed, as the ox "is driven to violent madness by a country mob while an elderly Protestant man tries to tell them that the ox was merely happy." The deep irony and the incongruous balance of urbanity and seething sarcasm of this satire cause it to become invective in its tone (Prescott 259).

In 1928, Coleridge wrote two poems about the foul odors that are to be found in the German city of Cologne, commenting on the irony that the same city that is famous for its perfume (cologne), could smell so bad. Coleridge is able to distinguish "two and seventy stenches, / All well defined, and several stinks!" The first of these twin poems is entitled "Cologne," and the second is entitled "On My Joyful Departure from the Same City" (Prescott 259).

"The Reproof and Reply" is one of four poems of the "Lightheartednesses in Rhyme" section first published in Friendship's Offering (1834). Coleridge prefaced the poem with the motto, "I expect no sense, worth listening to, from the man who never does talk nonsense." This poem is like his parodic sonnets, in that it warns against too much seriousness. The poem is about when Coleridge was caught stealing flowers on a Sunday morning in May, and begins, "Fie, Mr. Coleridge!--and can this be you? / Break two commandments? and in church-time too!" This is the "Reproof" of the title, and it is followed by the forty-seven line "Reply" written in neo-classical style. The poem is entirely ironic, and can be placed into the category of burlesque (Prescott 259).

Coleridge said that "poetry gives most pleasure when only generally and not perfectly understood" (Richards 177). The reader is meant to be somewhat perplexed, therefore when he reads "On a Volunteer Singer" (1800) which says,

Swans sing before they die--'twere no bad thing
Should certain persons die before they sing. (Browne 133)

Coleridge wrote more than eighty epigrams, and in November of 1833, eight months before his death, he even wrote his own epitaph in which the light and casual tone of the style is contrasted with the gravity of the subject. One of the stanzas of the poem reads as follows:

> Stop, Christian passer-by!--Stop, child of God,
> And read with gentle breast. Beneath this sod
> A poet lies, or that which once seem'd he.
> O, lift one thought in prayer for S.T.C. (Prescott 260).

Robert Prescott feels that Coleridge's light verse, his epigrams, his satires, and his conversational witticisms were "the lifelong products of one of the most complex and diverse wits of the nineteenth century" (Prescott 260).

Samuel Taylor Coleridge Bibliography

Browne, William H. Witty Sayings by Witty People. New York, NY: Arno Press, 1974.

Coleridge, Samuel Taylor. Collected Works, Volume XII. Princeton, NJ: Princeton University Press, 1980.

DeCiccio, Albert Carl. "The Wisdom of the Father is Visited Upon the Son: Philosophical and Literary Metaphors." WHIMSY 4 (1986): 55-59.

Holland, Norman N. Laughing: A Psychology of Humor. Ithaca, NY: Cornell University Press, 1982.

Levin, Harry. Veins of Humor. Cambridge, MA: Harvard University Press, 1972.

Morris, Scot. "In Search of the Perfect Pun." Omni 8.2 (November, 1985): 128-129.

Newlyn, Lucy. "Parodic Allusion: Coleridge and the 'Nehemiah Higgin-Bottom' Sonnets, 1797." Charles Lamb Bulletin 56 (1986): 255-259.

Prescott, Robert A. "Samuel Taylor Coleridge." Encyclopedia of British Humorists, Volume I. Ed. Steven H. Gale. New York, NY: Garland, 1996, 256-262.

Richards, I. A. Speculative Instruments. New York, NY: Harcourt, Brace, and World, 1955.

Robert Southey (1774-1843)

Southey's particular style of humor in his minor poems can be seen in "The Filbert" where Southey pleads the causes of the pig, the dancing bear, and even the maggot:

> Nay gather not that filbert, Nicholas,
> There is a maggot there; it is his house--
> His castle--oh! commit not burglary!
> Strip him not naked; 'tis his clothes, his shell. (L'Estrange 164)

Southey is also able to give humorous descriptions of monkeys, bears, codfish, and oysters. And he can see humorous resemblances, as in, "Would not John Dory's name have died with him, and so been long ago dead as a door-nail, if a grotesque likeness for him had not been found in the fish, which being called after him, has immortalized him and his ugliness?" (L'Estrange 166). Southey's Joan of Arc (1796) is a "would-be epic" the heroine of which Coleridge called "a Tom Paine in petticoats." It is a provocative political manifesto that extols the French ideal of liberté, egalité, and fraternité (Raimond 1042). In his Letters Written during a Short Residence in Spain and Portugal (1797), and in his Journals of a Residence in Portugal (1800-1801), and his Journal of a Tour in the Netherlands (1815), and his Journal of a Tour in Scotland (1819), and his Visit to France (1838), Southey proves to be "an attentive and often humorous observer of men and manners (Raimond 1043). Many critics consider "The Inchcape Rock" (1805) to be a masterpiece of comic invention in which the villains are always published, either in this world or the next. Sir Ralph is a pirate who unintentionally causes his own death by maliciously removing a bell from a submerged reef and then a year later smashing his ship against it. Much of the grim humor of the poem stems from the fact that Sir Ralph meets the same end as that which he has inflicted upon his unfortunate victims (Raimond 1042). Southey's "The Surgeon's Warning" (1805) is a burlesque parody of "The Woman of Berkeley" and demonstrates that Southey wanted to integrate humor into his ballads (Raimond 1042).

Napoleon is referred to as "Emperor Nap" and is the target of the satire in "The March to Moscow" (1813). Here Southey has fun making up pseudo-French swear words like "morbleu," "Sacrebleu," and "Ventrebleu." He also makes up Russian names ending in "-itch," "-off" and "-offsky." In Southey's "A True Ballad of St. Antidius, the Pope, and the Devil," the Devil becomes a laughing stock (Raimond 1042), but so does the Pope. When the Devil hears that the Pope has committed a deadly sin,

> He wagg'd his ears, he twisted his tail,
> He knew not for joy what to do,
> In his hoofs and his horns, in his heels and his corns,
> It tickled him all through. (Raimond 1043).

Jean Raimond said that Southey was afraid of the supernatural, and he used humor as a means of escaping from its hold. By mocking his own anxiety, he is able to control this anxiety (Raimond 1043). It was Robert Southey's A Vision of Judgement (1816) that was the inspiration to George Gordon, Lord Byron's devastating parody A Vision of Judgment (1822). Jean Raimond said that Southey's Vision of Judgement is so dull that it deserves little more than sarcasm (Raimond Encyclopedia 1042).

According to Edgar Allan Poe, the wit and the humor of The Doctor, etc. (1834) "have seldom been equalled." Walter Bagehot says that The Doctor is "a lengthy and elaborate jest;" George Saintsbury says that it is "one of the most delightful books in English" (Raimond 1043). Robert Southey also commented on this work: "I see in the work a little of Rabelais, but not much; more of Tristram Shandy, somewhat of Burton, and perhaps more of Montaigne; but methinks the quintum quid predominates." M. H. Fitzgerald said that "Southey delights us, in The Doctor, with his displays of curious learning, his brave and cheerful outlook upon life, his meditative wisdom; now and again with some quaint stroke of humour which hits the mark." The Doctor is about Dr. Daniel Dove of Doncaster, and contains a revised story of the Three Bears, and a recounting of the Cats of Greta Hall, and an account of Joseph Glover's statues. There are also the blue gothic letters enigmatically dedicated to "the Bhow Begum Kedora Niabarma." In addition to these clownish tricks, Southey also has the three successive question and exclamation marks of chapter VI.A.I, and the descending pagination of the seven chapters that precede the ante-preface and the preface, and then there is the "initial chapter" which is distinct from Chapter I.

Reading The Doctor one often feels as if the handling of so many words-- English, foreign, or coined--made him giddy. He coins substantives (potamology, felisofy, kittenhood), adjectives (unipsefying, farraginous, bablative) and verbs (to crabgrade, to impossibilitate). He has a penchant for such barbarous terms as agathokakological, Prothesis, Epenthesis, Antiptosis, Ischnotesism, and Plateasm. He takes pleasure in actually juggling with words as in the following sentence, "Secondly, the flea which came upon my paper was a real flea, a flea of flea-flesh and blood, partly flea-blood and partly mine, which the same flea had flea-feloniously appropriated to himself by his own process of flea-botomy." (Raimond 1044) Jean Raimond considers such "verbal pirouettings" to be typical of Southey's humor in The Doctor, and says that the ultimate example is Southey's "Aballiboozobanganorribo," which is "the utmost limit reached by a language the function of which is less to mean than to be." What Southey is doing here is parodying himself. Southey has a genuine sense of humor. Maria Edgeworth once said to Robert Southey, "Take my word for it, Sir, the bent of your genius is for comedy" (Raimond 1044).

Robert Southey Bibliography

L'Estrange, Alfred Gu. "Southey." History of English Humour. New York, NY: Burt Franklin, 1878, 164-174.
Raimond, Jean. "Humour et Romantism: Le Cas de Robert Southey." Unpublished Paper. Clermont, France: Université de Clermont Centre du Romantisme Anglais, 1974.
Raimond, Jean. "Robert Southey." Encyclopedia of British Humorists, Volume II. Ed. Steven H. Gale. New York, NY: Garland, 1996, 1041-1046.

Jane Austen (1775-1817)

Esther Smith says that even though Jane Austen writes in the comic mode, there is a wide range to this writing. Much of her juvenilia tends to be broad parody. Her letters often contain biting wit. and Her novels contain subtle irony. "Austen skillfully uses reversal, literalization, protraction, condensation, and exaggeration to mock conventions that have become artificial (Smith 63). Denise Marshall considers such Austen juvenilia as "The Journal of Mistress Joan Martyn" (1806), "Friendship's Gallery" (1807), and "A Society" (1821) to be "comic satire, burlesque, and fantasy shot through with hard-nosed reality." She also considers Virginia Woolf's juvenilia to have these same qualities (Marshall 151-152). In contrast, Jane Austen's adult novels are about marriage and money. Almost all of Austen's antagonists of her heroines exhibit what Esther Smith calls the "Midas mentality." Austen's adult novels are also about marriage in particular, and about the role of women in Victorian Society in general (Smith 62).

Rachel Brownstein says that although Jane Austen has been remembered, read, and even canonized as a stunning authority on the woman's perspective, she is a problem for feminists, because in the power struggle between radical and conservative critics, she has been claimed over the years by both parties (Brownstein 57). Kate Fullbrook suggests that in most of Austen's writing she assumes a paradoxical stance. "She speaks precisely in the voice of the culture she mocks--hers is one of the most civilized voices in English fiction, and one of the most subversive" (Fullbrook 41). What appears on the surface of a Jane Austen novel is very often not the real message of the author. Regina Barreca says that Austen's novels are written in disguise, and "to read her works without taking the disguise into account is to misread refusal as inability, irony as sentiment, considerable contempt as pleasant affection, and women's comedy for men's" (Barreca Untamed 58). Barreca suggests that Austen writes about certain conventions not to reinforce them, but to expose and undercut them, and this places Austen's work clearly within the tradition of women's comedy. Austen's novels are written from a feminist perspective. In fact, Austen had no way of knowing how young men talk to one another, and it is an essential quality of her writing that she not stray outside of her range of knowledge and experience. "Jane Austen's men are of little consequence apart from how they function in the lives of the female characters, so that, in fact, the only important things about men are their marital status, income, rank, and looks". According to Barreca, "Men, in Jane Austen, are at their best when they are out of the room" (Barreca Untamed 59).

Since in the end of all of Jane Austen's novels love triumphs, and since none of her villains and fools are treated worse than they deserve to be treated, all of her novels can be considered to be comedies (Smith 63). A. N. Kaul considers Austen's novels to be "the central achievement of English comedy." He continues, "She sums up and perfects a tradition that goes back through Fielding and Shakespeare and whose history includes that internal split which resulted in the opposing movements of Restoration Drama and Sentimental Drama and, later, such minor and indeterminate figures as [Oliver] Goldsmith and [Richard Brinsley] Sheridan" (Kaul 193). Julia Prewitt Brown makes finer distinctions as she catalogues Jane Austen's novels. She says that three of them are ironic comedies, Northanger Abbey, Pride and Prejudice, and Emma. Her other three novels are classified as satiric realism, the difference being that in satiric realism the "misery is real." In Sense and Sensibility when it becomes apparent that Marianne will marry Colonel Brandon, the voluble Mrs. Jennings asserts that "they had in fact nothing to wish for, but the marriage of Colonel Brandon and Marianne, and rather better pasturage for their cows" (qtd in Smith 63).

Robert Polhemus considers Jane Austen to be the first woman to write great comic fiction in the English language (24). David Demarest considers one of Austen's most effective rhetorical devices to be the "ironic second-look" by which the minor characters are used as mirrors to distort, exaggerate, or minimalize our views of the major characters. Demarest gives this rhetorical device the name of "reductio ad absurdum."

> Behind the foreground figures--Elinor, Emma, Sir Thomas, Fanny--stands a gallery of strange reflections--Miss Steele, Mrs. Jennings, Mrs. Elton, Miss Bates, Lady Bertram, Aunt Norris. One raison d'être of these hobbyhorsical minor figures is their function as comic qualifiers adjusting our attitudes toward the major characters, adjusting our attitudes toward Austen's most serious themes. (54)

Sense and Sensibility (1811) was written to expose the silliness of the sentimental and Gothic novels that were popular during Austen's day. It was originally entitled Elinor and Marianne, and these title characters remained in the newly named novel. Elinor always exercised common sense and hides her suffering. Marianne, on the other hand, reacts to her surroundings much the way a heroine of a Gothic or Sentimental novel would react, effusively, and melodramatically (Smith 61). In Sense and Sensibility, Marianne Dashwood must not marry the man she loves--Willoughby, who is described in the novel as "a gentleman carrying a gun" (Barreca Untamed 53). Instead, she must marry Colonel Brandon, who is described in the novel as "neither very young nor very gay" (Barreca Untamed 54). Although Willoughby is an exile, his life nevertheless contains some happiness:

> That he was forever inconsolable, that he fled from society, as contracted an habitual gloom of temper, or died of a broken heart, must not be depended on--for he did neither. He lived to exert, and frequently to enjoy himself. His wife was not always out of humour, nor his home always uncomfortable; and in his breed of horses and dogs, and in sporting of every kind, he found no inconsiderable degree of domestic felicity. (Sense and Sensibility 367)

Sense and Sensibility, which of all of Austen's novels best fits into the comedy-of-manners genre, uses the device of reductio ad absurdum very effectively. "Nowhere else is Austen so preoccupied with social appearances, and, except for Northanger Abbey, nowhere else so concerned with a superficial vogue--here the cult of sensibility" (Demarest 54). In this novel, Austen makes a sharp contrast between Marianne Dashwood, who is guided by feeling, or sensibility, and her sister Elinor Dashwood, who is guided by reason, or sense. Marianne's ardor and passion are contrasted with Elinor's coolness of judgment (Demarest 55). "In contrast to Marianne, Elinor plays a cautious detective, examining appearances in order to learn the truth about the lover Marianne has so carelessly accepted, and in order to discover the full character of Edward Ferrars, the man she herself is interested in.... One of Elinor's investigative modes is eavesdropping, or spying" (Demarest 56). The readers of Sense and Sensibility may feel that Elinor's behavior is sometimes "dangerously close to snooping," but Austen has introduced the character of Miss Steele as a foil, in order to distinguish between the prudent (Elinor) and the grotesque (Miss Steele). The prototypical gossip of Sense and Sensibility is Mrs. Jennings. Demarest feels that her actions are so exaggerated to suggest that Austen is here parodying the eavesdropping detective motif (Demarest 58). Demarest contrasts Elinor with Mrs. Jennings in terms of the caution with which they evaluate their information by saying that "Mrs. Jennings listens to 'confirm her hopes'; Elinor gathers evidence in full consciousness that she must guard against 'partiality.' This comic echo of the norm serves, then, to define by contrast that norm" (Demarest 59).

A. N. Kaul suggests that many critics feel that the central theme of Sense and Sensibility is the contrast of opposites suggested between Elinor (Sense), and Marianne (Sensibility); however, "the contrast does not in fact hold in the novel. The two sisters are more alike than one would suppose, not merely from the title but from a good deal that happens and is said in the novel itself. The novel, indeed both supports and at the same time plays ironically against the simple antithesis implied in its title" (Kaul 213).

Demarest suggests that in Sense and Sensibility, Austen is setting the stage for her later novels where the readers will again see the heroine as spy, detective, and judge. Austen is also anticipating her later novels by parodying the serious theme, since with varying degrees of tomfoolery the minor characters imitate Elinor. Part of the effect can be described as simple, hi-jinks comedy, in this attempt to guide the readers' feelings about Elinor. The satiric treatment of theme, and the ironic second-look, which will be used masterfully in the later novels, is first introduced in Sense and Sensibility (Demarest 57).

For David Demarest both Fanny and Lady Bertram represent what he calls "reductio ad absurdum or fixity of character." Here, a moral good, when pushed to its extreme, becomes a hollow negative. Fanny has gotten a headache picking flowers on a hot day, and Lady Bertram laments, "I am very much afraid she caught the headache there, for the heat was enough to kill anybody. It was as much as I could bear myself. Sitting and calling to pug, and trying to keep him from the flower beds, was almost too much for me." (Demarest 68)

Esther Smith says that Pride and Prejudice (1813) is noted for its liveliness of characterization, its high comedy, its ethical standards, and its cleverness (Smith 60). In Chapter One, Mrs. Bennet explains to her husband that after a person has five grown daughters she ought to give up thinking about her own beauty. Mr. Bennet sarcastically replies, "In such cases a woman has not often much beauty to think of" (Pride 4). Darrel Mansell contributes Mr. Bennet's dignified manner to his detachment. "His study door gives him distance from the family problems that would threaten his detachment by requiring moral decisions, some commitment to a truth" (Mansell 81).

From the very beginning of Pride and Prejudice, there is a subversion of the idea of consensus. The novel begins, "It is a truth universally acknowledged, that a single man in possession of a good fortune, must be in want of a wife" (Pride and Prejudice 1). Virginia Woolf praised this novel as opening with "a woman's sentence." In talking about this opening sentence, Rachel Brownstein says, "far from describing the real state of things in society, the novel's first sentence expresses a gossip's fantasy that women exchange or traffic in men." This is how Mrs. Bennet perceives things (Brownstein 64). Regina Barreca notes that this sentence "undermines its own authority by asserting it so unequivocally" (Barreca Untamed 55). This first sentence of the novel is expanded in the last sentence of Chapter 1, which explains how Mrs. Bennet views the world, "She was a woman of mean understanding, little information, and uncertain temper. When she was discontented she fancied herself nervous. The business of her life was to get her daughters married; its solace was visiting and news" (qtd. in Brownstein 64).

In Pride and Prejudice, the Bennet girls know that there is a law that gives

Longbourn, their home, to a distant male relative by the name of William Collins as soon
as Mr. Bennet dies. This causes Mr. Collins to assume that any one of the of the Bennet
girls would be more than happy to accept his proposal of marriage thereby ensuring her
future position as mistress of Longbourn.   Austen contrasts Collins's long-winded
pomposity with Mrs. Bennet's hysterical protests, and with Mr. Bennet's laconic cynicism
in the following excerpt:

> "Come here, child," cried her father as she appeared. "I have sent for you
> on an affair of importance. I understand that Mr. Collins has made
> you an offer of marriage. Is it true?"
> Elizabeth replied that it was. "Very well--and this offer of marriage you
> have refused?"
> "I have, sir."
> "Very well. We now come to the point. Your mother insists upon your
> accepting it. Is it not so, Mrs. Bennet?"
> "Yes, or I will never see her again."
> "An unhappy alternative is before you, Elizabeth. From this day you must
> be a stranger to one of your parents. Your mother will never see
> you again if you do not marry Mr. Collins, and I will never see you
> again if you do. (qtd. in Smith 62).

According to Donald Bloom, Elizabeth Bennet in Pride and Prejudice, is a
prototypical witty heroine in a romantic comedy, comparable to Rosalind in Shakespeare's
As You Like It, Florimell in Dryden's Secret Love, Doralice in Dryden's Marriage à la
Mode, and Millamant in Congreve's The Way of the World (Bloom 53).

> For the romance to work she must have a powerful character, an inner self
> that is worth exploring, that we can view in heroic terms, and that can make
> the idea of Love profound instead of pedestrian. For the comedy to work,
> she must be lighthearted yet true, able to provide a point of stability in the
> conflict of societies or ideals that interferes with the marriages that will form
> the new society. But at the same time, she must be a wit, an intelligent,
> insightful, and verbally skillful person who can express truths vividly. It is
> a rare author (male or female) who can bring off such a character (male or
> female). But when we find one, we should enjoy her to the fullest. (Bloom
> 77)

Elizabeth is sharp witted, and to some extent, uncontrolled. In the novel she is described
as "almost wild" on a number of occasions. Elizabeth resists the idea that there are certain
things (such as Mr. Darcy) which are not to be laughed at (Barreca Untamed 55). "Mr.
Darcy is not to be laughed at! That is an uncommon advantage, and uncommon I hope it
will continue, for it would be a great loss to me to have many such acquaintances. I dearly
love a laugh.... I hope I never ridicule what is wise or good. Follies and nonsense, whims
and inconsistencies do divert me, I own, and I laugh at them whenever I can" (Pride 102).
Mr. Darcy is so proud a man that even at the moment of declaring his love to Elizabeth,
he doesn't allow humility or modesty into his speech. Instead, he is proud and arrogant
in his proposal. "And this is all the reply which I am to have the honor of expecting! I
might, perhaps, wish to be informed why, with so little endeavor at civility, I am thus
rejected. But it is of little importance" (Pride 180). This statement is entirely ironic.
Darcy is accusing Elizabeth of being uncivil while he himself is acting like a pompous ass.
Both Elizabeth and Mr. Bennet have an uncanny ability to be just as snobbish as the people
they scorn as being snobbish. As Darrel Mansell states it, "we find Elizabeth again and
again assuming a position superior to her surroundings. She is proud as well as prejudiced.
Caroline Bingley is not altogether wrong when she says that in Elizabeth there is 'a little
something, bordering on conceit and impertinence' " (Mansell 81). Mansell suggests that

the hypocritical sides of Elizabeth and her father add an extra comic dimension to the pre-existing comedy of manners of the novel.

Female bonding, and women's laughter are important elements in the happy ending of Pride and Prejudice, but Barreca considers these devices to be a subtle subversion of the conventional romantic genre (Barreca Last Laughs 67). At the beginning of Pride and Prejudice, the reader is told that Elizabeth "had a lively, playful disposition, which delighted in anything ridiculous" (Barreca Last Laughs 58). But although there is much female bonding in Austen's novels, Austen was nevertheless critical of women authors, and often mocked these novels for their moralizing. The maxims related to the attitude of patriarchal authority on sex and marriage, the main subject of such novels, are parodied in Pride and Prejudice where Elizabeth lifts up her eyes in amazement while her sister Mary moralizes about Lydia's running away: "That loss of virtue in a female is irretrievable--that one false step involves her in endless ruin--that her reputation is no less brittle than it is beautiful" (Pride 289).

In her novels, Austen attacks sentimentalism, romanticism, and the "terrorism of the Gothic Novel" (Kitchin 248). She also likes to satirize the mania for the romantic tour, especially the tour to the wilder parts of England. "Gilpin and a host of others had written up Wales and the Highlands. The Cumberland district was soon to become embarrassingly popular before people had reconciled themselves to the modern mania of view hunting. In Mansfield Park (1814), for example, we can find the following account: "While our father is fluttering about the streets of London, gay, dissipated and thoughtless at the age of fifty-seven, Matilda and I continue secluded from mankind in our old and moldering castle which is situated two miles from Perth, on a bold projecting rock, and commands an extensive view of the town and its delightful environments" (Kitchin 249).

Mansfield Park contains a number of humours characters. Aunt Norris is unnecessarily nasty, and Lady Bertram is unreasonably dull. "Both seem close allies to positive themes in the novel--Mrs. Norris to a system of authoritarian training of the young, Lady Bertram to an affirmation of permanence, stability, fixity" (Demarest 65). There are other humours characters as well, and a number of them illustrate important points about the educational process Austen wants to make:

> "Self-denial" and "humility" are, of course, exactly the attitudes which Fanny has had drummed into her since her arrival at Mansfield Park. Timid by nature, she has been over-awed by Sir Thomas, scolded by Aunt Norris, railed at by Maria and Julia and preached to by Edmund. Such has not been a pleasant education, but Austen is clearly attacking a view of education that would indulge children. Austen's view is traditional--children are not inherently good; they must be civilized by education. (Demarest 66)

Mary and Fanny contrast as humours characters. Mary declares, "I must move...; resting fatigues me." In contrast, Fanny must remain stationary. And when Susan takes over Fanny's place at Mansfield Park, Austen states that "Susan became the stationary niece" (Demarest 67).

In an article entitled "Mary Crawford and the Comic Heroine," Michael Tatham examines the reversal of the virtues of Mary Crawford and Fanny Price in Mansfield Park (Smith 66). Many critics view Mary Crawford as Jane Austen's alter-ego. Regina Barreca views her as an "anti-heroine," and as "a nasty little piece of work generally." But Mary is a compelling character because of her sense of humor. Mary is able to parody a parody, and she can compose her own satiric verse about the local families. Mary makes jokes about the clergy, about the aristocracy, and about society in general. She even jokes about the possibly fatal illness of her beloved's elder brother, "upon my honor, I never bribed a physician in my life" (Barreca Untamed 52). An important paradox of Mansfield Park involves Aunt Norris. Even though readers must condemn Aunt Norris harshly, they must also acknowledge that quite by accident she has played an important role in the education of the heroine. "Austen manages to have it both ways: she attacks the authoritarian abuse that may grow out of the parental role, but she affirms authority itself as the chastening agent basic to education." Austen believes in a principle which Demarest calls "moral realism" (67).

Robert Polhemus feels that what makes Emma (1816) both important and original is the comic vision and sense of humor (24). Austen had a deep passion both for reverence, and for ridicule, and these are somehow reconciled in Emma (25). The reason for this paradox is that Austen admired her father and her brother, who were both clergymen. Austen herself had a keen intellect, and "a deep pastoral concern for the moral well-being of people," and she would have liked to have been a clergyman herself, but the Anglican Church would not allow it. There would have been, therefore, no outlet for her ethical imagination or talents if she had not developed an excellent sense of the ridiculous. Austen's sense of the ridiculous, sense of irony, and sense of humor were her reactions to a male-dominated, parochial moral order. For Austen, it was what Robert Polhemus called a kind of "feminine lawlessness."

Critics such as Suzanne Langer and Northrop Frye feel that the basic function of comedy is to present "the rhythm of life overcoming obstacles and renewing itself" (Stovel 463). This is certainly what Emma is concerned with. In this novel, the obstructing society is within Emma herself, for she is the character who "frustrates nature's plans for marriage and erects insuperable barriers between social classes." Therefore, any renewal of the novel's society will have to be the result of a change within Emma herself. Only at the end of the novel can Emma's desires to be herself, and her love for Mr. Knightley, and her desire to be good all coincide. This is because Emma finally forsakes her fanciful schemes and is able to see the vain motives which had prompted them. Emma must discover that the deepest 'source of pleasure to herself' is to be in the real world with the man she respects and loves. And the novel thus ends with the comically fulfilling words, "the perfect happiness of the union" (Stovel 464).

Emma is a "moral comedy." But of course morality for Austen includes a comic understanding of things. Life without a sense of humor has little value for Austen, because for her, comedy is indispensable. Robert Polhemus suggests that marriage is for comedy what death is for tragedy, and this is certainly true in Emma. In the same way that King Lear allows us to feel the awfulness of death, Emma allows us to feel the wonder of marriage, and the species which invented it. Marriage is good because it institutionalizes sex and because it provides the means of regenerating the race. It is something of "a comic compromise between self-gratification and social responsibility. In it, biology, psychology, theology, anthropology, and economics are wed. Austen makes marriage the aim and end of her fiction" (Polhemus 58). Polhemus feels that the "happy ending" of Emma is the result of the "necessary union of the moral and the comic imagination." No word more explains the significance of the novel than the last one, "union" (24). According to Polhemus, this word gives the novel a "happy ending" (24).

David Demarest considers the final comic irony of Emma's listening to Harriet's evidence and finally understanding that she--Emma--must have Mr. Knightley. At this point, Emma jumps to the opposite extreme. She will believe nothing that her heart tells her. She now must have evidence for everything. "Without contradicting her central theme, Austen at the end of Emma characteristically takes the ironic second-look: sometimes the wisdom of the heart makes the truth self-evident" (Demarest 64).

Austen's Emma satirizes the impact that the reading of romantic novels can have on real life. However, real life can also have an important impact on the development of a novel. "If marriage is so important to Austen," the reader may ask, "then why did Jane Austen herself never marry?" Robert Polhemus suggests that Jane Austen did marry, as she tells us that "Emma, the striving, kinetic, lucky, ironic, ridiculous subjective comic heroine weds Knightly" (Polhemus 59).

In 1837, John Henry Newman wrote, "Everything Miss Austen writes is clever...., but there is a want of body to the story; the action is frittered away over little things" (Stovel 458). Bruce Stovel relates this statement to Austen's Emma (1816): "But underneath the over-little things is a single large one, their cause and successor: her response to Mr. Knightley" (Stovel 459). Stovel continues,

> Mr. Knightley, in fact, functions as Emma's deepest or true self throughout the novel. For instance, Emma expresses a stern view of Frank Churchill's procrastinations to Mrs. Weston, but, a few pages later, she perversely claims more sympathy for Frank than she actually feels; she thus finds herself in the ironic position of "making use of Mrs. Weston's arguments against herself," while Mr. Knightly expresses "her real opinion." (Stovel 462)

Emma prides herself on having a sense of humor (Barreca Untamed 57), and like Austen's other heroines Emma uses passivity to gain power. "The heroines seem to submit as they get what they both want and need" (Gilbert and Gubar 163). David Demarest suggests that Austen perfected several rhetorical techniques in Emma that had been introduced in her earlier novels. There is an adjustment of reader attitude toward the heroine; there is a sense of the universality of the problems presented; there is an ironic qualification of Austen's central theme; and there is a discovery of reasons for tolerance in surprising places. There are two kinds of characters in Emma. Emma, Frank Churchill, and Mr. Knightley are what Demarest terms "complex characters." Mr. Woodhouse, Miss Bates, and Mrs. Elton, on the other hand are what Demarest terms "hobbyhorsical characters."

> Austen deliberately plays upon our inclination as readers to write off the simple characters as predictable stick figures, good for little more than a laugh.... One of Austen's modes of satiric perspective in Emma is to put into the mouths of apparent fools better insights than Emma's; sometimes, in fact, the simple characters use Emma's very words with better sense than Emma herself had intended. (60)

Nevertheless, the minor characters representing various "humours" are used by Austen as "reductive mirrors."

> The "humours" characters see everything in the extreme of their ruling passion: Mr. Weston, the sanguine, can scarcely think ill of anyone; the hypochrondiac Mr. Woodhouse likes his germs and gruel; Mrs. John Knightley can no more understand anything not related to the welfare of her children than Mrs. Elton can look beyond Maple Grove and the barouche-landau.... Austen's use of minor characters in Emma dramatizes the universality of the problem of proper perception. (62)

During the course of the novel, Emma evolves. Earlier in the novel, she jumps to conclusions on the basis of imaginative premises, but later she collects and examines the evidence much more carefully. She changes from a deductive reasoner who assumes conclusions to an inductive reasoner who arrives at conclusions on the basis of the evidence (Demarest 62).

The novel Emma is a comedy in the tradition of Much Ado About Nothing, The Way of the World, and Tom Jones. In such comedies, "the conflicts and characters are simple and fixed: what interests us is the intricate design, the complex and surprising pattern, into which these elements fall" (Stovel 453). Emma is what Paul H. Fry calls "Georgic Comedy," which he defines as "the teaching of useful and sociable skills against the backdrop of a farm" (129). Austen writes much about the house and grounds of

Donwell. The houses in Austen's fiction are much like the houses in Gothic fiction; they are impressive, and they are symbolic, and they are thus appropriate for their inhabitants; in the case of Donwell, one of these inhabitants is Mr. Knightly. The novel is concerned with the unravelling of the "mystery of false properties" (132).

In Chapter 3 the reader is given a description of Harriet Smith: "She was a very pretty girl, and her beauty happened to be of a sort which Emma particularly admired. She was short, plump and fair, with a fine bloom, blue eyes, light hair, regular features, and a look of great sweetness." Since Emma herself is tall and elegant, and has hazel eyes, Harriet provides a perfect foil for Emma's charms (Stovel 454). Bruce Stovel suggests that in the ironic development of the novel there are three main threads to Austen's web: One is the hidden love that Emma and Mr. Knightley have for each other; another is the counterpoint of the secret love and secret engagement of Frank Churchill and Jane Fairfax; and the third is the use of other characters in the novel to compare and contrast with various aspects of Emma herself. Emma doesn't tell anyone that she is in love with the appropriately named Mr. Knightly. She doesn't even allow herself to realize it, and the major irony of the novel is that Emma, who is so frequently teaching other people how to know themselves better, and who so much cultivates detachment, is herself so radically misconceived in her own true personal attachment (Stovel 455).

Jane Austen's position on women's novels is clearly stated in Northanger Abbey (1818): She considers women's novels to be more original than most of what's published. She also says that even though their characters are often stereotyped and their plots are frequently implausible, these novels are nevertheless both pleasurable and accurate (Brownstein 60-61). In these novels, "the greatest powers of the mind are displayed, in which the most thorough knowledge of human nature, the happiest delineation of its varieties, the liveliest effusions of wit and humour are conveyed to the world in the best chosen language" (Northanger Abbey 38).

The narrator in Northanger Abbey considers "history" to be no less important than "poetry and plays and things of that sort." The narrator then goes further, showing that "history" is a domain of males: "The quarrels of popes and kings, with wars or pestilence, in every page; the men all do good for nothing, and hardly any women at all--it is very tiresome" (Northanger Abbey 84).

Northanger Abbey is a satire which directly targets the sentimentalism which was so much the part of a girl's education during Austen's time. It also targets the "terror" or "Gothic" novel. It is more specifically a parody of Ann Radcliffe's The Romance of the Forest (1791), which gave the suggestion for the excruciating thrill when Catherine Morland discovered the laundry bill in the closet, and Sicilian Romance (1790), which provided her with the dire suspicions which she harboured about General Tilney's involvement in his wife's death (Kitchin 250).

Northanger Abbey is about Catherine Morland, an ordinary girl who is quite plain and tomboyish in childhood and comes from a commonplace family background. But in her mind she feels that she is destined to become a future heroine of romance. "Showing above all no aptitude for drawing or music or any of the other required accomplishments, her mind seems definitely "unpropitious for heroism"--up to the age of fifteen. But at fifteen appearances suddenly start mending, and Catherine, despite her disqualifications, considers herself from this point on as avowedly 'in training for a heroine'" (Kaul 207). In Northanger Abbey Catherine Morland is a rebel. In the opening pages of the novel, Catherine is described in the following way:

> noisy and wild, hated confinement and cleanliness, and loved nothing so well in the world as rolling down the green slope at the back of the house....
> As if this were not bad enough, later in life, when her mysterious sweetheart fails to show up at a ball, Catherine returns home in her disappointment not

to weep or toss sleeplessly in bed, but instead to "appease" her "extraordinary hunger," and then to fall asleep early, for nine refreshing hours. (Northanger Abbey 164)

Northanger Abbey is a parody of the romantic novel in general, and the Gothic novel in particular. Austen's parodic and mocking tone comes out strongly in the following excerpt from the beginning of the novel.

She [Catherine] had reached the age of seventeen without having seen one amiable youth who could call forth her sensibility; without having inspired one real passion, and without having excited even any admiration but what was very moderate and very transient. This was strange indeed! But strange things may generally be accounted for if their cause be fairly searched out. there was not one lord in the neighbourhood; no--not even a baronet. There was not one family among their acquaintance who had reared and supported a boy accidentally found at their door--not one young man whose origin was unknown. Her father had no ward, and the squire of the parish no children. (Austen 40)

Catherine reasons, "When a young lady is to be a heroine, the perverseness of forty surrounding families cannot prevent her. Something must and will happen to throw a hero in her way" (Kaul 207). Catherine begins her heroine training in Bath, where Isabella Thorpe is in charge of educating Catherine's mind, and Henry Tilney, as her potential lover, is in charge of her romantic training (Kaul 208). Isabella tells Catherine about a romantic novel entitled Udolpho, and reading this novel greatly influences Catherine's perceptions. When she visits Northanger Abbey, the family seat of the Tilney's, she sees General Tilney as a villain, and she sees his dead wife as his victim. At midnight, she explores Northanger Abbey, and finds a manuscript which she takes to be a cryptic record of secret crimes committed and suffered in the Abbey, but on closer examination, this manuscript turns out to be an inventory of linen needing to be washed. Henry Tilney admonishes Catherine for not thinking things through carefully and for coming to the wrong conclusion:

Consult your own understanding, your own sense of the probable, your own observation of what is passing around you. Does our education prepare us for such atrocities? Do our laws connive at them? Could they be perpetrated without being known in a country like this, where social and literary intercourse is on such a footing?... Dearest Miss Morland, what ideas have you been admitting? (Kaul 209)

What is especially ironic about Henry Tilney's admonition is that Catherine's "education" and "social and literary intercourse"--that is, the reading of the romantic novel, Udolpho-- are precisely the factors that have brought her to the wrong conclusions (Kaul 209).

Misunderstandings abound throughout Northanger Abbey. One such misunderstanding involves Catherine Morland and Henry Tilney. In this misunderstanding, Catherine says to Henry: "I do not understand you," to which Henry responds, "Then we are on very unequal terms, for I understand you perfectly well." To this Catherine responds, "Me?--yes; I cannot speak well enough to be unintelligible," and Henry finally responds, "Bravo!--an excellent satire on modern language" (Austen 142). This dialogue demonstrates Catherine's ingenuousness. As Joy Rutter explains, Catherine's "I cannot speak well enough to be unintelligible" is not an example of biting satire, but it is rather meant to be taken at face value. "It requires Henry's ready wit to turn it into an 'excellent satire on modern language'" (Rutter 4-5).

Although many critics feel that Northanger Abbey is an attempt to write a realistic novel which contrasts the Gothic and the domestic worlds, or the imaginary and the real worlds, or the literary and the natural worlds, Jan Fergus suggests that the novel is attempting to do something else, as he argues that Austen's interest is "more playful; she wants to bring up a tour de force, to expose her readers to everything absurd in a convention or genre and then to make the convention 'work' all the same" (Fergus, 1983, 20). Marvin Mudrick, for example, criticizes the inconsistency in Austen's development of Catherine. Mudrick says that Catherine is unimaginative and incredulous in the Bath section, yet in the Northanger section, she is suddenly both credulous and imaginative (Mudrick 57). Fergus counters by saying that Austen deliberately makes Catherine shrewd or naive as the situation requires, endowing her with whichever quality will yield the most humorous situation (Fergus, 1983, 17-18).

Kate Fullbrook believes that the final joke in Northanger Abbey is not on Catherine, but is on "those who are so unimaginative as to think Catherine completely misguided in the horrors she fancies lurking within the Abbey walls." She continues, "In many ways, Catherine, even in her delusions, is more correct in her view of the world than Henry" (Fullbrook 48). Regina Barreca continues that when Catherine admits to Henry that she doesn't understand him, his response is a haughty one: "Then we are on very unequal terms, for I understand you perfectly well" (Northanger Abbey 103). Barreca notes that Henry is firm in his belief that he knows everything, while Catherine is uncertain about what constitutes truth, and then she asks, "Who is wiser?" (Barreca Untamed 51).

David Demarest feels that characters play off from each other in intricate, and sometimes ironic and paradoxical ways in Austen's novels:

> In characters like Mrs. Jennings, Miss Bates, Harriett Smith, Aunt Norris, and Lady Bertram, Austen manages double effects--satiric second looks at her heroines and at her own positive themes, and tolerant insistence that all human beings deserve acknowledgement. The result of this double effect is the flexible common sense typical of the neoclassicists. Neat logical systems on the one hand and passive amoral acceptance of life on the other are both inadequate responses; proper morality lies in the illogical yet commonsensical ability to judge and accept at the same time. (68)

Jane Austen's novels are written from a feminine perspective. In Northanger Abbey (1818) Henry Tilney says that the very idea of instruction makes women wary. "I use the verb 'to torment,' as I observed to be your own method, instead of 'to instruct,' supposing them to be now admitted as synonymous" (Northanger Abbey 85). Regina Barreca notes that these female pupils "resist believing in what they are instructed to accept as the 'truth.'" Barreca compares Jane Austen with Charlotte Lennox saying that for both of these authors, "the system of values shared by reader and author are not those of the didactic male teachers who appear in the novels, but rather the values espoused by the uninitiated female protagonists" (Barreca Untamed 44). In Austen's and Lennox's novels there is a "metanarrative of refusal" at the heart of the laughter. "The comedy works not against the renegade woman-reader-heroine, but against those who would confine her to the attic of 'acceptable' behavior" (Barreca Untamed 45).

Jane Austen is often criticized for having ignored the large events of her day, such as the French Revolution and the Napoleonic Wars. It has also been said that her ironic humor lacked the intensity, the passion, or the "high seriousness" that Matthew Arnold and his contemporaries required (Southam 25). Some critics have accused her of failure to provide vivid detail, fresh metaphors, and symbols, even going so far as to suggest that the reason she omitted specific detail was that she was nearsighted. Nevertheless, Esther Smith considers Austen to have been a "careful observer who could laugh at the Human Comedy without bitterness or a betrayal of basic morality" (Smith 61).

Jane Austen Bibliography

Austen, Jane. Emma. London, England: John Murray, 1815.

Austen, Jane. Northanger Abbey. (1818) Ed. Anne Henry Ehrenpreis. London, England: Penguin, 1972.

Austen, Jane. Pride and Prejudice. (1813) Ed. Donald J. Gray. New York, NY: Norton, 1964.

Austen, Jane. Sense and Sensibility. (1811) London, England: Penguin, 1967.

Barreca, Regina. "Dearly Loving a Good Laugh: Humor in Charlotte Lennox and Jane Austen." Untamed and Unabashed: Essays on Women and Humor in British Literature. Detroit, MI: Wayne State University Press, 1994, 34-60.

Barreca, Regina, ed. Last Laughs: Perspectives on Women and Comedy. New York, NY: Gordon and Breach, 1988.

Bizzaro, Patrick. "Global and Contextual Humor in Northanger Abbey." Persuasions: The Jane Austen Society of North America. (7 December, 1985): 82-88.

Bloom, Donald A. "Dwindling into Wifehood: The Romantic Power of the Witty Heroine in Shakespeare, Dryden, Congreve, and Austen." Look Who's Laughing: Gender and Comedy. Ed. Gail Finney. New York, NY: Gordon and Breach, 1994, 53-80.

Bradley, A. C. "Jane Austen as Moralist and Humorist." Pride and Prejudice. Ed. Donald J. Gray. New York, NY: Norton, 1964.

Brower, Reuben A. "Irony and Fiction in Pride and Prejudice." Pride and Prejudice. Ed. Donald J. Gray. New York, NY: Norton, 1964.

Brown, Julia Prewitt. Jane Austen's Novels: Social Change and Literary Form. Cambridge, MA: Harvard University Press, 1979.

Brown, Lloyd W. "The Comic Conclusion of Jane Austen's Novels." Publication of the Modern Language Association. 84 (1969): 1582-1589.

Brownstein, Rachel M. "Jane Austen: Irony and Authority." Last Laughs: Perspectives on Women and Comedy. Ed. Regina Barreca. New York, NY: Gordon and Breach, 1988, 57-70.

Demarest, David P., Jr. "Reductio Ad Absurdum: Jane Austen's Art of Satiric Qualification." Six Satirists. Ed. Austin Wright. Pittsburgh, PA: Carnegie Mellon University Press, 1965, 51-68.

Fergus, Jan. "The Comedy of Manners." Modern Critical Interpretations: Pride and Prejudice. Ed. Harold Bloom. New York, NY: Chelsea House, 1987.

Fergus, Jan. Jane Austen and the Didactic Novel. London, England: McMillan, 1983.

Fry, Paul H. "Georgic Comedy: The Fictive Territory of Jane Austen's Emma." Studies in the Novel 11 (1979): 129-146.

Fullbrook, Kate. "Jane Austen and the Comic Negative." Women Reading Women's Writing. Ed. Sue Rose. Brighton, Sussex, England: The Harvester Press, 1987, 39-57.

Gallon, D. N. "Comedy in Northanger Abbey." Modern Language Review 63 (1968): 802-809.

Gilbert, Sandra M., and Susan Gubar. The Madwoman in the Attic: The Woman Writer and the Nineteenth Century Literary Imagination. New Haven, CT: Yale University Press, 1984.

Kaul, A. N. "Jane Austen." The Action of English Comedy: Studies in the Encounter of Abstraction and Experience from Shakespeare to Shaw. New Haven, CT: Yale University Press, 1970, 193-249.

Kitchin, George. "Modern Prose Parody--Jane Austen to Bret Harte." Survey of Burlesque and Parody in English. London, England: Oliver and Boyd, 1931, 247-282.

McCormick, Marjorie. "Occasionally Nervous and Invariably Silly: Mothers in Jane Austen." Mothers in the English Novel: From Stereotype to Archetype. New York, NY: Garland, 1991, 47-76.

Mansell, Darrel. The Novels of Jane Austen: An Interpretation. Bristol, England: Macmillan, 1973.

Marshall, Denise. "Slaying the Angel and the Patriarch: The Grinning Woolf." Last Laughs: Perspectives on Women and Comedy. Ed. Regina Barreca. New York, NY: Gordon and Breach, 1988, 149-177.

Mudrick, Marvin. Jane Austen: Irony as Defense and Discovery. Princeton, NJ: Princeton University Press, 1952.

Polhemus, Robert M. "Austen's Emma: The Comedy of Union." Comic Faith: The Great Tradition from Austen to Joyce. Chicago, IL: Univ of Chicago Press, 1980, 24-59.

Rutter, Joy. "Irony in Jane Austen's Northanger Abbey." Unpublished Paper. Tempe, AZ: Arizona State University, 1994.

Smith, Esther M. G. "Jane Austen." Encyclopedia of British Humorists, Volume I. Ed. Steven H. Gale. New York, NY: Garland, 1996, 59-66.

Southam, B. C. ed. Jane Austen: The Critical Heritage. New York, NY: Barnes and Noble, 1968.

Spacks, Patricia Meyer. "Austen's Laughter." Last Laughs: Perspectives on Women and Comedy. Ed. Regina Barreca. New York, NY: Gordon and Breach, 1988, 71-86.

Stovel, Bruce. "Comic Symmetry in Jane Austen's Emma." Dalhousie Review 57 (1977): 453-465.

Tatham, Michael. "Mary Crawford and the Comic Heroine." New Blackfriars: A Monthly Review. 60 (1979): 11-26.

Trickett, Rachel. "Jane Austen's Comedy and the Nineteenth Century." Critical Essays on Jane Austen. Ed. B. C. Southam. New York, NY: Barnes, 1968, 162-181.

Charles Lamb (1775-1834)

B. W. Proctor considered Charles Lamb to be something of a chameleon, as he spoke to different people in very different ways:

> With Hazlitt he talked as though they met the subject in discussion on equal terms; with Leigh Hunt he exchanged repartees; to Wordsworth he was almost respectful; with Coleridge he was sometimes jocose, sometimes deferring; with Martin Burney fraternally familiar; with Manning affectionate; with Godwin merely courteous; or if friendly, then in a minor degree. (Proctor 173-174).

Charles Lamb was something of a practical joker. In 1800, Lamb sent a letter to his landlord and former school mate, James Matthew Gutch, saying that a clerk had stolen all of Gutch's money and that his partner had fled. On the back of the letter Lamb added that he had only been teasing. On Christmas Day, 1815, Lamb wrote to Thomas Manning who at the time was in China, and told him that all of Manning's friends, including Coleridge, Wordsworth, Godwin, and Mary Lamb were all dead. He further informed Manning that St. Paul's Cathedral had been reduced to ruins, and that the Monument to the Great Fire of London had shrunk to less than half of its former height (Rosenblum 638).

Lamb was famous for his hyperbole. In his "Dissertation on Roast Pig" he wrote that this dish is so delectable that people often burned down their houses to enjoy the taste. In "Mrs. Battle's Opinions on Whist" he considers the game of Whist to be one of life's primary concerns. Mrs. Battle considers Whist her "duty," it is "the thing she came into the world to do--and she did it." Lamb considered all people who did not take the game of Whist seriously to be "insufferable triflers" (Rosenblum 638). It is ironic that this is an expression that is usually used for people who spend too much of their time playing cards (Rosenblum 639).

Robert Lynd notes that Charles Lamb was very precocious as an infant. It was commonly said of Lamb that he "knew his letters before he could talk." One day as a child Charles was walking through a cemetery with his sister, Mary, and Charles was reading the epitaphs on the headstones. He noted that all of these epitaphs said wonderful things about the people who were buried there, so as they were leaving the cemetery, Charles turned to Mary and asked, "Mary, where are the naughty people buried?" Lynd notes that although this anecdote was widely told as a joke, it was not a joke to the small child who had asked a legitimate question. Nevertheless, Lynd notes that "this is the kind of observation out of which humour grows" (151).

Lamb grew up as the son of a Cockney scrivener. His sister Mary had fits of madness, and in one of these fits she stabbed their mother in the heart. For this crime, Mary would have been confined permanently to an asylum, but Charles could not allow this, so he gave his solemn agreement that he would take her under his care for the rest of her life (151-152).

In his youth, Lamb was appointed the official jester for the <u>Morning Post</u>. He was paid sixpence a joke, and he had to furnish six jokes a day. He "depended upon this remuneration for all of his supplementary livelihood--everything beyond mere bread and cheese." He hated the job, however, and he said,

> No Egyptian task-master ever devised a slavery like to that, our slavery. No fractious operants ever turned out for half the tyranny, which this necessity exercised upon us. Half-a-dozen jests in a day, (bating Sundays too,) why, it seems nothing! We make twice the number every day in our lives as a matter of course, and claim no Sabbatical exemptions. But then they come into our head. But when the head has to go out to them--when the mountain must go to Mohamet. Readers, try it for once, only for some short twelvemonth. (L'Estrange 176-177)

Alfred Gu L'Estrange suggests that Lamb's humor and poetry gleam one through the other, and often "leave us in pleasant uncertainty whether he is in jest or earnest." L'Estrange further suggests that "no one ever so finely commingled poetry and humour as Charles Lamb" (175). Valentine Le Grice describes Lamb's wit as "flashing out of his melancholy." It was further described as "the summer lightning, playing innocuously round the very cloud that gave it birth." For Lamb, "a pun may discharge a whole load of sorrow: the sharp point of a quibble or a joke may let out the long-gathered waters of bitterness" (qtd. in Lynd 153).

Lamb did not believe in living under patronage, and he was even resentful when he felt that Samuel Taylor Coleridge tried to protect him by referring to him as "my gentle-hearted Charles," three times in a single poem, as he thought that the phrase was not only patronizing but even libellous. He responded to this situation by writing, "For God's sake, don't make me ridiculous any more by terming me gentle-hearted in print, or do it in better verses.... In the next edition of the 'Anthology'...please to blot out <u>gentle-hearted</u> and substitute drunken dog, ragged-head, self-shaven, odd-eyed, stuttering, or any other epithet which truly and properly belongs to the gentleman in question" (Lynd 153-154).

In this context, it is interesting to note Lamb's witty description of Coleridge as "an archangel a little damaged" (Lynd 153). Lamb had a close relationship with Coleridge, but he was often annoyed by Coleridge's tendency to engage him in long conversations, so he told a story about one day when he was on his way to the City, and he met Coleridge "brimful of some new idea."

> He took me by the button of my coat, and closing his eyes commenced an eloquent discourse, waving his right hand gently, as the musical words flowed an unbroken stream from his lips. I listened entranced; but the striking of a church-clock recalled me to a sense of duty. I saw it was of

no use to attempt to break away, so taking advantage of his absorption in his subject, I, with my penknife, quietly severed the button from my coat, and decamped. Five hours afterwards, in passing the same garden, on my way home, I heard Coleridge's voice, and on looking in, there he was with closed eyes,--the button in his fingers,--and his right hand gracefully waving, just as when I left him. He had never missed me!" (Lynd 155)

About this story, Robert Lynd remarks that it may not have had the truth of history, but it certainly had the truth of caricature (Lynd 155).

Lamb had an excellent ability at light conversation, but his serious conversation was even better, ranging from sheer nonsense and puns to wit and humor much like that found in his letters and essays. The three most important qualities of his letters were their sincerity, their sympathy, and their wit (Rosenblum 639). "His puns were not particularly good, and few of them would have been recorded if they had not been uttered by Charles Lamb" (Lynd 155). Max Eastman described his puns as "hard, shallow bumps in the fluid texture" (70).

But Lamb loved puns, and on one occasion when he met a countryman on the Strand carrying a hare, he asked him, "Prithee my good fellow, is this thy own hare, or a wig?" (Levin 111). Lamb also loved practical jokes. On one occasion he found himself in a drawing-room after dinner, and he noticed a gentleman standing in the middle of the room in a stooped position with his shoulders bent forward. He was in a position which British schoolboys called "making a back." Lamb took advantage of the situation by placing his hands on the unaware victim and flying over his head as if he were playing leapfrog. Some of the guests who witnessed the event were amused; some were indignant; but all were astonished (Lynd 166).

Charles Lamb hated travel, and in a letter to William Wordsworth, he says, "Separate from the pleasure of your company, I don't much care if I never see a mountain in my life. I have passed all my days in London, until I have formed as many and intense local attachments, as any of you mountaineers can have done with dead nature" (Priestley 141). Lamb had mixed feelings about the Quakers. They had attractive qualities for him, but he could never endure their "mystical quietude." "I am all over sophisticated, with humours, fancies, craving hourly sympathy. I must have books, pictures, theatres, chit-chat, scandal, jokes, ambiguities, and a thousand whim-whams, which their simpler taste can do without. I should starve at their primitive banquet" (Priestley 143).

Charles Lamb considers the best drama to be a "breeze of sunshine." in which the moralistic paranoid attempts to protect himself by "wrapping up in a great blanket surtout of precaution" (Heller 153). Lamb feels that realism is appropriate in drama, in such places as Shakespeare's tragedies and comedies; however, Lamb feels that realistic interpretations of Congreve's and Sheridan's dramatis personae are ill-conceived. For Lamb, "the actor in an artificial comedy should play not only to the other characters but also to the audience, thus shattering the illusion of reality." For Lamb, comedy of manners is like a plant in being a living organism. Like a plant, therefore, it "needs a sympathetic soil to grow in." In his Guide Through the Romantic Movement (1930), Ernest Bernbaum calls Lamb a "laughing philosopher," suggesting further that Lamb "supplemented Wordsworth's message by disclosing how one's life could come into contact with ideal values in the city as well as in the country; how urban life might mean something finer than an alternation of toil and frivolity" (Heller 155).

Lamb insisted on dramatic morality by which the audience was forced to recognize the difference between reality on the one hand and imaginative artifice on the other. Lamb uses this distinction in evaluating the literary achievements of the sixteenth and seventeenth centuries, and in attacking the "artistic and critical orthodoxy of the late eighteenth century with its weakly liberal humanitarian emphasis." Lamb considered the relieving of poverty by the purse, and the restoration of a young man to his parents by methods prescribed by the "Humane Society" as amiable subjects. While they are "pretty things to teach the first rudiments of humanity; they amount to about as much instruction as the stories of good boys that give away their custards to poor beggar-boys in children's books. But, good God! is this <u>milk for babes</u> to be set up in opposition to Hogarth's moral scenes, his <u>strong meat for men</u>?" (Park 228-229).

Lamb's essay on old actors was written as an apology for audiences who were delighted and applauded the drama of plays rather than their messages. In this essay, Lamb is making essentially three points:

> Firstly, that the stage performance of Restoration Comedy is great fun. Secondly, that our enjoyment is even greater when the plays are acted with proper attention to an <u>imperfect</u> dramatic illusion, with the emphasis falling on what he calls the "acted villainy" of the characters. Finally, that literature, and art in general, has suffered too much in the past from the improper transference of realistic criteria. (Park 241)

When Charles and Mary Lamb were quite old, Cowden Clarke was once listening to them talking with each other. Charles said to his sister, "You must die first, Mary." Mary responded with a quiet nod and a sweet smile, "Yes, I must die first, Charles." According to Robert Lynd, this story gives us "a glimpse of the harrowed soil from which Lamb's wit and humour were harvested" (168).

Charles Lamb loved to pun. Just before he proposed to actress Fanny Kelly, he wrote to ask her for theatre passes, which at that time were made of bone. In a letter dated July 9, 1819, he said, "If your Bones are not engaged on Monday night, will you favor us with the use of them? I know, if you can oblige us, you will make no bones of it." He continued to extend this pun, and then ended with, "I am almost at the end of my bon-mots." Lamb once said that he hoped to inhale his last breath through a pipe and exhale it with a pun (Rosenblum 639).

Charles Lamb Bibliography

Eastman, Max. The Sense of Humor. New York, NY: Octagon Books, 1972.

Heller, Janet Ruth. "The Breeze of Sunshine: A Study of Lamb's Essay 'On the Artificial Comedy of the Last Century.' " Charles Lamb Bulletin 16 (1976): 149-156.

Houghton, Walter E., Jr. "Lamb's Criticism of Restoration Comedy." Journal of English Literary History 10 (1943): 61-72.

Jerrold, Walter, ed. Bons-Mots of Charles Lamb and Douglas Jerrold. London, England: J. M. Dent, 1893.

L'Estrange, Alfred Gu. "Lamb." History of English Humour. New York, NY: Burt Franklin, 1878, 175-183.

Levin, Harry, ed. Veins of Humor. Cambridge, MA: Harvard Univ Press, 1972.

Lynd, Robert. "Charles Lamb." English Wits. Ed. Leonard Russell. London, England: Hutchinson, 1940, 149-168.

Park, Roy. "Lamb and Restoration Comedy." Essays in Criticism 29 (1979): 225-243.

Polhemus, Robert M. Comic Faith: The Great Tradition from Austen to Joyce. Chicago, IL: University of Chicago Press, 1980.

Priestley, J. B. "Charles Lamb. English Humour. New York, NY: Longmans, 1929, 138-149.

Proctor, Bryan W. (Pseudonym of Barry Cornwall). Charles Lamb: A Memoir. Boston, MA: Roberts Brothers, 1866.

Rosenblum, Joseph. "Charles Lamb." Encyclopedia of British Humorists, Volume II. Ed. Steven H. Gale. New York, NY: Garland, 1996, 635-642.

William Hazlitt (1778-1830)

According to Hugh Walker, the satire of Hazlitt targeted the extravagances of the court of Henry VIII, a court which furnished abundant material for satire against men and against women as well; the result is seen in Hazlitt's Early Popular Poetry of England. Hazlitt's book includes poems which accuse women of pride and excessive love of fine clothing. In A Merry Jeste of a Shrewde and Curste Wyfe lapped in Morrelles Skin, the "curste wife" is tamed in much the same way as Kathryn is tamed in Shakespeare's The Taming of the Shrew. The Boke of Mayd Emlyn tells about women who have many husbands and who betray and abuse them all, in the tradition of Chaucer's The Wife of Bath. The wife's reaction to the death of the third husband is as follows:

> She was than stedfast and stronge,
> And kepte her a wydowe veraye longe,
> In faythe almoost two dayes. (Walker 35)

The Proud Wyves Pater Noster tells about petitions turned into prayers for fine raiment. And The Schole-house of Women maintains that there is a "salve for every sore except marriage, and the gout" (Walker 35-36).

William Hazlitt Bibliography

Ready, Robert. "Hazlitt as an English Comic Writer." The Wordsworth Circle 6 (1975): 109-114.
Walker, Hugh. English Satire and Satirists. New York, NY: E. P. Dutton and Co. 1925.

Thomas Moore (1779-1852) IRELAND

See Nilsen, Don L. F. **Humor in Irish Literature: A Reference Guide**. Westport, CT: Greenwood, 1996.

William Hone (1780-1842)

In the late 1810s and early 1820s, William Hone published a number of topical parodies and satires. These satires caught the attention of an enormous readership. Between 1819 and 1822 alone, Hone sold over 250,000 copies of his political squibs, making Hone the best-selling author in Britain at the time. In his writings, Hone exposed the foibles of the establishment and thus he helped to consolidate his audience's antigovernment sentiments (Grimes 532).

Most of the parodies which Hone wrote in 1817 were written in the form of the Catechism, the Litany, and the Athanasian Creed from the Book of Common Prayer. The Late John Wilkes's Catechism (1817), for example is about "Lick Spittle," a member of government, who frequently rehearses his "articles of faith." These "articles of faith" are in fact a declaration of support for Tory politics. When Spittle is asked the set question, "What dost thou chiefly learn in the Articles of thy Belief?" he answers, "First, I learn to forswear all conscience, which was never meant to trouble me, nor the rest of the tribe of Courtiers. Second, to swear black is white, or white black, according to the good pleasure of the Ministers. Thirdly, to put on the helmet of impudence, the only armour against the shafts of patriotism." Hone also rewrites the "Lord's Prayer," renaming it the "Minister's Memorial," so that it begins with "Our Lord who art in the Treasury," and continues in this same vein until the conclusion, which says, "Turn us not out of our Places; but keep us in the House of Commons, the land of Pension and Plenty; and deliver us from the People. Amen."

Hone got into trouble by parodying various sacred texts in his The Late John Wilkes's Catechism (1817)(a parody of the sanctification of catechism), The Political Litany (1817)(a parody of the Litany or General Supplication), and The Sinecurists' Creed (1817)(a parody of the Athanasian Creed) (Kitchin 262). In December of 1817, The Attorney General officially charged Hone with blasphemous libel, and he had to go to court. His defence was both simple and clever. He should be acquitted because there was no precedence for anyone ever having been convicted for parodying Holy Writ or any of the Sacred Writings. In fact, Hone's trial was "merely a belated attempt to get at political opponents through the blasphemy laws" (Kitchin 264). Thus Hone successfully defended himself by arguing that "parody does not necessarily impugn the quality or the validity of the original text from which it takes its form." These acquittals were a major embarrassment for the government, and the acquittals made Hone pretty much immune from further libel prosecution. It was at this time that he wrote Buonapartephobia (1817), a parody based on Laurence Sterne's Tristram Shandy (Grimes 533).

The Political House That Jack Built (1819) was one of the most popular parodies which Hone wrote, since it sold more than one hundred thousand copies in a single year. Hone's comic text criticizes government actions that threaten to plunder the "wealth" that lay in the house that Jack built. This wealth consisted of the Magna Carta, the Bill of Rights, and Habeas Corpus. What made this pamphlet even more popular was that it was illustrated by Hone's friend and collaborator, George Cruikshank (Grimes 533).

Non Mi Ricordo! (1820) is a parody based on a very famous cross-examination of an Italian witness the government had brought to England to testify against Caroline. The Queen's Matrimonial Ladder (1820) brings to mind a children's toy which is now called "Jacob's Ladder." Hone had seen the toy in a shop window. Both of these pieces are written to "chastise the hypocrisy of the English Church as it kowtowed to the demands of political expedience" (Grimes 533). In The Man in the Moon (1820), the speaker is taken to the moon, where he listens to the "Prince of Lunataria" as he delivers his annual address to the Lunar Parliament. The speech which the Prince of Lunataria gives is a parody of the English Regent's Parliamentary address (Grimes 533).

The Political Showman--At Home! (1821) contains Cruikshank's caricatures of prominent political figures of Hone's day. These visual caricatures are supplemented by Hone's text, which is written in imitation of the language of a carnival barker. The speaker presents the various political figures as if they were dangerous zoo animals. They are "curiosities and creatures" exhibited for the "horror and fascination of the onlookers" (Grimes 534). A Slap at Slop and the Bridge-Street Gang (1822) is a parody directed against Hone's arch-rival John Stoddart (Hone's "Dr. Slop"), the Tory propagandist who edited and wrote for The New Times. And Facetiae and Miscellanies (1827) is a collection of many of Hone's most popular parodies and other comic works. Most of Hone's writings satirize famous political figures of his day, but "perhaps the most prominent theme in all of Hone's parodies and satires concerns the political function of the press itself" (Grimes 534).

William Hone Bibliography

Grimes, Kyle. William Hone." Encyclopedia of British Humorists, Volume I. Ed. Steven
 H. Gale. New York, NY: Garland, 1996, 531-535.
Kitchin, George. Survey of Burlesque and Parody in English. London, England: Oliver and
 Boyd, 1931.

Sikes, Herschel M. "William Hone: Regency Patriot, Parodist, and Pamphleteer." The Newberry Library Bulletin 5 (1961): 281-294.

Ebenezer Elliott (1781-1849)

Elliott's most famous and greatest work is entitled Corn-Law Rhymes (1831). This is a fierce condemnation of the fiscal system as it then was, and although it is satire, it also has a lyrical fervor which transcends the satire (Walker 282).

Ebenezer Elliott Bibliography

Walker, Hugh. English Satire and Satirists. New York, NY: J. M. Dent, 1925.

(James) Leigh Hunt (1784-1859)

"On the Combination of Grave and Gay" appeared in Leigh Hunt's Wit and Humour Selected from the English Poets (1846). This was later to appear in Leigh Hunt's Literary Criticism edited by L. H. Houtchens and C. W. Houtchens (1956). In "On the Combination of Grave and Gay," Hunt tries to show that both gravity and gaiety are necessary aspects of the best literature. "To the amusement which is given our brains, is added the approbation of the heart. What might have seemed nothing but levity, is found accompanied with the best kind of gravity. The man whom we might have feared as a satirist, we think we might count upon as a friend" (Hunt 559; Martin 75).

Hunt says that the basis of both wit and humor seems to be incongruity. He also says that the pleasure of wit derives from the intellect, and is neither superior, malicious, nor condescending. For Hunt, what separates humor from wit is not so much attitude as it is the nature of the subject matter. Humor "deals in incongruities of character and circumstances, as Wit does in those of arbitrary ideas" (Hunt 12; qtd. in Martin 72). With wit the triumph is not insolent, but congenial. The triumph is not to anyone's disadvantage, but is to the listener's own "joy and assurance" (Hunt 7). In reaction to Hunt's assertion, Robert Martin notes that there is a touch of Lewis Carroll in a situation where triumph is congenial, a situation where everyone wins and no one loses. In saying that wit is congenial, Hunt is reacting to the theory of superiority which was being preached at the time. Hunt is redefining "superiority" to mean "incongruity." "Two ideas are as necessary to Wit, as couples are to marriages. They must both remain separate and become one" (Hunt 10; qtd. in Martin 73).

Hunt felt that Chaucer was "entertaining, profound, and good-natured" (Hunt 75; qtd. in Martin 74); "Shakespeare had as great a comic genius as tragic" (Hunt 122; qtd in Martin 74); Samuel Butler had "little humour," but he was nevertheless "the wittiest of English poets." In Hudibras the "wit is pure and incessant" (Hunt 242; qtd. in Martin 74). Hunt says that Pascal, Saint Francis of Sales, Thomas More, Martin Luther, and Socrates are all good examples of the union of wit, dignity, and reverence (Hunt 561; qtd. in Martin 75). Hunt says that Shakespeare could write as Milton wrote. Shakespeare could think with equal seriousness and express himself with Miltonic nobility; however Milton, because he lacked a sense of humor, "could not write like Shakespeare" (Hunt 560; qtd. in Martin 75).

(James) Leigh Hunt Bibliography

Martin, Robert Bernard. "Chapter V: Sydney Smith, Leigh Hunt, and Thackeray." The Triumph of Wit: A Study of Victorian Comic Theory. Oxford, England: Clarendon Press, 1974, 67-81.

Thomas De Quincey (1785-1859)

De Quincey loves the incongruous, and makes much use of this device in his writing. He also enjoys the various techniques of burlesque, especially anachronism. In 1821 De Quincey published his Confessions of an English Opium-Eater, and Jean-Jacques Mayoux feels that the fun of this piece "hangs on successive and interlaced motives. One of them is the letter to Monsieur de Quincey, scribbled in the illegible hand which is supposed to be the mark of French penmanship" (Mayoux 113). Robert Martin considers De Quincey's wit and intellect to be amoral, or possibly even immoral. But De Quincey's humor was moral. This is because De Quincey made a distinction between "wit" which is intellectual, and "humour" which "has an influx of the moral nature" (qtd. in Martin 30).

De Quincey's "Jeu d'Esprit," which was first published as an article in Blackwood's Quarterly, was probably based on Erasmus's Praise of Folly. Here, De Quincey tries to please the readers by writing in a style that was reminiscent of the learned burlesques of the past, but the Blackwood's Quarterly setting also helped establish the piece as burlesque. The chief ingredient in his humor is "the witty parade of obscure learning, which brings the pleasantry into line with the great sixteenth-century burlesques" (Kitchin 261). De Quincey's Murder Considered as One of the Fine Arts (1827) is another De Quincey burlesque, and is to some extent the culmination of his burlesque technique (Kitchin 261).

Jean-Jacques Mayoux indicates that it is very clear that De Quincey is not only a humorist, but a "conscious humorist." "What seems to be much less certain is that he knows the way his humor is going, or that he guides it." There are often lengthy digressions and endless digressive notes in De Quincey's texts, and these are often followed by apologies. De Quincey just could not help digressing, and his digressions were caused by many different things--a provocative subject, a particular theme, a mere word. "As soon as he has stepped aside, not only has all sense of proportion been lost, but the main subject is as if it did not exist any more. There is an interlude, which may be short or long, what he would call a trance, in the conscious personal time, during which an irrepressible fascination takes over" (Mayoux 123-124).

Thomas De Quincey Bibliography

Kitchin, George. Survey of Burlesque and Parody in English. London, England: Oliver and Boyd, 1931.
Martin, Robert Bernard. The Triumph of Wit: A Study of Victorian Comic Theory. Oxford, England: Clarendon Press, 1974.
Mayoux, Jean-Jacques. "De Quincey: Humor and the Drugs." Veins of Humor. Cambridge, MA: Harvard Univ Press, 1972, 109-131.

Thomas Love Peacock (1785-1866)

Thomas Love Peacock targets such timeless satiric subjects as vanity, hypocrisy, and greed, but he also targets contemporary intellectual, political, social and artistic pretensions in his poetry, essays, and novels (O'Connor 835). Peacock produces such humors characters as Moley Mystic of Cimmerian Lodge, and Mr. Feathernest, and Mr. Paperstamp of Mainchance Villa. He satirized Samuel Taylor Coleridge's "obscurity," and Robert Southey's and William Wordsworth's "turncoat conservatism" (O'Connor 837). Peacock satirized the intellectual, artistic, political, and social excesses of his day, and he attacked radical liberalism with the same vigor as he attacked reactionary conservatism. He found absurdity in both the cult of the primitive and in the cult of progress (O'Connor 840).

Peacock spoofs the excesses of Romantic visionaries, and is able to build comedy out of a person's total inability to effect change in modern society (Henkle 63). Robert Polhemus considers Peacock's comedy to be "mundane, not divine, but it is reverent." In the Gothic tradition, country houses often become the titles of his novels, as in Headlong Hall (1816), Melincourt (1817), Crochet Castle (1931), and Gryll Grange (1860). Polhemus says these are all "neo-Bacchic temples of communion." According to William Allan Neilson, Peacock's satiric novels have scanty plots, but are filled with odd characters. Nightmare Abbey is all of this and more. "Like a church, it serves as both a sanctuary from the urgencies of the world and a gathering place for the world" (Neilson 157).

The Monks of St. Mark (1804) is written in the mock Gothic genre (O'Connor 834). The monks of the title struggle not so much with Satan as with Bacchus, so that the story is not so much a tale of terror as it is a tale of drunken revelry. It is filled with punning and unbridled slapstick. "Peacock's love of witty buffoonery, and his use of outrageous humor to mock a literary fashion foreshadows much of the satire to come" (O'Connor 835). Sir Proteus: A Satirical Ballad (1814) is one of Peacock's best attempts at extended poetic satire. Here he attacks Robert Southey, Sir Walter Scott, William Wordsworth, Samuel Taylor Coleridge and others. Sir Proteus is also a high-spirited poetic lampoon of "Germanic supernaturalism, brooding egotism, insipid sentimentalism, false primitivism, and other literary barbarisms" of Peacock's age (O'Connor 835).

Headlong Hall (1816) employs conversational humor in its development of Jonsonian humours or single-minded characters, who are drawn together at Headlong Hall. Headlong Hall is about Harry Headlong , Esquire, an amiable but self-indulgent aristocrat of ancient Welsh lineage. Harry Headlong has invited a group of eccentrics to visit his ancestral home (O'Connor 835). Robert O'Connor describes the guests as "a panoply of crack-brained thinkers, writers, artists; and dilettanti, each of whom talks incessantly of his personal hobby-horse." The limited perspective of Mr. Foster is that he thinks that all things work toward the world's ultimate perfection. Mr. Escot, on the other hand, sees only constant deterioration. Mr. Jenkison is in constant equivocation, and The Reverend Dr. Gaster sees everything in terms of gastronomy. To Mr. Cranium, it is phrenology that is the "key to truth." Finally, Mr. Milestone likes to improve landscapes by leveling them with gunpowder (O'Connor 836).

In Melincourt (1817), Anthelia Melincourt believes in modern chivalry, and requires that anyone who is to win her hand must be a proper suitor. One of Anthelia's suitors is Mr. Derrydown, a caricature of Sir Walter Scott, who is more fascinated by the antiquarian shadow of chivalry than he is in its substance. Sylvan Forester is another suitor; Forester is chivalric in his nature, but he has to be drawn out of his retirement at Redrose Abbey if he is to be united with Anthelia and achieve his full potential. Another character who represents the chivalric tradition is Sir Oran Haut-ton, whom Forrester describes as "a specimen of the natural and original man" (O'Connor 836). In a reversal of the Pygmalion myth, Sylvan Forester cultivates this orangutan by the name of Oran Haut-ton, and puts him up for election as a member of Parliament. Oran Haut-ton is well-bred and his manners are impeccable, and he is an accomplished performer both on the French horn and the flute. He is also the ideal dinner companion except for the fact that he is not able to converse (Henkle 67). "Sir Oran is both a satiric tool for belittling the more extreme notions of the primitivists, particularly Lord Monboddo, and an embodiment of an active instinctive heroism" (O'Connor 836).

Nightmare Abbey (1818) is set at the Gothic home of Christopher Glowery, Esquire, who has gathered a bunch of "cranks and crochets" representing early nineteenth-century English literati.   Christopher's son, Shelleyan Scythrop, immerses himself in "the distempered ideas of metaphysical romance and romantic metaphysics", and at the same time develops a "passion for reforming the world." Mr. Flosky is reminiscent of Coleridge, as he is addicted to metaphysical obscurity, and has lost faith in human progress. He wants to reconstruct the oppressive past. Mr. Cypress is reminiscent of Byron, as he is destined to an exile's hopeless quest for perfection in an imperfect world. Like Childe Harold, Mr. Cypress is drawn "to the ruins of the past." "Nightmare Abbey is the most devastating of contemporary attacks on Romantic pretension, but it lampoons its targets with such disarming good humor that even its victims, particularly Shelley and Byron, could enjoy its exuberant wit" (O'Connor 837).

Robert Polhemus says that wine is a controlling image in Bacchic rites, in the Eucharist, and in Peacock's novels. This is especially true of Nightmare Abbey, where wine is not shown to be the cause of inebriation or hangovers, but is rather the symbol of "enduring, festive being." In the novel, the most important events happen "when the characters drink, almost ritually, celebrating a comic mass in which they are at one with each other and with all humanity." The wine flows freely in every chapter, and as the novel progresses, the reader becomes more and more aware of its central role (Polhemus 76-77).

> In the chanting, the singing, and the transformation of gloom and dispute into play and exhilaration, Peacock shows the magical properties of wine to create solidarity. For him, as for Hilary, it symbolizes perfect life. It is, as Flosky says, an "objective fact," connoting pleasure, companionship, the continuity of human culture through ages and--not least--the metaphorical power of the race. (Polhemus 78)

Scythrop shouts that wine is "the only styptic for a bleeding heart," and in fact the last words in Nightmare Abbey are "Bring some Madeira."

"Wine" is the controlling metaphor of Nightmare Abbey, but "women" and "song" are also important. The two girls in the novel function as humours characters. Celinda is a "Romantic bluestocking," and Marionetta is a coquette. "Their casting-off of Scythrop helps form the pattern of humours blending into humor." "Music" is also important in the novel. It draws the dissonant company together and it provides a paradigm for human harmony. These three major themes fuse together in the novel to show how much people have in common, and in their fusion they reveal that shared experience (Polhemus 81).

Northrop Frye considers Nightmare Abbey to be one of the most original and thought-provoking works of the English Romantic Period. Because Peacock parodied the works of Coleridge, Wordsworth, and Shelley, Robert Polhemus calls him an "ugly duckling among the Romantic swans" (Polhemus 61). Although Nightmare Abbey started out as a parody, it ended up as more than that, since it attempts "to make sense of our lives through a genuinely religious sense of humor" (Polhemus 62).

> Nightmare Abbey makes fun of several early nineteenth-century intellectual humors that would become very influential, among them cultivation of the emotional self (Scythrop), popular transcendentalism (Flosky), pessimism, nostalgia, and degeneration-of-the-world theories (Mr. Toobad, Cypress), natural science (Asterias), privileged-class feminism (Celinda), bourgeois pseudo-revolutionary fervor (Scythrop), reactionary passion (Mr. Glowry, Flosky). The great humor of the age that Peacock dramatizes--primarily in Scythrop, Glowry, and Flosky--is the tendency to disassociate thought and feeling from material reality. (Polhemus 64)

Robert Polhemus notes that Peacock has been severely criticized for parodying Shelley and

Coleridge with his characters of Scythrop and Flosky (Polhemus 64).

Mr. Toobad is the millenarian doomsayer in Nightmare Abbey. He slouches around proclaiming that "The Devil is among us, having great wrath," but the novel's protagonist, Scythrop, makes the same statement much more eloquently: "Evil, and mischief, and misery, and confusion, and vanity, and vexation of spirit, and death, and disease, and assassination, and war, and poverty, and pestilence, and famine, and avarice, and selfishness, and rancour, and jealousy, and spleen, and malevolence...all prove the accuracy of [Toobad's] views" (Abbey 17). Mr. Toobad also says, "The world being a great theatre of evil..., laughter and merriment make a human being no better than a baboon" (qtd. in Henkle 58).

George Kitchin compares Peacock's Nightmare Abbey with Jane Austen's Northanger Abbey, calling them both "pure burlesque." This is a much better burlesque than is The Misfortunes of Elphin, where "we are never quite sure if he is writing with romantic zest or in sheer mockery" (Kitchin 256). Nightmare Abbey satirizes the craze for the "Gothic" novel. "The satire on German metaphysics is perhaps new, and certainly the bringing of actual persons on the stage (Coleridge, Byron, and the hero, Shelley) is an innovation. Coleridge is burlesqued by a character named Mr. Flosky, and this character is generally to be the best parody. Mr. Cypress, who represents Byron is also an effective burlesque. Mr. Scythrop represents Shelley, and this character is sufficiently exaggerated to make the burlesque inoffensive. "Mr. Scythrop is indeed a compost of all the crazy horror mongering and utopianism of the age. The youthful Shelley was perhaps rather like this" (Kitchin 257).

Polhemus notes that Nightmare Abbey's Scythrop Glowry is a significant Peacock character, since he is the tool which Peacock uses to "turn humours into humor." "Peacock creates in him a figure whose destiny is the sum meaning of all the other characters, the persistence of communal life, which is inevitably renewed in particular folly." The last chapter is a comic vision of humanity's fate. Scythrop says that if his father has not returned with one of his loves by a particular time, he will kill himself. This fatal time approaches, and there is no sign of his father, so Scythrop rings for his servant, Raven:

"Raven..., the clock is too fast."

"No, indeed," said Raven...; "if anything, it is too slow."

"Villain!" said Scythrop, pointing the pistol at him; "it is too fast."

"Yes--yes--too fast, I meant," said Raven, in manifest fear.

"How much too fast?" said Scythrop.

"As much as you please," said Raven.

"How much, I say?" said Scythrop, pointing the pistol again.

"An hour, a full hour, sir," said the terrified butler.

"Put back my watch," said Scythrop." (Polhemus 67-68)

Shortly thereafter, the father returns, but he has not brought Scythrop's love with him. Nevertheless, the father easily convinces Scythrop that there is no point in killing himself, since the appointed time for it is long past (Polhemus 68).

"The Four Ages of Poetry" (1820) was published in Ollier's Literary Miscellany. In poetic form, it gives the history of mankind. The first age in the history of mankind is the Iron Age. Then comes the Age of Gold, the Age of Silver, and finally, the Age of Brass. In the Iron Age, Peacock praises those who are presently in power. In the Golden Age, Peacock looks back to the glories of the Age of Iron, and "magnifies the grandeur of this misrepresented past." The Silver Age is the age of poetry, during which truth is so much polished and imitated that it becomes lost. During the Brass Age all of the civilized polishing of the Silver Age is rejected. The Brass Age regresses to the period of barbarisms and crude traditions of the Iron Age. The Brass Age is an attempt to return to nature, and to revive the age of gold (O'Connor 838).

Maid Marian (1822) is a satire based heavily on the legend of Robin Hood. In the times of Maid Marian the wealth flows from the powerless to the powerful, but there are those who want to have the world's riches redistributed, and they realize that in order for this to happen there must first be a redistribution of the world's power (O'Connor 838). The Paper Money Lyrics (1825) parodies a number of Peacock's favorite targets, including not only Wordsworth and Coleridge, but also the suffering produced by the British financial system (O'Connor 838). The Misfortunes of Elphin (1829) is the second of Peacock's "historical romances." Here again, the economic theme appears. The Misfortunes of Elphin is set in Wales at the time of King Arthur and the Celts (O'Connor 838).

Crochet Castle (1831) is a conversational novel in which Ebenezer MacCrochet enjoys the company of such obsessed eccentrics as Mr. Firedamp, who is afraid of some sort of water-borne contagion, and Mr. Henbane, who has killed a number of cats with his experiments with poison, and Mr. Skionar, who is an unflattering portrait of Coleridge, and Mr. Toogood, who believes in Utopia, and M. Chainmail, who wants to revive the Middle Ages, and Mr. MacQuedy (pronounced "Mac Q.E.D.") who is an avant-garde political economist arguing that man is a product of his education (Henkle 67). Mr. McQuedy judges everything in terms of profit and loss, and being Scottish, he held to a number of theories of political economy which Peacock abhorred. "Throughout the novel, MacQuedy argues for using monetary value as the measure of all things and for making financial calculations the arbiter of every human decision" (O'Connor 839).

Gryll Grange (1861) is Peacock's last conversational novel. In this novel the proprietor brings together a bunch of eccentric characters whose interactions develop the novel's satiric concerns. Gregory Gryll is so satisfied with the comforts of his present life that he is very resistant to change. His neighbor, Algernon Falconer, however, is even more addicted than Gregory Gryll is to "ritualized stability." The novel has an excessive nine marriages, and Robert O'Connor describes this as follows: "In this final statement of Peacock the humorist, then, the comedian speaks his message of unconquerable joy while the satirist folds his arms in skeptical amusement" (O'Connor 840).

Robert Polhemus feels that Peacock had a genuinely religious sense of humor. "By that I mean that his comedy, like religion, tries to convey a sense of well-being and immortal life by changing the perspective in which we see ourselves. He is one of the few "amiable humorists" who manage to avoid sentimentality; he does not make moral claims for the goodness of man and does not base his vision of communication on conscious human sympathy" (87).

Roger Henkle suggests that Thomas Peacock's books provide very little social context, since they are "comic symposia," in which clusters of people assemble for a weekend or else they are thrown together, and talk about human nature or philosophical issues far into the night, being totally oblivious to the living world that exists around them. Thus Henkle says that Peacock helped to develop a new genre called "comedy of ideas" the principal objective of which was the presentation and spoofing of various current philosophies and social and political positions. Henkle traces this genre from Peacock all the way to Evelyn Waugh in the twentieth century (Henkle 60-61).

> Peacock believes that the plethora of theories about the nature of man and the state of things produces nothing in the way of concrete effects. His fictional characters pop off at each other like champagne corks and contain mostly fizz. Lord Feathernest speaks for us all when he cries out in the midst of a pompous debate about whether the poem "Chevy Chase" or "Paradise Lost" gives a deeper insight into the truth of things: "I do not know what you mean by the truth of things."

and this discussion is followed by one of the conversants remarking, "A dry discussion. Pass the bottle, and moisten it" (Henkle 62).

Thomas Love Peacock Bibliography

Butler, Marilyn. Peacock Displayed: A Satirist in His Context. Boston, MA: Routledge and
    Kegan Paul, 1979.
Dawson, Carl. His Fine Wit: A Study of Thomas Love Peacock. Berkeley, CA: University
    of California Press, 1970.
Henkle, Roger B. "Peacock, Thackeray, and Jerrold: The Comedy of 'Radical'
    Disaffection." Comedy and Culture--England--1820-1900. Princeton, NJ: Princeton
    University Press, 1980, 58-110.
Kitchin, George. Survey of Burlesque and Parody in English. London, England: Oliver and
    Boyd, 1931.
Neilson, William Allan. Webster's Biographical Dictionary. Springfield, MA: G. and C.
    Merriam, 1971.
O'Connor, Robert H. "Thomas Love Peacock." Encyclopedia of British Humorists, Volume
    II. Ed. Steven H. Gale. New York, NY: Garland, 1996, 832-841.
Peacock, Thomas Love. Nightmare Abbey. New York, NY: Capricorn, 1964.
Polhemus, Robert M. "Peacock's Nightmare Abbey (1818)." Comic Faith. Chicago, IL:
    University of Chicago Press, 1980, 60-87.
Schmid, Thomas H. Humor and Transgression in Peacock, Shelley, and Byron. Lewiston:
    The Edwin Mellen Press, 1992.

Eaton Stannard Barrett (1786-1820) IRELAND

See Nilsen, Don L. F. **Humor in Irish Literature: A Reference Guide**. Westport,
CT: Greenwood, 1996.

James Silk Buckingham (1786-1855)

Alfred Gu L'Estrange feels that although Buckingham wrote poetry, his humour was
of very poor quality (L'Estrange 293). In The Rehearsal, Buckingham and others "applied
their wit to ridicule in heroic couplets the rant and fustian which frequently marred the
rhymed heroic drama" (Walker 146). Despite its poor quality, The Rehearsal was very
much approved, because it was aimed at Dryden in particular, and the heroic drama in
general. In this work, Buckingham made a distinction between the effect of humor in the
plot and the effect of humor in the dialogue of a play. (L'Estrange 294)

James Silk Buckingham Bibliography

L'Estrange, Alfred Gu. "Rochester--Buckingham--Dryden--Butler." History of English
    Humour. New York, NY: Burt Franklin, 1878, 271-302.
Walker, Hugh. English Satire and Satirists. New York, NY: J. M. Dent, 1925.

Richard Whately (1786-1863)

Richard Whately was an Archbishop who wrote that "jests are mock fallacies, i.e.
fallacies so palpable as not to be able to deceive anyone, but yet bearing just the
resemblance of argument which is calculated to amuse by contrast." He also wrote, "There
are several different kinds of jokes and raillery, which will be found to correspond with the

different kinds of fallacy." One of these classes of jokes is the "manufactured" class. Whately considered the pun to be, in most cases, "a mock argument founded on a palpable equivocation of the middle term" (L'Estrange 322-323).

Richard Whately Bibliography

L'Estrange, Alfred Gu. History of English Humour. New York, NY: Burt Franklin, 1878.

Mary Russell Mitford (1787-1855)

According to James Agate, Mary Mitford has four claims to fame: "Our Village," her letters, her wit, and the care she gave to father, a man very much like Charles Dickens's character, Harold Skimpole (332). Mary Mitford was responsible for many short and insightful statements. She compared great authors to the Alps: "Great authors are great people--but I believe they are best seen at a distance. The Alps are only fit for the background of a picture, and not always for that" (347).
James Agate suggests that Mitford might have developed her wit to compensate for her physical plainness and awkwardness. About dancing, she said, "What, indeed, should I do at a dance with my dumpling of a person tumbling about like a cricket-ball on uneven ground, or a bowl rolling among nine-pins--casting off with the grace of a frisky Yorkshire cow, or going down the middle with the majesty of an overloaded hay-wagon passing through a narrow lane? What should I do at a ball?" (Agate 347).

Mary Russell Mitford Bibliography

Agate, James. "Mary Russell Mitford." English Wits. Ed. Leonard Russell. London, England: Hutchinson, 1940, 329-349.

Richard Harris Barham (Thomas Ingoldsby) (1788-1845)

Barham possessed a great natural facility for humor, as can be seen in his "Ingoldsby Legends." The humor of these legends relates to common subjects, and is of a lower character, but it provides a laugh, and affords a distraction, and has made the "Ingoldsby Legends" highly successful (L'Estrange 206).

Richard Harris Barham (Thomas Ingoldsby) Bibliography

L'Estrange, Alfred Gu. History of English Humour. New York, NY: Burt Franklin, 1878.

George Gordon, Lord Byron (1788-1824)

Throughout his life, George Gordon, Lord Byron's letters sparkled with wit, enthusiasm, and a profound interest in public literature. Many of these letters foreshadowed the comic genius that was to come (Riley 192). In a letter written in 1813, Byron wrote about his natural love of contradiction and paradox (Riley 193). Byron loved to write poetry. On January 22, 1821, on the occasion of his thirty-third birthday, he wrote:
> Through life's road, so dim and dirty,
> I have dragged to three and thirty.

What have these years left to me?
Nothing--except thirty-three. (Riley 200)
Sometime later he wrote a letter to Thomas Moore about the Chivalric tradition:
To do good to mankind is the chivalrous plan,
And is always as nobly requited;
Then battle for freedom wherever you can,
And, if not shot or hang'd, you'll get knighted. (Riley 200)
          Lord Byron believed in the doctrine that "the petty, the contemptible and the base
will always be found close to the heroic and the pathetic" (Walker 271). Even in his
earliest writings, Byron showed a love of humor. In speaking of his college choir he says:
          Our choir would scarcely be excused,
               Even as a band of raw beginners:
          All mercy, now, must be refused
               To such a set of croaking sinners.
          If David, when his toils were ended
               Had heard these blockheads sing before him,
          To us his psalms had ne'er descended;
               In furious mood, he would have tore 'em. (L'Estrange 186)
Byron also wrote a poem about a lady who had maligned him to his wife which shows that
Byron may not always have known where humor ends and the ludicrous begins:
          With a vile mask the Gorgon would disown
          A cheek of parchment and an eye of stone,
          Mark how the channels of her yellow blood
          Ooze at her skin, and stagnate there to mud.... (L'Estrange 187)
By considering such examples as this, it is easy to see why Byron's humor was often
misapprehended. "His letters abound with jests and jeux d'esprit, which were often taken
seriously as admissions of an immoral character" (L'Estrange 187). Edwin Sturzl notes that
Byron's double vision allowed him to lead the reader's mind in a particular direction, and
then twist it back on itself, as when he wrote about a writer that "he had written much
blank verse, and blanker prose." Byron also wrote about "four Honourable Masters, whose
/ Honour was more before their names than after" (Sturzl 18). There was a sting barb of
satire in much of Byron's writing. X. J. Kennedy quotes the following poem written by
Byron:
          Who killed John Keats?
          "I," said the Quarterly,
          So savage and Tartarly,
          "'Twas one of my feats." (Kennedy 157)
          "English Bards and Scotch Reviewers, A Satire" (1809) is a satire in the Eighteenth-
Century mode. Here Byron assesses the literary merit of English poets and critics in a way
that is reminiscent of Pope's Dunciad (Riley 192). Childe Harold's Pilgrimage, A Romaunt
(1812) contains little or no humor. What it does contain, however is a sweeping
perspective, interrupted by prolonged and cynical meditations about particular scenes or
particular characters, a style that would later be developed in Byron's most effective satire,
Don Juan (Riley 193). Byron wrote to his friend Thomas Moore that in the third canto of
Childe Harold he was "half mad during the time of its composition." He was so mad in
fact, that on many a "good day" he could have blown his brains out, except for the thought
that this might have given pleasure to his mother-in-law (Riley 194).
          Manfred, A Dramatic Poem (1817) is a poetic drama with vivid paradoxes. The
title character is a magician who wants to escape from the inevitable contradictions of
human life (Riley 194). Byron's first effective satire was Beppo, A Venetian Story (1818).
Hugh Walker notes that here, as in Don Juan (1819-1823), "the story is the smallest part

of the piece. It is merely a peg on which to hang the poet's humorous and satirical criticisms of life" (263). Beppo mocks the inconsistent Venetian moral code and in fact mocks human inconsistency in general. Byron is despondent as he writes, "My pen is at the bottom of a page, / Which being finished, here the story ends; / 'Tis to be wished it had been sooner done, / But stories somehow lengthen when begun" (Riley 195).

Byron was himself something of a "Don Juan." "The women adored him. He was young (just twenty-four), spectacularly handsome, aristocratically pale, a genuine Lord, the proprietor of the 'Gothic pile' of Newstead Abbey, haughty and aloof in manner, his charm enhanced by a deliciously terrifying reputation for evil. What more could they ask?" (Wright 71). But Byron's style changed dramatically from the serious writing of his early poems to the less serious writing of Don Juan. Byron explains this transition in Don Juan.

> As a boy, I thought myself a clever fellow,
>   And wish'd that others held the same opinion;
> They took it up when my days grew more mellow,
>   And other minds acknowledged my dominion.
> Now my sere fancy "falls into the yellow
>   Leaf," and Imagination droops her pinion,
> And the sad truth which hovers o'er my desk
> Turns what was once romantic to burlesque.
> (Canto IV, Stanza 3)

In an article entitled, "Old Gentlemanly Vice: Humorous Metaphors of Aging in Byron's Don Juan," Deborah Gutschera suggests that Byron uses the contrast between youth and age as a distancing device in Don Juan. She indicates further that, "the imagery he uses to underline this contrast reveals Byron's characteristic strategy as a humorous poet: He combines an occasional use of new and unusual metaphor with the regular use of metaphors which are familiar and conventional, and which derive their comic effect from the ironic, often inappropriate, context in which they are placed" (74). Between youth and old age, there is middle age, which Byron attacks rather ferociously:

> Of all the barbarous ages, that
>   which is most barbarous is the middle age
> Of man! It is--I really scarce know what;
>   But when we hover between fool and sage. (Gutschera 73)

In Don Juan (pronounced "Jew-on"), Byron presents European civilization as being thoroughly decadent and irredeemable. Don Juan, the "hero" is more acted upon than acting. Byron calls Don Juan an "epic satire" because he wanted his readers to see this piece as part of the epic tradition. Byron planted reminders like "my poem's epic" in some of the most farcical passages to suggest that "a slapstick epic was the only sort possible for his own degraded era." Don Juan begins with a seventeen-stanza "Dedication" to Robert Southey, the Poet Laureate of England during Byron's time, and to Southey's fellow "Lake Poets," William Wordsworth, and Samuel Taylor Coleridge. Byron's lines are in the spirit of "English Bards and Scotch Reviewers," but they are highly satiric (Riley 195). Don Juan assaults not only poets, but also scientists, philosophers, politicians, critics, and other people who wrote public discourse. It is written in "ottava rima," which requires that the first sestet be in an ABABAB rhyme scheme thereby encouraging, or sometimes almost forcing word play to happen. This is partly because of the rhyme scheme itself, and partly because the rhythm of the ballad, which this is very close to, is often a vehicle for humor in English poetry. Furthermore, the stanzas require resourcefulness; this type of stanza lends itself to wit rather than to sustained philosophical commentary (Riley 196).

Don Juan is not an epic; rather it is a mock epic in the tradition of the "picaresque," a satiric form that goes back several centuries in European literature (Riley 197). This picaresque narrative is built around a series of adventures encountered by a wanderer (Don

Juan). These adventures or episodes are "clearly designed to reveal the hypocrisy and vanity of human behavior." Nevertheless, the hero "remains idealistic in the face of all human venality." Don Juan is thus written in the tradition not only of Miguel Cervantes's Don Quixote, but also in the tradition of such eighteenth century picaresque satires as Henry Fielding's Tom Jones, Tobias Smollett's Roderick Random, François Voltaire's Candide, and especially of Lawrence Sterne's Tristram Shandy. In these picaresque novels, the protagonist has no real character of his own, but rather acquires his character from his ever-changing environment. In an 1823 conversation with Lady Blessington, Byron said, "If I know myself, I should say, that I have no character at all...I am so changeable, being everything by turns and nothing long." Thus the main character in Byron's Don Juan is very much like Byron himself (Riley 198).

Don Juan supports Suzanne Langer's contention that in "The Comic Rhythm" "it is the nature of comedy to be erotic, risqué, and sensuous if not sensual, impious, and even wicked" (O'Connor 74). In the beginning of Don Juan, the reader meets Donna Inez, Don Juan's mother. Her sexually vigorous and unfaithful husband, Don José, has died, and she vows to make Don Juan as different from his father as possible. Therefore, she does everything in her power to sap Don Juan of his vitality. "She makes sure he learns dead languages, abstruse sciences, and useless arts; she exposes him to literature expurgated of every hint of sexuality; and above all, she shields him from every fact of 'natural history.' She wishes him to be moral: in other words, to be docile and sexually repressed" (O'Connor 74). Robert O'Connor interprets Don Juan in the following way:

> The convention of comic renewal has, in fact, been turned on its head, and what Byron expresses in the opening cantos of Don Juan is the comic message reversed. In normal comedy, the sexual triumph of the virile young man is a figurative representation of the vigorous health of humanity; an occasional, temporary sickness may occur, but the life force at the heart of man's existence will ultimately reassert itself, and all will be well. The view of Don Juan exactly contradicts this. Mankind is unregenerate and society incurably corrupt. The enemies of vitality and freedom are in control of man's fate, and the life force, although it may achieve its temporary victories, is too weak to bring about a true rejuvenation. (75)

The name "Don Juan" is therefore intended to be interpreted ironically, since Don Juan is meant to be "the comic spirit in defeat, the power of rejuvenation in a world that refuses to be renewed" (O'Connor 76). In the second canto, Don Juan is ship-wrecked and is discovered by Haidée on the beach. When he regains consciousness, he gazes up into Haidée's eyes, but although these are the eyes of an angel, he nevertheless at the same time longs for a beefsteak (McCartney 67-68). Hugh Walker notes that in the harem cantos, Byron "simply wallows in vice," adding that "in the moral sense they are radically bad" (276). Such scenes were so frequently misunderstood that on October 10th of 1822, Byron wrote a letter to his publisher, John Murray, saying that "Don Juan will be known by and by, for what it is intended--a Satire on abuses of the present states of society, and not a eulogy of vice" (Walker 276).

In Don Juan, the protagonist is at first presented as a heartless rake, but it later becomes clear that he is a hapless victim of circumstances. Byron said that Don Juan was intended to be "a little quietly facetious about everything" (Wright 74). This is consistent with the satires which Byron wrote for Blackwood's which treated "well-nigh with equal derision the most pure of virtues, and the most odious of vices" (Wright 75). Byron considers Don Juan to be a "jocose burlesque." Northrop Frye interprets Don Juan as a "comic acceptance of the world rather than a satiric rejection of it" (Beaty 147).

Austin Wright notes that in Don Juan there are echoes of Alexander Pope's The Rape of the Lock and The Dunciad, but in Wright's opinion, the poem is even more closely related in style to Henry Fielding's Tom Jones. "There is the same mock-heroic burlesque, the same fondness for witty and sardonic digression on the characters in the story and on human follies and vices; and both Byron's hero and Fielding's are more the victims of seduction than the architects of it, good-hearted lads who fall into error through impulse rather than viciousness" (74).

Don Juan was written in "ottava rima," which employs six lines rhyming alternately and a final couplet providing the opportunity for a satiric thrust, for an ironic anticlimax, for a deflating surprise, or for a comic double or triple rhyme (Wright 75). Byron's effectiveness in the use of this form can be seen in a stanza of Canto I in which the first four lines are lifted from the works of Robert Southey, poet laureate to George III. Southey's sentimental lines were written as part of a command-performance in celebration of the marriage of Princess Charlotte, and aesthetically, they are patently absurd.

> Go, little book, from this my solitude!
> I cast thee on the waters--go thy ways!
> And if, as I believe, thy vein be good,
> The world will find thee after many days.

This is followed by Byron's reaction to Southey's "poetry":

> When Southey's read, and Wordsworth's understood,
> I can't help putting in my claim to praise--
> The first four rhymes are Southey's, every line:
> For God's sake, reader! take them not for mine! (Wright 78)

One of the techniques which Byron uses for satiric effect is inconsistency:

> At one moment the agony of a woman's heart--at the next, the fripperies and trivialities of feminine daintiness. In the same spirit the pathos of Juan's farewell to Spain is made ridiculous by his sea-sickness. It is by such juxtapositions that Byron barbs his satire; the root of his cynicism is the doctrine that the petty, the contemptible and the base will always be found close to the heroic and the pathetic. (Walker 271)

Byron had difficulty figuring out an ending for Don Juan, so he wrote to John Murray, his publisher, that he had been unable to finish the poem. "I had not quite fixed whether to make [Juan] end in Hell, or in an unhappy marriage, not knowing which would be the severest" (Wright 79). With the possible exception of Robert Burns, Hugh Walker considers Byron to have been the author most successful in the intermingling of satire with pure poetry and irony and wit (Walker 268).

Byron's The Vision of Judgement, Suggested by the Author of Wat Tyler, Liberal (1822) is an ottava rima satire containing 106 stanzas in which Lucifer is arguing with Michael the Archangel outside the gates of Heaven about what should happen to the soul of George III of England, who had died just two years earlier (Riley 200). The Vision of Judgement also satirizes Southey's panegyric which has the same title (Walker 264). Since Southey had made himself the official panegyrist of the king, Byron considered Southey to be an equally legitimate target of his satire (Wright 265). The Vision of Judgement employs a wide range of satirical tools, one after another--jibing, irony, humor, invective, and contempt. "and they alternate with passages of a tempestuous imagination" (Previté-Orton 202). James Kingsley notes that Southey's A Vision of Judgement is purely emotive, while Byron's version is consistently ironic (Kingsley). The middle of stanza 96 reads, "He [Southey] meant no harm in his scribbling; 'twas his way / Upon all topics; 'twas, besides, his bread, / Of which he buttered on both sides" (Kingsley 204).

In his various satires, Lord Byron appears to target bad writing, the lusts of an old queen, and the inert minds of his native peers but in truth he almost always has the same target--language. He is fascinated by cant, and he is also fascinated by multiple senses and duplicity of meaning.

Byron is attracted to cant because of its curious connections with satire. To begin with, the modes of cant and satire are exact mirror-images of each other. A rhetoric designed to conceal while seeming to reveal is met and countered by a rhetoric designed to expose, to be so incisive that it not only finds all the membranes in the façade but opens them up with varying degrees of gentility and gentleness. Cant and satire are modes of language which lock into place with each other because each is all that the other is not. Together they make a whole.... (Garber 36)

Frederick Garber explains Byron's preoccupation with cant by suggesting that the chief tool of satire is irony, and he adds that irony, like cant, is "heavily dependent on duplicity. In both there is a structure in which surface utterance and depth of intention stand at variance with each other" (36). Garber considers irony to be just as "double-dealing" as is cant, but with irony the doubleness <u>must</u> show through, whereas with cant it <u>cannot</u> show through (37). Byron considers satire to be the complement of cant, "standing against it in symmetrical opposition. Irony is the parody of cant, mimicking the order of its duplicitous cousin" (Garber 37).

In a letter to Thomas Moore, Byron said that he is not the misanthropical and gloomy person which most people take him to be. Rather, he describes himself as "a facetious companion, as loquacious and laughing as if I were a much cleverer fellow" (Wright 74). It was nevertheless Byron who said, "If I laugh, 'tis that I may not weep" (Levin 9). Frederick Garber considered both Lord Byron and Thomas Moore to have been "ferociously witty" about Viscount Castlereagh's ineptness in the use of metaphor, especially his inability to resolve tenors and vehicles or to follow a metaphor through to its logical conclusion (39-40). Byron also wrote that Samuel Taylor Coleridge was often "explaining metaphysics to the nation," but then he adds, "I wish he would explain his Explanation" (Wright 77).

Byron used as much care in choosing his format of writing as he did in the language that he chose. The form which Byron chose for three of his "most highly esteemed" satiric works, Beppo, The Vision of Judgement, and Don Juan, is the ottava rima. William Tenant first used this poetic form in English, and Hugh Walker credits Frere with inspiring Byron to use it humorously (Walker 260-261). According to Frederick Beaty, this discovery gave Byron an outlet for his "natural exuberance" (Beaty 14). The stanzaic format of six alternately rhyming lines ending with a couplet "provides opportunity for satiric thrust, for ironic anticlimax, for deflating surprise, for comic double and triple rhymes" (Wright 75). The ottava rima also allowed Byron to mix sentiment with satire; the two-part form is perfect for changing mood abruptly and providing what is known as "Byronic irony" (Beaty 6). Lord Byron wrote satirical works ranging from the comical Beppo (1818) to the serious Don Juan (1824), but the general consensus is that his best poem was The Vision of Judgement (1821)(Kingsley 170).

George Gordon, Lord Byron Bibliography

Beaty, Frederick L. Byron the Satirist. DeKalb, IL: Northern Illinois University Press, 1985.
Cunningham, John. The Poetics of Byron's Comedy in Don Juan. Salzburg, Austria: Institut für Anglistik und Amerikanistik, 1982.
Garber, Frederick. "Self and the Language of Satire in Don Juan." Thalia: Studies in Literary Humor 5.1 (1983): 35-44.
Gutschera, Deborah A. " 'Old Gentlemanly Vice'--Humorous Metaphors of Aging in Byron's Don Juan." WHIMSY 2 (1984): 73-74.

Kennedy, X. J. Tygers of Wrath. Athens, GA: University of Georgia Press, 1981.

Kingsley, James, and James T. Boulton. "The Vision of Judgement." English Satiric Poetry. London, England: Edward Arnold, 1966, 169-208.

L'Estrange, Alfred Gu. History of English Humour. New York, NY: Burt Franklin, 1878.

Levin, Harry. Playboys and Killjoys. New York, NY: Oxford Univ Press, 1987.

McCartney, Robert. "The Parody of Universal Analogy in Death's Jest-Book by Beddoes." WHIMSY 2 (1984): 67-69.

O'Connor, Robert H. "Sexuality without Renewal: The Undoing of the Comic Metaphor in the Opening Cantos of Byron's Don Juan." WHIMSY 2 (1984): 74-76.

Previté-Orton, C. W. "The Elevated Satire of the Nineteenth Century." Political Satire in English Poetry. New York, NY: Russell and Russell, 1968, 193-232.

Ridenour, George M. The Style of "Don Juan." New Haven, CT: Yale University Press, 1960.

Riley, Terrance. "Lord George Gordon Byron." Encyclopedia of British Humorists, Volume I. Ed. Steven H. Gale. New York, NY: Garland, 1996, 190-202.

Schmid, Thomas H. Humor and Transgression in Peacock, Shelley, and Byron. Lewiston, NY: The Edwin Mellen Press, 1992.

Sturzl, Edwin A. Stylistic Media of Byron's Satire. Salzburg, Austria: University of Salzburg, 1982.

Thackeray, W. M. The English Humorists, Charity and Humour, The Four Georges. London, England: Dent, 1912.

Walker, Hugh. "The New Satire: Burns and Byron." English Satire and Satirists. New York, NY: J. M. Dent, 1925, 252-277.

Wright, Austin. "The Byron of Don Juan." Six Satirists. Ed. Austin Wright. Pittsburgh, PA: Carnegie Mellon University Press, 1965, 69-84.

Theodore Edward Hook (1788-1841)

Theodore Hook's father was a music composer, and Theodore's first employment was writing songs for his father. He became very proficient as a composer, and at parties he would sit down at the piano and extemporize two or three hundred lines of humorous remarks about everyone present. At one of these parties Sir Roderick Murchison was present, and he wondered if Hook would be able to bring his name into a rhyme. Hook immediately composed the following couplet:

And now I'll get the purchase on,
To sing of Roderick Murchison.... (L'Estrange 196-197)

Hook would be introduced to new guests, and would be given their names and their occupations or some other salient facts about them, and he would not hesitate in composing such lyrics as the following:

Next comes Mr. Winter, collector of taxes,
And you must all pay him whatever he axes;
And down on the nail, without any flummery;
For though he's called Winter, his acts are all summary. (L'Estrange 197)

In view of such verses, it is ironic that Hook also wrote cautionary verses against punning, such as

My little dears, who learn to read, pray early learn to shun,
That very silly thing, indeed, which people call a pun. (L'Estrange 197)

The Soldier's Return; or What Can Beauty Do? (1805) is a comic opera in two acts. Exchange no Robbery; or, The Diamond Ring (1820) is a comedy in three acts. And Killing no Murder (1809) is a farce in two acts which ran for thirty-five performances.

This play was controversial because of its ridicule of the Methodists, so a law was passed whereby the objectionable lines were omitted. Hook figured out a way to get around the law, however. He merely distributed the printed copies of the suppressed scene to members of the audience (Parascandola 541).

In Sayings and Doings (1824-1828), Hook was able to create a number of striking humours characters. In the second series of Sayings and Doings (1825), for example, Mrs. Rodney from "Passion and Principle" was described as "a lady exemplary and domestic," who was "as methodical and mechanical in all her movements, as if she had been wound up at seven o'clock in the morning to go through certain evolutions until eleven o'clock in the evening" (Parascandola 541).

The works which Hook wrote after 1833 utilized farce more heavily than did his earlier works, and his subjects shifted from the aristocracy to the middle classes, whom he generally cast in a rather unfavorable light. Gilbert Gurney (1836) is probably Hook's best work. It is a string of anecdotes, some of which are autobiographical. Hook's stories include many real-life people, such as George Gordon Lord Byron and Richard Brinsley Sheridan. In one scene, Sheridan loses a play that had been sent to him for his comments. Sheridan apologizes to the author for losing the play, and then shows the author a drawer stuffed with other plays that have been sent to him for his comments. He offers the playwright any three plays that he has been sent in consolation for the piece which he has lost (Parascandola 541).

Hook had a sharp wit, and he was an animated story teller. His combination of humor and realism had an effect on the writings of Charles Dickens, William Makepeace Thackeray, and Anthony Trollope. Samuel Taylor Coleridge went so far as to claim that Hook was "as true a genius as Dante" (Parascandola 542). But A. J. A. Symons notes that Hook was a troubled man: "The punning, the gambling wit, the reckless jester, the madcap boon-companion, was a circumscribed and self-tormented moralist. True, he never married, though once at least he might have won beauty and companionship. But if he did not marry, neither did he desert his mistress" (Symons 127). Symons did not consider Hook to be a wit, but he did consider him to be very witty. The point that Symons is making here is that the power of Hook's jests, puns, and improvisations was based on the rapidity of thought and expression. Wits, on the other hand were noted for the didactic weight of their epigrams (Symons 147).

Alfred Gu L'Estrange notes that there is a kind of polite social satire which runs through all of Hook's works. He also notes that Hook's best humor was political, and reflected Hook's strong Tory leanings (L'Estrange 198-199). Hook frequented the coffee room of The Athenaeum, and he usually sat in a particular corner of this room, from which he would make jokes, and rhymes, and repartees. And whenever he wanted to refresh himself with some brandy or gin, he would call out for "another glass of toast and water," or "a little more lemonade." Because of this, the corner where Hook sat became known as "Temperance Corner" (Symons 126).

Theodore Edward Hook Bibliography

L'Estrange, Alfred Gu. "Theodore Hook, Sydney Smith, Thomas Hood, et al." History of English Humour. New York, NY: Burt Franklin, 1878, 196-206.

Parascandola, Louis J. "Theodore Edward Hook." Encyclopedia of British Humorists, Volume I. Ed. Steven H. Gale. New York, NY: Garland, 1996, 540-543.

Symons, A. J. A. "Theodore Hook." English Wits. Ed. Leonard Russell. London, England: Hutchinson, 1940, 125-148.

Thomas Ettingsall (c1790-1850) IRELAND

See Nilsen, Don L. F. Humor in Irish Literature: A Reference Guide. Westport, CT: Greenwood, 1996.

Joseph O'Leary (c1790-c1850) IRELAND

See Nilsen, Don L. F. Humor in Irish Literature: A Reference Guide. Westport, CT: Greenwood, 1996.

Jeremiah O'Ryan (c1790-1855) IRELAND

See Nilsen, Don L. F. Humor in Irish Literature: A Reference Guide. Westport, CT: Greenwood, 1996.

Frederick Marryat (1792-1848)

The Naval Officer: or, Scenes and Adventures in the Life of Frank Mildmay (1829) is a series of adventures that are based on Marryat's life at sea. On the sea, death may come at any time, so there is a grim side to the humor in Marryat's novels. In The Naval Officer there is a scene in which a well-dressed man is walking along a beach, and the captain of a ship in the distance orders his men to fire a gun as a test. As a joke, the gunners aim at the man on the beach knowing that there is very little chance they could hit such a small target. They do hit him, however, and the ball cuts him in two. It is Frank Mildmay, the protagonist, who recounts the story and then tells us that the book which the man had been reading before he was hit was Ovid's Metamorphoses (Parascandola 726).

As the title implies, Peter, the protagonist in Peter Simple (1832-1833) is an Innocent; nevertheless much of the humor in this novel is rather ribald. When Peter encounters a prostitute, he is unaware of her profession. "I had arrived opposite a place called Sally Port, when a young lady, very nicely dressed, looked at me very hard and said, 'Well, Reefer, how are you off for soap?' I was astonished at the question, and more so at the interest she seemed to take in my affairs. I answered 'Thank you, I am very well off; I have four cakes of Windsor, and two bars of yellow for washing'" (Parascandola 726).

Japhet has an obsession in Japhet, in Search of a Father (1836), and that obsession is to find his father. But his monomania often leads him on false quests. At one point, for example, he follows a bishop around because the Bishop's nose resembles his own, and he therefore concludes that the Bishop might be his father. Eventually, Japhet finds his father, who is by now a wealthy retired general from India. After the two of them have a somewhat farcical argument, Japhet wins his father over (Parascandola 726).

According to Louis Parascandola, Mr. Midshipman Easy (1836) abounds in lighthearted humor and puns. "Mr. Nicodemus Easy was a gentleman who lived down in Hampshire: he was a married man, and in very easy circumstances. Most couples find it very easy to have a family, but not always quite so easy to maintain them" (Parascandola 727). In Percival Keene (1842), Keene has a teacher who threatens his students with a "blow-up" if they make him too angry. It is ironic, then, when Keene sets fire to some fireworks near the teacher, and he actually does "blow-up," but in a very different sense from the one he had predicted (Parascandola 727).

Frederick Marryat Bibliography

Parascandola, Louis. "Frederick Marryat." Encyclopedia of British Humorists, Volume II. Ed. Steven H. Gale. New York, NY: Garland, 1996, 725-728.

Percy Bysshe Shelley (1792-1822)

Along with Byron, Shelley was considered a "fellow-poet of the Satanic school." Shelley wrote very little specific satire; however he loved to make general denouncements of aspirations. His truest satire is The Mask of Anarchy. It has "admirable qualities of imagination and style (Previté-Orton 213). Shelley also wrote such comic satires as Swellfoot the Tyrant, but these are "dreary failures." "He was only at home in higher realms of the imagination, where he himself seems to move, a 'glorious phantom,' among the dreams he created (Previté-Orton 215).

"To Wordsworth" is one of Shelley's most amusing works. It is Shelley's response to the poems of William Wordsworth, and was originally written as a letter to addressed to Wordsworth himself circa 1815. The first quatrain is in the form of a sonnet, and it reads:

> Poet of Nature, thou hast wept to know
> That things depart which never may return;
> Childhood and youth, friendship and love's first glow
> Have fled like sweet dreams, leaving thee to mourn.

Here Shelley is implying that Wordsworth is ignorant of the ways of the world (Coleman 483). In analyzing this poem, Julia Taber reminds the reader:

> We must remember that the focus in the Romantic Period was the connection with God, nature, memory and remembrance. Here Shelley is telling Wordsworth that memory means nothing, remembrance means nothing, everything departs and it should be left at that instead of dwelling on complex harmony. He should move on and find realistic tranquility. (qtd. in Coleman 483).

Shelley is telling Wordsworth to "wake up and smell the coffee," as can be seen in his concluding couplet, "Deserting these, thou leavest me to grieve, / Thus, having been, that thou shouldst cease to be" (Coleman 483). Here Shelley is mocking Wordsworth by not using the "language of real men," but instead by using such words as "shouldst" and "leavest," words which Wordsworth passionately detested (Taber 4-5).

Percy Bysshe Shelley Bibliography

Coleman, Elliott. Poems of Byron, Keats, and Shelley. Garden City, NY: Doubleday, 1967.
Previté-Orton, C. W. "The Elevated Satire of the Nineteenth Century." Political Satire in English Poetry. New York, NY: Russell and Russell, 1968, 193-232.
Schmid, Thomas H. Humor and Transgression in Peacock, Shelley, and Byron. Lewiston, NY: The Edwin Mellen Press, 1992.
Taber, Julia. "Irony among the Romantics." Unpublished Paper. Tempe, AZ: Arizona State University, 1997.

William Maginn (1793-1842) IRELAND

See Nilsen, Don L. F. Humor in Irish Literature: A Reference Guide. Westport,

CT: Greenwood, 1996.

William Carleton (1794-1869) IRELAND

See Nilsen, Don L. F. Humor in Irish Literature: A Reference Guide. Westport, CT: Greenwood, 1996.

Charles O'Flaherty (1794-1828) IRELAND

See Nilsen, Don L. F. Humor in Irish Literature: A Reference Guide. Westport, CT: Greenwood, 1996.

Thomas Carlyle (1795-1881) SCOTLAND

Carlyle considered humor to be a characteristic of the highest order of mind. According to Carlyle, a man could be a "humorist" only if he possessed the creative gift that is the "special characteristic of genius" (Lilly 5). Much of the appeal of Carlyle's The History of Frederick the Great is that it is written in the style of a comedy of humours (Lilly 123).   According to William Lilly, Carlyle was "eminently human," and it was this humanness that made his work of value, for without it he would not have been so "acutely sensitive, so hasty in temper, and so quick to express his grievances, real or imaginary" (Lilly 119).   Lilly considers Carlyle to be a humorist "in the fullest sense of the word." Carlyle uses his humor to gain insights and inspiration that allows him to make accurate prophecies. His humor allows him to correctly read and interpret the signs of his times (Lilly 123-125).   Carlyle uses his humor to expose the political and social lie which he describes as the right of all men, whatever their capacity or incapacity, to an equal share of political power. He also uses humor to expose the lie of economic systems that promises the greatest happiness to the greatest number of people (Lilly 152). Carlyle took the ironic stance that human freedom is attainable only in obedience to laws which respect the nature of things, and that the only real liberty a person has is the freedom to find one's appointed work in the world and to do it (Lilly 158). Carlyle agreed with Socialists in believing that work is a social function and a social trust. He did not believe that the economic benefits of hard work should be "scrambled for by the law of the strongest, law of supply-and-demand, law of Laissez-faire, and other idle laws and unlaws" (Lilly 163).
Sartor Resartus: The Life and Opinions of Herr Teufelsdrockh (1836) is a satire which is both earnest and comic at the same time.   Sartor Resartus has many levels of humor and incongruity as the basis for its "structure," a structure that is derived in large part from James Beattie's An Essay on Laughter and Ludicrous Composition (1776) (Athey 210). It is also based on Johann Wolfgang von Goethe's statement that can be translated to "true humour springs not more from the head than from the heart." Using Beattie and Goethe as sources, Carlyle therefore wrote his Sartor Resartus not in the tradition of social corrective humor that would later be developed by George Meredith, but rather in the tradition of "comedy of incongruity."   Sartor Resartus thus contains neologisms, Germanisms, intentional misspellings, appositions, inversions, out-of-place Biblical injunctions, and "an imperative rhetoric that parallels its torrent of ideas and combative spirit." Carlyle called this style of writing "a kind of Satirical Extravaganza on Things in General." Sartor Resartus is a biography of Professor Diogenes Teufelsdrockh whose name means "God-born Devil's-excrement." He teaches at the University of Weissnichtwo,

which means "Know-not-where." Sartor Resartus is an allegory on clothes. It is also a parody on scholarship written in a mock-heroic prose style. It contains such outrageous visual images as when the Duke of Windlestraw addresses a naked House of Lords in Chapter 9 of Book 1 (Athey 211).

Carlyle's characters are very much like those in a Dickens novel. They include the Duke of Windlestraw, Sir Jabesh Windbag, Mr. Facing-both-ways (a name first used in John Bunyan's Pilgrim's Progress), and Viscount Mealymouth. Sir Windbag is described in Chapter 14, Book 3 as "a Columbus minded to sail to the indistinct country of Nowhere" (Athey 211). The Duke of Windlestraw is also a character in Past and Present (1843). Another character in this novel is the hatter that is found in the Strand of London. Instead of making better felt hats than other hatters make, this hatter decides to make a single huge lath-and-plaster hat that is seven-feet high and must therefore be mounted on wheels (Athey 211).

Leslie Stephen considered Carlyle to be largely responsible for the belief in the necessity of having a sense of humor. "His humour is so genuine and keen and his personality so vigorous that he has fairly bullied us into accepting this view" (Stephen 319). Robert Martin suggests that Stephen's point is ironic, for he makes the following statement about Carlyle: "Yet those qualities most antithetic to true humour--priggishness, platitude, belief in cliques--have never flourished more vigorously" (Martin 86). But although Carlyle's humor is somewhat enigmatic and paradoxical for Martin, it is possible to resolve the incongruities. "All the Romantic and Victorian distrust of the intellect is implicit in Carlyle's praise of 'true humour', which 'springs not more from the head than from the heart; it is not contempt, its essence is love; it issues not in laughter, but in still smiles, which lie far deeper' " (qtd. in Martin 28). Martin says that Thomas Carlyle, and probably George Eliot as well, considered humor to be reflective of the imagination. For them it was one of the more creative forms of comedy, a form which penetrated more deeply than wit into the meaning of subjects that were being considered (Martin 37).

Joel Athey considers Thomas Carlyle's tone to be unsettling. His writing contains Biblical injunctions such as "For the night cometh wherein no man can work," and irony, as in "Is it possible to have god-ordained priests?" and sarcasm, as in "his university the worst, except of course England's." Carlyle's style and tone are so distinct that he can be easily parodied. Carlyle was parodied in Punch magazine. And in Anthony Trollope's The Warden (1855), Carlyle was Dr. Pessimist Anticant. Probably the best Carlyle parody appears in the "Oxen of the Sun" episode of James Joyce's Ulysses. Many of Charles Dickens's eccentrics are grounded in Carlyle, and Carlyle referred to his own writing as "this piebald entangled hyper-metaphorical style of writing, not to say of thinking" (Athey 212).

Thomas Carlyle Bibliography

Athey, Joel. "Thomas Carlyle." Encyclopedia of British Humorists, Volume I. Ed. Steven H. Gale. New York, NY: Garland, 1996, 209-213.

Lilly, William Samuel. "Thomas Carlyle: The Humourist as Prophet." Four English Humorists of the Nineteenth Century. London, England: Norwood, 1978, 117-175.

Martin, Robert Bernard The Triumph of Wit: A Study of Victorian Comic Theory. Oxford, England: Clarendon, 1974.

Stephen, Leslie. "Humour." Cornhill Magazine 33 (March, 1876): 318-326.

Tennyson, George. "Parody as Style: Carlyle and His Parodists." Carlyle and His Contemporaries Ed. John Clubbe. Durham, NC: Duke University Press, 1976.

Thomas Chandler Haliburton (1796-1865) CANADA

Although Thomas Haliburton spent most of life in Nova Scotia, Canada, he was strongly attached to Britain, and was more at home in England than in Canada. In addition, most of his books were written for a British audience (Panofsky 495).

Haliburton is best known for having created the character of Sam Slick, a Yankee clock salesman who is constantly uttering "wise saws," and "soft sawder," and who has a keen grasp of "human natur" (Panofsky 496). In the nineteenth-century, Thomas Haliburton's Sam Slick rivaled Charles Dickens's Sam Weller in popularity. Like Charles Dickens's Mr. Pickwick and Sam Weller, Sam Slick encountered many eccentric characters, regional dialects, and interesting episodes. Like Dickens, Haliburton used a sophisticated narrative technique to entertain and engage his readers (Panofsky 497).

The Clockmaker; or The Sayings and Doings of Samuel Slick, of Slickville (1837) is a picaresque novel of episodic sketches filled with humor, satire, and irony. Sam Slick had two foils, the Squire Poke, and the Reverend Hopewell, both of whom articulated the imperialistic views of God. Sam Slick was, then, an American, traveling through the Maritime provinces and selling his clocks to arrogant Blue Noses. "He could visit Nova Scotia, offer scathing commentary, partake in controversial political discussion, temper it with flattery, and leave comfortably to return upon his next whim." In the process, Sam Slick presented many contradictions, sly witticisms, aphorisms, epigrams, and metaphors in making his political points about the British: "Whoever gave them [the British] the name of John Bull, knew what he was about, I tell you; for they are bull-necked, bull-headed folks, I vow; sulky, ugly-tempered, vicious critters, a-pawin' and a-roarin' the whole time." But in spite of this apparent criticism of Britain and her colony, the Sam-Slick series upheld the virtues of imperialism.

> The Clockmaker beguiled the English with its praise of their country. While British readers would feel superior to the Nova Scotians whom Slick derided, they could enjoy the entertainment and elucidation provided by the work. Conversely, American readers would take a certain pride in Slick's ambition and intelligence. They too, would feel superior to the colonial neighbors and would not loathe Slick's exploitation of the Nova Scotians. (Panofsky 497)

The character of Sam slick figured into many of Thomas Haliburton's novels. He is in The Attache; or, Sam Slick in England (1843-1844), and in Sam Slick's Wise Saws and Modern Instances; or, What He Said, Did, or Invented (1853), and also in Nature and Human Nature (1855). But Thomas Haliburton wrote other humorous works as well, including The Letter Bag of the Great Western; or, Life in a Steamer (1840), and The Season-Ticket (1860). The Letter Bag is an epistolary telling of a steamship voyage, and it was probably influenced by Tobias Smollett's The Expedition of Humphry Clinker (1771). Haliburton's The Old Judge; or, Life in a Colony (1849) is a series of sketches which is nostalgic in tone. It is filled with quiet understatement, and some realism, and is about Stephen Richardson, a native Nova Scotian. Richardson is droll, and is filled with inexhaustible good humor. He is quick in perception, and also quite shrewd (Panofsky 498). The development of the Nova Scotian Stephen Richardson helps to explain the great irony of Thomas Haliburton's humorous writing. In his day, Haliburton was rejected by his fellow Nova Scotians because he had treated them so harshly, and because he published his books in England, wrote them for a British audience, and was considered to be a "British humorist." Ironically, however, today Haliburton is regarded by Canadian scholars as "the foremost nineteenth-century writer of histories, political tracts, and fiction" (Panofsky 498).

Thomas Chandler Haliburton Bibliography

Blair, Walter, and Raven I. McDavid, Jr. "Thomas Chandler Haliburton." The Mirth of a
    Nation: America's Great Dialect Humor. Minneapolis, MN: University of Minnesota
    Press, 1983, 11-16.
Engle, Gary. "Thomas Chandler Haliburton." Encyclopedia of American Humorists. Ed.
    Steven H. Gale. New York, NY: Garland, 1988, 189-191.
Haliburton, Thomas Chandler, ed. Traits of American Humor, by Native Authors, 3
    Volumes, London, England: Colburn, 1852.
Nilsen, Don L. F. "Thomas Chandler Haliburton." Humor in American Literature: A
    Selected Annotated Bibliography. 48-49.
Panofsky, Ruth. "Thomas Chandler Haliburton." Encyclopedia of British Humorists,
    Volume I. Ed. Steven H. Gale. New York, NY: Garland, 1996, 495-499.
Waldron, Edward E. "Thomas Chandler Haliburton." Dictionary of Literary Biography,
    Volume 11: American Humorists, 1800-1950. Ed. Stanley Trachtenberg. Detroit,
    MI: Gale, 1982, 169-175.

James Robinson Planche (1796-1880)

Peter Hall suggests that James Planche's burlesque "Extravaganzas" are an important
(but often ignored) transition between the burlettas of the eighteenth century, such as John
Gay's The Beggar's Opera (1728), and the comic operas of the late nineteenth century,
such as Gilbert and Sullivan's HMS Pinafore (1878). The gentle satire, and the plain
comedy of Planche's Extravaganzas mark them as clear antecedents of the light opera of
the 1870s and 8880s (Hall 864). One of the important clues of the importance of Planche's
writings is the effect that they had on other writers. When Gilbert wrote a burlesque of
Donizetti's opera L'elisir d'Amore entitled, Dulcamara, or the Little Duck and the Great
Quack (1866), Gilbert was pleased that it was favorably compared to the writings of
Planche.

Planche's Amoroso, King of Little Britain: A Serio-Comick Bombastic Operatick
Interlude in One Act (1818) uses both verse and song to burlesque the tragedy and opera
of the theatrical repertoire of Planche's time. Shakespeare's Hamlet is parodied when
Roastanda enters and says, "Ah! Coquentinda slain!--Die tyrant die!" and stabs the king.
Then she asks, "Who falls the next?" The King answers, "You, sir, as well as I" as he
stabs the Cook, and dies." Then Roastanda says, "I'm pepper'd--Nature fades upon my
sight, I go, I toddle, so might sir, good night," and dies (Hall 864).

James Robinson Planche Bibliography

Fletcher, Kathy. "Aristophanes on the Victorian Stage: J. R. Planche's Adaptation of 'The
    Birds.'" Theatre Studies 26.7 (1980): 89-98.
Fletcher, Kathy. "Planche, Vestris, and the Transvestite Role: Sexuality and Gender in
    Victorian Popular Theatre." Nineteenth Century Theatre 15.1 (1987): 9-33.
Hall, Peter C. "James Robinson Planche." Encyclopedia of British Humorists, Volume II.
    Ed. Steven H. Gale. New York, NY: Garland, 1996, 862-865.
MacMillan, Dougald. "Planche's Early Classical Burlesques." Studies in Philology 25
    (1928): 34-45.

Joseph Augustine Wade (1796-1845) IRELAND

See Nilsen, Don L. F. **Humor in Irish Literature: A Reference Guide.** Westport, CT: Greenwood, 1996.

Samuel Lover (1797-1868) IRELAND

See Nilsen, Don L. F. **Humor in Irish Literature: A Reference Guide.** Westport, CT: Greenwood, 1996.

Henry Labouchere (1798-1869)

One day Henry Labouchere was sitting in his London Club, talking loudly and candidly with his friend James McNeill Whistler. Whistler was amused at Labouchere's performance; however there was an old gentleman near-by who overheard Labouchere's observations, and strongly objecting to their tone he arose and with a reddened face and announced that he could bear such comments no longer. "Young man, I knew your grandmother." At that point, Labouchere also arose, and responded, "Perhaps, sir, I have the honour of addressing my grandfather" (Pearson 178).

Henry Labouchere's wit was natural and unforced, and an integral part of his personality from childhood to old age. It appeared in his writings, his speeches, and especially in casual social intercourse. "When he wrote of his own variegated adventures it was with an engaging air of taking the reader into his special confidence" (Hadley 237). Labouchere was trained and performed as an actor, and "when he ceased to be an actor the need for self-expression ceased, and he was unlikely to feel any call to amuse a posterity that would not amuse him." He therefore never bothered to collect the articles he wrote for his own paper, Truth, nor did he bother to revise his articles; that would have bored him. He did, however, write a series of "Labby" stories which were quite witty (Hadley 237-238).

Labouchere also had a number of witty encounters with various people. There is a story that one morning as a child he made an illicit visit to Town, and happened to meet his father in the Strand.

> Once, when strolling in the Strand, he came face to face with his father, who exploded with indignation and demanded the reason for his absence from the University. Altering his normal expression and looking as little like himself as possible, Henry assured his parent that it was a case of mistaken identity and walked on. But he took care to leave by the next train to Cambridge, which his father also caught. At journey's end he jumped from the carriage and dashed out of the station, being discovered by his irate parent some minutes later surrounded by books, his brow furrowed with studious application. (Pearson 164)

On another occasion, a proctor caught Labouchere walking arm in arm with a lady of pleasure. When he was asked to account for his company, he said she was his sister. The proctor didn't buy Labouchere's story, and shouted with indignation that she was one of the most notorious courtesans in the town, but Labouchere looked saddened and responded, "I know that, sir, but is it kind to throw my family misfortunes in my face?" (Pearson 165).

On still another occasion, Labouchere was taking an examination, and the proctors were suspicious that he was cheating. One of the proctors asked to see what Labouchere was constantly looking at which was located beneath his blotting paper. Labouchere was reluctant to reveal what was underneath, but was given a peremptory order to do so, at which point he produced a photograph of a music-hall "star," at the same time explaining that "her beauty inspired him to persevere with his work" (Pearson 165).

Labouchere was conservative in his leanings, and was one of the staunchist opponents of votes for women. His reputation in this regard became well known, and a delegation of two ladies searched him out in his hotel room in Northampton, and Labouchere received them in his sitting room. Each lady in turn stated the reasons why women should have the vote, and Labouchere listened with total attention, considering each of their points very carefully. Then there was a period of silence, and Labouchere turned toward the ladies, leaned forward, and murmured, "Pretty dears!" (Hadley 252-253).

On the day before he died, Labouchere was lying in his bed, and Thorold (his nephew and biographer) was sitting beside him. There was a spirit lamp burning beside the bed, and this was accidentally overturned and caused a small fire. Labouchere opened his eyes, muttered the words, "Flames?--not yet I think", laughed, and went back to sleep. He died the next day (Hadley 255).

Henry Labouchere Bibliography

Hadley, W. W. "Henry Labouchere." English Wits. Ed. Leonard Russell. London, England:
    Hutchinson, 1940, 237-255.
Pearson, Hesketh. Lives of the Wits. New York, NY: Harper and Row, 1962.

Thomas Hood (1799-1845)

Thomas Hood's themes include infidelity, physical disabilities, family relations, inebriation, and bodily handicaps (Brummer 536). Nevertheless, Hood is chiefly remembered as a humorist; in fact, he is one of the notable figures in the humor tradition (Henkle "Hood" 190). According to Roger Henkle, Hood was cheerful, funny, compassionate, and resilient. He was an excellent illustration of the old expression that "great men of humor lead lives of melancholia and tragedy." In Hood's poetry there is evidence of the intensity of his anguish. His poems tend to be "somber, impassioned pleas against the injustice of the hard lot of common folk" (Henkle "Hood" 188). Hood's humor was morbid, but there was also a jaunty comic disjunction, and constant word play, and shifts of register, all of which reflect the slippage in Victorian urban discourse and some of the social processes underlying that slippage. Roger Henkle wrote an article entitled, "Comedy as Commodity: Thomas Hood's Poetry of Class Desire," in which he investigated the "...topical stories, news events, and patterns of life, recasting them into a formulaic "story" such as that of the ballad, and then situating them in the cultural continuum. Hood, like the others in his circle--Jerrold, the early Punch group, and Dickens--is highly reflexive, always on the lookout for shifts in the wind" (Henkle "Comedy" 306).

"A Discovery in Astronomy" is a satiric poem in which Hood gently chides the astronomers of his day (Brummer 537). The "Discovery" which Hood has made is that the spots on the sun have resulted from the fact that the sun is so hot that it has "freckled" itself. Hood is not afraid to approach delicate subjects in his poetry. His "Tim Turpin," is subtitled "A Pathetic Ballad," and it deals with blindness.

> Tim Turpin he was gravel blind
> And ne'er had seen the skies:
> For Nature, when his head was made,
> Forgot to dot his eyes. (Brummer 538).

"Mary's Ghost" is about a ghost who appears before "young William" because grave robbers have dismembered her body for scientific purposes. This poem shows Hood's tendency for the macabre and the grotesque:

> Don't go to weep upon my grave,
> And think that there I be;
> They haven't left an atom there,
> Of my anatomie. (Clubbe 86)

Humor was a very important element in Thomas Hood's "Song of the Shirt" and "Address of the Laundresses to the Steam Washing Company." "Song of the Shirt" was based on a police report in the Times about a wretched seamstress named Biddell who had a "squalid, half-starved infant at her breast." This lady was hauled before a magistrate because she had illegally pawned some of her piece-work materials in order to obtain bread for herself and her children (Henkle "Comedy" 307).

Humor was also an important element in Hood's "Drop of Gin," which contains the following verse:

> Gin! gin! a drop of gin!
> What magnified monsters circle therein,
> Ragged and stained with filth and mud,
> Some plague-spotted, and some with blood. (L'Estrange 202)

About "Faithless Nelly Gray, A Pathetic Ballad" Roger Henkle remarked, "The reader delights in the poem as in a plaything: in the way it 'works' so cleverly, is so neatly put together, and yet carries out its symbolic operations on such a relatively simple level" (Henkle "Comedy" 304). The careful structuring of Hood's poetry to get maximal comic effect, and the linguistic playfulness of his very-dark humor can be seen in verses 1, 5, 7-8, 11-12, and 13-14.

> Ben Battle was a soldier bold,
>> And used to war's alarms;
> But a cannon-ball took off his legs,
>> So he laid down his arms!
>
> But when he called on Nelly Gray,
>> She made him quite a scoff;
> And when she saw his wooden legs,
>> Began to take them off!
>
> Said she, "I loved a soldier once,
>> For he was blythe and brave;
> But I will never have a man
>> With both legs in the grave!
>
> Before you had those timber toes,
>> Your love I did allow,
> But then, you know, you stand upon
>> Another footing now!"
>
> "O, false and fickle Nelly Gray!
>> I know why you refuse:--
> Though I've no feet--some other man
>> Is standing in my shoes!
>
> I wish I ne'er had seen your face;
>> But, now, a long farewell!
> For you will be my death:--alas!

You will not be my Nell!"

Now when he went from Nelly Gray,
    His heart so heavy got--
And life was such a burthen grown,
    It made him take a knot!

So round his melancholy neck,
    A rope he did entwine,
And, for the second time in life,
    Enlisted in the Line! (Henkle "Comedy" 303-304)

In this poem the singsong lightheartedness of the form is contrasted with the brutal humor
of the subject (Henkle "Hood" 189).

Even darker and more witty than "Faithless Nelly Gray" is a poem entitled, "Sally
Simpkin's Lament." In this poem, John has been spurned by Sally because he is too fat,
and Sally is lamenting the fact that her lover, in attempting to drown himself, has been
bitten in two by a shark. In this poem, John is pleading with Sally.

"You know I once was all your own,
    But now a shark must share!
But let that pass--for now, to you
    I'm neither here nor there.

"Alas! death has a strange divorce
    Effected in the sea,
It has divided me from you,
    And even me from me!" (Henkle "Comedy" 308)

The ending of the poem is especially dark, and especially humorous:

"But now, adieu--a long adieu!
    I've solved death's awful riddle,
And would say more, but I am doomed
    To break off in the middle!" (Clubbe 98-100)

Henkle remarks that dismemberment, violent death, and morbid, disintegrating self-pity set
the tone for Hood's poems. "Their obsession with the macabre as the site of wit and thus
of intellectual engagement signals an intensity that has not been modulated" (Henkle
"Comedy" 309).

Thomas Hood's literary reputation is based mainly on a comic verse which
"crackles with puns often playing upon grotesqueries of dismemberment, and that produces
jolting shifts of register" (Henkle "Comedy" 301). Hood had an important influence not
only on Lewis Carroll, Edward Lear, and W. S. Gilbert, but also on the poets who wrote
for Punch and the New Yorker. Hood was the compiler and principle author of his Comic
Annual, which ran from 1829 until 1839. It is through this work that he became known
as the "quintessential topical comic writer, who could run any current social event through
the gamut of puns and witty turns of the phrase" (302). Hood's humor was grounded in
pain. He had a rheumatic heart, and he suffered medical complications as well, which put
him out of action for long periods of time. Late in life he said, "No gentleman alive has
written so much Comic and spitted so much blood" (Henkle "Comedy" 302).

Hood's Comic Annual is a collection of humorous verse and prose which for ten
years was characteristically published around Christmas time. By 1844 he was editing and
writing his own humorous magazine entitled Hood's Monthly Magazine and Comic
Miscellany, in which many of his comic poems appeared, carrying direct social messages.

These poems were a series of odes which "assailed the earliest expressions of Victorian cant, self-aggrandizement, and narrow social or religious prescription; and this is where a long poem entitled "Miss Kilmansegg and Her Precious Leg" appeared, a poem which satirized the crassness of the nouveau riche, and a prototype for the nonsense verse of Lewis Carroll, W. S. Gilbert, Edward Lear, and C. S. Calverly that would follow. Hood's poem "displays one of the most curious conflicts of tone and content in English literature" (Henkle 188).

Hugh Wood considers Hood's Miss Kilmansegg and her Golden Leg to be the "best satirical poem of the nineteenth century after Byron" (Walker 280). In the poem, Miss Kilmansegg is the daughter of one of the richest men in England. Banker, the horse she is riding, shies at the sight of a city beggar in rags, bolts, runs amok, and damages Miss Kilmansegg's leg. As an artificial leg, Miss Kilmansegg will accept only one made out of solid gold, and this makes her the most sought-after damsel in the Western world. She has to reject suitor after suitor, until she is finally approached by a foreign Count, who is hounded by his creditors, and who in desperation seizes Miss Kilmansegg's golden leg, and during a struggle, he bashes her head in (Henkle "Comedy" 312). This is a poem about class differences, a poem in which the satire is skillfully blended with the humor, and "the fantastic rhymes and puns rather show up than hide the depth of feeling and the seriousness of the thought." The poem targets the love of wealth as an end in itself, as distinct from the love of wealth as a means towards an end. Miss Kilmansegg is buried under mountains of wealth. "By Gold her spirit is stifled in infancy; her last sleep on earth is filled with dreams of 'golden treasures and golden toys,' and the crash of the Golden Leg upon her skull ends her life. Vanity of vanities!" (Walker 280).

Hood's A Sentimental Journey from Islington to Waterloo Bridge, in March, 1821 was influenced by Laurence Sterne's Sentimental Journey through France and Italy by Mr. Yorick (1768). Ross Brummer considers this work to be "amusing" (Brummer 538). Odes and Addresses to Great People (1825) is the first book-length compilation of Thomas Hood's comic poetry; it was co-authored by Thomas Hood and John Hamilton Reynolds, Hood's brother-in-law. It was in the poems of this compilation that Hood became famous for his wonderful use of the pun. Whims and Oddities (1826) is the second book-length compilation of Hood's comic poetry. The comic verse of this collection soon became Hood's trademark, and of course the pun was his most potent tool. In his ballad to Sally Brown, he wrote:

> His death, which happened in his berth,
> At forty-odd befell:
> They went and told the sexton, and
> The sexton toll'd the bell (Clubbe 80)

"The Last Man" in Whims and Oddities was described by a reviewer for Blackwood's Edinburgh Magazine as "a sort of absurd sailor-like insolent ruffian, sitting with arms a-kimbo, cross-legged and smoking his pipe on the cross-tree of a gallows (Reid 75). Ross Brummer says that this poem "anticipates the more modern black, or sick, humor popular in America today" (Brummer 536).

Hood's National Tales is said by Ross Brummer to contain stories that have "Gothic, romantic, tragic, comic, and moralistic concepts." His Tylney Hall is considered by Brummer to be well liked for its humorous content. Brummer considers Hood's Literary Reminiscences (1839) to be "pleasant, witty, and light." In Hood's "Johnsoniana" (1833), and in his "Queries in Natural History" (1839), and "Speculations of a Naturalist" (1839), the puns are rampant, and can be illustrated by "an Oyster is very anomalous, because you must take it out of its bed before you can tuck it in!." In both "The Schoolmistress Abroad: An Extravaganza" (1839) and "Fishing in Germany" (1840), there are again "ample morsels of Hood's humor" (Brummer 538).

During his lifetime, Thomas Hood was often associated with comic journals. He published a great deal of his work in The Comic Annual (1830-1839), and this gave him the grounding to establish Hood's Own which was very popular in his day, and influenced the comic output of a number of important authors of his day. Hood was also the first editor of Punch which lasted from Hood's day until its demise in 1992. Because of all of Thomas Hood's punning, Lloyd Jeffrey refers to, "A Lively Hood for a Livelihood" (Jeffrey 68), and Ross Brummer continues, "What better epitaph can one have for a man who, like William Shakespeare, dignified the pun and made it respectable?" (Brummer 540).

Thomas Hood Bibliography

Brummer, Ross. "Thomas Hood." Encyclopedia of British Humorists, Volume I. Ed. Steven H. Gale. New York, NY: Garland, 1996, 535-540.

Clubbe, John. Selected Poems of Thomas Hood. Cambridge, MA: Harvard University Press, 1970.

Henkle, Roger B. "Comedy as Commodity: Thomas Hood's Poetry of Class Desire." Victorian Poetry. 26.3 (1988): 301-318.

Henkle, Roger B. "Hood, Gilbert, Carroll, Jerrold, and the Grossmiths: Comedy from Inside." Comedy and Culture--England--1820-1900. Princeton, NJ: Princeton University Press, 1980, 185-237.

Jeffrey, Lloyd N. Thomas Hood. New York, NY: Twayne, 1972.

L'Estrange, Alfred Gu. "Theodore Hook, Sydney Smith, Thomas Hood, et al." History of English Humour. New York, NY: Burt Franklin, 1878, 196-206.

Reid, J. C. Thomas Hood. London, England: Routledge and Kegan Paul, 1963.

Walker, Hugh. English Satire and Satirists. New York, NY: J. M. Dent, 1925.

Rev. Thomas Hamblin Porter (c1800-c1890) IRELAND

See Nilsen, Don L. F. **Humor in Irish Literature: A Reference Guide.** Westport, CT: Greenwood, 1996.

Winthrop Mackworth Praed (1802-1839)

C. W. Previté-Orton notes that some of Praed's light satires are like earlier ballads and that others are somewhat modern in tone. Praed's poetic satire is filled with humor, wit, and good sense, and is preëminently English in nature. Although there is some foreign influence, the motives, purposes, and ideals of Praed's satires are all drawn on national circumstances; furthermore, it developed in close conjunction with the development of the political party system (236).

Winthrop Mackworth Praed Bibliography

Previté-Orton, C. W. Political Satire in English Poetry. New York, NY: Russell and Russell, 1968.

Edward George Earle Bulwer-Lytton (1803-1873)

According to Scott Rice, Edward Bulwer-Lytton was a prolific Victorian novelist and all-round man of letters. During his lifetime, he was second in popularity only to Charles Dickens. "He has been an inspiration to generations of untalented writers, the most famous of whom is Snoopy in the Peanuts comic strip. It was Bulwer-Lytton in his novel Paul Clifford (1830) who introduced the notorious opening line, "It was a dark and stormy night." This is, of course, the line with which Snoopy always opens his novels" (Rice, 1984, viii). "The enmity to Bulwer had begun in the early 1830s in circles associated with Fraser's Magazine--notably including Thackeray. In curiously bitter attacks, these critics had expressed irritation with Bulwer's personality, his dandy mannerisms, and the pompous seriousness with which he took his literary vocation." They considered what Bulwer-Lytton did to be "vulgar sensationalism" (Christensen 82-83).

William Makepeace Thackeray was always fascinated by the works of Bulwer-Lytton. He was annoyed by Bulwer-Lytton's snobbish Francophilia and forced elegance in Pelham (1828). He also disliked the presumptuous invented dialogue between great historical figures and literary figures in Bulwer-Lytton's fiction, and the glorification of vice in Bulwer-Lytton's portrayal of the glamorous criminal. "All of these Bulwerisms are exaggerated and ridiculed in George de Barnwell, but the most amusing and telling aspect of the parody is Thackeray's imitation of Bulwer-Lytton's style which seeks at the same time to be dramatic and philosophical, sublime and picturesque, classical and modern--all things to all readers" (Kiely 161). Thackeray parodies Bulwer-Lytton's inflated language, his meaningless strings of abstractions, his apostrophes, and his forced alliterations by presenting them in a long string of clichés. Thackeray suggests that Bulwer-Lytton is "writing in the mock-heroic vein without knowing it" (Kiely 161).

In Pelham; or, The Adventures of a Gentleman (1828), Bulwer-Lytton's hero is an attractive dandy whose adventures comically expose some of the foibles of men in nineteenth-century English society.   Pelham was such a successful novel that the protagonist's wearing of black as the color of his evening dress revolutionized European men's fashion. The protagonist in Pelham only pretended to be flippantly trivial, and that is one of the clues that Pelham is a satire; the novel conveyed the impression that fashionable dandyism was an absurdity. It is on this level, however, that Henry Pelham's adventures and the amusing outrageousness of many of the remarks in the book can still delight today's readers (Christensen 77).

Paul Clifford (1830), like Pelham, stirred some controversy, and this controversy added to its commercial success. In the case of Paul Clifford, Bulwer-Lytton even encouraged the controversy by implying that there were many parallels between eighteenth-century highwaymen and nineteenth-century politicians. The difference was that politicians were able to conceal their moral corruption with civilized appearances and manners (Christensen 78).

Bulwer-Lytton's The New Timon (1846) is one of the few long poems in the nineteenth century which is an attempt at satire. It is a satire of literature, of the laws of England, of England's social system, and above all, it is a satire of the evils of the factory system. But it is more than a satire; it is a romance as well, as can be seen by the subtitle, "A Romance of London," and the romantic tone weakens the satire. Hugh Walker suggests that the poem "is sentimental and gushing, and gush and sentimentality will no more mingle with satire than oil with water" (Walker 279).

In is in Lucretia; or, The Children of Night (1846) that Bulwer-Lytton views each country to actually be two countries that are hostile to each other, much like the "Two-Nations" dichotomy of Disraeli; here Bulwer-Lytton coins the terms "the haves," and "the have nots," and says that of these two, the ruling-class haves may be the guiltier nation, but both nations are made up of "craftily selfish and unscrupulous predators" (Christensen 81).

Between 1849 and 1858, Bulwer-Lytton published three "Caxton" novels. The first was The Caxtons: A Family Picture (1849); the second was "My Novel," by Pisistratus Caxton: or, Varieties in English Life (1852); and the third was What Will He Do With It? by Pisistratus Caxton (1858). In the three Caxton novels, Bulwer-Lytton conveyed his own good-humored sympathy for ordinary people in spite of their flaws and absurdities. He wanted to strengthen the latent humanity and tolerance of his readers. The Caxton novels are comical in tone. They are intended to counteract the Marxist doctrine, and other doctrines that were breeding class hatreds; they were intended to heal the fragmentations that earlier tragic novels had caused (Christensen 83).

The Coming Race (1871) is a utopian satire which tells about a new race that is peaceful but appallingly materialistic. It is a classless race that stresses harmonious integration with the physical environment. Bulwer-Lytton must have thought that sensitive and thoughtful people must lose the "motive-power" necessary to life (Christensen 84).

Edward George Earl Bulwer-Lytton Bibliography

Christensen, Allan C. "Edward Bulwer-Lytton." Victorian Novelists Before 1885. Eds. Ira
     B. Nadel and William E. Fredeman. Detroit, MI: Gale, 1983, 73-87.
Kiely, Robert. "Victorian Harlequin: The Function of Humor in Thackeray's Critical and
     Miscellaneous Prose." Veins of Humor. Ed. Harry Levin. Cambridge, MA: Harvard
     University Press, 1972.
Rice, Scott, ed. Bride of Dark and Stormy: Yet More of the Best (?) from the Bulwer-
     Lytton Contest. New York, NY: Penguin, 1988.
Rice, Scott, ed. It Was a Dark and Stormy Night: The Best (?) from the Bulwer-Lytton
     Contest. New York, NY: Penguin, 1984.
Rice, Scott. Son of "It Was a Dark and Stormy Night": More of the Best (?) from the
     Bulwer-Lytton Contest. New York, NY: Penguin, 1986.
Walker, Hugh. English Satire and Satirists. New York, NY: J. M. Dent, 1925.

Gerald Griffin (1803-1840) IRELAND

See Nilsen, Don L. F. **Humor in Irish Literature: A Reference Guide**. Westport, CT: Greenwood, 1996.

Douglas William Jerrold (1803-1857)

Richard Kelly points how much Douglas Jerrold borrows on previous fiction to develop the satires and ironies, and the grotesque flavor of his own works (Kelly Works 97). Jerrold live in a time of extreme patriotism, of comic defiance, of some unreasonable authority, of sentimental values, of the triumph of virtue over vice, of crime, and of grotesque humor (Worth 580). Richard Kelly felt that between 1842 and 1848, Jerrold was "the unrivalled genius of comic journalism" (Kelly Best 5). Jerrold's writings for Punch were very biting, creative, and funny. Jerrold contributed to Punch in its running jokes, its short parodies, its cartoons, its reviews, and its miscellanies. Jerrold's longer fiction tended to be episodic, satiric, and fantastic. He wrote to amuse, but he also wrote to draw attention to abuses and injustices (Worth 581).

After many years of writing farces under contract to various theatre managers, and after having developed an abiding sense of the social injustices imposed by the higher classes on the lower classes, Douglas Jerrold became one of the founders of Punch. His satiric assaults on received ideas and on the sanctified institutions of the Victorian

Establishment were constant (Henkle 102). In <u>Punch</u>, Jerrold wrote a series entitled, "Mrs. Caudle's Curtain Lectures," which were written in the Victorian tradition of "Comedy of Ordinary Living Experiences." As a moralist, Jerrold was interested in the nature of social relationships. He wrote about the pressures of class and position, and about the tensions experienced by an ordinary man living an ordinary life (Henkle 219). "Mrs. Caudle's Curtain Lectures" are the harangues of a lower middle-class housewife, Mrs. Caudle, who meets her hapless spouse every night at bedtime. Her primary grievance is that Mr. Caudle insists on having a pint each evening at the neighborhood pub with some of the boys. Mrs. Caudle doesn't like the idea of sitting around "like Cinderella by the ashes whilst her husband can go drinking and singing at a tavern." One of the more ludicrous flaps occurs when Mr. Caudle joins the Masonic Order and Mrs. Caudle "writhes in anguished speculations of what must go on in 'secret' meetings." Henkle notes the irony that "there could hardly be a more socially conservative way to take one's 'mysteries' than in lodge meetings" (Henkle 222).

During Jerrold's times, public hangings were common in order for the fates of the condemned to be "morally instructive," and Jerrold responded as follows:

> If we might suggest an enlargement of Newgate hospitalities, we could propose that all ladies admitted to the condemned sermon should be invited to behold the galvanic battery applied to the corpse of the murderer as early as possible after execution. Certain we are that the exhibition would be equally interesting, equally pleasurable to the nervous system.... And more, what a wholesome, moral fillip it would give them, if, at midnight, they were to attend the burial of the assassin, and, to show their horror of his deeds, were to cast within his humblest, unsanctified grave, a handful or so of lime.... They would--bless their delicacy!--scatter their lime, as the <u>Queen</u> in <u>Hamlet</u> scatters the flowers upon <u>Ophelia</u>'s tomb--with the same tenderness, the same pathos! ("Old Bailey" 240)

It was Jerrold's method to carry the outrage to its furthest extreme in order to penetrate the thick hides and thick skulls of his contemporaries (Henkle 103).

One critic said that every jest of Jerrold's was "a gross incivility made palatable by a pun," but Alfred Gu L'Estrange believes that this is not true, though L'Estrange does admit that "as a humourous writer he is almost unique in his freedom for verbal humour" (208). Along with Gilbert A-Beckett and Mark Lemon, Douglas Jerrold was one of the founders of <u>Punch,</u> which was a periodical designed to expose all kinds of hypocrisy, and fraud. Another function of <u>Punch</u> was to attack the strongholds of Toryism (L'Estrange 208).

In <u>Mr. Paul Pry</u> (1827), Jerrold translates the ordinary comedy of John Poole into an energetic and funny farce by expanding Poole's leit-motif phrase for Paul Pry, which is "I hope I don't intrude." This catch phrase is so extended that it helps Jerrold to develop Paul Pry as a "grotesquely memorable caricature" (Worth 579).

<u>Black Ey'd Susan: or All in the Downs</u> (1829) is a melodrama in which a man named William protects the virtue of his wife by giving a drunk and jovial sailor a black eye. The husband later finds out that the man he hit is not only a Captain in the Royal Navy, but is the husband's commanding officer. The punishment for William's action is death, and a gruesome execution ceremony follows. But at the darkest point in this drama it is discovered that some time ago William had asked for a discharge from the Navy, and his request had been granted, and in fact, his request had been granted before his unfortunate altercation, so he was not, after all, guilty of a capital offense (Worth 580).

Part of the development of the satire of <u>The Rent Day</u> (1832) comes from the comic characterization of Bullfrog, the bailiff, who is successful in his job, but unsuccessful in his courtship. The phrase that is very often heard from his lips is "Business is business"

(Worth 580). Bubbles of the Day (1842) is a farce which sardonically comments on the emptiness of London society. Here there are a number of effective caricatures, and some clever deceptions, as well as frequent asides (Worth 580). Punch's Letters to His Son and Punch's Complete Letter Writer (1842) is a witty parody of Lord Chesterfield's Letters. It satirizes the hypocrisy, the self-interest, and the worldly wisdom of modern life by saying such things as "My son, in conclusion, it is well to drink from your own bottle; but it is still better to drink from another man's" (Kelly Works 472). Punch's Complete Letter Writer (1844) contains letters which are mostly comic. An example is the letter from a home-owner which is designed to check the references of a servant, and the letter from a servant which is designed to check the references of the potential employer (Worth 581).

Mrs. Caudle's Curtain Lectures (1845) are warm and comically inventive. They are also filled with sympathy for ordinary human frailties. Mrs. Caudle's Curtain Lectures are designed to amuse at the same time as they expose the audience's prejudices. They contain many familiar stereotypes, such as the hen-pecked husband. Many of his jokes are good examples of casual sexism: "Women are all alike. When they are maids they're as mild as milk: once make 'em wives, and they lean their backs against their marriage certificates and defy you." It may be true that Mrs. Caudle is a figure of fun as she engages in her nightly tirades. But it is also true that she is bigger than life, and that her sheer presence makes her "memorably triumphant" (Worth 582).

Jerrold's The History of St. Giles and St. James (1845) is filled with quaint and humorous moralizing. St. James, in his brocade, is contrasted with St. Giles in his tatters (L'Estrange 209). Jerrold's Mrs. Robinson Crusoe is a rather obvious burlesque or parody of Daniel Defoe's Robinson Crusoe. One clue to the parody is that Robinson Crusoe has been changed to Mrs. Robinson Crusoe; also, Robinson Crusoe's Bible has been changed to the Complete Art of Cookery in Jerrold's version. Like the original Robinson Crusoe, Mrs. Robinson Crusoe does a debit-and-credit column of her situation. In the "Evil" column she has, "I am thrown upon a desert island without a blessed soul to speak to," and "I am singled out to be a single woman, when I might have been a wife and a parent." In the "Good" column she has "Then I have this consolation--there's nobody to scandalize me," and "I might have been married early to a brute, and been a grandmother at eight and thirty" (Kitchin 277).

The satiric target of A Man Made of Money (1849) is the entire world of consumerism. The man of the title was able to tear £100 notes off from his body. "Truly he was a Man made of Money. Money was the principle of his being; for with every note he paid away a portion of his life" (Kelly Works 80). The "Jenkins Papers" (published posthumously in 1859) are described by Christopher Worth as pompously reporting on fashionable society "through exaggeration, burlesque, and heavily ironic commentary" (Worth 582).

Jerrold was able to keep his friends or his fellow writers in fits of laughter over long periods of time. The regular editorial meetings of Punch, for example, were frequently dominated by Jerrold's stream of witticisms. He said things like, "Dogmatism is puppyism come to full growth," or "jokes are the luxury of beggars; men of substance can't afford them" (Worth 582). Jerrold's prose freely utilized grotesque imagination, fantasy, satire, parody, and vicious verbal humor. Jerrold used comic parody, satire, caricature, and wit to expose hypocrisy, poverty, and exploitation. Many of Douglas Jerrold's contemporaries considered Jerrold to have been one of the wittiest people they had ever met. But his wit served a serious purpose as well (Worth 583).

Douglas William Jerrold Bibliography

Henkle, Roger B. "Hood, Gilbert, Carroll, Jerrold, and the Grossmiths: Comedy from

Inside." Comedy and Culture--England--1820-1900. Princeton, NJ: Princeton University Press, 1980, 185-237.

Henkle, Roger B. "Peacock, Thackeray, and Jerrold: The Comedy of 'Radical' Disaffection." Comedy and Culture--England--1820-1900. Princeton, NJ: Princeton University Press, 1980, 58-110.

Jerrold, Douglas. "Old Bailey Holidays." Punch 11: 240.

Jerrold, W. Blanchard, ed. The Wit and Opinions of Douglas Jerrold. London, England: W. Kent, 1859.

Jerrold, Walter, ed. Bons-Mots of Charles Lamb and Douglas Jerrold. London, England: J. M. Dent, 1893.

Jerrold, Walter. Douglas Jerrold, Dramatist and Wit, 2 Volumes. London, England: Hodder and Stoughton, 1914.

Jerrold, Walter, ed. Douglas Jerrold and "Punch." London, England: Macmillan, 1910.

Kelly, Richard M. ed. The Best of Mr. Punch: The Humorous Writings of Douglas Jerrold. Knoxville, TN: University of Tennessee Press, 1970.

Kelly, Richard M. The Works of Douglas Jerrold. New York, NY: Twayne, 1972.

Kitchin, George. Survey of Burlesque and Parody in English. London, England: Oliver and Boyd, 1931.

L'Estrange, Alfred Gu. "Douglas Jerrold." History of English Humour. New York, NY: Burt Franklin, 1878, 207-215.

Worth, Christopher G. "Douglas William Jerrold." Encyclopedia of British Humorists, Volume I. Ed. Steven H. Gale. New York, NY: Garland, 1996, 579-585.

James Clarence Mangan (1803-1849) IRELAND

See Nilsen, Don L. F. **Humor in Irish Literature: A Reference Guide**. Westport, CT: Greenwood, 1996.

Benjamin Disraeli (1804-1881)

Hesketh Pearson notes that by the age of twenty Benjamin Disraeli had already dropped both the apostrophe from his surname (D'Israeli), and the study of law, saying, "The Bar: pooh! law and bad jokes till we are forty; and then, with the most brilliant success, the prospect of gout and a coronet." Disraeli wanted to become great, and he believed that in order to enter high society a person needed to be born well, have a million pounds, or be a genius (144).

Since Disraeli wasn't born especially well, and didn't have a million pounds sterling, he decided to develop his genius. Disraeli lived in the great age of burlesque, an age which George Kitchin describes as follows: "We are now approaching the great age of burlesque--burlesque of the ballad and legend chivalrous, and burlesque of the classical drama or legend. The mock classical play was indeed to make the fortunes of several managers and actors at the Haymarket, culminating as it did in the capital fun of the Savoy operas" (Kitchin 268). Disraeli was burlesquing the classics when he wrote Ixion in Heaven. Ironically, William Aytoun was offended by Disraeli's burlesque, and Aytoun wrote a burlesque of Disraeli's piece which he called Endymion: or a Family Party of Olympus. Both Disraeli's Ixion, and Aytoun's Endymion describe the love of a mortal for a goddess; nevertheless, whereas Ixion was impudent and had langourous elegance, Endymion had an additional coarseness and modish impertinence, both of which signalled the parody form. According to George Kitchin, Aytoun was satirizing the language of society in his own day (Kitchin 268-269). Kitchin evaluates the two types of parodies: "If the classical mythology is to be burlesqued let it be in Disraeli's way, and if that species of burlesque is to be parodied, it cannot very well be in any other way than that adopted in Endymion; or a Family Party of Olympus" (Kitchin 269).

It was Thomas Peacock who developed the tradition of inserting real people as characters in his fiction, but Disraeli continued this tradition.   Croker in Disraeli's Coningsby is burlesqued by the intriguing and heartless politician Rigby. Disraeli also writes a severe burlesque of Thackeray in Ixion; the character's name is St. Barbe, and the character's development is viewed by many critics as revenge for Thackeray's earlier parody of Coningsby (Kitchin 275).

Disraeli had a reputation as a wit, and the following dialogue once took place between Benjamin Disraeli and William Gladstone:

> GLADSTONE: I understand, sir, that you are a witty fellow.
> DISRAELI: Some people are under that impression.
> GLADSTONE: I'm told that you can make a joke on any subject.
> DISRAELI: That is quite possible.
> GLADSTONE: Then I challenge you--make a joke about Queen Victoria.
> DISRAELI: Sir, Her Majesty is not a subject. (Espy 313)

Benjamin Disraeli Bibliography

Espy, Willard. Another Almanac of Words at Play. New York, NY: Clarkson N. Potter, 1980.
Kitchin, George. Survey of Burlesque and Parody in English. London, England: Oliver and Boyd, 1931.
Pearson, Hesketh. "Benjamin Disraeli." Lives of the Wits. New York, NY: Harper and Row, 1962, 143-162.

Rev. Francis Sylvester Mahony (1804-1866) IRELAND

See Nilsen, Don L. F. Humor in Irish Literature: A Reference Guide. Westport, CT: Greenwood, 1996.

Elizabeth Barret Browning (1806-1861)

Elizabeth Barret Browning was a faithful admirer of Napoleon III, as can be seen in her excellent satire entitled, An August Voice (Previté-Orton 221).

Elizabeth Barret Browning Bibliography

Previté-Orton, C. W. Political Satire in English Poetry. New York, NY: Russell and Russell, 1968.

Charles James Lever (1806-1872) IRELAND

See Nilsen, Don L. F. Humor in Irish Literature: A Reference Guide. Westport, CT: Greenwood, 1996.

Lady Dufferin (1807-1867) IRELAND

See Nilsen, Don L. F. Humor in Irish Literature: A Reference Guide. Westport, CT: Greenwood, 1996.

Mark Lemon (1809-1870)

Mark Lemon said about himself, "I was made for Punch and Punch was made for me." Mark Lemon's humor was rather thin, like loading the first part of a poem entitled "Taking the Veil" with images of "vespers," and "melting into the night," and "fading from human sight," but then, someone shouts, "Policeman, here's a wench," and the policeman comes and arrests the lady because she has been shoplifting. Another of Lemon's poems, "Songs for the Sentimental" (1840) is about a young man who tells his love that his refusal to dance is not because he lacks passion for her, but is rather because he has broken his "braces." Lemon's writing is hearty, jolly, and sentimental to a fault. But even though Lemon's humor and wit were not overly sophisticated, he nevertheless had the ability to surround himself with writers whose humor and wit were indeed sophisticated. Craig Howes said, that although Lemon was "not especially witty himself," as editor of Punch he had to be the cause of wit in other men (Howes 653). John Andrew Hamilton described Mark Lemon as follows: "In person robust, handsome, and jovial, humorous rather than witty in his conversation, indefatigable and prolific in production" (Hamilton 910). According to Craig Howes, Mark Lemon lifted comic journalism "out of political vendetta and scurrility and up to the level of universal humor." It was largely because of Lemon that violent cruel humor, libelous attacks, and smut were now allowed in the pages of Punch (Howes 654).

Mark Lemon Bibliography

Fisher, Leona Weaver. Lemon, Dickens, and Mr. Nightingale's Diary: A Victorian Farce. Victoria, BC, Canada: English Literary Studies, 1988.
Fisher, Leona Weaver. "Mark Lemon's Farces on the 'Woman Question.'" Studies in English Literature: 1500-1900. 28 (1988): 649-670.
Hamilton, John Andrew. "Mark Lemon." The Dictionary of National Biography: From Earliest Times to 1900, Volume 11. Ed. Sir Leslie Stephen and Sir Sidney Lee. Oxford, England: Oxford University Press, 1922, 909-910.
Howes, Craig. "Mark Lemon." Encyclopedia of British Humorists, Volume II. Ed. Steven H. Gale. New York, NY: Garland, 1996, 650-656.
Lemon, Mark. The Jest Book. London, England: Macmillan, 1864.

Alfred, Lord Tennyson (1809-1892)

James Kincaid considers the central theme of Tennyson's major poems to be the conflict between the comic and the ironic modes. Kincaid considers no other nineteenth-century writer to be more responsive to the intense presence and distancing effect of the comic life, which makes life possible in its promise of continuity but at the same time turns the writing into a mockery of genuine life, because ironically, the masque of death is glimmering through the portrayal of life (3).
The Poems by Two Brothers and the volumes of 1830, 1832, and 1842 all

contain a few comic poems but show, in the main, a steady development toward more compact and rich ironic statement. Beginning with The Princess, however, and continuing through In Memoriam and Maud, Tennyson tries various and often unique comic strategies, only to return to irony in the late poems, and particularly in Idylls of the King, surely the major ironic work of art of the century. This development is neither simple nor pure--comic and ironic forms are used throughout his career--but the main outlines seem reasonably clear. (Kincaid 3)

James Kincaid considers In Memoriam to be Tennyson's version of The Divine Comedy. However, it entirely lacks "the total confidence and the resultant easy coherence of Dante's poem," because Tennyson is always "turning over the comic coin, seeing if the affirmation can stand its own negation. This ironic tendency in his comedy is both remarkable and unsettling" (Kincaid 10).

Tennyson juxtaposes antithetical and contradictory concepts in his development of ironic tension. He depicts

> dominant opposites which cannot be coordinated or made to cancel, but which demand equal and contradictory responses. The tension between the religious, hopeful symbol on the one hand, and the tragic or melancholic symbol on the other, marks the center of Tennyson's poetry, the point being that his irony is not merely gloomy, almost never simply macabre. The contraries exist together, as brothers, an early poem says, stealing "symbols of each other." (Kincaid 6)

Thus, Tennyson's ironic vision insisted on the paradox of alternate truths: "All Things Will Die," and "Nothing Will Die" (Kincaid 6).

Although irony doesn't dominate all of Tennyson's poems, it does dominate the early poems (up to 1842), and many of the later ones, especially Idylls of the King. Tennyson's middle period, however, is more concerned with transcendentalism than with irony. It was during this period that Tennyson said, "Nothing worth proving can be proven," and "Poetry is truer than fact." But James Kincaid feels that Tennyson's liberation was achieved not only by his ability to transcend but by his discovery of the possibilities of comedy as well. Tennyson found that comedy could provide a happy surprise. "Tennyson sought to forge a unique and lasting comic vision" (Kincaid 7).

C. W. Previté-Orton considers Tennyson to be the king of Victorian literature, and notes that he was a satirist as well, though he wrote only one true politic satire. This was entitled The Third of February 1852, and it was a political attack on the policies of Napoleon, though the argument of the attack did not conform totally to party lines (222).

Tennyson had a zest for experience which he himself expressed as follows: "Only one joy I know, the joy of life." But at the same time, Tennyson was obsessively preoccupied with death, the negative aspect of his insatiable life-zest that informed so much of his poetry His craving for immortality resulted in his leading a happy life: "Very little comedy is as dubious of its own affirmations as is Tennyson's. This very distrust, however, can make the affirmations all the more striking" (Kincaid 9).

Alfred, Lord Tennyson Bibliography

Gesali, Esteban Pujals. "En Defensa del Lector: 'The Charge of the Light Brigade,' de Tennyson, Pieza de Humor Negro." Literary and Linguistic Aspects of Humour. Barcelona, Spain: Univ of Barcelona Dept of Languages, 1984, 205-210.
Kincaid, James Russell. Tennyson's Major Poems: The Comic and Ironic Patterns. New Haven, CT: Yale University Press, 1975.
Previté-Orton, C. W. Political Satire in English Poetry. New York, NY: Russell and

Russell, 1968.

John Francis Waller (1809-1894) IRELAND

See Nilsen, Don L. F. Humor in Irish Literature: A Reference Guide. Westport, CT: Greenwood, 1996.

Sir Samuel Ferguson (1810-1886) IRELAND

See Nilsen, Don L. F. Humor in Irish Literature: A Reference Guide. Westport, CT: Greenwood, 1996.

Gilbert Abbott à Beckett (1811-1856)

George Kitchin considers Gilbert à Beckett's Comic History of England (and of Rome), and his The Comic Blackstone to have been written when à Beckett was at his best as a writer. They represent the time of boisterous merriment when Victoria ascended to the throne. These books are a very comical form of burlesques. There was a rumor at the time, probably started by Douglas Jerrold, that à Beckett had written a "comic Bible." This rumor was probably the result of Jerrold's remark that he "supposed that à Beckett would next write a parody of the Sermon on the Mount" (Kitchin 278).

In 1831 Gilbert Abbott à Beckett joined forces with Henry Mayhew to establish Figaro in London a very successful one-penny, four-page quarto magazine which came out every Saturday. Between 1831 and 1834 à Beckett was the editor (Galbreath 748). Along with Douglas Jerrold and Mark Lemon, Gilbert A-Beckett was one of the founders of Punch, which was a periodical designed to expose all kinds of hypocrisy, and fraud. Another function of Punch was to attack the strongholds of Toryism (L'Estrange 208).

Gilbert Abbott à Beckett Bibliography

Galbreath, Rebekah N. "Henry Mayhew." Encyclopedia of British Humorists, Volume II. Ed. Steven H. Gale. New York, NY: Garland, 1996, 747-752.
Henkle, Roger B. "Hood, Gilbert, Carroll, Jerrold, and the Grossmiths: Comedy from Inside." Comedy and Culture--England--1820-1900. Princeton, NJ: Princeton University Press, 1980, 185-237.
Kitchin, George. Survey of Burlesque and Parody in English. London, England: Oliver and Boyd, 1931.
L'Estrange, Alfred Gu. History of English Humour. New York, NY: Burt Franklin, 1878.

William Makepeace Thackeray (1811-1863)

Early in his writing career, Thackeray developed a great ability to establish a relationship with his audience, which would respond to him with laughing, sneering, or growling. He developed this ability by serving an extensive apprenticeship as a journalist and writer of comic sketches for The Morning Chronicle, Punch, The Corsair, Fraser's, and a number of other magazines, newspapers, and journals (Henkle 71). Thackeray wrote not only under his own name, but also under the pen names of Michael Angelo Titmarsh, Charles James Yellowplush, George Savage Fitzboodle, Jeames, Mr. Brown, and Theophile

Wagstaff. Robert Martin notes that the irony in Thackeray's novels was fine and astringent, and displayed a cool wit (Martin 81). Like Fielding and many other masters of irony, Thackeray started out as a parodist. For example, he wrote a burlesque poem entitled "Timbuctoo" in the undergraduate paper at Cambridge University named The Snob. This poem parodied Tennyson's prize poem, as can be seen in the first couplet:
                In Africa--a quarter of the world--
                The men are black, their locks are crisp and curled.
George Kitchin says that Miss Tickletoby's Comic History was not very good, and realizing that, Thackeray never finished it. Thackeray's first sustained satire formed a link with the Anti-Jacobins and was entitled Elizabeth Brownrigge: A Tale (1832) (Kitchin 268). The Yellowplush Papers (Memoirs of Mr. C. J. Yellowplush) written for Fraser's Magazine were probably Thackeray's first relatively successful attempts at burlesque; these were written between 1842 and 1854 (Kitchin 270).

        M. Taine considered both Charles Dickens and William Makepeace Thackeray to be humorists even though their styles were very different. Dickens's writing style was
                more ardent, more expansive, wholly given up to verve, an impassioned
                painter of crude and dazzling pictures, a lyric prose-writer, all powerful in
                provoking laughter or tears, plunged into fantastic invention, painful
                sensibility, vehement buffoonery; and by the boldness of his style, the excess
                of his emotions, the grotesque familiarity of his caricatures, he has displayed
                all the forces and weaknesses of an artist, all the audacities, all the
                successes, and all the oddities of the imagination. (qtd. in Lilly 37)
Thackeray's style, in contrast to that of Dickens was "more self-contained, better instructed and stronger." Thackeray was
                a lover of moral dissertations, a counselor of the public, a sort of lay-
                preacher, less bent on defending the poor, more bent on censuring man. [He]
                has brought to the aid of satire a sustained common-sense, great knowledge
                of the heart, consummate cleverness, powerful reasoning, a store of
                meditated hatred, and has persecuted vice with all the weapons of reflection.
                (qtd. in Lilly 37)
Taine did not like Thackeray's judgmental style, (which was similar in its misanthropy, its imperturbable gravity, its solidity of conception, and its talent for illusion to Jonathan Swift's style), and complained that instead of viewing the passions as poetic forms, Thackeray viewed them as moral issues (Lilly 37, 39).

        Thackeray defined himself as a humorist; he often compared himself and his subjects to clowns and jesters, and one of his favorite words was "quack." Furthermore, his most typical guises were those of Harlequin and Punchinello, because for Thackeray, all people (including himself) are actors and frauds, since all people show sides of themselves in public which are different from their true natures. In The English Humourists (1851), Thackeray tells a story about a man who is in a deep depression. This man asks his physician for a cure, and the physician advises him to visit the theater, where Harlequin is playing. This advice is useless, because it is the patient himself who plays Harlequin (Kiely 148). Robert Kiely considers Thackeray to have been a droll caricaturist with an excellent ability to detect buffoonery. He had a silly side which fit in well with his concept of the humorist as a "compassionate moralist" (Kiely 150).

        In The English Humourists, Thackeray gives an insightful description of the role of the humorous writer, who should awaken the reader's love, and pity, and kindness, and scorn for untruth or pretension, and tenderness for the weak. "To the best of his means and ability he comments on all the ordinary actions and passions of life almost. He takes upon himself to be the weekday preacher, so to speak" (Lilly 3-4). For Thackeray, as for Charles Lamb, humor pervaded all of his works, but it was unsustained humor: "He adorned with it [humor] almost everything he touched, but did not enter into it heart and soul, like a man of really joyous mirth-loving disposition. His pages teem with sly hits and insinuations, but he never develops a comic scene, and we can scarcely find a single really laughable episode in the whole course of his works" (L'Estrange 216). Alfred Gu L'Estrange says that all of Thackeray's descriptions are satiric in nature. "He was always making pincushions, into which he was plunging his little points of sarcasm, and owing to his confining himself to this kind of humour he avoids the common danger of missing his mark" (L'Estrange 224). L'Estrange says also that most of Thackeray's humor tended to produce a grin rather than a smile, and sometimes the grin was more of a grimace because of the bitterness from which his humor sprang (L'Estrange 217).

Thackeray plays the role of humorist not only when he is an author, but when he is a critic as well. In The English Humourists, Thackeray deals with other authors as if they were characters in his novels. He treats them with a mixture of whimsy, compassion, respect, ridicule, and affection.

> The crucial question for the critical biographer to ask about his subject is not "what are his works like?" but "would we have liked to live with him?" In the early pages of The English Humourists he is up to his familiar trick of trying on various roles, imagining what it would be like to have been the friend of Swift, of Fielding, of Dr. Johnson. Warming to the idea, he writes: "I should like to have been Shakespeare's shoeblack--just to have lived in his house, just to have worshipped him--to have run on his errands." (Kiely 159)

Thackeray's first novel is entitled Catherine (1839), and it has a light-hearted beginning: "At that famous period of history when the seventeenth century (after a deal of quarrelling, king-killing, reforming, republicanizing, restoring, rerestoring, play-writing, sermon-writing, Oliver-Cromwellizing, Stuartizing, and Orangizing, to be sure) had sunk into its grave..." (Catherine 431). The entire novel is written in this same humorously irreverent tone, "If Miss Cat, or Catherine Hall, was a slattern and a minx, Mrs. Score was a far superior shrew.... Yet...Mrs. Score put up with the wench's airs, idleness, and caprices, without ever wishing to dismiss her from the Bugle. The fact is, that Miss Catherine was a great beauty; and for about two years since her fame had begun to spread, the custom of the inn had also increased vastly" (Catherine 438).

The basic premise of Paris Sketch Book (1840) is that art uniquely communicates the nature of social life (Henkle 76). Here it is argued that the novel Tom Jones "gives us a better idea of the state and ways of the people, than one could gather from any more pompous or authentic histories" (Henkle 77).

During 1846 and 1847 Thackeray wrote a series of articles for Punch entitled "The Snobs of England, by One of Themselves," which helped to refine his writing style. It is an extensive mock categorization of the various English social strata. There are essays to satirize "the Snob Royal, Great City Snobs, Clerical Snobs, Political Snobs of various persuasions, Continental Snobs, Country Snobs--the gamut of snobbery" (Henkle 77-78).

William Lilly considers Thackeray's Book of Snobs to be a masterpiece of humor, filled with satiric playfulness, and adds that "the keen vivacious satire of an accomplished man of the world is Thackeray's distinctive note as a humourist" (Lilly xvi). The normal expression of the snobs in Thackeray's Book of Snobs is one of "intense gloom and subdued agony." Thackeray gives these snobs "the kind of grave, pungent, forcible satire they delight in" (Lilly 38).

Thackeray defines "humorist" as a "literary man, pretty sure to be of a philanthropic nature, to have a great sensibility, to be easily moved to pain or pleasure, keenly to appreciate the varieties of temper of people round about him, and sympathize in their laughter, love, amusement, tears. Such a man is philanthropic, man-loving by nature, as another is irascible, or red-haired, or six feet high" (Levin 15).

In Novels by Eminent Hands (1847) Thackeray was learning his art as an author at the same time that he was lampooning the habits of other writers. "Though each author parodied by Thackeray obviously possessed traits which he found amusing, each also provided him with techniques he adapted to his own purposes in his fiction. The burlesques are entertainments, but they are also critical statements and laboratories in which Thackeray tested his powers" (Kiely 160).

Among those parodied are Benjamin Disraeli, and James Fenimore Cooper, and Catherine Gore, and George James, and Charles Lever, and Edward Bulwer-Lytton, and Sir Walter Scott. "Thackeray's collection starts with Lytton, whose poetical drama, The Sea Captain, he had already pulverized in his parody entitled, Memoirs of Yellowplush. "George de Barnwell" is introduced inartistically with a broad sneer at Lytton's manner. The author might have left it to the parody to expose the heated nonsense, the dandyism, and the boring transcendental chatter of the victim" (Kitchin 273). Charles Lever is also satirized in Novels by Eminent Hands. The point of this satire is the "devil-may-care manner of his roaring boys and lively belles." Thackeray also parodies Lever's amusing trait of having a surprising intimacy in his adventures with the great and famous (Kitchin 273).

One year before he had written Novels by Eminent Hands, Thackeray had written Proposals for the Continuation of Ivanhoe (1846), and this was followed in 1850 by Rebecca and Rowena which is described by George Kitchin as "knock-about burlesque." Here Thackeray "does not seem to be aware of anything in the species outside tushery and tourneying" (Kitchin 274). Rebecca and Rowena is a parody of Scott's Ivanhoe. Robert Kiely, however, considers this to be a sequel and a meditation as well as a parody. "The terms takeoff and put-on--which sound like opposites, but aren't--suggest the nature of Thackeray's peculiar approach to Scott. There is an air of whimsy and fraud throughout the piece" (Kiely 163). "If Ivanhoe had any sense, for example, he obviously would not have settled for the bloodless and vapid Rowena but would have married the intelligent, virtuous, and beautiful Rebecca. The piece contains a good deal of fun at the expense of Scott and the fashion of Romantic medievalism, but it also contains many passages of straightforward adventure narrative" (Kiely 164).

Kiely suggests that Thackeray did not think that Scott had adequately solved the problems involved in writing historical novels. The author had to evoke the atmosphere of an earlier era while at the same time making characters and events credible and understandable to contemporary readers. "Scott's habit of mixing archaic and pseudo-archaic language with colloquial expressions of his own time was to Thackeray a constant source of amusement. Rather than endowing the past with an authentic vitality, it created a stage setting peopled by characters who seemed to forget their lines from time to time and say things in their own words and accents" (Keily 164).

In his Codingsby, Thackeray wrote a parody of Benjamin Disraeli's Coningsby. George Kitchin considers Disraeli's novel to be an easy mark for Thackeray, and adds that "the Jewish oddity and love of the bizarre are done to a hair in Codingsby" (Kitchin 273). Thackeray's Barbazure parodies, mocks, and insults the historical novel in general, and the works of G. P. R. James in particular (Kitchin 274).

Ironically, however, Thackeray incorporated into his own novels many of the traits he most enjoyed lampooning in the works of Bulwer-Lytton and Sir Walter Scott. "But then, he would have been willing to admit that the humorist must be a persistent and shameless scavenger if he is to keep his devices varied and changing. Almost any old trick will do if it is not allowed to stand so long as to become stale" (Kiely 166). For Thackeray, humor is not a cover-up or an oversimplification of reality, but the opposite. Humor evokes a number of complex and even contradictory responses. Thackeray feels that "the seriousness and sadness of the true humorist show through his best jokes, not in spite of them, but in subtle combination with them." For Thackeray, humor appeals more to the heart than to the mind. It is related to love, pity, tenderness, and scorn, but it is not so much related to reasoned disapproval. Since Thackeray "feels the truth" he feels obligated to become a "week-day preacher." For Thackeray, the humorist is a compassionate moralist. "The humorist...is just like everybody else, only more so. His art depends more on his power to create bond with the readers than on his power to surprise or impress them" (Keily 149).

Some of Thackeray's readers are irritated by his travel books because he liked to mimic accents and expressions and to exaggerate the modes of dress and social intercourse of these foreigners. He appeared to be ridiculing the customs, beliefs, habits, and dress of these people simply because they were not British. These tendencies can be seen very clearly in The Irish Sketch Book (1843) and From Cornhill to Grand Cairo (1846).

Paris Sketch Book (1840) illustrates the process of cultural assimilation as Thackeray sees it. The first stage is one of detachment, where French ways are criticized on moral grounds. The second stage is one of amiable warming to the color and vivacity of the French culture; during this stage there are often such wishful ejaculations as "Would that we English had their wit, their museums, their elegance!" The third stage is one of self-conscious exaggerated imitation of French ways; the jokes are double-edged because they are based on the incompatibility of the French and the English temperaments. The fourth stage returns to the sensibility and comfort of the English perspective, but with a difference; although the tone is still one of moralizing, it is more knowing and less strident than was the original tone (Kiely 153).

One the first characters introduced in Paris Sketch Book is Sam Pogson. He illustrates the second stage in the model above, as he imitates French ways (or what he thinks are French ways) as soon as he is in Calais. He flirts with every woman in sight; he constantly drinks champagne; and he drops "fashionable French phrases" on every occasion possible (Kiely 151). "Pogson's folly is not so much in wanting to enter into the spirit of things by imitating foreign ways, but in his adoption of a self-congratulatory tone in the midst of his failure to see the difference between his copy and the real thing" (Kiely 152).

Robert Kiely feels that for Thackeray, imitation, role-playing, and mimicry are essential to humor. Kiely notes that the wit is constantly distinguishing himself from others, while the humorist seeks a common ground and therefore risks looking like the fool himself. Thackeray, like his character Sam Pogson, is not a wit, but a humorist (Kiely 152).

One of Thackeray's functions as an author is to show how comic fiction can perform the traditional functions of religious faith. He considered humorists (himself included) to be "week-day preachers," saying of these "satirical moralists" that, "Our profession seems to me to be as serious as the Parson's own" (Polhemus 126). For Thackeray, the purpose of the comic was to establish faith, hope, and charity (Polhemus 130).

> We can imagine "heaven;" we can and do imagine a scheme of things, better than reality, by which to measure the folly of our lives; but this standard, this something better, which allows for the implicit comparison inherent in satire, exists only in our minds, and no divine intervention can attain it for us. Nothing exists beyond this world. There is no God, only comic insight, to judge the world and offer salvation. (Polhemus 149)

The title-page illustration in Thackeray's Vanity Fair (1848) is described by Robert Lougy as follows:

> In the illustration's foreground is Thackeray's "friend in motley," sitting on

a plank stage, resting his shoulders against an opened stage trunk, a wooden sword by his side. Dressed in rather tattered clothing, he is gazing into a mirror in his right hand. He grips the mirror by the frame rather than by the handle, as if he had intended to pick it up for just a moment; his gaze, however, is so steady and so intense that we must believe he has been gazing into the mirror for quite a while, either at something new or at a rediscovery of something old. (Lougy 58)

The foreground is filled with the ironic tensions. The player appears to be in a state of physical relaxation, but his expression is tired and melancholy, and he is staring into the mirror intensely. According to Lougy, Thackeray's player is neither comic nor heroic. In the picture there is also the tension which results from the contrast of the foreground and the background. There is a split-rail fence which separates the player and the stage from the shaded background.

And in the distance is a gothic cathedral surrounded by dwellings which are themselves almost hidden by thick clusters of foliage. Within the illustration, we see two Englands suspended in space: in the foreground is the stage and on it, the nonheroic soldier, the noncomic buffoon; in the background is a strong and serene England, one of gothic architecture, cottages, and protective trees. These two worlds are divided by a meager split-rail fence. (Lougy 58)

Karen Gindele says that in Vanity Fair the violence that attaches to the laughter is surprising even for someone who already knows the violence is there. "Nearly everybody at some point 'bursts out' laughing in a sudden uncontainable impulse. One character usually takes pleasure at the expense of another's humiliation, if not downright pain" (Gindele 145).

The full-bodied laughs of men in the novel most often mark the common man in the middleclass or the outsider in the upper class--the isolated rogue or rebel, who does not wield power within the established system-- mysteriously not the working man who in 1848 was threatening. Women, in contrast, when they reach a certain volume, are threatening because they represent either the revolt and violence of a mob or the superficial, artificial, inauthentic pleasure of the upper crust, who assume that wit is their luxury and the sign of their class position. (Gindele 146)

Amelia is totally feminine. Her narrow limits are normally bounded "between her two customs of laughing and crying." In contrast to Amelia, there is Dobbin, who is debonair, but with a certain gracelessness and awkwardness of the body that show he is not in control of his body's power. Dobbin laughs at himself, thereby transforming self-criticism into self-denial (Beach 5). Becky demonstrates many different kinds of laughter. She can have a "comical and good-humour air," or she can laugh "with a cordiality and perseverance" at Mr. Sedley's jokes. Or she can make "sweet little appeals, half tender, half jocular" to Jos. Or she can let out a scream and giggle at Rawdon's cigar. Furthermore, Becky is able to switch from laughter to fury in an instance, and she is also able to produce tears at will (Beach 22-25, 105). Then there is Jos who has the large body of the bourgeoisee. Jos is both the object and the subject of a great deal of laughter. Amelia and Becky have a "fit of laughter" at the fact that Jos makes arrangements for homosocial pairs to connect with each other. Jos says, "I believe I'm very terrible, when I'm roused." Jos makes a grimace "so dreary and ludicrous, that the captain's politeness could restrain him no longer, and he and Osborne fired off a ringing volley of laughter" (Beach 56).

Robert Lougy contrasts the beginning of Vanity Fair with the end. At the beginning of the novel, Thackeray's role as artist and moral satirist are traditional and nonthreatening. Thackeray's Vanity Fair is like Bunyan's "Vanity Fair." In Chapter 8, Thackeray describes

Vanity Fair as a "vain, wicked, foolish place, full of all sorts of humbugs and falsenesses and pretensions," and Thackeray must "have at them...with might and main" using his wit and laughter as weapons "to combat and expose such as those [quacks and fads] no doubt, that Laughter was made" (Lougy 64). But in Chapter 51, Vanity Fair has changed, and Robert Lougy explains why.

> because laughter and satire cut through and destroy those façades and social forms upon which civilization so precariously rests, they are properly seen as anarchic forces. Thus we see the satirist who, because he sees the dangers of his own satire, has become an apologist in defense of the status quo: "all the delights of life...would go to the deuce, if people did but act upon their silly principles, and avoid those whom they dislike and abuse."
> (Lougy 65)

Lougy suggests that the power of Vanity Fair comes in large part from Thackeray's struggle to resolve the tension between the vision of the social satirist/critic, and that of the visionary prophet (Lougy 81).

Although the title and the concept of the Vanity Fair come from the Vanity-Fair passage in The Pilgrim's Progress from This World to That Which Is to Come (1678) by John Bunyan, Thackeray may be closer to Edward FitzGerald than to John Bunyan in his own philosophy, for it was FitzGerald who said in his Rubáyát of Omar Khayyám, "make the most of what we yet may spend, / Before we too in the Dust descend." Thackeray states it this way in Chapter 51 of Vanity Fair: "It is all vanity to be sure: but who will not own to liking a little of it? I should like to know what well-constituted mind, merely because it is transitory, dislikes roast-beef? That is a vanity; but may every man who reads this, have a wholesome portion of it through life.... Yes, let us eat our fill of the vain thing, and be thankful therefore" (Lougy 60).

Vanity Fair is not only mock epic; it is mock scripture as well. "Thackeray, the narrator, much more resembles Zeus or some trickster deity than Jehovah, as he takes different shapes to seduce and work his will on us." He is "a comic preacher interpreting comic creation for a comic congregation" (Polhemus 151). Vanity Fair allows readers to contemplate the sin of vanity in themselves and in other people. Vanity Fair is "a very vain, wicked, foolish place, full of all sorts of humbugs, falsenesses, and pretensions" (Vanity Fair 80), and it is Thackeray's intention to walk the reader through this fair, "to examine the shops and the shows there; that we should all come home after the flare, and the noise, and the gaiety, and be perfectly miserable in private" (Vanity Fair 181). Vanity Fair is what Thackeray calls his "little world of history." Robert Polhemus considers it to be an epic, but an epic with a difference since it mocks and mimics. It is therefore a "comic epic" in the tradition of Henry Fielding (Polhemus 127).

The narrator in Vanity Fair is flexible in his consciousness. This narrator may not know everything; however, he is able to strike various poses. "He is by turns cynical, ironical, credulous, witty, startlingly wise, and fatuous" (Polhemus 152). This narrator takes on all of the stances of the modern comedian--"the poses, the direct appeals to the audience, the confessional mode, the 'inside' jokes, which create a special sense of fellowship--these traits of Thackeray are now the property of the best comic monologist" (Polhemus 155). Time in the novel is also dynamic rather than static. There is often "a movement from anticipation and expectation to some form of disillusionment or resignation," and the conclusion is not so much a happy ending as a parody of a happy ending (Polhemus 158). Thackeray's rhetoric is also dynamic: "The style is equivocal, allusive, rapid, ironic, subversive, and tough-minded. It allows for many moods and shifts in tone, and, because it defines Vanity Fair, it is often hostile and bitter" (Polhemus 161). Thackeray's irony, like that of Jane Austen, gives the reader many different perspectives, and shows that these perspectives are logically in conflict to each other. "His irony questions the ultimate value of life itself, as hers [Austen's] does not. It points to an incoherence that is inevitable in the tyranny of materialism and possession. Much more than Austen, Thackeray directs his irony against his audience and himself" (Polhemus 164). Whereas Austen's irony reveals contradictions that are neither perceived nor understood, Thackeray's irony reveals the "innate illogic in being."

> The "truth" is that conditions may be both tolerable and intolerable, statements true and false, our beliefs and assumptions somehow wrong and right at the same time. The style is like a verbal equivalent of those trick badges that, from one angle, show a woman fully clothed but, from another, show her naked. His irony says that, in this world of vanity, reflections, and multiple perspectives, whatever we may think, the opposite may also be true. That is unsettling but, on reflection, comic, since it undercuts intellectual affectations and dogmatism and frees us from the hobgoblin of foolish consistency. (Polhemus 165)

In Vanity Fair, Amelia Sedley is the practicing Christian, and Becky Sharp is the practicing comedian.

> Amelia is a parody of the myth of goodness, the legend of the patient Griselda, selfless virtue-rewarded-and-rewarding. Becky parodies the myth of advancement and success, the Cinderella-Pamela myth of deserved rise from humble to high station. People actually base their lives on these fictional patterns, but Thackeray finds them sentimental and deceiving. The new Cinderella turns out to be a comic avatar of the wicked stepsister; the new Griselda proves a hapless saint of ignorance and misplaced love. Becky can see reality, but she cannot see love. Amelia can see love, but cannot see the truth. (Polhemus 129)

But Becky is more than Cinderella and Pamela; she is Thackeray himself, and furthermore, she is Napoleon Bonaparte (Polhemus 130). Becky's life, like that of Napoleon can be seen as an experiment in egoism. Both lives ask the question of how far the single individual can go in breaking free of traditional authority (Polhemus 131). But while Napoleon's life is serious, Becky's life is comic, and what Becky does is meant to lampoon everything which Napoleon stands for (Polhemus 132).

Although Becky is full of spite against the mistresses of property she nevertheless assumes all of the traditional roles to become a mistress of property herself. Robert Polhemus interprets this by saying, "Resentment may be the sincerest form of flattery, because it so often leads to imitation" (Polhemus 135). Becky scorns marriage and motherhood. In unladylike fashion, Becky schemes, gambles, carouses, flaunts her sexuality, jokes, and meets setbacks and danger with courage.

> This behavior can look very much like liberty in a world that smothers or channels the potential of women's lives. But the fact that Becky's career has the scope of a man's makes the failure of her constricting "success" only that much more biting and relevant as satire. Equal opportunity in the age of individualism can lead finally to that gilded cage of hypocrisy, a dull stall in Vanity Fair. (Polhemus 135)

The character of Becky projects more hope than do the other characters in Vanity Fair. Becky has a capacity for pleasure, and the reader sees her as "having the most fun just when she ought to be down and out, disgraced" (Polhemus 135).

Other characters in Vanity Fair are humours characters; however, Rawdon Crawley (Becky Sharp's husband) is more complex. He was probably originally conceived as the hard-living and not especially bright soldier-husband, "but by the time he departs for almost certain death on Coventry Island, he has become an individual who is, given the right circumstances, capable of great affection and courage" (Lougy 61). There is a similarity between Rawdon Crawley and Henry Fielding's Tom Jones in that "both reach the nadir of their existence in jail and emerge from it with discoveries about themselves and their place within their respective worlds" (Lougy 61).

Jos Sedley is a humours character; he is a fat, pompous, "gourmandizer," who is obsessed with his neuroses and who is inspired only by rack punch and a copious table. He is "the grand comic epitome of hapless self-entrapment. He is a bolster, stuffed with his vanities, playing the charade of a personality" (Henkle 85). He is in fact a "fleshbag of conspicuous consumption," and he "mirrors the grotesque side of British imperialism" (Polhemus 141). Dobbin is the best that this world has to offer; he is a gentleman (Polhemus 145). Each character is consistent to his or her particular humor. Becky is greedy; Amelia is loving; Dobbin is kind, and the narrator is constantly praising virtue. All of these characters "help shape the world into an emblem of vanity to the superlative degree: Vanitas Vanitatum (Polhemus 144). Ironically, Thackeray shows that the strongest vanity of them all is pride in personal virtue. The novel ends with the Dobbin family meeting Becky at a fair and refusing to speak to her.

> Emmy, her children, and the Colonel, coming to London some time back, found themselves suddenly before her.... She cast down her eyes demurely and smiled as they started away from her; Emmy scurrying off on the arm of George (now grown a dashing young gentleman), and the Colonel seizing up his little Janey, of whom he is fonder than of anything in the world-- fonder even than of his "History of the Punjaub." (Polhemus 145)

Vanity Fair is a confirmation of the fact that there is not really much difference between the honest man and the scoundrel. Vanity Fair is a mocking representation of what life is like in a capitalistic world. It is a ridiculous depiction of the vanities of a commercial and competitive society, and the novel ends in the following way: "Ah! Vanitas Vanitatum! Which of us is happy in this world? Which of us has his desire? or, having it, is satisfied?--Come children, let us shut up the box and the puppets, for our play is played out" (Polhemus 124).

In 1851 Thackeray delivered a series of six lectures which would later be collected and published in his English Humourists of the Eighteenth Century. A year later in New York, Thackeray spoke on the subject of "Charity and Humour" (Martin 76). Thackeray's "Charity and Humour" suggests that charity and humour have the same purpose (Martin 79). Thackeray introduced English Humourists by saying that he wanted to speak "of the men and of their lives, rather than of their books" (Humourists 3). Their books were to be dealt with "only in as far as they seem to illustrate the character of the writers" (Humourists 146). Robert Martin suggests that the reason that Thackeray concentrated on biography is that he had a "sentimental view of humour..., a belief that humour is the attempt to make sympathetic contact with other characters" (Martin 77). Martin also suggests that this "sentimental view of humour" distorted Thackeray's vision, and forced him to have an inaccurate perception of such writers as Jonathan Swift, for Thackeray criticized Swift's "A Modest Proposal," saying that it exposed Swift's "unreasonableness of loving and having children" (Humourists 30).

> To Thackeray comedy was tolerable only when it warmed the heart of both writer and audience. Fielding's "moral sense was blunted by his life," which is proved by his "evident liking and admiration for Mr. [Tom] Jones." It was absurd, he said to create "a hero with a flawed reputation; a hero sponging for a guinea; a hero who can't pay his landlady, and is obliged to let his honour out to hire." (Humourists 215; qtd. in Martin 78-79)

In his evaluation of Fielding's wit, Thackeray nevertheless admitted that it was "wonderfully wise and detective," and that "it flashes upon a rogue and lightens up a rascal like a policeman's lantern" (Martin 79).

Thackeray believes that humorous writers are "our gay and kind week-day preachers," and asks whether or not they have been active in the cause that drew their audience together for that particular night. Thackeray says that Addison, Steele, Fielding, Goldsmith, Hood, and Dickens all "confer benefit by their sermons." And Thackeray slights such humorous writers as Swift, Sterne, and Congreve because they fail to fit his definition. For Thackeray, humor is "wit and love." For Thackeray, "the best humour is that which contains most humanity" (Humour 270).

William Makepeace Thackeray Bibliography

Beach, Joseph Warren, ed. Vanity Fair: A Novel Without a Hero by William Makepeace Thackeray (1848). New York, NY: Modern Library, 1950.

Burch, Mark H. "The World is a Looking-Glass": Vanity Fair as Satire." Genre 40.3 (1982): 281-302.

Collins, Philip. "A Twinkle in the Narratorial Eye: Dickens, Thackeray and Eliot." Literary and Linguistic Aspects of Humor. Barcelona, Spain: University of Barcelona Department of Languages, 1984, 9-25.

Gindele, Karen C. "When Women Laugh Wildly and (Gentle)Men Roar: Victorian Embodiments of Laughter." Look Who's Laughing: Gender and Comedy. Ed. Gail Finney. Amsterdam, Netherlands: Gordon and Breach, 1994, 139-160.

Henkle, Roger B. "Peacock, Thackeray, and Jerrold: The Comedy of 'Radical' Disaffection." Comedy and Culture--England--1820-1900. Princeton, NJ: Princeton University Press, 1980, 58-110.

Kiely, Robert. "Victorian Harlequin: The Function of Humor in Thackeray's Critical and Miscellaneous Prose." Veins of Humor. Ed. Harry Levin. Cambridge, MA: Harvard Univ Press, 1972, 147-166.

Kitchin, George. Survey of Burlesque and Parody in English. London, England: Oliver and Boyd, 1931.

Levin, Harry. Playboys and Killjoys. New York, NY: Oxford Univ Press, 1987.

L'Estrange, Alfred Gu. "Thackeray." History of English Humour. New York, NY: Burt Franklin, 1878, 216-225.

Lilly, William Samuel. "William Makepeace Thackeray: The Humourist as Philosopher." Four English Humorists of the Nineteenth Century. London, England: Norwood, 1978, 37-72.

Lougy, Robert E. "Vision and Satire: The Warped Looking Glass in Vanity Fair." William Makepeace Thackeray's Vanity Fair. Ed. Harold Bloom. New York, NY: Chelsea House, 1987, 57-82.

Martin, Robert Bernard. "Chapter V: Sydney Smith, Leigh Hunt, and Thackeray." The Triumph of Wit: A Study of Victorian Comic Theory. Oxford, England: Clarendon Press, 1974, 67-81.

Polhemus, Robert M. Comic Faith: The Great Tradition from Austen to Joyce. Chicago, IL: University of Chicago Press, 1980.

Thackeray, William Makepeace. Catherine (1839). New York, NY: Hurst n.d.

Thackeray, William Makepeace. The English Humourists of the Eighteenth Century; Charity and Humour: The Four Georges. New York, NY: Henry Holt, 1900.

Thackeray, William Makepeace. Vanity Fair. Boston, MA: Houghton, Mifflin, 1963.

3

Humor in Middle Nineteenth-Century British Literature

NINETEENTH-CENTURY MONARCHS OF GREAT BRITAIN:		
George III (William Frederick)	Hanover	1760-1820
George IV (Augustus Frederick)	Hanover	1820-1830
William IV (Silly Billy)	Hanover	1830-1837
Victoria (Alexandrina)	Hanover	1837-1901

Robert Browning (1812-1889)

Curtis Dahl says that Browning's humor can be found in Browning's subjects, his style, his characterization, his action, his situations, and his construction. In his best poems there is always some element of humor, whether playfulness, wit, comedy, caricature, irony, self-satire, ambiguity, amusingly exaggerated melodrama, or comic grotesque (Dahl 163).

Some of Robert Browning's poems are light, but even more of his poems are wry, dark, grotesque, ironic, and humorous. Much of Browning's humor borders on the horrible and the macabre (Dahl 159). Curtis Dahl says that Robert Browning's poetry anticipates the "madhouse world of Franz Kafka," or the theater of the absurd, and the black humor of the twentieth century. The reader doesn't laugh at Browning's humor; rather the reader chuckles inwardly. Browning's humor is serious humor. It is based on incongruity that "causes the mind to laugh while the heart feels sympathy as the mind confronts serious, even tragic problems." Many of the titles of Browning's work promise humor. One of his volumes is entitled Jocoseria (1883), and another is entitled Asolando (1889), which is a pun on the name of the town Asolo and the Italian verb "asolare" which means "to amuse oneself at random." One of the reasons that Browning used humor is that by so doing he could present his most personal and unorthodox opinions and when he was challenged he could back away and say that what he was proposing had only been said in fun (Dahl 158). The characters in Robert Browning's poems range all the way from the light, almost trivial Mr. Sludge the Medium, who is a "delightfully clever and engagingly witty rascal" to Fra Lippo Lippi, the friar who is caught by the local vice squad at night in the red-light district of Florence, and all the way to Johannes Agricola, an extreme egotist who is a strong believer in predestination (Dahl 159).

Many of Browning's poems are humorous. "My Last Duchess" (1842) contains dark and ironic humor. Here the Duke is talking about his "last duchess" to an envoy who has come to help arrange for the Duke's marriage to the "next duchess." The irony is that the entire purpose of telling about the "last duchess" is to warn the next duchess that she must be very careful not to be like the last one. Here "the Duke really reveals more about himself than about her. By attempting to blacken his former wife's character, he blackens his own." "Porphyria's Lover" (1842) tells about the moment of ecstacy when Porphyria completely and passionately belongs to her lover. Her lover winds her hair "in one long yellow string... / Three times her little throat around, / And strangled her." Curtis Dahl says about "Porphyria's Lover" that "the psychology is grim and mad and grotesque, but the exaggerated situation is also comic. The tone of "The Soliloquy of the Spanish Cloister" (1842) is playfully humorous. It begins with the word "Gr-r-r." The speaker snaps off Brother Lawrence's prize lilies. He piously drinks his orange juice in three gulps in order to frustrate the Arians. He lusts after the dark-haired Dolores. And he thinks up ways to stop Brother Lawrence while at the same time cheating the Devil out of his own soul. All of these devices are basically comic. "The Glove" (1845) is humorous in tone even though it is deeply serious in intent. The grim comedy of "The Laboratory" (1845) is making a jibe at France (Dahl 159). "How It Strikes a Contemporary" (1855) tells about a poet who is "God's spy" and who writes letters back to his master. But the townspeople do not know that the poet is so holy. They think that he is in his secret bower eating his supper in a room that blazes with lights and has four Titians on the walls, and around him are twenty naked girls who are assigned to change his plate (Dahl 161). The humor and absurdity of this poem are based not only on the townspeople's lack of perception of the truth, but it is also based on their foolish fancyings. Ironically, Raphael, the artist in "One Word More" (1855) writes a poem rather than painting a picture. And Dante, the author, paints a picture rather than writing poetry (Dahl 162). "Transcendentalism: A Poem in Twelve Books" (1855) is ironically a short poem. Here Browning appears to be vigorously attacking didacticism in poetry, but Curtis Dahl suggests that Browning is "playing both sides of the field; he is having fun with the reader" (Dahl 161). "A Light Woman" (1855) contains humor of situation as the speaker, in order to save his friend from a designing female must seduce her himself. In "The Heretic's Tragedy" (1855), John the Templar argues that he should not be burnt for heresy. He argues that it is impossible for him to be a heretic since he has "roasted three Turks" (Dahl 159).

In "Caliban on Setebos" (1864), Browning "launches a double-pronged satiric attack on the proponents of Deistic 'natural philosophy' and on the Calvinists." Caliban is half a man. He is the Darwinian "missing link." "It is funny to hear this grotesque brute-man in his rough jargon mouthing sophisticated religious ideas" (Dahl 162). In "Mr. Sludge, 'The Medium'" (1864) Sludge turns and twists his words in an attempt at self-justification, but his twistings and turnings only send him deeper and deeper into guilt Sludge is a despicable charlatan, but he is also amusing and almost likable (Dahl 161). "Gold Hair" (1864) is very dark. The girl's golden hair is thought by the villagers to be a sign of her purity; however, when her corpse is dug up years later, her golden hair proves to be not a halo, but rather a crown of golden coins that she had earned through sin (Dahl 160). The title of "A Forgiveness" (1876) is darkly ironic. As long as the wife has a lover, he scorns her. But when she convinces him that she really loves him (her husband) and sinned only because he had ignored her, his scorn turns to hatred, and he kills her. The title of the poem, therefore, refers to the fact that after he kills her, he forgives her (Dahl 162). "Shop" (1876) is intentionally vulgar, and uses an amusingly doggerel rhythm. "Pan and Luna" (1880) is about how Luna modestly plunges into a clowd to keep Pan from seeing her nakedness, but Pan goes into the clowd with Luna, and instead of being indignant, Luna chases Pan into the woods to continue the game (Dahl 159). "Doctor--" (1880) is a comic story about how a wife can be so bad that she can cheat even the Devil (Dahl 159). The mouth referred to in the poem, "Muckle-Mouth Meg" (1889) is not especially large, and is actually quite beautiful. But her lover gives her the nickname of "Muckle-Mouth Meg" because he vows to kiss her so long and so hard that her mouth will widen into a "muckle-mouth".

Talking of Robert Browning's poem entitled "Fra Lippo Lippi," Donald Hair said that there are several kinds of discrepancies. One discrepancy is that between what is said and what is meant by the speaker; this results in an inner conflict. Another discrepancy is that between what is said by the speaker and what is understood by his/her listener; this results in a communicative conflict. Still another discrepancy is that between what is said by the speaker, and what is understood by the reader; this results in a literary conflict (Hair 104). The beginning of "Fra Lippo Lippi" is very apologetic since Fra Lippo has been placed in a defensive position. Another monk has seized him by the throat because Fra Lippo Lippi has been discovered late at night in a red-light district. Fra Lippo tries to account for being in such a place at such a time, but his account arouses much suspicion. Kim says that this opening is symbolic because the street and the monastery represent contradictory forces, and Lippo is being forced to reconcile this contradiction (Kim 4). Readers of Browning's poem may feel inclined to blame Fra Lippo, but they also love him because they see him as a man and an artist who is filled with a passion for life and art. In Lippo's monologue, the reader overhears a person who embraces both the ideal and the real of the world in which he lives. Thus Browning forces the reader to see Fra Lippo either as a bad monk, or as an authentic man, or both (Hackett and Ferns 117).

Donald Hair says that the irony in "Fra Lippo Lippi" suggest the comic realization of a particular outlook on life and art, and that these ironic manners can also be seen in other Browning characters. In "Pictor Ignotus" there is a man who doesn't understand himself. And the gap that exists between what Pictor Ignotus says of himself, and what the readers know to be true of him creates much of the irony (Hair 107). Consider also the irony of the Bishop in "The Bishop Orders His Tomb at Saint Praxed's Church." This irony is the result of the Bishop's inability to understand himself and his situation. Also consider Karshish in "An Epistle Containing the Strange Medical Experience of Karshish, the Arab Physician." Here the poem shows an inconsistency between Karshish's knowledge and his faith (Walsh 218).

Many of Browning's longer works are humorous as well. In Aristophanes' Apology (1875), Balustion argues that "truth may lurk in jest's surprise," and Aristophanes (who also speaks for Browning) "defends laughter as a cleansing agent and contends that the best writing incorporates both the comic and the serious" (Dahl 158). In Fifine at the Fair (1872), the villain Don Juan is ironic in that he expresses so many of Browning's own ideas in spite of the fact that he is a deep-dyed villain. The Inn Album (1875) is a very amusing and quizzical self-satire which the reader must pay attention to or miss the comic point. In these pieces, Browning demonstrates that he has the ability to laugh at himself (Dahl 163).

C. W. Previté-Orton suggests that Browning's Prince Hohenstiel-Schwangau, Saviour of Society is a political satire targeting Napoleon III (224-225). Browning's "Caliban upon Setebos: Natural Theology in the Island" is also a satire, about which Thomas Wolfe says, "to view the poem primarily as religious satire is to ignore 'all that life and fun and romping' it affords" (7). This poem not only fits Robert Langbaum's definition of the dramatic monologue, but in the eyes of Thomas Wolfe, it is a comic masterpiece as well. In the poem, Caliban is "infantile" in a number of ways. Caliban is dominated by the instinctual life or the pleasure principle. "The governance of the pleasure principle implies self-indulgence instead of restraint of pleasure; immediate instinctual gratification instead of delayed gratification; play instead of work" (Wolfe 8). Caliban is preoccupied with his body, which is the locus or center of sensation. "Instinctual gratification and ego glorification are hardly separable here. The body is the special most personal 'me,' to be pampered and pleasured" (Wolfe 9). Wolfe believes that criticism relating to this poem has tended to be much too restricted:

> I think it limits our appreciation of "Caliban" to view it primarily as religious satire, as a satire of Calvinism, or Natural Theology, or the Higher Theology, or of Darwinism. If there is an object satirized, surely it is anyone given to interpreting the world to answer to the needs of the will; and I do not think anyone can properly read the poem without discovering himself to be an object of its ridicule. (Wolfe 18)

Wolfe agrees with Langbaum who states that "the most successful dramatic monologues deal with speakers who are in some way reprehensible" (Wolfe 19), and Wolfe adds that these reprehensible speakers are also usually "irresistibly funny," for he feels that dramatic monologue is essentially a comic form. Wolfe notes that there are striking parallels between Langbaum's definition of dramatic monologue and Freud's description of the comic experience in Wit and Its Relation to the Unconscious. The Caliban poem nicely conforms to both of these definitions, as Caliban is seen flat on his belly in the mire looking out at particular objects which have for him particular meanings. Langbaum says that the facts in the dramatic monologue are "looked at, limited and distorted by the view of a particular person in a particular time and place" (Wolfe 19). In the dramatic monologue, there is not only the "particular perspective;" there is also the "disequilibrium between sympathy and judgment." These are both necessary for maximum monologue effect. Wolfe again compares this with Freud's description of the comic experience:

> It is characteristic of the comic situation as Freud describes it to compare the psychic expenditures of ourselves and another ego by "the putting of one's self into the psychological process of another" in the "desire to understand him," so in the dramatic monologue, as Langbaum describes it, we participate in the monologuist's particular perspective and suspend judgment "for the sake of understanding." (Wolfe 21)

Wolfe notes that "there is something immediately comic about the association of a person of religious authority with instinctual striving, because there is such an immediate and strong cultural inhibition against it." Wolfe applies this to the Browning poem by noting that Caliban's self-indulgent body stroking, and his fantasies of omnipotence, dreaming of wish-fulfillment, and even his cruelty is more immature than it is reprehensible. "We do not say of a four-year-old terrorizing an ant pile that he is immoral or sub-human; we say, with amusement, that he is a child" (Wolfe 22-23).

Robert Browning Bibliography

Babington, Percy L. Browning and Calverley; or Poem and Parody. London, England: John Castle, n.d.

Chakraborty, S. C. Robert Browning's Ironic Gaze. Calcutta, India: KLM, 1977.

Dahl, Curtis. "Robert Browning." Encyclopedia of British Humorists, Volume I. Ed. Steven H. Gale. New York, NY: Garland, 1996, 157-164.

Dornberg, Curtis Leon. "Genial Humor, Comic Irony, and Satire in the poetry of Robert Browning." Ph.D. Dissertation. Ames, IA: Iowa State University, 1965.

Hackett, Susan, and John Ferns. "A Portrait of the Artist as a Young Monk: The Degree of Irony in Browning's 'Fra Lippo Lippi.'" Studies in Browning and His Circle 4.2 (1976): 105-118.

Hair, Donald S. Browning's Experiments with Genre. Toronto, Canada: University of Toronto Press, 1997.

Kemper, Claudette. "Irony and Browning's 'Fifine at the Fair.'" Ph.D. Dissertation. Philadelphia, PA: University of Pennsylvania, 1965.

Kim, Hae Ri. "Comic Irony in Robert Browning's "Fra Lippo Lippi." Unpublished Paper. Tempe, AZ: Arizona State University, 1997.

Nichols, Ashton. "'Will Sprawl' in the 'Ugly Actual': The Positive Grotesque in Browning." Victorian Poetry 21 (1983): 157-170.

Previté-Orton, C. W. Political Satire in English Poetry. New York, NY: Russell and Russell, 1968.

Priestley, F. E. L. "Some Aspects of Browning's Irony." Browning's Mind and Art. Ed. Clarence Rupert Tracy. London, England: Oliver and Boyd, 1968.

Ryals, Clyde de L. "Browning's Irony." The Victorian Experience: The Poets. Athens, OH: Ohio University Press, 1982, 23-46.

Walsh, Cheryl. "The Voice of Karshish: A Bakhtinian Reading of Robert Browning's 'Epistle.'" Victorian Poetry 31.3 (1993): 213-226.

Wolfe, Thomas P. "Browning's Comic Magician: Caliban's Psychology and the Reader's." Studies in Browning and His Circle 6.2 (1978): 7-24.

Charles (John Huffam) Dickens (1812-1870)

On April 2, 1836, Charles Dickens married Catherine Hogarth. Charles was born nine months after their marriage. Over the next fifteen years came nine more children, some of whom were named after writers Dickens especially liked. The names of Charles's and Catherine's children were Mary, Kate, Walter Landor, Alfred Tennyson, Sydney Smith Haldemand, Henry Fielding, Dora Annie, and Edward Bulwer-Lytton (Diedrick 83).

Elton Smith notes that for Charles Dickens, "everyone is larger than life or smaller than life, but never just life-size" (Smith 312). Charles Dickens had an excellent eye for the eccentric or humours character. Some of Dickens's Innocents are what Smith calls "Perfect Innocents," which makes them "invulnerable to violence, theft, hunger, and seduction--in short, experience." These Perfect Innocents include Little Nell, Oliver Twist, Smike, Kate Nickleby, Mr. Wilfer, and Mrs. Boffin. We are not allowed to laugh at these "Perfect Innocents." "We may suffer with them, weep for them, but we know from chapter 1 that they will die closing innocent blue eyes upon a world that taught them nothing." We are allowed to laugh at the other Innocents, because they have a capacity for knowledge of the world, and a potential for growth. In this category are David Copperfield, Pip, and Mr. Pickwick. Dickens's Villains are usually the types of Villains that we are allowed to laugh at, though we may feel a bit squeamish doing so. Scrooge is a Villain who mistreats his employees, but we are allowed to laugh at him because he is scared into change by the ghosts. Likewise, Wackford Squeers enjoys beating boys and girls but "his hypocritical sense of his great scholarship and his innate respectability are hilarious." Jew Fagin victimizes children, but he is at the same time a surrogate parent. Uriah Heep has many qualities of villainy, but he also assumes obsequious humility at times, and in addition, he has twining double-jointed legs. Silas Wegg is an ingrate who "bites the hands that feed him," but he also is able to burst out irrepressibly into an "idiot survey of British poetry." We are also generally allowed to laugh at Dickens's Monsters, even though they may be physically, mentally, or emotionally handicapped. Miss La Creevy as a "miniature," likes to dress up ordinary citizens in splendid uniforms, as it is her way of reducing them down to her own dimensions as miniatures. There is also Mr. Lillyvick, "whose giant self-esteem sees him through a humiliating and disastrous marriage and abandonment." There is also Jenny Wren, who makes dresses for little dolls. She is pathetically crippled, but she is also "irresistibly funny" when she calls her father her "bad child," and develops that kind of a relationship with him (Smith 311). Related to the "Monsters" are the "Pathetics," from which Dickens extracts both tears and laughter. The daughter in the Vincent Crummles Travelling players, who is referred to as "the Infant Phenomenon" is one of these Pathetics. "Her proud, loving parents, always more appreciative of drama than life, kept her up late every night, fed her little, and gave her an unlimited allowance of gin-and-water from infancy to protect the Infant Phenomenon from the blight of growth." As Mr. Sleary says in his lisp, "People mutht be amuthed" (Smith 312).

H. P. Sucksmith feels that Charles Dickens's viewed life is "an ironic tragi-comedy of deception" (Smith 315). In his satires, Dickens targets Chancery, Poor Houses, boys' boarding schools, the lack of education for women, the tyrannies of family life, the reliance upon alcohol, and the effects of poverty. His narratives are filled with wonderful coincidences, "fausse denouements," and total reversals, but they all emphasize the ultimate triumph of goodness over evil (Smith 309). James Kincaid said that Dickens's "rhetoric of laughter" was "simply a technique of persuasion," as he varied his humor from verbal to farcical to situational to melodramatic (Smith 310).

Charles Dickens was often appalled at the ineptitude of various political leaders, and he was more apt to portray them as funny than as dangerous. In an early sketch entitled "The House," he said that the House of Commons was like a pantomime that was "strong in clowns." Dickens said that the members of Parliament "twist and tumble about, till two, three and four o'clock in the morning; playing the strangest antics, and giving each other the funniest slaps on the face that can possibly be imagined, without evincing the smallest tokens of fatigue." He says that they often can be found "talking, laughing, lounging, coughing, oh-ing, questioning, or groaning," and that they present a "conglomeration of noise and confusion to be met with in no other place in existence, not even excepting Smithfield [the cattle market] on a market-day, or a cock-pit in its glory" (Ford 93).

Sylvia Bank Manning dedicates her Dickens as Satirist to Peter, her husband, "whose undying hostility to Dickens provided an invaluable sounding board." In this book, Manning discusses the satire in the following Dickens novels: Pickwick Papers, Barnaby Rudge, Martin Chuzzlewit, Dombey and Sons, David Copperfield, Bleak House, Hard Times, Little Dorrit, A Tale of Two Cities, and Great Expectations. She also discusses the "modified satire" of Our Mutual Friend. But some of Dickens's earliest satire did not appear in his novels. In 1839, Dickens told John Forster that he planned to begin writing a series of "satirical papers." This led to Master Humphrey's Clock, which started as satire, but was soon diverted. In 1855 Dickens again had an idea for a "fine little bit of satire", and this culminated in his "The Thousand and One Humbugs" which appeared in Household Words on April 21, April 28, and May 5 of 1855. Manning contends that "for Dickens, satire is not necessarily literary: it is any form of truthful, ironic, and other bitter commentary upon life" (6). Manning contends that not only the scene, the plot, and the characters in Dickens's novels are satiric, but the rhetoric is satiric as well (15).

> In the earlier books, the satire is generally very close to comedy and its anger diverted to laughter, though this does not make the exposure less complete or the contempt engendered less pure. Mrs. Gamp is an example. Later the tone changes. There is less humor and a strong undertow of bitterness in a character like Mr. Vholes. His own distance from humanity is frightening, but the full horror lies in his being but part of an extensive network of evil that threatens to strangle all forces opposing it. (Manning 22-23)

Under the pen name of "Boz," Dickens wrote his Sketches by Boz: Illustrative of Every-Day Life and Every-Day People (1836-1837). These sketches were illustrated by George Cruikshank, and were Dickens's freewheeling and comic impressions of Victorian culture. In contrast to his earlier work, Dickens's later work "betrays the sense of paradox and extreme alienation that we find in Oscar Wilde" (Henkle 111). Dickens was very much impressed by his visit to America, and he later wrote accounts of New York's Tombs prison, and the Philadelphia penitentiary. He used his mordant wit to satirize "the Tombs," saying that while he was visiting this prison his guard told him that a particular boy he saw in a cramped cell was there for "safe keeping" because he was a witness in the trial of his father, which would soon be on the docket. Dickens asked if this was not a hard treatment for a witness, and the guard replied, "Well, it ain't a very rowdy life, and that's a fact!" (Diedrick 85).

Some of Dickens's early sketches told a story. Others were simply descriptions of various parts of London, such as Newgate Prison, or Monmouth Street (a shopping center for secondhand clothing). Still others were portraits of taxi drivers, circus clowns, or other picturesque characters (Ford 96). The pen-name of "Boz" has an interesting history. The nickname that Dickens devised for his youngest brother, Augustus, was "Moses" after one of the Primrose children in Goldsmith's Vicar of Wakefield. But Augustus was not able to say "Moses," so he said "Boses" instead. This later shortened to "Bose," and further shortened to "Boz" which rhymes with "laws" and not with "foes" (Ford 96). Dickens's Sketches caught the eye of a number of important reviewers of the nineteenth century, one of which recommended that Sketches should be promoted in America because they would save these readers "the trouble of reading some hundred dull-written tomes on England, as it is a perfect picture of the morals, manners, [and] habits of a great portion of English society" (Ford 96).

Dickens started having The Posthumous Papers of the Pickwick Club, Edited by "Boz" published in 1836 and continued until 1837. The first edition of The Pickwick Papers sold only 400 copies, but the last edition, printed in October of 1837, sold 40,000 (Diedrick 83). The Victorians valued Pickwick Papers for two reasons: they thought they were funny, and they thought they were true (Newman 33). It was Number Four of the Pickwick Papers that radically changed the circulation, because it was in Number Four that two strikingly colorful Cockney characters were introduced, Sam Weller, and his father, Tony, the fat coachman. Sam was impudent, but he was warmhearted. His worldly-wise anecdotes were told in a strong Cockney accent that made him an ideal foil for Mr. Pickwick's innocence and benevolence. "Dickens had recreated an endearing pair like Sancho Panza and Don Quixote." It was this type of contrastive characterization that made Pickwick Papers so popular, as they appealed to all classes of readers from the highly educated to those who had very little education (Smith 99).

Mr. Pickwick's innocent faith in the benevolence of man and nature is contrasted by Sam Weller's wry suspicion of both. "I only assisted natur' ma'am; as the doctor said to the boy's mother, arter he'd bled him to death" (Newman 35). According to S. J. Newman, Sam's offering of paradoxical criticisms is a way that Dickens had of anticipating the readers' objections and defusing them in a witty manner (Newman 36).

Joseph Priestley notes that Dickens created an incredible number of "drolls," further noting that there are nearly a hundred characters in Pickwick Papers alone, nearly all of them comic (150). Steven Marcus suggests that Pickwick Papers is the only Dickens novel in which wickedness, although it exists, is not a threat. Walter Allen continues this line of thought:

> It makes, of course, all the difference in the world. It means that in Pickwick Papers we are in the realm of pure humour as in no other book ever written except perhaps Alice in Wonderland. As a comic work, it is almost wholly devoid of satire. It has, admittedly, its rogues and villains-- Mr. Jingle and Job Trotter, Dodson and Fogg, the Rev. Mr. Stiggins. But we do not think of them as rogues and villains. We think of them as purely comic creations; and so they are. (21)

James Kincaid considers <u>Pickwick Papers</u> to be one of the great English comedies, so important that it helped to define the genre (9). This novel is a burlesque of the touring and sporting club in general, and of a number of social customs in particular. The burlesque qualities of the book are most noticeable at the beginning, the founding of the club, but throughout the novel there is a joyous medley of burlesque in which many public institutions are lightly ridiculed. George Kitchin says that both Mr. Pickwick and Don Quixote run about eagerly trying to redress evils, and both, through their naivité, invariably end up looking ridiculous. This comparison of Mr. Pickwick with Don Quixote is made more complete by the further comparison of Mr. Weller with Sancho Panza, his speech being as full of farcical comparisons as was Sancho Panza's speech full of proverbs (Kincaid 280).

In the preface to the reprinted <u>Pickwick Papers</u>, Charles Dickens admits that Mr. Pickwick undergoes a decided change in character during the course of the novel, and that he has become a better and more sensible man: "I do not think this change will appear forced or unnatural to my readers, if they will reflect that in real life the peculiarities and oddities of a man who has anything whimsical about him, generally impress us first, and that it is not until we are better acquainted with him that we usually begin to look below these superficial traits, and to know the better part of him" (qtd. in Martin 29).

S. J. Newman considers <u>Pickwick Papers</u> to be more of a "funny book" than a "comic novel." "The comic novel expresses a governing outlook, whether conciliatory, satirical, or absurdist. The funny book, on the other hand, is reflexive, unpremeditated, almost physical, even cheerful" (36). Pickwick's funny and cheerful world is especially achieved in the two Wellers, father and son. Sam's mind is witty, sane, and down-to-earth. He is not himself pretentious, but at the same time, nothing that <u>is</u> pretentious survives his scrutiny. "When John Smauker condescendingly describes the taste of the Bath waters as 'killibeate,' Sam answers, 'I don't know much about that 'ere.... I thought they'd a very strong flavour o' warm flat irons.' " Newman notes that about eighty per cent of the "Wellerisms" in <u>Pickwick Papers</u> are either morbid, or else they deal with such things as debt, unhappy marriage, misanthropy, or general social discomfort. Newman uses such Wellerisms as "There; now we look compact and comfortable, as the father said ven he cut his little boy's head off, to cure him o' squintin," and "That's what I call a self-evident proposition, as the dog's meat man said, when the housemaid told him he wasn't a gentleman" to classify Sam Weller as a "Cockney Augustan" (37). Roger Henkle considers <u>Pickwick Papers</u> to have been "the great culminating work of the English humor tradition of the eighteenth and early nineteenth centuries" (Henkle 117).

One of Dickens's imprints is that he takes a long time to tell a story. Orwell cites another example of this tendency in Sam Weller's story about the obstinate patient in Chapter 44 of <u>The Pickwick Papers</u> (1836-1837). Sam Weller is telling a story which in the original Greek took about six lines, but as Sam Weller tells it, it becomes about a thousand words. "Long before getting to the point we have been told all about the patient's clothes, his meals, his manners, even the newspapers he reads, and about the peculiar construction of the doctor's carriage, which conceals the fact that the coachman's trousers do not match his coat" (Orwell 61).

<u>The Life and Adventures of Nicholas Nickleby</u> (1837-1939) contains a gallery of colorful eccentrics filled with vitality and energy, the best-known of which is Wackford Squeers, who is a semiliterate master of a school in Yorkshire (Ford 104). Dickens describes Squeers as follows:

> Mr. Squeers's appearance was not prepossessing. He had but one eye, and the popular prejudice runs in favor of two. The eye he had was unquestionably useful, but decidedly not ornamental: being of a greenish grey, and in shape resembling the fan-light of a street door. The blank side

of his face was much wrinkled and puckered up, which gave him a very sinister appearance, especially when he smiled, at which times his expression bordered closely on the villainous. His hair was very flat and shiny up from a low protruding forehead, which assorted well with his harsh voice and coarse manner. He was about two or three and fifty, and a trifle below the middle size; he wore a white neckerchief with long ends, and a suit of scholastic black; but his coat sleeves being a great deal too long, and his trousers a great deal too short, he appeared ill at ease in his clothes, and as if he were in a perpetual state of astonishment at finding himself so respectable. (31)

In Nicholas Nickleby, Dotheboy's Hall is almost a situation comedy in itself as the new boys and the new master become butts of the savage humor and fantastic jokes. There is a ferocious administration of brimstone and treacle, after which Mrs. Squeers casually tells a boy to come forward so that she can wipe her sticky fingers on his curly hair. This is evidence of her casual, or maybe even her callous, insensitivity (Smith 310).

Irony is a key element in a particular scene prior to the placement of Mrs. Snawley's step-sons at Dothsboys Hall. Mr. Snawley and Mr. Squeers are talking to each other, and Mr. Snawley says, "They are not great eaters." Mr. Squeers replies, "Oh! that doesn't matter at all. We don't consider the boys' appetites at our establishment." The narrator then remarks, "This was strictly true; they did not." (34)

In the preface of Nicholas Nickleby, Dickens justifies Mr. Squeers as follows: "Mr. Squeers is the representative of a class, and not of an individual. Where imposture, ignorance, and brutal cupidity, are the stock in trade of a small body of men, and one is described by these characteristics, all his fellows will recognize something belonging to themselves, and each will have a misgiving that the portrait is his own" (Manning 12). Northrop Frye considers the hero's mother to be the silliest character in Nicholas Nickleby. She is a romancer who dreams of impossible happy endings for her children (81).

Gamsfield, in Oliver Twist; or, The Parish Boy's Progress, by "Boz." (1838-1839), is the overseer of the chimney-sweeps., and he makes readers laugh by lighting dry straw fires while the boys are in the chimneys. "Boys is wery obstinit, and wery lazy, gen'lmen, and there's nothink like a good hot blaze to make 'em come down vith a run. It's humane too, gen'lmen, acause, even if they've stuck in the chimbley, roasting their feet makes 'em struggle to hextricate theirselves" (Smith 312).

In Oliver Twist, there are a number of "humours characters." Bill Sikes is a very brutal thief and housebreaker who has an intimidating ruffian's scowl, is stockily built, and has an abused dog named "Bull's-Eye." The rascal Fagan is the person who trains the thieves and receives the stolen goods. Although Fagan has many repulsive traits, he seems to watch over Oliver and the other young apprentices, as a sort of surrogate father. Steven Marcus has traced this befriending back to the time when Dickens himself worked in a dismal blacking warehouse, and was befriended by an older boy named "Bob Fagin" (Benstock and Staley 107).

In Chapter 17 of Oliver Twist, Dickens comments on the fact that he merged comedy with tragedy. "It is the custom on the stage, in all good murderous melodramas, to present the tragic and the comic scenes, in as regular alternation, as the layers of red and white in a side of streaky bacon" (Ford 102). Walter Allen notes that in Oliver Twist, the modern reader does not see Fagan as comic. But Fagan sees himself as comic, and he succeeds in making even Oliver laugh. Allen suggests that there is a reason that Fagan is called "the merry old gentleman." And in fact, Fagan's merriment makes him all the more sinister. One of the things which Dickens was satirizing in Oliver Twist was the New Poor Law that was enacted in 1834. This law held to the "statistical view of man," in which man is seen as "a machine that can be kept in working order, i.e., alive, by the injection into it of a carefully calculated minimum of energy-producing fuel--calories." Mr. Bumble expresses this attitude very well when he is summoned by the Sowerberries to deal with Oliver after his attack on Noah Claypole. Bumble says, "It's not Madness, ma'am.... It's Meat." When Mrs. Sowerberry says that she doesn't understand, Mr. Bumble continues, "You've over-fed him, ma'am. You've raised a artificial soul and spirit in him, ma'am, unbecoming a person of his condition.... If you had kept the boy on gruel, ma'am, this would never have happened." "Dear, dear!" ejaculated Mrs. Sowerberry, piously raising her eyes to the kitchen ceiling: "this comes of being liberal!" Allen notes that Mr. Bumble is Dickens's first instance of a savage caricature. He notes further that Mr. Bumble is not simply a caricature of a beadle; rather he represents "any unimaginative and corrupt underling to whom bureaucracy has given power" (Allen 23).

Mr. Bumble may be frightening, but he is a figure of fun as well, as in the scene when he proposes marriage to Mrs. Corney. Later in the novel, Mr. Bumble becomes a stock comic figure representing the henpecked husband with a domineering wife (Ford 102). When he is told that "the law supposes that your wife acts under your direction," Mr. Bumble responds, "If the law supposes that, the law is a ass--a idiot." A scene from Oliver Twist which even more comic than the one with Mr. Bumble is when the Artful Dodger is in court demanding his "priwileges" as an Englishman. He admonishes the judges that "this ain't the shop for justice" (Ford 103). Many of Dickens's plays were adapted in various ways before they reached the stage, and there is a story that during one performance of Oliver Twist, Dickens became so outraged that he lay down on the floor of the box during the first scene, and refused to get up until the show was over (Allen 77).

It is remarkable how many of Dickens's heroes and heroines are children, or are described in ways associating them to childhood. Dickens's heroines, even when they are fully grown, are described as "little," or are compared to fairies. In Alice-in-Wonderland fashion, many of Dickens's girl-child characters are described in a grotesque world. In his preface to The Old Curiosity Shop (1841), Dickens describes his fascination with the beauty-and-beast archetype, and Dickens's girl-child characters are often surrounded by monsters, some of them amiable like Kit, others sinister like Quilp. "Little Nell descends to this grotesque world and then rejoins the angels" (Frye 71). Other girl-child characters who find themselves among grotesques include Florence Dombey, who is protected by Captain Cuttle, and Maggie, who is mothered by Little Dorrit. Frye considers some of the places in Dickens's novels to have the same kind of special magic as can be found in Lewis Carroll's looking glass.

> We may also notice the role of the old curiosity shop itself: it plays little part in the story, but is a kind of threshold symbol of the entrance into the grotesque world, like the rabbit-hole and mirror in the Alice books. Its counterparts appear in the Wooden Midshipman shop in Dombey and Sons, the Peggotty cottage in David Copperfield, the bone-shop of Venus in Our Mutual Friend, and elsewhere. (Frye 72)

Dickens writes melodramas, and in this genre, private worlds of dreams and death are created. These hidden worlds are not necessarily better or worse than the ordinary world of experience, but in these worlds the powers of good and evil appear as much stronger and less disguised countervailing forces. "We may protest that its moods are exaggerated, its actions unlikely, its rhetoric stilted and unconvincing. But if it were not there nothing else in Dickens would be there. We notice that the mainspring of melodramatic action is, like that of humorous action, mainly obsession" (Frye 76).

Dickens's humor had a liberating effect, which Robert Polhemus describes as follows: "Again and again it seems to say, 'Look! Here is your world, where moral imperatives, in one form or another, are constantly being thrust at you and various moral judgments can seem so daunting.' Yet, prescribing morality is nothing but a vocation of self-interest followed by people who, in their presumption, are fit only to be the butt of jokes" (112).

In The Old Curiosity Shop, Dickens's visual imagery is effective. Kit Nubbles, for example, is described as follows:

> Kit was a shock-headed shambling awkward lad with an uncommonly wide mouth, very red cheeks, a turned-up nose, and certainly the most comical expression of face I ever saw. He stopped short at the door on seeing a stranger, twirled in his hand a perfectly round old hat without any vestige of a brim, and, resting himself now on one leg, and now on the other, and changing them constantly, stood in the doorway, looking into the parlour with the most extraordinary leer I ever beheld. The lad had a remarkable manner of standing sideways as he spoke, and thrusting his head forward over his shoulder, as if he could not get at his voice without that accompanying action. (Davis 164)

A most memorable character in the Old Curiosity Shop is Quilp. In Chapter 48 of the novel he takes a carriage ride with Mrs. Nubbles:

> It was some gratification to Mr. Quilp to find, as he took his place upon the roof, that Kit's mother was alone inside; from which circumstance he derived in the course of the journey much cheerfulness of spirit, inasmuch as her solitary condition enabled him to terrify her with many extraordinary annoyances; such as hanging over the side of the coach at great risk of his life, and staring in with his great goggle eyes, which seemed in hers the more horrible from his face being upside down. (Henkle 125)

The death of Nell in The Old Curiosity Shop was something of a phenomenon. Francis Jeffrey was a sophisticated, and sometimes severe critic of Dickens's works, but even he was affected, as he likened the young Dickens to Shakespeare in the writing of great tragedy, and added that there had been "nothing so good as Nell since Cordelia." During this episode, sales soared to an unprecedented 100,000 copies. Nevertheless, in the late Victorian period, there was a reappraisal whereby Nell was no longer appreciated. Oscar Wilde went so far as to say that a person "must have a heart of stone to read the death of little Nell without laughing" (Ford 106). Little Nell was important not only as a character in her own right, but also as a transition device to other characters. Little Nell discovers that her grandfather, the keeper of the Old Curiosity Shop, has become an obsessive gambler. The chief moneylender for the grandfather is Daniel Quilp, a dwarf with the head of a giant. He is a combination of a prankster and a villain, and he is a significant part of some of the most haunting scenes of terror and of fun in the novel (Ford 106).

Robert Polhemus says that of all English novels, only Joyce's Ulysses compares with Dickens's The Life and Adventures of Martin Chuzzlewit (1842-1844) in the fantastic, suggestive, and astonishingly original comic use of language, and he gives an example of this effective comic use of linguistic humor by quoting a section from Martin Chuzzlewit, in which Mark Tapley says the following: "A Werb is a word as signifies to be, to do, or to suffer (which is all the grammar, and enough too, as ever I wos taught); and if there's a Werb alive, I'm it. For I'm always a-bein', sometimes a-doin', and continually a sufferin'." Polhemus compares this statement with a similar statement in the Gospel of John: "In the beginning was the Word, and the Word was with God, and the Word was God," noting that Dickens's statement has a tinge of blasphemy about it, and mocks not only constricting rationalism in particular but academic logic in general (88-89). One segment of Martin Chuzzlewit involves a scene with Mr. Tapley which is highly reminiscent of a Chevy Chase comedy routine. Mr. Tapley stands behind an old man with a napkin under his arm and finds it difficult to resist the temptation of casting sidelong glances at him.

>The extraordinary things Mr. Tapley did with his own face when any of these detections occurred, the sudden occasions he had to rub his eyes, or his nose or his chin, the look of wisdom with which he immediately plunged into the deepest thought or became intensely interested in the habits and customs of the flies upon the ceiling or the sparrows out of doors, or the overwhelming politeness with which he endeavoured to hide his confusion by handing the muffin may not unreasonably be assumed to have exercised the utmost power of feature that even Martin Chuzzlewit the elder possessed. (Davis 165)

In Martin Chuzzlewit, Montague Tigg is a con man who makes the following linguistically enigmatic statement: "'Life's a riddle: a most infernally hard riddle to guess, Mr. Pecksniff. My own opinion is, that like the celebrated conundrum, 'Why's a man in jail like a man out of jail?' there's no answer to it. Upon my soul and body, it's the queerest sort of thing altogether--but there's no use in talking about it. Ha! ha!" (Polhemus 92). Even the choice of the title for Martin Chuzzlewit was a linguistic event for Dickens. Forster notes that the name was chosen only after a great deal of hesitation and discussion. The first names considered were "Sweezleden," "Sweezleback," "Sweezlewag," and then his mind went off on a different tack to consider "Chuzzletoe," "Chuzzleboy," "Chubblewig," and "Chuzzlewig," before the perfect name of "Chuzzlewit" was finally chosen, and once the name was chosen, he used it to open the novel (Polhemus 93). In the fourth chapter of the novel, there is a greedy reunion of the Chuzzlewits and their relatives and friends, the Pecksniffs, Slyme, Spottletoes, and Tigg. Polhemus describes this event as "a gathering of funny words" (93-94).

The Mrs. Malaprop of Martin Chuzzlewit is named "Sairey Gamp." She says things like "Rich folks may ride on camels, but it ain't so easy for them to see out of a needle's eye," and she talks about the "witness for the persecution," and the "torters of the imposition." At one point Sairey Gamp says, "We never knows wot's hidden in each other's hearts; and if we had glass winders there, we'd need keep the shetters up, some of us, I do assure you!" According to Robert Polhemus, Sairey "blends, imaginatively old sayings, biblical saws, Christian teaching, church history, and tags and phrases from literature into her life, but, unlike Mrs. Malaprop, she ingeniously shifts and transforms their meanings into something rich and strange" (98, 120). When Sairey Gamp is irritated she can use vivid, but strangely inept metaphors, as when her bell rings and she responds, "What is it? Is the Thames a fire and cooking its own fish, Mr. Sweedlepipes?" Fantastic images like this permeate the language and life of Martin Chuzzlewit (Polhemus 119).

Mrs. Gamp is a strange character: "With innumerable leers, winks, coughs, nods, smiles, and curtseys and all leading to the establishment of a mysterious and confidential understanding between herself and the bride, Mrs. Gamp, invoking a blessing upon the house, leered, winked, coughed, nodded, smiled, and curtseyed herself out of the room" (Davis 165).

There are also some very dark-but-humorous visual images in Martin Chuzzlewit.

>Dickens is full of so-called "black" and "sick" humor, which, despite moralists, is for many people, almost by definition, the funniest kind. When a subject that normally resists humorous treatment can be made comic, the release of psychological pressure can be very exhilarating. No comedy could be more macabre, savage, and "orgiastic," or further from the traditions of "amiable humor," than the linguistic flights of Dickens's great comic speakers, such as Gamp, Pecksniff, Sam Weller, and Mr. Micawber. In Chuzzlewit, Dickens, for some, makes wildly funny such images as bottled dead babies, gagging and smothered children, husbands laid out dead

with pennies on their eyes and wooden legs beside them, [and] pregnant women frightened into labor by dogs and locomotives. (Polhemus 121)

Sairey Gamp and Pecksniff have the most powerful, and the funniest voices in Martin Chuzzlewit (Polhemus 99). Edgar Johnson considers America to be "a land of Pecksniffian manifest destiny." America had the same function for Dickens as Lilliput had for Swift. It was "a place where he could isolate and satirize major developments and coming distractions of his world" (Polhemus 101). Polhemus explains further that "the surging new patriotism of America and the nineteenth century is the first cover for confidence men of all types--power-hungry political exploiters, money-grubbers, land speculators, public-opinion merchants, and the like," and in his satire, Dickens liked to exploit these tendencies (Polhemus 103). An excellent example is when Martin and Mark first arrive in New York and hear the cries of the newsboys: "'Here's this morning's New York Sewer!' cried one. 'Here's this morning's New York Stabber!' 'Here's the New York Family Spy!' 'Here's the New York Private Listener?' 'Here's the New York Peeper!' 'Here's the New York Plunderer!' 'Here's the New York Keyhole Reporter!' 'Here's the New York Rowdy Journal!'" (Polhemus 104) George Ford characterizes the American scenes in Martin Chuzzlewit as "open-stopped satire" all the way from the newsboys shouting the names of their various newspapers to the swampy land development called "Eden" which is very reminiscent of Gulliver among the Yahoos. Thomas Carlyle described this scene as "all Yankee-Doodle-Dum blew up like one universal soda-bottle" (Ford 109). Dickens is here satirizing an aspect of American society because of which an individual's life tends to be made public and political, and because of which private personal matters, if they are interesting enough, are soon turned into public acts (Polhemus 104).

Dickens also views America as a land of driving, insatiable hungers, and describes a particular American boarding-house scene as follows:

> All the knives and forks were working away at a rate that was quite alarming...; everybody seemed to eat his utmost in self-defence, as if a famine were expected to set in.... The poultry...disappeared as rapidly as if every bird had the use of its wings, and had flown in desperation down a human throat.... Great heaps of indigestible material melted away as ice before the sun. (Polhemus 113)

Mr. Pecksniff in Martin Chuzzlewit is a complex character. He professes to be a teacher of architecture, but here, as in other aspects of his life, he is a colorful and eloquent fraud. He is "the archembodiment of the hypocrite--and also, it must be added, a great comic creation." Jonas Chuzzlewit, a greedy businessman who murders his father, is much less of a comic figure. The motto of Jonas is "Do other men, for they would do you" (Ford 108). Mrs. Gamp is a gin-drinking nurse who is able to receive praise from an imaginary spokesman she has invented by the name of Mrs. Harris. She quotes this Mrs. Harris with "pleasurable relish."

Walter Allen considers Mr. Pecksniff to be one of Dickens's supreme comic achievements. He is more than just a hypocrite; he is an absolutely selfish man. He is "the complete embodiment and dramatization of solipsism" (15). After he has bilked John Westlock out of his funds, he remarks that "Money, John, is the root of all evil." Once the having of money is deemed as immoral, Mr. Pecksniff's act can no longer be considered a bad action (Polhemus 108). Referring to this and similar acts in Martin Chuzzlewit, Polhemus says, "The devil loves to use Scripture--even comic scripture" (111).

Pecksniff is more than merely a rubbishy figure, a figure of hypocrisy with a tuft of hair. He is more than this because of his language, which is gloriously absurd. "What are we...but coaches? Some of us are slow coaches--Some of us...are fast coaches. Our passions are horses; and rampant animals, too!...and Virtue is the drag. We start from The

Mother's Arms, and we run to The Dust Shovel." Dickens follows the language with a description. "When he had said this, Mr. Pecksniff, being exhausted, took some further refreshment. When he had done that, he corked the bottle tight, with the air of a man who had effectually corked the subject also; and went to sleep for three stages" (Priestley 153-154).

Northrop Frye compares Pecksniff to a university professor "attempting to extract a discussion from a group of clammed-up freshmen" in the dialogue with Mr. Pecksniff saying, "The name of those fabulous animals...who used to sing in the water, has quite escaped me." Mr. George Chuzzlewit suggested "Swans," to which Pecksniff responded, "No, Not swans, Very like swans, too. Thank you." Then the nephew suggested "Oysters," to which Pecksniff responded, "No, nor oysters. But by no means unlike oysters: a very excellent idea; thank you, my dear sir, very much." Then Mr. Pecksniff arrives at the correct answer himself, "Wait! Sirens. Dear me! Sirens, of course" (Frye 59).

Walter Allen considers the comic, the caricature, and the grotesque to be closely related for Dickens. Dickens uses fascinating visual imagery to describe Mr. Scadder in Martin Chuzzlewit. He was

> ...swinging backwards and forwards in a rocking-chair, with one of his legs planted high up against the door-post, and the other doubled up under him, as if he were hatching his foot.... He was a gaunt man in a huge straw hat, and a coat of green stuff. The weather being hot, he had no cravat, and wore his shirt collar wide open; so that every time he spoke something was seen to twitch and jerk up in his throat, like the little hammers in a harpsichord when the notes are struck. Perhaps it was the truth feebly endeavouring to leap to his lips. If so, it never reached them. (Allen 7)

Harry Levin suggests that Dickens considered himself and other humorists to be "weekday preachers"; and asks if there has ever been a better charity sermon preached in the world than Dickens's A Christmas Carol (1843) (Levin 15).

Roger Henkle notes that what is most stunning about the comic characterizations in Dombey and Sons (1846-1848) is that almost all of the characters are broken, stunted, and/or discarded (Henkle 148). "Joe, Josh, old Joey Bagstock hobbles apoplectically about, with his lobster eyes and his purple face, gorging himself like a boa constrictor." In Chapter 7, he considers himself to be "Tough, sir, tough, and devilish sly!" but in fact he has "arrived at what is called in polite literature the grand meridian of life, and [is] proceeding on his journey downhill with hardly any throat, and a very rigid pair of jaw-bones." He wheezes, and he wrenches spasmodically as he goes along, "waggling his walk stick about until his blue veins throb" (Henkle 149). Cousin Feenix is another humours character in Dombey and Sons. Forty years before, Feenix had been a man about town, but now he "only retains a certain juvenility of manner." Cousin Feenix suffers from "ataxia," which is the inability to control his body movements. He's "not exactly certain when he walks across a room, of going quite straight to where he wants to go." At the Dombey's wedding, he turns to the wrong page of the Church register, and enters his name as having been born on that day. Other humours characters in Dombey and Sons are Major Bagstock, who complains about apoplexy, and Mrs. Skewton, who has aphasia (Henkle 149).

David Copperfield (1850) is normally read during childhood, and can be considered to be a children's classic. It is memorable because of the kinds of fears that it arouses, such as the scenes with Mr. Murdstone, or Mr. Creakle, or even of the "gargoylelike menacings of Uriah Heep." But David Copperfield is also memorable for its fun, and is a classic not only for children, but for adults as well (Ford 113). In David Copperfield, Dickens uses a great deal of visual imagery in describing Mr. Micawber's physical appearance:

I went in, and found there a stoutish middle-aged person in a brown surtout and black tights and shoes, with no more hair upon his head (which was a large one, and very shining) than there is upon an egg, and with a very extensive face, which he turned full upon me. His clothes were shabby, but he had an imposing shirt-collar on. He carried a jaunty sort of a stick, with a large pair of rusty tassels on it; and a quizzing glass, hung outside his coat, for ornament, I afterward found, as he very seldom looked through it, and couldn't see anything when he did. (Davis 163-164)

Mr. Micawber's moods fluctuate radically, and he is often "caught in the muddle of his own impecuniousness and financial irresponsibility" (Henkle 154).

David Copperfield compares Mrs. Micawber to her husband. In Chapter 11, he says, "Mrs. Micawber was quite as elastic. I have known her to be thrown into fainting fits by the king's taxes at three o'clock, and to eat lamb-chops breaded, and drink warm ale (paid for with two tea-spoons that had gone to the pawnbroker's) at four." Roger Henkle considers this resilience to be the "essence of the comic spirit. The Micawbers always snap back" (Henkle 155).

Uriah Heep is another humorously significant character in David Copperfield. In Chapter 16, he says, "I am well aware that I am the umblest person going, let the other be where he may. My mother is likewise a very umble person. We live in a numble abode, Master Copperfield, but have much to be thankful for." When David Copperfield shakes hands with Uriah Heep, he says that his handshake feels as if he had just "grasped a frog, his lizardlike spasticity, his involuntary writhing and screwing up of the face, and his red, shadowless eyes, Heep embodies the self-abasement that accompanies the obsequiousness by which he wriggles up the social ladder" (Henkle 171).

Lionel Stevenson calls the 1850s and 1860s Charles Dickens's "Dark Period" because of such novels as Bleak House (1852-1853), Hard Times (1854), Little Dorrit (1855), and Our Mutual Friend (1864-1865). These dark novels tended to be very critical of social institutions of the time, and one reviewer by the name of Fitzjames Stephen became so irritated at Dickens's account of the Circumlocution Office in Little Dorrit that he wrote what George Ford considers to be the nastiest review of a Dickens novel ever to appear in England during Dickens's lifetime. Stephen went so far as to call Dickens's writing "puppy pie and stewed cat" (Ford 113).

Mademoiselle Hortense, Lady Dedlock's French maid, is the villain of Bleak House (1852-1853). Although she dresses tastefully, she speaks broken English and is quite impatient and excitable. Mademoiselle Hortense's speech and mannerisms are very similar to the speech and mannerisms of the real-life Maria Manning, who had murdered Patrick O'Connor, her lover. Hortense was able to camouflage her evil "through all the good taste of her dress and little adornments." "She seems to go about like a very neat She-Wolf imperfectly tamed." Playing off from Mademoiselle Hortense is Inspector Bucket, who had the habit of "employing his fat forefinger for emphasis." Inspector Bucket is genial, friendly, charismatic, talkative, and confidential, "but he is all those things only to the extent he wants to be" (Benstock and Staley 107). Inspector Bucket had one quality that made him invincible--his dogged and unrelenting persistence. Dickens said the following about him, "Time and place cannot bind Mr. Bucket. Like man in the abstract, he is here to-day and gone to-morrow--but very unlike man indeed, he is here again the next day" (Benstock and Staley 109).

Sylvia Manning considers Bleak House to be a prototypical satire as outlined by Alvin Kernan. It contains "massive amounts of foolishness and villainy, and a jumble of material things pressing in a disorderly fashion upon, and threatening to obliterate, the remnants of sanity and decency" (7). Manning goes on to say that Dickens's characters can be justified only if they are viewed as largely satiric, and this is reinforced by the grotesqueness and the caricature. Harold Skimpole, for example is a parody of Leigh Hunt. "Hunt has been one of the most burlesqued writers in our literary history, but Dickens clearly went over the score in representing him as a heartless and almost imbecile dilettante" (Kitchin 275).

In Bleak House, Harold Skimpole lives more on his comic imaginative spirit than any of the other characters. He takes his breakfast at noon, and his breakfast consists of a peach, claret, and coffee, all of which remind him of the sun. Skimpole is a humors character--a harmless eccentric who is good natured, and sensitive, but who is not a man of this world (Henkle 156). In Chapter 18, Skimpole says, "I lie in a shady place like this, and think of adventurous spirits going to the North Pole, or penetrating to the heart of the Torrid Zone, with admiration. I dare say theirs is an unpleasant experience on the whole; but, they people the landscape for me, they give it a poetry for me, and perhaps that is one of the pleasanter objects of their existence" (Henkle 157).

Mr. Bounderby, the factory owner in Hard Times: For These Times (1854), was a bully, and Mr. M'Choakumchild, the school teacher was crammed with facts, but was nevertheless uneducated. And Mr. Gradgrind, the hardware merchant, believed in the "exclusive values of fact and rational calculation. Mr. Gradgrind is in conflict with the ideology that values affection and imagination, which view is held by Mr. Sleary, with his circus and its horse riders (Ford 115).

Northrop Frye notes that sometimes when Dickens is most involved in developing his plots he becomes careless, perhaps even contemptuous of the inner logic of the story. Frye cites the mysterious rumblings and creakings in the Clennan house throughout Little Dorrit (1855-1857) as an example. This is foregrounding meant to convey to the reader that the house is about to fall down. "What this in turn means is that Dickens is going to push it over at a moment when the villain is inside and the hero outside." Another example is the spontaneous combustion of Krook in Bleak House. According to Frye, this happens when Dickens is finished with this particular character (51). "Everyone realizes that Dickens is a great genius of the absurd in his characterization, and it is possible that his plots are also absurd in the same sense, not from incompetence or bad taste, but from a genuinely creative instinct" (Frye 52).

In Little Dorrit, Tattycoram has been adopted into the household of the Meagleses. They treat her partly as a child, and partly as a servant-companion to their real daughter, Pet. "Tattycoram" is not her real name. When she came to live with the Meagleses, her name was Harriet, but "Harriet" was changed into "Hattey," and "Hattey" became "Tatty," and so on. "We thought even a playful name might be a new thing to her, and might have a softening and affectionate kind of effect." The Meagleses live near a pretty little stream in a pretty suburban cottage, and their house is furnished with memorabilia from their numerous tours abroad (Henkle 177). "There were...bits of mummy from Egypt (and perhaps Birmingham); model gondolas from Venice; model villages from Switzerland; morsels of tesselated pavement from Herculaneum and Pompeii, like petrified minced veal; ashes out of tombs...rosaries blest all round by the Pope himself, and an infinite variety of lumber" (Henkle 178).

In a letter written to John Forster, Dickens said that the pivot on which the story turns in Great Expectations (1861) is "the grotesque tragicomic conception that first encouraged me." Dickens added, "You will not have to complain of the want of humour, as in The Tale of Two Cities" (Talon 6). This tragicomic conception can be seen in some lines uttered by Pip.

> My sister must have had some general idea that I was a young offender whom an Accoucheur Policeman had taken up (on my birthday) and delivered over to her, to be dealt with according to the outraged majesty of the law. I was always treated as if I had insisted on being born, in

opposition to the dictates of reason, religion, and morality and against the
dissuading arguments of my best friends. (Talon 7)

In Great Expectations, Joe's awkwardness is also depicted in the tragicomic tone.
He is dressed in his Sunday best when he visits Satis House in Chapter 13, and Pip says,
"I could hardly have imagined dear old Joe looking so unlike himself or so like some
extraordinary bird; standing, as he did, speechless, with his tuft of feathers ruffled and his
mouth open as if he wanted a worm" (Talon 8). In Chapter 27, Joe visits Barnard's Inn
and when he is asked for his hat Joe is too uncomfortable to give it up. " 'I am glad to
see you, Joe. Give me your hat.' But Joe, taking it carefully with both hands, like a bird's
nest with eggs in it, wouldn't hear of parting with that piece of property, and persisted in
talking over it in a most uncomfortable way" (Talon 8). Henri Talon says that away from
his forge, Joe "seems to be hampered by his body, and this is always funny." However,
the narrator is constantly reminding us of Joe's kindness, even while he is making fun of
him (Talon 8).

Miss Havisham is also a tragicomic figure in Great Expectations. It is ironic that
a romantic and visionary Victorian boy would perceive a person who looked like a witch
as a fairy god-mother. "Pip must have fancied that he was behaving like 'the young Knight
of romance' as he went down on his knee and put Miss Havisham's hand to his lips"
(Talon 10). Writing about Dickens's tragicomic vision, P. J. M. Scott refers to the
"apparent dichotomy which exists between Dickens's confident genial voice, his tone of (as
it were) suppressed high spirits or ebullition just held in check, and the darkness, the
recalcitrant and impassable human agonies which he deliberately discovers for us" (3).

Great Expectations (1861) was written at the end of Dickens's "dark period," and
contains many elements of dark comedy. Because of this timing, "many of his Victorian
readers welcomed this novel for its humor." Dickens's readers also enjoyed Pip's growth
from an "ugly duckling" into a "proud swan" (Ford 118). Nevertheless, George Ford states,
"Most critical discussions since 1950 argue that the Victorians were misled by some of its
great comic scenes such as Mr. Wopsle's playing Hamlet, and also by Pip's career. Unlike
the Victorians, modern critics see Great Expectations as a brilliant study of guilt (Ford
120).

From early childhood on, Dickens was like most Victorians in being fascinated by
crime. At bedtime, Mary Weller, his nursemaid, told him stories about dreadful murderers,
and he parodied these "Nurses' Stories" in The Uncommercial Traveller (1861) (Benstock
and Staley 106). Charles Dickens can produce powerful metaphors. The Podsnap soiree
in Our Mutual Friend (1865), for example involves a haunch of mutton that produces such
a steam-bath of moist odors that the diners are described as bathers (Smith 310). George
Ford says that some of the humor in Our Mutual Friend comes from its being a satire. An
example of this humor is at the dinner-party scenes at the homes of Mr. and Mrs. Podsnap
and of Mr. and Mrs. Veneering (Ford 121).

Edgar Johnson notes that under the pen name of "Boz," Dickens edited the
Memoirs of Joseph Grimaldi (1870), a comic English actor. Grimaldi had a great impact
on Dickens life, even when he was in America. One evening, he attended a dinner at the
Parker House in Boston, Massachusetts with other notables like James Russell Lowell,
Oliver Wendell Holmes, Henry Wadsworth Longfellow, and Charles Eliot Norton. Some
of Dickens friends went with Dickens to his room when he retired in the evening, and
Dickens was still in a very talkative mood. He started to draw himself a bath, at the same
time entertaining his companions by imitating the clown Grimaldi on the rolling edge of
the tub. While performing this complicated feat, he lost his balance and with a "tidal wave
of a splash, he fell into the bath tub, evening dress, boutonniere, gold chains, brilliantined
earlocks, and all." It was a magnificent pratfall (Collins 56).

Charles Dickens was writing The Mystery of Edwin Drood (1870) when he died.

He never finished it, and there has been much speculation as to how he would have ended it. "There are shelfloads of books with The Mystery of Edwin Drood as their subject, but they are not critical studies; instead, they are attempts to solve the mystery by conjecture or by simply inventing six more books of the story as Dickens might have written them" (Ford 121). In January of 1914, a group of famous writers and attorneys held a mock trial for John Jasper. The mock trial was held in London, and G. K. Chesterton took on the role as judge, just as George Bernard Shaw functioned as the foreman of the jury. The jury found Jasper guilty; however, Chesterton fined them for contempt of court and pronounced the case unsolvable (Benstock and Staley 108).

Judy Little suggests that in Dickens's novels a person's class, profession, eccentricities, obsessions, dress, and mannerisms all come in for much comic ridicule. "The ruthless or fawning social climbers in Dickens's novels are characterized largely by reference to these features of social and economic life" (Little 15). The villains of Charles Dickens's early books provide readers with some of the most splendid comic moments in all of literature. G. K. Chesterton says that he hates to see a Dickens villain leave; "if only the scoundrel could stick his head back into the doorway and make one more atrocious remark" (qtd. in Henkle 123). But this does not mean that such villains as Quilp or Carker are meant to prevail over the instruments of good in Dickens's novels. Nevertheless, "we cannot be so false to our own reading experience as to deny the fascination and pleasure that such scoundrels bring." Roger Henkle asks, "Who can resist thumbing ahead to see when the next Quilp passage occurs in The Old Curiosity Shop?" (Henkle 123). George Orwell said that before he was ten years old he was having Dickens ladled down his throat by schoolmasters who had a strong resemblance to Mr. Creakle. English lawyers delight in Dickens's portrayals of Sergeant Buzfuz, and Little Dorrit is enjoyed by many English politicians. On the basis of such evidence, George Orwell concludes, "Dickens seems to have succeeded in attacking everybody and antagonizing nobody" (Orwell 3).

Orwell considers the most salient feature of Dickens's writing to be his "unnecessary detail." Mr. Jack Hopkins is telling a story at Bob Sawyer's party about a child who had swallowed its sister's necklace:

> Next day, child swallowed two beads; the day after that, he treated himself to three, and so on, till in a week's time he had got through the necklace--five-and-twenty beads in all. The sister who was an industrious girl and seldom treated herself to a bit of finery, cried her eyes out at the loss of the necklace; looked high and low for it; but I needn't say, didn't find it. A few days afterwards, the family were at dinner--baked shoulder of mutton and potatoes under it--the child, who wasn't hungry, was playing about the room, when suddenly there was heard the devil of a noise, like a small hailstorm.... (Orwell 59-60)

George Orwell asks, how "a baked shoulder of mutton and potatoes under it" advances the story, and then he answers that it doesn't. "It is something totally unnecessary, a florid little squiggle on the edge of the page; only, it is by just these squiggles that the special Dickens atmosphere is created" (Orwell 61).

Dickens suffered from spasmodic attacks, and he was such a sickly child that he could not take part in the games of other boys. Nevertheless, he enjoyed watching their games as he peered over whatever book he happened to be reading. He would sit with a book in his left hand, clasping this same left wrist with his right hand. His body would sway back and forth while sucking sounds would utter from his mouth. Every spare minute of his time was spent reading Roderick Random, Peregrine Pickle, Humphry Clinker, Tom Jones, The Vicar of Wakefield, Don Quixote, Gil Blas, Robinson Crusoe, The Arabian Nights, and other books (Pearson 3-4).

His characters came from his reading, and from real life, but they were always presented with a great deal of creativity and originality. At one time he was looking for a harsh magistrate for a police court scene, and he had heard that there was a rather unpleasant specimen named Mr. Laing at Hatton Garden, so he entered the court there and made a brief study of him. Mr. Laing had a reputation of having a bad temper in court, and the authorities had already received many complaints in this regard, one from a clergyman who was later convicted of stealing a silver spoon at a charity dinner he was in charge of. Dickens talked to local authorities, talked to people who had visited Mr. Laing's court, and talked as well to Mr. Laing himself. "Dickens certainly caught him in a peevish mood. Perhaps he was drunk, or, worse still, sober. Dickens leaves it an open question":

> Mr. Fang was a lean, long-backed, stiff-necked, middle-sized man, with no
> great quantity of hair, and what he had, growing on the back and sides of
> his head. His face was stern, and much flushed. If he were really not in the
> habit of drinking rather more than was exactly good for him, he might have
> brought an action against his countenance for libel, and have recovered
> heavy damages. (Pearson 69)

Shortly thereafter, Mr. Laing was discharged from his position of trust. Pearson notes that "nowadays a paragraph like that would have brought its writer into court, not sent its victim out of one" (Pearson 69).

Many of Dickens's characters were grounded in real life. The character of Little Nell in The Old Curiosity Shop was based on Mary Hogarth, Dickens's sister-in-law, who died in Dickens's arms at the age of seventeen. When the character Little Nell died, all of England wept. Mr. Micawber was based on his father, and Mrs. Nickleby was based on his mother. Mrs. Nickleby speaks in loquacious monologues that are filled with delightful absurdities (Ford 105). Mr. Squeers, the schoolmaster in Nicholas Nickleby was also taken from real life, and the portrait was painted so well, and so close to real life that the person on whom the sketch was based suffered from a premature death. Hesketh Pearson notes that Dickens's portrayal of the Yorkshire schools was so devastating that the school system drastically changed, and schools like the ones he described were ridiculed out of existence (Pearson 72-73). Dickens's mother did not realize that she was the model for Mrs. Nickleby, and Dickens once wrote about "Mrs. Nickleby herself, sitting bodily before me in a solid chair [who] once asked me whether I believed there ever was such a woman." J. W. T. Ley, although he was a zealous Dickensian, felt that "this lampooning of his mother was in the worst taste" (Pearson 74). As a last example of Dickens's effect on the reality which he drew his figures from, consider Mrs. Gamp of Martin Chuzzlewit, a satirical character based on what Joseph Priestley calls the "pre-Nightingale type of nurse, a drunken, grasping, ignorant, elderly woman, hardly fit to tend a sick dog. The deplorable habits of Mrs. Gamp were those, apparently of a whole generation of so-called nurses, and Dickens's satirical portrait hastened the extinction of the type" (155).

S. J. Newman considers Balzac, Dickens, Dostoevsky, and Tolstoy to be the greatest novelists in the history of Europe, and in a book entitled Dickens at Play, he suggests that for Dickens, comedy always had precedence over the idea. Dickens wrote to his friend Bulwer-Lytton that it was his "infirmity to see odd relationships in things," and Newman notes further that "this irrepressible comic energy goes deeper, stranger, more anarchic modes of vision than in any other artist" (1). Newman considers in depth Dickens's sense of play, in terms of fancy, language, and theatre, "in order to set against Coleridgean, Arnoldian, Jamesian, and Leavisite principles--which are unitary, critical, responsible, and adult--the value of an art which is discrete, creative, irresponsible, and young" respectively. "In the early novels the imagination is rampant. Even these works can be skimmed for moral instruction or sociological information, but their information is random and their instruction undesirable. What they testify to is simply the shocking brilliance and gusto of Dickens's creativity" (Newman 3). Dickens's novels have what Joseph Priestley calls a "genuine creative force, a fountain of high spirits, a gushing spring of absurdity." Dickens had remarkable powers of imagination. "It is significant that highly poetical people, such as Swinburne, have always delighted in the humour of Dickens; whereas stoutly prosaic persons, like Trollope, have never felt at home with it" (Priestley 152).

In 1872, G. H. Lewes said of Dickens that he was a "seer of visions." "And his visions were of objects at once familiar and potent. Psychologists will understand both the extent and the limitations of the remark, when I say that in no other perfectly sane mind (Blake, I believe, was not perfectly sane) have I observed vividness of imagination approaching so closely to hallucination" (Allen 11-12). Lewes goes on to say that when Dickens imagined a street, a house, a room, or a figure, he saw it not in the vague schematic way that the rest of us imagine it, but rather, in his mind's eye he saw "all the salient details obtruding themselves on his attention" (Allen 12).

Joseph Priestley says that the most significant aspect of Dickens's humor is his humorous characterizations. Often his readers are able to remember Dickens's comic characters more readily than they can remember the books that contain them. Priestley notes that few people could assign such characters as Mr. Peter Magnus, Mr. Sapsea, Mr. Guppy, Mr. Jack Hopkins, Mrs. Todgers, Mr. Toots, Mrs. Gamp, Mr. Pumblechook, or Miss Nipper to their appropriate novels without hesitation (150). Furthermore, during Dickens's time, and to some extent later as well, people communicated personality traits by giving each other such names as Mr. Pecksniff, or Mr. Tapley. But there is an irony in this regard: "It was then pointed out these were exactly the reasons why such characters were not great creations, that we knew so much about them precisely because they were not like human beings, that Pecksniff or Tapley merely meant hypocrisy and a gallant optimism." They were thus considered merely "gross caricatures" (151). Priestley agrees that these are caricatures; however, he states that literature is full of caricatures, "but literature is not full of Dickens characters, and if anybody imagines that they are easy to do, let him try" (151). In this regard, Mrs. Sapsea's epitaph is appropriate, "Stranger, pause. And ask thyself this question, Canst thou do likewise? If not, with a blush retire" (151).

Dickens's characters are odd, and idiosyncratic, and these qualities are "manifest not only in his comic characters, whether purely humorous like Pickwick, the Wellers, and Micawber, or satirical, as with Pecksniff and Podsnap, but also through a wide spectrum of characters from the purely humorous to the monstrous and melodramatically wicked" (Allen 9). Walter Allen notes that even the characters which Dickens most admires are odd and idiosyncratic. Tom Pinch, for example is described as "an ungainly, awkward-looking man, extremely short-sighted, and prematurely bald."

> Seeing that Mr. Pecksniff sat with his back towards him [Tom Pinch], gazing at the fire, [he] stood hesitating, with the door in his hand. He was far from handsome certainly; and was drest in a snuff-coloured suit, of an uncouth make at the best, which, being shrunk with long wear, was twisted and tortured into all kinds of odd shapes; but notwithstanding his attire, and his clumsy figure, with a great stoop in his shoulders, and a ludicrous habit he had of thrusting his head forward, by no means redeemed, one would have been disposed...to consider him a bad fellow by any means. (Allen 8)

Walter Allen notes that whenever Dickens doesn't describe his characters as odd or idiosyncratic, his characterizations fail, and this is true especially of Dickens's young women, like Rose Maylie, Kate Nickleby, and Ruth Pinch. "It is as though they are sacrosanct by virtue of their youth, sex, innocence and class, qualities that inhibit criticism and the external approach that is the expression of criticism.... They lack idiosyncracy; it seems that if they were in any way odd they would be less than perfect" (9).

Northrop Frye suggests that the structure which Dickens uses for his novels is "New

Comedy." This is a genre which comes to us from Plautus and Terence through Ben Jonson and Molière.

> The main action is a collision of two societies which we may call for convenience the obstructing and the congenial society. The congenial society is usually centered on the love of hero and heroine, the obstructing society on the characters, often parental, who try to thwart this love. For most of the action the thwarting characters are in the ascendant, but toward the end a twist in the plot reverses the situation and the congenial society dominates the happy ending. (Frye 52)

Thus, according to the traditions of New Comedy, the plot reversal and resultant happy ending is a form of festivity. There are often several marriages, the dispensing of money, and/or the dispensing of a great deal of food. Such characteristics have remained constant in the New Comedy tradition since Greek times (Frye 55). The plot-reversal, which is an important characteristic of this genre is frequently the result of the discovery that one of the main characters, often the heroine, was born into a better family than had been previously thought (Frye 53). Frye contrasts the salient mystery of Dickens's novels with the salient mystery of modern mystery novels, saying that the mystery in a Dickens novel often deals with birth, while the mystery of a whodunit deals with death (54).

Another important feature of New Comedy is the humours characters. Frye considers Dickens characters to be neither realistic portraits in the tradition of Anthony Trollope, nor caricatures. Rather, they are humours characters in the tradition of Ben Jonson. "The humour is a character identified with a characteristic, like the miser, the hypochondriac, the braggart, the parasite, or the pedant, and he is obsessed by whatever humour he represents. Frye notes that these humours characters are very consistent with Henri Bergson's statement that our superiority to an obsessed person, someone bound to an invariable ritual habit, is one of the chief sources of laughter (Frye 56). There are two kinds of humours characters, the genial, generous, and lovable ones, and the absurd or sinister ones. Typically the characters in the congenial society have amiable and harmless eccentricities, while the humours characters of the obstructing society reinforce the false standards and values of that society (Frye 56-57). In Bleak House Smallweed is the miser, Chadband is the hypocrite, Skimpole and Turveydrop are the parasites, and Mrs. Jellyby is the pedant. In The Pickwick Papers, Mr. Winkle is the duffer sportsman, whose pretensions go far beyond his performance. Mr. Winkle, however represents another humour as well--"the pleasant young man who breaks down family opposition on both sides to acquire a pleasant young woman" (Frye 57). Other humours characters in The Pickwick Papers include Mr. Tupman the incautious lover, Mr. Snodgrass, the melancholy poet, and Mr. Pickwick himself, the pedant (Frye 57). But Mr. Pickwick is a complex character, and one whose humour changes. In the tradition of New Comedy, there is a reversal in the direction of the plot of Pickwick Papers, and Mr. Pickwick in the debtors' prison becomes a man of principle, "and the humour of pedantry is transferred to the law which entraps him" (Frye 58).

Associated with many of the humours characters in Dickens's novels are particular phrases, or ways of speaking, and Frye calls this "tagged humor." Walter Allen says that "all of Dickens's successful characters, major and minor alike, speak in idioms uniquely personal to them as individuals. They are as intensely realized in their speech as their external appearance and mannerisms" (14). Thus Mrs. Micawber is constantly saying that she will never desert Mr. Micawber, and Major Bagnet in Bleak House says that he admires his wife but must never tell her so because "discipline must be maintained." Mr. Jingle is identified by his disjointed phrases, and Mrs. Nickleby and Flora Finching by their asyntactic babble. Uriah Heep always insists on his "umble" qualities, and then there is the squeezing landlord in Little Dorrit, the beggarly whine of Chadband, and the Parliamentary flourishes of Mr. Micawber. Victorian prudery is a humour well represented by Podsnap of Our Mutual Friend, and by Mrs. General (the prunes-and-prisms woman) of Little Dorrit (Frye 61). Frye compares the repetition of the tagged humor with other types of repetition in Dickens, such as the emphasis on Carker's teeth in Dombey and Son; this is appropriate for a villain like Carker, because it dehumanizes him, and cuts off sympathy. "We cannot feel much concern over the fate of a character who is presented to us mainly as a set of teeth" (Frye 58).

In Dickens, the obstructing society has two important features; it is parasitic, and it is pedantic (Frye 66). Frye suggests that humour comedy has a natural affinity to the morality play, since humours are viewed by the audience as good if they are on the side of the congenial, and bad or ridiculous if they are on the side of the obstructing society. This is reinforced by the allegorical names which Dickens often gives to such minor characters as "Pyke" and "Pluck," in Nicholas Nickleby, or "Bar," "Bishop," and "Physician," who all turn up at Merdle's dinners in Little Dorrit. Frequently these names appear in contrasting good-bad pairs: "We have a "good" major in Bleak House and a "bad" one with a very similar name in Dombey and Son; we have a villainous Jew in Oliver Twist and a saintly Jew in Our Mutual Friend, and so on. Within Dombey and Son itself the "bad" major is paired against a "good" navy man, Captain Cuttle" (Frye 60). There are also humours characters who either try to disguise their humours, or effectively change them. Thus Boffin is generous but he pretends to be a miser. And Scrooge goes through the reversal process, as does Mercy Pecksniff who changes from the feather-head to the faithful ill-used wife. The most common type of metamorphosis results in a character's releasing his humour or obsession at the end of the novel. Martin Chuzzlewit escapes from his selfishness, Mark Tapley from his compulsion to seek difficult situations in order to "come out strong," and Tom Pinch from his innocence (Frye 60).

Alfred Gu L'Estrange notes that prior to Dickens's time people had regarded the poor and uneducated with a great deal of contempt. "Their language and stupidity had formed fertile subjects for the coarse ridicule of the humorist.... With Dickens, the poor man was not a mere clown or blockhead; but beneath his 'hodden gray' often carried good feeling, intelligence, and wit" (226-227). According to Stephen Leacock, Dickens had the ability to "change a cheat and a crook into a charming character, a criminal imposter into a delight--that is Dickens and that is no one else.... It is as if the world itself were transformed and its worse sins seen in the light of a kindly and amused tolerance that is higher than humanity itself" (125). Dickens is remarkably gentle when his humor relates to the poor. He may treat their ignorance and simplicity with amusement, but he always throws in some sterling qualities as well, for his treatment is usually good-natured and sympathetic. Sam Weller is pleasant as is Boots at the Holly Tree Inn. Mrs. Jarley, who travels about to fairs with wax-works, is also kindly and hospitable (L'Estrange 229). This is consistent with William Lilly's calling Dickens "the humourist as democrat." What he means by this is that Dickens, more than any other author, tried to deliver the common people from being considered debased and vulgar. Dickens fought strenuously to enfranchise and elevate the masses (Lilly 29-30). It should be noted, however, that Dickens was criticized for doing this. Richard Barham (Thomas Ingoldsby) wrote, "There is a sort of Radicalish tone about Oliver Twist which I don't altogether like." Thackeray was even harsher, saying that men of genius had "no business to make these characters interesting or agreeable" (Pearson 70).

All of Dickens's novels contain a great deal of humor, but each novel offers a humor of a different sort as can be seen by the chapter headings in James Kincaid's Dickens and the Rhetoric of Laughter: "Chapter 2: The Pickwick Papers: The Vision from the Wheelbarrow," "Chapter 3: Oliver Twist: Laughter and the Rhetoric of Attack," "Chapter 4: The Old Curiosity Shop: Laughter and Pathos," "Chapter 5: Barnaby Rudge:

Laughter and Structure," "Chapter 6: Martin Chuzzlewit: The Comedy of Accommodation,"
"Chapter 7: David Copperfield: Laughter and Point of View," "Chapter 8: Little Dorrit: The
Attack on Comedy," and "Chapter 9: Our Mutual Friend: Mr. Pickwick in Purgatory" (ix).

James Kincaid says that Dickens has a special talent for evoking strong emotions
that result in laughter, terror, and/or pathos. These emotions are used to support his
dominant themes and effects, and although the earlier novels tend to be lighter in tone and
the later novels more serious, there is a seriousness in his humor throughout his writing
career. "Generally speaking, as Dickens progressed he used humour for perhaps more
serious purposes, attacking and persuading the reader more and more subtly" (4).

In order to support his books, Dickens did many readings. There is a story about
a lady at one of these readings who stopped Dickens and asked if she could "touch the hand
that has filled my house with many friends." Dickens had a special ability to form an
emotional bond with his readers. In his letters, he said that what excited him most about
his readings was the particular warmth and personal response of his audience. Dickens felt
that if his rhetoric was to be successful, the reader had to play a very active role. He felt
that the reader had to participate equally with the writer in the experience and in the theme,
and Dickens accomplished this task very well. Dickens described his readings as follows:
"The affectionate regard of the people exceeds all bounds and is shown in every way. The
audiences do everything but embrace me, and take as much pains with the readings as I do"
(Kincaid 19).

Once, late in life, after he had given a public reading in Portsmouth, he was
strolling with his agent through the streets and he noticed the name of a particular terrace.

"By Jove!" he exclaimed: "here is the place where I was born." But he
could not locate the number. They walked up and down. Dickens pointing
to one house and saying that he must have lived there because it looked so
much like his father; then he favoured another because it looked like the
birthplace of a man who had deserted it; then he picked on a third because
it had obviously been the home of a puny weak child such as he had been;
and so on, until it appeared that he had been born at every house in the
terrace. (Pearson 1-2)

The comedy of Dickens's late novels comes from his personal, and psychological
concerns rather than from his broad and categorizing vision. "The forms of comic
expression are those that accommodate internalized anxieties and aspirations. They are
consequently more ambivalent, more convoluted in expression, more paradoxical" (Kincaid
5-7). James Kincaid considers the most salient aspects of Dickens's humor to be his
peculiar perspective, his use of concrete details, his use of the idiom and vernacular
language, his savagery and his darkness (Kincaid 5-7). It has been noted that much of
Dickens's humor depends on making light jests in a solemn manner. John Ruskin once
said, "I believe Dickens to be as little understood as Cervantes, and almost as mischievous"
(Kincaid 7). Dickens frequently asks his reader to laugh at the very subjects which he
describes in other parts of the novel with sympathy or anger--death, loneliness,
improvidence, rigidity, spontaneity, cruelty. But Dickens was also preoccupied with such
traditional comic values and symbols as freedom, justice, rebirth, and flexibility. In his
obituary notice in the Spectator, Charles Dickens is described as "the greatest humourist
whom England ever produced--Shakespeare himself certainly not excepted" (Kincaid 8).

Charles Dickens Bibliography

Allen, Walter. "The Comedy of Dickens." Dickens 1970: Centenary Essays. Ed. Michael
    Slater. New York, NY: Stein, 1970, 3-27.
Barickman, Richard. "The Comedy of Survival in Dickens's Novels." Novel 11 (1978):

128-143.

Benstock, Bernard and Thomas F. Staley, eds. Dictionary of Literary Biography, Volume Seventy: British Mystery Writers, 1860-1919. Detroit, MI: Gale, 1988, 102-111.

Borowitz, Albert. "Charles Dickens." Dictionary of Literary Biography, Volume Seventy: British Mystery Writers, 1860-1919. Eds. Bernard Benstock and Thomas F. Staley. Detroit, MI: Gale, 1988, 102-111.

Collins, Philip. "A Twinkle in the Narratorial Eye: Dickens, Thackeray and Eliot." Literary and Linguistic Aspects of Humor. Barcelona, Spain: University of Barcelona Department of Languages, 1984, 9-25.

Collins, R. G. "Dickens and Grimaldi." Thalia: Studies in Literary Humor 1.2 (1979): 55-73.

Cross, Barbara M. "Comedy and Drama in Dickens." Western Humanities Review 17 (1963): 143-149.

Davis, Jim. " 'Like Comic Actors on a Stage in Heaven': Dickens, John Liston and Low Comedy." Dickensian 74 (1978): 161-166.

Dickens, Charles. Nicholas Nickleby. London, England: Dent, 1977.

Diedrick, James. "Charles Dickens." Dictionary of Literary Biography 55: Victorian Prose Writers before 1867. Ed. William B. Thesing. Detroit, MI: Gale, 1987, 80-90.

Fanger, Donald. "Dickens and Gogol: Energies of the Word." Veins of Humor. Ed. Harry Levin. Cambridge, MA: Harvard Univ Press, 1972, 131-146.

Fisher, Leona Weaver. Lemon, Dickens, and Mr. Nightingale's Diary: A Victorian Farce. Victoria, BC, Canada: English Literary Studies, 1988.

Ford, George H. "Charles Dickens." Victorian Novelists before 1885. Eds. Ira B. Nadel, and William E. Fredeman. Detroit, MI: Gale, 1983, 89-124.

Frye, Northrop. "Dickens and the Comedy of Humors." Experience in the Novel: Selected Papers from the English Institute. Ed. Roy Harvey Pearce. New York, NY: Columbia Univ Press, 1968, 49-71.

Henkle, Roger B. "Early Dickens: Metamorphosis, Psychic Disorientation, and the Small Fry." Comedy and Culture--England--1820-1900. Princeton, NJ: Princeton University Press, 1980, 111-144.

Henkle, Roger B. "Later Dickens: Disenchantment, Transmogrification, and Ambivalence." Comedy and Culture--England--1820-1900. Princeton, NJ: Princeton University Press, 1980, 145-184.

Kincaid, James Russell. Dickens and the Rhetoric of Laughter. New York, NY: Clarendon, 1971.

Kitchin, George. Survey of Burlesque and Parody in English. London, England: Oliver and Boyd, 1931.

L'Estrange, Alfred Gu. "Dickens." History of English Humour. New York, NY: Burt Franklin, 1878, 226-240.

Leacock, Stephen. Humor: Its Theory and Technique. Toronto, Canada: Dodd Mead, 1935.

Levin, Harry, ed. Veins of Humor. Cambridge, MA: Harvard Univ Press, 1972.

Lilly, William Samuel. "Charles Dickens: The Humourist as Democrat." Four English Humorists of the Nineteenth Century. London: Norwood, 1978, 3-30.

Little, Judy. Comedy and the Woman Writer: Woolf, Spark, and Feminism. Lincoln, NE: University of Nebraska Press, 1983.

McKenzie, Gordon. "Dickens and Daumier." University of California Publications: English Studies, 8.2 (1941): 273-298.

Manning, Sylvia Bank. Dickens as Satirist. New Haven, CT: Yale Univ Press, 1971.

Martin, Robert Bernard. The Triumph of Wit: A Study of Victorian Comic Theory. Oxford, England: Clarendon Press, 1974.

Miller, J. Hillis. "The Sources of Dickens's Comic Art: From American Notes to Martin

Chuzzlewit." Nineteenth-Century Fiction 24 (1970): 467-476.

Newman, S. J. Dickens at Play. London, England: Macmillan, 1981; also New York, NY: St. Martin's, 1981.

Orwell, George. Dickens, Dali and Others. New York, NY: Harcourt, Brace, Jovanovich, 1946.

Pearson, Hesketh. Dickens: His Character, Comedy, and Career. New York, NY: Harper and Brothers, 1949.

Priestley, J. B. "Dickens." English Humour. New York, NY: Longmans, 1929, 150-162.

Priestley, J. B. "The Wonderful World of Dickens." English Humour. New York, NY: Stein and Day, 1976, 66-77.

Pritchett, V. S. "The Comic World of Dickens." The Dickens Critics. Eds. George H. Ford and Lauriat Lane, Jr. Ithaca, NY: Cornell Univ Press, 1961, 309-324.

Rasponich, Beverly J. "Charles Dickens and Stephen Leacock: A Legacy of Sentimental Humour." Thalia: Studies in Literary Humor 3.2 (1981): 17-24.

Scott, Peter James Malcolm. Reality and Comic Confidence in Charles Dickens. New York, NY: Barnes and Noble, 1979.

Simpson, Evelyn M. "Jonson and Dickens: A Study in the Comic Genius of London." Essays and Studies 29 (1943): 82-92.

Smith, Elton E. "Charles Dickens." Encyclopedia of British Humorists, Volume I. Ed. Steven H. Gale. New York, NY: Garland, 1996, 307-315.

Sucksmith, H. P. The Narrative Art of Charles Dickens: The Rhetoric of Sympathy and Irony in His Novels. Oxford, England: Clarendon, 1970.

Talon, Henri. "On Some Aspects of the Comic in Great Expectations." Victorian Newsletter 42 (1972): 6-11.

Edward Lear (1812-1888)

Lear once wrote, "Nonsense is the breath of my nostrils." Vivien Noakes commented that nonsense was inseparable from Lear's life as it "expresses both his merriment and his most deeply held beliefs" (1812-1888 13). Noakes notes that it is now difficult to determine whether Lear's success as the author of the Book of Nonsense (1846) detracted from or added to his reputation as a serious painter. It is interesting to note, however, that he published the first two editions of his book anonymously as Old Derry down Derry; only the third edition bore his real name (1812-1888 14). It should be further noted that in English tradition, the Old Derry down Derry was the stereotypical fool of the mummers (Lear Book of Nonsense v).

In 1846, Lear gave drawing lessons to Queen Victoria. In this same year, Lear published A Book of Nonsense (1846). He later published A Book of Nonsense Second Edition (1861), Nonsense Songs, Stories, Botany and Alphabets (1871), More Nonsense, Pictures, Rhymes, Botany, etc. (1872), Laughable Lyrics, A Fourth Book of Nonsense Poems, Songs, Botany, Music, Etc. (1877), and Nonsense Songs and Stories (1895). Even Lear's travel journals were entertaining and fresh in their observations, and filled with humor (Lehmann 8, 119). In the February 1886 edition of The Pall Mall Magazine, John Ruskin wrote, "I don't know of any author to whom I am half so grateful for my idle self as Edward Lear. I shall put him first [in the list] of my 'hundred authors'" (Lear Exhibition 2, 4).

Lear spent a number of years as the official artist at Knowsley Manor, where he was employed to draw the animals of the Earl of Derby's menagerie, and he became a close friend of the Earl's children and their friends, and he entertained them with nonsense drawings and impromptu rhymes (Mégroz 7). Lear didn't like the adults at Knowsley

Manor, and about high society he said, "The uniform apathetic tone assumed by lofty society irks me dreadfully; nothing I long for half so much as to giggle heartily and to hop on one leg down the great gallery--but I dare not." At various Knowsley social gatherings Lear enjoyed mingling with the children rather than with the adults, and Vivien Noakes suggests that while some critics have considered Lear's characters to be deceptive, they are instead childlike, as they display "carelessness, greed, despair, generosity, and humour" (Lear Book of Nonsense vi).

Lear dedicated his First Book of Nonsense (1846) to "the Great-Grandchildren, Grand-Nephews, and Grand-Nieces of Edward, 13th Earl of Derby." It was the 13th Earl of Derby who was the Lord of Knowsley Manor (Mégroz 6). One day, Lear was in a passenger car of a train traveling from London to Guilford, and across from him were an elderly gentleman and two ladies, accompanied by two little boys reading a copy of Lear's Book of Nonsense. One of the ladies remarked that the author of the book was "Edward Lear," but the gentleman responded, "Ah, so it is printed; but that is only a whim of the real author, the Earl of Derby. 'Edward' is his Christian name, and as you may see, LEAR is only EARL transposed." When the lady countered with "But, here is a dedication to the great-grandchildren, grand-nephews, and grand-nieces of Edward, thirteenth Earl of Derby, by the author, Edward Lear," the gentleman calmly replied, "That is simply a piece of mystification; I am in a position to know that the whole book was composed and illustrated by Lord Derby himself. In fact, there is no such a person at all as Edward Lear." Edward Lear, who had heard this entire conversation without saying a word knew that his hat, and his handkerchief and stick were all marked with his name, and that in addition he had a number of letters in his pocket addressed to Edward Lear. Since the temptation was too great to resist, he flashed all of these articles at once at the gentleman, and thus doing, "I speedily reduced him to silence" (Lear Book of Nonsense xii-xiii).

In More Nonsense (1861), Edward Lear developed his own brand of limerick. Lear had a stock cast of characters. The limerick tended to be an Old Man, a Young Lady, an Old Person, or a Young Person. This was followed by the name of a place (a particular town, city, or country). Elton Smith tells why Lear's limericks are considered to be humorous in tone: "The repetition of a refrain tends to make the limerick sound like a ballad, the seesaw rhythm like a nursery rhyme. The basic absurdity of character and action creates the aura of nonsense." Smith further notes that Lear's limericks tend to fall into topical groupings. In the early limericks, Lear's Old Men tend to become victimized. Lear's Young Ladies tend to be serenely in charge of all situations. In later limericks the Old Men tend to be furious, frenzied, or threatening, while the Young Ladies have aged considerably, and have lost their earlier ability to entrance. Lear's limericks, like his paintings, also made reference to many different types of animals, with the animals in his first limericks being either menacing or charmed, and with those in the later limericks becoming like Lear himself. From his careful observations of the birds and animals in the Knowsley menagerie, Lear remembers and mentions in his limericks such animals as ravens, larks, wrens, crows, parrots, ducklings, geese, cranes, owls, hens, carps, pigs, frogs, Bluebottle flies, bears, mice, rabbits, apes, cats, horses, cows, and calves. But Lear never mentions (or paints) dogs, because he seems to have been afraid of dogs for his entire lifetime (Smith 647).

Many of Lear's poems are romantic quests."The Owl and the Pussy-cat" (1867) was written for Janet, the daughter of John Addington Symonds. Lear composed his own music for the piece, and he often played and sang it as a court jester in the country houses which he visited.. The song is in the tradition of romantic love, and is a quest for a wedding ceremony and marital bliss. It is odd, however, that the Cat is the groom, and the Owl is the bride, as this is a reversal of expectations. Also, it is the female who steers the boat, and it is the male who sits in the bow of the boat and sings expressions of flattery. She is the one who proposes, and he is the one who bashfully gets the ring from a pig's nose while she stairs critically at his ineptitude. "The Owl and the Pussy-cat" is similar in structure to "The Duck and the Kangaroo." Again Lear has an ill-matched pair, with the male-Kangaroo being fastidious and hypochondriacal, while the female-Duck smokes her cigar and is resourceful and decisive. This time the quest is to make it three times around the world, which seems a bit excessive (Smith 648).

"The Dong with a Luminous Nose" is another romantic quest with vivid visual imagery, and with sexual innuendo (Smith 648). The Dong has gone in search of the Jumbly girl, but though he does find Paradise, he does not find love, so the Dong weaves a luminous nose and goes through live always seeking but never finding. "The Pobble Who Has No Toes" is still another romantic quest. This is a wonderfully daring adventure in which the Pobble sets out to find Aunt Jobiska's Runcible Cat. After he sacrifices his toes, he comes back to be consoled by his Aunt's insistence that "everybody knows a Pobble is happier without his toes." "But, does the Pobble know that?" (Smith 649).

Edward Lear was popular enough to be invited to the homes of many important people, and on one afternoon in 1879 he was invited to the home of the British Vice-Consul at San Remo, where he met the sons and daughters of the Vice-Consul and his wife, Mrs. and Mrs. Bevan. One daughter was especially witty and vivacious, and later she collaborated with Edward Lear to write "How Pleasant to Know Mr. Lear!" (Smith 646). Lear later wrote this poem about himself in a letter to Hallam Tennyson. The poem is written in the mock-heroic style:

How pleasant to know Mr. Lear!
    Who has written such volumes of stuff!
Some think him ill-tempered and queer,
    But a few think him pleasant enough.

His mind is concrete and fastidious,
    His nose is remarkably big:
His visage is more or less hideous,
    His hair it resembles a wig....

He has many friends, laymen and clerical,
    Old Foss is the name of his cat;
His body is perfectly spherical,
    He weareth a runcible hat....

He reads but he cannot speak Spanish,
    He cannot abide ginger-beer:
Ere the days of his pilgrimage vanish,
    How pleasant to know Mr. Lear. (Wells 88-89)

Lear loved to play with language and with culture. In "The Story of the Four Little Children Who Went Round the World" (1895) a wide range of nonsense devices is employed. There is a mirroring or inversion in which an island made of water is surrounded by earth; there is play with imprecise boundaries, as when they bought a large boat to sail around the earth by sea, but they had to come back on the other side of the earth by land; there is play with incongruity, infinity or seriality, as when the island was filled with two-thousand veal-cutlets and a million chocolate drops, but nothing else; there is play with simultaneity as when they pursue their voyage "with the utmost delight and apathy"; there is play with arbitrariness, as when the significance of the story is both affirmed and denied at the same time. The story ends with a number of ironic contradictions, or at least paradoxes.

Thus, in less than eighteen weeks, they all arrived safely at home, where they were received by their admiring relatives with joy tempered with contempt; and where they finally resolved to carry out the rest of their travelling plans at some more favourable opportunity. As for the Rhinoceros, in token of their grateful adherence, they had him killed and stuffed directly, and then set him up outside the door of their father's house as a Diaphanous Doorscraper. (Tigges, 1988, 149)

W. H. Auden wrote the following about Lear.

Left by his friend to breakfast alone on the white
Italian shore, his Terrible Demon arose
Over his shoulder; he wept to himself in the night,
A dirty landscape-painter who hated his nose.

Auden ended his tribute to Lear with the line "And children swarmed to him like settlers. He became a land" (qtd. in Lehmann 6). John Lehmann described Lear as follows:

He was tall, with a slight stoop, no doubt caused partly by having to peer very closely through his strong spectacles at whatever he was drawing, and also by his extremely delicate health. He was not in any way good-looking, but his sensitively pleasing expression and the humorous twinkle in his eye made up for a general plainness and the large, shapeless nose of which he was painfully conscious all his life. (Lehmann 7)

After the publication of his More Nonsense in 1861, Lear wrote, "It is queer (and you would say so if you saw me) that I am the man as is making some three or four thousand people laugh in England all at one time" (Noakes Wanderer 7).

George Orwell uses an Edward Lear nonsense limerick to illustrate how non-violent language can be used to present a very violent image:

There was an old man of Whitehaven
Who danced a quadrille with a raven;
But they said, "It's absurd
To encourage this bird!"
So they smashed that old man of Whitehaven. (qtd. in Henkle 216)

Orwell notes that "To smash somebody just for dancing a quadrille with a raven is exactly the kind of thing that 'They' would do." Roger Henkle continues with Orwell's reasoning: "We know very well who 'they' are--the Establishment, the self-appointed moral arbiters of society. And what are they smashing? Harmless adult play, whimsy, dancing. Lear's verse is slight, hardly serious, yet its underlying resentment is perfectly communicated" (Henkle 216).

Edward Lear was the twentieth of twenty-one children. From the age of seven onward, Lear suffered acute bouts of depression, about which he says,

The earliest of all the morbidnesses I can recollect must have been about 1819--when my Father took me to a field near Highgate, where was a rural performance of gymnastic clowns etc., and a band. The music was good--at least it attracted me--and the sunset and twilight I remember as if yesterday. And I can recollect crying half the night after all the small gaiety broke up-- and also suffering for days at the memory of the past scene. (Noakes 1812-1888 13)

Lear was sad that this pleasant scene was so ephemeral. It was a number of years before Lear discovered that he could recreate this clownish gaiety himself through his Nonsense. He was especially fond of limericks, a form which probably derived from an early eighteenth-century form of nursery rhyme. During the eighteenth century, this form was used for political squibs. But it was Lear's adoption and adaptation of the form that has caused it to survive (Mégroz 6).

Edward Lear received very little formal education, and Peter Levi writes that Lear's youthful accomplishments were like those of "a vicar's daughter" in that he turned to the drawing of birds, flowers and shells, and the writing of occasional verses and songs. Although this may seem to be a limiting environment, it nevertheless laid the foundations of Lear's career and fame. Lear enjoyed the power of nonsense. He enjoyed getting his audience involved in the adventures of his Uncle Arly, knowing that this name was created by misspelling the word "unclearly" (Tigges, 1988, 164).

A number of Victorian authors had an uncanny concern with language. Although many contemporary authors have this same concern for language, there is an ironic difference between the Victorian and modern perspectives.

> This concern with language is one of the major links between Victorian nonsense and modern art and philosophy, for in a time when many felt that "no words are entirely right any more," even nonsense begins to make sense, or at least it offers a potential explanation of why sense is no longer available to us. For these and other reasons, certain recent critics have examined nonsense with a seriousness and intensity which most Victorians, including Lear and Carroll, would have found absurd. (Ede "Introduction" 47)

Lisa Ede suggests that Edward Lear's poems are controlled more by sound than by sense, for how else could we get such nonsense juxtapositions as "There was an Old Person of Tartary, / Who divided his jugular artery," or "There was an Older Person of Gretna, / Who rushed down the crater of Etna" ("Introduction" 52).

Or consider Lear's

> A was once an apple-pie,
>> Pidy
>> Widy
>> Tidy
>> Pidy
> Nice insidy
> Apple-pie.

About this, Ede suggests that "the complexity of nonsense, its power to disturb intellectually and emotionally, results in part from the constant redefinition and sudden jarring illuminations inherent to the dialectec technique." Lear produces a kind of "nightmare of logic," with his "surreal logic of dreams. This is perfectly consistent with Johan Huizinga's definition of "play" ("Introduction" 58). "Play is a voluntary activity or occupation executed within certain fixed limits of time and place, according to rules freely accepted but absolutely binding, having an aim in itself and accompanied by a feeling of tension, joy and the consciousness that it is 'different' from 'ordinary life.'" (Huizinga 28). Thus "play" is in fact very structured, and the language play of human beings is even more structured, so structured, in fact, that Huizinga has suggested that humans be classed as "Homo Ludens" rather than "Homo Sapiens."

Because they are operating in a framework of play, games, and nonsense, Lear and Carroll have more poetic license than they would normally have. They can treat such serious issues as physical violence, death, and madness as if they were non-serious matters. The sting is removed from such issues in the death jokes that appear in the <u>Alices</u>, and in "The Hunting of the Snark," and in the scenes of annihilation in Lear's "History of the Seven Families" and "Mr. and Mrs. Discobbolos." And Lear can with immunity write such non-violent limericks as the following:

> There was an Old Person of Buda.
> Whose conduct grew ruder and ruder,
>> Till at last, with a hammer,

They silenced his clamour,
By smashing that person of Buda.

Where sense rules over sound in Lear's writings, it is a strange kind of sense. Edmund Miller has a suspicion that Lear's writings are filled with allusions to sex. "When the Pobble protects his toes by wrapping up his nose in scarlet flannel, for example, Mr. Miller solemnly announces: 'The suggestion of displacement becomes at this point unescapable. The male genitalia are at the root of the Pobble's problems.'" ("Introduction" 56). Ede comments that it is alright to present Lear as a man with a narrow range of rather explicit obsessions--noses, beards, eating, growth, and age, as Miller does. And it is also alright to point out that there is such a thing as a runcible spoon, a kind of fork with two short blunt prongs and one long, curved pointed one--a virtual sculpture of the male genitalia, but Ede believes that using this information to draw the conclusion that sex is "never far from Lear's mind" seems to be unsubstantiated ("Introduction" 56-57). But the real power of much of Lear's writing lies in his illustrations, or rather in the ironic and paradoxical incongruities resulting from the understated verse contrasted with the overstated illustrations. Many readers have criticized Lear's limericks for their mildness, and for their failure to build to a climax. But often such readers fail to realize that this is the power of Lear's writing, for this anticlimax reinforces the understatement and therefore the incongruity with the illustration, and it also forces the energies of the limerick back upon itself. Lisa Ede says about Lear's illustrations that "it would be wrong to view these drawings as illustrations in the modern sense--appendages to the word, slavish visual imitations or recreations of a literary event" ("Limericks" 104). It may in fact be the reverse which is true--the limericks are appendages to the illustrations, for it is the illustrations, and not the limericks which contain the real climax. Consider, for example, the following:

There was an Old Man with a nose,
Who said, "If you choose to suppose,
That my nose is too long, you are certainly wrong!"
That remarkable Man with a nose. (104)

This poem is totally prosaic and un-newsworthy. There are many old men, and they <u>all</u> have noses. And the nose of this poem must be of a normal size, for some people say it is too long, and others say it is not too long. There is, in fact, nothing about the old man which could justify the suggestion in the last line that he is "remarkable." But now consider Lear's illustration to accompany this limerick. The nose in question is drawn considerably longer than the man is tall, and the twist in the nose makes it even longer and more remarkable. The "Old Man" is a typical Lear drawing--"large head, round body, arms flung back like a bird, one foot off the ground." His nose is disfigured and very long.

Here, for example, the illustration clarifies just how extraordinarily long the old Man's nose is, and it shows that the "you" of the verse are three young boys. The drawing seems reminiscent of a child's rope game, where one person swings the rope evenly but at increasingly higher levels, while the others try to jump above it as it twirls around; only here the rope is a nose, and the boys appear surprised and upset at being included in such a strange sport. The Old Man's feelings are less clear, but the intensity of his gaze and his somewhat malicious smile seem to indicate that he is taking great pleasure in revenging himself against those who maligned him.

The effect of the illustration is to give a great deal of ironic force to the meek charge in the verse that anyone who chooses to suppose that his "nose is too long" is "certainly wrong" ("Limericks" 105).

Another irony in the relationship between Lear's limericks and his illustrations is that he tends to draw characters so that they look like the animals with which they are

involved, even though there is no explicit mention of the similarity in the verse itself.
Consider the following:

> There was an Old Man with an owl,
> Who continued to bother and howl;
> He sate on a rail, and imbibed bitter ale,
> Which refreshed that Old Man and his owl. (Ede "Limericks" 110)

Lisa Ede explains the relationship between the limerick and the drawing in the following
way:

> Lear generally creates his "doubles" by manipulating facial features and
> general body position, and the illustration for the "Old Man with an owl" is
> no exception. In this case Lear perches man and owl on the rail, stiffening
> the Old Man's coattails and shortening his legs so that his body mimics that
> of the owl. But the major alterations involve the man's face; his eyes are
> deepened and made rounder; his nose is lengthened so that it resembles a
> beak; he even has two tufts of hair which approximate the owl's ears.
> Lear's distortions of these features do more than make him look like the
> owl, however; they also give the Old Man a mad, frenzied look--one which
> contrasts markedly with the limerick's last line, "Which refreshed that Old
> Man and his owl." (Ede "Limericks" 111).

Another visual trick which Lear uses in his illustrations is infinite regress to
represent the tedious total conformity that is often present when groups are in conflict with
individuals.

> There was an Old Man with a gong.
> Who bumped at it all the day long;
> But they called out, "O law! you're a horrid old bore!"
> So they smashed that old Man with a gong. (Ede "Limericks" 114)

There are so many smashers that they fade off into the distance, each a perfect mirror
image of every other. And the smashers are annoyed and unhappy, while the individual
old man displays obvious joy, as he is suspended high above the floor buoyed up by his
own enthusiasm ("Limericks" 115).

Consider still another understated and uninteresting Lear limerick:

> There was an old Person whose habits,
> Induced him to feed upon Rabbits;
> When he'd eaten eighteen, he turned perfectly green,
> Upon which he relinquished those habits. (Ede "Limericks" 112)

Here again the illustration must be considered along with the limerick if the irony is to be
understood. The old person is shown eating a rabbit, but the expression on the face of the
rabbit is a smirk, while that on the face of the old man is one of horror or surprise. The
rabbit seems to know that the old man is going to become ill, and maybe the old man
suddenly realizes this as well. And all of the rabbits who have seen their fellow rabbits
eaten, and are about to be eaten themselves are happily playing very close to the old man,
and in fact one of the rabbits is perched on its hind legs in a position that suggests he is
going to jump into the old man's mouth as soon as the other rabbit is finished. The rabbits
seem to know that they are causing the old man a great deal of distress, even though this
is an odd relationship between an eater and his meal. There is poetic justice as the
"predator has become the victim of those he feeds upon" (Ede "Limericks" 112-113).

Wim Tigges points out that even when Lear's limericks, or their illustrations are
viewed autonomously there is often an ironic contradiction or paradox. There is a clash
between the "Romantic" and the "Absurd" in the following limerick:

> There was an old person of Putney,
> Whose food was roast spiders and chutney,

Which he took with his tea, within sight of the sea,
That romantic old person of Putney. (Tigges, 1988, 142)

But this clash between the "Romantic" and the "Absurd" is only partially developed in the limerick itself; it is much more fully developed in the illustration, or what Tigges calls the "doodle."

> Note that, just as the left half of the doodle is "romantic," and the right half "absurd," the top half, so to speak, of the text is absurd, and the bottom half romantic.... In the picture, with only a few lines of the pen, Lear has drawn a similar collocation of domesticity (the tea-urn and cup on a three-legged table) and its opposite, travel by sea (the sail on the horizon--a recurrent theme in Lear's nonsense). The same collocation is presented in that of exotic (but edible) chutney, and domestic (but inedible) spider. (Tigges, 1988, 142)

Later in life, Lear's eyesight started to go, and he became a landscape painter because he no longer was able to accomplish the close observation that was needed for his natural history studies. At this time he remarked that "no bird under an ostrich shall I soon be able to see and do" (Hyman 14). Lear traveled to Europe in order to view interesting landscapes, and Alfred Lord Tennyson wrote about Lear's experiences in Greece in a poem entitled "To E.L. on his Travels in Greece."

> Illyrian woodlands, echoing falls
> of Water, sheets of summer grass,
> The long divine Peneian pass,
> The vast Akrokeraunian walls,
>
> Tomohrit, Athos, all things fair,
> With such a pencil, such a pen,
> You shadow forth to distant men,
> I read and felt that I was there.

Lear later wrote a lampoon of Tennyson's poem, mocking Tennyson's lofty praise and his own elevated aspirations:

> Delerious Bulldogs; echoing calls
> My daughter--green as summer grass:--
> The long supine Plebeian ass,
> The nasty crockery boring falls;
>
> Tom--Moory Pathos;--all things bare,--
> With such a turkey! Such a hen!
> And scrambling forms of distant men,
> O!--ain't you glad you were not there!

Lear had earlier done the illustrations for a book of Tennyson's poems. Lear had become capricious and prickly with his editors about various technical problems, and about the Tennyson illustrations, he wrote "I go on irregularly at the A. T. illustrations, seeking a method of doing them by which I can eventually multiply my new designs by photograph or autograph or sneezigraph or any other graph" (Lehmann 113).

Ann Colley considers many of Lear's limericks to be syllogisms. In "There was an old person in gray," for example, she considers the first two lines to be an announcement of the subject matter, or in other words the major premise: "There was an old person in gray, / Whose feelings were tinged with dismay." According to Colley, the third line offers the details associated with a minor premise: "She purchased two parrots, and fed them with carrots." And in regular syllogism fashion, the last line renders a conclusion based on the preceding major and minor premises: "Which [therefore] pleased that old person in gray"

(Colley 293). Colley suggests that Lear got the idea of the syllogistic limerick from various verses which he read, such as,

> There was an old Captain of Dago,
> Liv'd long on rice-gruel and sago;
> But at last to his bliss,
> The physician said this--
> To a roast let of mutton you may go.

Lear was a very careful artist. When Lear was revising the two hundred landscapes to be used as illustrations for Tennyson's poems, he thought of them as evolving from eggs (the original sketches) into the full-grown chrysalis state (the drawings ready for painting). The originals (the eggs) were done in black and white and were only about four inches long. Next to the eggs Lear sketched larger drawings and roughed in the light and the shade; he called these his "newly hatched caterpillars." These drawings were then increased to double their size in order to exaggerate the effects, but they were still artistically very rough; Lear considered these to be his "full grown caterpillars." Finally Lear was able to finish the set of drawings to a form ready to be copied by a lithographer; Lear considered these final drawings to be in the "Chrysalis state." Lear's art was such a careful and painstaking task that during the last fifteen years of his life he feared that his failing health might prevent him from bringing the Tennyson project to conclusion. Lear did not, however, suffer the same anxieties over the illustrations that accompanied his limericks, "for these Lear was content to let the metamorphoses remain unresolved." The illustrations for Lear's limericks were much more spontaneous and less carefully prepared than were his "serious" drawings.

> The facile, syllabic character of the nonsense drawings reflects the ease with which nonsense resides within a disjointed world. Within the context of the limerick, there is no need to fill in the empty spaces, to join the disparate parts, or come to a metaphoric closure. The limericks mock the reader's impulse to find a resting place in congruity. They remind him of the ever-present and visible gaps in his own experience. (Colley 297)

The pleasure of Lear's nonsense is that "nonsense removes the reader (and, indeed, its author) from the anxiety of difference and lets him safely explore the gaps between events" (Colley 298).

The rhymes in Lear's poetry tend to bring together things which are generally not associated. He rhymes "Rhodes" with "toads," "Prague" with "plague," and "Coblenz" with "immense." Such rhymes are not so much a feature of poetry as they are a feature of poetry parodies. Such rhymes give "an illusion of a metaphoric frame, the rhyme momentarily holds and brackets the separated images" (Colley 294). The last lines of these limericks add to the illusion of the metaphoric frame rather than resolving the frame itself. Lear wrote such enigmatic last lines as "That intrinsic Old Man of Peru," "That ombliferous person of Crete," "that mendacious Old Person of Gretna," "That oracular Lady of Prague," and "You luminous person of Barnes." "Lear gathers all the force of the limerick into the adjectives. Like siphons, they draw off the free-floating pieces into a single container" (Colley 294). It is only through this method that the ability of the "Young Lady of Welling," to "play the harp and catch carp" qualifies her for the last line proclaiming her to be an "accomplished Young Lady of Welling" (Colley 294). But the verbal clashes in Lear's poetry are different from the artistic clashes.

> No matter how frequently the words of the verses of the limericks describe a collision of one object or figure with another, the drawings refuse to carry the intended violence through. Always a gap intervenes. Rarely does a figure touch another, and rarely do the instruments of harm reach their victim. Instead, they hang suspended and unconnected. For instance, the

knife with which an Old Person of Tartary divides his jugular artery floats blissfully free of his extended fingers and his screeching wife's hands; the large stones which "several small children" throw at an old Person of Chester hang like bubbles over the man's right side, and the oversize puppy which is supposed to snap up an Old Man of Leghorn fails, as if blocked by the intervening space. (Colley 295)

In an article entitled "An Anatomy of Nonsense," Wim Tigges defines nonsense poetry as "a genre of narrative literature which balances a multiplicity of meaning with a simultaneous absence of meaning. This balance is effected by playing with the rules of language, logic, prosody and representation, or a combination of these" (Tigges 166). Edward Lear loves to explore opposition and antithetical relationships in his nonsense literature. Lisa Ede says that nonsense, like the Victorian age, maintains "a tension between extremes," a basic dichotomy between "illusion and reality and order and disorder, with such further contrasting pairs as fantasy and logic, imagination and reason, the child and the adult, the individual and society, words and their linguistic relations...denotation and connotation, and form and content" ("Introduction" 57).

In summary, Ede considers the relationship between Lear's limericks and his drawings to be paradoxical, or even subversive, "for their apparent naiveté and simplicity mask an underlying design of great subtlety and force." There is an interaction which accounts for much of their density. "Lear's limericks turn in upon themselves, inviting further consideration--in effect refusing, Peter Pan-like, to leave the nonsense world" ("Limericks" 116).

Edward Lear Bibliography

Anderson, Jorgen. "Edward Lear and the Origin of Nonsense." English Studies: A Journal of English Letters and Philology 31 (1950): 161-166.

Byrom, Thomas. Nonsense and Wonder: The Poems and Cartoons of Edward Lear. New York, NY: Dutton, 1977.

Colley, Ann C. "Edward Lear's Limericks and the Reversals of Nonsense." Victorian Poetry 26.3 (1988): 285-299.

Davidson, Angus. Edward Lear: Landscape Painter and Nonsense Poet. London, England: John Murray, 1938.

Ede, Lisa S. "Edward Lear's Limericks and their Illustrations." Explorations in the Field of Nonsense. Ed. Wim Tigges. Amsterdam, Holland: Rodopi, 1987, 103-116.

Ede, Lisa S. "An Introduction to the Nonsense Literature of Edward Lear and Lewis Carroll." Explorations in the Field of Nonsense. Ed. Wim Tigges. Amsterdam, Holland: Rodopi, 1987, 47-60.

Fromkin, Victoria, and Robert Rodman. An Introduction to Language. 3rd edition. New York, NY: Holt, Rinehart and Winston, 1983.

Henkle, Roger B. Comedy and Culture: England 1820-1900. Princeton, NJ: Princeton University Press, 1980.

Huizinga, Johan. Homo Ludens: A Study of the Play Element in Culture. Boston, MA: Beacon, 1950.

Hyman, Susan, ed. Edward Lear in the Levant: Travels in Albania, Greece and Turkey in Europe 1848-1849. London, England: John Murray, 1988.

Jackson, Holbrook, ed. The Complete Nonsense of Edward Lear. London, England: Faber, 1947.

Lear, Edward. A Book of Nonsense. London, England: J. M. Dent, 1859.

Lear, Edward. Edward Lear 1812-1888: A Loan Exhibition of Oil Paintings, Watercolours and Drawings, Books and Prints, Nonsense Works. London, England: Gooden and

Fox, 1968.

Lear, Edward. Nonsense Books. Boston, MA: Little, Brown, 1888.

Lehmann, John. Edward Lear and his World. New York, NY: Charles Scribner's Sons, 1977.

Levi, Peter. Edward Lear: A Biography. New York, NY: Scribner, 1995.

Mégroz, Rudolphe L. Ed. A Book of Lear. Harmondsworth, England: Penguin, n.d.

Noakes, Vivien. Edward Lear: 1812-1888. London, England: Royal Academy of Arts, 1985.

Noakes, Vivien. Edward Lear: The Life of a Wanderer. London, England: Ariel, 1985.

Schiller, Justin G., ed. Nonsensus. New York, NY: Justin G. Schiller, 1988.

Sewell, Elizabeth. The Field of Nonsense. London, England: Chatto and Windus, 1952.

Smith, Elton E. "Edward Lear." Encyclopedia of British Humorists, Volume II. Ed. Steven H. Gale. New York, NY: Garland, 1996, 642-650.

Strachey, Lady, ed. Queery Learn Nonsense. London, England: Mills and Boon, 1911.

Tigges, Wim. An Anatomy of Literary Nonsense. Amsterdam, Holland: Rodopi, 1988.

Tigges, Wim. "An Anatomy of Nonsense." Dutch Quarterly Review of Anglo-American Letters 16.3 (1986): 162-185.

Wells, Carolyn, Ed. A Nonsense Anthology. New York, NY: Scribners, 1915.

Henry Mayhew (1812-1887)

Henry Mayhew was an editor of comic magazines, and he was also a popular writer of comic novels and fairy tales. In the 1830s and 1840s his farces and burlesques had a wide audience. In 1831 Henry Mayhew joined forces with Gilbert Abbott à Beckett to establish Figaro in London a very successful one-penny, four-page quarto magazine which came out every Saturday. Between 1831 and 1834 à Beckett was the editor, and then Mayhew became the editor from 1835 until 1838. Figaro in London was one of the most successful satirical magazines of the 1830s. The satire focused on politics and political events. It poked fun at the pomposity of the aristocracy, and at the obsession with appearances that is so much a part of the English upper-middle class. In an article entitled "Candour of the Times," Mayhew responds to an article that had earlier appeared in the Times about the issuance of paper currency, by saying, "The Times is opposed to a paper issue, which it calls a depreciated currency. It is at least candid of our contemporary to admit, that it believes no good can arise to the country from a large paper circulation." Rebekah Galbreath says that it was the success of Figaro in London that paved the way for Punch (Galbreath 748).

In 1835, Henry Mayhew, Douglas Jerrold, and William Makepeace Thackery met in Paris and discussed the need for a good comic journal like the Parisian Charivari (Galbreath 748). Only a few years later, in 1841, Punch was founded. Punch was a weekly magazine that used humor to demonstrate the absurdities of pompous political figures, or ineffective institutions (Galbreath 749). Henry Mayhew was co-founder of Punch, and is credited with having given the journal its "original genial tone and pleasant and philosophical wit" (Spielman 28).

In 1850 and 1851, Mayhew edited The Comic Almanack, another highly successful comic magazine, partly because George Cruikshank was the illustrator. The Comic Almanack was filled with good-humored satire, frequently targeting the "Blue-stockings" in particular, and the pomposity of the upper-middle class in general. William Makepeace Thackeray, Albert Smith, Robert Brough, and Henry and Horace Mayhew were all contributors to The Comic Almanack (Galbreath 749).

The Wandering Minstrel (1834) is Mayhew's first play. It is a farce about mistaken identity and about courtship intrigues, and there is a great deal of witty wordplay. Mrs. Crincum wants to arrange a marriage between Julia and an aristocrat who, according to the local newspaper, will soon be "travelling through the country under the guise of a wandering minstrel." But at the appointed time, a vagabond by the name of Jem Baggs happens to be playing a violin outside of Mrs. Crincum's house, and of course she mistakes the vagabond for the wandering minstrel (Galbreath 749). Much of the humor of The Wandering Minstrel is derived from Mayhew's presentation of the different dialects spoken by the different classes. "Baggs's vulgar speech is the target of ridicule, and when he is brought in contact with the upper-class Crincums, who speak well, the cultural and linguistic distance between the characters incites laughter." But what incites even more laughter is that Mrs. Crincum and her upper-class friends, even though they are so class conscious, and place such a high premium on social standing, are totally unable to recognize that Baggs is a tramp rather than an aristocrat (Galbreath 750).

But however-- (1838) is Mayhew's second farce; Mayhew wrote it in collaboration with Henry Beylis. It is quite a physical farce in which characters hide in closets and stumble over furniture. Again there is a case of mistaken identity, in this case the landed gentry and members of the upper-middle class cannot tell the difference between a squire who is supposed to arrive from India in order to claim his bride and his recently inherited estate, and a common thief. There is a great deal of punning that is intended to provoke bawdy laughter. In one scene, Chizzler, a small-time swindler, is able to see a case of mistaken identity as an opportunity to make some quick cash. He plays the role of a concerned aristocrat, saying to Mrs. Juniper, "You are a lone unprotected female,--I a private single gentle-man--you endowed with every charm--I not particularly bad looking-- you possessed of a snug little income--and I--but however--" (Galbreath 750). "Peter Punctilio: The Gentleman in Black" is Mayhew's third farce, and it first appeared in Bentley's Miscellany (1838).

Henry Mayhew's comic novels are gentle satires of the attitudes and customs of the middle and the upper-middle classes. In effect, Mayhew is asking the readers to laugh at themselves (Galbreath 750). The Greatest Plague of Life; or, the Adventures of a Lady in Search of a Good Servant (1847) is a comic novel written by Henry and Augustus Mayhew. The narrator of The Greatest Plague is a young, middle-class housewife in search of a good servant. The novel "satirizes the stereotypically sweet naiveté of a young Victorian housewife." After he becomes fed up with his wife's ineffectual behavior, the more sophisticated husband is forced to take matters into his own hands (Galbreath 751).

Whom to Marry and How to Get Married! or, the Adventures of a Lady in Search of a Good Husband (1848) is also a comic novel written by Henry and Augustus Mayhew. In this novel, the heroine goes on a series of amusing adventures to discover what kind of wretchedness happens to people who don't obey their fathers or their mothers. Against her parents' wishes, the heroine marries an older man, and her husband turns out to be mean, selfish, and miserly. The novel has a typical Mayhew sweet-and-sentimental ending, however (Galbreath 751).

Henry Mayhew Bibliography

Bradley, John L. "Henry Mayhew: Farce Writer of the 1830's." Victorian Newsletter 23 (1963): 21-23.
Galbreath, Rebekah N. "Henry Mayhew." Encyclopedia of British Humorists, Volume II. Ed. Steven H. Gale. New York, NY: Garland, 1996, 747-752.
Spielman, M. H. The History of "Punch." New York, NY: Cassell, 1895.

William Edmonstoune Aytoun (1813-1865) SCOTLAND

Aytoun's Endymion; or a Family Party of Olympus is a burlesque of a burlesque, often printed together with the piece which it parodies, Benjamin Disraeli's Ixion. Both Ixion and Edymion describe the love of a mortal for a goddess, "Ixion with langourous elegance and impudence, Endymion as befits a parody, with an added coarseness and modish impertinence. Aytoun is satirizing the language of society in his own day" (Kitchin 269).

William Edmonstoune Aytoun Bibliography

Kitchin, George. Survey of Burlesque and Parody in English. London, England: Oliver and
   Boyd, 1931.

Joseph Sheridan Le Fanu (1814-1873) IRELAND

See Nilsen, Don L. F. **Humor in Irish Literature: A Reference Guide**. Westport, CT: Greenwood, 1996.

James McKowen (1814-1889) IRELAND

See Nilsen, Don L. F. **Humor in Irish Literature: A Reference Guide**. Westport, CT: Greenwood, 1996.

Anthony Trollope (1815-1882)

Anthony Trollope had the ability to combine comedy with pathos (Jones 1148). He also used humor for subversive purposes. His narrator's wit deflates pretentions by exposing the differences between appearance and reality. Marnie Jones feels that Christopher Herbert's Trollope and Comic Pleasure is "the most informed and persuasive book examining how Trollope's comedy subverts the assumptions of his age" (Jones 1142). Anthony Trollope considered the work of a writer to be mainly concerned with attention to detail. He likened himself to a diligent shoemaker, and many of his critics seeing his deep-dyed conventionality consider him a typical representative of the Victorian bourgeois spirit. Most of Trollope's contemporaries, however, considered him to be just the opposite. They saw him as a "recklessly innovative writer whose career was a series of hazardous experiments" (Herbert 2).

Trollope's novels exhibit two distinct types of humor. The "rhetorical humor" is based on the fact that the narrator has control of everything in the novel. In contrast, the structural humor resides in the characters, and in the explicit and sometimes outrageously comic scenes. Of the two, it is the rhetorical humor which is more subtle. The narrator's voice is very biting, but is at the same time bemused and tolerant, as Trollope "finds humor in the very fabric of life" (Jones 1143).

Trollope felt that a novel should "give a picture of common life enlivened by humour" (Polhemus 170). The dialogue in Trollope's novels is subtle and full of nuances. Understatement is a common British device for slipping things past the moral censors (internal or external), but it is also a way of making light of life's outrageousness, of not being a bore by taking everything too seriously. For Trollope, understatement is a mode of irony, but an indirect mode, since it "assumes a bond of communication and a superior understanding and sympathy between like-minded people attuned to recognizing and putting down crude hyperbole and self-dramatization. Understatement relies on, and encourages, a community of shared perspective" (Polhemus 193).

Anthony Trollope wrote a series of six novels in his Chronicles of Barsetshire. They include The Warden (1855), Barchester Towers (1857), Doctor Thorne (1858), Framley Parsonage (1861), The Small House of Allington (1864), and The Last Chronicle of Barset (1867). These novels all deal with the social happenings in a small cathedral city (Neilson 1486). The humor in the Barsetshire novels changes from novel to novel. In The Warden (1855), the satire is sharp and the mock-heroic rhetorical device is extended. Marnie Jones feels that in The Warden, "the mock-epic perspective dominates," as Trollope "burlesques the obsession with reform by employing a grand rhetorical style" (Jones 1143).

Dr. Proudie of Barchester Towers (1857) "may well be said to have been a fortunate man, for he was not born to wealth, and he is now bishop of Barchester" (qtd. in Jones 1144). In the Proudie household, it is Mrs. Proudie who reigns supreme in all domestic matters. Furthermore, as it states in Chapter 3, she "stretches her power over all his movements, and will not even abstain from things spiritual. In fact, the bishop is henpecked." Marnie Jones says that the comic punch of Barchester Towers comes from the simplicity of such sentences as this one about Mrs. and Mr. Proudie (Jones 1144). Mr. Slope is another humors character, who is described in Chapter 4 as follows: "His nose...is his redeeming feature; it is pronounced, straight, and well-formed; though I myself should have liked it better did it not possess a somewhat spongy, porous appearance, as though it had been cleverly formed out of a red coloured cork." La Signora Madeline Vesy Neroni is described by Trollope as a beautiful and bewitching woman who is not only witty, but who also possesses the "fire of passion." "Her beauty is made more tantalizing by a self-induced paralysis. Injured while riding, she chooses never to walk again rather than reveal her physical imperfection." Madeline is the object of much of the humor in Barchester Towers, but she also orchestrates some of the humor, as when she comically undoes Mr. Slope. James R. Kincaid says that Madeline uses "a kind of Freudian humour to transform her pain into clever parody and continual witty victories" (Kincaid, 1980, xviii).

Slope is attracted to Madeline, and this attraction alienates him from a potential supporter, the bishop's wife. It is when Slope starts acting independently of Mrs. Proudie that much of the humor of the novel occurs, since this creates a tense and uncomfortable situation resulting from three conflicting powers, as the husband, the wife, and Mr. Slope all compete to run the diocese. At one point in the novel it is the physical comedy that takes over, as Madeline's sofa is accidentally shoved across the room. As it travels at great speed, it picks up Mrs. Proudie's train, and "gathers were heard to go, stitches to crack, plaits to fly open, flounces were seen to fall and breadths to expose themselves" (Jones 1145). Madeline and Mrs. Proudie are the two strongest women in the novel. One gets her power through her beauty, the other gets her power through renouncing her femininity. But although they are generally in competition with each other, Madeline and Mrs. Proudie agree on one thing--that Slope must be destroyed. Mrs. Proudie is so outraged by Slope's flirtations with Madeline, and with his attempts to exert his own power against her, that she battles him for control of her husband. As Trollope described the situation in Chapter 3, "Mrs. Proudie was the Medea of Barchester; she had no idea of not eating Mr. Slope.... She would pick him to the very last bone" (Jones 1146).

In Barchester Towers, the formal rituals of Septimus Harding's High Church is contrasted with the religious enthusiasm of Mrs. Proudie's Low Church. This novel is a scathing but humorous attack on the young, and on the agents of reform (Jones 1143). These agents of reform are blind to the good that they are destroying. The primary symbol of reform is The Jupiter, which finds Parliament always to be wrong. In contrast, The

Jupiter finds that "it is a fact amazing to ordinary mortals that The Jupiter is never wrong." Trollope finds both good and bad in both the Parliament, and in The Jupiter. "'Tis a pity that he [Dr. Anticant, who represents Thomas Carlyle] should have recognized the fact, that in this world no good is unalloyed, and that there is but little evil that has not in it some seed of what is goodly." Trollope is different from Carlyle, as he recognizes that characters are neither "purely good" or "purely bad," but they are purely funny (Jones 1144).

Robert Polhemus considers Trollope's Barchester Towers to be at the very heart of the "great comic tradition," as it juxtaposes prayer and laughter. He considers this novel to be "self-effacing, disingenuous, shifty, playful, and differential" and he adds that Trollope had to be very careful because he is making fun of many of the pieties of his age (Polhemus 197).

> Trollope uses a mock-epic style to describe a meeting of the Grantly forces. He parodies Paradise Lost and tacitly compares Religion and Church in Miltonic England with their role in Barchester: "Then up rose Dr. Grantly; and, having thus collected the scattered wisdom of his associates, spoke forth with words of deep authority. When I say up rose the archdeacon, I speak of the inner man.... His hands were in his breeches pockets." The narrator's mock-heroic voice works to ridicule those who would claim their experience to be extraordinary and elevated above the social norms that govern the world of the reader. (Polhemus 198)

Humorous understatement and irony can be seen in Arabin's internal dialogue about Eleanor.

> He asked himself whether in truth he did love this woman; and he answered himself, not without a long struggle, but at least honestly, that he certainly did love her. He then asked himself whether he did not also love her money; and he again answered himself that he did so. But here he did not answer honestly. It was and ever had been his weakness to look for impure motives for his own conduct. (Polhemus 195)

But Arabin's looking for impure motives in his own conduct is a strength, not a weakness of character as it appears on the surface, for it allows Arabin to progress (Polhemus 195).

Mrs. Proudie is one of the most genuinely religious people in the novel. "With her sense of moral duty, her reforming obsession, her earnest inner certitude, and her utter lack of humor, she represents that oppressive, puritanical side of religion, which just asks to be ridiculed. In her unctuous language, Trollope parodies the offensive tone of certainty that marks the smug proselyte of a 'higher morality.'" (Polhemus 177). In Barchester Towers, Mrs. Proudie is a "would-be priestess" who wants to be bishop of Barchester. At the beginning of the novel there are three or four people contending with each other to fill the vacated Bishop's position, but even though it is Mr. Proudie who is ordained to the position, it becomes clear as the novel progresses that it is in fact Mrs. Proudie herself who has become the Bishop. "She comes across as a figure of modern comic myth inspired by social change and male anxiety; she is a caricature of militant feminism" (Polhemus 189).

> In his burlesque of the would-be career woman, Trollope parodies male careerism and projects a comic switch on one of the common sins of male professional ambition. She tyrannizes over her male and in her drive for power tramples on his dignity and self-esteem. She treats him, in other words, like a long-suffering hapless wife. The satire on her expresses the incipient fear of women set loose to compete, but it also contains Trollope's basic criticism of all careerists. (Polhemus 190)

Madeline in the same novel expresses aggressive behavior, witty talk, and sardonic laughter. She is what George Meredith would call a "Comic Spirit."

> Whenever people wax out of proportion, overblown, affected, pretentious,

> bombastical, hypocritical, pedantic...; whenever it sees them self-deceived...,
> drifting into vanities, congregating in absurdities..., plotting dementedly;
> whenever they are at variance with their professions; are false in humility
> or mined with conceit, individually, or in bulk; the Spirit...will look
> humanely malignant, and cast an oblique light on them, followed by volleys
> of silvery laughter. (Meredith 47-48)

This is a description of Madeline, who like Becky Sharp, "excels at badinage and at playing charades with the sentimental idiocies of her time. She uses role-playing and jesting to make fun of contradictions, hidden immoralities, and unconscious motives in the world" (Polhemus 178). Because of her constantly probing, iconoclastic wit, Madeline is one of the most interesting figures in the novel (Polhemus 179).

> Madeline and her Bohemian brother Bertie don't take life seriously; they
> keep looking for amusement, and they work in dialectical fashion to give the
> Barchester world what it lacks: skepticism, flash, drama, a love of pleasure,
> and a touch of frivolity. Trollope stresses their good nature, but he calls
> them "heartless," which means as he uses the word, that they cannot love or
> feel deeply. That lack distances them from us and makes them subjects as
> well as instruments of satire. (Polhemus 180)

Bertie shows that bohemianism has both good and bad qualities. As a lazy dilettante, he exhibits comic gaiety, unexpected insight, and tolerance, but he also exhibits irresponsible arrogance and a well-cultivated ego. "Through Bertie, Trollope expresses something that endures in the British comic tradition and, I may say, in any lively society, and that is a hedonistic longing for pleasure and jokes, for idylls of irresponsibility" (Polhemus 180-181).

Polhemus notes the balance in Barchester Towers. Trollope balances the disrespectful and campy humor of the Stanhopes with another brother-sister pair, the anachronistic Thornes of Ullathorne. Trollope also balances the church and the parties; however, in this novel the parties predominate, for he devotes about a third of the book to them (Polhemus 181-182). The last chapter of Barchester Towers begins, "The end of a novel, like the end of a children's dinner-party, must be made up of sweetmeats and sugar-plums." This sentence mocks our craving for happy endings, saying that they are childish. It also implies that our fantasies of fiction may bring us real pleasure as long as we don't take them too seriously (Polhemus 199).

Polhemus feels that Henry Fielding's Parson Adams, Oliver Goldsmith's Vicar Primrose of Wakefield, and Laurence Sterne's Yorick and Dr. Slope may all have influenced Trollope's Barchester Towers. Trollope was also greatly influenced by Jane Austen, from whom he learned how to develop a comic dialectic between the character and the community, and how to present the intensity of interpersonal relationships. From Austen he learned that "a community without comic imagination can be stagnant, empty, and dangerous." From William Makepeace Thackeray's Vanity Fair, he learned how to shift comic perspective. Furthermore, "As Thackeray shrinks Napoleon into Becky and the nineteenth century into his Vanity Fair, reducing and controlling them in his comedy, so Trollope shrinks the religious controversy, church factionalism, and secularization of his age into Barset" (Polhemus 168).

Lily Dale is wooed and won by Adolphus Crosbie from London in The Small House of Allington (1864). Marnie Jones feels that Trollope's satiric depiction of Crosbie comically diminishes him. He has pretensions to be grand, but Trollope describes his actions as follows: "He had set himself down before the gates of the city of fashion, and had taken them by storm; or, perhaps, to speak with more propriety, he had picked the locks and let himself in." In this way, Trollope deflates Crosbie's pretensions. In one of the subplots of the novel Johnny Eames is in love with Lily, but Johnny is also in love with

Amelia, and he makes the mistake of writing about his love for Amelia. From this and other examples, it can be seen that Trollope frequently views love as war. He "paints the London boardinghouse scenes with a broad brush. He casts the vying feminine wiles of Amelia and Mrs. Lupex, a married woman with a notoriously loose reputation as a navel battle, as, is illustrated by the point in the plot "when Amelia carried the greater guns, and was able to pour in heavier metal than her enemy could use." There is physical humor in The Small House of Allington, as when Johnny rescues the Earl De Guest. De Guest has a red handkerchief in his pocket, and a bull who sees the handkerchief has attacked him. But Trollope undercuts Johnny's heroism by focusing his attention on how bewildered the bull is when Johnny jumps into the fray. The bull gave up the fight "when the animal saw with what unfairness he was treated, and that the number of his foes was doubled" (Jones 1147).

In The Last Chronicle of Barset 1867), Johnny continues his amorous dallyings with dangerous women. The Last Chronicle of Barset is a comedy of manners in which Madalina Demolines, a cunning actress, wants to catch Johnny as a husband. In one farcical scene, she is so cunning that he has to get the aid of a policeman in order to escape unscathed. Trollope brings the Chronicles of Barsetshire to a close by gathering together all of the characters from the early novels. "The lives of Lily, Crosbie, and Johnny become intertwined with those of Mr. Harding, his daughter Eleanor, Archdeacon Grantly, and the Proudies." Mrs. Proudie is in a "dress of awful stillness and terrible dimensions," as she displays the "awful face of the warrior, always ready for combat." In Chapter 17, Trollope says that Mrs. Proudie carries with her "her armor all complete, a prayer book, a bible, and a book of hymns." Even though Mrs. Proudie wins her victory against her husband, she realizes that she has really lost the victory, for "she had loved him dearly, and she loved him still.... At the bottom of her heart she knew that she had been a bad wife. And yet she had meant to be a pattern wife! She had meant to be a good Christian; but she had so exercised her Christianity that not a soul in the world loved her" (Jones 1148).

There are seven novels in Trollope's series entitled, The Palliser Novels. They include Can You Forgive Her? (1864), Phineas Finn (1869), The Eustace Diamonds (1873), Phineas Redux (1874), The Prime Minister (1876), The Duke's Children (1880), and An Autobiography (1882). This is a series of political novels also called the "Parliamentary Series" and also includes The Three Clerks (1858), Orley Farm (1862), and Dr. Wortle's School (1881) (Neilson 1486).

It is Lizzy Eustace, the pretty, rich, clever, and "bad" heroine who dominates the novel The Eustace Diamonds (1873) rather than Lucy Morris, the "good" heroine. Frank Greystock, the "bad" hero also plays an important role. Frank doesn't suffer from the "vulgar vices." Rather he suffers from ambition, luxury, self-indulgence, pride, and covetousness, and these are qualities which for Trollope are excellent sources of humor (Jones 1149).

In The Prime Minister (1876), Glencora is irritated with Plantagenet for not attending her lavish and successful parties in support of his coalition government. In Chapter 11, she approaches this topic with humor, "I feel myself to be a Lady Macbeth, prepared for the murder of any Duncan or any Daubeny who may stand in my lord's way. In the meantime, like Lady Macbeth herself, we must attend to the banqueting (Jones 1150).

There are many independent women in The Palliser Novels. In the two Phineas books alone there is the spirited Lady Laura, the witty Violet Effingham, and the strong Madame Max and Glencora Palliser. Perhaps the most interesting woman in The Palliser Novels is Marie (Madame Max) Goesler. She is very wealthy, very beautiful, and very intelligent (Jones 1149). She has been called by Shirley Letwin, "the most perfect gentleman in Trollope's novels" (Letwin 74). Madame Max has an adventurous spirit.

"Her integrity and her respect for herself do not make her the object of Trollope's wit but rather an eloquent advocate for an appreciation of life." In The Palliser Novels, Trollope tells the story of Lady Gelencora Palliser, who became the Duchess of Omnium, from her first passionate relationship with Burgo Fitzgerald and her subsequent prudent marriage all the way to Plantagenet Palliser. Lady Glencora is a battler, and she uses her wit to win many of her battles. But she can also get physical, as she says during one of her battles in Chapter 43. "You must hold your ground, and show your claws--and make [the old cat] know that if she spits, you can scratch.... She'll find I'm of the genus, but of the tiger kind, if she persecutes me." The characters say many humorous things, but it is probably the narrator's witty and ironic explorations of the political world outlined in this series where the reader finds the most subtle and effective on-going humor (Jones 1150).

The central plot of Trollope's He Knew He Was Right (1870) is a tragedy; however there are a number of subplots which make this novel a comedy and a farce as well. Even the central plot is a comedy seen in reverse, since it has a happy beginning rather than a happy ending. The main plot of the novel is Louis Travelyan's descent into madness. But this main plot is more of a parody of tragedy than a real tragedy (Nardin 304).

> In order to underscore the fact that comedy and tragedy move in different directions, Trollope opens his quasi-tragic main plot with an ominous parody of comedy's usual conclusion: a celebratory marriage creating a new society of the young. The rich, intelligent, independent Louis Trevelyan wins the love and hand of the beautiful Emily Rowley in the very first paragraph of the story.... Thus in its first four pages, the novel recreates the situation which typically concludes stage comedy. (Nardin 304)

Trollope's tragedy is also parodying comedy in another important respect. Unlike what could be expected in comedy, Trollope's protagonists have absolutely no difficulty to overcome in order to become married. In Chapter 1 of the novel, "the marriage arouses no opposition from the older generation, for Louis is a parent's ideal lover. He is 'well connected...had been ninth wrangler at Cambridge...had already published a volume of poems...possessed £3,000 a year of his own,' a conventional young man of whom his elders 'said all good things...a man sure to be honored and respected.'" (Nardin 305).

But although the novel has a happy beginning, it does not have a happy ending.

> Louis is destroyed by two forces: one, the excessive leisure with which the nineteenth-century gentleman of fortune must deal, the other, his old-fashioned sense of his powers and prerogatives as a man. Believing that he has a right to complete submission and obedience from his wife..., Louis becomes obsessed by Emily's friendship with Col. Osborne, an old crony of her father's, and his descent toward madness and death commences. (Nardin 305)

The great irony of Louis's descent and destruction is that by the middle of the novel, Emily's objectionable friendship with Col. Osborne has ceased to happen; yet Trevelyan begins at this point to ask Emily for a confession of her unfaithfulness. Trevelyan could end his quarrel with Emily, but he does not. At any point, almost to the moment of his death, he could change his mind and not require an admission from Emily, and if he were to do this, Trollope's tragedy would become a comedy. But this doesn't happen. According to Jane Nardin, He Knew He Was Right cannot be a tragedy, because

> tragedy freely chosen is not real tragedy and thus Trevelyan's increasing sufferings, instead of deepening our sympathy for him, tend to seem more pointless and ridiculous as it becomes clear that his tyrannical rigidity alone prevents a happy conclusion. And if rigid, mechanical, or inappropriate behavior is, as Bergson suggests, the essence of farce or low comedy, then we can see why Trollope presents the last stages of Trevelyan's decline in

terms which are at least partly farcical. (Nardin 308)

When Trevelyan delivers his ultimatum concerning Emily's behavior, the narrator of the novel comments that he did so "with an air that would have been comic with its assumed magnificence had it not been for the true tragedy of the occasion. His indignant anger is described as 'almost grotesque' " (Nardin 308).

Trevelyan compares his own tragedy to the tragedies of Lear and Hamlet, but he especially sees himself as Othello. He sees Col. Osborne as the tragic villain. Trevelyan sees Col. Osborne as if he were Iago; however, Nardin sees the Colonel as a very inadequate Iago. When Iago heard that Othello was jealous, his pleasure was enhanced, but Col. Osborne, unlike Iago, "does not intend to deceive--he is merely drifting on a tide of flirtatious vanity" (Nardin 306).

In addition to the quasi-tragic main plot, which deals with the descent of Louis Trevelyan, there are four subplots, three of them joyous and satisfying romantic comedies, and the fourth, a farce dealing with Reverend Gibson's absurd difficulties in selecting a wife. One subplot concerns Nora Rowley's rejection of the Honorable Charles Glascock, heir to Lord Peterborough's title and immense fortune in favor of marrying a journalist by the name of Hugh Stanbury, for love. A second subplot deals with Mr. Glascock's on-the-rebound romance with an "unsuitable" American woman by the name of Caroline Spalding. A third subplot traces the development of Hugh's sister, Dorothy, as she changes from a weak and insecure girl into a mature and capable woman, able to assert her right to marry the man she loves even though she is opposed by members of the older generation. "The interweaving of these subplots allows Trollope to play with the conventions of stage comedy." Furthermore,

> the three romantic comedies in this novel are so handled as to develop an ultimate defense of comedy: these subplots suggest that comedies do not end happily simply because the happy ending is an arbitrary convention of the genre, but rather that the lives of the people who can learn how to live will inevitably take comic form. People who can learn create their own happiness and are seldom doomed by cosmic forces to tragic or farcical fates. (Nardin 310)

The fourth comic subplot involves Reverend Gibson, who provides a comic reflection of Trevelyan in the main plot.

> In Trevelyan's case excessive rigidity produces tragedy, but in Gibson's an inability to take a firm stand on even the most vital issue creates farce. Because Gibson does not rely on his own judgment, but simply allows himself to be driven hither and thither by circumstances and by other people, his behavior is every bit as mechanical and inappropriate--as comic in the Bergsonian sense--as is Trevelyan's obsessive rigidity. (Nardin 308)

The Gibson subplot is like many comedies which reverse the tables by showing a male figure being humiliated by women. "In this respect it is in striking contrast to the novel's main plot, in which women are poignantly powerless. Gibson, a prosperous clergyman, is first publicly shamed by an old maid acquaintance, then menaced by a virago, Camilla French, and finally forced into marriage by the most unlikely candidate of all: the aging, foolish, unattractive, and meek Arabella French" (Nardin 309). Animal metaphors abound. The French sisters are described as "two pigs...at the same trough;" when he is unable to make a decision, Gibson is described as "a donkey between two bundles of hay," and Arabella's desire to attach herself to a man is reminiscent of other animals--the rat, the toad, the slug, and the flea (Nardin 310).

Jane Nardin makes the point that the interplay of five plots, one tragic, three comic, and one farcical, implies that tragedy and farce, by their very natures, "must deal with characters who are unable to learn and therefore have only negative lessons to teach, while comedy is the genre that teaches us how to live" (Nardin 304). Henri Bergson would say that what differentiates the comic characters from the tragic and farcical characters is that tragic and farcical characters are obsessed, while comic characters have the ability to decide when to yield and when to be firm (Nardin 311).

Anthony Trollope Bibliography

Herbert, Christopher. Trollope and Comic Pleasure. New York, NY: Penguin, 1987.
Jones, Iva G. "Patterns of Estrangement in Trollope's The Way We Live Now." Amid Visions and Revisions: Poetry and Criticism on Literature and the Arts. Baltimore, MD: Morgan State University Press, 1985.
Jones, Marnie. "Anthony Trollope." Encyclopedia of British Humorists, Volume II. Ed. Steven H. Gale. New York, NY: Garland, 1996, 1141-1152.
Kincaid, James R. Barchester Towers. Oxford, England: Oxford University Press, 1980.
Kincaid, James R. "Barchester Towers and the Nature of Conservative Comedy." Journal of English Literary History 37 (1970): 595-612.
Langford, Thomas A. "Trollope's Satire in The Warden." Studies in the Novel 19 (1987): 435-447.
Letwin, Shirley Robin. The Gentlemen in Trollope: Individuality and Moral Conduct Cambridge, MA: Harvard University Press, 1982.
Meredith, George. "Essay on Comedy." Comedy Ed. Wylie Sypher. Baltimore, MD: Johns Hopkins University Press, 1956, 3-60.
Nardin, Jane. "Comic Tradition in Trollope's Rachel Ray." Papers on Language and Literature: A Journal for Scholars and Critics of Language and Literature 22 (1986): 39-50.
Nardin, Jane. "Conservative Comedy and the Women of Barchester Towers." Studies in the Novel 18 (1986): 381-394.
Nardin, Jane. "Tragedy, Farce, and Comedy in Trollope's He Knew He Was Right." Genre 15 (1982): 303-313.
Neilson, William Allan. Webster's Biographical Dictionary. Springfield, MA: G. and C. Merriam, 1971.
Polhemus, Robert M. "Trollope's Barchester Towers (1857)." Comic Faith: The Great Tradition from Austen to Joyce. Chicago, IL: University of Chicago Press, 1980.
Wall, Stephen. "Trollope, Satire, and The Way We Live Now." Essays in Criticism: A Quarterly Journal of Literary Criticism 37 (1987): 43-61.
West, William A. "The Last Chronicle of Barset: Trollope's Comic Techniques." The Classic British Novel. Eds. Howard M. Harper, Jr., and Charles Edge. Athens, GA: Univ of Georgia Press, 1972, 121-142.

Philip James Bailey (1816-1902)

The Age (1858) was written by Philip James Bailey as a "colloquial satire" (Walker 279). It is a criticism of literature all the way from the Greeks up to the author's own time. It also targeted social and political subjects such as the ballot, the extension of the suffrage, the abuses of the press, and the evils of war (Walker 279-280).

Philip James Bailey Bibliography

Bailey, Philip James. The Age: A Colloquial Satire. New York, NY: Garland, 1986.
Walker, Hugh. English Satire and Satirists. New York, NY: J. M. Dent, 1925.

Charlotte Brontë (1816-1855)

When Jane is still a child in Jane Eyre, Brocklehurst quizzes her to make sure that she knows that the good go to Heaven, while the wicked go to Hell. Brocklehurst says to Jane, "No sight [is] so sad as that of a naughty child, especially a naughty little girl. Do you know where the wicked go after death?" Jane responds, "They go to hell." Then Brocklehurst continues, "And what is hell? Can you tell me that?" "A pit full of fire." "And should you like to fall into that pit, and to be burning there for ever?" "No, sir." "What must you do to avoid it?" And then comes Jane's coup de grace: "I must keep in good health, and not die." Of course Jane's lateral thinking doesn't impress Brocklehurst who is not able to see the humor in such a response. Brocklehurst is here a target of Brontë's satire. The confrontation between Jane and Brocklehurst continues, as Jane tells Brocklehurst that she doesn't like to study the psalms and Brocklehurst tells Jane about a little boy he knows who is younger even than Jane is. And when this little boy is asked if he would rather have a ginger-bread-nut, or a verse of a Psalm to memorize, he responds, "Oh! the verse of a Psalm! Angels sing Psalms. I wish to be a little angel here below." And then the young child is given not one, but two ginger-bread-nuts because of his "infant piety" (Jane Eyre 65). Barreca notes that the boy gets two nuts to reward him for his hypocrisy, but Jane gets nothing but a "lash of disapproval" for her honest answer (Barreca 65).

Regina Barreca says that in Jane Eyre it is Jane's defiant wit which captivates Rochester's admiration. She says that competitive humor is an important part of the relationship between Jane and Rochester (Barreca 61). She says that their romance is both formed and maintained by repartée, and that "Jane matches Rochester in pride and outstrips him in insight." In support of her contention Barreca points to the place where Rochester talks about Jane's beauty: "'I will make the world acknowledge you a beauty, too,' [Rochester] went on, while I really became uneasy at the strain he had adopted, because I felt he was either deluding himself or trying to delude me. 'I will attire my Jane in satin and lace, and she shall have roses in her hair; and I will cover the head I love best with a priceless veil.'" But Jane responds simply, "And then you won't know me, sir; and I shall not be your Jane Eyre any longer, but an ape in a harlequin's jacket--a jay in borrowed plumes" (Jane Eyre 288). Later Jane mockingly threatens to create a revolution among the harem of women which Rochester mockingly threatens to buy. Rochester says, "And what will you do, Jane, while I am bargaining for so many tons of flesh and such an assortment of black eyes?" And Jane responds, "I'll be preparing myself to go out as a missionary to preach liberty to them that are enslaved--your harem inmates amongst the rest. I'll get admitted there, and I'll stir up mutiny" (Jane Eyre 298).

In Jane Eyre, Bertha is the madwoman in the attic, and while it is true that Bertha is not associated with humor, she certainly is associated with laughter. Bertha's laughter echoes through the halls, and haunts the bedrooms of Thornfield. Her laughter is described as "tragic" and "preternatural" (Jane Eyre 138), and it is the sound which Jane was least expecting when she first explored the mansion. Jane describes it as "a curious laugh-- distinct, formal, mirthless" (Barreca 63). Even though Bertha herself is physically confined to parts of the mansion, her laugh is ubiquitous. "the 'clamorous peal' of her laughter is indicative of Bertha's uncontrolled and uncontrollable presence in the text" (Barreca 64), and Bertha's "thickly loud laughter is in contrast to Jane's "dryly ironic [smiling] humor" (Barreca 64).

At one point in Villette, Lucy Snowe was waxing poetic and romantic as she said she felt a "divine delight," and said, "I drew from the heaving channel-waves," and "the quiet, yet beclouded sky," and "in my reverie, methought I saw the continent of Europe, like a wide dream-land, far away," and "tiniest tracery of clustered town and snow gleaming tower." But then Lucy did a second-take, and addressed the audience directly, saying, "Cancel the whole of that, if you please, reader--or rather let it stand, and draw thence a moral--an alternative, text-hand copy." Using a self-mocking voice, Lucy said that in the earlier version she had been "creating" rather than "describing" the scene (Barreca 68). Lucy then gives a more realistic accounting of the scene: "Becoming excessively sick, I faltered down into the cabin" (Villette 118).

Lucy Snowe makes wry observations, has a satiric perspective and expresses many humorous insights even though she gives the appearance of being an unlaughing character. But Lucy does indeed laugh during those times when, in her own words, it becomes "impossible to do otherwise" (Villette 148). Although Lucy does laugh, she tries to hide her laughter because she knows that women are not supposed to laugh. "Indeed, I confess, for my part, I did laugh till I was warm; but then I bent my head, and made my handkerchief and a lowered veil the sole confidants of my mirth" (Villette 396). Jane Eyre behaved in much the same way. In fact, Lucy Snowe has many of the same qualities that Jane Eyre has. She is able to be the teller of her own tale, a tale marked by much irony. She is involved in a romantic relationship characterized chiefly by wit and repartée. She is also alone and has no money (Barreca 69).

Much of the humor in Villette is witty and understated; however there is slapstick as well, as when Lucy confronts her first classroom filled with adolescent girls. These girls are ruthless in their misbehavior, and the three worst offenders are ironically named "Blanche, Virginie, and Angelique" (Villette 143). Although Lucy usually used her wit to take control of such situations, she realized that her wit would be of little benefit in this particular situation in helping her gain the control and respect of the students. Lucy noted that one of the ring leaders was sitting next to a little door which she knew opened into a small closet where books were stored.

> I measured her stature and calculated her strength. She seemed both tall and wiry; but, so the conflict were brief and the attack unexpected, I thought I might manage her. Advancing up the room, looking as cool and careless as I possibly could..., I slightly pushed the door and found it was ajar. In an instant, and with sharpness, I had turned on her. In another instant she occupied the closet, the door was shut, and the key in my pocket. (Villette 144)

Lucy is not the kind of character who can allow traditions to go unchallenged. When she visits an art museum, she hears "a gentleman viewer's ritual appreciation of the museum's holdings." She describes him as follows: "How daintily he held a glass to one of his optics! With what admiration he gazed upon the Cleopatra...! Oh, the man of sense! Oh, the refined gentleman of superior taste and tact! I observed him for about ten minutes and perceived that he was exceedingly taken with this dusk and portly Venus of the Nile" (Villette 281), and then Lucy gives her own evaluation:

> This picture, I say, seemed to consider itself the queen of the collection. It represented a woman, considerably larger, I thought, than life. I calculated that this lady, put into a scale of magnitude suitable for the reception of a commodity of bulk, would infallibly turn from fourteen to sixteen stone. She was, indeed, extremely well fed: very much butcher's meat--to say nothing of bread, vegetables, and liquids.... (Villette 275)

Lucy refuses to elevate art to the whispered, spiritual heights society says it deserves to be elevated to. On the other hand, Lucy does elevate hairdressing to exactly this level, as she "describes the ceremonial aspects of coiffure in terms decidedly religious" (Barreca 73).

> Sacrilegious to state (the hairdresser) fixed his head-quarters in the oratory, and there, in presence of beniter, candle, and crucifix, solemnized the

mysteries of his art. Each girl was summoned in turn to pass through his hands; emerging from them with head as smooth as a shell, intersected by faultless white lines, and wreathed about with Grecian plaits that shone as if lacquered. I took my turn with the rest...the lavish garlandry of woven brown hair amazed me--I feared it was not all my own, and it required several convincing pulls to give assurance to the contrary." (Villette 199) Lucy is able to "braid the vain with the venerable" in such a way as to make them barely distinguishable. In doing this she is suggesting that the vain and the venerable are much closer than usually acknowledged. "The danger Lucy poses to the system is not so much the danger of challenge, but that of disinterest" (Barreca 73).

Later in the novel, Lucy's lover Graham is seduced by a charming and attractive flirt by the name of Ginevra Fanshawe. Graham sees Ginevra as young and lovely, as basically good and unspoiled, and he expects Lucy to see her in the same way. He tells Lucy, "She is so lovely, one cannot but be loving towards her. You--every woman older than herself, must feel for such a simple, innocent, girlish fairy, a sort of motherly or elderly-sisterly fondness. Graceful angel! Does not your heart yearn towards her when she pours into your ear her pure, child-like confidences?" Lucy does not see Ginevra the same way that Graham sees her, and when Graham asks Lucy if she is "not a little severe" on Ginevra, she responds, "I am excessively severe--more severe than I choose to show you. You should hear the strictures with which I favour my 'beautiful young friend,' only that you would be unutterably shocked at my want of tender considerations for her delicate nature" (Villette 222).

Then Lucy continues by saying, "But excuse me, Graham, may I change the theme for one instant? What a god-like person is that de Hamal! What a nose on his face--perfect! Model one in putty or clay, you could not make a better, or straighter, or neater; and then, such classic lips and chin--and his bearing--sublime" (Villette 222). Lucy is repeating Graham's litany almost word for word, except that she is applying it to the young man who is Graham's rival (Barreca 74). Lucy is employing Graham's own words against him, thereby perfectly illustrating "the humorous, mocking voice that characterizes the woman writer." Lucy is suggesting that as an older man, Graham should have "a sort of admiring affection, such as Mars and the coarser deities may be supposed to have born the young, graceful Apollo." But of course Lucy knows that this is absurd--but no more absurd than Graham's wanting her to adore the "pure, child-like confidences" of Ginevra (Barreca 75).

Brontë does a good job of exploring the "gendered nature of language" by showing how words spoken by men have very different meanings than these same words when spoken by women (Barreca 76). Furthermore, men's social roles differ from women's social roles as much as men's language differs from women's language. Brontë gives a satiric treatment of Mr. Emanuel's male-constructed curriculum. Mr. Emanuel will not give Lucy, his younger female colleague, a book without first taking out his penknife and editing the text. "After looking over the two volumes he had brought and cutting away some pages with his penknife (he generally pruned before lending his books, especially if they were novels." Sometimes the people he lent books to were "provoked at the severity of his censorship, the retrenchments interrupting the narrative" of the novels (Villette 435). Thus it was proper at the time for men to control women's reading because those sections which contained "contraband appetite for unfeminine knowledge" had to be removed (Barreca 77).

Charlotte Brontë Bibliography

Barreca, Regina. Untamed and Unabashed: Essays on Women and Humor in British

Literature. Detroit, MI: Wayne State University Press, 1994.
Brontë, Charlotte. Jane Eyre. London, England: Penguin, 1988.
Brontë, Charlotte. Villette. London, England: Penguin, 1980.
Jones, Robin. "The Goblin Ha-Ha: Hidden Smiles and Open Laughter in Jane Eyre." New
    Perspectives on Women and Comedy. Ed. Regina Barreca. New York, NY: Gordon
    and Breach, 1992, 201-211.

Arthur Hugh Clough (1819-1861)

Arthur Hugh Clough's "The Latest Decalogue" provides a strong and apparent
illustration of social satire aimed at moral hypocrisy. The poem presages George Orwell's
Animal Farm, by listing each of the ten commandments with each commandment followed
by an ironic and sarcastic remark by the poet, in the following manner:
    Thou shalt have one God only;
        who would be at the expense of two?
    No graven images may be worshipped;
        except the currency.

    Honor thy parents;
        that is, all from whom advancement may befall.
    Thou shalt not kill;
        but need'st not strive officiously to keep alive. (Knowles 140)

Arthur Hugh Clough Bibliography

Knowles, Frederick. A Treasury of Humorous Poetry. New York, NY: Books for Libraries
    Press, 1902.

George Eliot (née Mary Ann Evans)(1819-1880)

William Lilly considers George Eliot's humorous poetry to be in the Socratic
tradition. He further feels that her best poetry is in her novels (84-86). In 1856 George
Eliot said that "humour, in its higher forms, and in proportion as it associates itself with
sympathetic emotions, continually passes into poetry; nearly all great modern humourists
may be called prose poets" (Kiely 149). Manuel Alvarez de Toledo Morenés notes that
irony explains George Eliot's humor, and human weaknesses explain her irony (Morenés
105).
Regina Barreca compares George Eliot's Maggie Tulliver with Jane Austen's
Elizabeth Bennet and Charlotte Brontë's Jane Eyre, saying that all three of these women
characters have grown up relying on their humor. Maggie can get away with refusing to
do patchwork and dragging her bonnet on the floor, much to her mother's displeasure,
because she can get her father to "laugh audibly" (Barreca 92). Barreca suggests that the
presence of humor in Middlemarch and in Mill on the Floss as well, has an "emancipatory
effect because of its challenge to the very idea of moral, religious, and social orthodoxy"
(Barreca 82). Eliot, like other women writers, challenges authority by parodying this
authority. "Eliot's heroines use humor to combat the restrictions of their roles. Their
defiance often cloaks itself in wit and their anger appears cross-dressed as laughter." Thus
Eliot uses a "deft and defiant wit," and "her humor shapes her metaphors and delineates her
central concerns" (Barreca 86). In contrast to Regina Barreca's assessment of Eliot's

humor there is that of Virginia Woolf, who is less kind in her analysis, saying that Eliot is not able to produce anything more than a simple, even simple-minded "commentary on the rustic." Woolf says that Eliot's humor "has shown itself broad enough to cover a wide range of fools and failures, mothers and children, dogs and flourishing midland fields, farmers, sagacious or fuddled over their ale, horse-dealers, inn-keepers, curates, and carpenters," but Woolf considers all of these comic characters to be stock-figures and buffoons (Woolf 156).

Since George Eliot is a serious writer, her humor is moral humor. "She laughs at the unveiled weaknesses of human minds in order to mend them. Some of these minds are simply weak and George Eliot understands them gently. Some of them strive to hide their weaknesses under the guise of virtues and George Eliot uncovers their nakedness" (Morenés 109-110). Joseph Beach notes that George Eliot often accompanies the thoughts of her characters with a dry humor, a mild sarcasm and irony, that "partake of the comic spirit" (Beach 12).

Often the target of George Eliot's satire is religion. She satirizes Adam, and she satirizes Noah as well:

> When the animals entered the ark in pairs, one may imagine that allied species made much private remark on each other, and were tempted to think that so many forms feeding on the same store of fodder were eminently superfluous, as tending to diminish the rations. (I fear the part played by the vultures on that occasion would be too painful for art to represent, those birds being disadvantageously naked about the gullet, and apparently without rites and ceremonies). (Coles 164)

George Eliot uses satire in Middlemarch to relentlessly mock the authoritative voice. For example, in this novel a poorly prepared speech is ridiculed merely by repeating the speaker's exact words until they lose all meaning: "The most innocent echo has an impish mockery in it when it follows a gravely persistent speaker, and this echo was not at all innocent; if it did not follow the precision of a natural echo, it had a wicked choice of the words it overtook" (Middlemarch 548).

Middlemarch is filled with the ironies, riddles, and enigmas of life. This novel in fact centers around the theme of life's "indefiniteness" (Coles 155).

> The novel's plot, its characters, its psychological and philosophical themes-- they all resist clear-cut definition. In the eight books that make up the author's study, stories give way to other stories; and unattractive individuals to our surprise demand our sympathy while those we have felt close to suddenly are found wanting. No central argument prevails, even as no one person dominates the narrative. (Coles 158)

Bulstrode is an important character in Middlemarch, and he gets very heated about God and God's will. Bulstrode is also very curious about what God is up to, and is able to understand God only through his own point of view. Bulstrode is "a devout banker, a man apprehensive not only about creditors but his own credit in God's universe" (Coles 190). With his credit-debit mentality, Bulstrode wonders how God can permit him, a man of avowed faith, to be destroyed by an obvious heathen. Bulstrode prays, whereas John Raffles, his enemy, drinks and has nothing to do with any church. And in his prayers, Bulstrode knows that he should say, "Thy will be done," and he said this often. "On the other hand, he hoped against hope that 'the will of God might be the death of that hated man' " (Coles 191).

Dorothea Brooke is another important character in Middlemarch, and Robert Coles notes that "it is a major irony in the novel that Dorothea, who has so much, can be at critical points in her life so self-effacing (if still proud), whereas Mary Garth, far lower down in Middlemarch society, is robustly protective of her independence" (Coles 178).

Mary Garth was a servant, but she also considered herself entitled to demand things of others in addition to waiting on them. Dorothea, on the other hand, had many servants at her disposal; however, she "aimed to please, if not serve. Life is ironic because, among other reasons, social class cannot determine one's attitude toward others or oneself" (Coles 180).

Morenés sees George Eliot's portrait of Mary Garth, sitting at night remembering the scenes of the day, as a self portrait. Robert Coles points out that Mary Garth represents the observant but uneducated lower classes.

> She sat to-night revolving, as she was wont, the scenes of the day, her lips often curling with amusement at the oddities to which her fancy added fresh drollery: people were so ridiculous with their illusions, carrying their fools' caps unawares, thinking their lies opaque while everybody else's were transparent, making themselves exceptions to everything, as if when all the world looked yellow under a lamp they alone were rosy. (Coles 177)

Morenés notes that George Eliot's lips, in fact, "often curl[ed] at human comedy, and her mischievous fancy adds some smart to the things she watches" (Morenés 108).

Rosamond Vincy's husband in Middlemarch was named Dr. Tertius Lydgate, and he was a man of misery and despair. "He has tempers to the very end, and they are directed at his wife. He refers to her as his basil plant, explaining that 'basil was a plant which had flourished wonderfully on a murdered man's brains' " (Coles 167). Reverend Edward Casaubon is portrayed as a completely pretentious and humorless person, and as he is dying, he is a jealous and melancholy man who has not been able to finish his pretentious treatise entitled "Key to All Mythologies." Robert Coles notes that this title is so pretentious that it would have "set Augustine into one of his rages" (Coles 164). Middlemarch is a novel of indeterminacy. The finale of the novel appropriately begins with the words, "Every limit is a beginning as well as an ending" (Coles 204).

Much of the satire of Middlemarch is concerned with differences between the male and female perspectives. "A man's mind--what there is of it--has always the advantage of being masculine--as the smallest birch-tree is of a higher kind than the most soaring palm-- and even his ignorance is of a sounder quality.... [A] kind Providence furnishes the limpest personality with a little gum or starch in the form of tradition" (Middlemarch 44). Here Eliot is questioning a system that automatically rates the masculine as more valuable than the feminine (Barreca 84).

The family that owns the mill in the Mill on the Floss are the Tulliver's, and all of the Tullivers are comic characters. Mrs. Tulliver is a character controlled by habit. Her mechanical movements prevent her from adapting to the world. She is therefore "a fit object for humor because she refuses to admit the possibility of change." Mrs. Tulliver had lived thirteen years with her husband, but she retained the ability she had in her early life of saying things "which drove him [Mr. Tulliver] in the opposite direction to the one intended. (Barreca 87) In Mill on the Floss, Mrs. Tulliver is compared to the goldfish which "retains to the last its youthful illusion that it can swim in a straight line beyond the encircling glass. Mrs. Tulliver was an amiable fish of this kind, and after running her head against the same resisting medium for thirteen years would go at it again to-day with undulled alacrity" (Mill 134).

Maggie is the girl of the Tulliver family who has limited horizons because she is a girl. Maggie was happy and playful rather than serious and glum. She controlled life rather than allowing life to control her. For this reason, she never finished some of the books she started. She never finished Corinne because she anticipated an ending that she could not approve of. She never finished The Pirate because "I went on with it in my own head, and I made several endings; but they were all unhappy. I could never make a happy ending out of the beginning" (Mill 401). Maggie was not supposed to read Defoe's History of the Devil because it was not deemed "the right book for a little girl" (Mill 67), but Maggie read it nevertheless. But she is puzzled by the old woman in the water who is being judged. "They've put her in, to find out whether she's a witch or no, and if she swims she's a witch, and if she's drowned--and killed, you know--she's innocent, and not a witch, but only a poor silly old woman." And then she asks, "What good would it do her then, you know, when she was drowned?" And she goes on to describe the Devil figure watching this scene, with "his arms akimbo, laughing" (Mill 67).

In Mill on the Floss, Maggie learns early that even though girls possess "a great deal of superficial cleverness," they are not able to "go far into anything. They're quick and shallow." Eliot describes Maggie's reaction to society's assessment of her abilities: "She had been so proud to be called 'quick' for all her little life, and now it appeared that this quickness was the brand of inferiority" (Mill 220). Maggie's "inferiority" was reinforced by the fact that she seemed unable to handle the serious and important things of life. She starved her brother's rabbits to death. She licked the paint off from his lozenge box. She let the boat drag down his fish line. And she pushed her head through his kite, "all for nothing" (Mill 88). But Regina Barreca says that this was not in fact done "all for nothing," and in fact suggests that Maggie's actions become comic precisely because this evaluation is clearly inaccurate (Barreca 84-85).

Because nothing that she does is taken seriously, Maggie has the play ethic; because everything he does is taken seriously, Tom, Maggie's brother, has the work ethic. "Tom's hated Latin grammar becomes, in Maggie's hands, a delightful toy; he hates it because it is imposed on him, and he is depressed by the weight of its authority. She adores it because she can both play with its language and refuse to acknowledge its weight." Thus, "her acquaintance with Latin is placed in a humorous frame" (Barreca 91). "It was really very interesting--the Latin Grammar that Tom had said no girls could learn: and she was proud because she found it interesting" (Mill 217).

"Maggie's refusal to comply with the ceremonies of femininity and her desire to triumph through her cleverness" are considered very unladylike. As an act of defiance to authority figures, Maggie begs Tom to cut her "mass of dark, unruly hair" (Barreca 92). Tom is delighted to cut her hair, and he becomes even more delighted when he sees the mess he makes out of the job. He laughs at Maggie and tells her she resembles "the idiot we throw our nutshells to at school." Maggie has "a bitter sense of the irrevocable" (Mill 121), and tells Tom not to laugh at her, but he refuses to stop. Maggie, with her rebellious attitude, illustrated especially by her having her feminine locks removed, is described as "a small Medusa with the snakes cropped" (Mill 161).

In Mill on the Floss, Tom appears to be noble, since he is "very fond of his sister," but this means that he is obliged "always to take care of her." When Tom talked about looking after his sister, what he intended was to "make her his housekeeper, and punish her when she did wrong" (Mill 92). Tom is only interested in learning the "authorized version" of things, and he therefore disparages Maggie's imaginative creativity as nothing more than "girls' stories." "My sister Maggie is always wanting to tell me stories but they're stupid stories.   Girls' stories always are" (Mill 237). Eliot is here using humor to remind the reader of "the need to examine, rather than purchase wholesale, such commodified, conventional wisdom" (Barreca 91).

Much of the humor of Mill on the Floss comes from the smallness and pettiness in the application of general principles. Mrs. Tulliver applauds Lucy Deane as "such a good child" but we later discover that this means "you may set her on a stool, and there she'll sit for an hour together and never offer to get off" (Mill 96). And Mr. Stelling, Tom's teacher, is described as "very far from being led astray by enthusiasm, either religious or intellectual" (Barreca 90). As Eliot wrote, "How should Mr. Stelling be expected to know that an education was a delicate and difficult business...any more than an animal endowed with a power of boring a hole through a rock should be expected to have wide views of excavation" (Mill 241).

Maggie's Uncle Glegg is also a comic stereotype, who is controlled by Biblical imagery. It is difficult for Uncle Glegg to understand how Mrs. Glegg, a creature made out of a man's rib, could so often be in a state of contradiction to even the blandest of propositions. This was a mystery that so much bothered Mr. Glegg that he often sought in vain for a clue in the early chapters of Genesis (Mill 187). As Barreca notes, "In Glegg's hands the bible becomes a marriage manual" (Barreca 91).

George Eliot's "German Wit: Heinrich Heine" was published in 1963 in Essays, edited by Thomas Pinney. Here George Eliot says, "Humour draws its materials from situations and characteristics," that are more rudimentary than are the "unexpected and complex relations" which account for wit. According to Eliot, "Schoolboys may joke, but they are not capable of comedy" (Eliot 217-218; Martin 83). For Eliot wit and humor were constantly overlapping and blending. She continues that "wit is apt to be cold, and thin-lipped, and Mephistophelean in men who have no relish for humour, while broad-faced, rollicking humour needs the refining influence of wit" (Eliot 220; Martin 84). Eliot quotes Goethe as saying that nothing is more revealing about a man's character as what he finds laughable. And then she adds wryly that "the truth of this observation would perhaps have been more apparent if he had said culture instead of character" (Eliot 217; Martin 85).

George Eliot Bibliography

Barreca, Regina. "Laughter as Reproof, Refutation, and Revenge in The Mill on the Floss and Middlemarch." Untamed and Unabashed: Essays on Women and Humor in British Literature. Detroit, MI: Wayne State University Press, 1994, 80-108.

Beach, Joseph Warren. The Comic Spirit in George Meredith: An Interpretation. New York, NY: Russell, 1963.

Coles, Robert. Irony in the Mind's Life: Essays on Novels by James Agee, Elizabeth Bowen, and George Eliot. Charlottesville, VA: University Press of Virginia, 1974.

Eliot, George. Middlemarch. New York, NY: Penguin, 1979.

Eliot, George. Mill on the Floss. New York, NY: Penguin, 1979.

Eliot, George. "Silly Novels by Lady Novelists." The Essays of George Eliot. Ed. Nathan Sheppard. New York, NY: Funk and Wagnalls, 1883.

Kiely, Robert. "Victorian Harlequin: The Function of Humor in Thackeray's Critical and Miscellaneous Prose." Veins of Humor. Ed. Harry Levin. Cambridge, MA: Harvard University Press, 1972.

Lilly, William Samuel. "George Eliot: The Humourist as Poet." Four English Humorists of the Nineteenth Century. London, England: Norwood, 1978, 75-102.

Martin, Robert Bernard. "Chapter VI: George Eliot, Leslie Stephen, and George Meredith." The Triumph of Wit: A Study of Victorian Comic Theory. Oxford, England: Clarendon Press, 1974, 82-100.

Morenés, Manuel Alvarez de Toledo. "George Eliot's Humour: Weaknesses in Middlemarch." Literary and Linguistic Aspects of Humour. Barcelona, Spain: University of Barcelona Literature Department, 1984, 105-110.

Pinney, Thomas, ed. Essays of George Eliot. New York, NY: Columbia University Press, 1963.

Thackeray, W. M. The English Humorists, Charity and Humour, The Four Georges. London, England: Dent, 1912.

Woolf, Virginia. "George Eliot." Collected Essays. Ed. Leonard Woolf. London, England: Chatto and Windus, 1967, 162-172.

Edward Vaughan Hyde Kenealy (1819-1880) IRELAND

See Nilsen, Don L. F. **Humor in Irish Literature: A Reference Guide**. Westport, CT: Greenwood, 1996.

Matthew Arnold (1822-1888)

Clyde de L. Ryals notes that few critics consider Arnold's poetry to be ironic. In his book about Arnold, Douglas Bush, for example concluded that although Arnold was a master of irony in prose, "he rarely approached it in verse." Ryals disagrees with Bush, saying that almost every contemporary account about Arnold testifies to his playfulness, his posturings, and his poses, further adding that Max Mueller said of Arnold that Arnold had such a reputation as a humorist that people were not able to take him seriously. "Jest and seriousness, artless openness and dissimulation--these same qualities define his poetry, which is to say, the poet is an ironist" (Ryals 91).

Arnold was a free spirit, with a flexible and elastic imagination. He was a "Romantic Ironist," who avoided closure, one who "deconstructs the invented fictional world." Arnold's mind was permeated by a sense of play, which allowed him to transcend to the creative self, to hover above the work and "glorify in its own self-activity." Ryals says that Arnold, like other Romantic Ironists, tended to "forego meaning for metaphysical and aesthetic play" (Ryals 92). As Arnold once said to Schiller, "lofty thought lies oft in childish play" (Ryals 96).

Ryals contends that "doubleness" and "dividedness" are common in Victorian literature, and that the reader should therefore not be surprised to find this feature in Arnold's writing. "Arnold is always splitting himself up into various 'selves'--the best self and the ordinary self, the buried self and the masked self," etc. (Ryals 97).

Arnold's elegiac poetry written after 1852 tended to be extremely ironic. "Lycidas is dead and we lament his loss as we celebrate his talents; but Lycidas is not dead; he lives on in another state" (Ryals 98). The point of Arnold's "The Scholar-Gipsy" is not the quest of the scholar gypsy, but rather it is the Romantic Irony, which allows Arnold to "rise above his finite subject matter to a realm of aesthetic consciousness" (Ryals 99). Likewise in Sohrab and Rustum the poem ends in an ironic situation where two people who love each other are frustrated by that desire and come together only as the result of conflict, when one slays the other and the dead son is transformed into art. "There is erected over his grave a giant pillar which also serves as a seal not only of the son but of the father too in that those who see it say, "Sohrab, the mighty Rustum's son, lies there, / Whom his great father did in ignorance kill" (Ryals 99-100).

In "Heine's Grave," Arnold elegizes Heinrich Heine. Heine, like Arnold, was an ironist, but Heine lacked love and charm, so his irony tended to be bitter. At one time Arnold had admired Heine, but he had to separate himself from Heine to keep from being infected by Heine's mocking laughter.

> Obviously Arnold has come to re-bury Heine and not to praise him. Yet near the end of his elegy, after 198 lines of mocking derision of the German writer, the poet decides not thus to take leave of him but "with awe / Hail, as it passes from earth / Scattering lightnings, that soul!" ...What Arnold repudiates in Heine is not his irony but his lack of playfulness and joy, characteristic of a higher irony. (Ryals 101)

Ryals believes that Arnold should not be dubbed "the poet of sincerity," but that instead he is the essence of "the Romantic Ironist that presents a self always in process and always relishing and extolling its own self-activity" (Ryals 101).

Matthew Arnold Bibliography

Ryals, Clyde de L. "Romantic Irony in Arnold's Poetry." Victorian Poetry 26.1-2 (1988): 91-102.

Dion Boucicault (1822-1890) IRELAND

See Nilsen, Don L. F. Humor in Irish Literature: A Reference Guide. Westport, CT: Greenwood, 1996.

Richard Dalton Williams (1822-1862) IRELAND

See Nilsen, Don L. F. Humor in Irish Literature: A Reference Guide. Westport, CT: Greenwood, 1996.

Timothy Daniel Sullivan (1827-1914) IRELAND

See Nilsen, Don L. F. Humor in Irish Literature: A Reference Guide. Westport, CT: Greenwood, 1996.

Charles Joseph Kickham (1828-1882) IRELAND

See Nilsen, Don L. F. Humor in Irish Literature: A Reference Guide. Westport, CT: Greenwood, 1996.

George Meredith (1828-1909)

In his "Essay on Comedy," George Meredith wrote, "The higher the comedy the more prominent part women play in it" (Meredith 14). Meredith was one of the first novelists to accurately depict the emancipation of women in the late nineteenth century in his novels. "The two major comic characters he treats in his "Essay on the Comic" are both women. This is Millament of The Way of the World and Célimène in Le Misanthrope. Both of these women are in charge of the action because of their superior wit and intelligence. Both of them are elevated above the men who surround them (Martin 95). Meredith said, "The heroines of Comedy are like women of the world, not necessarily heartless from being clearsighted: they seem so to the sentimentally-reared only for the reason that they use their wits, and are not wandering vessels crying for a captain or a pilot" ("Essay" 14-15).

Meredith goes so far as to suggest that in a novel, on the stage, or in a poem, comedy flourishes only where the women and the men are on equal footing. Robert Martin responds to Meredith's suggestion. "It may be, as Meredith suggests, that equality of the sexes is a prerequisite for the culture that can produce comedy. Yet this was certainly not true of the Greek civilization from which sprang Aristophanes and Menander, to both of whom Meredith pays tribute." But then Martin adds that Meredith is overstating his case only because he is repudiating the common Victorian view that laughter and comedy are inappropriate for well-bred women (Martin 96).

For George Meredith, "pure comedy" is an unrealized ideal. "Good comedies are such rare productions [precisely because the] great comic poet [is] repelled [by] a state of marked social inequality of the sexes." Meredith believed that comedy can only flourish in a society where "men...consent to talk on equal terms with women, and to listen to them." And of course Victorian England is not that type of society (McWhirter 195). Virginia Woolf considered Meredith to be "a great innovator whose experimental comic fictions anticipate her own quest for a fictional form capable of fusing detachment and penetration, pattern and contingency, abstraction and empathy--the imperatives of comic form and novelistic insight" (McWhirter 197).

In The Comic Spirit in George Meredith (1963), Joseph Beach succinctly describes Meredith's humor. "Taking humor as an inclusive term for all varieties of the ludicrous, we may distinguish two functions of humor. The primary function is to make one laugh, the secondary function is to make one think. With most English humorists, the primary function has prevailed, largely to the exclusion of the secondary. With Meredith the secondary function is all-important" (Beach 5). Meredith's comedy is "comedy of mind." It is a lean humor "divested of those appurtenances of the sensuous, of sentimentality, of naturalistic detail, of material accident, of waggish impertinent wit, that make so fat and succulent the work of most English humorists" (Beach 6).

Beach notes that Meredith had an abiding interest in the comic spirit. All of his novels have this comic spirit, and it pervades most of his novels like an atmosphere (Beach 4). Meredith himself explicitly describes three of his novels as comedies, and he further describes the leading characters in another of his novels as "tragic comedians." In addition, he wrote a treatise on comedy in the prelude to The Egoist (1879), published a lecture entitled "On the Idea of Comedy and the Uses of the Comic Spirit" (first delivered in 1877); he also wrote "The Ode to the Comic Spirit," and "Two Masks" (Beach 2-3, 11). In these various places, Meredith explained what he meant by the "comic spirit." "Always he [the comedian] is a hunter, an executioner, an agency of correction and discipline. We learn, for example, that comedy 'watches over sentimentalism with a birch rod.' Comedy is not hostile to honest feeling, but to that false sentiment that turns its back on truth and prefers to bask in the rose-pink light of illusion" (Beach 11).

In a chapter entitled "Comedy and Tragedy: The Paradox of Ironic Vision" of his The Novelist as Comedian: George Meredith and the Ironic Sensibility (1983), Joseph Moses says that in all of his novels, George Meredith forces a union of comedy and tragedy, but that this is especially true in The Tragic Comedians (1880). Meredith has a distrust of the purely comic transcendence, and therefore an ironic ambivalence often emerges. This can be easily seen in The Shaving of Shagpat (1856) for example, and also in The Adventures of Harry Richmond (1871), which contain "a gallery of tragic comedians and of histories which, first precipitated into tragic event, are then reviewed by a common perusal." Squire Beltham is a tragic comedian who is trapped into a pattern of life he is not able to rise above. Moses continues, "The Princess Ottilia's marriage into safety, like Julia Rippinger's marriage which does not keep her safe, are both instances of tragic waste enforced by social stupidity upon individual weakness" (Moses 213-214).

> The forced conjunction of comedy and tragedy thus represents Meredith's most audacious and comprehensive irony. As The Shaving of Shagpat can be translated into an instance of ironic interplay between comic and tragic meanings, so the comedy of style in One of Our Conquerors [1891] can be understood as a comic use of language, as in Joyce, incessantly battering against a traditional story of misfortune and defeat. (Moses 215)

George Meredith gave the English humorists a cosmopolitan tinge by making honorary Englishmen out of Cervantes and even Rabelais and Aristophanes (Levin 5). Meredith was also greatly influenced by Molière's comedy of manners, but since he wrote novels rather than plays, the "comedy of manners" became for Meredith a "comedy of narrative." Meredith was also "the first major British novelist explicitly to reject and ridicule the dogmas of Christianity and to set up comedy as a rival to religion" (Polhemus 204).

The Shaving of Shagpat (1856) is an "Arabian Entertainment," and Farina (1857) is "a "Legend of Cologne." Both are experiments in comic-burlesque modes and "jeux d'esprit" (Stevenson "Innovations" 311). The Shaving of Shagpat is a parody of Oriental romances many of which were inspired by The Arabian Nights. It is also a parody of the works of Thomas Carlyle. It features a barber by the name of Shibli Bagarag, who sets out on a "heroic" quest to shave the head of Shagpat, a tailer who is wealthy and powerful because he has a single, magical hair. Shibli is naive and egotistical, and he undergoes many "thwackings" and other difficulties as he comes to understand his own foolishness (Ives 753).

In The Ordeal of Richard Feverel (1859), Meredith explores the link between tragedy and comedy. Because Austin Feverel is so embittered by his own failed marriage, he provides an education for Richard by which Richard is systematically isolated from other children, especially girls. But Richard nevertheless falls in love with the daughter of a neighboring farmer named Lucy Desbrough and he marries her in spite of his father's attempts to keep them apart. At this point readers see the novel as what Northrop Frye calls "New Comedy," and they assume that the lovers will live happily ever after, but there is a reversal of this theme, and the son's marriage ends as disastrously as did the father's marriage (Ives 753).

Richard Stevenson considers The Ordeal of Richard Feverel to be all at the same time a farce, a comedy, a romance, and a tragedy. Furthermore, these four elements are "all important components of this extraordinarily ambitious...novel" ("Spirit" 214). Stevenson points out that Meredith resolved the difficulty of the somber elements of The Ordeal of Richard Feverel by dividing the novel into two parts--the tragedy of Richard and Lucy, and the comedy of Sir Austin and his System (Stevenson "Spirit" 206). J. B. Priestley says that Richard Feverel is presented as a comedy, but "has a tragic ending thrust upon it, quite arbitrarily" (Stevenson "Spirit" 207). Joseph Moses points out that the title of The Ordeal of Richard Feverel (1859) is ironic, since the novel in fact tells about the "ordeal" of Richard Feverel's father, Sir Austin Feverel (Moses 226). Moses further agrees with Priestley that Richard Feverel is presented as a comedy; however, it has a tragic ending thrust upon it (Moses 216). "It seems almost possible that, were the author willing to leave certain matters of character, responsibility, and consequence unresolved, the novel could end happily. And this appealing possibility is what makes the catastrophic ending so forceful, what has caused so many readers to complain of its gratuitous brutality" (Moses 229).

In Richard Feverel, Meredith sets out to show how comedy and tragedy could play off from each other, and in the novels which followed Richard Feverel he continued to investigate this interplay. Thirty-six years later, in The Amazing Marriage, he is still working with the ironies, and paradoxes inherent in the mixing of tragedy with comedy (Moses 234). J. B. Priestley suggests that this mixture of tragedy and comedy is what defines the modern novel, saying that, "The modern novel began with the publication of The Ordeal of Richard Feverel in 1859. In that novel, and those following, Meredith presented us, as we have seen, with a world radically different from those of contemporary novelists, a world bathed in a dry intellectual light occasionally coloured by outbursts of Romantic Comedy" (qtd. in Moses 235). Priestley continues by saying that Meredith's idea of Comedy "contrived to bring together romantic figures and an intellectual background, a sympathetic interest coupled with a detached point of view" (Moses 235).

Lucy in Richard Feverel has a well-developed sense of humor, and in fact she has an important effect on the tone of the novel. Before Lucy's appearance in the novel, the laughter is distorted, and unhealthy. There are Adrian's cynical asides and Richard's and Ripton's raucous guffaws at the expense of Farmer Blaize. In contrast, Lucy's laughter is very healthy. She laughs at Richard's excessive and sentimental behavior in the "Ferdinand and Miranda" chapter.

> Her blue eyes lightened laughter out of the half-closed lids.
> "I cannot help it," she said, her mouth opening and sounding harmonious bells of laughter in his ears. "Pardon me, won't you?"
> His face took the same soft smiling curves in admiration of her.
> "Not to feel that you have been in the water, the very moment after!" she musically interjected, seeing she was excused.
> "It's true," he said; and his own gravity then touched him to join a duct with her, which made them no longer feel strangers, and did the work of a month of intimacy. ("Spirit" 216)

Stevenson feels that Lucy's good-natured humor is contagious, and further suggests that it allows Richard to see himself as she sees him ("Spirit" 216). Stevenson notes that there are a number of devices used by Meredith to undercut the novel's comic tone and to foreshadow the tragic outcome. There is Richard's disastrous duel with Mountfalcon. There are the recurring images of the cypress, there is the constant reminder of the role played by the System, there is the narrator's foreboding comments, and there is also the motif of knight errantry.

According to Roger Henkle, The Ordeal of Richard Feverel is influenced by Meredith's father-in-law, Thomas Peacock and his friends. The Peacockian figure in Feverel is a prematurely cynical young man named Adrian Harley, "a fat Wise Youth, digesting well: charming after dinner, with men or with women: soft, dimpled, succulent-looking as a suckling pig: delightfully sarcastic: perhaps a little too unscrupulous in his moral tone" (Cline Feverel 25). In other words, Adrian Harley is a figure who "could have adjourned from a dinner at Peacock's Crochet Castle" (Henkle 239).

Evan Harrington, He Would Be a Gentleman (1860) is conventionally comic in its design. It is written as a satire against social pretensions and sentimentality. Here Meredith used clothing and tailoring as a motif to explore social and personal posturings as Thomas Carlyle had done earlier in his Sartor Resartus. Maura Ives considers the Countess in Evan Harrington to be "one of Meredith's finest comic characters." She compares the Countess with Thackeray's Becky Sharp, in that "her manipulations are so outrageous that the reader is compelled to admire her" (Ives 754).

Evan Harrington is Meredith's "first work that can be consistently called a 'comedy' with any fidelity to his later use of that term in the famous Essay on Comedy." According to Meredith, "The Comic poet is in the narrow field, or enclosed square of the society he depicts; and he addresses the still narrower enclosure of men's intellects with reference to the operation of the social world upon their characters" (Stevenson "Innovations" 311). In Evan Harrington, Meredith sets out to write "a pure comedy of manners in narrative," in an attempt to avoid the problems of mixture he had come across in writing Richard Feverel. Evan Harrington may be a novel, but the structure, the characterization, and the theme are all very reminiscent of the theatre (Stevenson "Innovations" 312). In Evan Harrington,

> The Countess de Saldar de Sancorvo provides the story with its real center of comic interest. As Evan's feminine counterpart, this "daughter of Shears" is the true Molièrian figure of comedy. The Countess de Saldar is a marvelous rendition of a Cinderella who has married nobility, albeit in the form of a middle-aged, impoverished, and exiled count, and then dedicated her life to covering the tracks leading back to her humble origin. (Stevenson "Innovations" 313)

In one scene, the Countess hears some young men laughing outside of her window, and when she looks out she sees that it is her brother who is the object of their amusement. Harry Jocelyn is the most prominent of the young men in the group, and she hears him say, "By Jove! This comes it strong. Fancy the snipocracy here--eh?" The Countess does not wait to hear what the others say. Instead, she hastily puts on her bonnet, effects a peculiar smile in the mirror, and lightly runs down the stairs.

> In a matter of minutes, the Countess detaches Harry from his friends, intrigues him into accompanying her on a fool's errand, and then, with a few sure words, plants the notion in his head that he is to be her protector and confidant. The most striking aspect of Meredith's portrayal of the Countess in her personal relations is that she almost invariably succeeds in making others look foolish. (Stevenson "Innovations" 318)

According to Richard Stevenson, Louisa in Evan Harrington is Meredith's first heroine who fulfills the dramatic percepts Meredith later set down in his Essay on Comedy of the Comic Spirit. She is a paradoxical blend of virtues and vices, and she posseses the intellectual capacities which Meredith associated with those feminine figures he wished his readers to admire. Because she is a supreme egoist, and because she demonstrates both vanity and hypocrisy, she is one of Meredith's most memorable comic creations, and "the strong sense one has of her 'presence' in Evan Harrington is due in no small part to the innovations of comic method--particularly the methods of the comic stage--that he was introducing in this novel" (Stevenson "Innovations" 315).

In his Essay on Comedy (1877), Meredith insists that comedy can only flourish in a cultivated society, by which he means a society that is based on common sense and in which women and men are social equals (Ives 754). Meredith furthermore states that "the impersonal attitude of the Comic Spirit separates it from humor and satire, forms of comedy that appeal to the emotions." Maura Ives says that Meredith's comedy appeals mainly to the intellect. Meredith has a way of looking at the world "without contempt and without illusions" (Ives 755). Although Essay on Comedy has been read widely, and widely quoted, there is still much confusion about the message. Here we have an extended statement of the theory of comedy by a major nineteenth-century comic artist. In Essay Meredith considers comedy to be the "ultimate civilizer," and he states that the English are overdue for dispassionate, cultivated comedy. Meredith also notes that the "comic spirit" is different from "humour" or "satire." "The laughter of comedy is impersonal and of unrivaled politeness, nearer a smile--often no more than a smile. It laughs through the mind, for the mind directs it; and it might be called the humor of the mind" ("Essay" 47). In Essay on Comedy, George Meredith said, "The humorist of mean order is a refreshing laughter, giving tone to the feelings, and sometimes allowing the feelings to be too much for him; but the humorist of high humor has an embrace of contrasts beyond the scope of the comic poet." Meredith's model of comedy was patterned after Cervantes.

> Heart and mind laugh at Don Quixote, and still you brood on him.... The Knight's great aims and constant mishaps, his chivalrous valiancy exercised on absurd objects, his good sense along the high road of the craziest of expeditions, and the compassion he plucks out of derision, and the admirable figure he preserves while stalking through the frantically grotesque and burlesque assailing him, are in the loftiest moods of humor, fusing the tragic sentiment with the comic narrative. (Moses 220-221)

But another pattern for Meredith's comedy was Molière. As Meredith himself says, "The source of Molière's wit is clear reason: it is a fountain of that soil; and it springs to vindicate reason, common sense, rightness and justice" (Stevenson "Spirit" 209). In his plays, Molière develops the archetype of the "raisonneur"--the spokesman for common sense. Molière's examples include Cléante in Tartuffe, Chrysalde in L'École des Femmes,

Philinte in <u>Le Misanthrope</u>, and Ariste in <u>L'École des Maris</u>. Examples of this same archetype from Meredith's novels include Austin Wentworth in <u>Richard Feverel</u>, Merthyr Powys in <u>Sandra Belloni</u>, Gower Woodseer in <u>The Amazing Marriage</u>, and Vernon Whitford in <u>The Egoist</u>. "They are all more or less uniformly predictable and dull. The reason for this is that in both Meredith and Molière the real artistic and moral interest is found less in the rational men than in the figure who is <u>déraisonnable</u>." The "raisonneur" nevertheless has an important purpose, for this is the character that the "déraisonneur" is measured against. "he helps to keep our eyes set clearly on the norm that is being violated" (Stevenson "Spirit" 212).

Very often for Meredith the "raisonneurs" are women: "Comedy lifts women to a station offering them free play for their wit, as they usually show it, when they have it, on the side of sound sense. The higher the comedy, the more prominent the part they enjoy in it" ("Spirit" 212). Meredith considers Molière's Célimène of <u>Le Misanthrope</u> to be the epitome of the "comic heroines whose wit is on the side of sound sense." Such characters as Princess Ottilia in <u>The Adventures of Harry Richmond</u>, Aminta Farrell in <u>Lord Ormont and His Aminta</u>, Carinthia Jane Kirby in <u>The Amazing Marriage</u>, Clara Middleton in <u>The Egoist</u>, and Lucy Desborough in <u>The Ordeal of Richard Feverel</u> demonstrate that the role of the heroine in Meredith's fiction is linked to the spirit of critical intelligence. And each of these heroines is a foil representing the norm. Princess Ottilia is a foil for Harry Richmond; Aminta Farrell is a foil for Ormont; Carinthia Jane is a foil for Fleetwood, and so on. In <u>The Egoist</u> the pattern is repeated at least three times, as Sir Willoughby Patterne's arrogance and utter lack of rational perspective are contrasted with Constantia Durham, Clara Middleton, and Laetitia Dale in various parts of the novel ("Spirit" 214).

In <u>Essay on Comedy</u>, Meredith explains that when the intellect predominates, humor gives way to satire or the grotesque. When feelings are primary, humor gives way to sentimentality, or capriciousness. The ideal is to avoid the extremes, which occur only in "high humor" (Craig 50). Christopher Herbert suggests that in <u>Essay on Comedy</u>, Meredith dwells on the need to purify comic writing of what he euphemistically calls "realism" and more pointedly calls "the gutters of grossness" (Herbert 4). In <u>Essay on Comedy</u>, Meredith also explores the importance of humor for the feminist movement, calling on "cultivated women to recognize that the comic Muse is one of their best friends." "Let them look with their clearest vision abroad and at home. They will see that, where they have no social freedom, comedy is absent.... But where women are on the road to an equal footing with men, in attainments and in liberty...there, and only waiting to be translated from life to the stage, or the novel, or the poem, pure comedy flourishes" ("Essay" 32).

Meredith's <u>An Essay on Comedy</u> and his "Prelude" to <u>The Egoist</u> (1879), treat comedy as if it were some sort of religion that needs to be defended.

> There is a hierarchy of comedy, and there is a proper comic mode. Meredith on what comedy should be is like a theologian on what religious faith should be. He is a Jesuit of comic faith seeking influential and talented converts, and, in their own fashion, Wilde, Butler, Beerbohm, Shaw, Firbank, and Joyce prove his success, though in their work they did not always follow his dogma for comedy. I think he meant his style to have a snob appeal. In a way, it is the equivalent of the in-joke, which turns its appreciators into a knowing elite. (Polhemus 241)

Maura Ives feels that the ideas expressed in Meredith's <u>An Essay on Comedy</u> are put to practice in <u>The Egoist</u> (1879). In fact, in the "Prelude" to <u>The Egoist</u>, Meredith reaffirms his statement that the purpose of comedy is "to illuminate the world of civilized men and women, and he identifies the Egoist as an English gentleman surrounded by "imps" that wait for him to reveal himself as a comic target." The Egoist in Meredith's novel is named Sir Willoughby Patterne, who has inherited Patterne Hall. Willoughby has become engaged to Clara Middleton, a young and intelligent, but inexperienced daughter of a classical scholar. Clara is to Willoughby "a parasite and a chalice." Willoughby feels that she is a vessel which he must fill with "knowledge of himself" (Ives 755).

Roger Henkle notes that Meredith's most significant comic novels, Feverel (1859) and The Egoist (1879) both deal with the most devastating experience of Meredith's life, the break-up of his marriage to Mary Ellen Peacock (Henkle 241). The Egoist is an example of what Richard Stevenson calls a "Comedy in Narrative." This genre is closely related to the comedy manners which Meredith treats in his Essay, but differs in that it is associated with the novel rather than with the play (Stevenson "Innovations" 205). In The Egoist, Crossjay is a sort of comic imp who has been plucked out of the soil of the earth like a root. He becomes a sort of metaphor for nature (Polhemus 235). Sir Willoughby Patterne in The Egoist is a representation of George Meredith himself.

> The inspiration for Sir Willoughby was surely autobiographical, as the story of Meredith's disastrous first marriage reveals. He wooed Mary Ellen Nicolls, Thomas Love Peacock's widowed daughter, and, refusing to take no for an answer, he finally won her. After a few unhappy years of marriage, she left him and their child for Henry Wallis.... He found a pattern of egoism in his own conduct and, surprisingly, a pattern of comic faith in his ability to criticize and mock himself. (Polhemus 220)

Like Don Quixote, Sir Willoughby enjoys reading sentimental fiction to the extent that his expectations about the world derive from the assumptions of such "fictional realities."

> He sees himself as a type of eighteenth-century patrician hero and center of society, envisioned in such figures as Richardson's Sir Charles Grandison and Burney's Lord Orville: He is the supercompetent hero who manages the lives of those around him, is treated with sycophantic deference by nearly every other character in the work, and evokes no pretensions of equality from the humble heroine. (Stewart 242)

In The Egoist, God, Sir Willoughby, and the reader are bound in a sort of trinity of human egoism. The book is a witty blasphemous parody of Christian theology (Polhemus 208). Sir Willoughby represents the humor of egoism incarnate. He is arbitrary and severe toward those beneath him, and he is vindictive whenever he can be. He is the prototype representing foolish ruling-class tyranny. In ridiculing Willoughby, Meredith is ridiculing the entire class system (Polhemus 211). Willoughby, the egoist, constantly criticizes others for doing what he himself does, and sooner or later people are able to see through him. "When Willoughby woos Laetitia [Dale] while still holding Clara [Middleton] to her vow and nevertheless talks of deceit and love, he convicts himself. See and hear, says Meredith, the contradiction between doing and saying and between the conflicting desires of egoism. Loving his own voice, the egoist records the tapes that lead to his own exposure" (Polhemus 216). Willoughby's aunts, Isobel and Eleanor, are two women who act the way Willoughby wants them to act. "They depend totally on him, talk only of him, and have no personal identity." They are wonderfully comic figures, and are highly representative, since at the time of the writing of The Egoist there were hundreds of thousands of such women in Victorian England (Polhemus 217).

Willoughby, the egoist, explains to Clara, his new fiancée that she must swear that she will not remarry if he should die. Willoughby envisions a ring of monkey-faces grinning at Clara if she does not make this oath. But there is an irony in Willoughby's actions. "Willoughby makes a self-defeating attempt to absorb the soul and individuality of a woman and in doing so teaches her the necessity of her independence for self-preservation (Polhemus 214).

Comedy for George Meredith was both a means and an evidence of feminine progress. The Egoist is about women's struggle toward freedom against the "imperium of male egoism" (Polhemus 225). Victorian society considered women to be morally superior to men; they were therefore held to a higher standard of morality and purity (Polhemus 226). Robert Polhemus considers Victorian spiritual pornography to be the reverse of sexual pornography. "It just as clearly shows the impulse to use another, without limit, for personal gratification. Moreover, it is just as demeaning. Wanting to seem attractively pure, women have had to neglect their potential of mind and spirit. They think they should be innately pleasant, innocent, and moral, but, knowing they are not, they sham" (Polhemus 227). Women were to be "machines of pleasure and virtuous ornaments as well."

> Laetitia begins as a relatively humorless character, but as she develops her powers of irony and playful mockery, she develops her independence. Clara uses her wit like a magic potion to relieve the pressures of her intolerable state and to steel her courage. And Mrs. Mountstuart Jenkinson, whose deadly wit and epigrams Sir Willoughby fears so much, is not accidentally a woman and a devotee of the comic spirit. (Polhemus 227)

Polhemus considers the major comic achievements of The Egoist to have been achieved through the speech patterns and rhythms of his particular characters--

> Dr. Middleton's charming and maddening pedantry, the chanted self-abnegation of the aunts, Colonel De Craye's gay banter, the jibing, rhythmic dialogue of Vernon and Clara. Above all, Willoughby's voice is a comic triumph of the highest order. His talks with Clara and Laetitia reveal a semantics of supreme selfishness and cry out that rhetoric is the inevitable instrument of the ridiculous ego. (Polhemus 244)

In The Tragic Comedians (1880), Meredith writes that "To have no sympathy with a playful mind is not to have a mind" (Stewart 245). The hero of The Tragic Comedians is described by I. M. Williams as being "handed over to the Comic Muse because he falls short of the 'nobleness' required of the tragic hero as described in Meredith's 1887 poem, 'The Two Masks' " (Stevenson "Innovations" 206). At the end of The Tragic Comedians, Meredith describes the prototypical tragic comedian as "a grand pretender, a self-deceiver, one of the lividly ludicrous, whom we cannot laugh at, but must contemplate" (Moses 215).

Anthony Trollope described the title character of Sandra Belloni (1885) as "a contrast of a girl of simplicity and passion and our English sentimental. socially-aspiring damsels" (Cline Letters 236). Sandra Belloni had been published earlier under the name of Emilia in England (1864), and was about Emilia Alessandra Belloni, who is contrasted with Arabella Pole, Adela Pole, Cornelia Pole, and Wilfrid Pole. The members of the Pole family are targets of Meredith's direct attack on middle-class hypocrisy. The Pole daughters are "sentimentalists," who have only a veneer of refinement and sensitivity, a veneer that only thinly hides their commonplace snobbery and social ambition. These sisters look down on Emilia's lack of sophistication, but they nevertheless exploit Emilia's musical talent to gain social prominence (Ives 754).

In Diana of the Crossways (1885), the space that Diana claims for laughter is "the breath of her soul" (Diana 7). This laughter depends on "the liberty she [allows] herself in speech and action" (Diana 6). Diana provokes peals of laughter from Emma over civilization and politics, and also laughs herself (Diana 118). It is also laughter which characterizes her relationship with her maid, Danvers. Danvers laughs so much that she thinks Diana to be "as good as a play." Laughter is also an important aspect of Diana's relationship with Thomas Redworth. There is a particular carriage ride which is filled with misadventure, but it is also filled with hilarity, as Diana has "some of her wildest seizures of iridescent humour" (Diana 102). In Diana of the Crossways, Andrew Hedger's favorite food is prime bacon. At one point, he says, "Ah could eat hog a solid hower!... Hog's my feed." This is the type of scene which Meredith praised in Cervantes. "The juxtaposition of railroad tycoon and country yokel, like that of knight and squire in <u>Don Quixote</u>, fuses the tragic sentiment with the comic narrative, and suggests why Meredith is a humorist as well as a comedian" (Craig 51). Victor Radnor in <u>One of Our Conquerors</u> (1891) may be admirable, but he is also ludicrous; he may be noble, but he is also mean; he may be generous, but he is also self-centered. This novel is filled with such paradoxes (Moses 218).

In 1908, Richard Curle wrote that the novelist must realize that tragedy is intensely personal, and that in order to grasp the tragedy the reader needs a great power of imagination and sympathy. He further noted that this is very different from the philosophical mind that is needed in order to grasp the comic spirit. Curle continues: "Meredith's profound greatness lies in his double grasp of the subject. The comic spirit has saved him from sentimentality, the human understanding from too cold a basis of logic. They have together given him the insight which sees the tragedy of tragedy but sees it from the hill of the optimist" (Moses 224). Meredith's comic stance is paradoxical since it recognizes both the tragic and the comic realities.

Meredith's "On the Idea of Comedy and of the Uses of the Comic Spirit" was published in 1910 in Volume 23 of <u>Miscellaneous Prose</u>. Meredith's "An Essay on Comedy" was published in Wylie Sypher's <u>Comedy</u> in 1956. In "Essay on Comedy" Meredith attempted to rid Victorian comic writing of the "incubus of sentimental humour" (Martin 90). Here Meredith distinguishes between the "agelasts" (non-laughers), the "misogelasts" (laughter-haters), and the "hypergelasts" (excessive laughers). For Meredith, the golden mean was to be found only in the play of wit, which brings a "slim-feasting smile", or at most a "volley of silvery laughter" (Martin 91). Meredith repeatedly makes the point that humor deals with the idiosyncratic and the accidental, while both wit and comedy deal with philosophic abstractions which are made concrete by example. "The laughter of comedy is impersonal." For Meredith, comedy is based not so much on specific incidents and characters as it is on the ideas that lie behind them. Comedy "laughs through the mind, for the mind directs it; and it might be called the humour of the mind" ("Essay" 46).

Meredith was in tune with the late-Victorian notion that the best Comedy is basically intellectual, witty, incongruous, poetic, symbolic, evocative, and divorced from contempt. The best comedy springs from the "totally engaged process of the mind" (Martin 98). According to Meredith, an excellent way to determine the civilization of a country is to test it against the notion of the Comic Idea and of Comedy. "The test of true Comedy is that it shall awaken thoughtful laughter" (Martin 99).

George Meredith Bibliography

Beach, Joseph Warren. <u>The Comic Spirit in George Meredith: An Interpretation</u>. (1911); New York, NY: Russell, 1963.
Brewer, Edward V. "The Influence of Jean Paul Richter on George Meredith's Conception of the Comic." <u>Journal of English and Germanic Philology</u> 29 (1930): 242-256.
Cline, C. L., ed. <u>The Collected Letters of George Meredith</u>. Oxford, England: Clarendon, 1970.
Cline, C. L., ed. <u>The Ordeal of Richard Feverel</u> by George Meredith (1859). Boston, MA: Houghton Mifflin, 1971.
Comstock, Margaret. "George Meredith, Virginia Woolf, and Their Feminist Comedy." Ph.D. Dissertation. Stanford University, 1975.
Craig, Randall Thomas. " 'Harmless Wine' and 'Prime Bacon': Meredith's Comic Cuisine." <u>WHIMSY</u> 6 (1988): 50-51.
Curtin, Frank D. "Adrian Harley: The Limits of Meredith's Comedy." <u>Nineteenth-Century</u>

Fiction 7 (1953): 272-282.

Henkle, Roger B. "Meredith and Butler: Comedy as Lyric, High Culture, and the Bourgeois Trap." Comedy and Culture--England--1820-1900. Princeton, NJ: Princeton University Press, 1980, 238-295.

Herbert, Christopher. Trollope and Comic Pleasure. Chicago, IL: University of Chicago Press, 1987.

Ives, Maura. "George Meredith." Encyclopedia of British Humorists, Volume II. Ed. Steven H. Gale. New York, NY: Garland, 1996, 752-757.

Landis, Joseph C. "George Meredith's Comedy." Boston University Studies in English 2 (1956): 17-35.

Levin, Harry, ed. Veins of Humor. Cambridge, MA: Harvard Univ Press, 1972.

McWhirter, David. "Feminism/Gender/Comedy: Meredith, Woolf, and the Reconfiguration of Comic Distance." Look Who's Laughing: Gender and Comedy. Ed. Gail Finney. New York, NY: Gordon and Breach, 1994, 189-204.

Martin, Robert Bernard. "Chapter VI: George Eliot, Leslie Stephen, and George Meredith." The Triumph of Wit: A Study of Victorian Comic Theory. Oxford, England: Clarendon Press, 1974, 82-100.

Mayer, Frederick P. "George Meredith: An Obscure Comedian." Virginia Quarterly Review 1 (1925): 409-422.

Meredith, George. Diana of the Crossways (1885). New York, NY: Charles Scribner's Sons, 1911.

Meredith, George. "An Essay on Comedy." (1877) Comedy. Ed. Wylie Sypher. Garden City, NY: Doubleday, 1956, 31-57.

Meredith, George. Poems and Lyrics of the Joy of Earth. London, England: Macmillan, 1883.

Meredith, George. The Tragic Comedians. London, England: Chapman and Hall, 1880.

Moses, Joseph. The Novelist as Comedian: George Meredith and the Ironic Sensibility. New York, NY: Schocken, 1983.

Polhemus, Robert M. "Meredith's The Egoist (1879): The Comedy of Egoism." Comic Faith: The Great Tradition from Austen to Joyce. Chicago, IL: University of Chicago Press, 1980, 204-244.

Priestley, J. B. English Humour. New York, NY: Stein and Day, 1976.

Pritchett, V. S. George Meredith and English Comedy. New York, NY: Random, 1969.

Robinson, E. Arthur. "Meredith's Literary Theory and Science: Realism vs. The Comic Spirit." Publication of the Modern Language Association 53 (1938): 857-868.

Stevenson, Richard C. "Comedy, Tragedy, and the Spirit of Critical Intelligence in Richard Feverel." The Worlds of Victorian Fiction. Ed. Jerome H. Buckley. Cambridge, MA: Harvard Univ Press, 1975, 205-222.

Stevenson, Richard C. "Innovations of Comic Method in George Meredith's Evan Harrington." Texas Studies in Literature and Language 15 (1973): 311-324.

Stevenson, Richard C. "Laetitia Dale and the Comic Spirit in The Egoist." Nineteenth-Century Fiction 26 (1972): 406-418.

Stewart, Maaja A. "Techniques of Intellectual Comedy in Meredith and Fielding." Genre 8 (1975): 233-247.

Thackeray, W. M. The English Humorists, Charity and Humour, The Four Georges. London, England: Dent, 1912.

Margaret Oliphant (1828-1897)

Nearly everybody laughs in Margaret Oliphant's Miss Marjoribanks (1866), everybody, that is, except the heroine, Lucilla--and many people laugh at Lucilla. Lucilla admits that she has no sense of humor, and that she often doesn't see what is ridiculous; however, when people laugh at her, they usually laugh with admiration and they attribute to her more wit, and more ironic double vision and distance than she in fact has. "Much of the comedy of the novel lies not in the accidents of failure, but in the astonishing serendipity of her successes" (Gindele 149). In Miss Marjoribanks, the laughter of the Doctor is significant. "He often chuckles to himself, he laughs softly, he sometimes laughs and sighs; he most often laughs when he is beaten by Lucilla--partly at himself, partly in admiration of her. He also provides an internal perspective of pleasure in her. There is a power struggle between Lucilla and the Doctor at the dinner table. When Lucilla returned from school, "He found her, to his intense amazement, seated at the foot of the table, in the place which he usually occupied himself." Of course he is angry at her boldness, but he is also "amused and pleased...to have so clever a daughter" (Fitzgerald 68). He is the type of person who credits Lucilla with wit when she is earnest (Gindele 151). Mrs. Woodburn is another of Lucilla's critics. Mrs. Woodburn doesn't have the same self-contained aloofness of Dr. Marjoribanks. Instead, her laughter is explosive. For Mrs. Woodburn, laughter is a "safety-valve" (Gindele 152).

Margaret Oliphant Bibliography

Gindele, Karen C. "When Women Laugh Wildly and (Gentle)Men Roar: Victorian Embodiments of Laughter." Look Who's Laughing: Gender and Comedy. Ed. Gail Finney. Amsterdam, Netherlands: Gordon and Breach, 1994, 139-160.
Fitzgerald, Penelope, ed. Miss Marjoribanks, by Margaret Oliphant (1866). New York, NY: Penguin/Virago, 1989.

4

Humor in Late Nineteenth-Century British Literature

Charles Graham Halpine (1829-1868) IRELAND

See Nilsen, Don L. F. Humor in Irish Literature: A Reference Guide. Westport, CT: Greenwood, 1996.

Charles Stuart (Blayds) Calverley (1831-1884)

Charles Calverley wrote parodies which targeted the stilted phrase, the pretentious claim, the deliberate obscurity, and the sickly sentimentality. Targets he especially liked included people he admired like Alfred, Lord Tennyson as well as people he deplored like Robert Browning. He also targeted such women poets as Anna Mastilda, Jean Ingelow, Felicia Dorothea Hemans, and Elizabeth Barrett Browning. In his "Memoir," John Seelye refers to Calverley's "elfish mockery, the exuberant playfulness of a powerful mind and tender, manly nature" (Smith 204).

In A Century of Parody and Imitation (1913), Walter Jerrold and R. M. Leonard anthologized ten of Calverley's parodies. He parodied Longfellow ("Ode to Tobacco"), Byron ("Beer"), Tennyson ("Wanderers"), Tupper ("Proverbial Philosophy"), Jean Ingelow ("Lovers, and a Reflection," and "Ballad"), and Browning ("The Cock and the Bull") (Smith 204). "The Cock and the Bull" may be Calverley's most celebrated parody. It is an attack of Browning's The Ring and the Book, which is 80,000 lines in length. Calverley mocked Browning's masculine bravado, his large chunks of technical language, the absence of the lyrical impulse in this piece, and Browning's intermingling of Latin and English phrases. Elton Smith says that Calverley's parodies of Browning, Tennyson, Virgil, and William

Morris provide amusement at the same time as they reveal the extravagant styles of these important writers. Calverley's "light, occasional verse is lean, disciplined, and exact. His comedic point of view is always the good-natured exposure of personal eccentricities, the Romantic 'agony,' and the sentimental fervor" (Smith 205).

Charles Stuart (Blayds) Calverley Bibliography

Babington, Percy L. Browning and Calverley; or Poem and Parody. London, England: John Castle, n.d.

Ince, R. V. "Calverley and Some Cambridge Wits of the Nineteenth Century." Athenaeum 2 (1885): 533.

Jerrold, Walter, and R. M. Leonard. eds. A Century of Parody and Imitation. London, England: Oxford University Press, 1913.

Smith, Elton E. "Charles Stuart (Blayds) Calverley." Encyclopedia of British Humorists, Volume I. Ed. Steven H. Gale. New York, NY: Garland, 1996, 203-206.

Lewis Carroll (né Charles Lutwidge Dodgson)(1832-1898)

Lewis Carroll's father may have been an earnest Victorian, but he also had a great sense of humor. At the age of seven, Carroll received the following letter from his father:
> You may depend upon it; I will not forget your commission. I WILL have a file and a screw driver, and a ring, and if they are not brought directly, in forty seconds, I will leave nothing but one small cat alive in the whole town of Leeds.... Then what a bawling and tearing of hair there will be! Pigs and babies, camels and butterflies, rolling in the gutter together--old women rushing up the chimneys and cows after them--ducks hiding themselves in coffee cups, and fat geese trying to squeeze themselves into pencilcases. (Nadel and Frederman 46)

From the time he was a child, words both attracted and repelled Carroll. He found words problematical, and he said that "it was their nature to be ambiguous (Nadel and Frederman 53). As a boy, Carroll had a "multitude of sisters," and for them, he was their master of ceremonies, an inventor of their games, a magician, a marionette theater manager, and editor of their family journals (Nadel and Frederman 45). Carroll started writing nonsense as a boy for his own amusement, and for the amusement of his brothers and sisters. He soon acquired a special skill at it, and his play developed into an art--an art which retained child's play as one of its qualities. To be successful, nonsense has to keep a precarious balance between childlike whimsy and the caprice of a trained artist exhibiting his skills. It is like caricature in that it appears to be casually rendered, "but it is often swept up in the exuberance of comic creation, the writer improvising and piling on richer and wilder creations and scenes for his own delight in them" (Henkle 204). Carroll was ambivalent in his feelings toward religion, and Roger Henkle notes that the Alice books can easily be read as critiques of various Calvinist tenets. In Through the Looking Glass, the dreaming king seems to be a satire about predestination, as is the policy of "punishment first, guilt later." The basic premise of the knave's trial is that there is always something that a person is guilty of, and that the purpose of a trial is to figure out what it is. This may be a satire of the idea of primordial sin (Henkle 213).

Linda Shires suggests that epistemological uncertainty was a prominent feature of nineteenth-century English literature, and that this epistemological uncertainty was manifested in terms of madness, hallucination, multiple divisions of the subject and in such modes as Gothic fiction, fantasy, and the literature of the marvelous. "Fantasy, nonsense, and parody each questions the status of the real in a different, and differently disturbing, way, pushing language and meaning toward dangerous limits of dissolution. Such flirtation with limits of sense-making and, in some works, such dissolution of sense, proves pleasurable because it terrifies" (Shires 267). Shires compares this tendency to uncertainty with the distorting mirror at the circus funhouse. "Fantasy is the mirror that sucks the body in, as it does Alice in Alice's Adventures in Wonderland and literally in Through the Looking-Glass. Parody is the placement of a distorted mirror image against an 'original' mirror image. Nonsense is that which cannot be seen, or known, or held onto: the broken mirror, the broken image" (Shires 268).

In a book entitled Lewis Carroll, Richard Kelly points out that philosophers have analyzed Lewis Carroll's ideas; linguists have analyzed his sentences; social critics have analyzed his environment; and psychoanalysts have analyzed his mind. "Yet both the man and his writings remain enigmas" (Kelly, 1977, 3). Appropriately enough, Lewis Carroll was born under the name of Charles Lutwidge Dodgson at Daresburg parsonage in Cheshire. In 1854, at the age of twenty-two, Dodgson began to establish himself as a freelance humorist by contributing humorous poems and stories to the Oxonian Advertiser and the Whitby Gazette. In 1855 he published the first stanza of "Jabberwocky" in his scrapbook Mischmasch, and contributed parodies to the Comic Times. In 1856, on the advice of Edmund Yates, he adopted "Lewis Carroll" as his nom de plume for publishing in a comic paper entitled The Train. Here he published a number of parodies, including "Upon the Lonely Moor." In February of 1863 he completed Alice's Adventures under Ground, and in April of 1864 he got John Tenniel to illustrate it. In June of that same year he changed the title to Alice's Adventures in Wonderland, and in 1865 Carroll sent a presentation copy of Alice's Adventures in Wonderland to Alice Liddell, for whom the book was written.

After Alice Liddell had grown up and become Mrs. Hargreaves, she gave her impressions of what it had been like to have been "Alice" at the time that Alice's Adventures in Wonderland were written:

> I believe the beginning of "Alice" was told one summer afternoon when the sun was so burning that we had landed in the meadows down the river, deserting the boat to take refuge in the only bit of shade to be found, which was under a new-made hayrick. Here from all three came the old petition, "Tell us a story," and so began the ever-delightful tale. Sometimes to tease us--and perhaps being really tired--Mr. Dodgson would stop suddenly and say, "And that's all till next time." "Ah, but it is next time," would be the exclamation from all three. (Nadel and Frederman 48).

Charles Dodgson was a teacher of Logic and Mathematics at Oxford University. He felt that mathematics was superior to the other sciences because of its certainty and lack of ambiguity (Pycior 162). But Carroll was caught in a dilemma, since he was both a scientist and an author. According to George Lakoff, scientists often claim to be totally objective. Authors on the other hand have a problem which is opposite to that of scientists. They admit that their field is subjective, interactional, and not quantifiable or replicable. But authors sometimes have problems with grounding, and this has happened in Lewis Carroll's writings (Nilsen "Limitations" 377). Some of Carroll's academic works could be described as "wittily serious." These include Euclid and His Modern Rivals (1879), The Game of Logic (1886), and Symbolic Logic, Parts I and II (1896). "Of the academic studies, the most notable are not the most serious in tone but are leavened with humor (Nadel and Frederman 45).

Charles Dodgson was both fascinated and disturbed by symbolic algebra, to the extent that it played on his imagination and appeared in many different guises in the Alice books. He was so bothered by lines multiplied by lines, and quantities less than nothing that he set about to create the world of Wonderland in which nonsense and arbitrariness prevailed (Pycior 163). Although Carroll never used the term "negative," he did talk about "quantities less than nothing" and "quantities obtained by taking a greater from a lesser" (Pycior 164).

In Alice's Adventures in Wonderland, the Mad Hatter says that it is impossible to subtract something from nothing. In the tea party scene, the March Hare offers Alice "more tea," and Alice responds that she has "had nothing yet [and] so...can't take more." At this point Hatter comments: "You mean you can't take less.... It's very easy to take more than nothing" (Carroll 101). Later in the same work, the Mock Turtle describes his early schooling, saying that his lessons lessened (decreased) day by day. On the first day, he studied for ten hours; on the second, nine hours; and so on. Alice asks whether he rested on the eleventh day, and he responded that he did, since ten hours minus ten hours equals zero hours. But Alice then pushes beyond the zero point, by asking: "And how did you manage on the twelfth?" (Carroll 130), thereby bringing the discussion around to the problem of the negatives. The Gryphon abruptly changes the subject of conversation from lessons to games (Pycior 164).

The Red Queen in Through the Looking-Glass, also introduces the problem of the negative numbers when she asks Alice to subtract nine from eight. Alice simply objects that is an impossible subtraction (Pycior 164). The absurdity of the question is reinforced by the fact that it was the arbitrary Red Queen who asked the question, and further reinforced by a series of preposterous pseudo questions involved with dividing a loaf by a knife, subtracting a bone from a dog, and so forth (Pycior 165).

> Subjected to the vagaries of her underground experience, such as changes in her size, Alice comes to question even her identity. She wonders if she is Ada or Mabel, two of her above-ground friends. In this epistemological crisis, reminiscent of Descartes's [crisis] in the Discourse on Method, Alice imitates the French philosopher by trying to establish what she knows with certainty. It is not surprising that Alice turns first to mathematics, given its privileged position in Victorian culture. "I'll try if I know all the things I used to know. Let me see; four times five is twelve, and four times six is thirteen, and four times seven is -- oh dear! I shall never get to twenty at that rate!" (Pycior 165)

According to Helena Pycior, the Multiplication Table doesn't signify. Furthermore, the meaningless and arbitrariness of symbolical algebra provide a key to the meaninglessness and arbitrariness of Carroll's underground world. "The parallels between Carroll's nonsense writings and symbolical algebra are striking; both stress form or structure over meaning, using words (or other symbols) with multiple possible interpretations" (Pycior 166).

> Critics sometimes ridiculed the symbolical approach by exploring the consequences of interpreting algebraic symbols as absolutely universal (standing for all possible mathematical entities). The Hatter applies the latter interpretation to words (rather than algebraic symbols) in sentences (rather than mathematical formulas). "You can draw water out of a water-well," the Hatter says, "so I should think you could draw treacle out of a treacle-well--eh, stupid?" (Carroll 102). The structure of the two sentences is the same (you can draw b out of a b-well), but the content is different.... The point of Carroll's humor now seems clear; structure does not guarantee meaning; emphasis on structure over meaning, so basic to the symbolical approach, can lead to nonsense. (Pycior 167)

Games are like symbolic algebra in this respect. They have their own rigid laws which cannot be questioned within the game itself (Pycior 169). The King, the Queen, and the attendants are playing cards. They are merely symbols, like a, b, and c, and as symbols they are abstract, manufactured, and arbitrary (Pycior 168).

> The facts that the Alices deal with a search for meaning in a meaningless world, that Dodgson's nonsense emphasizes structure over meaning, that the analogy of a game is appropriate to his literature, and that Dodgson was acquainted with and yet uneasy about the symbolical approach all point to symbolical algebra as a major influence on the Alices. The Alices were, at least partly, expressions of Dodgson's anxiety over the loss of certainty implicit in the mathematicians' acceptance of the symbolical approach. Alice's bewilderment in Wonderland paralleled Dodgson's bewilderment in the mathematical world of the symbolical algebraist. (Pycior 170)

In her Play, Games, and Sport: The Literary Works of Lewis Carroll, Kathleen Blake notes that the play impulse underlies games and sport. Blake says that play is spontaneous, disinterested, nonutilitarian, and characterized by "a fundamental urge to mastery through incorporation of experience to the ego rather than by adjustment or accommodation of the ego to experience." The difference between play and work is the difference between eating up life--for the pleasure of it, and being digested by life--for the hunger of it (Blake Play 18).

In much of his writing, Carroll alludes to actual people, places, and events. In the scene of the painting of the roses, for example, one of the cards accuses another card of "bringing the cook tulip roots instead of onions" (Carroll Alice 75). Michael Gardner says that here Carroll may be referring to an incident that happened in Holland, where tulips are a valued possession. An English traveler mistook a rare species of tulip roots for an onion and began to peel and eat it. It turned out that this root was worth 4000 florins, and the traveler was arrested and thrown into jail until he could pay back the owner of the root (More Annotated 94). Carroll is also playing a similar game of allusion when he has the White Rabbit continually calling Alice by the name of Mary Ann, which makes Alice assume that he has mistaken her for his maid (Carroll Alice 28). In fact, "Mary Ann" is a British euphemism for a servant girl, but in addition to this, the name of "Mary Ann" has a variety of other innuendos. It is the term used to refer to a dressmaker's dress stand. It is the term used to refer to the women of Sheffield who attacked sweatshop owners. "Mary Ann" was also slang for guillotine, and is probably an allusion to the obsession of the Duchess and the Queen for having people beheaded. During the French Revolution, "Mary Ann" became a French symbol of republican values. This is comparable to England's "John Bull," and America's "Uncle Sam" (Gardner More Annotated 43).

At the point where it takes two people to play, and one of these people will win, we have a game. Lewis Carroll loved games, and in 1858 he purchased a copy of Hoyle's Games, and from that point on lived his life "according to Hoyle." In Victoria through the Looking-Glass, Florence Becker Lennon said, "His life was a game, even his logic, his mathematics, and his singular ordering of his household and other affairs. His logic was a game and his games were logical" (Blake Play 60). In his writings, Carroll has many games relating to geometry, logic, language, and communication. Games are especially well developed in the Alice books, which are structured on the rules of games, but with these rules running wild. In a letter to May Forshall, one of Carroll's childhood friends, Carroll wrote, "Do you ever play at games? Or is your idea of life "breakfast, lessons, dinner, lessons, tea, lessons, bed, lessons, breakfast, lessons, and so on? It is a very neat plan of life and almost as interesting as being a sewing machine or a coffee grinder" (Blake Play 11).

Carroll loved children, and John Pudney quotes a poem which Carroll wrote:
> I'd give all wealth that years have piled,
> The slow result of Life's decay,

To be once more a little child
For one bright summer-day. (Pudney 37)
Lewis Carroll loved to play games and he in fact invented a number of games like "Rules for Court Circular," "Croquet Castles," "Puzzles from Wonderland," "A Charade," "Word Links," "Doublets," "A Game for Two Players," "Lanrick," "Mischmasch," "The Game of Logic," "Circular Billiards," "Syzygies: A Word-Puzzle," and "Arithmetical Croquet." He also invented a game named "Symbolic Logic," the playing of which required a playing board and gray and red counters. He also invented "Blot-Backgammon," in which each player scores the other player's points, and "Thirdie Backgammon" which uses three rather than two dice, and "Co-operative Backgammon" where two of the three dice determine the player's moves, and the third moves the opponent's pieces. " 'Co-operative' is a strange term for the relation between the players here, as they must certainly cooperate in no sense of the word except by their mutual endeavors to set each other back."
Blake considers the Alice books to be "famously nondidactic and playful."

> Games abound in them, at various levels: there are the jokes and riddles, aimed as much at the reader as at Alice: "Jam tomorrow and jam yesterday-- but never jam to-day"; "How is a raven like a writing desk?" The creatures share a mania for play, from the caucus-race on. Humpty-Dumpty treats conversation itself as a game. Cards, croquet, and chess establish the narrative frameworks of the novels. (Blake Play 12)

Although the Alice books have often been searched for scatological content by Freudian critics, Blake notes that there are no phalluses, toilets, cannibals, wombs, or amniotic fluids in the Alice books, though there are games (Blake Play 13). In talking about the nature of play, Johan Huizinga notes that make-believe is very different from delusion. "In a tribal ritual there exists the knowledge that what is being enacted is not "real." But there is also the knowledge that it is not "unreal" at the same time (Blake Play 15).

In his writing, Carroll "retreats into juvenility and dream states, reverts to play and nonsense, toys with language, avoids any overtly didactic or practical purpose, and escapes from society, history, and 'reality' into the fantasy of his own mind." But by doing this, Carroll "appears before us as a comic prophet and a father of modernism in art and literature" (Polhemus 245). In referring to Lewis Carroll as a "comic prophet," Polhemus is aware that the Reverend Charles Dodgson was an ordained cleric, and that he used his comic fantasy to "preserve the possibility of Christian faith, since it undercuts those very forces that were undermining Christianity: rationalism, science, positivism, utilitarianism, materialism, and the worship of progress." However, Polhemus adds that "the main effect of his comic vision is surely to render an absurdist world that makes ridiculous all authority, all dogma, including the traditional Christian brand" (Polhemus 247). Polhemus sees a relationship between jokes, humor, literature, and religion in that they are all forms of regression, though often positive, socially approved forms of regression. "Culture needs an institutionalized fantasy life--be it religion, art, myth, or sports--as a mind needs to dream" (Polhemus 249). Robert Higbie agrees with Polhemus, suggesting that Alice's Adventures in Wonderland and Through the Looking Glass are both in search of a kind of religious certainty. In fact, they deal with the problem of finding certainty of any kind, but the kinds of doubt expressed here are in Higbie's opinion an expression of Carroll's uncertainty about God (Higbie 21). Carroll once said about God, "If all-powerful, then how also all-good?" (Nadel and Frederman 54). Higbie compares a number of events in Alice's Adventures in Wonderland to events in the Bible:

> She [Alice] is denied entry into an Edenlike garden because she has eaten enchanted food. Then she survives a flood that to her is as all-encompassing as the Biblical deluge. She wanders in the wilderness and is given laws by various self-appointed prophets. At one point she even rises up toward the

heavens and is accused of being a serpent, as though she were being called sinful for aspiring to godlike status. At the end, the trial, her persecution and her transformation resemble Christ's. But though she may be Christlike, when she looks up into the heavens, she sees--not a figure of divine love-- but a mocking face, the Cheshire cat's. (Higbie 24)

In his Explorations in the Field of Nonsense, Wim Tigges explains some of the special linguistic attributes of nonsense:

> Nonsense is, in a unique and special way, a world of words come to life, a world whose insistently self-defined reality is almost completely linguistic. In nonsense, words often exercise a creative power similar to that granted to language in some primitive cultures. Lear's nonsense botanies and Carroll's Looking-Glass insects, for example, represent objects created from attributes of language itself. Thus what is in Alice's world a butterfly becomes in Looking-Glass Land a "Bread-and-Butter-Fly," whose wings are made of bread and butter, while its body is a crust and its head a lump of sugar. (Explorations 51-52)

This sets up a death joke for children, for when Alice asks how a Bread-and-Butter-Fly stays alive, she is told that it lives on weak tea with cream in it.

> "Supposing it couldn't find any?" she suggested.
>
> "Then it would die, of course."
>
> "But that must happen very often," Alice remarked thoughtfully.
>
> "It always happens," said the Gnat. (Polhemus 271)

Polhemus continues, "Joking about death is one of the most sophisticated ways that we have of combating its menace--of accepting it and defying it at the same time" (Polhemus 271).

Carroll viewed nonsense and parody as being closely connected not only with humor, but with death as well (Shires 276). Linda Shires notes that Alice's Adventures in Wonderland begins with Alice's fear of killing someone underneath her as she falls. The book ends with Alice's destruction of her fantasy world (Shires 277). There is much death in Through the Looking-Glass, where Humpty Dumpty falls and breaks, and Alice is fading (compare the Cheshire cat and the gnat). And the White Knight faces death every time he falls from his horse. (Shires 278)

In his An Anatomy of Literary Nonsense, Wim Tigges points to many critics who have contrasted the nonsense of Edward Lear with that of Lewis Carroll. G. K. Chesterton, for example, says that Lear's nonsense is poetical and even emotional, whereas Carroll's nonsense is purely intellectual--a blend of the mathematical and the logical. Emile Cammaerts said that Lear's nonsense discards all of the rules, except for those of verse structure, whereas Carroll's nonsense "obeys rules, but rules which are different from our normal ones." Elizabeth Sewell says that Carroll's nonsense is much more concerned with the process of language itself than is Lear's nonsense; this is why Carroll has so many puns. Carroll is breaking rules of number and logic, while Lear is moving us in the direction of dreams and nightmares. Rolf Hildebrandt says that Lear's nonsense is that of language play, absurd reasoning, exaggeration, logical and material indifference, free association, and total lack of direction, whereas Carroll's nonsense is what he calls the "nonsense of the ratio." Lisa S. Ede contrasts Lear's and Carroll's nonsense according to their literary genres, and their treatment of motifs. She feels that Carroll's nonsense is more concerned with ideas, while Lear's is more concerned with action. Stephen Pickett says that "whereas Lear's nonsense is one of emotion, nostalgia, and sheer buffoonery, Carroll's is one of undeviating rationality pushed to its furthest and wildest extremes" (Anatomy 81-84). Tigges summarizes by saying that Lear's nonsense is based on linguistic and logical imagination, while Carroll's nonsense is based on linguistic and logical fallacies

(Anatomy 150). The White King tells Alice, "There is nothing like eating hay when you're faint," to which Alice responds, "I think throwing cold water over you would be better." In a totally literal mindset, the White King then says, "I didn't say there was nothing better; I said there was nothing like it" (Carroll Through 76). The White Knight is also being perfectly literal when he tells Alice about a long and beautiful song. "Everybody that hears me sing it--either it brings tears to their eyes, or else--." "Or else what?" Alice asked when the Knight paused. "Or else it doesn't, you know" the White Knight continued (Paulos 49).

The White Queen engages in the same type of logical fallacy, as she offers Alice jam "every other day" in payment for her being her Lady's Maid. The dialogue continues:

> ALICE: Well, I don't want any to-day, at any rate.
>
> WHITE QUEEN: You couldn't have it if you did want it. The rule is, jam to-morrow and jam yesterday--but never jam to-day."
>
> ALICE: It must come sometimes to "jam to-day."
>
> WHITE QUEEN: No, it can't. It's jam every other day: to-day isn't any other day, you know. (Carroll Through 53)

Compare this to Alice's encounter with the White King. When Alice says, I see nobody on the road," the White King replies, "I wish I had such eyes, to be able to see Nobody!" (Carroll Through 74). Later when the White King asks his messenger who he had passed on the road, the messenger replies, "Nobody," to which the White King responds, "Quite right. This young lady saw him too" (Carroll Through 76; Tigges Explorations 52).

Lewis Carroll wrote Alice's Adventures in Wonderland (1866) to entertain children. Nevertheless, it has become an important work for philosophers, literary scholars, biographers, clergymen, psychoanysts, linguists, mathematicians, theologians, logicians, and the general public--both children and adults alike (Kelly Encyclopedia 215). Alice's recitations of poems turn into parodies in the same way that his baby turns into a pig, or a cat turns into a grin, as time, space and objectivity become fluid rather than static (Kelly Encyclopedia 216).

Alice's Adventures in Wonderland is a surreal novel in which the stability of being, the consistency of rules to allow fair play, the rational constructs, and even the words themselves flow around among riddles, puns, conversational misconstructions, and constant plays upon semantic and grammatical anomalies (Nadel and Fredeman 53). Alice's Adventures in Wonderland tells about a Wonderland where the conventional can't be found. The characters are more concerned with literal usage of words than their in-context meanings. Games are treated with respect, while serious events, like a courtroom trial, are treated with open disrespect. Derek Hudson compares Alice's Adventures with a Marx Brothers movie: "Both have been based largely on a play with words, mixed with judicious slapstick, and set within a framework of an idiosyncratic view of the human situation; their purpose is entertainment" (Hudson 23). Richard Kelly points out that Carroll was satirizing the Victorian Age which emphasized earnestness of nature, moral puritanism, and respectability by writing about Wonderland, a place where all of the opposites of these virtues reigned supreme.

> In an age when technological advance and urban industrialization in England threatened to "de-humanize" mankind, Carroll presented a world where one of the most humane of characteristics still held sway: a sense of humor. Predictably, "Alice" was not received with much enthusiasm upon its initial publication. The Victorian ideal of a "children's book" was one that instructed the child in religion and morals, not one that openly parodied the didactic and proper customs of contemporary [Victorian] society. (Kelly, 1977, 23)

Alice's Adventures in Wonderland contains twelve chapters each of them concerned with particular kinds of rules and ways of breaking these rules. Lisa S. Ede points out that the opening chapters of this book "focus primarily on Alice's frequent and confusing changes of size" (Ede 91). Chapter I is entitled "Down the Rabbit-Hole," and is concerned with the order of nature, and disruption of that nature. Chapter II is entitled "The Pool of Tears," and is concerned with how body size is affected by perceptions (of a child) and by eating and maturing. In Chapter II, Alice is nearly drowned in a pool of her own tears which she had wept when she was nine feet tall.

Chapter III is entitled "A Caucus-Race and a Long Tale," and is concerned with the breaking of the rules of games and sports, and the breaking of rules of language. In Chapter III Alice is saved from drowning by a mouse who is swimming in the water. Upon reaching shore, this mouse proposes to dry off Alice and the other creatures by relating to them a piece of dry history. When this doesn't work, the Dodo bird comes up with a remedy which does work. It proposes that everyone should become engaged in a "caucus race," in which prizes are to be awarded to everybody. Not only does everyone win a prize, but everyone also gets dried off in the process as well (Kelly, 1977, 84).

Chapter IV is entitled "The Rabbit Sends in a Little Bill" and is concerned with habitation. Chapter V is entitled "Advice from a Caterpillar" and is concerned with the breaking of the rules of communication.

Chapter VI is entitled "Pig and Pepper" and is concerned with the breaking of the rules of social conventions. In Chapter VI, Alice asks the Cheshire Cat for directions. When the Cat wants to know where she is going, she replies, "I don't much care where." The Cheshire Cat then replies, "Then it doesn't matter which way you go" (Gardner Annotated 89).

Chapter VII, "A Mad Tea-Party" begins with what appears to be a normal tea-party. Six o'clock is the time of the tea party, but here it is always six o'clock. Since it is always time for tea, the only thing that changes is the position of the guests at the table (Jannuzzi 5). Chapter VII is concerned with the breaking of the rules of time. At the end of this chapter, so many rules are broken that Alice walks off in disgust. Here and elsewhere, Alice is yearning for companionship, and she is disappointed when the March Hare and the Mad Hatter don't call after her when she leaves, but rather occupy themselves by putting the Dormouse into a Teapot (Tigges Anatomy 158).

Chapter VIII is entitled "The Queen's Croquet-Ground," and is concerned with the breaking of the rules pertaining to play, games, and sports. Throughout this chapter, the Queen of Hearts is constantly shouting "Off with his/her/its/their head(s)," and Wim Tigges suggests that Carroll is here taking the viewpoint of a child whose mother or governess is constantly shouting, "Off to your bed!" (Anatomy 158). Carroll is also taking the viewpoint of the child in reference to the rules of the game. Why should adults be allowed to make up all of the rules? Justice is one of the main concerns of children--Alice included--and Alice at one point remarks, "I don't think they play at all fairly" (Anatomy 159). In "The Queen's Croquet-Ground" Alice discovers that card games and croquet have different rules from what she had been accustomed to (Tigges Anatomy 158). "Alice thought she had never seen such a curious croquet-ground in her life...: the croquet balls were live hedgehogs, and the mallets live flamingos" (Gardner Annotated 111).

In Alice's Adventures in Wonderland, when the Duchess tells Alice "If everybody minded their own business, the world would go around a deal faster than it does," Alice responds that she didn't think that would be any advantage. "Just think what work it would make with the day and night!" You see, the earth takes twenty-four hours to turn round on its axis--" At this point, the Duchess raises her voice to say "Talking of axes, chop off her head!" What the Duchess says is not a non-sequitur; rather it illustrates egocentric speech, which is usually associated with small children, but which is here the property of an adult--the Duchess. Alice and the Duchess here have different mind sets, and what is going on here is not a single dialogue, but rather two somewhat distinct monologues. If this exchange were analyzed according to the rules of Script-Model Grammar, we could say that what we have here is a double script, with "axis-axes" being the trigger that takes the reader from one script to the other (Carroll Alice's 76).

    Chapter IX of Alice's Adventures in Wonderland is entitled "The Mock-Turtle's Story" and is concerned with the breaking of rules relating to ethics and education. Chapter IX discusses various ideas of ethics and education. "The Mock Turtle's Story" is a story about morals and lessons. The Mock Turtle explains to Alice that a "real tortoise" is educated in "reeling," "writhing," "ambition," "distraction, "uglification," and "derision." Carroll's puns of reading, writing, addition, subtraction, multiplication, and division are still another example of nonsensical methods used to infer to a particular theme (Gardner Annotated 129).

    Chapter X is entitled "The Lobster-Quadrille," and is concerned with breaking the rules of dance. There is an interesting kind of antithesis that goes on in Chapter X. In the song that the Turtle dances to, the term "whiting" is used. When Alice wants to know what it means, the Gryphon tells her that it is what is done to shoes and boots. Alice corrects him, saying that she thinks this is called "blacking," but the Gryphon says that under the sea, boots and shoes are done with "whiting." He then extends the pun by telling her that under the sea the shoes are made of "soles" and "eels" (Gardner Annotated 136-137).

    Chapter XI is entitled "Who Stole the Tarts?" and is concerned with the breaking of the rules of justice. In this chapter many of the characters who have been met earlier in the novel are reintroduced in various roles in the court room. The White Rabbit becomes a herald or an usher, the Mad Hatter is a witness; Bill the Lizard is a juror, and so on (Anatomy 159). And finally, Chapter XII is entitled "Alice's Evidence," and is concerned with the breaking of rules of etiquette; it is also concerned with leaving the strange rules of Wonderland and reëstablishing the rules of the real world. Alice reëstablishes her true identity, her true size, and her true judgement, and has an epiphany which shocks her into the real world: "You're nothing but a pack of cards!" (Anatomy 160).

    Carroll's ability to transcend in his writing has resulted in much conflicting criticism:

> Read what has been written about Carroll and you will find a zoo of interpretation. It has been seriously argued, for example, that Alice equals a phallus, that her pool of tears represents the amniotic fluid, that Alice's Adventures in Wonderland may contain a secret history of the Oxford Movement, that the "pig and pepper" chapter is a description of toilet training, that the White Queen stands for John Henry Newman, that these tales are dangerous for children, that they are literally nonsense and do not refer to the real world, that Alice is an existential heroine, that Carroll was a latent homosexual, an atheist, and a faithful Christian.... Something in the nature of the writing itself sparks a wide variety of reactions. (Polhemus 249)

Alice's Adventures in Wonderland contains a number of nonsense verses, many of them parodies of earlier verses. In his A Book of Nonsense, Edward Lear lists the following: "Fury and the Mouse," "How Doth the Little Crocodile," "You Are Old, Father William," "Speak Roughly to your Little Boy," "Twinkle, Twinkle, Little Bat," "Will You Walk a Little Faster?" "'Tis the Voice of the Lobster," "Beautiful Soup," "The Queen of Hearts," and "They Told Me You Had Been to Her" (Lear 111-117). Richard Kelly feels that Carroll's nonsense verse is much more complex and paradoxical than is his serious poetry. These poems are all rebellious in exactly the way that children are rebellious. But they are also parodies. "Speak Roughly to Your Little Boy" is a parody of G. W. Langford's popular poem entitled "Speak Gently." It mocks the Victorian "sentimental glorification of the child." It opens with the stark advice, "Speak roughly to your little boy, / And beat him when he sneezes: / He only does it to annoy, / Because he knows it teases." It is ironic that the boy in question is sneezing not because he pleases, or because he teases, but rather because the room is full of black pepper (Kelly Encyclopedia 215).

The White Knight's song in Through the Looking Glass is also a 'parody--of William Wordsworth's "Resolution and Independence" (Shires 276). Carroll's poem is quintessentially Wordsworthian as the White Knight pushes parody to the limits. Carroll's poem "mutes the humor gained by the signifiers of the Knight's poem bearing little resemblance to those of "Resolution and Independence" (Shires 280).

Carroll also parodies Wordsworth's "Leech Gatherer," though he "alters the content of the Wordsworth poem so that the narrator, who in the original had been able to grow happy from his encounter with the leech gatherer, becomes entirely alone and self-absorbed, unable to relate in an adult world. And Carroll alters the speech of the leech gatherer so as to make him absurd" (Shires 281).

All of the parodies written by Lewis Carroll can stand on their own as good literature. When it is discovered that they are parodies, however, they become even more impressive, for now they also illustrate in addition what a good ear Lewis Carroll had for language (Nilsen "Linguistic" 38).

Isaac Watts wrote poetry in the tradition of nineteenth century didacticism. One of his poems reads as follows:

> How doth the busy little bee
>> Improve each shining hour,
> And gather honey all the day
>> From every open flower!

Carroll's parody of Watts's poem reads as follows:

> How doth the little crocodile
>> Improve his shining tail,
> And pour the waters of the Nile
>> On every golden scale! (Shires 275)

The moral of Watts's poem is "Be hardworking and dutiful!" But in Carroll's parody, the words attain a quite different meaning. By mocking Watts, and by supplying new words for his poetic formula Carroll calls the words into question. Carroll not only mocks the moral, he parodies the entire process of moralizing. In Carroll's parody there is a collision of two antithetical kinds of discourse--moral and amoral. The moral of Carroll's poem is quite different from that of Watts--poetry should not be didactic; it should be fun (Shires 276).

Alice's Adventures in Wonderland ends as follows:

> "Who cares for you?" said Alice (she had grown to her full size by this time). "You're nothing but a pack of cards!" At this the whole pack rose up into the air, and came flying down upon her; she gave a little scream, half of fright and half of anger, and tried to beat them off, and found herself lying on the bank, with her head in the lap of her sister, who was gently brushing away some dead leaves....

The logic of Alice's Adventures in Wonderland (1866), and the logic of Through the Looking Glass, and What Alice Found There (1871) are not the same. Although Wonderland undermines Alice's sense of time, space, and common-sense logic, Looking-Glass Land questions her very reality. It is Tweedledum and Tweedledee who express the Berkeleyian view that all material objects exist only in the mind of God. In Through the Looking Glass, Alice only exists in the mind of the Red King (God), who is asleep. They warn Alice that if the Red King were to wake up, she would "go out like a candle." The story ends, in fact, with the perplexing question of who it was who dreamed up the entire story. Was it Alice, or the Red King? "Presumably, Alice dreamed of the King, who is dreaming of Alice, who is dreaming of the King, and so on" (Kelly Encyclopedia 216).

Concerning the writing in Carroll's Through the Looking Glass, Cass Falardeau makes the following statement:

> An early influence on Carroll's life that affected his thought processes and was generally believed to be responsible for his lifelong speech affliction of stammering, was the numerous attempts to correct his left-handedness. The idea that he was somehow morally "backward" because he was left-handed led to Carroll's preoccupation with contradictory images of symmetry like mirrors, cameras, and words spelled backwards. (Falardeau 3)

The creatures in Looking glass land tend to be governed by "relentless logicality, neither understanding the loose statement characteristic of Alice's world, nor allowing her to get by with it. Alice is constantly made to see the illogicality of the conventions by the use of English" (Terente 201).

Through the Looking Glass is a parody of Thomas Huxley and Alfred, Lord Tennyson; it is a parody of both science and of literature, and Carroll's main weapon is "reductio ad absurdum." He takes the words of Huxley and Tennyson literally, as a child would take them, and he imagines their full implications by showing how ridiculous they are. The chess-game pattern that structures Through the Looking Glass is a general parody of the trite proposition that life is like a chess game, but it is also a more particular parody of Huxley's "A Liberal Education and Where to Find It," which used the chess-game analogy, and which was published in 1868, the year in which Carroll began to write Through the Looking-Glass. In the book, Humpty Dumpty is Carroll's farcical version of the "egghead." Humpty Dumpty embodies "the brittle vulnerability of hubris" (Polhemus 276), but he represents more. Polhemus suggests that Humpty Dumpty is a "fantasy projection of Carroll himself. Like his author, Humpty studies logic and semantics; he, too, is obsessed with mathematical problems. He has at times a brilliant Carrollian skepticism that cuts through stupid convention to a profound truth" as when he defines "glory" as "a nice knock-down argument." When Alice protests that he can't use words just anyway he wants to, he responds, "When I use a word, it means just what I choose it to mean--neither more nor less." When Alice says, "The question is, whether you can make words mean so many different things," Humpty Dumpty echoes back, "The question is, which is to be master--that's all" (Polhemus 285).

The book also parodies Tennyson's Maud, in which the flowers spoke rapturously.

> The red rose cries, "She is near, she is near"
> And the white rose weeps, "She is late"
> The larkspur listens, "I hear, I hear"
> And the lily whispers, "I wait." (Polhemus 257)

Tennyson's flowers sigh and weep for the entrance of Maud, as the lover waits in the garden. In Carroll's parody, the expressiveness of the flowers is exaggerated to make fun of Tennyson's brooding, narcissistic lover by feminizing him into a lonely little girl named Alice, as Carroll's flowers wait not for the jewel-like Maud, but rather for the frenetic Red Queen. Carroll is suggesting that Tennyson was guilty of the pathetic fallacy, a kind of "eloquent bullying, a rhetorical and emotional self-indulgence, that seeks to make all beings conform to the bard's sensibility" (Polhemus 257).

Jane Anderson notes that Carroll demonstrates the illogicality of the conventions of the use of English when he creates an entire series of looking-glass insects and names them with nonsense compounds such as Rocking-horse-fly, Snap-dragon-fly, and the Bread-and-butter-fly. Here, Carroll is poking fun at the English language, because the true names of these insects didn't make sense in the first place: "Horse-flies" are nothing like horses; "butterflies" contain no butter and are not flies, and the relationship between "dragon-flies" and true dragons requires a creative stretch of the imagination (Anderson 6).

Polhemus suggests that many of the fantastic creatures of Through the Looking Glass are forerunners of modern fantastic creatures that are seen on television and elsewhere. He feels that Humpty Dumpty, the Walrus and the Carpenter, Tweedledum and Tweedledee, the White Knight, the White Queen, and the Red Queen are forerunners of Donald Duck, the Road-runner, the Pink Panther, and other creatures "from the happy realm of innocuous cruelty and miraculous regeneration that is so popular in comic animation" (Polhemus 273). There is violence, futility, death, and/or disaster in every chapter of Through the Looking Glass, and Alice emerges from each chapter as a refugee, a survivor, the only figure with a real future (Polhemus 260).

The White Knight in Through the Looking Glass is a Don Quixote figure. Like Quixote, he has a habit of falling, as he shows the ridiculousness of the Victorian idea that the body and the mind can be separated. He "instantly rolled out of the saddle, and fell headlong into a deep ditch.... "what does it matter where my body happens to be?" he said. "My mind goes on working all the same" (Polhemus 278). The White Knight also illustrates the British tolerance for cranks. The White Knight "champions the informal institution of British eccentricity, and the main point of comic eccentricity lies in its effect on others. It makes people realize how daffy life can be, and it reminds them how relatively well adjusted and tolerant they themselves are" (Polhemus 279). The White Knight is a symbol of freedom. When he falls off his horse and gets stuck in his helmet he remarks to Alice, "I was as fast as--as lightning, you know." Alice objected that was a different kind of fastness, but the White Knight just shook his head and said, "It was all kinds of fastness with me, I can assure you!" (Polhemus 288). The White Knight gives readers the message that they have "the right to be different, even goofy."

The Gnat in Through the Looking Glass is a joke-maker, and a punster. The Gnat speaks to Alice in a very small voice, saying, "You might make a joke on that--something about 'horse,' " and 'hoarse' you know." When she mentions the "wood," he says, "You might make a joke on that...something about 'you would if you could' you know." The conversation between Alice and the Gnat ends with the Gnat's humor, his lack of confidence, his sorrow, and finally, his demise:

> "Well, if she said 'Miss,' and didn't say anything more," the Gnat remarked, "of course you'd miss your lessons. That's a joke. I wish you had made it."
>
> "Why do you wish I had made it?" Alice asked. "It's a very bad one."
>
> But the Gnat only sighed deeply, while two large tears came rolling down its cheeks.
>
> "You shouldn't make jokes," Alice said, "if it makes you so unhappy."
>
> Then came another of those melancholy little sighs, and this time the poor Gnat really seemed to have sighed itself away, for, when Alice looked up, there was nothing whatever to be seen on the twig. (Polhemus 279-280)

For the Gnat everything is a pun, a joke, or a witty statement, and he appropriately ends his existence on a pun, for he is losing "sighs" (i.e. size) until he finally disappears (Polhemus 286).

The Red Queen in Through the Looking Glass is Carroll's prototypical authority figure. In Annotated Alice, he calls her "pedantic to the tenth degree, and the concentrated essence of governesses" (Gardner 258).

> She has no self-doubt, no disinterested wonder, no hesitancy that might humanize her. Contradictory and rude, like so many of the cocksure characters Alice meets, she asks questions but then gives orders before they

can be answered. "Where do you come from? ...And where are you going? Look up, speak nicely, and don't twiddle your fingers all the time." (Gardner 258)

When the Red Queen asks Alice to sing her a "soothing lullaby" Alice replies that she doesn't know any. This being the case, the Red Queen decides to provide her own.

Hush-a-bye lady, in Alice's lap!
Till the feast's ready, we've time for a nap.
When the feast's over, we'll go to the ball--
Red Queen, and White Queen, and Alice and all! (Carroll Through 99)

What is interesting about this "soothing lullaby" is that it brings to mind the not-so-soothing original, which begins with a baby snoozing in a tree, and ends with the baby's fall-- possibly even a fatal fall--from the tree.

Chapter 3 of Through the Looking Glass satirically targets capitalism and industrialization. Here there is a railway, and a chorus of characters are shouting at Alice, "Don't keep him waiting, child! Why, his time is worth a thousand pounds a minute!" Everything is measured in terms of money. The land is worth a thousand pounds an inch; the smoke of the train is worth a thousand pounds a puff, and language is worth a thousand pounds a word. The surreal and noisy mixing of prices and steam are presented in much the way that a child would perceive these incongruous and incomprehensible facts (Polhemus 259).

Through the Looking Glass is a dream world, and it is filled with dream logic, and dream distortion. It has been created by a dreaming mind, and it has a kaleidoscopic kind of coherence. In his last chapter, Carroll "carefully refers to motifs, characters, imagery, subjects, and words from all the previous chapters and gives the book a greater unity than it is usually credited with."

> The snore of the Red King reappears as the snore of the two queens; the pudding course, invented by the White Knight, now banters with Alice; the White Queen talks of Humpty; Tweedledee's "shrill voice" welcomes Alice to her banquet; the Gnat's pun on "horse" turns up in the Frog's throat; the Bread-and-butter-fly and the "Brown bread and butter" of "The Lion and the Unicorn" become a part of Alice's "examination" dream; and, of course, the "dream-rushes" turn, by wordplay, into the rushing of the dream. (Polhemus 275)

Alice wins the chess match for her side by upsetting the Queen's banquet, thereby eliminating the Red Queen and putting the Red King in checkmate (Polhemus 292). As Alice comes out of her dream, the Red Queen becomes her kitty, to whom she continues to speak, but who only purrs in answer. Alice remarks, "How can you talk with a person if they always say the same thing?"

Robert Polhemus considers the humor of Through the Looking Glass like that of Alice's Adventures in Wonderland to be "the comedy of regression." Polhemus says that "the child" is for Carroll what "marriage" is to Austen, what "nature" is to Meredith, and what "community" is to Trollope: "It sets off thoughts and feelings that bind us to the future" (Polhemus 265). And Polhemus feels that the qualities of childhood which Carroll most admires include "curiosity, courage, kindness, intelligence, courtesy, dignity, a sense of humor, humility, sympathy, propriety, respect, imagination, wonder, initiative, gratitude, patience, affection, thoughtfulness, integrity, and a sense of justice in the face of an outrageous universe" (Polhemus 265). Carroll investigates role reversals as Alice meets Tweedledum and Tweedledee. It is Alice, the child, who demonstrates the maturity and wise judgement that only parents are supposed to have. Alice does not, however, have the parent's authority or influence (Polhemus 260).

Polhemus suggests that the Red King in Through the Looking Glass represents God.

If God really is omnipresent, and omniscient, and omnipotent, then in a way our minds are controlled by God's mind; we are created by God; we are part of God's dream in one sense or another. This thought fascinated Carroll as he developed the character of the most powerful figure of <u>Through the Looking Glass</u>, the Red King. Tweedledum says to Alice that she is part of the Red King's dream. "If that there King was to wake, you'd go out-- bang!--just like a candle!" Alice responded "I <u>am</u> real!" and she began to cry. Tweedledee said, "You won't make yourself a bit realler by crying." Alice responded, "If I wasn't real, I shouldn't be able to cry," at which point Tweedledum said, in a tone of great contempt, "I hope you don't suppose those are <u>real</u> tears." (Polhemus 262-263). As Tweedledum and Tweedledee talk about the Red King's dream, they are parodying Bishop Berkeley who felt that all material objects are only "sorts of things in the mind of God." "In fact, I think Carroll means to associate the Tweedles particularly with Berkeley" (Polhemus 292).

"Jabberwocky," a poem which appears in <u>Through the Looking Glass</u>, is a beautifully structured hero tale, with the first verse (introduction to a mythical atmosphere) balanced against the last (seventh) verse (denouement--same as the first verse), the second (warning) is balanced against the sixth (praise), and the third (pursuit) against the fifth (defeat of the Jabberwock). The fourth verse is the middle verse, and is the center of the poem since it involves the actual encounter between the hero and the jabberwock.

> The final verse returns the scenes to the past of the introduction--for although much has happened, nothing has changed.... The danger of evil is clear and eternal. Though the Jabberwock is dead, the monsters of the second verse--the Jubjub bird and the Bandersnatch--remain, and the possibilities are endless. Carroll was not mocking or parodying the heroic tales, but, like a true mathematician, he was formulating them, bringing them down to their common denominator. (Alkalay-Gut 30)

But even though "Jabberwocky" is not a parody, it is nevertheless mock heroic. In fact, Karen Alkalay-Gut calls it a

> ...perfectly constructed mock heroic poem, using the structure of the epic, but enveloping it in nonsense in order to prove the ridiculousness of all the heroic tales. But it is also possible to conclude the opposite, that the nonsense takes on special significance in the light of the epic structure and lends it a higher meaning.... By using nonsense words, the poem deflects the reader from transient details and allows him to focus on the eternal human conflict with the forces of evil. (Alkalay-Gut 28)

Alkalay-Gut indicates that the nonsense-nature of the poem serves a very important purpose; it dislodges the reader from the fixed and limited world, thereby providing the possibility of limitless associations. The freedom of the unstructured nonsense contrasts markedly with the tight structure, the parallel verses, and the tight grammar of the poem's surface structure (Alkalay-Gut 28). The function of the nonsense is not only to disorient, but it is to reorient as well, since it removes the reader from the world of "limited reality," and places the reader into an enervating mythical context. (Alkalay-Gut 29-30). Carroll was not interested in closure; he was interested in being suggestive and imaginative. This is why Humpty Dumpty explains the poem as he does: "'<u>Brillig</u>'...means four o'clock in the afternoon--the time when you begin <u>broiling</u> things for dinner. 'Slithy' is defined by the same source as 'lithe and slimy.' 'Lithe' is the same as 'active.' You see it's like a portmanteau--there are two meanings packed up in one word. '<u>Mimsy</u>' by this definition, means 'flimsy' and 'miserable'" (Alkalay-Gut 29). Marshall McLuhan considers Lewis Carroll's "non-use" of time in the Alice stories to be an "infinitely better way to mark time" because it is a "kind of space time which had its own space and its own time" (qtd. in Carlson 80). Carroll had written the original quatrain of "'Twas brillig" in 1855 in <u>Misch-Masch</u>, a family journal he wrote, handlettered, and illustrated for his brothers and sisters.

Here he gave quite different interpretations to the words than did Humpty Dumpty. For example, here Carroll gives "gyre" the meaning "to scratch like a dog," whereas Humpty Dumpty says it means "to go round and round like a gyroscope." (Imholtz 212). Imholtz evaluates the poem as follows:

> Carroll's imaginative compound words and astute use of syntax have made "Jabberwocky" a classic in the narrow genre of English nonsense poetry. Ordinary language word order and inflectional marks, like the "s" plurals and the adjectives ending in "y," define the approximate function of the poem's nonsense words. Words with adjective, noun, and verb inflections occur precisely where one would expect adjectives, nouns, and verbs to be. (Imholtz 213)

One of the amazing things about "Jabberwocky" is that even though it is total nonsense, it can be translated into other languages. According to Alexander Francis Tytler, three rules must be followed in order to render a good translation of this poem:

> I. The translation should give a complete transcript of the ideas of the original work.
> II. The style and manner of writing should be of the same character with that of the original.
> III. The translation should have all the ease of the original composition. (Tytler 15)

The Dean of Rochester, Robert Scott, translated the poem into German and called it "Der Jammerwoch."

> Es brillig war. Die schlichte Toven
> Wirrten und wimmelten in Waben;
> Und aller-mümsige Burggoven
> Die mohmen Räth' ausgraben. (Imholtz 214)

Hassard Dodgson, Master in the Court of Common Pleas, and Lewis Carroll's uncle provided the Latin translation, rendering the poem into elegiac couplets:

> Hora aderat briligi. Nunc et Slythaeia Tova
> Plurima gyrabant gymbolitare vabo;
> Et Borogovorum mimzebant undique formae,
> Momeferique omnes exgrabuere Rathi. (Imholtz 218)

The French version, "Le Jaseroque" is equally interesting, but very different not only in terms of the French words, but in terms of the nonsense words as well:

> Il brilgue: les toves lubricilleux
> Se gyrent en vrillant dans le guave,
> Enmimes sont les gougebosquex,
> Et le momerade horsgrave. (Nilsen 98)

August Imholtz indicates that few English nonsense verses have been translated into as many foreign languages as "Jabberwocky," and in fact Warren Weaver compiled a bibliography of translations in which he listed forty-two such translations in sixteen different languages. Imholtz adds that "Jabberwocky" is very English not only in its language, both real and invented, and in its tone, but in its figures as well (such as the St. George motif). Imholtz adds that every translation of "The Jabberwocky" into a foreign language extends the effect of the parody of the poem, which was originally written as a parody of the heroic ballad. "The translators play a game with Carroll's poem just as Carroll plays a game with the readers throughout the Alice books" (Imholtz 224-225).

Many of the episodes in Through the Looking Glass have an abrupt, or even a violent conclusion. There is a giant crow which chases off Tweedledum and Tweedledee. Humpty Dumpty falls off a wall with a crash. The Lion and the Unicorn are drummed out of town. "In each case the conflict has become so unresolvable that the situation explodes.

The way Carroll changes scenes by having Alice jump over brooks is equally arbitrary; each scene is a dream she wakes from.... The series of rejections throughout each book leads up to the climactic rejection at the end" (Higbie 25).

> "I can't stand this any longer!" she cried, as she jumped up and seized the tablecloth with both hands: one good pull, and plates, dishes, guests, and candles came crashing down together in a heap on the floor. "And as for you," she went on, turning fiercely upon the Red Queen, whom she considered as the cause of all the mischief--but the Queen was no longer at her side--she had suddenly dwindled down to the size of a little doll....
> (Higbie 25)

In a chapter on "Sport," Kathleen Blake discusses the sports to be found in The Hunting of the Snark (1876), in Sylvie and Bruno (1889), and in Sylvie and Bruno Concluded (1889) (Blake Play 6). Ira Nadel and William Frederman say that The Hunting of the Snark has attracted a great deal of attention and admiration as a "nonsense epic in verse," or as an "absurdist quest poem." They call it a "Moby-Dick of the nursery" (Nadel and Frederman 44). The Hunting of the Snark (1876) is about a voyage on board ship of a company of incongruous characters all of whose names begin with a B. The Barrister's dream is about a travesty trial. The Snark is the lawyer for the defense, but the Snark is also the jury and the judge who in the end condemns and sentences his own client (Nadel and Frederman 56). Most critics consider The Hunting of the Snark to be a "quest" rather than a "hunt," but Kathleen Blake would disagree, "for the poem suggests again Carroll's sense of the destructive part of play, which may turn back on the player." "The turning of the tables of the hunted upon the hunter as is described in the Snark, turning out to be a Boojum, causes the utter destruction, in fact, the vanishing away, of the Baker, one of the hunters" (Blake Play 177). "The epic ends with the complete physical destruction of one of the hunters, as prefigured in his dream fight with the Snark. The Baker, 'in the midst of his laughter and glee,' just when he has found the Snark to the 'delight' of the others-- their worst fear is 'that the chase might fail'--suddenly becomes its victim. 'For the Snark was a Boojum, you see'" (Blake Play 179). Like the Alice books, The Hunting of the Snark ends with an explosion which cancels out all that has come before. "The works then turn against themselves, making us pull away from the imaginary world, as if suddenly waking from a nightmare" (Higbie 21).

The Hunting of the Snark is a long poem which is a comic defense against the terrible idea that life might be meaningless. It is a way that Carroll has of dealing with his fear of annihilation after death. In this poem, the Bellman leads his madcap crew out after the Snark. Baker, the hero in this mock epic tale, has been warned that he will be annihilated if the Snark turns out to be a Boojum. On the adventure, the Bellman constantly rings his bell, reminding the crew that time is passing, and also reminding them of their mortality. The crew is to believe as true only those things which the Bellman repeats three times. In the end, the Snark does turn out to be a Boojum, and the Baker vanishes away forever (Kelly Encyclopedia 215).

In Sylvie and Bruno (1889), and in Sylvie and Bruno Concluded (1889), there are "random flashes of thought," and "dream suggestions" which are strung together as if on the thread of a consecutive story. The dream experiences are based on real-life experiences, and the Narrator is often confused as to what is reality, and what is fantasy: " 'So, either I've been dreaming about Sylvie,' I said to myself, 'and this is the reality. Or else I've really been with Sylvie, and this is a dream! Is Life itself a dream, I wonder?'" (Blake Play 153). Many critics consider these novels to be "schizophrenic," with the good part of Sylvie and Bruno representing Carroll, and the bad part representing Charles Lutwidge Dodgson (Blake Play 150). The humor of the Sylvie books is considered shallow by some critics: "Too often humor turns to cuteness as the jokes are hint-hintingly explained: Uggug has been dragged from the room by the ear, and his mother says to the Lord Chancellor, 'Your Lordship has a very taking way with children! I doubt if any one could gain the ear of my darling Uggug so quickly as you can!'" (Blake Play 153). But the humor of the event is redeemed by the narrator's remark that "For an entirely stupid woman, my Lady's remarks were curiously full of meaning, of which she herself was wholly unconscious" (Blake Play 153). Carroll's Eight or Nine Wise Words about Letter-Writing (1890) humorously explores the proposition that if anything can misfire in a communication, it will misfire (Nadel and Frederman 53).

Throughout his lifetime, Lewis Carroll had a preoccupation with food. His writings contain allusions to cakes, pills, mushrooms, and bottles which say "drink me."

> Oral aggressiveness is found everywhere. Some examples include: the Walrus and the Carpenter eating the oyster, Alice mentioning a mouse-eating cat to the Mouse, the owl being devoured by the panther, little fish by the crocodile. Schilder concludes from his brief survey of these "preponderant oral sadistic trends of cannibalistic character" that the book is perhaps too reinforcing of destructiveness to be safe for children. (Blake Play 24)

But Joseph Wood Krutch would disagree, noting that he had never heard of a child dangerously terrified by Alice, and further noting that "far from inculcating destructiveness, the book merely demonstrates that a child is never too young to laugh at those morbid fears which psychoanalysts tell us he is never too young to fear" (Blake Play 24). But the preoccupation with food was probably a fact, for in 1884, Carroll delivered a lecture in Alfreton in Derbyshire entitled, "Feeding the Mind," in an attempt to develop the analogy between feeding the body with food and feeding the mind with ideas. "I wonder if there is such a thing in nature as a FAT MIND? I really think I have met with one or two: minds which could not keep up with the slowest trot in conversation; could not jump over a logical fence to save their lives; always got stuck fast in a narrow argument; and, in short, were fit for nothing but to waddle helplessly through the world" (Blake Play 22).

Lewis Carroll loved play, and he loved children, but he didn't get along well with adults. Alexander Woolcott describes Dodgson, as "a fussy, fastidious, didactic bachelor who was almost painfully humorless in his relations with the grown up world around him" (qtd. in Dodgson 4-6). Even when his works became famous, Carroll tended to relate more to children than to adults, and when Queen Victoria became one of his fans, and asked him to dedicate his next book to her, he did. Unfortunately, however, his next book was entitled An Elementary Treatise on Determinants (Dodgson 4-6). Lewis Carroll had a tremendous impact on twentieth century writers, and in his Finnegans Wake, James Joyce refers to him as "Dodgfather, Dodgson and Coo," or "Father, Son, and Holy Spirit" (Kelly Encyclopedia 217).

Lewis Carroll Bibliography

Alkalay-Gut, Karen. "Carroll's 'Jabberwocky.' " Explicator 46.1 (1987): 27-31.
Anderson, Jane. "Making Sense of Nonsense in Through the Looking Glass." Unpublished Paper. Tempe, AZ: Arizona State University, 1991.
Baum, Alwin L. "Carroll's Alices: The Semiotics of Paradox." Lewis Carroll: Modern Critical Views. Ed. Harold Bloom. New York, NY: Chelsea House, 1987, 65-81.
Bjarkman, Peter C. "Carroll's Language of Non-Sense: Mere Humor or Philosophical Dialectic?" WHIMSY 4 (1986): 54-55.
Blake, Kathleen. "Lewis Carroll." Dictionary of Literary Biography, Volume Eighteen: Victorian Novelists After 1885. Eds. Ira B. Nadel and William E. Fredeman. Detroit, MI: Gale, 1983, 43-61.
Blake, Kathleen. Play, Games, and Sport: The Literary Works of Lewis Carroll. Ithaca,

NY: Cornell University Press, 1974.

Carlson, Richard S. The Benign Humorists. New York, NY: Archon, 1975.

Carroll, Lewis. Alice's Adventures in Wonderland and Through the Looking Glass (1865). Ed. John Tenniel. Cleveland, OH: William Collins/World, 1974.

Carroll, Lewis. Humorous Verse of Lewis Carroll. New York, NY: Dover, 1960.

Carroll, Lewis. Through the Looking Glass (1872). New York, NY: Maidenhead/Purnell, 1970.

Clark, Anne. Lewis Carroll: A Biography. New York, NY: Schocken Books, 1979.

Dodgson, Charles L. The Complete Works of Lewis Carroll. New York, NY: The Modern Library, 1964.

Ede, Lisa S. "The Nonsense Literature of Edward Lear and Lewis Carroll." Unpublished Ph.D. Dissertation: Ohio State University, 1975.

Falardeau, Cass R. "A Nonsense Universe." Unpublished Paper. Tempe, AZ: Arizona State University, 1992.

Gardner, Michael, ed. The Annotated Alice. New York, NY: New American Library, 1974.

Gardner, Michael, ed. More Annotated Alice: Alice's Adventures in Wonderland and Through the Looking Glass. New York, NY: Random House, 1990.

Gray, Donald J. "The Uses of Victorian Laughter." Victorian Studies. New York, NY: Crowell, 1976.

Guiliana, Edward, ed. The Complete Illustrated Works of Lewis Carroll. New York, NY: Crown, 1982.

Henkle, Roger B. "Hood, Gilbert, Carroll, Jerrold, and the Grossmiths: Comedy from Inside." Comedy and Culture--England--1820-1900. Princeton, NJ: Princeton University Press, 1980, 185-237.

Higbie, Robert. "Lewis Carroll and the Victorian Reaction against Doubt." Thalia: Studies in Literary Humor 3.1 (1980): 21-28.

Hudson, Derek. Lewis Carroll. London, England: Longmans, 1958.

Imholtz, August A., Jr. "Jam Sempiterne: A Note on Time in 'Through the Looking-Glass.' " Jabberwocky: Journal of the Lewis Carroll Society 8.1 (1979): 13-15.

Imholtz, August A., Jr. "Latin and Greek Versions of 'Jabberwocky' Exercises in Laughing and Grief." Rocky Mountain Review 41.4 (1987): 211-228.

Jannuzzi, Karen. "Nonsensical Devices Used in Alice in Wonderland." Unpublished Paper. Tempe, AZ: Arizona State University, 1995.

Kelly, Richard. Lewis Carroll. Boston, MA: Twayne, 1977.

Kelly, Richard. "Lewis Carroll." Encyclopedia of British Humorists, Volume I. Ed. Steven H. Gale. New York, NY: Garland, 1996, 213-219.

Kibel, Alvin C. "Logic and Satire in Alice in Wonderland." American Scholar 43 (1974): 605-629.

Lear, Edward. A Book of Nonsense. London, England: J. M. Dent, 1959.

Nilsen, Don L. F. "Dithyrambs: The Humor of Folk Poetry." Mississippi Folklore Register 17.2 (Fall, 1983): 95-107.

Nilsen, Don L. F. "The Limitations of Objectivist Semantics for Analyzing Literature: The Humanization of the Writings of Lewis Carroll." HUMOR: International Journal of Humor Studies 4.3-4 (1991): 375-389.

Nilsen, Don L. F. "The Linguistic Humor of Lewis Carroll." Thalia: Studies in Literary Humor 10.1 (1989): 35-42.

O'Hare, Tommie J. Perception, Conception, Cognition, and Language: Towards a Revised Theory of Linguistic Relativity. Unpublished Paper. Tempe, AZ: Arizona State University, 1985.

Paulos, John Allen. I Think, Therefore I Laugh: An Alternative Approach to Philosophy. New York, NY: Columbia University Press, 1985.

Polhemus, Robert M. Comic Faith: The Great Tradition from Austen to Joyce. Chicago, IL:
    University of Chicago Press, 1980.
Pudney, John. Lewis Carroll and his World. New York, NY: Charles Scribner's, 1976.
Pycior, Helena M. "At the Intersection of Mathematics and Humor: Lewis Carroll's Alices
    and Symbolic Algebra." Victorian Studies 28.1 (1984): 149-170.
Sewell, Elizabeth. The Field of Nonsense. London, England: Chatto and Windus, 1952.
Shaw, John Mackay. The Parodies of Lewis Carroll. Tallahassee, FL: Florida State
    University Press, 1960.
Shibles, Warren. Humor: A Critical Analysis for Young Children. Whitewater, WI: The
    Language Press, 1978.
Shires, Linda M. "Fantasy, Nonsense, Parody, and the Status of the Real: The Example of
    Carroll." Victorian Poetry 26.3 (1988): 267-283.
Terente, Ines Praga. "The Humour of Lewis Carroll." Literary and Linguistic Aspects of
    Humour. Barcelona, Spain: University of Barcelona Language Dept, 1984, 199-203.
Tigges, Wim. An Anatomy of Literary Nonsense. Amsterdam, Netherlands: Rodopi, 1988.
Tigges, Wim, ed. Explorations in the Field of Nonsense. Amsterdam, Netherlands: Rodopi,
    1987.
Tytler, Alexander Fraser. Essay on the Principles of Translation. London, England: T.
    Cadell and W. Davis, 1797.
Wakefield, Jody. "A Trip through Wonderland: Lewis Carroll's Satire of Victorian
    England." Unpublished Paper. Tempe, AZ: Arizona State University, 1992.

Sir Leslie Stephen (1832-1904)

Leslie Stephen's "Humour" appeared in 1876. Robert Martin describes this essay as "a brilliant, quirky sapping of the very foundations of the conceptions supporting sentimental humour" (Martin 85). Here Stephen investigates the difference between the virility of comedy of the eighteenth century and the feebleness of the sentimental comedy that had overtaken English in Stephen's day. Employing an ironic tone, Stephen alternates between his own views about humour and his ironic treatment of those views held by the contemporaries he was attacking. One by one, Stephen dismissed the humor of the Scots, the French, the Germans, the Irish, and the Americans leaving only the true kindly genial flavour of English humor to be worth further treatment. The rest of the essay shows how "nothing could be further from a true humour than what passes under that name in England" (Martin 86).

Stephen is wickedly accurate in his parody of contemporary descriptions of the humorist--"the man who laughs through tears":

> In the fabric of his emotions the warp of melancholy is crossed by the woof of cheerfulness. (I am not acquainted with warps and woofs in common life, but they are mentioned in Gray's Ode, and seem to be specially intended for literary use.) His writing is a play of cross lights, sunshine, and shadow dexterously intermingled or completely fused into a contradictory unity.... You cannot tell whether a cathedral will most affect him with an awe of the infinite or an exhibition of tumblers at a pantomime. He will even laugh at the Social Science Association. (qtd. in Martin 87)

Martin feels that the importance of Stephen's essay is that he "is demanding that the comic be taken seriously." His assertion is much more than a "plaything for idle hours" (Martin 89).

Sir Leslie Stephen Bibliography

Martin, Robert Bernard. "Chapter VI: George Eliot, Leslie Stephen, and George Meredith."
  The Triumph of Wit: A Study of Victorian Comic Theory. Oxford, England:
  Clarendon Press, 1974, 82-100.
Stephen, Leslie. "Humour." Cornhill Magazine 33 (March, 1876): 318-326.

George Du Maurier (1834-1896)

Through his entire lifetime, George Du Maurier went by his childhood nickname
of Kicky, or Kiki (Parris 338). Henry James found much "soft irony" in Du Maurier's
work. In the May 1883 issue of Century Magazine, James wrote, "No one has rendered
like Du Maurier the ridiculous little people who crop up in the interstices of that huge and
complicated London world...the snot, the cad, the prig, the duffer" (James 55).

In Social Pictorial Satire: Reminiscences and Appreciations of English Illustrators
of the Past Generation (1898), Du Maurier describes his own work, and the work of other
Punch cartoonists such as John Leech and Charles Keene as "the craft of portraying, by
means of little pen-and-ink strokes, lines and scratches, a small portion of the world in
which we live; such social and domestic incidents as lend themselves to humorous or
satirical treatment." Du Maurier also admired William Hogarth, "For he was not merely
a light humorist and a genial caricaturist; he dealt also in pathos and terror, in tragic
passion and sorrow and crime" (Du Maurier 99). The targets of Du Maurier's satire tended
to be the middle and the upper classes. Along with Charles Keene, George Du Maurier
"hated and despised the bloated aristocracy" (Parris 338). Du Maurier's cartoons tried to
catch high society "trying its best to be...civilized." Du Maurier created such characters as
Maudle, the painter, and Jellaby Postlewaite, who bears a striking resemblance to Oscar
Wilde, and Mrs. Cimabue Brown, who is artistically pretentious, and Mrs. Ponsonby de
Tompkyns, who has social ambitions, and Sir Gorgius and Lady Midas, who represent the
nouveau-riche (Parris 339).

Du Maurier's novels are late-Victorian romances. They are love stories that are
often spiced with the supernatural. In these novels, Du Maurier uses humor for comic
relief. He also creates many Dickensian humors characters "whose exaggerated appearances
and behaviors contrast with the trials and triumphs of the good-looking lovers" (Parris 339).
Peter's schoolmaster in Peter Ibbetson (1891), for example, is described as a man with a
green tail coat, and with a stiff shirt collar, and with thick flat thumbs stuck in the armholes
of his nankeen waistcoat, with long flat feet turned inward, with reddish mutton-chop
whiskers, with his hat on the back of his head, and with a clean, fresh, blooming, virtuous,
English face. He then goes on to describe this English face in more detail, as having,
"prominent front teeth, a high nose, a long lower lip, a receding jaw..., dull, cold, stupid,
selfish green eyes, like a pike's, that swerved neither to right nor left, but looked steadily
over people's heads as it stalked along in its pride of impeccable self-righteousness" (qtd.
in Parris 339-340).

Trilby (1894) is about a couple of penniless but jolly British painters named Taffy
and Sandy, who share a studio in Paris with the young hero. Svengali is the villain of the
story. Du Maurier's imagery in describing Svengali is as powerful as is his visual imagery
in describing Ibbetson's schoolmaster. Svengali "...was very shabby and dirty, and wore
a red beret and a large velveteen cloak, with a big metal clasp at the collar. His thick,
heavy, languid, lustreless black hair fell down behind his ears on to his shoulders, in that
musicianlike way that is so offensive to the normal Englishman" (qtd. in Parris 340).

Du Maurier's last novel is entitled, The Martian (1896). Except for the narrator's
occasional whimsical and ironic attitude, this novel does not tend to be comic. There is
some unintentional humor, however, in what Richard Kelly calls "a farcical and

melodramatic conclusion" (Kelly 132).

George Du Maurier Bibliography

Du Maurier, George. Social Pictorial Satire: Reminiscences and Appreciations of English
    Illustrators of the Past Generation. New York, NY: Harper and Brothers, 1898.
James, Henry. "Du Maurier and London Society." Century Magazine 4 (1883): 49-65.
Kelly, Richard. George Du Maurier. Boston, MA: Twayne, 1983.
Parris, P. B. "George Du Maurier." Encyclopedia of British Humorists, Volume I. Ed.
    Steven H. Gale. New York, NY: Garland, 1996, 337-340.

James McNeill Whistler (1834-1903)

On July 10, 1834, a boy was born in Lowell, Massachusetts, and was christened James Abbot. Some years later, this same boy stated in a court of law that his name was James McNeill Whistler, that he was born in St. Petersburg, Russia, and that he was seven years younger than his real age. According to Hesketh Pearson, Whistler had a "love of inaccuracy" (Pearson 178-179). Whistler was also filled with vanity, conceit, and arrogance. When asked "Do you think genius is hereditary?" he replied, "I can't tell you; heaven has granted me no offspring" (Pearson 181).

In middle life, Whistler presented a short, slight, dapper, even perky appearance. He wore a monocle, a tall silk hat, and carried yellow gloves in one hand and a wandlike cane in the other. He said the cane was "for the critics" (Pearson 181). Whistler's wit was considered cantankerous or bellicose to some critics, but was considered mere drollery to other critics. His comment on the foundation of the Bath Club in England was that this was "the latest incarnation of the British discovery of water." During a sea voyage on the P. and O. Liner, he observed that the British first class passengers were sick every night, but that they nevertheless were always attired in "correct evening clothes." He said, "You might as well dress to ride in an omnibus" (Lewis 75).

In reviewing a book by Tom Taylor, Whistler wrote, "Why squabble over your little article? You did print what I quote, you know, Tom; and it is surely unimportant what more you may have written of the Master. That you should have written anything at all is your crime" (Lewis 94). Based on such evidence as this, Sir Max Beerbohm called Whistler a man "choking with hate," however, Wyndham Lewis found it "impossible to believe that a man of Whistler's temperament hated his stockish enemies. They drove him wild with rage; he kicked them savagely in the stern; he bespattered them with abuse and ridicule; he drove them with derisive hootings back to cover;" but with all of this, he was a great droll and nothing more (Lewis 95).

James McNeill Whistler was a contemporary of William Schwenck Gilbert, and during their time, Whistler and Gilbert were known as the two most acerbic wits in Victorian England. They didn't like each other, however, and actually met each other only on one occasion. Hesketh Pearson explains why:

> Wits have one thing in common with bores: they recognize at sight and avoid one another, fearing competition. The wit, like the bore, must have an audience, and dislikes being kept on his toes by too keen a rivalry.... The two most biting wits of their time kept apart. Evidence of one meeting exists in Gilbert's diary: "Sunday, 24 Nov. Breakfast with Whistler." Not another word except that his own wife and Albert Moore were present. (Pearson 191)

But although there is no record of Whistler and Gilbert ever meeting each other again,

Gilbert did write Whistler into one of his comic operas. In Patience there is a character named "Bunthorne" who wore a white lock of hair and called himself "A greenery-yallery, Grosvenor Gallery, Foot-in-the-grave young man." Bunthorne furthermore sang a ditty which made fun of Whistler's well-known tastes: "Such a judge of blue-and-white and other kinds of pottery--From early Oriental down to modern terra-cotta-ry" (Pearson 192).

Whistler's wit grew not out of hatred, but out of anger. According to Wyndham Lewis, on every page of his ironic "The Gentle Art" Whistler's insults were dictated by anger, "a virile, merry anger mixed with truculent mirth at the eternal foolishness of fools" (Lewis 96). Whistler's "Art and the Art-Critics," and his "Ten O'Clock" are typically Whistler. Lewis is a bit turned off by Whistler's "addiction to alliteration for its own sake," but he nevertheless suggests that these pieces "are entirely admirable--strong, flexible, clear, sharp-cut, masterly in choice and grouping and sound..., broadly and boldly set down in slashing words." In summary, Lewis suggests that Whistler does not so much exhibit the British sense of "wit," as he exhibits the subtler French sense of "esprit" (Lewis 97).

James McNeill Whistler Bibliography

Lewis, D. B. Wyndham. "Whistler." English Wits. Ed. Leonard Russell. London, England: Hutchinson, 1940, 73-97.
Pearson, Hesketh. Lives of the Wits. New York, NY: Harper and Row, 1962.

Samuel Butler (1835-1902)

Hugh Walker suggests that dogmatic Christianity is the core target of Butler's satire, as can be seen in the chapter on the Musical Banks, "an unsparing exposure of the difference between the professions of the Church and the actual beliefs of the laity and clergy alike." Walker feels that Butler's satire of religion is a great deal sounder than is his satire of the family (314-315). Walker also makes a more general assessment of Butler's contribution to the field of satire:

> Butler stands clearly at the head of the satire of the later nineteenth century; but not in the first rank of satire, and still less in the first rank of literature. Swift, with whom his affinities are most obvious, is far superior in breadth and range, in force of thought, and in keenness of wit. On the other hand, Butler is much more humane; but this unfortunately is an advantage which diminished with time. The Way of All Flesh is far less pleasant and humane than Erewhon. (316)

Erewhon and Erewhon Revisited are described by Betty Richardson as being in the tradition of Utopian fiction (Richardson 186). In a book entitled Satiric Allegory: Mirror of Man, Ellen Leyburn considers Butler's Erewhon, or Over the Range (1872) to be a "high-hearted mocking of all Victorian complacencies." She continues that it had a youthful zest and exuberance, as it targeted such subjects as education, religion, law, convention, health, evolution, and technology. The satire is written tongue-in-cheek; the style is the same style as that of true narrative of exploration, and many of the details are authentic (Leyburn 92). One of the clues that it is satire is the reversal of names. Thus "Erewhon" comes from "nowhere," "Yram" is "Mary," "Thims" is "Smith," and "Senoj Nosnibor" is "Robinson Jones." "Arowhena" is an example of more sophisticated language play, as it suggests, but does not exactly transliterate to "anywhere," and "anywhen" (Leyburn 96). The process of spelling reversals was a constant amusement to Butler, and in the revised version of the chapter on the Colleges of Unreason, he talks about "a city whose Erewhonian name is so cacophonous that I refrain from giving it" (Butler 219; Leyburn 96). In this same chapter, he had no hesitation in presenting the names of "Drofxo," and "Egdirbmac," (Oxford and Cambridge), so this other city must have been cacophonous indeed (Leyburn 96). Butler reverses not only spellings, but also concepts, and in order to do this he must allude to passages that are known in the original. He reverses a Bible quotation by saying,

"Woe unto you when all men speak well of you"

Yes, and "Woe unto you when you speak well of all men." (Leyburn 96) and in "The Rights of Vegetables," he again reverse-quotes from the Bible: "Consider the Solomons in all their glory; they toil not, neither do they spin, yet verily I say unto you that not a lily among you is arrayed like one of these" (Leyburn 96). Butler has written not only "The Rights of Vegetables," but "The Rights of Animals" as well, and in these two pieces he presents some strategies of rationalization whereby common sense can appear to support fanatical views. For example the judge finds that although animals may not be killed in ordinary circumstances, they <u>may</u> be killed in self-defense. "Hardly had this decision become known before a number of animals hitherto harmless, took to attacking their owners with such ferocity, that it became necessary to put them to a natural death" (Butler 267; Leyburn 106). It is interesting that the distorted notions of the Erewhonians sometimes parallel the English ideas Butler is ridiculing, and sometimes reverse them (Leyburn 96). <u>Erewhon</u> is a dystopian satire of Butler's society, where Butler makes "unluckiness a crime, because that is what it amounts to in real life" (Henkle 277).

<u>Erewhon</u> was first published anonymously, and had an unnamed protagonist. The author was later identified as Samuel Butler Jr., and the protagonist as Thomas Higgs. Higgs sometimes made insightful observations about human follies, but at other times he was himself a fool. The main target of this novel is Christianity, and Butler's treatment is both satiric and bitter. There are frequent interruptions of the narration, as the tracts by Erewhonian philosophers are presented about the rights of animals or vegetables, or on the evolution of machines. "Apart from the religious satire, the satire is directed at theories of evolution, of penality, of education, and of zealous reformers concerned with issues such as the rights of animals" (Richardson 186). It is because animals have certain inalienable rights that Erewhonian slaughterhouses have been abolished. The consequences of this abolition, however, are strange, as there resulted a wave of suicides whereby various sheep and cattle would "scent out a butcher's knife if there was one within a mile of them, and run right up against it if the butcher did not get it out of their way in time" (Butler <u>Erewhon</u> 266). In <u>Erewhon</u>, not only do the animals have rights, but the vegetables have rights too, so that the only vegetables that Erewhonians are able to eat are those that have died from natural causes. In the "Book of the Machines" chapter of <u>Erewhon</u>, Butler explains that machines are simply part of human evolution. He reasons that a man with a shovel or a man in a train is more highly evolved than is a man who must work in a garden with his bare hands, or a man who must go from place to place on his feet (Richardson 187).

In <u>Erewhon</u> the hospitals and penal institutions are also reversed. Here, the criminals are hospitalized, and the victims of illness are imprisoned, and are harshly reprimanded and severely punished by judges. Butler's humor is both wry and bitter as he has a judge berate a patient for having tuberculosis, but the comedy should not obscure Butler's very serious point--"that it is absurd to blame a man for being the product of his environment and heredity" (Richardson 187).

Butler's <u>The Fair Haven</u> (1873) is a satiric attack on the types of evidence that are used to "prove" the crucifixion and the resurrection. Butler's father claimed that <u>The Fair Haven</u> caused the death of Samuel's mother, and this may have been why Samuel Butler Jr. did not have <u>Ernest Pontifex</u> published during his lifetime (Richardson 186). In 1898

Butler translated the Iliad, and in 1900 he translated The Odyssey. In doing research for these translations, Butler collected evidence that The Odyssey had been written by a woman, and he published this evidence in The Authoress of the Odyssey (1897).

Betty Richardson believes that Erewhon Revisited (1901) has a more coherent narrative, and is more wickedly humorous than is Erewhon, but the main satiric target of Erewhon Revisited remains the same--organized religion. After having left Erewhon in a hot air balloon, Thomas Higgs decides later in life to return to Erewhon in the name of Christianity, so that he can enslave the Erewhonians. Higgs is by now, however, a mellower man, and he is horrified at what the Erewhonians have created in his name. The Erewhonian priests have elevated Higgs's departure in a hot air balloon so that it has by now become a "heavenward journey in a chariot drawn by four black and white horses." Such Erewhonian priests and scholars as Professor Hanky and Professor Panky are now in control, and not only is Higgs now revered, but so are "his horses." Higgs is worshipped as the "Sunchild," and the alleged droppings from his horses are preserved in reliquaries. On holidays, the children buy sweets that are made to look like horse droppings. Earlier, when Higgs had been in Erewhon on his first trip, he had left Yram pregnant when he returned to England and married a young society girl named Arowhena. And when Yram gave birth to a son, this son was taught that he had two fathers, one on earth (the person whom Yram had married), and one in heaven (Higgs). Butler denied that he is here making any references to Christianity, but Betty Richardson feels that "the ridicule of Christianity is again unmistakable" (Richardson 188).

Butler's Ernest Pontifex, or The Way of All Flesh (1903) is autobiographical (Richardson 186). It was published posthumously, has been described as "a time bomb, set in the last decades of Victorianism, ticking away and in Butler's aggrieved mind through the 1870s, 1880s, and 1890s." This novel is a serious self-examination, and a spiritual conversion in reverse, since the novel describes a spiritual struggle and a conversion against religion toward self-regarding pleasure. Ernest Pontifex, the protagonist "wades through a slough of temptations just as did Christian in John Bunyan's Pilgrim's Progress. As a further ironic note, Butler had originally planned to give Ernest the name of Christian. The novel warns about the "temptations of the hypocritical religiosity of his parents and his society. He must be tested against his weak-willed inclinations to become an Evangelical reformer and a God-fearing, home-worshipping prig. He must constantly guard himself against the lures of earnestness and avoid backsliding into solemnity" (Henkle 276). Ernest Pontifex is a satire about a boy (Ernest Pontifex) who has a promising character until it is deformed by religion, education, and his parents. Theobald and Christina are Ernest's parents. They are "caricatures of religious priggishness and self interest disguised as pious zeal." Ernest Pontifex is not only an important novel in its own right, but it is also important because it influenced the satiric styles of James Joyce, Virginia Woolf, E. M. Forster, and Aldous Huxley (Richardson 188).

The Note-Books of Samuel Butler (1912) were also published posthumously, and represent notes which Samuel Butler took between 1874 until his death in 1902. These note-books contain brief essays, aphorisms, and paragraphs with many witty insights (Richardson 186). Betty Richardson says that Butler's Note-Books sparkle more with wit and spontaneity than anything else he has written. His aphorisms here are very memorable: "Our ideas are for the most part like bad sixpences, we spend our lives trying to pass them on one another" (Keynes and Hill 60), "Death is only a larger kind of going abroad" (Keynes and Hill 144), "All progress is based upon a universal innate desire on the part of every organism to live beyond its income" (Keynes and Hill 191), and "Life is the art of drawing sufficient conclusions from insufficient premises" (Keynes and Hill 222).

Samuel Butler Bibliography

Butler, Samuel. Erewhon. London, England: Trübner, 1872.
Henkle, Roger B. "Meredith and Butler: Comedy as Lyric, High Culture, and the Bourgeois
    Trap." Comedy and Culture--England--1820-1900. Princeton, NJ: Princeton
    University Press, 1980. 238-295.
Keynes, Geoffrey, and Brian Hill, eds. Samuel Butler's Note-Books. New York: Dutton,
    1951.
Leyburn, Ellen Douglass. "Satiric Journeys II: Erewhon." Satiric Allegory: Mirror of Man.
    Cambridge, MA: Yale University Press, 1956, 92-106.
Richardson, Betty. "Samuel Butler." Encyclopedia of British Humorists, Volume I. Ed.
    Steven H. Gale. New York, NY: Garland, 1996, 185-190.
Walker, Hugh. English Satire and Satirists. New York, NY: J. M. Dent, 1925.

Francis Cowley Burnand (1836-1917)

Francis Burnand had a talent for punning, parody, and light comic essays (Howes 171). He wrote more than one hundred farces, burlesques, light musicals, pantomimes, and melodramas. Some of the more important ones are Alonzo the Brave; or, Faust and the Fair Imogene (1857); The Deal Boatman: A Serio-Comic Drama in Two Acts (1863); Black-Eyed Susan (1867), a parody of Douglas Jerrold's play; Cox and Box, or the Long-Lost Brothers (1867), a parody of J. Maddison Morton's farce Box and Cox which Burnand co-authored with Arthur Sullivan; and The Frightful Hair; or Who Shot the Dog? (1867). Burnand was famous as a writer, but he was even more famous for his ability to rattle off hundreds and hundreds of jokes and puns. M. H. Spielmann called Burnand "probably the most prolific punster," and this was in an age that was addicted to the practice of punning (Howes 169). Alonzo the Brave; or, Faust and the Fair Imogene (1857) is a parody of Faust in which Burnand laughs at some of the stage conventions of his day. He describes it as "a tragical, comical, demoniacal, or whatever-you-like-to-call-it burlesque" (Howes 169).

Burnand's predictable comicalities, and his constant punning make Burnand's longer works tedious for today's reader. His fondness for burlesque and wordplay, however, made Burnand a natural choice for Punch. "When extended only through a paragraph or two, such joking can be lively and clever." In Punch, Burnand's "Makeanna, or the White Witness" (1863) was a successful parody of the sensational fiction that was then appearing in the London Journal. Mark Lemon, the editor of Punch not only accepted Burnand's article, but he even persuaded some of the artists who had done the original illustrations to do parody illustrations for Burnand's parody. These artists included Sir John Millais, "Phiz" (Hablot Knight Browne), John Gilbert, Charles Keene and George du Maurier and they all lampooned their own original illustrations (Howes 170).

As an author for Punch, Burnand also wrote a series called "Happy Thoughts," which began in 1866, and which was described by R. G. G. Price as "a humorous classic in the pages of Punch that lives on outside them (Price 91). The "absurd young man" which Burnand developed in this series was "undeniably an ancestor of the "Little Men" created later by Robert Benchley, S. J. Perelman, Stephen Leacock, and P.G. Wodehouse, and may even have had in influence on such performers as Jack Benny and Woody Allen (Prager 144). Burnand became the editor of Punch in 1880, taking over the editorship from Tom Taylor. Burnand revitalized Punch. To such artists as Keene, Tenniel, and du Maurier, whom he inherited, he added Harry Furniss, Phil May, E. T. Reed, and Bernard Partridge. He also added such important writers as Henry Lucy (who wrote "Essence of Parliament: The Diary of Toby, M.P.," and E. J. Milliken, who created the popular cad named "Arry," and Owen Seaman, who later became Punch's editor. During Burnand's editorship in the 1880s, <u>Punch</u> maintained a tone which Prager described as "scholarly, avuncular, mild, and middle aged" (Prager 141).

The Frightful Hair; or Who Shot the Dog? (1867) is a travesty of Edward Bulwer-Lytton's <u>The Rightful Heir</u>. Punning on the dog's name, Burnand says, "He was my Tray for breakfast, lunch, and dinner, / The good dog Tray--<u>tray bon</u>-- to cheer up my life." He then continues, "Together we made up the day's repast, / I bringing viands, he his little whine" (Howes 170).

The Real Adventures of Robinson Crusoe (1893) is a parody in which the main character is named Jack Robinson. But since he is a blackmailer and a thief, he needs to change his name:

> No matter what weather,
> We're jolly together
> And Jolly we've been, though it blew so,
> This Cruise--you may bet it;
> We'll never forget--
> We called it our Robinson Cruise, O! (Burnand <u>Crusoe</u> 79)

This pun provided the new name for "Robinson Crusoe." As an adventurer, Robinson Crusoe is quite shrewd. One reason that he preferred to wear clothing is that this made him less delectable for man-eating animals, since such animals prefer their food to be raw. "The most determined and voracious man-eating animal likes his food raw and rather objects to man dressed; whether well dressed or badly dressed doesn't matter" (Burnand <u>Crusoe</u> 120).

Francis Cowley Burnand Bibliography

Burnand, Francis Cowley. <u>The Real Adventures of Robinson Crusoe</u>. London, England: Bradbury, Agnew and Co., 1893.
Howes, Craig. "Francis Cowley Burnand." <u>Encyclopedia of British Humorists, Volume I</u>. Ed. Steven H. Gale. New York, NY: Garland, 1996, 168-172.
Prager, Arthur. <u>The Mahogany Tree: An Informal History of Punch</u>. New York, NY: Hawthorn Books, 1979.
Price, R. G. G. <u>A History of PUNCH</u>. London, England: Collins, 1957.

Sir William Schwenck Gilbert (1836-1911)

At the age of two, William Schwenck Gilbert was captured by two Neapolitan brigands and his parents had to pay the sum of 25 pounds to get him back. This was the foundation for one of Gilbert's later comic operas (Pearson 193). While he was a clerk for the Education Department of the Privy Council Office, Gilbert enjoyed playing practical jokes on the people who lived with him at the Pimlico boarding house. There he gave the impression that he was an influential figure in the theatrical world, so one of his fellow lodgers asked if he would write an order for seats for a particular play. Gilbert asked whether he would like stalls or a box, and when the friend said that he would prefer a box, Gilbert wrote the order. When the friend took the order to the box office, they laughed at the request. The friend told Gilbert that at the box office they had not honored his request, and Gilbert merely said, "You asked me whether I could write you an order for the play. I replied that I could, and I did, but I never said it would be of the least use to you" (Pearson 193).

W. S. Gilbert was called the "king of Victorian jesters, and he was a master of what he called "Topsy-turvydom." When Gilbert filled out a questionnaire for the <u>Strand</u>

Magazine, and was asked to give his birth place, Gilbert answered, "17 Southampton Street, Strand, in the house of my grandfather, who had known Dr. Johnson, Garrick, and Reynolds, and who wore Hessian boots and a pig-tail" (Swanson 445). Even though Gilbert's name is frequently associated with Sullivan's name, both Gilbert and Sullivan had established reputations in their respective fields before they actually met. Gilbert was a cartoonist, a writer of comic poems, and a lyricist; and Sullivan was a composer, a performer, and a conductor (Swanson 447).

W. S. Gilbert had a reputation for his ready wit and sharp remarks. It is said that one day Gilbert was waiting for a friend when a gentleman with bad eyesight mistook him for a servant and asked Gilbert to call him a cab. Gilbert looked at the man and said, "You're a four-wheeler." When the man angrily responded to Gilbert's "insult," Gilbert made the insult even worse by saying, "Well, you asked me to call you a cab--and I couldn't call you 'hansom.'" Another story has Gilbert standing outside of his club when a man came up to him and asked him if he knew a person with one eye called Mathew?" Gilbert said that he didn't know the man, but then he thought a while and asked, "And what was his other eye called?" Gilbert's conversations were sprinkled with such impromptu remarks as this. He was always "sensitive to the potential absurdities of language and of situation," and this sensitivity carried over into his poems, cartoons, stories, and works for the stage. Donald Swanson suggests that Edward Lear, Lewis Carroll, and W. S. Gilbert were all parodying, and making fun of the seriousness with which Victorian society took itself. According to Swanson, they couldn't have written what they wrote at any other period of history (Swanson 449). From 1861 until 1871, Gilbert regularly contributed humorous material to Fun, to Punch, to Illustrated Times and to other humorous publications (Swanson 446).

One of Gilbert's "Bab" Ballads: Much Sound and Little Sense (1869) was entitled "The Yarn of the 'Nancy Bell,'" and told about an elderly naval man who was very much like Samuel Taylor Coleridge's ancient mariner. He says, "I am a cook and a captain bold, / And the mate of the Nancy brig, / And a bo'sun tight, and a midshipmite, / And the crew of the captain's gig." Just exactly how he became all of the people listed above is that after a shipwreck he turned to cannibalism, and in the end was the sole survivor, because he "contained within himself all of the others." In the "Bab" Ballad entitled "General John," Gilbert tells how General John is an officer because of his high birth. And Private James is a Private because of his low birth. But the private has a "glimmer" that he and the general were cruelly switched at birth. Of course the General sneers at this suggestion, but Private James reasons that "No true gentleman would sneer at his inferior's "glimmer." The General, being a Gentleman, has to admit that what the Private says is true, and so the two must exchange positions with each other, and they become General James, and Private John. This is exactly the type of situation which Gilbert calls "Topsy-turvydom" (Swanson 450).

The "Bab" Ballads are Gilbert's first sustained comic works. These "Bab" Ballads which began appearing during the 1860s in various journals (especially Fun) and are illustrated by the author are short comic poems which gave Gilbert a popularity that was almost independent of his collaboration with Arthur Sullivan on Comic Operas (Henkle 193). One of these "Bab" Ballads is named "Absent Husband." It reads as follows:

Tell me, Edward, doest remember
    How at breakfast often we,
Put our bacon in the tea-pot
    While we took and fried our tea?

How we went to evening parties
    On gigantic brewer's drays?

> How you wore your coats as trousers,
>> In those happy, happy days? (Ellis 65)

Another of the "Bab" Ballads is entitled "Tempora Mutantur." It is about the Reverend Rawston Wright "who parts his hair down the middle, does his linen up with care, and is praised by congregation and bishop alike for his moderation, seriousness, and stern demeanor. Yet every once in a while, at night, he strikes a gigantic gong, tears his hair, leaps furiously about, and then sings this strange refrain" (Henkle 196).

> Oh, fan an aesthetical flame,
>> And sing to the moon so bright,
> For piggy-wigs worry and maim,
> And my highly respected name
>> is the REVEREND RAWSTON WRIGHT. (Ellis 82)

> Roger Ellis, editor of "Bab" Ballads had this to say about W. S. Gilbert's writing. He made his reputation from comic verse and his fortune from comic opera, yet thought of himself primarily as a serious writer. He who contrived some of the most whimsical lords of misrule in all literature lived scrupulously by the rule himself and demanded that others do so, too. He who placed so many insubstantial fairy realms upon the stage lived himself in a world of strict business and high finance in which he amassed a fortune and prided himself upon his houses, his yachts, his art collection, his telephones, and his automobiles. (Ellis 17-18)

Roger Henkle says that Gilbert's nonsense poems satirically target the more refined social anxieties of Gilbert's times--the pressures of conformity and respectability, the burdens of adult responsibilities, and the vague causes of dissatisfaction. These comic poems are "curiously self-critical, for they portray anticonventional impulses as bizarre, inhumane, manic" (Henkle 199).

Gilbert's "Rosenkrantz and Guildenstern" (1874) is a parody of Shakespeare's Hamlet, and it was first published in Fun. In Gilbert's version, King Claudius, when he was young, wrote a five-act tragedy, which was received with extreme hilarity. Although Claudius could have tolerated hisses, he could not tolerate laughter as a reaction to his tragedy, so he made any reference to his play a capital offense. All of the copies of the play were destroyed except for the one owned by Polonius, who had to have a copy because he was the Royal Censor. So Hamlet obtain's Polonius's copy of the play and arranges to have it performed, saving all of the silly soliloquies for himself. Everyone is amused, except for King Claudius, who becomes furious. Of course Hamlet is guilty of a capital crime, but the King commutes his sentence, and banishes him to the country of "Engle-land," "where people might tolerate such stuff" (Swanson 451).

Gilbert and Sullivan comic operas include Thespis (1871), Trial By Jury (1875), HMS Pinafore (1878), Princess Ida (1884), The Sorcerer (1884), The Mikado (1885), Ruddigore (1887), Pirates of Penzance (1888), The Yeomen of the Guard (1888), and The Gondoliers (1889) (Swanson 448). Gilbert's Thespis is the first work on which Gilbert and Sullivan collaborated. It is a satire which targets both classical myth and current Victorian stage conventions (Swanson 451). Trial By Jury pokes fun at the British court system; HMS Pinafore satirically targets the absurdities of the Royal Navy, and Pirates of Penzance rather than targeting the Royal Navy, targets instead the Army and the Police. Although these pieces are very critical, few people ever took offence because the criticism is always leveled with such good humor (Swanson 451).

Although Gilbert and Sullivan's comic operas are sometimes called satires, and although they resemble satires in their mocking of the social system, Robert Higbie suggests that they lack the seriousness that underlies satire. These comic operas lack the implicit moral standard by which society is condemned. They furthermore lack the anger or disillusionment that motivates the satirist's attack. "We can see most of the Savoy operas as offering a way of making the world's unfulfillingness bearable--even pleasing." Unlike the satirist, Gilbert absolves us of the need to take these bothersome matters too seriously. "We see they are unresolvable, but they do not arouse anxiety in us because we are made to feel that we need not try to resolve them" (Higbie 66). Gilbert doesn't offer us solutions; he offers us comic evasion. It is true that in these comic operas there is a "satirical edge;" the comic operas also present an attitude as negative as that of a satirist. Even though, the basic conflict in Gilbert's plots is usually between the individual and the social system, the real antagonist is not the individual, but the law itself, the rules and regulations which all of the characters, even the villains, must obey (Higbie 66).

Gilbert's Topsyturvydom (1874) was a comedy which dealt with the inversion of standard codes of conduct so that vice becomes virtue, beauty becomes ugliness, etc. His Engaged (1877) contains sardonic characters who engage solely in the pursuit of money. These characters raise hypocrisy to the level of an art. The deliberate cynicism, and the inversion of the Victorian codes of duty and respectability make Engaged resemble the early comedies of manners. Michael R. Booth says that Gilbert writes "deeply ironic, graceful, and witty comedy." Gilbert not only had an important influence on the comedies of Sir Arthur Wing Pinero, but on the comedies of George Bernard Shaw and Oscar Wilde as well (Ronning 54).

Gilbert was trained as a lawyer, but as a lawyer he was able to attract few clients, little money, and no fame. One of the ladies he defended unsuccessfully threw a boot at his head. A Frenchman, whose case he won, publicly hugged and kissed him so much that he wished he had lost the case (Pearson 193). But although Gilbert was not successful as a lawyer, he was nevertheless skilled at translating his knowledge of the law into successful lyrics in his comic operas.

> Laws are often harshly punitive; in Iolanthe [1882] there is constant talk of penal servitude, and The Mikado [1885] is about beheading. And like the laws governing the trial in Alice in Wonderland laws here are as pointless as they are harsh. The social system thus seems to exist merely for the sake of controlling people, not to enable them to reach any positive fulfillment. Instead of serving human needs, its regulations are arbitrary forms, existing simply as ends in themselves. In Iolanthe, for example, the whole political system exists to do "nothing in particular." And in Pinafore [1878] social advancement is a mere matter of form; all one need do to become the Ruler of the Queen's Navy is polish up the handle on the big front door. (Higbie 66)

The worlds represented by Gilbert's comic operas are split into opposing irreconcilable factions such as the fairies vs. the Lords in Iolanthe (1882, the military vs. the poetic in Patience (1881), the mortal vs. the divine in the burlesque in Thespis (1871), men vs. women in Princess Ida (1884), law-breakers vs. law-enforcers in Pirates of Penzance (1879). At a higher level of abstraction, each of these conflicts can be seen as representing the same conflict--the real vs. the ideal, or stated another way, the anti-romantic vs. the romantic (Higbie 67). The worlds in Gilbert's comic operas also place the individual in conflict with social order, and again the conflicts are irreconcilable. The policemen in Penzance are individuals with "feelings" that are "difficult to smother." The Lord Chancellor in Iolanthe has "two capacities, and they clash." Strephon in the same opera is half immortal, and thus embodies a romantic ideal half and a mortal half. Pooh-Bah in The Mikado has a number of personas and they all conflict with each other, but in general his conflict is between the id and the super ego. His dilemma is that "he has a duty to give himself into his own custody" (Higbie 67-68).

Higbie notes that there are many clues that Gilbert's comic operas are not satire in the judgmental sense of the word, and all of these clues relate to the fact that the operas are not written in the seriousness of typical satire. For one thing, Gilbert does not allow his audiences to identify too closely with his characters. Their problems don't seem to bother them very much, and the audience is therefore not required to feel sorry for them. "Instead of trying to resolve their conflicts, they often take evident pleasure in self-contradiction, jumping from one self to another without seeming to be bothered by any need to reconcile the two or justify their inconsistency (Higbie 68).

The "villains" in Gilbert's comic operas are not villains at all. These characters usually represent society's repressive control which keeps lovers apart. Such characters include the First Lord of the Admiralty, the Lord Chancellor, the Mikado, and the Lord High Executioner. "They seem like children playing at being grown-ups. Gilbert makes us feel they are playful by exaggerating them, making them absurdly, pointlessly strict, and by making them take delight in the opportunity to release energy which that exaggeration provides them, as when the Mikado sings with relish of all the punishments he wants to inflict" (Higbie 69-70).

Another clue that these conflicts are comic is that Gilbert takes neither side in the conflict seriously. "Although his plots ostensibly oppose good and bad characters, those characters do not really seem to represent any moral values. Since neither side attracts us enough to make us feel serious involvement, we can laugh at both" (Higbie 70). Furthermore, although Gilbert's characters sing that the punishments must fit the crimes, in the operas themselves this is seldom the case. Ko-Ko's flirting is very trivial. The audience cannot therefore believe that for such a trivial crime she would be punished by being beheaded, and this lack of belief is especially true in the world of a Gilbert and Sullivan comic opera, where the characters always seem able to evade such serious consequences (Higbie 71).

Another comic technique which Gilbert uses is to undercut the poetic and the sentimental with language that is ridiculous and inappropriate. Thus, "The Flowers that Bloom in the Spring" in The Mikado "have nothing to do with the case" (Higbie 72-73). Also, the language of Gilbert's characters tends to be a bit silly. In singing about her upcoming execution, for example, Ko-Ko describes her feelings by saying that she is "Awaiting the sensation of a short, sharp shock / From a cheap and chippy chopper on a big black block!"

> Although the ostensible subject here is quite grisly, the actual effect is comic, for we feel that what matters is not what the words mean but rather how they sound.... Gilbert, somewhat like the Victorian nonsense writers, is less concerned with meaning than with word-play. Thus here again he prevents our taking content too seriously. It might be said that his real subject here is his own playfulness. (Higbie 73)

This is true because Gilbert stresses form over meaning. In order to call attention to such surface-structure features as rhymes, he uses unlikely ones, especially feminine rhymes. He also uses incongruous rhymes, joining words whose meanings clash, in order to highlight the disparity between form and meaning. He furthermore, frequently juxtaposes a sentimental and an anti-sentimental word such as rhyming "passion intense" with "common sense."

> Often Gilbert rhymes poetic language based on a belief in an ideal, traditional, hierarchical order with social language, terms from the practical modern, urban middle-class world, the world which prevents attainment of a poetic ideal and in which traditional codes have lost their function. In Iolanthe he rhymed "bang the sounding brasses" with "lower middle classes," "fairy" with "Ladies' Seminary," and "pure and fair" with "Belgrave Square." The words with special social connotations puncture the vagueness

of the sentiment preceding them, exposing it as mere convention unrelated to social reality. In <u>Penzance</u> he rhymes "sentiment" with "Emollient," juxtaposing the poetic with the world of advertising, and rhymes "glory" with "gory," pointing out the physical reality the sentiment tries to ignore. (Higbie 74)

Gilbert and Sullivan's comic operas are filled with irony, contradiction and paradox. Gilbert is able to resolve irresolvable conflicts by the mere fact that if neither side of the conflict is worth taking seriously, there is no real conflict. "Thus Gilbert can bring about a happy ending simply by pointing out the absurdity of both sides" (Higbie 75).

Sir William Schwenck Gilbert Bibliography

Ellis, James, ed. <u>"Bab" Ballads by W. S. Gilbert</u>. Cambridge, MA: Harvard University Press, 1970.

Henkle, Roger B. "Hood, Gilbert, Carroll, Jerrold, and the Grossmiths: Comedy from Inside." <u>Comedy and Culture--England--1820-1900</u>. Princeton, NJ: Princeton University Press, 1980. 185-237.

Higbie, Robert. "Conflict and Comedy in W. S. Gilbert's Savoy Operas." <u>South Atlantic Review</u> 45.4 (1980): 66-77.

Pearson, Hesketh. "William Schwenck Gilbert." <u>Lives of the Wits</u>. New York, NY: Harper and Row, 1962, 191-208.

Ronning, Robert. "The Eccentric: The English Comic Farce of Sir Arthur Pinero." <u>The Quarterly Journal of Speech</u> 63.1 (1977): 51-58.

Swanson, Donald R. "W. S. Gilbert." <u>Encyclopedia of British Humorists, Volume I</u>. Ed. Steven H. Gale. New York, NY: Garland, 1996, 445-452.

Thorndike, Ashley H. "Sir William Schwenk Gilbert." <u>English Comedy</u>. New York, NY: Macmillan, 1929, 540-559.

James Joseph Bourke (1837-1894) IRELAND

See Nilsen, Don L. F. <u>Humor in Irish Literature: A Reference Guide</u>. Westport, CT: Greenwood, 1996.

John Francis O'Donnell (1837-1874) IRELAND

See Nilsen, Don L. F. <u>Humor in Irish Literature: A Reference Guide</u>. Westport, CT: Greenwood, 1996.

Algernon Swinburne (1837-1909)

C. W. Previté-Orton feels that Algernon Swinburne was "perhaps the first great poet to show a gutsy, emotional tendency, as he was the most sustained in passion and noblest in form of the new school" (Previté-Orton 226). Swinburne's verse satire was a satire of irony and scorn, but it also had a stirring quality (Previté-Orton 227). Swinburne was an Imperialist, but he was also a liberal, and "No one has written fierier verse in support of the Navy; or more fervently declared for the Union with Ireland" (Previté-Orton 228).

Algernon Swinburne Bibliography

Algernon Swinburne (1837-1909)

Previté-Orton, C. W. "Algernon Swinburne." <u>Political Satire in English Poetry</u>. New York, NY: Russell and Russell, 1910, 226-229.

Wilfrid Scawen Blunt (1840-1922)

W. S. Blunt's <u>Satan Absolved</u> is a play which shows much rhetorical skill. In this play, Satan and God are hearty combatants, and their censures are unreserved. God and Satan are engaged in satiric warfare about the English, and Satan says, "Their poets who write big of the 'White Man's Burden.' Trash! / The White Man's Burden, Lord, is the burden of his cash" (Previté-Orton 230).

Wilfrid Scawen Blunt Bibliography

Previté-Orton, C. W. "Algernon Swinburne." <u>Political Satire in English Poetry</u>. New York, NY: Russell and Russell, 1910, 226-229.

Thomas Hardy (1840-1928)

Much of Thomas Hardy's earliest humor was based on the contrasts between country life and urban life. This type of humor is most evident in <u>Under the Greenwood Tree</u> (1872), and <u>Far from the Madding Crowd</u> (1874). In his later writings, Hardy's humor became more subdued, but it was rekindled in <u>A Few Crusted Characters</u> (1894). In his early novels the reader can find many Wessex clowns and wits. Regarding his humor, Annie Macdonnel says that Hardy "has his eye always on the comedy of circumstances. Some of the novels, like <u>Two on a Tower</u> (1882), lack humor in the detail, but have it in the central conception" (Macdonnel 130). Satire in Thomas Hardy's novels usually has a secondary role, but in three novels it occupies a prominent position. These three novels are <u>The Hand of Ethelberta: A Comedy in Chapters</u> (1860), <u>The Well-Beloved</u>, and <u>Two on a Tower</u> (1882).

The focus of the satire in <u>The Poor Man and the Lady</u> (1867-1668)is on the more affluent urban aspects of society (Brummer 515). Glen Irvin suggests that Hardy's <u>Under the Greenwood Tree: A Rural Painting of the Dutch School</u> (1872) has a comic plot, with romance at its center.

> The young couple overcome the obstacles and marry, their bungling antics, fear, and hesitations providing ample humor. The tone is sustained by the narrator and the comic background characters. The conclusion resolves the issue of social inequality and the conflict of the choir and Fancy, of old and new. In form, tone, plotting, and resolution, this story is the purest example of Hardy's concept of the comic novel. (Irvin "Comic Archetype" 164)

Fancy Day in <u>Under the Greenwood Tree</u> says, "I like Dick, and I love him; but how plain and sorry a man looks in the rain, with no umbrella, and wet through." This is "plain-folks" humor. The "humor is revealed in the novel's rustic setting" (Brummer 515). <u>A Pair of Blue Eyes</u> (1873) is a romantic tragedy which again utilizes rustic humor, as the provincial characters act out a drama that is both humorous and macabre. Elfride Swancourt, the female protagonist, here again provides much of the humor (Brummer 515).

Beatriz Villacañas considers <u>Far from the Madding Crowd</u> (1874), <u>The Return of the Native</u> (1878), <u>Tess of the d-Urbervilles: A Pure Woman Faithfully Presented</u> (1891), and <u>Jude the Obscure</u> (1895) to be the most interesting and most characteristic of Hardy's novels, further noting that in these four novels Hardy uses three basic comic techniques.

1. He expresses things in humorous ways through his comments and his descriptions; 2. he uses humor in the development of conversational patterns of his rustic country people, the people of Hardy's native Dorset; and 3. he develops a prevailing irony contrasting the futility of people's struggle to master their own lives with fate, or chance which always seems to complicate matters and always has the final say (Villacañas 273).

Gabriel is the shepherd hero in Far from the Madding Crowd (1874). According to Noorul Hasan, Gabriel is presented in "a comic-realistic perspective." Even the description of Gabriel's watch seems to Hasan to be a "deliberate comic deflation" (Hasan 15). The entire first chapter is of a humorous design, as an analogy is drawn between Gabriel's hut and Noah's Ark. Gabriel's lack of tact is another humorous element, especially in his romantic encounters with Bathsheba, as when Bathsheba throws milk on the unconscious Gabriel in an attempt to bring him back to life. Gabriel's and Bathsheba's inability to communicate with each other is also comic, and so are Bathsheba's oxymorons (Brummer 514). Bathsheba says she wouldn't mind being a bride at a wedding, "if I could be one without having a husband." Part of the humor of Far from the Madding Crowd comes from the antithetical behavior of the two protagonists. She is a very saucy misogynist, and he is "the conventional swain" (Brummer 515). Noorul Hasan also considers Boldwood to be a humorous character, and describes him as being "so dominated by a single 'humor' that he seems a kind of pasteboard figure of sexual obsession unable by definition to attain full tragic stature while carrying about him a portentous air of tragedy" (Hasan 35).

Irony pervades many of Hardy's novels, and much of this irony is poignant. In Far from the Madding Crowd, for example, one of most significant ironies is that Bathsheba and Gabriel meet at the beginning of the novel, and have ample opportunities of marrying each other and living happily ever after; yet they don't marry until the very end of the novel, approximately 400 pages after they first meet (Villacañas 274-275). In Far from the Madding Crowd, Hardy uses humor in his description of Farmer Oak: "When Farmer Oak smiled, the corners of his mouth spread till they were within an unimportant distance of his ears, his eyes were reduced to chinks, and diverging wrinkles appeared round them, extending upon his countenance like the rays in a rudimentary sketch of the rising sun" (Villacañas 274). A further irony is that while this description of Farmer Oak seems trivial, and presents a humorous visual image of him, this is not at all in contradiction with his moral depth as a character. In this same novel, Mark Clark is described as "a genial and pleasant gentleman, whom to meet anywhere in your travels was to know, to know was to drink, and to drink was, unfortunately, to pay for" (Villacañas 274). Beatriz Villacañas points out that the country people in Hardy's novels provide most of the humorous situations and the funniest ones as well. Although Thomas Hardy was an educated man, he was a member of a rural community and a rural family, and he was able to thoroughly enjoy the hearty humor of his neighbors and his relatives. In fact, Hardy joined his father and other fiddle players and played at parties which were filled with joviality and playful joking (Villacañas 276).

As an example of Hardy's ability to amuse his readers with humorous conversation, consider Chapter 8, "The Malthouse" of Far from the Madding Crowd.

"A clane cup for the shepherd" said the master commandingly. "No--not at all" said Gabriel in a reproving tone of considerateness. "I never fuss about dirt in its pure state and when I know what sort it is." Taking the mug he drank an inch or more from the depth of its contents, and duly passed it to the next man. "I wouldn't think of giving such trouble to neighbours in washing up when there's so much work to be done in the world already." (Villacañas 274)

Beatriz Villacañas points out that Hardy himself was a countryman, and was well versed in the rural dialect of his neighbours. This was the native dialect of many of his friends, his neighbours, his parents, and, of course, himself. So even though the rural speech that Hardy presents is funny, there is also a feeling of respect, tenderness, and warmth (Villacañas 274).

Another example of humorous conversation appears in Return of the Native (1878) as Granfer Cantle is talking with his youngest son, Christian. Granfer is an "elderly man of more than considerable vitality, always ready for a joke, a good meal and, of course, a drink":

> "What be ye quaking for Christian?"
> "I'm the man."
> "What man?"
> "The man no woman will marry."

After they discuss the justification of this pronouncement, Granfer asks, "Well, what did the last one say to yee?" and Christian responds, "Get out of my sight, you slack-twisted, slim-looking maphrotight fool!" (Villacañas 276).

The most significant irony in The Return of the Native "lies in the gloomy fact that in wanting to do his best for his fellow neighbours, Clym Yeobright, the native who has come back home full of good intentions, destroys the hopes and life of his wife and...his mother. It is the irony of the impossibility of doing good to some without doing evil to others, including, perhaps, our dearest ones" (Villacañas 276). Hardy's humor is not so evident in The Return of the Native as in some of his other novels, except that the overall conception of this novel does create circumstances or human conditions from which fools tend to emerge (Brummer 514).

Two on a Tower (1882) addresses a serious theme comically, as its satirical attack on the established Church is grafted onto a complementary and ironic love story. Late in the story, Viviette protests that she can't accept the Bishop's proposal because she doesn't love him. Her brother Louis scoffs that "a woman who at two-and-twenty married for convenience, at thirty talks of not marrying without love." Hardy says that what is happening here is the "rule of inverse..., in which more requires less, and less requires more" (Irvin "High Passion" 79). According to Glenn Irvin, "Hardy constructs the romance through opposition! Swithin's celestial interests, Viviette's more earthy ones; his paganism, her Christianity; his youth, her age; his inexperience, her sophistication; his fairness, her darkness; his Adonis, her Venus--his seeming social and economic inferiority and their mutual secrecy in the complication" (Irvin "High Passion" 79). Irvin says further that under the pretense of wishing to learn about the stars, Viviette visits Swithin's tower, and Swithin rambles interminably on to her, in the best tradition of the comic pedant. He is oblivious to her requests for council regarding her husband. Swithin in fact becomes so distracted that he knocks his newly acquired telescope lens over the parapet. Irvin suggests that the tower in Two on a Tower is the novel's central symbol, and it is, of course, a phallic symbol, and he concludes his article that "with exquisite comic irony, Hardy makes the Bishop the butt of a ribald and all-too-human joke" (Irvin "High Passion" 80).

Wessex Tales (1888) is a collection of short stories many of which have elements of humor, irony, and satire (Brummer 515). Other Hardy collections of short stories which exhibit humor, irony, and satire include A Group of Noble Dames (1891), Life's Little Ironies (1894), and A Changed Man and Other Stories (1913). In all of these collections, the stories are mostly anecdotal. One of the stories is entitled "The Three Strangers," and this story contains a number of comic episodes, especially one in which an escaped convict "sings a counterpart to the hangman's grisly song while waving cups with him" (Brummer 516).

Thomas Hardy also wrote much humorous poetry in such collections as Wessex Poems (1898), Poems of the Past and the Present (1902), Time's Laughing Stocks (1909),

<u>Satires of Circumstance</u> (1914), <u>Moments of Vision</u> (1917), <u>Late Lyrics and Earlier</u> (1922). <u>Human Shows</u> (1925), and <u>Womter Words</u> (published posthumously in 1928). Hardy wrote more than 900 poems, and Ross Brummer feels that many of these poems tended to be humorous, sardonic, and even gruesome from time to time (Brummer 516). Hardy's <u>Times Laughing Stocks</u> (1909) is lyric poetry that expresses the rustic humor of various Dorset villagers (Brummer 514). His <u>Satires of Circumstance</u> (1914) exhibits a satiric type of humor that tends to be gentle and was often piquant. A very good example of Hardy's humor is "In the Room of the Bride-Elect" where a young lady who is about to get married chides her parents for not insisting that she marry her former boyfriend, since the person she is about to marry is a dolt (Brummer 516).

An example of humorous language which occurs in <u>Tess of the d'Urbervilles</u> (1891) is when the dairy man wants to prove his theory that bulls are more moved by music than cows are. He relates the story of a man named William Dewy who, when he was chased by a bull, pulled out his fiddle as he ran and struck up a jig: "The bull softened down and stood still, looking hard at William Dewy, who fiddled on and on; till a sort of a smile stole over the bull's face. But no sooner did William stop his playing and turn to get over the hedge than the bull would stop his smiling and lower his horns towards the seat of William's breeches." William Dewy, however, figures out a way to get out of this dilemma. "He broke into the 'Tivity Hymn, just as at Christmas carol singing; lo and behold, down went the bull on his bended knees, in his ignorance, just as if 'twere the true 'Tivity night and hour" (Villacañas 277).

Beatriz Villacañas suggests that irony is the prevailing sort of humor in Hardy's <u>Jude the Obscure</u> (1895). Villacañas agrees with Terry Eagleton, who says in his <u>Literary Theory: An Introduction</u> that "the irony is that Jude's labour-power is exploited literally to prop up the structures which exclude him." In other words, the world of Christminster, the city of learning is a society that uses Jude's physical work, but ignores him and his aspirations (Villacañas 276).

According to Ross Brummer, <u>The Dynasts: A Poetic Drama in Three Parts</u> (1904-1908) "traverses the human condition from pathos to satiric realism." Hardy's humor is especially evident in the satiric realism of the Prince Regent. The humor is also evident in the conversations of the servants. Josephine falls ill, and the servants speculate on her successor. This successor must have certain qualities:

FIRST SERVANT: She must be young.
SECOND SERVANT: Good. She must. The country must see to that.
FIRST SERVANT: And she must be strong.
SECOND SERVANT: Good again. She must be strong. The doctors will see to that.
FIRST SERVANT: And she must be fruitful as the vine.
SECOND SERVANT: Ay, by God. She must be fruitful as the vine. That, Heaven help him, he must see to himself. (Brummer 516).

Thomas Hardy Bibliography

Brummer, Ross. "Thomas Hardy." <u>Encyclopedia of British Humorists, Volume I</u>. Ed. Steven H. Gale. New York, NY: Garland, 1996, 513-518.
Hardy, Thomas. <u>Satires of Circumstance: Lyrics and Reveries with Miscellaneous Pieces</u>. London, England: Macmillan, 1914.
Hasan, Noorul. <u>Thomas Hardy, The Sociological Imagination</u>. London, England: Macmillan, 1982.
Irvin, Glenn W. "Hardy's Comic Archetype: <u>Under the Greenwood Tree</u>." <u>WHIMSY</u> 1 (1983): 163-164.

Irvin, Glenn W. "High Passion and High Church in Hardy's Two on a Tower." WHIMSY 2 (1984): 78-80.

Macdonell, Annie. Thomas Hardy. New York, NY: Dodd, Mead, 1895.

Villacañas, Beatriz. "Thomas Hardy: The Humour of a Tragic Novelist." Literary and Linguistic Aspects of Humour. Barcelona, Spain: Univ of Barcelona Dept of Languages, 1984, 273-278.

Ambrose Bierce (1842-c1914)

One critic wrote that Ambrose Bierce "is probably the most rediscovered writer in American literary history" (Davidson 4). In The Devil's Dictionary, Bierce defined "selfish" as "Devoid of consideration for the selfishness of others" (Bier 163). In this same dictionary he defined "hippogriff" as follows: "n. An animal (now extinct) which was half horse and half griffin. The griffin was itself a compound creature, half lion and half eagle. The hippogriff was actually, therefore, only one-quarter eagle, which is two dollars and fifty cents in gold. The study of zoology is full of surprises" (Bier 177).

Stuart Woodruff describes Bierce to have been a bizarre person who "indulged in anti-Christian orgies in cemeteries, pulled down holy crosses, exhumed corpses, loved snakes as he loathed dogs, and enjoyed meditation in graveyards, where he had once contracted asthma by sleeping on a tombstone" (Woodruff 7). Bierce's parents were solid Congregationalists, and in addition, his father was a devout Calvinist. Stuart Woodruff notes that Bierce had rejected the religion of his New England ancestors and he also rejected his Puritan upbringing. But at the same time, the code that he retained was almost as metaphysical as was the Calvinism that he denied. He had merely replaced a "harshly personal God" with a "harshly impersonal Fate." For Bierce, every man's slightest action was preordained, and it was man's duty to submit to the mysterious workings of the Supernatural (Woodruff 52). With such a background as this, it is no wonder that Bierce viewed religion in a somewhat nonconventional way. In "The Holy Deacon," Bierce tells about an itinerant preacher who after working hard in the world's "moral vineyard" approached the Holy Deacon of the local church and said, "Brother, these people know you and your active support will bear fruit abundantly. Please pass the plate for me, and you shall have one fourth." The Holy Deacon did pass the plate, and put all of the money into his own pocket. When the Itinerant Preacher asked the Holy Deacon for his share of the money he had collected, the Holy Deacon responded that there was no money collected for the Itinerant Preacher. "The Adversary has hardened their hearts and one fourth is all they gave" (Kiley and Shuttleworth 307).

Bierce had a fascination with the many ironies of life. He said,

> We set apart a "reservation" for a tribe of Indians, formally pledging ourselves to observe the treaty by which they are to have it for the land which they relinquish. After a time it is found to contain gold, or good agricultural land, or something that we need in our business and they do not in theirs. The region is straightway "invaded" by white miners, or settlers, in such numbers that the difficulty and cost of expelling them are a public burden. It is easier and cheaper to expel the Indians. (qtd. in Berkove 132)

Ambrose Bierce Bibliography

Berkove, Lawrence I., ed. Skepticism and Descent. Ann Arbor, MI: Delmas, 1980.

Bier, Jesse. The Rise and Fall of American Humor. New York, NY: Holt, Rinehart, and Winston, 1968.

Davidson, Cathy N. "Introduction." Critical Essays on Ambrose Bierce. Ed. Cathy N.
    Davidson. Boston, MA: G. K. Hall, 1982, 1-12.
Kiley, Frederick, and J. M. Shuttleworth, eds. Satire from Aesop to Buchwald. New York,
    NY: Collier/Macmillan, 1971.
Vasantkumar, N. J. C. "The 'Devil' in Mr. Bierce." WHIMSY 7 (1989): 61-62.
Woodruff, Stuart. The Short Stories of Ambrose Bierce. Pittsburgh, PA: University of
    Pittsburgh Press, 1964.

Arthur Seymour Sullivan (1842-1900)

One of the most comic and ironic elements of Gilbert and Sullivan's comic operas
is that Sullivan's music emphasizes regularity, and therefore often contradicts the sense of
the words. "The music tends toward the martial, implying a heroic social order comically
at odds with Gilbert's unheroic characters; and it also tends towards the sentimental, which
of course is also incongruous" (Higbie 74).

Arthur Seymour Sullivan Bibliography

Higbie, Robert. "Conflict and Comedy in W. S. Gilbert's Savoy Operas." South Atlantic
    Review 45.4 (1980): 66-77.

Alfred Perceval Graves (1846-1931) IRELAND

See Nilsen, Don L. F. **Humor in Irish Literature: A Reference Guide**. Westport,
CT: Greenwood, 1996.

George Grossmith (1847-1912)

Roger Henkle considers George and Weedon Grossmith's The Diary of a Nobody
(1894) to be the "classic nineteenth-century comedy of the ordinary man's ordinary
experiences." It began appearing in serial form in Punch on May 26, 1888, was later
published as a book, and has remained in publication to the present day. The Diary is a
recollection of events in the daily life of Charles Pooter, a small-time suburban clerk. It
begins with Charles Pooter asking himself, "Why should I not publish my diary? I have
often seen reminiscences of people I have never even heard of, and I fail to see--because
I do not happen to be a 'Somebody'--why my diary should not be interesting." Entries in
the diary include a conversation with the butcher, and a debate over the shade of chocolate
brown that would be required to touch up the stairs. The entries are humorously mundane
and understated, "Planted some mustard-and-cress and radishes, and went to bed at nine"
(Henkle "Comedy from Inside" 227). One entry involves the trying out of Pinkford's new
red enamel, which is advertised to "work wonders." Pooter is so impressed with what it
does to the flower pots that he goes on to paint everything in the maid's room red. From
there, he goes on to paint the coal scuttle, the backs of his Shakespeare collection, and then
the inside of his bathtub (Henkle "Pooter" 117). This is the life that the Pooters lead.
Even their vacations are spent at the same resort every year, with their old friends, the
'Gowings' and the 'Cummingses' " (Henkle "Comedy from Inside" 228). When the
families meet, conversations like the following are likely to occur:
        GOWING: Hullo, Pooter, why your trousers are too short!

POOTER: Very likely, and you will find my temper <u>short</u> also.

GOWING: That won't make your trousers longer, Juggins. You should get your missus to put a flounce on them.

POOTER: (<u>aside</u>) I wonder why I waste my time entering his insulting observations in my diary. (Grossmith 118)

At one point, Pooter has an opportunity to impress his wife's friends from the country, the Jameses, by taking them to a play with some tickets he has been given by Merton. But Merton's tickets turn out to be worthless and Mr. James has to go to the box office and buy tickets for the four of them. At the play, Pooter leans so far out of the box that his little black bow tie falls into the pit below, and a man puts his foot on it, and feeling the bump he reaches down and finds the tie, and throws it under another a nearby seat in disgust. But now Pooter doesn't have a tie, so he has to keep his chin down for the rest of the evening, and this gives him a pain in the back of his neck (Henkle "Pooter" 179).

Evelyn Waugh called <u>The Diary of a Nobody</u> "the funniest book in the world." In 1907, George Orwell wrote about this novel at some length, noting that it was a favorite in Russia, and further tracing the protagonist, Charles Pooter, back to Cervantes's Don Quixote. For some people, Mr. Pooter has become a generic term and symbol for a nonentity-type person (Moseley 53). Merritt Moseley considers Mr. Pooter to be one of the most exquisitely funny creations in English writing. "One major vein of Pooter humor comes from his haplessness. He is one of those people to whom things are always happening" (Moseley 54). This is ironic because one of Mr. Pooter's provincial qualities is that he is himself totally humorless. He never seems to understand what other people find so funny, nor does he understand that they are often laughing at him rather than with him. He considers himself a very funny man, and is proud of his witty remarks, usually bad puns, as when his wife Carrie brings down some shirts and advises him to take them to Trillip's cleaners. She tells Charles, "The fronts and cuffs are much frayed," and he responds without a moment's hesitation, "I'm <u>frayed</u> they are." Although Carrie almost always laughs dutifully at Mr. Pooter's humor, other people do not. On one occasion, Mr. Pooter is introduced by a friend who asks him if he knows Mr. Short. Charles Pooter responds, smiling, that he had not had that pleasure, but he hoped it would not be <u>long</u> before he knew Mr. <u>Short</u>, then Mr. Pooter continues, "He evidently did not see my little joke, although I repeated it twice with a little laugh" (Moseley 54).

Moseley suggests that in <u>The Diary of a Nobody</u> much of the humor is based on a dual perspective, as the reader relates to the story both from the inside and from the outside. Most of the time the readers feel superior to Mr. Pooter. They laugh at him because of his misfortunes and his pose of superiority; this is the outside humor. But at the same time that readers are laughing at Mr. Pooter, they realize that they themselves have many of Mr. Pooter's qualities; this is the inside humor. "We are of course insiders, in that we are reading Pooter's diary; and we understand it even better than he does." With Mr. Pooter, readers recognize a kind of shared humanity. We feel an affectionate identification with this comical character (Moseley 55).

See also "(Walter) Weedon Grossmith"

George Grossmith Bibliography

Grossmith, George, and Weedon Grossmith. <u>The Diary of a Nobody</u>. (1894). London, England: Collins, 1968.

Henkle, Roger B. "Hood, Gilbert, Carroll, Jerrold, and the Grossmiths: Comedy from Inside." <u>Comedy and Culture--England--1820-1900</u>. Princeton, NJ: Princeton University Press, 1980, 185-237.

Henkle, Roger B. "From Pooter to Pinter: Domestic Comedy and Vulnerability." The Critical Quarterly 16.2 (1974): 174-189.

Moseley, Merritt. "The Diary of a Nobody and the Humor of Suburban Life." WHIMSY 6 (1988): 53-55.

Moseley, Merritt. "George Grossmith." Encyclopedia of British Humorists, Volume I. Ed. Steven H. Gale. New York, NY: Garland, 1996, 491.

William Hurrell Mallock (1849-1923)

The humor of Mallock's The New Republic (1877) and his later satire The New Paul and Virginia, or Positivism on an Island (1878) are examples of what George Meredith calls "laughter of the mind." Mallock himself noted that his novels were patterned after those of Thomas Peacock, but with one significant difference. While Peacock's most important theme was that his visionaries and thinkers were not able to translate their ideas into action, Mallock's body of intellectuals are not in the least concerned with the realm of action. "His people are contented with their ideas and sometimes with just the sounds of their ideas" (Henkle 266).

William Hurrell Mallock Bibliography

Henkle, Roger. Comedy and Culture: England 1820-1900. Princeton, NJ: Princeton University Press, 1980.

Robert Lewis Stevenson (1850-1894) SCOTLAND

In 1879 Robert Louis Stevenson wrote his first book. It was a travel book entitled Travels with a Donkey in the Cevennes. In his introduction to this book, Robin Neillands describes the Stevenson's eccentric choice of equipment,

> He decided to do without a tent and settled instead for a sleeping sack into which he stowed some books, a leg of cold mutton, a bottle of Beaujolais, an egg-beater, and a considerable quantity of black and white bread. The size and weight of his supplies called for a beast of burden, and for this he purchased Modestine for sixty-five francs and a glass of brandy. (17)

One hundred years after Stevenson's trek, Robin Neillands and a group of writers walked the trail again, and received official sanction for the "Robert Louis Stevenson Trail." They had originally decided to take a donkey with them, more for companionship and for color than as a beast of burden, "but a small test during the reconnaissance revealed that, like Stevenson's Modestine, modern donkeys have an all-out speed of one mile an hour, and a mind of their own. Stevenson, by his own admission, treated Modestine abominably in order to keep her moving, but having no heart for that, we decided to go without one" (24).

Robert Lewis Stevenson Bibliography

Stevenson, Robert Louis. Travels with a Donkey in the Cevennes. London: Chatto and Windus, 1988.

Henry Arthur Jones (1851-1929)

Henry Arthur Jones (1851-1929)

Henry Arthur Jones wrote the following plays: The Silver King (1882), Saints and Sinners (1884), The Tempter (1893), The Masqueraders (1894), Michael and his Lost Angel (1896), Mrs. Dane's Defence (1900), The Hypocrites (1906), Mary Goes First (1913), Cock o' the Walk (1915), and The Pacifists (1917). Henry Arthur Jones, like Sir Arthur Pinero, Oscar Wilde and George Bernard Shaw, wrote plays with eccentric characters, though of these four playwrights, Jones tended the most in the direction of melodrama.   All four authors, however, delighted in devising comic and dramatic situations in which their characters inverted the standard codes of Victorian and Edwardian society (Ronning 55).

Henry Arthur Jones Bibliography

Ronning, Robert. "The Eccentric: The English Comic Farce of Sir Arthur Pinero." The Quarterly Journal of Speech 63.1 (1977): 51-58.

George Moore (1852-1933) IRELAND

See Nilsen, Don L. F. **Humor in Irish Literature: A Reference Guide**. Westport, CT: Greenwood, 1996.

Max Beerbohm (H. Beerbohm Tree) (1852-1917)

Max Beerbohm's major claim to fame is as an actor. It is said that Sir William Schwenck Gilbert once remarked that Beerbohm Tree's Hamlet was "funny without being vulgar." Gilbert denied having made this statement; however a statement he did make (in a letter) is that he [Gilbert] had a way to resolve the debate over whether it was Shakespeare or Bacon who wrote Hamlet. "They are going to dig up Shakespeare and dig up Bacon; they are going to set their coffins side by side, and they are going to get Tree to recite Hamlet to them. And the one who turns in his coffin will be the author of the play" (Pearson 209). It was on Monday, May 20, 1878 that Max Beerbohm adopted his stage name of H. Beerbohm Tree. In one week in 1878, seven plays were presented by the Bijou Comedy Company, and Tree appeared in all of them, mostly in leading parts. On two occasions during this week, Tree gave his "inimitable Dramatic and Mimictic Recitals" in which he imitated Irving, Toole, Salvini, and other famous actors of the London theatre (Pearson 210-211).

Max Beerbohm (H. Beerbohm Tree) Bibliography

Pearson, Hesketh. "Beerbohm Tree." Lives of the Wits. New York, NY: Harper and Row, 1962, 290-221.

William Boyle (1853-1874) IRELAND

See Nilsen, Don L. F. **Humor in Irish Literature: A Reference Guide**. Westport, CT: Greenwood, 1996.

Francis Arthur Fahy (1854-1935) IRELAND

See Nilsen, Don L. F. <u>Humor in Irish Literature: A Reference Guide</u>. Westport, CT: Greenwood, 1996.

William Percy French (1854-1920) IRELAND

See Nilsen, Don L. F. <u>Humor in Irish Literature: A Reference Guide</u>. Westport, CT: Greenwood, 1996.

(Walter) Weedon Grossmith (1854-1919)

<u>The Diary of a Nobody</u> (1892) was written jointly by George and Weedon Grossmith, and it was illustrated by Weedon. It was first published in serial form in <u>Punch</u>, and then later appeared in book form. Evelyn Waugh called it "the funniest book in the world" (Gallagher 85). <u>The Diary of a Nobody</u> is a record of fifteen months in the life of Charles Pooter, who lives in a noisy house by the railroad tracks, and who has difficulty getting his garden to grow, and who suffers humiliations with tradesmen and failures of home repair, and the snobberies of his various neighbors. Mr. Pooter has encounters with his wife, Carrie, and with his two good friends, Mr. Cummings and Mr. Gowing, and with his son Willie, who has renamed himself "Lupin." The Pooters live lives of insignificance. Their only significant events are domestic parties, and holidays by the sea, and their minor domestic arguments. Mr. Pooter is very proud of the bad jokes which he makes, and Carrie is obligated to laugh at them. The mundane existence of the Pooters is sometimes broken by unsuccessful forays into high society, as when they are invited to the Lord Mayor's Ball, given at his Mansion House, or to the Volunteers Dinner and Ball given by the East Acton Rifle Brigade in honor of an American journalist named Hardfur Huttle. But when they get to the Mansion House, they discover that almost everyone was invited. They are especially upset to discover that their ironmonger is one of the guests. The Pooters are also humiliated because they don't know how to behave in high society. Mr. Pooter drinks too much and crashes to the floor with Carrie at the Mansion House. When they dine with the American journalist, they are forced to listen in silence as the American goes on denouncing the very types of people they are and the very kinds of lives they live. Their son, Lupin, earns some money on investments, and in general lives a much higher speed of life than his father lives (Moseley 492). Lupin has flashy clothes, and has show-business aspirations, and has friends who affront the Pooters, because of the Pooters's concern with "respectability." Pooter is the narrator of the story, but he is always an unreliable narrator. He thinks that he and his wife are special; but they are common people. He and his wife think that their ugly house is handsome, and they aren't very smart, and they take pride in the wrong things. According to Merritt Moseley, "Charles Pooter, has given the English language the eponym 'a Pooter' and the adjective 'Pooterish.'" <u>Diary of a Nobody</u> was so popular that the British humorist Keith Waterhouse has done take-offs entitled, <u>Mrs Pooter's Diary</u> (1983), and <u>The Collected Letters of a Nobody</u> (1986), and the genre of diary humor has affected such recent popular books as Sue Townsend's <u>The Secret Diary of Adrian Mole</u> (1984)(Moseley 493).
    See also "George Grossmith"

(Walter) Weedon Grossmith Bibliography

Gallagher, Donat, Ed. <u>The Essays, Articles, and Reviews of Evelyn Waugh</u>. Boston, MA: Little, Brown, 1984.

Moseley, Merritt. "Walter Weedon Grossmith." Encyclopedia of British Humorists, Volume I. Ed. Steven H. Gale. New York, NY: Garland, 1996, 491-494.

Oscar Wilde (1854-1900) IRELAND

Oscar Wilde wrote in a genre which many critics have dubbed "satire of manners" (Robinson 1200). Other critics have called them "aesthetic satires." "He paradoxically makes virtue a vice and desanctifies society's accepted standards, eliminating society's mediating role; consequently, the individual is left free to develop and to adhere to his own or her own standards." Bonnie Robinson feels that "the one unifying feature which Wilde's satire shares with that of other satirists is its humor, its comicality." Wilde's humorous devices range very widely, and include both wit, and humorous symbol (Robinson 1201). Oscar Wilde's tone is amoral, flippant, skeptical, and exaggerated. The structure of his writing is staccato and abrupt. Much of his humor is based on paradox, which for him is the essence of "transvaluation." He uses situational humor, epigrams, paradoxes, repartee, parody, and symbol in his plays. He satirizes "over-crusted, fossilized, and fossilizing sentiment," but in addition, he satirizes the style in which such people express these sentiments. His epigrams include, "Work is the curse of the drinking classes," "Don't be led astray into the paths of virtue," and "He hasn't a single redeeming vice" (Pearson 101).

In A Picture of Dorian Gray (1890), Lord Henry Worton speaks almost continuously in epigrams, and these epigrams are well integrated into the dialogue. Lord Worton apologizes to Dorian for being late, and then he says, "I went to look after a piece of old brocade in Wardour Street, and had to bargain for hours for it. Nowadays people know the price of everything but the value of nothing" (Robinson 1202).

There are many running jokes in Wilde's plays which involve characters commenting on other characters which are absent or rarely scene. Such running jokes are about Agatha in Lady Windermere's Fan, a Comedy (1892), whose effusive "clever talk" continually repeats "Yes, mama"; Mrs. Daubeney in A Woman of No Importance, a Comedy (1893), who is the English stoic who is blind, deaf, and bedridden, but who nevertheless manages to be "so very cheerful"; and Lord Bracknell in The Importance of Being Earnest, a Comedy (1895), who remains docilely at home, because "the home seems to be the proper sphere for the man." "These characters represent a society which complacently accepts stereotypic and superficial behavior without truly understanding the philosophy of the superficial, a philosophy which promotes Wilde's concept of individualism" (Robinson 1202). Such characters fail to be individuals not because they don't choose a self-expressive style or because of their superficiality, bur rather because they conform to conventions and by so doing they suppress their individuality (Robinson 1202).

Richard Foster points out that in The Importance of Being Earnest (1895), Wilde used exaggeration to parody many of the literary clichés of his day. It is a paradox when Cecily accepts Algernon's evil past, saying, "I hope you have not been leading a double life, pretending to be wicked and being really good all the time. That would be hypocrisy." In the same, play, Lord Illingworth excuses himself to Mrs. Allonby by saying, "I'll be back in a moment. People's mothers always bore me to death. All women become like their mothers. That is their tragedy." To this Mrs. Allonby responds, "No man does. That is his." One of the important concepts developed in The Importance of Being Earnest is "Bunburyism." This can be defined as the "escape from convention," and is "the artistic mask from behind which a person may express his/her true self." Bonnie Robinson says that "'Bunburyism' is the individual's response to 'Victorianism'" (Robinson 1203).

Being a true maternal hero, Lady Berwick in Lady Windermere's Fan (1892) throws her daughter Agatha into the arms of Agatha's first available suitor, saying, "Of course, we should be very sorry to lose her, but I think that a mother who doesn't part with a daughter every season has no real affection" (Robinson 1204). Lord Illingworth of A Woman of No Importance (1893) exposes English aristocratic society by saying, "You should read the Peerage.... It is the best thing in fiction the English have ever done" (Robinson 1205). In Lord Arthur Savile's Crime, Wilde's protagonist is told by a chiromantist that he is destined to commit murder, and since Lord Arthur was "too conscientious to set pleasure above principle," he tries to poison his second cousin, Lady Clementina. Since this doesn't work, he tries to blow up his uncle, the Dean of Chichester. He finally achieves his predestined fate to tipping Mr. Podgers, the chiromantist who had originally made the prediction, into the Thames. After that Lord Savile (but not Mr. Podgers) lives happily ever after (Robinson 1204). An Ideal Husband (1895), like Lady Windermere's Fan, A Woman of No Importance, The Importance of Being Earnest, and Lord Arthur Savile's Crime is a comedy because it ends like a comedy. In The Importance of Being Earnest, Wilde explains what such a comic ending is like: "The good ending happily, and the bad unhappily. That is what fiction means" (Robinson 1205).

Wilde was very critical of "Puritan values," and in a letter written on November 28, 1897 to Leonard Smithers, Wilde wrote, "I never came across anyone in whom the moral sense was dominant who was not heartless, cruel, vindictive, log-stupid, and entirely lacking in the smallest sense of humanity" (Robinson 1203). In "The Soul of Man Under Socialism" (1908), Wilde asserts that "selfishness is not living as one wishes to live; it is asking others to live as one wishes to live. And unselfishness is letting other people's lives alone, not interfering with them" (Robinson 1201). Oscar Wilde is generally considered to be one of England's greatest wits. His epigrams and paradoxes can be found in his conversations, his essays, his short stories, his novel, and in his comedies. These comedies directly link Wilde with William Shakespeare, William Congreve, Richard Brinsley Sheridan, and George Bernard Shaw (Robinson 1206).

See also Nilsen, Don L. F. Humor in Irish Literature: A Reference Guide. Westport, CT: Greenwood, 1996.

Oscar Wilde Bibliography

Foster, Richard. "Wilde as Parodist: A Second Look at The Importance of Being Earnest." College English. 18 (1956): 19-25.

Jordan, Robert J. "Satire and Fantasy in Wilde's The Importance of Being Earnest." Ariel 1.3 (1970: 101-109.

Pearson, Hesketh. Oscar Wilde: His Life land Wit. New York: Harper and Brothers, 1946.

Reinert, Otto. "Satiric Strategy in The Importance of Being Earnest." College English 18 (1956): 14-18.

Robinson, Bonnie J. "Oscar Wilde." Encyclopedia of British Humorists, Volume II. Ed. Steven H. Gale. New York, NY: Garland, 1996, 1199-1207.

Index

Burton, Robert (Democritus Junior) (1577-1640), 110
Business, See "Economics"
Buss, Robert William, 9, 81
Butler, Marilyn, 134
Butler, Samuel (c1613-1680), 17-18, 65, 79
Butler, Samuel (1835-1902), 259-262
Butterick, George F., 63
Byrom, Thomas, 206
Byron, George Gordon, Lord (1788-1824), 79, 96, 99, 110, 131-132, 135-142, 144, 237

Calhoun, Randall, 65-66
Calverley, Charles Stuart (Blayds)(1831-1884), 237-238
Calvin, John (1509-1564), 16-17, 24, 238, 273
Cammaerts, Emile, 243
Campbell, Dowling G., 57-58
Canada, 147-148
Canning, George (1770-1827), 100
Carey, Henry (c1687-1743), 42-43
Caricature, 81-82, 124, 127, 156-158, 164, 177-197, 198-207, 238-256, 262-263, 274-276
Carleton, William (1794-1869), 145
Carlson, Richard S., 96-99, 251, 255
Carlyle, Thomas (1795-1881), 96, 145-146, 185
Carnochan, W. B., 27-28
Carroll, Lewis (1832-1898), 96-98, 101-102, 128, 179, 182, 201, 238-256,
Carruthers, Gerard C., 82-83
Cartooning, See "Caricature"
Case, A. E., 27-28
Cashe, Arthur H., 65
Castlereagh, Robert Stewart (1769-1822), 141
Castillo, Rosa, 58
Catholicism, See "Religion"
Cazamian, Louis, 1, 3, 9, 34, 63, 91
Celtic, See "Ireland," "Scotland," and "Wales"
Centlivre, Susanna (1667-1723), 21-22
Cervantes, Saavedra Miguel de (1547-1616), 54, 67, 96, 138, 180, 190, 227, 232-234, 249, 275
Chakraborty, S. C., 176

Charles I (1600-1649), 17
Charles V (Charles le Sage)(1337-1380), 17
Chatten, Elizabeth N., 69
Chaucer, Geoffrey (1340-1400), 18, 39, 128
Chesterfield, Lord Philip Dormer Stanhope (1694-1773), 50
Chesterton, Gilbert Keith (1874-1936), 190, 243
China, 74-75, 122
Christ, Jesus, See "Religion"
Christenson, Allan C., 155-156
Churchill, Charles (1731-1764), 2, 76
Cibber, Colley (1671-1757), 8, 31-32, 45-46
Clark, Anne, 255
Clark, John R., 6-7, 9, 47-48, 67
Clark, Roy Peter, 2
Clarke, Cowden, 125
Cline, C. L., 229-234
Clinton-Baddeley, V. C., 2, 9, 43
Clough, Arthur Hugh (1819-1861), 220
Clubbe, John, 151-154
Coleman, Elliott, 144
Coleridge, Samuel Taylor (1790-1850), 81, 107-109, 122-124, 129-132, 140, 142, 191
Coles, Robert, 221-222, 224
Coley, William, 13, 58

Colley, Ann C., 204-206
Collins, Philip, 172, 189, 196
Collins, R. G., 189-196
Collins, William (1721-1759), 68
Colloquial Humor, See "Vernacular Humor"
Colman, George (1732-1794), 7
Comedy of Humours, 115, 117, 177-197, 257, 263-268, 280
Comedy of Manners, 4, 19-21, 29-31, 38-39, 95-96, 172, 177-197, 263-268, 280
Comstock, Margaret, 234
Congreve, William (1670-1729), 4, 19, 29-31, 172, 280
Cope, Kevin L., 37, 59-60, 86-87
Corneille, Pierre (1606-1684), 46
Cowley, Hannah (1743-1809), 80-81
Cowper, William (1731-1800), 76-78
Craig, Randall Thomas, 234

About the Author

DON L. F. NILSEN is Professor of English at Arizona State University and Executive Secretary of the International Society for Humor Studies. He is an officer of various humor societies and actively contributes to a number of publications. His previous books include *Humor in Irish Literature: A Reference Guide* (Greenwood, 1996), and *Humor in British Literature, From the Middle Ages to the Restoration: A Reference Guide* (Greenwood, 1997).

ISBN 0-313-29705-3

90000>

EAN

9 780313 297052

HARDCOVER BAR CODE